BERNARD SHAW'S BOOK REVIEWS

BERNARD SHAW'S BOOK REVIEWS

Originally Published
in the
PALL MALL GAZETTE
from 1885 to 1888

Edited and with an Introduction
by
Brian Tyson

The Pennsylvania State University Press
University Park and London

Library of Congress Cataloging-in-Publication Data

Shaw, Bernard, 1856–1950.
    Bernard Shaw's book reviews : originally published in the Pall
Mall gazette from 1885 to 1888 / edited and with an introduction by
Brian Tyson.
        p.   cm.
    Includes bibliographical references and index.
    ISBN 0-271-00721-4
    1. Books—Reviews. I. Tyson, Brian, 1933– . II. Title.
PR5364.B47   1991
028.1—dc20   90–39579
                                                                  CIP

It is the policy of The Pennsylvania State University Press to use acid-free
paper for the first printing of all clothbound books. Publications on uncoated
stock satisfy the minimum requirements of American National Standard for
Information Sciences—Permanence of Paper for Printed Library Materials,
ANSI Z39.48–1984.

CONTENTS

ACKNOWLEDGMENTS

First, I am deeply indebted, as are all Shavians, to the pioneer efforts of those scholars who have revealed the facts of Shaw's life and documented his early labors, in particular Stanley Weintraub, Dan H. Laurence, and Michael Holroyd.

My thanks are also due to the Society of Authors for permission to quote from Shaw's printed works and to edit these reviews, and to Michael Holroyd, who waived a prior claim on the project.

Next, I should like to thank the SSHRCC and the University of Lethbridge for their financial assistance in the early days, and my wife Jill for her continued help and encouragement in subsequent stages of the project.

After a determined but vain effort to locate copyright owners of the five illustrations in the book, I conclude that the work of those artists is now in the public domain. However, I am grateful to their ghosts.

Finally, my gratitude is due to those whose detective work has helped to track down the many authors. That there are still a few "missing persons" in the manuscript I regret; but there would be many more were it not for the generous assistance rendered by John V. Howard, the Reverend R. D. Howe, Robert N. Smart, Dr. Shaun Tyson, Dr. John Wall, and Carolyn Willms.

INTRODUCTION

In this volume I have confined myself to reproducing and annotating the book reviews of Bernard Shaw that appeared in the *Pall Mall Gazette* (subtitled *An Evening Newspaper and Review*) between the years 1885 and 1888, during which time he was one of that newspaper's regular book reviewers. Occasionally he intruded a theatrical review or notes on the meeting of a society, which I have seen fit to pass over in order to present a clearer picture of Shaw's fiction and nonfiction reviewing. The reviews in question are buried deep enough in the archives to have lain almost undisturbed by a century of literary scholars. Although they are (with one exception) unsigned, we know they *are* by Shaw because his diaries for the years in question contain a note of each review written, and because he himself collected them and pasted them in a scrapbook of press cuttings.

In presenting these book reviews for the press, I have had to walk a fine line. On the one hand I wished to preserve as far as possible their journalistic appearance insofar as it faithfully reflects Shaw's developing style during the 1880s. On the other hand I wished to present a volume of which the mature Shaw himself would have approved, and this required compromise. To achieve the first objective, I have—like Dan H. Laurence before me—"chosen to follow the safe method of reproducing the texts exactly as they originally appeared, except for the occasional correction of obvious typographical errors,"[1] presenting

---

1. Bernard Shaw (ed. Dan H. Laurence), *Selected Non-Dramatic Writings of Bernard Shaw* (Boston: Houghton Mifflin, 1965), xvi.

each one (including the occasional illustration) under its date and newspaper headline, with only the addition of the Laurence Biblio-graphical Code (e.g., [C520]) in brackets. To accommodate the second objective, and to prevent the reviews from being, in Shaw's words, "absolutely unintelligible now they can no longer be read with the context of the events of the week in which they appeared,"[2] I have fully annotated the text, hoping with Shaw that "Thirst for knowledge might overcome the reader's natural objection to stand being treated as if he were 'little Frank' "! Evidence that Shaw himself at some point in his long career had intended to reprint the following reviews is to be found in the scrapbook of cuttings in which he carefully pasted them, writing above each one, with a fine pen, the date of its publication, and occasionally making shorthand corrections, or notes, in the margin. These last I have included among the endnotes of each review; endnotes which I have not numbered, because I wished to earn the praise Shaw himself gave to Pitt Cobbett, whose edition of his father's *Rural Rides* betrayed "no tampering with the text, . . . [or] editorial impertinences."

With the endnotes I have possibly erred on the side of inclusion. Many of the authors whose work Shaw reviewed either have been omitted by biographical dictionaries as too insignificant for inclusion or accorded the minimum of attention. Some have clearly been dis-missed too readily. It is my hope that as a consequence of Shaw's discerning eye and critical appraisal they will be rediscovered. At the moment, however, too many are shadowy figures whose known biogra-phies lack dates and details. This last I have tried to remedy. Occasion-ally, however, tracing the very identity of authors has proved down-right impossible: "Fayr Madoc," for example, has for a hundred years preserved an impenetrable pseudonymity, as has "Esca," whose slim volume *Albynne, a Dramatic Medley* seems to have been this poet's sole effusion. With a writer like Shaw, who was so immersed in the culture of his day, further endnotes are necessary to identify writers, artists, musicians, and scientists mentioned in his text who are no longer the common currency of cultural reference or comparison. And in the case of everyday topicalities in the reviews, I have tried to strike a balance between the inessential and what a reader today must know about the England of 1885.

For Shaw himself England was still new. It had been less than a

2. Bernard Shaw, letter to Archibald Henderson, 30 June 1904, in *Bernard Shaw: Col-lected Letters 1898–1910* (ed. Dan H. Laurence) (New York: Dodd, Mead, 1972), 425.

decade since he had, in his own words, "exported himself" from Dublin to London where, at the beginning of 1885, he was living at 36 Osnaburgh Street, near Regent's Park, with his mother and surviving sister, on a pound a week sent from his estranged father in Dublin, on the interest on an Irish mortgage, which came to as much again, and on the small proceeds from Mrs. Shaw's singing lessons. During this time he had made next to nothing by his pen, although he had "ghost-written" musical articles for his mother's mentor, Vandeleur Lee, written five novels (two of which had been serialized in a journal), produced the bulk of a glossary and index for an edition of the works of Thomas Lodge, edited Gronlund's *Co-operative Commonwealth* for the Modern Press, and written pamphlets for the newly formed Fabian Society. When, on 19 April 1885, Shaw's father expired, and with him the paternal pound, Shaw was in desperate straits financially and needed regular employment. He was rescued by a recent acquaintance, William Archer, the Scottish literary critic and translator of Ibsen, who,

> finding me full of literary ability but ridiculously incapable of obtaining literary employment and desperately in need of it, . . . set me on my feet as a critical journalist by simply handing me over a share of his own work, and making excuses for having deputed it until the Pall Mall Gazette and The World, then in the van of fashionable journalism, accepted the deputy as a principal.[3]

The job on the *Pall Mall Gazette* came as a godsend to Shaw, who was paid, according to Frank Harris (and Shaw proofread this book, so its accuracy may be assumed), "two guineas per thousand words."[4] Moreover, according to Hesketh Pearson, Shaw had just been turned down as book reviewer for the *St. James's Gazette* because its editor, Frederick Greenwood, to whom Hyndman had recommended Shaw as "another Heine," was horrified by the indifference to the death of his wife displayed by a character in one of Shaw's novels (*An Unsocial Socialist*).[5] Frederick Greenwood had been the original editor of the *Pall Mall Gazette* when it had first appeared under its proprietors

3. Bernard Shaw, *Pen Portraits and Reviews* (London: Constable, 1932), 29.

4. Frank Harris, *Frank Harris on Bernard Shaw: An Unauthorised Biography Based on Firsthand Information, with a Postcript by Mr. Shaw* (London: Victor Gollancz, 1931), 110.

5. Hesketh Pearson, *Bernard Shaw: His Life and Personality* (London: Reprint Society, by arrangement with William Collins and Co., 1948), 107.

G. Smith, Elder, and Co. in 1865. Its politics at that time were predictably conservative. However, in 1880 a new proprietor, Henry Yates Thompson (Smith's son-in-law), appointed a new editor, John (later Viscount) Morley, and the political color of the journal changed dramatically.[6] Nevertheless, when Shaw presented Morley in the summer of 1880 with examples of his journalistic craftsmanship, he was told that "in my opinion you would do well to get out of journalism."[7] It was not until Morley was elected M.P. for Newcastle-upon-Tyne in 1883 and the assistant editor William Thomas Stead was promoted to the editorship that the *Pall Mall Gazette*—which up to that point had been a dignified recorder of daily happenings—became clamorous in its support of social reform and a leading example of what Matthew Arnold called "the New Journalism." It was now ready to receive Bernard Shaw. Although the *Gazette* continued until 1923, Shaw's claim for it to have been "in the van" of fashionable journalism in 1885 is no more than the truth: the golden years of the *Pall Mall Gazette* were those under the fiery editorship of W. T. Stead.

Shaw's new editor, who, incidentally, left the *Pall Mall Gazette* in the same year as Shaw, initiated numerous social and political movements, which made his newspaper highly controversial. In October 1883, for example, the *Gazette* had reviewed *The Bitter Cry of Outcast London: An Inquiry into the Condition of the Abject Poor,* a penny pamphlet prepared by nonconformist ministers exposing the frightful conditions of the housing of the working classes. Immediately, it reported, the newspaper received "an almost unmanageable number of letters" from all parts of the kingdom. "On no question that has been raised for many years," they announced on 22 October, "does public interest appear to be so keen and deep." Their correspondents included William Booth, the Earl of Shaftesbury, and Gertrude Toynbee, while other columns in the *Gazette* contained investigations into and reports on the rehousing of outcast Glasgow, the housing of outcast Liverpool, the homes of the poor in Dublin, and the living conditions of the poorer classes in Germany and France. Shaw helped himself freely to this information when he began his first play the following year, just as he later plundered the pages of his old

6. On 20 May 1880, John Morley wrote to Auberon Herbert, "I have been induced for a time to take command of the *Pall Mall Gazette*—with a view to its transformation into a genuinely liberal paper" (Harris S. Hutchinson, *Auberon Herbert: Crusader for Liberty* [London: Williams & Northgate, 1943], 224).

7. John Morley, quoted in *Bernard Shaw: Collected Letters. 1874–1897* (ed. Dan H. Laurence) (London: Max Reinhardt, 1965), 32.

newspaper when he wrote *Mrs Warren's Profession* in 1893; for, having exhausted the possibilities of slum-landlordism, Stead launched another press crusade in July 1885, this time under the heading "The Maiden Tribute of Modern Babylon" to bring to public attention the prevalence of prostitution and "white slave traffic" in Europe. This crusade was so successful that the *Pall Mall Gazette* was accused of "flooding London with filth and obscenity," the Prince of Wales stopped his copy, and W. H. Smith and Son, the booksellers, refused to carry it. Ultimately Stead himself became involved in litigation concerning a young girl he had "bought" in order to prove that young girls were habitually sold, and was given a three-month prison sentence; and what began as a campaign for moral reform ended as a minor scandal. Whatever may have been the truth of the matter—and Stead was no doubt as misunderstood as Gladstone in his attempts to correct public vice—he expiated his sins in a unique way: he was one of the passengers who went down on the *Titanic* in 1912. He was sixty-three. In 1885, however, Stead remained unabashed, and during Shaw's critical tenancy conducted courageous crusades on behalf of battered brides like Mrs. Langworthy and convicted criminals like Israel Lipski. With such an employer, it is clear that Shaw felt free to tilt at the establishment without offending editorial sensibilities.

Although he had at his fingertips the enormous resources of the British Museum Reading Room, the books Shaw received for review supplied him, in his impecunious state, with what must have been his first personal library. And in them he occasionally found seeds that were to blossom in his later plays. For example, in his review of Butler's *Luck, or Cunning?* we sense an interest beyond the evident admiration of one stylist for another:

> Let it suffice to acknowledge his skilful terseness and exactness of expression, his frank disdain of affected suavity or imperturbability, his apparently but not really paradoxical humour, his racy epigrams, and the geniality of his protest against "a purely automatic conception of the universe as of something that will work if a penny be dropped into the box."

Here in fact begins Shaw's conversion from Darwin's theory of natural selection to the creative evolutionary creed of Lamarck and the vitalism of Butler, which will animate *Man and Superman* and *Back to Methuselah*. His reviews reveal other influential works. Field's *The*

Greek Islands and Turkey after the War provides clues to *Arms and the Man*. A review of a book on the Irish question contains the germ of *John Bull's Other Island*. Names and attitudes of physicians and surgeons in *The Life of Sir Robert Christison, Bart* find their way into *The Doctor's Dilemma*. Thomas Tyler's edition of Shakespeare's *Sonnets* contains *l'idée mère* for *The Dark Lady of the Sonnets*. Even the two books on physiognomy, Francis Warner's *Physical Expression* and Rosa Baughan's *Handbook of Physiognomy,* supplied Shaw with ideas that he later incorporated into his plays in the meticulous care he took with the facial descriptions of his characters.[8]

About half of Shaw's book reviews are of nonfiction: volumes of biography, musical history, spiritualism, and ghost stories (the Society for Psychic Research had made its popular appearance in 1882), plus sundry volumes on ethics, economics, folklore, physiognomy, travel, and Socialism. As this last had been the "living centre of all Shaw's interests" (since Henry George had "switched him over" from atheism in 1882), there is, as one might expect, a goodly admixture of political propaganda in Shaw's reviewing. A book on gambling is Shaw's excuse for an attack on capitalism. So is Walter Besant's desire to obtain for authors "an unfairly large return" from copyrighting their work: Shaw admonishes him to "stand aside until millions of other workers, whose needs are far more pressing, and whose utility is far less questionable than yours, are served." In another review he even praises the "resurrection man" in his bodysnatching for making the "Henry Georgian distinction" between the human body and the shroud—which last is a "product of human industry." Socialism was also one stick with which he beat romantic fiction during these years, even when the heroes of the novels thought they believed in it. In his very first review he claims that

> The adept Socialist of to-day, with his economic fatalism, his "iron laws," and his prophets, Marx, Lassalle, and Engels, will repudiate Trajan Gray's very novelistic Socialism with ineffable disdain.

In the same way he attacks the heroine of *Othmar* for her ignorance of Marx. And he has no patience with "reformers" like George Moore, who, seeking to be politically "modern," simply recruited Capital and

---

8. See Brian Tyson, *The Story of Shaw's SAINT JOAN* (Kingston and Montreal: McGill–Queen's University Press, 1982), 120 n. 32, and 50 below.

Labor as the latest fashion in melodramatic villains and heroes. When novelists ignored the political scene (as the majority of them did), Shaw still brought it home to them in his reviews. His outline of George Fleming's *Andromeda* begins,

> Certain idle ladies and gentlemen are represented as unproductively consuming wealth while travelling in the Tyrol and in Italy. They are heedless of Mr. Ruskin's classification of persons who are not workers as beggars or thieves. They have not even heard of Mr. Chamberlain: the shadow of "ransom and restitution" has not yet fallen on them, nor has the threat of a graduated income tax roused them from a chronic dejection which, if it were a little more philosophical, might be dignified with the title of pessimism.

He solves the problem of Mrs. Oliphant's *The Second Son* by simply saying that we should "give up throwing our counties as private property to country gentlemen and their heirs to play pitch and toss with." He reminds William Black that his heroine, who has nothing to do but wear delicious dresses and break hearts, involves an extra dose of drudgery somewhere for "unlovely people" who stitch "her tailor-made dresses at three farthings an hour." And in his review of Mrs. Alexander's *A Second Life,* to the reader's surprise, Shaw attacks not the villain of the piece but both the author and her heroine, Mildred Carr, who is thrown into poverty by the death of her father.

> An opportunity of recovering her lost creature comforts by a marriage with an elderly bill discounter, of coarse exterior and detestable character, offers itself to her. She embraces it without the least scruple, and without a word of remonstrance from her mother.

Welby, the bill discounter, makes her feel that she has no claim to be mistress of his house, and his tyranny and loathing force her to leave him and begin the second life of the book's title.

> Even then, though she admits that she has done wrong in breaking her vows, which, under the circumstances, is absurd, she has still not the least remorse for making them, nor any suspicion that her treatment by Welby was no more than she richly deserved.

Shaw here attacks the author for blindly accepting the social status quo. He objects to Mildred Carr's cheerfully selling herself to the highest bidder apparently without the least idea that what she is doing is only a refined form of prostitution, or proletarianism, as he would have said. Shaw's play *Mrs Warren's Profession* was written eight years later to reinforce public awareness of the problem faced by women in a society of buying and selling, where all that most women have to sell is themselves.

The fact is that by 1885 fiction was having a hard time coping with the effects of the rise of capitalism in Europe, which, through a hundred years of industrial expansion, cheap raw materials, and huge markets, had increased production and profits for the few, while it had reduced the many to squalor, poverty, drunkenness and disease. As J. I. M. Stewart points out,

> A literature of protest or outcry, such as Mrs. Gaskell's or Charles Kingsley's, was not enough; nor did pietistic solutions—the gospel of a change of heart—hold water. Political science must be mastered in the interest of political morality, and the resultant findings brought home to the people alike by rational persuasion and the resources of art.[9]

Shaw, who had arrived in London to become a novelist—that being the accepted way to literary eminence in those days—had written just such a novel informed by economic theory, called *An Unsocial Socialist;* but it had not proved commercially acceptable. There had, however, been one response to the changed social scene from the so-called realistic school of novelists, who, however ignorant of political science, were yet well equipped to describe the unpleasant symptoms of unbridled industrial expansion, which were spreading through society. The "realists" caused both a rift in literary criticism, and a public outcry. Leslie Stephen spoke of the first in a lecture on "English Novels" he gave at the University College Literary Society on 3 May 1887:

> When I read our reviews it seems to me that we are in rather a chaotic state as regards our principles. There are several schools of critics who seem to carry on an internecine warfare with each other. . . . We have a contest between the idealists

9. J. I. M. Stewart, *Eight Modern Writers* (Oxford: Clarendon Press, 1963), 1.

and the realists. In the realistic novel, the facts may be painful, even revolting, but the whole interest of the novel is in its representation of truth, and we cannot have too much truth. The existence of wrong in the world is a justification for its use in fiction. Opposed to these realists are other persons, who hold that fiction should be fictitious, and should represent some ideal world in which the fancy may have full swing. Realism is not, however, properly opposed to idealism at all.[10]

The wisdom of that final comment was not immediately apparent to many Victorians, who publicly denounced a novelist like Emile Zola as though, in describing the visible symptoms of poverty and crime, he was responsible for both. Sadly, Zola was considered as vulgar and disgusting by the much-lettered Wilde as he was by the unlettered mob; and even Ibsen separated himself from the Frenchman's reputation by saying, "Zola descends to the sewer to take a bath: I do [so] in order to scour it." The leaders of the establishment were alarmed that this kind of literature was on the increase, its production and distribution a triumphant example of the same industrial expansion that marked other areas of the economy. As Shaw remarked of one of the authors he reviewed:

It would be impertinent to compliment him on his ability to write a novel: that much is expected from everybody nowadays.

Thus it was that on 8 May 1888, Mr. Smith rose in the House of Commons to move "That this House deplores the rapid spread of demoralizing literature in this country, and is of opinion that the law against obscene publications . . . should be vigorously enforced and, if necessary, strengthened." He specifically had Zola in mind:

Mr. Vizetelly stated that he had a sale of 1,000 a week of the writings of Zola, which had been faithfully translated into English. In this state of things nothing was to be gained by preserving silence upon the unrestricted issue of books than which nothing more diabolical had ever been written by the pen of

10. Leslie Stephen, "English Novels," lecture presented at the University College Literary Society, London, 3 May 1887 (reported in the *Pall Mall Gazette* on 4 May 1887).

man. These works were commonly described as "realistic," which he took to mean nothing short of sheer beastliness.[11]

It was unfortunate that the *Pall Mall Gazette* relegated Shaw to the discussion of minor works; for on this matter his was the voice of truth. Shaw alone of the *Gazette's* reviewers had inspected the economic underpinnings of the society that produced the horrors described, could distinguish between the symptoms of poverty and oppression and the disease itself, and was capable of prescribing a cure. Other reviewers were only capable of cries of agreement or disagreement at the revelations of the realists: in this they were no better than most of their readers, who, shocked when the miners in *Germinale* spit black because their lungs are corrupted by coal dust (though such a fact was observable by anyone who happened to live within spitting distance of a mining town), felt that Zola was intent upon displaying to all and sundry unpleasant facts that everyone knew about, but which should not be mentioned in polite company. As an admirer of Zola (and he read Zola's novels and critical articles for pleasure during his reviewing days at the *Pall Mall Gazette*), Shaw shared the Frenchman's interest in scientific realism;[12] but he was less interested in presenting facts that everyone knew but did not mention than he was in revealing underlying truths that very few people knew about at all. In this he was a true "realist." As Stuart E. Baker has said

> At heart, the realist's secret is a simple knack for always making the distinction between what is inside and what is outside, while insisting on the importance—and the reality—of each.[13]

In consequence, Shaw, in his reviews, had little patience with novelists who presented romance disguised as realism. When George Moore, in *A Mere Accident,* pretends to psychoanalyze rapist and vic-

11. *The Times* (London) 9 May 1888, 7.
12. Shaw, in his own novels, had considered himself a realist. Macmillan and Co., rejecting *Immaturity,* had nevertheless described it as "the work of a humourist and a realist." Shaw's reply to them confirmed his intention. "This design was to write a novel, scrupulously true to nature, with no incident in it to which everyday experience might not afford a parallel." His remaining novels were conceived in the same spirit. During his years as a reviewer he also read for his own pleasure Emile Zola's novels and critical articles; he frequently discussed the topic of realism with William Archer; and on 8 January 1888, at the Blackheath Essay and Debating Society, Shaw moved that "Realism is the Goal of Fiction."
13. Stuart E. Baker, "Shavian Realism," in *Shaw: The Annual of Bernard Shaw Studies,* vol. 9, *Shaw Offstage: The Nondramatic Writings,* ed. Fred D. Crawford (University Park and London: Pennsylvania State University Press, 1989), 84.

tim, Shaw responds by "psychoanalyzing" the author. The reason Moore's book deals with rape is that it affords him the opportunity for

> one of his favourite sham clinical lectures on morbid sexual conditions. Let it be freely admitted that these discourses would, if truly realistic, have a scientific value sufficient to fortify Mr. Moore against prudish critics. But as they are realistic only as symptoms of the condition of Mr. Moore's own imagination, which hardly deserves a set of volumes all to itself, they have no more claim on our forbearance than the gratuitously romantic passages in a shilling shocker. The objection, in fact, to Mr. Moore is not that he is realistic, but that he is a romancer who, in order that he may take liberties, persuades himself that he is a pathologist.

On the other hand, Shaw praised Trollope as an honest realist—albeit one who was unaware of the slums; and he attacked those novelists who thought that, since Zola's realistic novels treated mostly of human and social disorder, the bleaker the picture you could paint, the more realistic you necessarily became. This confusion is discussed at length in the review of W. E. Norris's *Major and Minor,* where Shaw claims that some novelists' understanding of realism has not got much further than

> an opinion that the romance of the drawing-room is less real than the romance of the kitchen, the romance of the kitchen than that of the slum, that of the slum than that of the sewer, and generally, that reality is always in inverse proportion to self-control, eduation, health, and decency. . . . [It] must not . . . be forgotten that the proper, the placid and the pleasant, even when quantitatively less than the improper, the hysterical, and the noisome, are quite as real. And when the separate question as to which is fitter for the three-volume treatment arises, it is to be considered that no born romancer can help imparting a certain attraction, morbid or healthy, to his subject matter; and that when he treats of the improper, the hysterical and the noisome, he must, whether he will or no, clothe them with the fascinations of his art.

In short, Shaw exposed the fake "realists" of the eighties, just as he was able to identify the fake Ibsen enthusiasts of the nineties.

But the majority of novelists whose work he reviewed—like their readers—treated the novel as pure escapism. Those suffering the effects of poverty—if they read at all—escaped into a fantasy land of their "betters": their "betters" escaped into the slums. The remarkable thing is the forbearance Shaw shows as a critical realist in directing the hose of commonsense onto the feeble fires of fantasy in the books that he reviews. He remains genial, even when he is making short work of them. His very first review sets the tone:

> [The hero's adventures] are by no means deficient in interest. A shipwreck, a man and bull fight, a war, the siege of Paris, and a revolt vary highly wrought domestic scenes, at the conclusion of which the gentlemen stagger, ghastly and despairing, from the premises, while the ladies are found prone on the carpet, with their hands clenched over the undone masses of their hair. Bouts of brain fever ensue; but all the characters are in good condition for the final massacre, which they manage to escape in sufficient numbers to ensure a happy ending amid the fire and carnage of the suppression of the Commune.

When the "shilling shocker" added violence to romance, Shaw made short work of that too:

> It seems hard that the heroine, an interesting and good-looking young woman, should be married over and over again, pitched from a bridge by the hardness of one husband, fished from under a barge by the heroism of another, and brought round in a hospital only to creep away to a desolate tower and stab herself, which final catastrophe could not have occurred but for her unaccountable habit of carrying a dagger.

And when the grinding formula of romance began to repeat itself from the "legion novelist," Shaw, in Aristotelian fashion, applied inductive reasoning to the "three volumes of pure silliness" that lay on his desk, simply reducing them to their constituent elements:

> There is the long-lost child, the long-lost sister, the trusting maiden, the smiling seducer, the cynical worldling, the honest and opportune rescuer whose roof is ready to shelter the betrayed, the recluse expiating a dreadful crime, the herculean dwarf whose misshapen shoulders heave with the throes of a

noble heart, the angel child with golden curls whom alone of all mankind he softens to, the madwoman who flits about the graves in the ghostly moonlight, the hidden hoard of gold which provides virtue with unlimited cash at a critical moment, the diary which explains everything, the duel which avenges everybody, the storm and fatal accident which clear the inconvenient people out of the way, the restoration of the long-lost ones, and the final epithalamium and chime of wedding bells. Just the thing, as Lincoln said, for the people who like that sort of thing. But not by any means the thing with which serious criticism has now anything to do.

Unfortunately, it *was* the thing with which Shaw's serious criticism too frequently had to do, in spite of the occasional relief afforded by Wilkie Collins and Paul Heyse. So while it is true to say that Shaw made short work of these romances, it might be truer to say that they made short work of him. As the number of books to be reviewed increased, Shaw was frequently driven to reviewing them two and three at a time. On one occasion he reviewed twenty volumes of deplorable verse in a single article: volumes that had presumably been collecting dust on his desk because he could not bring himself to write about them. And after two or three years of this, Shaw had had enough. It is impossible to locate the precise straw that broke the camel's back, but the note of exasperation in his review of Hall Caine's *A Son of Hagar* in February 1887 suggests a reviewer coming to the end of his tether. He proposes to form a guild of nineteenth-century authors who will swear to abandon romance. They will write according to rules: for example "That the heroine shall not be subject to fainting fits" and "That if the hero be incurably addicted to using his hands when irritated, he shall be thrashed by the villain in a fair stand-up fight at least once in the third volume." They will not be allowed to dispose of unwanted characters by the use of railway and colliery accidents, or use ghosts, wills, and solemn oaths; and "if [the characters] know any important secret they shall out with it at once to save trouble." The most significant rule, however, is that "books shall not be written at all except under irresistible provocation." Under such conditions, he claims, "a civilized school of novel and drama might be formed, and the lives of reviewers almost indefinitely prolonged." Finally, in September 1888, exasperated by the "long continuance of the silly season in the publishing trade," Shaw wrote a letter to C. Kinloch-Cooke, the subeditor:

Why condemn me to read things that I can't review—that no artistic conscience could long survive the reviewing of? Why don't you begin notices of boots, hats, dogcarts and so on? They would be fifty times as useful and interesting as reviews of the last novel by Miss Braddon, who is a princess among novel manufacturers. There ought to be legislation against this sort of thing—on the lines of the Factory Acts. I believe the mortality in hospitals is perceptibly increased by the books distributed through reviewers by the Kyrle Society.

The industrial metaphor is exact: the mass production of novels was leading to cruel working conditions for reviewers! As he remarked later, "Journalistic criticism, after the first years, becomes necessarily for the most part repetitive breadwinning."[14] It comes as no surprise to find that Shaw's last book review appeared in the *Pall Mall Gazette* just three months after the publication of the above letter, on 26 December 1888.[15]

In fact, of course, Shaw could now afford to move on. When he began reviewing for the *Pall Mall Gazette* he was scarcely published and practically unknown. Three and a half years later, thanks largely to William Archer, he had become a regular contributor to a dozen journals, had had articles in three American publications, one translated into French, and had built the beginnings of a powerful reputation and an unmistakable style. Though the reviews were unsigned, Shaw's hallmarks, wit, balance, polish, incisiveness, are to be found in each sentence:

An autobiography is usually begun with interest by writer and reader alike, and seldom finished by either.
Every Englishman believes that he is entitled to a ghost after death to compensate him for the loss of his body, and to enable him to haunt anybody that may have murdered or otherwise illused him in the days when he was solid.
The pessimists have ever been the heroes of literature, and

14. Bernard Shaw, *Pen Portraits and Reviews* (London: Constable and Company, 1932), 216.
15. So far as I can tell, St. John Ervine is the only person to retail the anecdote about Shaw losing his job at the *Pall Mall Gazette* because it took him a year to review a book by Henry Sidgwick. According to Ervine, the publishers complained to the editor, who stopped sending Shaw any more books! This is not true, although he did stop recording in his diary books sent to him for review after 1887. He reviewed numerous books published in 1888.

damnation has made more preachers popular than salvation. It is the last weakness of the individual artistic mind to believe that art work which displeases it is bad work.

The crispness of style is all the more remarkable when one considers the speed with which most of the essays were produced and the other engagements with which Shaw's diary for those years is burdened. It is also worth remembering that of the more than four hundred Shavian articles published between 1885 and 1888, 65 percent were submitted to journals other than the *Pall Mall Gazette!* Shaw's most celebrated days as a critic were just beginning. And since his greatest critical interest lay with the performing arts, it was natural that he should abandon fiction, moving first into musical and finally into theatrical criticism.

Nevertheless, his book reviewing on the *Pall Mall Gazette,* if it is only a first, is still a firm, step on Shaw's road to discovering his true vocation as a dramatist. There was both negative and positive reinforcement in the experience. Negatively, it not only cured him of the desire to review novels; it also cured him of the desire to write any. In one sense this is surprising; for he was just beginning to enjoy some success as a novelist;[16] and his diary records the beginning of one more novel—his sixth—during his reviewing period. The work, however, was untitled and remains unfinished.[17] The negative aspects of the romantic novel's formulaic writing and escapism, which drove Shaw away from fiction, were balanced by the greater immediacy and anonymity afforded him by journalism, which, in its turn, was a subtle inducement towards the drama. Occasionally, for example, the *Gazette* published indignant letters from authors whose works had been attacked. Shaw's review of *A Mere Accident* prompted a squeal of protest from George Moore; Richard Proctor replied at length to Shaw's humorous attack on *Chance and Luck;* Edmund Gurney com-

16. The serialization of *An Unsocial Socialist* in *To-Day* in 1884 led to its publication in a cheap edition by Swan Sonnenschein & Co in 1887, and the serialization of *Cashel Byron's Profession* in the same journal in 1885/6 led to that novel's being published shortly thereafter.

17. Of course, in Shaw's desertion of the novel for the play, we see an example of what was to become fairly common at the turn of the century, when the intellectual pendulum was swinging back from the page to the stage, just as a hundred years before it had deserted the drama for the novel. In the wake of Ibsen, many fiction writers tried writing for the theater. One thinks of the highly successful Chekhov and Wilde, of the less successful Henry James and George Moore, even of Thomas Hardy, who, when he abandoned novel writing in 1893, joined—albeit briefly—the Independent Theatre Association (of which Shaw was a member), presumably with a view to writing plays. Shaw's movement in the same direction is prefigured in his book reviews.

plained about Shaw's derisive review of *Phantasms of the Living;* and, when Shaw tried to separate the art of the recently deceased author of *For a Song's Sake* from the maudlin sentimentality that surrounded his blindness, H. E. Clarke wrote:

> in the name of common decency, and for the sake of many relatives and friends, to whom it will give the bitterest pain, I protest against this brutal, wanton and cowardly personal attack upon a dead man.

Shaw sometimes found time in his column to write rebuttals to these complaints, no doubt enjoying the exchange. Less enjoyable, however, was the response of Grant Allen, who preferred guerrilla warfare to open confrontation, and persuaded his friends at the *Pall Mall Gazette* to remove the offensive portions of Shaw's reviews of his work before they were printed. As time went by, Shaw occasionally began to use a persona in his reviews, slanting the angle of his attack to sharpen the irony. On one occasion, he becomes the Rev. C. W. Stiggins, Jr., of Box Hill to consider disparagingly a collection of *Wellerisms;* on another, to review George Sims's gossipy belowstairs novel *Mary Jane's Memoirs,* which purports to be the actual diary of a kitchenmaid, Shaw startlingly assumes the persona of "An English Mistress" (the girl's employer) and manages an amusing exposé of the class system through her disapproving remarks about Mary Jane. Again, when reviewing Proctor's book *Chance and Luck,* Shaw wears the mask of an inveterate gambler, ironically pretending that since reading the book by Proctor—who is against gambling—he has won more than ever at the gaming tables. And once more, when Shaw was debunking the proceedings of the Society for Psychical Research, his review, signed "A Firm Believer," is written with owl-faced solemnity, while destroying the pretensions of the book. At the same time, to provide the other half of the dialogue, as it were, Shaw contributed letters to the press on a variety of topics under such aliases as George Bunnerd, Jesse Dodd, Redbarn Wash, W. Chalks ("a milkman"), Amelia Mackintosh, and William Walker Smyth of the Christmas Day Abolition Society. It is only a short stride from pretending that you are the son of a hypocritical clergyman, an English mistress, an inveterate gambler, or a firm believer in ghosts to writing plays in which you make yourself each in turn. The dialogue is already magnificent, compressive, succinct—as it must be for a journalist who has to budget his words. All it needs is a play to put it in. And four years later Shaw completed one.

BERNARD SHAW'S BOOK REVIEWS

*TRAJAN** [C111]

IN this novel Mr. Henry F. Keenan, like a good American, devotes to the paradise of his countrymen 642 pages, most of them superfluous, but all readable without exceptional effort by leisured persons of a romantic turn. Adopting the Imperial policy of "Frappe fort, et frappe vite," he at once seizes the reader's attention by putting the climax of his novel in the first chapter, in which the hero, Trajan Gray, an American artist with a Chinese taste in suicide, is starving himself to death. From this point the novel is written backward until, by the time we reach page 200, we are thoroughly informed as to Trajan's ancestry, career previous to attempted suicide, and motive for the attempt, which is of course a disappointment in love. We now start fair with him, and follow his adventures in their natural order. They are by no means deficient in interest. A shipwreck, a man and bull fight, a war, the siege of Paris, and a revolt vary highly wrought domestic scenes, at the conclusion of which the gentlemen stagger, ghastly and despairing, from the premises, while the ladies are found prone on the carpet, with their hands clenched over the undone masses of their hair. Bouts of brain fever ensue; but all the characters are in good condition for the final massacre, which they manage to escape in sufficient numbers to ensure a happy ending amid the fire and carnage of the suppression of the Commune. Trajan is everything that is romantic and irresponsible—handsome, American, an artist, and a special correspondent. He occasionally, inspired by love, retires to his studio for a week or so to paint a masterpiece; but ordinarily he neglects his business and philanders or philosophises according to the sex of his company. He is a Socialist of an obsolete school, quoting Rousseau, and actually citing England and America as examples of free government. "The aspirations of the rights of man," he says, "have made in America a great people, and in England a powerful and well ordered one." The adept Socialist of today, with his economic fatalism, his "iron laws," and his prophets, Marx, Lassalle, and Engels, will repudiate Trajan Gray's very novelistic Socialism with ineffable disdain; but the public at large will probably not be very much concerned about the quality of his chrematistics. There are plenty of other people in the book, each with an extensive family history; and the reader will require all his

---

*"Trajan: a Novel." By Henry F. Keenan. (London: Cassell and Co. 1885.)

presence of mind at first to remember who is who. Their conversation is occasionally somewhat overpowering. Among the first remarks made by one of the heroines to her brother—a young man who came from Harvard "in the flush of a brilliant graduation"—is the following: "I am surprised that the dragons of propriety permitted you into such disreputable dissipation." A woman who can say this without stammering is evidently no ordinary person. When the splendours of the empire are his theme, Mr. Keenan allows the relish of the American to temper the rancour of the Republican. We read of "the glittering floor," with "a thousand lights dazzling from the pyramids of crystal candelabra overhead, the glories of France looking down from the priceless panels on which the pencil of Paul Vernet had set the lineaments of marshals, generals, admirals, and statesmen." Some of the descriptions of natural scenery have a refreshing dash of novelty. Thus the nightingale and the dove, of which we are growing tired, are supplanted in this fashion: "A melancholy cat-bird sent forth its plaintive refrain in the thick shade above." It is impossible to say, without research, what a cat-bird is; but any addition to the monotonous ornithology of romance is welcome. Later in the novel we have abundance of second-hand French revolution, with the hackneyed mob and the hackneyed heroine queen, and a general clatter of the imagination working furiously in a worn-out groove. But the interest, such as it is, does not flag; and the book, though it will not make its author famous for judgment or profundity of thought, is likely to make him highly popular with readers who like plenty of such exciting incidents and highly-coloured scenes as will not wear out their thinking apparatus too rapidly. It may be added that they must be persons whose time is of comparatively small value.

Editor's Notes

- The first mention of this novel appears in Shaw's diary on Sunday, 3 May 1885: "Read part of *Trajan: A Novel* given me by Archer to review for the *Pall Mall*" (*Bernard Shaw: The Diaries 1885–1897. With early autobiographical notebooks and diaries and an abortive 1917 diary*, 2 vols., edited and annotated by Stanley Weintraub [University Park and London: The Pennsylvania State University Press, 1986], 81. Hereafter, the regular references to this valuable resource will be labeled simply *Diary*). The following day he notes, "finished review of *Trajan* in the forenoon at home." And on the fifteenth he

"corrected and sent off to *PMG* proofs of review of *Trajan*—my first job with them" (*Diary*, 81, 84).
▪ Henry Francis Keenan (1850–1928), American novelist. Born in Rochester, New York, he became a journalist on the staff of the *Rochester Chronicle* in 1868 and freelanced on other newspapers in New York and elsewhere. As a novelist he is best remembered for *The Money-Makers* (1885), subtitled *A Social Parable*, attacking the corrupting influence of capitalism (an anonymous response to John Hay's 1884 attack on labor unions in *The Breadwinners*). He also wrote *The Aliens* (1886), *The Iron Game* [a tale of the American Civil War] (1891), and *The Conflict with Spain: a history of the* [Spanish-American] *war, based upon official reports and descriptions of eye-witnesses* (1898), in addition to short fiction for *Harper's Weekly*.
▪ Shaw himself had been a convert to Socialism for less than three years at this time, and had been acquainted with the works of Karl Marx (1818–83) for an even shorter period. He also was friendly with Marx's youngest daughter, Eleanor Marx-Aveling (1855–98), with whom he shared an interest in Ibsen. Friedrich Engels (1820–95), co-founder with Marx of scientific socialism, was at this time acting as midwife to Marx's theories, two years after the latter's death. The German Socialist Ferdinand Lassalle (1825–64), least well known of the Communist triumvirate, had projected a number of state socialist views that differed markedly from those of Marx and Engels. Shaw himself was to differ with Marx later.

4 June 1885

*VIA CORNWALL TO CAIRO** [C115]

THIS book must not be confused by unthinking readers with Thackeray's "From Cornhill to Cairo." It is Miss Gordon Cumming's latest book of travel, and is quite free from the egotism which confines most travellers to descriptions of their direct personal experiences. It appears that the Guion steamship *Montana* went aground five miles from Holyhead on the 13th of March, 1880, with Miss Gordon Cumming on board, and the catastrophe struck her as "an episode in the shipping annals of A.D. 1880 surely worthy of record." She has, therefore, recorded at considerable length not only what actually did happen, which

*"Via Cornwall to Cairo." By C. F. Gordon Cumming. (London: Chatto and Windus. 7s. 6d. 1885.)

was not very tragic, but what might have happened had a tempest been raging at the time; and this hypothetic shipwreck was dreadful indeed. But this by no means exhausts Miss Gordon Cumming's interest in the subject. Among the shipwrecked passengers, she says, "were a family"; and this family had once sailed from New York to Hull in the steamship *Hindoo,* of the Wilson line. The *Hindoo,* like every ship in which Miss Gordon Cumming has travelled, or in which there was a human being that ever subsequently made her acquaintance, was lost; and the details of this calamity, which are most harrowing, are narrated circumstantially. But, "by a singular coincidence," Miss Gordon Cumming had herself started from England seven years previously in this very *Hindoo.* "Perhaps," she suggests modestly, "some notes of that eventful trip may not be wholly without interest." It is scarcely necessary to add that on that occasion the vessel all but foundered before it got as far as Portland Harbour, in which it took refuge. While the necessary repairs were in progress, Miss Gordon Cumming went ashore, only to learn that "within two days two vessels had been wrecked at this very place, and a third had come ashore, forsaken of her crew." A faithful account of these events, the second of which was of unparalleled awfulness, occupies several interesting pages. Eventually the *Hindoo* started again, with the traveller-authoress on board. It had better have entertained Jonah or Vanderdecken unawares. When, on a Friday night, they left the peaceful harbour, "it was to experience such a tempest as the most experienced old sailors declared they had never seen the like of in the English Channel." But Miss Gordon Cumming bears a charmed life: she always lives to tell the tale. After drifting at the mercy of the winds and waves in a heartrending manner, all hands working at the pumps and expecting each hour to be their last, the vessel at last escapes into Plymouth Harbour, where it came within six inches of running down a man-of-war, nearly ran upon the breakwater, and did not land its passengers safely until they were saturated with terror as well as with sea water. Once on shore, Miss Gordon Cumming varied her surfeit of horrors by a visit to Plymouth dockyards and St. Michael's Mount, and went overland to Cornwall. Some of the other passengers went by sea in the *Agra;* and, as might have been expected, the weather presently became such that a "weather-beaten man" remarked to Miss Gordon Cumming, "Well, if there *be* any ships off our coast to-night, they're bound to go down!" The *Agra,* however, returned disabled to Plymouth. The same misfortune had happened to it on two previous occasions, details of which are given. Both Plymouth and Falmouth harbours were found by the passengers of the *Hindoo* to be "mere shipping hospitals," and many maritime disasters are cursorily mentioned; but there are only two more really frightful wrecks—those of the *Louisa* and the *Flower of Loch Leven*—chronicled at full length. Miss Gordon Cumming at last sailed for Gibraltar. Of the *Hindoo* we hear nothing more than that "once off Halifax, and once off Hull, she was in imminent danger of foundering, and had to be towed into port in a disabled condition." Delightful as Miss Gordon Cumming's narratives of the sea are, the prudence of underwriting the bottoms in which she voyages, or indeed any shipping whatsoever in her neighbourhood, is likely to become a vexed question at Lloyd's.

Her passage through the Bay of Biscay was uneventful, only one man falling overboard and being drowned. Her accounts of Gibraltar, where "imagination conjured up" (at some length) the story of Elliot's famous cannonade of red hot balls; of Alexandria before it was "ruthlessly destroyed by Arabi Pasha;" of Cairo, where she refused to ascend the Great Pyramid, but nevertheless gives a capital description of the view from the top of it, and of Aden and the Red Sea, are all interesting and instructive in matters that we all pretend to have at our fingers' ends, but which few of us could pass an examination in. Even the paragraphs on the prevalence of the prefixes Tre, Pol, and Pen in Cornwall, and on the love of the cat for valerian, may surprise many young students. Miss Gordon Cumming never overrates the information of her readers, and her style is pleasant and easy. Her allegations that coastguard and lifeboat authorities do not attend to signals of distress except on rather special occasions, and that our dwellers by the sea are apt to receive shipwrecked refugees with sticks and stones, suggests reflection and even official inquiry.

Editor's Notes

- Shaw wrote this review on 29 May 1885 (*Diary*, 87), correcting the proofs on 3 June. His exhortation to the reader not to confuse the book with Thackeray's is ironic, since he himself erroneously calls it *Via Cornwall to Cairo*. Its correct title is *Via Cornwall to Egypt*. Thackeray's *Notes of a Journey from Cornhill to Grand Cairo* from the pen of one of his famous pseudonyms, "Mr. M. A. Titmarsh," had first appeared in 1846.
- C[onstance] F[rederica] Gordon Cumming (1837–1924), English traveler and writer. She was the daughter of Sir William Gordon Cumming and youn-

ger sister of Roualeyn Gordon Cumming (who was known as the "Lion-hunter of South Africa"). A visit to a married sister living in the Himalayas was followed by twelve years of almost continuous traveling, resulting in a number of travel books, illustrated in some cases by her own watercolors. Her output included *From the Hebrides to the Himalayas* (1876), *At Home in Fiji* (1881), *A Lady's Cruise in a French Man of War* (1882), *Fire Fountains: the Kingdom of Hawaii: its Volcanoes and the History of its Missions* (1882), and *Granite Crags* (1883). Such a lady traveler may have given Shaw the idea for Lady Cicely Waynflete in *Captain Brassbound's Conversion*.

- (Sir) George Augustus Eliott (1717–90), afterward Lord Heathfield, was the "gallant defender" of Gibraltar during its siege by the combined land and sea forces of Spain during the years 1779–83. The misspelling of his name as "Elliott" is either Shaw's or the *Pall Mall Gazette*'s; Ms. Gordon Cumming accurately renders it with one "l."
- Valerian is a drug (used as a stimulant) derived from the rootstock of the wild valerian plant.

27 June 1885

A REGULAR PICKLE [C122]

"A Regular Pickle." By Henry W. Nesfield. One vol. (George Redway. 10s. 6d.) This novel, entirely free from plot, heroine, or style, is as fresh and unembarrassing as might be expected under the circumstances. The author's aim is to amuse at any cost, and with readers who are naturally of an exceedingly mirthful disposition, and not intellectually thirsty, he is likely to succeed. The novel is replete with purpose, many pitfalls in the way of rich young gentlemen without developed aptitude for anything but vicious excitement of one kind or another being earnestly pointed out. Mr. Nesfield, in the course of his travels in Egypt was much impressed by the efficiency of government by the kourbash. "Certain natures," he observes, "are incapable of understanding any other argument save that which applies directly to their outward senses. Pain, judiciously inflicted, is a most admirable corrective, and it is to be regretted that flogging is not more universally resorted to, both in England and elsewhere." Mr. Nesfield is to be congratulated on the fact that critics are not permitted to apply "arguments" to the "outward senses" of these "certain natures" which are not unrepresented among literary offenders.

Editor's Notes

- The full title of this book is actually *A Regular Pickle: How he Sowed his Wild Oats.*
- Shaw's longhand comment, written above his scrapbook copy of this review states, "Date lost—Early in 1885." In fact his diary reveals that he wrote it on 21 June 1885 ("Wrote short review for *PMG*" [*Diary,* 92]). It was published a week later.
- Henry W[   ] Nesfield (1846–?), English adventurer and writer. After an undistinguished education at Eton, followed by ten months with a private tutor in Strasbourg, Germany, and a failed attempt to begin a career in a London ship brokerage, Nesfield emigrated to New Zealand in 1865 on the ship "The Star of Greece." Here his occupations were various, including cook on a coasting vessel, hired hand on a sheep station, and, after a very brief return visit to England, manager of a canteen, livery-stable proprietor, actor, agent, groom and coachman, attendant in a private asylum, and storekeeper in the outback of Australia. Finally, after fifteen years in the bush, all recounted most humorously in his book *A Chequered Career* (1887), Nesfield returned to England to stay.
- The kourbash was a hide whip used as an instrument of punishment in Egypt and Turkey.

15 July 1885

TWO NOVELS OF MODERN SOCIETY* [C127]

"A Second Life"

WHEN the heroine of a novel behaves very improperly and gets into trouble in consequence, and when the novelist says nothing in repre-

---

*"A Second Life." By Mrs. Alexander. Three vols. (London: R. Bentley and Son. 1885.)
"Who was then the Gentleman?" By Compton Reade. Three vols. (London: L. and R. Maxwell. 1885.)

hension of her misconduct and much in sympathy with its retributive sorrows, the reader cannot but wonder occasionally whether the author saw anything censurable in her proceedings. Mildred Carr, whose second life is the subject of Mrs. Alexander's last novel, is thrown into poverty at the outset of her career by the death of her father. An opportunity of recovering her lost creature comforts by a marriage with an elderly bill discounter, of coarse exterior and detestable character, offers itself to her. She embraces it without the least scruple, and without a word of remonstrance from her mother. The two women, indeed, congratulate themselves upon the legalized infamy of the younger; and there is not a word in Mrs. Alexander's three volumes that indicates any sense on her part that it was in the least discreditable to them. On the contrary, Mrs. Carr is presented as a type of refined English womanhood, and all her daughter's misfortunes are attributed, not to her crime, but to the villainy of Welby, the bill discounter, who having purchased Mildred, soon makes her feel, not unnaturally, that she has no claim to be mistress either of his house or of herself. His tyranny and her loathing soon becoming unendurable she escapes from him by an extraordinary stratagem, and begins the second life to which the title of the book refers. Even then, though she admits that she has done wrong in breaking her vows, which, under the circumstances, is absurd, she has still not the least remorse for making them, nor any suspicion that her treatment by Welby was no more than she richly deserved. Her subsequent intercourse with a remarkable old blind lady to whom she becomes reader and companion is of some interest; but the greater part of the second and third volumes consists of afternoon calls which are nearly as dull and as like one another as real afternoon calls usually are. In the end, having wounded and invalided the hero to no purpose (he having already gained Mildred's sympathy and extracted a confession of love, from her), Mrs. Alexander grows tired of her work, makes Welby drop dead, and fastens or snips off the loose threads of the narrative anyhow. The book is promising at first, because Mildred's marriage, revolting as it is, is no worse than others contracted in actual life every day by delicately nurtured ladies without any qualms of conscience or any reproaches from without. Her situation, like that of Gwendolen Harleth and Grandcourt in "Daniel Deronda," seems to have been constructed to point a personal and social moral of great scope and interest. When the reader at last discovers that there was no such stuff in the author's thoughts, it is too late to re-estimate the book by the ordinary time-killing standard, and the general impression left is one of disappointment.

"Who Was Then the Gentleman?"

Mr. Compton Reade pays to Charles Reade, whom he claims as his relative, friend, and benefactor, the compliment of a dedication and some injudicious imitation. Charles Reade earned a certain exemption from idle ceremony with his readers by the great pains which he took to master his subjects, and the exactitude with which he fitted them with words. The weight of his work gave force to his style; and he never sought to obtain force on any cheaper terms. Mr. Compton Reade does not seem to understand this. In misguided emulation of his great namesake, he rides roughshod through his story, and with a swaggering disregard not merely of ceremony but of ordinary good manners invents such names for fictitious lawyers as "Messrs. Buggins and Flease," and speaks of a Hibernian lady of spare figure as "skinny Irish Fiddle." His style recalls that of the admiral who, when remonstrated with for his profanity by the bishop, declared that he hated nonsense, and liked to call a spade a spade. To which the bishop replied that he too approved of calling a spade a spade; but that to call it a damned shovel was neither as accurate nor as sensible as calling it an agricultural implement. Much of Mr. Compton Reade's ostentatious downrightness is slovenly rhetoric of the damned shovel order. That his hotheadedness is not wholly an affectation is, however, proved by the want of verisimilitude in many portions of the narrative. A writer must indeed be boiling with indignation at the corruptness of modern society when he represents ladies and gentlemen openly planning and discussing mean villainies and even capital crimes with an impudent consciousness of and indifference to their own guilt, worthy of Wainwright the poisoner. From the pessimist's point of view there is something to be said for the implied opinion that our family affection, honesty, disinterested love, and chivalry are for the most part shams; but no acute pessimist believes that they are hypocritical shams; we are ourselves imposed on no less than we impose on others. In "Who was then the Gentleman?" the fault is not that the characters are for the most part vile scoundrels, but that they are conscious of being scoundrels, and feel towards themselves much as the author feels towards them, barring only his indignation. There is, for example, a vivisector in the story who dissects living animals because their agony is a luxury to him. Granting that this infernal emotion is really active in the laboratory, is it conceivable by any observant person that it is recognized and avowed there, and that physiologists speak of themselves to one another as deliberate voluptuaries in torture? Granting further that even this may be the case, what has it to do with the morality of vivisection? Animals dislike being vivisected, but they also dislike be-ing forced to bear burdens and draw loads. The difference is not in the pain endured by the animal, but in the fact that whereas there is no doubt that an intelligent horse would consent to do a reasonable quan-tity of work for its living if it were capable of economic reasoning, just as men do, it is equally certain that no horse would on any terms submit to vivisection. On this ground the vivisector violates the moral law; and on this ground he may be called hard names. But Mr. Comp-ton Reade does not give any reasons: he proceeds at once to immoder-ate vituperation. Hence he will be dismissed by all advocates of vivisec-tion as an abusive sentimentalist. Nor is he a perfectly successful advocate from an artistic point of view. He writes with all the vigour of indignant conviction on the labour question, the land question, the drink question, the vivisection question, the Church question, and the Irish question; but his labourers, his landlords, his drunkards, his vivisectors, his parsons, and his Paddies are cooked and carved to fit his moral and economic doctrine. If the doctrine were sound and the fig-ures truthfully drawn, they would need no carving; their natural fit-ness to one another would prove the accuracy of the author's reasoning and verify his observation at one stroke. But as a matter of fact the figures have been so denaturalized to make them fit that in some instances—notably those of the aristocratic female characters—they are starkly impossible. Either the reasoning or the observation must be faulty; and no reader will hesitate to condemn the observation. The book, though not excellent as a work of art, is refreshing as a vigorous explosion of what is called "Christian Socialism." The plot turns on a change of babies, whereby a labourer's son takes the place of the heir to a baronetcy; but the reader is not plagued by any of the stock mystifica-tions of this useful old theme. Lady Marmyon, Flaymar the dema-gogue, and Conolly the Irish dynamitard belong to the failures of fic-tion. The other persons concerned are, if not quite lifelike, plausible enough for the ordinary reader to make believe with.

Editor's Notes

▪ Shaw's diary records that he may have begun writing this review on 8 June 1885, continued it on 7 July, and finished it on the ninth. He revised it again on 12 July and revised the proofs on the fourteenth (*Diary*, 95–96).

- "Mrs. Alexander," [pseudonym for Mrs. Annie Hector French] (1825–1902), Irish novelist. She was born in Dublin, and began to write at an early age. She abandoned her literary career on her marriage, but resumed it on the death of her husband. Her output was prodigious, and included verse, *The Legend of Golden Prayer* (1872), and about fifty novels of varying lengths. Some of her most popular were *Which Shall It Be?* (1866), *The Wooing o't* (1873), *The Heritage of Langdale* (1877), *The Admiral's Ward* (1883), *A Life Interest* (1888), *Snare of the Fowler* (1893), and *Mrs. Crichton's Creditors* (1897). In an obituary notice, the New York *Critic* said, "Her stories were not profound, but they were human and sparkled with a wit that must have been her Irish heritage" (*Critic*, [New York], 5:4, October 1902).
- *Daniel Deronda* (1876) was the last of George Eliot's novels. Its heroine, Gwendolen Harleth, marries the arrogant, selfish, yet wealthy Henleigh Grandcourt to save her mother and herself from destitution. Shaw's diary reveals that he read this novel in the British Museum on 20 March 1880 (*Diary*, 40). George Eliot is said to have based the character of Daniel Deronda himself on Edmund Gurney [see page 221].
- Shaw's rebuke to both the heroine and her mother is the seed from which blossoms Tanner's outburst against "fashionable society" in *Man and Superman:*

> What is it? A horrible procession of wretched girls, each in the claws of a cynical, cunning, avaricious, disillusioned, ignorantly experienced, foul-minded old woman whom she calls mother, and whose duty it is to corrupt her mind and sell her to the highest bidder.

- [The Reverend T.] Compton Reade (1834–1909), English author. He graduated from Magdalen College, Oxford, in 1857, and was ordained the same year. From 1867 to 1869 he was vicar of Cassington in Oxfordshire, and subsequently rector of Elton, Durham, of Eldon, Hampshire, and of Kenchester, Herefordshire. His published output was not great, but it included verse, *Basilissa* (1869) and *Pictura Picturæ* (1871); fiction, *Take Care Whom You Trust* (1872); social commentary, *The Pollution of Rivers* (1882), *The Exodus, and other poems* (1883), and a book more descriptive of his prejudices than its subject, *The Smith Family* (1903). Mutual dislike existed between Shaw and Compton Reade, reflected in an exchange of shots (over "sacred music") in *The Dramatic Review* in September of this year.
- Charles Reade had died the previous year. Born in 1814 and educated at Oxford, he began his literary career as a dramatist, his most popular piece being *Masks and Faces,* which was performed at the Haymarket Theatre in 1852. He also wrote numerous novels, his greatest, perhaps, being *The Cloister and the Hearth* (1861). Later he authored the well-known melodrama frequently produced by Sir Henry Irving under the title *The Lyons Mail.*
- Thomas Griffiths Wainewright (1794–1852), who wrote art critiques for *The London Magazine* in the 1820s and exhibited at the Royal Academy, was both a forger and a poisoner, and died a convict in Tasmania. He was the

original of Varney in Bulwer Lytton's fiction *Lucretia* (1846) and suggested to Dickens (who visited him in Newgate prison) his sketch *Hunted Down*. He was a friend of Charles Lamb and the subject of Oscar Wilde's Memoir "Pen, Pencil and Poison," published in *Intentions* (1891).

▪ Shaw's opinion of the practice of vivisection was unwavering. His first printed pronouncement on the subject of cruel experiments on animals in the name of Science occurs just three months before this review, in the April 1885 episode of *To-Day*'s serialization of Shaw's novel *Cashel Byron's Profession*, where Byron, the boxer, defends his profession by contrasting its cleanliness with that of a French doctor who "bakes dogs in ovens." In the present review Shaw tackles the common rebuttal that the antivivisectionist is merely an "abusive sentimentalist." Eight years later, putting his preaching into practice, Shaw, in *The Philanderer*, attacks vivisection on moral grounds; and, no doubt remembering his own censure of Compton Reade, he anticipates and outwits his critics by making the vivisector himself the sentimentalist.

27 July 1885

COBBETT'S *RURAL RIDES** [C130]

WILLIAM COBBETT was so deficient in our national inordinate capacity for living in a fool's paradise that he was probably more dangerous to corrupt Governments than any single man known to English history, excepting only Jonathan Swift. Not that he was, like Swift, a pessimist, or, like Thackeray, a disappointed optimist. He had no appetite for anything but the truth, to the weight of which, when expressed in clear language, he ascribed the convincing power of his writings. Had he been able to see all the pregnant facts of his time as clearly as he saw many that the politicians of his day were blind to, and had he also been able to make a synthesis of his facts in the manner of Ricardo and Marx, or Darwin, he would almost have brought about the millennium single-handed; for he had not only the common readiness to say what he thought, but the far rarer courage to ignore nothing that he saw. When the nation swept its dust out of sight under the State

---

*"Rural Rides in the Counties of Surrey, Kent, &c., &c., during the Years 1821 to 1832, with Economical and Political Observations." By the late William Cobbett, M.P. for Oldham. (London: Reeves and Turner. 12s. 6d. 1885.)

furniture, and then pretended that the country was clean, Cobbett, destitute of good taste, which he quite clearly saw to be an apologetic name for moral cowardice, repudiated the fiction, raked the dust out, and clamoured for its removal. He reminds us of the boatswain in "The Tempest," who, declining to soften the fact that the sea was likely to swallow up the king without the slightest regard for his rank, was cursed by the king's brother as "a bawling, blasphemous, incharitable dog." Cobbett was as plain spoken and irrefutable as the boatswain, and was accordingly rewarded by "thirty years of calumnies poured out incessantly from the poisonous mouths and pens of three hundred mercenary villains called newspaper editors and reporters." "But," he says, "I did not sink, no, nor bend, beneath the heavy and reiterated blows of the accursed system, which I have dealt back, blow for blow; and, blessed be God, I now see it reel."

Cobbett was nearly sixty when he began to write descriptions of his rural rides. They bring him before us as still fiercely resentful of his ruinous imprisonment for "sedition," which in 1810 was as useful for the muzzling of inconveniently progressive editors as "blasphemy" and "obscenity" are at present. No private enmities seem to have troubled him; but at the foes of the commonweal (and he generally concluded that a foe of Cobbett must be a foe to the commonweal) he loses no chance of dealing either a sarcasm with the slyness duly accentuated by italics, a volley of hearty vituperation, or even a round oath. "I see," says he, "that Mr. Curteis has thought it necessary to state in the public papers that *he* had nothing to do with my being at the dinner at Battle! Who the d—— thought he had?" To the subject of the war taxation, the suspension of cash payments by the Bank, and the over-issue and consequent depreciation of inconvertible paper money, Cobbett alludes at every opportunity with studied extravagance, attributing to it not only the growth of "wens" or suburbs upon towns by the villas built for persons living unproductively on the interest of the national debt, but also many deplorable evils in the condition of the agricultural labourer which the resumption of cash payments has certainly done nothing to remove. This, and his apparent belief that the stoppage of outdoor relief would, by compelling the farmers to raise wages, benefit the labourers whose pay had to be supplemented by it to raise it to subsistence point, seems to prove that Cobbett never succeeded in plunging deep enough through the scum of political abuses to get to the bottom of the labour question. Hence it is not surprising to find him speaking contemptuously of William Petty, Robert Owen, and Ricardo, whom he dubbed "The Oracle." That any man who had been a stockbroker could possibly have anything to teach honest William Cobbett evidently never occurred to him: he displays quite a high Tory instinct of revolt against the spectacle of English statesmen condescending to defer to the utterances of a man who had amassed wealth "by watching the turn of the market." It is noteworthy that against Ricardo as an economist he has nothing to say. But his eloquence on the subject of "beastly Malthus and his nasty disciples" would, if it were now available, considerably enliven an emigration meeting at the Mansion House. He rages against "the folly, the stupidity, the inanity, the presumption, the insufferable emptiness and insolence and barbarity of those numerous wretches who have now the audacity to propose to transport the people of England upon the principle of the monster Malthus, who has furnished the unfeeling oligarchs and their toad-eaters with the pretence that man has a natural propensity to breed faster than food can be raised for his increase." He proceeds to combat "this mixture of madness and blasphemy" on the ground recently reoccupied by Mr. Henry George. Another favourite topic of his is the Reformation, which he harped on in the interests of Catholic emancipation. With no prevision of Mr. Froude, he dwells on "the infamy of that ruffian, Henry VIII"; launches all the invective of Billingsgate at the memory of Elizabeth; and glorifies not only Catherine of Arragon, but all her relatives, Ferdinand and Isabella the Catholic included. "Tom Cranmer" is "a perfidious hypocrite and double-apostate"; and a book still venerated by all good Evangelicals is described as "Fox's Book of Liars." These opinions seem to have satisfied Cobbett as strictly logical deductions from the fact that the Reformation was practically a wholesale confiscation of the property of the people, administered more or less honestly in their interests by the Church, for the benefit of the nobles of Henry's court.

It is impossible to cite here a tithe of the deliverances of Cobbett on questions that are still burning. On most of them he says the right thing (so far as we, fifty years after his death, can pretend to have ascertained it) at least once, even when he elsewhere says the wrong thing, or rather the irrelevant thing, half a dozen times. In treating of free trade, his exposure of the absurdity of relieving the country by prohibiting the importation of foreign corn might serve the Cobden Club for the text of a new pamphlet. But, on the other hand, his contemptuous repudiation of the Manchester school Free Trade as a panacea for poverty, and his appreciation of the motives that tempted "the cotton lords" to advocate it, would content even Mr. Hyndman. His happy phrase, "Reciprocity all on one side," is likely to come into fashion again. Neither fair trade nor free trade (as he knew it) could make a monomaniac of him. Only in contemplating the desperate inconveniences of the suspension of cash payments and the spread of the funding system does he seem to have mistaken the smoke for the fire. Like most Radicals of his time, too, he expected too much from the Reform Bill.

The reprint of the "Rural Rides" has been edited by the Rev. Pitt Cobbett very sensibly and faithfully. There is no tampering with the text, no Bowdlerization, no editorial impertinences. Mr. Pitt Cobbett evidently considers that his author went rather fast in one or two places; but he does not complain nor interfere, he simply hints that he does not endorse. The additional information is given in the right quantity and at the right place. There is an excellent sketch of the author's life; and there is an index in which there is only one odd entry. That one is "*Mr.* Johnson," alluded to in the text as "old dread-death and dread-devil Johnson," a "teacher of moping and melancholy," and "a time-serving, mean, dastardly old pensioner." The editor seems to have been unable to believe that this could refer to the famous doctor. But it is not less appreciative than the editor's own note elsewhere about Robert Owen. Men of all ranks and occupations, from statesmen to private soldiers, gardeners, and labourers, will find the "Rural Rides" still full of interest. It is usually the fate of the journalist-agitator to lose all power of writing otherwise than polemically and on the politics of the hour. Cobbett, after decades of such warfare, had as much to say about methods of cultivating mangel wurzel as about Lord Liverpool; and he gave as much prominence to his opinion of women and shoemakers (favourable in both instances) as to his estimate of Sidmouth, whom he charges with his imprisonment and ruin. His creed, deficient in scientific accuracy from the point of view of modern sociology, but sound as far as it goes, is contained in his reply to the bountiful Sir Thomas Baring: "Amongst the labouring people," he says, "the first thing you have to look after is common honesty, speaking the truth, and refraining from thieving; and to secure these the labourer must have his belly-full and be free from fear; and this belly-full must come to him from out of his wages, and not from benevolence of any description."

Editor's Notes

- According to his diary, Shaw wrote "part of" this review on 21 July 1885 and finished it the following day (*Diary*, 98).

- William Cobbett (1763–1835), English politician and social reformer. The self-educated son of a country laborer, he served as a soldier in St. John, New Brunswick, from 1785–91. After his discharge, he brought an action of peculation against some of his former officers and, in 1792, to avoid prosecution, retired to America, where he wrote pro-British pamphlets, under the pseudonym of "Peter Porcupine." He returned to England in 1800, becoming first a Tory journalist, and, four years later, a writer in the radical interest. He published "Parliamentary Debates" (afterwards taken over by Hansard), wrote an English grammar, and numerous books on economics and other subjects. In 1832 he became a member of Parliament. His *Rural Rides*, originally collected in 1830, are today the best known of his writings.

- David Ricardo (1772–1823), English writer on economics and politician. Born in London, he left school at the age of fourteen to join a brokerage house. By his mid-twenties he had made a fortune on the London Stock Exchange, and then devoted himself to the study of economics. His major work *Principles of Political Economy and Taxation* (1817) is primarily concerned with the causes determining the distribution of wealth. In this his famous theory of rent (which influenced Marx) played an important part. Simply put, Ricardo believed that wages are determined by the price of food, which is determined by the cost of production, itself determined by the amount of labor required to produce the food; in other words, labor determines value. For the last four years of his life Ricardo was an influential member of Parliament in London.

- (Sir) William Petty (1623–87), political economist and friend of Hobbes. For the Commonwealth he carried out the Down Survey of forfeited lands in Ireland, perhaps the first attempt on such a scale to carry out a scientific survey. After the Restoration, Petty was knighted, and in 1662 became a founding member of the Royal Society. He published economic treatises, the chief of which, *Political Arithmetic* (1690), dealt with what today would be called statistics.

- Robert Owen (1771–1858), Welsh social reformer. In spite of little schooling (he began work in a textile shop at the age of ten) at nineteen he was manager of one of the largest cotton-spinning mills in Lancashire. In 1799, he and his associates bought the spinning mills in New Lanark, an area of great poverty in Scotland, where he put into practice the social theories for which he later became famous, establishing schools (including the first nursery school in Great Britain), improvements in housing and sanitation, and a store at which goods could be purchased for little more than cost. When the Factory Act of 1819 contained only a few of his proposals, he became disillusioned with reform schemes and sought instead to change the social structure of society by establishing cooperative communities in which members would share the products of their labor. However, establishment of union-owned industries in 1832 provoked such government opposition that Owen was forced to dissolve the movement in 1834, and he withdrew from active participation in labor affairs. Nevertheless, for the rest of his life, Owen promoted his socialist and educational theories, adding to *A New View of Society*, which had appeared in 1813, *Revolution in Mind and Practice* (1849) and his autobiography in 1857–58.

- Thomas Robert Malthus (1766–1834), English economist. In 1798 he published *An Essay on the Principle of Population* in which he argued that population increases faster than the means of its subsistence, with the result that living standards are depressed to a bare minimum. Whenever there is a relative gain in production over population growth, Malthus argued, it merely stimulates the latter; whereas if population overtakes production, its growth is checked by famine, disease, or war. Malthus's theories caused a storm of controversy, contradicting, as they did, the optimistic theories of the nineteenth century; but they received support from many who were opposed to bettering the conditions of the poor, or who embraced Malthus's solution of "moral restraint" to keep down the population. His theories influenced Ricardo, whose theory of the distribution of wealth contains Malthusian elements; while, for Darwin, Malthus's phrase "the struggle for existence" found an echo in his own discoveries and, when applied to all organic life, provided the numerical surplus necessary for natural selection. From 1805 until his death, Malthus was professor of political economy at the College of the East India Company at Haileybury. His later writings include *An Inquiry into the Nature and Progress of Rent* (1815) and a treatise on *The Principles of Political Economy* (1820). Almost a year after writing the above review, Shaw was reading Malthus again, in preparation for a lecture he was to give on 20 June 1886, entitled "Socialism and Malthusianism," in which he found the two incompatible.

- Henry George (1839–97), American economist. In 1871, George wrote a pamphlet *Our Land and Land Policy*, in which he argued that the boom in the West, resulting from railroad development, was actually impoverishing most people and making only a few rich, because land ownership was concentrated in the hands of the few. The answer, according to George, was the imposition of a single tax on land values. He proposed to retain private ownership, requiring only that society appropriate the socially created value of land, which increases in value largely as a result of community growth. These ideas (influenced in part by those of Ricardo) were set out in his book *Progress and Poverty* (1879), which made him famous as an opponent of injustice in modern capitalism. In the 1880s George wrote and lectured on his ideas, touring the United States, Ireland, and Great Britain. During one of these tours on 5 September 1882, he was the author of Shaw's conversion to Socialism when he lectured at the Memorial Hall, Farringdon Street, London, on "Land Nationalization and the Single Tax." In 1886, Henry George came second in a three-man race for the mayoralty of New York city. He had enjoyed the support of both labor and liberal groups; indeed, Shaw himself attended a meeting at St. Andrews Hall, London, on 1 November 1886, to support George's candidacy. Two years later, at the request of the Christian Socialist Stewart Headlam, Shaw sent George a copy of his paper "The Transition to Social Democracy," published in Annie Besant's magazine *Our Corner* in November 1888; and the following year he met George personally and reported in *The International Review* on the debate held in July of that year between George and H. M. Hyndman, "Single Tax vs. Social Democracy." In 1897, running as an Independent Democrat, George again made a bid for the mayoralty of New York, but died during the campaign. His other writings include *Social Problems* (1884), *Protection or Free Trade* (1886), and *The Science of Political Economy* (1897). Shaw maintained his respect for George, briskly dismissing Gronlund's attempted demonstration of the insufficiency of his theory [see pages 436–39 below].

▪ James Anthony Froude (1818–94), English historian. From 1856 to 1870 he published his *History of England from the Fall of Wolsey to the Defeat of the Spanish Armada*. Presumably it is to the notorious inaccuracies in this work that Shaw is referring. Much of Froude's writing, including *The English in Ireland in the Eighteenth Century* (1872–74), and even his work as Carlyle's literary executor, met with severe criticism. Nevertheless, he was appointed Regius Professor of Modern History at Oxford, two years before his death.

▪ Richard Cobden (1804–65), English radical. His public career was launched by the publication in 1835–36 of two pamphlets advocating free trade and a foreign policy of peace and nonintervention. He entered Parliament in 1841 and was instrumental in the repeal of the Corn Laws. He was opposed to Factory legislation, believing in a "laissez-faire" policy. The Cobden Club was founded in London in 1866 to promote free-trade economics, and it became a center for political propaganda on those lines. Significantly, an engraved portrait of Richard Cobden hangs in Roebuck Ramsden's study in *Man and Superman*.

▪ Henry Mayers Hyndman (1842–1921), English pioneer Socialist. He came from a wealthy, well-educated family, receiving his own education first from private tutors and later at Cambridge. As a young man he traveled in Italy (assisting Garibaldi's forces in the conflict with Austria), and then in Australia and Polynesia. Returning to London, he worked as a political journalist in the 1870s, contributing articles to the *Pall Mall Gazette* criticizing the incompetence of the British authorities in India. In 1880, on a trip to Utah in the United States, he was finally converted to Socialism by reading a French translation of Marx's *Das Kapital*. Back in England, he struck up an acquaintance with Marx himself, but when he wrote a book (*England for All*) in which he borrowed, without acknowledgment, many of Marx's views, a breach developed between the two men. On 8 June 1881, Hyndman started the Democratic Federation. William Morris was an early recruit, as was Edward Pease. Two years later the name had been changed to Social Democratic Federation (SDF for short), and its manifesto *Socialism Made Plain* advocated the overthrow of the Capitalist system. From the SDF a splinter group, wishing to form an association "whose ultimate aim shall be the reconstruction of Society . . . to secure the general welfare and happiness," gave rise to the Fabian Society in January 1884. On 5 September of that year, Shaw formally joined the Fabians. The two societies were not initially rivals, and Shaw was for a time a "candidate member" of the SDF, but he soon became irritated by Hyndman's rancorous and revolutionary speeches and disagreed with him over what Shaw considered a fatal flaw in Marx's derivation of surplus. The two men seem to have regarded one another with admiration, notwithstanding their political differences, and Shaw later turned his friend's mannerisms to good use, according to Henderson, who claimed,

> The mannerisms of Craven [in *The Philanderer* (1893)] "now really," in especial, are taken directly, Mr. Shaw once told me, from Mr. H. M. Hyndman, the English Socialist leader. (A. Henderson, *George Bernard Shaw: His Life and Work* [London: 1911], 298).

25 August 1885

FOLK LORE, ENGLISH AND SCOTCH* [C137]

"'Twixt Ben Nevis and Glencoe"

THE banished Duke in "As You Like It," who found sermons in stones, has probably often been envied on Saturday afternoons by ecclesiastics at a loss for the morrow's discourse. He also found books in the running brooks, but on this point, and probably on the other too, he is equalled by Dr. Alexander Stewart, who finds articles in streams, storms, rats, mice, birds, and fishes; and strings them into books well padded with anecdotes which, to turn his favourite phrase, he makes no apology for quoting at full length. Such books are not fair game for the reviewer: they are addressed to children of all ages who are willing to shut their eyes and open their mouths. In this attitude the grown-up children will presently be gratified by some startling flattery. "Unrivalled as a soldier, and almost faultless as a man," says the author, "you will have some difficulty, if you try, in finding any one entitled for an instant, and on any claims whatever, to stand with the slightest pretensions to equality of stature besides the, perhaps, greatest man of his age—James Graham, Earl and Marquis of Montrose." The reader, thus liberally blarneyed, may modestly disclaim the military skill attributed to him; but he cannot be insensible to the assurance

---

*"'Twixt Ben Nevis and Glencoe." By the Rev. Alexander Stewart, LL.D., F.S.A. Scotland. (Edinburgh: William Paterson. 1885.)
  "The Gentleman's Magazine Library—English Traditions and Foreign Customs." Edited by George Laurence Gomme, F.S.A. (London: Elliot Stock. 1885.)

that he is "almost faultless as a man," though the compliment must fall somewhat flat on lady readers, who will possibly contend that Dr. Stewart has made a slip and that the superlative soldier and excellent man referred to is none other than Montrose. In some instances the author's appreciation of the details of a subject overbalances his judgment of it as a whole. For example, in discoursing on rats, he opines that "the scene in 'Hamlet' would lose much of its grim humour and effectiveness if it were not for the rat behind the arras." This almost reminds one of Mr. Wopsle's dresser, who maintained that the secret of all great actors of "Hamlet" was that they never permitted their tights to be seen in profile. Again, when Dr. Stewart saw an old woman cure a bad case of colic by administering water in which a redhot flat-iron had been plunged, he seems to have believed that the charm lay in the flat-iron, and that a pint of water warmed in the usual way in a kettle would have been of no avail. Dr. Stewart, in fact, has the faults of his qualities. His love of legend stretches his credulity, just as his love of animals impairs his grasp of Shakspearean tragedy. His admiration of the great poets is frank hero-worship; and he esteems himself fortunate in having seen an aërolite exactly corresponding to the meteoric phenomenon described by Homer in the famous passage in the fourth book of the Iliad, which tells of the descent of Pallas from Olympus to the plains of Troy. Pope translated it as a comet, and Professor Blackie more cautiously calls it a meteor star; but Dr. Stewart has identified the genuine article as what the Highlanders call a *drèag*. He proposes that it shall henceforth be called "a Minervalite," and engages to call it so himself "in all time coming." The name is not a handsome or very convenient one, but it may be forgiven to an amiable and chatty naturalist, who, by acting as a sort of scientific and literary ragpicker, has managed to provide us with a miscellany free from sensationalism, and yet full of interest for the snapper-up of unconsidered trifles.

"THE GENTLEMAN'S MAGAZINE LIBRARY"

The Psychical Society will find plenty of ghost stories in Mr. G. Laurence Gomme's selection of such of these notes and anecdotes as relate to English traditional lore and the customs of foreign countries and peoples. The classification is not always as happy as the selection. "Ghosts" seems hardly the proper heading for the following:—"At the Council of Trent, the Legate Crescentio, having long laboured at his despatches, rose from his chair and thought he saw an ugly dog advance and run under the table. In haste he called for his servants, but no dog could be found. The Legate took to his bed and died of fright." Notwithstanding the respect due to the memory of Crescentio, Mr. Gomme might, without impropriety, have put this case under the heading "Delirium Tremens." The story of the mysterious red man who haunted Napoleon is a genuine—that is, not a true—ghost story. "Who the red man really was has never been known; but that such a person obtained an interview with Napoleon seems to have been placed beyond a doubt." This modest comment is in the finest manner of the ghost-storyteller, whose audience would doubtless be disappointed beyond measure if the red man were reduced to fact as prosaically as the once equally mysterious black man who ordered Mozart's requiem. The accounts of the bite of the tarantula are masterpieces of flagrant mendacity; and it is greatly to be feared that Stephen Storage, who in 1753 obliged the *Gentleman's Magazine* with a "distinct detail" of how he had been "instrumental" (the instrument was his violin) "at the cure of a poor plowman that was bit by that insect," is now wishing that he had restrained his invention within reasonable bounds. During the eighteenth century tourists were evidently not only permitted to tell lies, but encouraged to do so. The *Gentleman's Magazine* must have acted as a powerful stimulus to the imagination of the travelled. This was hardly needed; for more than a century before the magazine was started we find so simple and frank a soldier as Othello confessing before the council at Venice that he had beguiled his father-in-law with tales of men whose heads beneath their shoulders grew.

Mr. Gomme, like Dr. Stewart, has furnished his book with an index, which will be of great service to persons in search of information on all sorts of subjects. The general reader, turning over the pages, will learn many things that are not of the slightest importance to him, but which he may, nevertheless, wish to know because other people occasionally write or speak of them.

Editor's Notes

- Shaw's diary for 21 August records simply that he "began review for *PMG*. Read rather discursively at Museum for it." He continued writing it the following day, and finished and sent it off on the twenty-third (*Diary*, 105–6).
- Alexander Stewart (1829–1901), Scottish scholar, naturalist, poet, and antiquary. He was born in Benbecula, the son of David Stewart, an Inland Revenue

officer, and educated at the University of St. Andrews. After obtaining his M.A., he was appointed missionary at Oban Chapel in 1849. He was ordained on 10 April 1851. Later he received an LL.D. from St. Andrew's University. He married Mary Janet Morrison on 24 November 1852, who bore him three children, a daughter, Fassifern Cameron (1854), and twins, a boy and girl, Kenneth Morrison and Christina Mary (1855). In addition to 'Twixt Ben Nevis and Glencoe reviewed above, he also edited (with a memoir) James Logan's The Scottish Gael (1876), and wrote Nether Lochaber: The Natural History, Legends, and Folk-lore of the Western Highlands (Edinburgh, 1883). His contributions to literature were written under the name "Nether Lochaber."

- Mr. Wopsle is a friend of Joe Gargery's in Great Expectations. At first a parish clerk, he afterwards becomes an actor in London under the stage name of Mr. Waldengarver.

- An aerolite is a meteroic stone, or meteorite.

- [Sir] George Laurence Gomme (1853–1916), English archaeologist, anthropologist, and antiquary. He was born in London, and educated at the City of London School. He became a lecturer at the London School of Economics, and was for a time Statistical Officer and Clerk to the London County Council. He edited the Gentleman's Magazine Library from 1888 to 1906. In his time he also edited The Antiquary, The Archæological Review, and the Folklore Journal. In fact he was the original founder and subsequent secretary of the Folklore Society, and later Secretary to the Lieutenancy of London. Among his publications are Primitive Folk-Moots (1880), Folklore Relics of Early Village Life (1883), The Literature of Local Institutions (1886), The Village Community (1889), Folklore as an Historical Science (1908), and The Making of London (1911).

3 September 1885

GHOST STORIES* [C140]

"I WANTS to make your flesh creep," said the fat boy in "Pickwick." This expresses the normal attitude of the ghost story teller. Cups of tea and pegs of brandy have wrecked our national nerve and made us afraid to go upstairs in the dark, afraid to look under the bed for a burglar, afraid to put out the candle without having looked, afraid to keep our eyes open lest we should see something, and afraid to keep

---

*"Woven in Darkness: Stories, Essays, and Dreamwork." By W. W. Fenn. Two vols. (London: Kelly and Co. 1885.)

them shut lest there should be something there to see. Yet we have writers who do not hesitate to begin at us in this fashion:—

"It was a quaint old house, with all sorts of mysterious corners, &c." We know that this will in the course of a page or two lead up to a blood-curdling bedroom, in which the writer assures us that owing to "an undefined uneasiness—a vague presentiment of something to come"—he could not sleep. "I have never," proceeds the narrator, judicially, "been a believer in the supernatural. I shall merely describe, as simply and faithfully as possible, what took place, without pretending to assign any reason or explanation, &c." Then comes a footstep; or a strange sensation of being no longer alone; or an overpowering dread such as seizes us at the culmination of a nightmare; or a blueish light; or "my name pronounced in a whisper that reached my ear distinctly and unmistakably, though it seemed to be wafted from an infinite distance;" or (coming to the point at once) a female form, through which the folds of the heavy black curtain were distinctly visible. Sometimes it is an old man instead of a young woman; but whichever it is, and whatever may be the matter with him or her—whether it is a buried chest with a will in it, or an unburied skeleton with a knife in it—the effect on the reader is the same: he passes the night in abject terror; and finds his heart beating up to 250 when the window rattles, and stopping dead when he catches sight of his dressing-gown hanging up on a nail in the door. The worst of it is that he knows perfectly well that his tormentor never really saw a ghost in his life, nor ever slept in anything quainter than a two-pair back within easy walking distance of the British Museum reading-room. Yet he asseverates the truth of his tale with a circumstantiality and solemnity which no mere novelist or the like dare affect. There must surely be an ethic even in fiction against which such bogey tales are an offence.

The writer cannot pretend ignorance of the suffering he causes. The terrors endured by himself in the past are his guide to the soft places in our nerve-centres when he tortures us. He has become like Macbeth, who once remarked to his armourer that the time had been when his senses would have cooled to hear a night-shriek, and his fell of hair would at a dismal treatise rouse and stir, as life were in't. Yet even the superstitious Scotchman became hardened by supping full of horrors; and so do the writers of the dismal treatises. Direness, familiar to their slaughterous thoughts, cannot once start them. But they ought to consider that other people are kept awake and frightened out of their wits by books about ghosts. It may be argued that they are not compelled to read such books unless they like them; but it is seldom possible to see the danger until the mischief is done. One cannot be expected to know what is in a book without a glance at the table of contents. That table, in the case of the two volumes by Mr. Fenn which suggested this remonstrance, contains the word "ghosts" in the very first line. Then come "In the Room with the Arras," "The Haunted Rock," "The Hand on the Latch," "The Face at the Window" (in such a connection this title alone would make a strong tea-drinker scream with terror), and "The Ghost on the Chain Pier."

Perhaps the reader is not imaginative enough to receive a suggestion of the supernatural from such a phrase as "In the Room with the Arras." But let him just take the reference—page twenty—and turn to the story. Here is the first line, as printed. "The Room with the Arras! And I was to sleep there!" After seeing so much, one may as well read on, since one's hair cannot well stand straighter on end than those two sentences have set it already. But the evil of the story does not end with the return of composure and the morning sun. The reader meets a friend next evening, and, if at a loss for conversation, as friends generally are, is as likely as not to mention a curious tale that he was reading last night. The friend receives the tale coldly, evidently not thinking much of it. Presently he remarks, "I know a strange circumstance" (or a rum thing, or a queer start, or a most extraordinary game, according to his habit of speech) "that really happened." He did not exactly see it himself; but he has it on unimpeachable authority—that (if you press him for the name) of Smith, who is incapable of mendacity. The reader admits Smith to be the soul of honour, as all ghost-story authenticators are, but suggests a merely natural explanation of the strange circumstance vouched for. His friend will instantly invent some particular to defeat the explanation. This is quite certain. Many a man is too truthful to invent or even exaggerate a ghost story; but let him once commit himself to one by relating it, and he will steep himself to the lips in falsehood sooner than allow it to be desupernaturalized by the substitution of natural causes for the alleged ghostly ones. Thus are ghost stories even more fatal to our candour than to our courage.

Mr. Fenn's book, if the above considerations might be waived, would be irreproachable in its kind. It's title, "Woven in Darkness," refers to the author's loss of sight, which he alludes to with perfect tact, gratifying that curiosity as to the sensations of the blind which most readers feel, but which they shrink from expressing because they cannot do so without alluding to a painful subject. Mr. Fenn has the gift of making all subjects pleasant. Even his ghosts are not harrowing; and he has, in "The Ghost on the Chain Pier," ingeniously used the conclusions of the Psychical Research Society as to apparitions of the living, to dissociate ghosts from the mortuary associations from which all their horrors spring.

Editor's Notes

- Shaw's diary reveals that he wrote this review on 31 August 1885 (*Diary*, 108).
- W(illiam) W(ilthew) Fenn (?1827–1906), English landscape painter and limner, a follower of Cox and Constable. From his first exhibition in 1848, his paintings were shown in the Royal Academy twenty-three times (as well as in the British Institute and in Suffolk Street). In his youth he had been a friend of Millais and Michael Halliday (the latter an enthusiastic but not very skilled artist), both of whom took an active part in encouraging Fenn into his new career as a writer, when his blindness came upon him in middle years. He died in London on 19 December 1906.
- The fat boy in *The Pickwick Papers* is Joe, servant to Mr. Wardle and a youth of enormous appetite and obesity. He expresses the desire to "make your flesh creep" in chapter 8 of Dickens's novel. However, he hopes to carry out his intention not by telling a ghost story, but by reporting to old Mrs. Wardle the amorous exploits of her daughter Miss Rachael and the susceptible Mr. Tracy Tupman.
- A two-pair back was a second story lodging at the back of a house.
- The Psychical Research Society, more properly called the Society for Psychical Research, was primarily the brainchild of Professor W. F. Barrett who, in 1876, offered the British Association a paper on his experiments in thought transference, which prompted considerable press interest. After this, Barrett conceived the idea that a group of spiritualists should take part with a group of scientists and scholars in a dispassionate investigation of psychical phenomena. On 5 and 6 January 1882 at 38 Great Russell Street, London, a conference was held at which the foundation of a society was proposed. The Society was formally constituted on 20 February 1882 with the philosopher Henry Sidgwick [see page 335 below] as its first president. In 1886 there were internal dissensions over the slate-writing feats of William Eglinton [see pages 112–13 below and 115] between the scientists and the spiritualists, resulting in the resignation of many of the latter from the society, which left Sidgwick and his friends in virtual control. Since he was a highly respected scholar (he became Professor of Moral Philosophy at Cambridge University in 1883), Sidgwick, who remained the Society's president for nine of its first eighteen years, exercised a beneficent influence on its reputation, particularly since he was himself known as a cautious man in the matter of accepting psychic

phenomena. The Society certainly flourished under his leadership: its membership grew from 150 in 1883 to 707 in 1890, its members including Gladstone, Balfour, and no less than eight Fellows of the Royal Society. Among the literati whose names were connected with the society in those years were Lewis Carroll, Tennyson, and Ruskin. In addition to its interest in apparitions and supernatural manifestations, the Society for Psychical Research concerned itself with thought transference, hypnotism, and extrasensory perception; thus, its investigations, though unorthodox by today's standards, bordered on more orthodox, yet still novel branches of study, such as psychology. That, in spite of his scepticism, Shaw took the Society seriously, at least until 1887, is clear from his *Diary,* which reveals that he attended meetings of the Society for Psychical Research on 26 June 1885 and again on 29 October 1885, on the second occasion to hear Myers [see page 104 below] on "Human Personality." On this occasion Podmore [see page 222 below] suggested he sleep in a haunted house in south London. Shaw did so that night, and had a "terrific nightmare" (*Diary,* 121). On 6 March 1886, Shaw listened to W. F. Barrett speak on "Certain Inexplicable Phenomena"; on 3 May, Mrs. Sidgwick on "Spiritualism"; and on 23 April 1887, Gurney [see pages 221–22 below] on "Recent Advances in Hypnotism." That the Society took Shaw's criticisms seriously is also clear from the angry response to his review of *Phantasms of the Living,* in their newspaper *Light* [see pages 329–30 below].

17 September 1885

*PHYSICAL EXPRESSION** [C144]

THIS fifty-second volume of Messrs. Kegan Paul and Trench's International Scientific Series is introduced by Dr. Francis Warner as the forerunner of a larger work to be addressed to a more select audience. It may therefore be regarded as a provisional arrangement of his views in the shape of some easy reading on the subject for the general public. It might have been rendered still easier by avoiding some unnecessary repetition, and omitting some clinical notes that are not much to the point. The book is indifferently put together, but it has been carefully written, and more than this can perhaps hardly be claimed from a busy physician who is only secondarily an author, and who, writing for a popular audience, is avowedly not putting his best leg foremost. Physi-

---

*"Physical Expression." By Francis Warner, M.D., Lond., F.R.C.P. (London: Kegan Paul, Trench and Co. 1885.)

cal expression is a subject full of interest in a society like ours. When we are young our inordinate fondness for theatricals and novel-writing leads us to simulate and describe emotions which we do not feel. Later, when the struggle for existence becomes too serious for such follies, real emotions come to us in battalions; but we take as much trouble to conceal them as we formerly did to affect them, imagining that our livelihood depends chiefly on the success of a systematic imposture which we call "keeping up appearances." Life comes to mean finance; and finance is regarded as a vast game of poker, in which fortunes are to be made by desperate and destitute men if they can bear themselves like millionaires. In such a society a knowledge of the symptoms of any particular state of mind will be turned to account by a clever comedian to simulate or dissemble that state of mind, as his interest may dictate; and the cleverest comedian, other things being equal, is likely to be the most successful man. But "other things" here includes knowledge of the symptoms—of expression, in short. How if the clever comedian gives a wrong reading of his part through ignorance of the science of expression? How if, through such ignorance, we are continually expressing the truth about ourselves unawares? Let us take the common case of A invited to dinner by B, whom he hates, envies, and fears. A, of course, accepts the invitation, and is careful to express himself verbally as an affectionately respectful admirer of his host. Facially, too, A can dissemble his feelings: his social training teaches him to keep his dog tooth covered even though he may never have read Darwin's admirable analysis of sneering. Yet B may discover the truth from A's hands. Hands, according to the researches of Dr. Warner, tell us so much that an applicant for a policy of life insurance generally wishes to conceal that by the time the subject is fully worked out mankind will, in self-defence, live with its hands in its pockets. Such rough classification as feeble hand, convulsive hand, energetic hand, nervous hand, and so forth, will in time lead to a subtle discrimination of incredulous hand, disparaging hand, or even hand expressive of doubts as to the price of the wine and the age of the hostess. It will be useless then to close the doors of speech and grimace against detection. For each of these closed doors there are, it appears, a hundred and fifty standing wide open to the man of science.

The legion novelist, too, hitherto subject only to reproaches for bad taste, must now prepare to face absolute condemnation on scientific proof of error. Hitherto writing a novel has been like spelling Mr. Weller's name, a matter of taste and fancy. The heroine has turned bright red or deathly pale quite arbitrarily. Her hands have clutched and waved, her arms tossed, her pupils dilated, and her voice sunk to a whisper or risen to a scream, her lips moved silently or compressed themselves into a thin red streak, just as the romancer ordained. But the criticism of the future will diagnose all such symptoms, and judge the work accordingly. The *Lancet* will devote a column to "novels of the week," and no novelist's library will be complete without the works of Sir Charles Bell, Darwin and Dr. Warner. The actor will be even worse off. He will be expected to determine Hamlet's diathesis from his acts and speeches. Given the diathesis and the transient condition, restful or convulsed, of the patient, the posture and movements of the hand, the average twitching per minute of the eyebrows, and the general kinetic action proper to the Prince of Denmark will be immutably fixed, leaving nothing to the actor's genius except the putting of it all into stage perspective. The new school, insisting on rigid determining causes for every tone, gesture, and colour, will recognize taste only in the choice of subject. The subject once chosen, the sole admissible treatment will be an accurate statement of the inevitable consequences. The interest will be in the complication of the problem. The novelty of this method is only apparent: critics and artists have always pursued it more or less blindly. Happily, art does not become less charming as she turns to science. Already the attitude of the Dying Gladiator has been accounted for by Sir Charles Bell, and the hand of the Venus de Medici classified by Dr. Warner. No falling-off in the attractiveness of either statue has yet been observed in consequence.

Dr. Warner has a chapter on art criticism at the end of his book; but his sympathies are those of the physician rather than the artist. The treatises of Leonardo da Vinci and Raphael Mengs, and Siddons's translation of Engel (whose work on stage gesture should, for the sake of the illustrations, be at least looked at in the original), are included in the bibliography which he gives; but it is evident that he is at heart less interested in the expression of the emotions than in the expression of those functions with the derangement of which the physician has to deal. To him the expression of nutrition is of far greater importance than the disposition of the features in rage, love, despair, and the rest. And from the point of view of the general welfare, intimately connected as that is with the general digestion, it cannot be said that his preference needs any apology. In his acceptance of the theory of evolution there is none of that reserve which disables many writers of an earlier generation from conciliating the large body of scientific amateurs who can hardly take in any subject that is not stated for them in terms of the Darwinian hypothesis. But, unlike the famous author of the "Expression of the Emotions in Man and the Lower Animals," Dr. Warner concedes to human vanity a certain reticence as to those remote ancestors of whom we are not proud. He is throughout almost morbidly careful to conciliate the metaphysicians by disclaiming all concern with consciousness as distinct from the modes in which consciousness is expressed. Nevertheless, there is a hint of the physicist's contempt for the distinction in his sceptical comment on Professor Tyndall's declaration that "when we endeavour to pass from the region of physics to that of thought, we meet a problem not only beyond our present powers, but transcending any conceivable expansion of the powers we now possess."

Editor's Notes

- Shaw read this book, whose full title is *Physical Expression: Its Modes and Principles,* for review on twelfth and thirteenth of September 1885 (while he was suffering from a bad cold), wrote the review on the fourteenth, and revised and sent it off on the fifteenth (*Diary,* 111). On the 15 April 1886, he sent a copy of the book to Bruce Joy, a sculptor whose studio he had visited the day before, and a paragraph about whose work he was to write for *The World* three days later.
- Francis Warner (1847–1926), English physician and surgeon. He was educated privately and at King's College, London. He graduated with an Honors M.B. in 1872, became an M.D. and a Fellow of the Royal College of Surgeons the following year, and a Fellow of the Royal College of Physicians in 1883. From 1877 to 1879 he worked at the London Hospital, where he was a lecturer in botany; and he was assistant physician at the East London Hospital for Children from 1878 to 1884 [for an account of the hospital, see page 344 below]. In 1887, he was made Hunterian Professor of Comparative Anatomy and Physiology at the Royal College of Surgeons. Later, he became a Fellow of the Royal Medical Society and was in residence at the London Hospital for war work during World War I. Among his other publications were *The Study of Children* (1897) and *The Nervous System of the Child: Its Health and Training* (1900).
- In the "memorable" trial of Bardell versus Pickwick, Sam Weller, asked by the judge whether his name begins with a V or a W, replies that that "depends upon the taste and fancy of the speller, my lord."
- (Sir) Charles Bell (1774–1842), Scottish surgeon and anatomist. He was born and educated in Edinburgh. In 1779 he became a member of the Edinburgh College of Surgeons and in 1836 Professor of Surgery at the University of Edinburgh. His contributions to the study of anatomy were remarkable, particularly in the area of the nervous system. His discoveries were treated in his books, including *A New Idea of the Anatomy of the Brain* (1811) and *The*

Nervous System of the Human Body (1830). However, it was in *Anatomy and Philosophy of Expression* (1842) that Bell "accounted for" the attitude of the Dying Gladiator.

▪ *The Literary Works of Leonardo da Vinci*, compiled and edited from the original manuscripts by Jean Paul Richter, had been published in English only three years before. Shaw no doubt refers to the anatomical studies therein. He also refers to the hypothesis of beauty in sculpture and painting by the German painter Anton Raphael Mengs (1728–79) and Henry Siddons's translation and adaptation to the English drama of Johann Jacob Engel's *Practical Illustrations of Rhetorical Gesture and Action* (1807).

▪ The correct title of Darwin's book is *The Expression of the Emotions in Man and Animals* (1872).

▪ John Tyndall (1820–93), British physicist and natural philosopher. In 1853 he became a professor of natural science at the Royal Institution and a colleague and friend of Faraday, whom he succeeded as superintendent in 1867. His views on the relationship between science and religion were made known in his presidential address to the British Association at Belfast in 1874—an event that occasioned much controversy at the time. Mrs. Whitefield (in *Man and Superman*) grieves to Jack Tanner

> It's a very queer world. It used to be so straightforward and simple; and now nobody seems to think and feel as they ought. Nothing has been right since that speech that Professor Tyndall made at Belfast.

And in *John Bull's Other Island* Father Dempsey is suspicious of the word "theory" because *theories are connected in his mind with the late Professor Tyndall, and with scientific scepticism generally*. Tyndall had retired to live in Surrey. And in the first draft of *Mrs Warren's Profession*, subsequently excised, a reason given for Vivie's late arrival back from a walk with Praed is that they have been

> inspecting the screen Professor Tyndall has put up to prevent people from looking at his house. (British Museum MS 50598A, 75)

23 September 1885

*A HANDBOOK OF PHYSIOGNOMY** [C147]

IT is refreshing at this time of day to meet with an astrologer, and decidedly surprising to meet with an intelligent one. The Theoso-

---

*"The Handbook of Physiognomy." By Rosa Baughan. (London: George Redway. 1885.)

phists, it is true, have made it fashionable to emulate the magic of Sir Boyle Roche's bird by means of "an astral self" and a confederate or two; but the old style of astrologer—the savant who classifies us and predicts our future by the planet we were born under—has been driven out of society and almost out of existence. There are still men to be found far away in Hammersmith or Holloway who will, for half a crown, cast your horoscope for you, with the help of an old almanack, and, if you ridicule them openly, revenge themselves by telling you that your planet will enter the house of death at twelve o'clock next day, and that you will do well to prepare yourself for a great misfortune just about that time. But these more or less venerable practitioners are mere survivals; and it is to be feared that they do not invariably believe in the efficacy of their art for any higher purpose than that of extracting coin from the modern Macbeths who consult them. Miss Rosa Baughan comes to the rescue of a decaying profession. She does not interfere with established practitioners by competing with them as a fortune-teller, but she gives countenance to their terminology by assuring the readers of her interesting little book on physiognomy that "the sanguine or choleric temperament is the result of the astral influence of Mars and Jupiter; the lymphatic of the moon and Venus, but more especially of the moon; the bilious, which is especially the intellectual temperament" (this statement ought to secure many favourable reviews for the book), "of Apollo and Mercury; and the melancholic temperament is the result of the dominance of the sad planet Saturn." There is also an impressive chapter on "The Signatures of the Planets on the Face." With this portion of the work no merely human critical faculty can grapple. A few readers may scoff at it; but candid and well-disposed persons will not ridicule what they do not understand. All that can be done is to be reverently mute as to astral science, to deal with the practice of guessing character from the features as an art, and to regard Miss Baughan as an empiric with a turn for observing faces, apologetically reminding her that after all the most strictly deductive reasoner can be reduced to much the same complexion if his process be considered too curiously.

The phraseology of Shakspeare comes unawares to the pen when Miss Baughan is the theme, not only because of her uncommon knowledge of character, but because she once reconstructed his works for the use of girls, and distinctly succeeded in making his tragedies more astonishing than he left them. She was evidently impressed far more cheerfully than Mr. Thomas Tyler, M. de Laveleye, and the pessimist critics, by the philosophy of the national bard; for she cites him against the objection that physiognomy, "by laying bare the vices and weaknesses, induces a cynical opinion of human nature." Shakspeare (she argues) knew all the weaknesses of our nature, yet he was no cynic. She even seems to consider that he was admittedly an optimist. In view of the estimate of human nature expressed in "Troilus and Cressida" and in "Hamlet," even when abridged for the use of girls, it must be concluded reluctantly that Miss Baughan is not so good a judge of a play as she is of a face. And she is conscious of where her strength lies; for when she comes to the subject of Sterne (the author, she reminds us, of "the inimitable though now little-read work 'Tristram Shandy'") she criticises his nose rather than his writings. The merit of her book consists in the admirable clearness of her descriptions of faces. So vivid is the impression produced by them that she is able to dispense with illustrations, the reader using the faces of his acquaintances for that purpose. The classification, too, is good, although the astrological headings may be regarded by the profane as merely fanciful.

Physiognomy may now be scientifically studied by means of composite photography, a process of which, as Miss Baughan makes no mention, she can hardly have grasped the importance, if she is even aware of its existence. But, after all, the method of visual observation is essentially that of composite photography, as is proved by our instant recognition of the types portrayed by it. Miss Baughan's eye is perhaps not so dispassionate as Mr. Francis Galton's camera; but it is an uncommonly sharp eye. Some of her points are put with startling force. For example, she describes a certain forehead that denotes sweetness and sensitiveness of nature; and adds that a woman with this sort of forehead could never be a shrew. But she slips in a tremendous parenthesis, thus: "A woman with this sort of forehead, unless her lips were thin, could never be a shrew." Could the fell significance of thin lips be more forcibly put? Such statements as that "a mole on the right side of the forehead or temple signifies that the person will achieve sudden wealth and honour," if they have any logical support at all, must hang on a chain of reasoning of such extreme and subtle tenuity as to render many of the links invisible to the uninspired eye. Hence they undeniably give the book an air of being a shillingsworth of quackery. This is a pity; for there is at least a good sixpenn'orth of shrewd observation of character and apt recollection and comparison of faces in it. And that must be admitted to be a generous proportion in an age of three-volume novels, containing on the average a pennyworth of observation to thirty-one and fivepence worth of matter in comparison to which astrology is respectable.

Editor's Notes

- On 18 September 1885, Shaw read this book, began writing the review the following day, and finished and despatched it on the twentieth (*Diary*, 112). Notwithstanding the gentle ridicule in this review, there is evidence that Shaw's own interest in physiognomy was in the ascendancy when he described the facial characteristics of many of the principal figures in his plays. I remark elsewhere that Joan shares her "resolute mouth" with Sartorius (of *Widowers' Houses*), Morell (of *Candida*), Violet Robinson (of *Man and Superman*), and Blanco Posnet (of *The Shewing-up of Blanco Posnet*). Perhaps more interesting, in view of Shaw's satirical account of the "certain forehead that denotes sweetness and sensitiveness of nature" in Baughan's book, is the succession of noble foreheads in his own work, from the "good forehead" of Morell and the "serene brow" of Candida, to the "imposing brow" of John Tanner, the "very presentable forehead" of Androcles, and the "finely domed" head of the Ancient in *Back to Methuselah*. We see that Shaw himself, whether convinced by Baughan's book or not, was equally prone to make value judgments on the basis of physical appearance.
- Rosa Baughan (n.d.), English (or Irish) writer. Her books covered many topics. Shaw in his review makes reference to her *Shakespeare's Plays Abridged for the Use of Girls* (1871) and her *Shakespeare's Works for Schools, Expurgated Edition* (1878); but she also wrote *The Leather-Work Book (containing Full Instructions)* (1879), *The Northern Watering Places of France: a Guide for the English People* (1880), and *Winter Havens in the Sunny South: A Complete Handbook to the Riviera: with a Notice of the New Station, Alassio* (1880). Increasingly, she seems to have turned her attention towards the mysterious and the occult, writing *Character indicated by Handwriting* (1880), *The Handbook of Palmistry* (1882), *Chirognomancy, Temperament, &c of Thumb and Fingers* (1883), and *The Influence of the Stars: a Book of Old World Lore* (1888).
- Although theosophy is a designation for any religio-philosophical system that purports to furnish knowledge of God and his relation to the universe by direct mystical intuition, in the nineteenth century the term was applied with particular reference to a system of occult philosophy expounded by Madame Helena Petrovna Blavatsky [see page 105 below]. She founded the Theosophical Society in New York City in 1875 and claimed to have received her teachings from Oriental religious teachers who had reached a higher plane of existence than other mortals. According to her belief the Deity is the source of both spirit and matter, and the former descends into the latter and the latter ascends into the former in cyclic fashion. Thus Man is seen as a being with a dual nature: the higher, consisting of mind, soul, and spirit, has been

contaminated by the lower—more physical—and must be purified through a series of reincarnations. Her many followers in England seem to have adhered rather loosely to her beliefs, those at one end of the scale claiming the existence of a great range of dubious psychic phenomena much of which was exposed as fraud in 1884 by the Society for Psychical Research, those at the other seeing the Society as a means of founding an egalitarian universal brotherhood and propagating a vague form of Pantheism.

▪ Sir Boyle Roche (1743–1807), Irish politician. He was allegedly the greatest perpetrator of that unconscious, self-contradictory form of humor known as the "Irish bull." Shaw's comment refers to the occasion when he is supposed to have said, "Mr. Speaker, how could I be in two places at once unless I were a bird?"

▪ Thomas Tyler [see pages 79–82 below].

▪ Emile Louis Victor, *baron* de Laveleye (1822–92), French socialist and political economist.

▪ (Sir) Francis Galton (1822–1911), scientist, born near Birmingham, England, and educated at the Universities of London and Cambridge, at which last he worked. He was a cousin of Charles Darwin, traveled in Africa; and although he is best known for his work in anthropology and heredity, and his pioneer work in eugenics, one example being his work *Hereditary Genius* (1869), he was also interested in photography and fingerprinting. In 1878 he published *Composite Portraits*. Shaw, in his work, used Galtonic ideas concerning genius and visions: in his preface to *Saint Joan* he put forward the possibility that Joan was a "Galtonic visualizer."

9 October 1885

ANDROMEDA; OR, A CASTLE IN THE AIR* [C151]

THERE is a sort of novelist whose art is the delightful one of building castles in the air and describing them to the public with intense affection and belief. High among these literary architects and master masons in the regions above the earth is "George Fleming." She is a landscape gardener, too, of no common skill, and can pile the clouds into rare semblances of the splendours of the southern shores or the

---

*"Andromeda." By George Fleming. Two vols. Price 21s. (London: Richard Bentley and Son. 1885.)

stark solitudes of the icebound mountains. (The feminine pronoun is here used advisedly in spite of the masculine name. Just as ladies put on tall hats when they go riding, they call themselves Tom, Dick, or Harry when they go novel-writing. Charlotte Brontë set the example of this disloyalty to her sex by calling herself Currer Bell. Marian Evans followed it, and became known throughout the English-speaking world as George Eliot. Their whim has become a custom; and now the usual reply to the question, "Have you read any of John Smith's novels?" is, "No, what is her real name?" Whether the literary Rosalind takes a swashing and a martial outside to defraud the public judgment, or merely to gratify a taste for masquerade, her counterfeiting is usually of the most transparent order, and does not deceive even a reviewer. No intelligent reader of "Andromeda," the latest work of the author of "A Nile Novel," will mistake George Fleming for a man. Probably no deception was seriously intended; and the matter should have passed without comment were it not that the spread of the practice suggests that it is time to remark with some emphasis that it is neither a sensible nor a sincere one.)

"Andromeda" is, as has been hinted, a castle in the air. Certain idle ladies and gentlemen are represented as unproductively consuming wealth while travelling in the Tyrol and in Italy. They are heedless of Mr. Ruskin's classification of persons who are not workers as beggars or thieves. They have not even heard of Mr. Chamberlain: the shadow of "ransom and restitution" has not yet fallen on them, nor has the threat of a graduated income tax roused them from a chronic dejection which, if it were a little more philosophical, might be dignified with the title of pessimism. "George Fleming" takes these tourists at a West-end valuation as highminded but unhappy people. She sees them in the light of their own dreams, and has no suspicion of that relation of theirs to the work-a-day world in view of which Dickens, in "Little Dorrit," made the Britisher abroad appear so deplorably futile and disreputable. But even in "Andromeda" the reader perceives with some weariness that since these unfortunate wanderers have no taste for gluttony or gambling, and since poetic landscape is only a stimulus to emotional activity, and in no sense an absorbent of energy, there is nothing for them but to fall in love with one another. This they accordingly do, more or less thoroughly. Lovely women and brave men come and go, philander and forget, declare themselves, depart, or die, for the most part not basely. Their words and reminiscences have a passably noble air, and to their amours out of doors there is always a background of crag and cloud or sea and sky, with green walls of pine, and a mountain torrent for mirror and music. Indoors there is no squalor: oaken chairs, tapestries, ranges of ancestral pictures, aged hounds stretched on the carpets, and curtains that are often raised by jewelled hands, make the settled melancholy of love stately if they cannot make it continuously interesting. At last all minor flirtations are weeded out, and two heroes, devoted friends, find themselves in the familiar predicament of being desperately in love with the same woman. Need it be said that she, after engaging herself to one of them, discovers that she is enamoured of the other? Subsequently, however, matters are arranged with the utmost magnanimity on all hands, and the parties resume their unprofitable travels.

Andromeda herself is a Miss Clare Dillon. All the gentlemen in the story fall in love with her, in which distraction they break out into uncouth scraps of French, and even address her as "Oh, my child," or as "Child" simply. "Child," says one of them, "love is the supreme good of life; but the supreme necessity is—liberty." She proves able to hold her own with them as far as epigrams are concerned. Here is one of her best:—"Justice is not popular. People are always more prepared for what they don't deserve than for what is owed to them." It will be seen from this that the dialogue is serious. Indeed, the characters introduced would be very good company if they were not all so low-spirited in consequence of having nothing to do but fall in love. And even for this one of the heroes is unfitted by his personal resemblance to Richard III, like whom he wears a cloak upon one shoulder to conceal its deformity. The account of the childhood of this unlucky gentleman, who is called the Marchese Riccardo di San Donati, is one of the best passages in the book. His sister Gina is incapable of affection, and the reader is induced by this trait to form large hopes of her; but she is crowded out of the story by her more amorous acquaintances. Some of the old people introduced are past love-making, but they have all had prehistoric turns at it, and are each carrying a sorrow to the grave in consequence. There is no villain, and no realistic unpleasantness of any sort; and as the economic vacuum of novel land remains perfect throughout, the personages being unhampered by pecuniary or social pressure, "Andromeda" is a capital book to forget the worries of real life with. The scenery is charming; and the constant employment of curious effects of light—candle-light throwing grotesque shadows on the white walls of mountain inns, torchlight shining on thick gold hair, lamplight on rich curtains, sunlight on the sea, lightning among the pine woods "à la Wagner," as the author says—all exercise the mind's eye without overtaxing the intellect. The figures thus variously illuminated are at least negatively virtuous, and they have noble instincts. No one will be any the worse for spending a few hours with them.

Editor's Notes

- Shaw received this book (with others) from the *Pall Mall Gazette* on 29 September 1885, began reading it the same day, the day following finished it and began his review, which he concluded and despatched on 1 October (*Diary,* 115).
- "George Fleming" [Mrs. Julia Constance Fletcher] (1858–1938), American novelist and playwright. She was the daughter of the Reverend James Cooley Fletcher, an American clergyman, but resided most of her life in Venice. In addition to the novel reviewed here, she also wrote *Kismet* (1877), later republished under the title *A Nile Novel, Mirage* (1878), *The Head of Medusa* (1880), *Notes on a Collection of Pictures by G. Costa* (1882), *Vestigia* (1882), and *The Truth About Clement Ker* (1889). In 1896, Shaw was highly critical of her stage play *Mrs. Lessingham.* Yet, ironically enough, when her comedy *The Canary* (starring Mrs. Patrick Campbell) appeared at the Prince of Wales Theatre in November 1899, she was described as "modelling herself to some extent upon Mr. George Bernard Shaw . . . (in finding) a pleasure in deriding her own creations and, it may almost be said, in burlesquing the action of her own play" (*The Athenæum,* no. 3761, 25 November 1899, 729). In 1900 she wrote an English version of Rostand's *Romanesques.*
- Joseph Austen Chamberlain (1836–1914), British statesman. Raised in London, in 1854 he migrated to Birmingham where he became mayor in 1873. He was a strong radical at this time, and Birmingham rapidly became a pattern of improvement for the whole country. Since he enjoyed controversy, and even seemed to delight in enraging his enemies, he enjoyed the reputation among Conservatives of being a revolutionary. In *John Bull's Other Island* (1904), Broadbent is *still smarting under Mr. Chamberlain's economic heresy.* When the Liberals returned to power in 1880, Gladstone appointed Chamberlain president of the Broad of Trade with a seat in the cabinet (though he had held no previous office). In 1886 he was president of the local government board; but when the Home Rule bill was introduced, he resigned his post and opposed the measure. Many followed him; this split the Liberal party, and at the next general election Chamberlain was returned as the leader of seventy-eight Liberal Unionists. For the next nine years he cooperated with the Conservatives, and became Colonial Secretary in Lord Salisbury's third administration in 1895. He was held responsible by many for the South African War in 1899, but his other foreign efforts on the whole strengthened the British Empire in Australia and South Africa, and he is credited with cementing Anglo–American relations. Two weeks before writing the above review (on 24 September) Shaw had attended a lecture by Chamberlain at the Victoria Theatre (*Diary,* 113–34).

21 October 1885

HISTORY FROM A GENTEEL POINT OF VIEW*
[C154]

THIS volume is capital reading for a county family. It is written about Kings and Courts by people who believed idolatrously in Kings and Courts, and who would sit or stand for hours in sweltering summer heat, marrow-piercing draughts, or numbing cold, in all manner of uncomfortable dresses and places, in loyal fulfilment of their mission to stare at Majesty in uniform and listen to military bands playing "God save the King." To be invited where Royalty was, was to them success and happiness: to be omitted from the Chamberlain's list was failure and disgrace. In these memoirs the proud country gentleman rejoices like a child when "a little dirty boy" is sent to tell him that if he will make haste to a kitchen in St. James's Palace he may peep through a window at an Emperor, a Grand Duchess, and a Prince passing with the Lord Mayor. Great ladies tell with triumph how they coaxed other great ladies to allow them to sit on the staircase while twenty-two princes of Royal Blood went up to dinner. Families make heirlooms of books from which Princesses, driven to desperation by "the sameness of the usual conversation," condescend to read aloud. A tender maiden rushes home from her first ball to write to the loved ones in the far away country house how the Prince of Orange, having accidentally trod on her toes, turned and apologized as the humblest unit of the mob would have done. Few records of that excess of honour which at once transports and terrifies the recipient are more thrilling than Miss Frampton's account of what happened to her in September, 1799. "We were sitting," she says, "at work in my little room with Mrs. Drax. I happened to look out, and actually saw the King and Princess Sophia, with their attendants, at my garden gate. I screamed out, threw down everything about me, and flew out to them. The King called out, 'Well run, Mrs. Frampton.' " This delirious Court life was not without its moments of discouragement. Mdme. de Lieven, when she came over from Russia, retained so much of the barbarism of that country that she shocked the Court by giving her opinion of everything with sincerity. The Elector of Cologne, though own brother to

*"The Journal of Mary Frampton from 1779 to 1846." Edited by her Niece, Harriot Georgiana Mundy. (London: Sampson Low and Co. 1885. 14s.)

an Emperor, cut off his queue and made himself look "like a vulgar English patriot." Useful tufthunters living in houses which overlooked Royal processions were corrupted by offers of fifty guineas for seats from commercial persons. Newly made knights were hardly presented at the levée when their blushes were changed to pallor by "a small star, and a large card containing a list of fees," which cards the naval knights at once deposited in the outer room, impiously swearing that they would not pay £108 each for an honour "not worth sixpence." But perhaps the deepest tragedy of all is described in a letter from Lady Elizabeth Feilding to Lady Mary Talbot, which must be quoted at length. The italics are Lady Elizabeth's. "What do you think of the Prince of Wales, at the Duke of Clarence's fête, handing out Mrs. Jordan *before* the *Countess* of Athlone and the *Duchess* of Bolton? I say that the Duchess and Countess were very well served for putting themselves in such company."

The faith of the Court devotees could not but suffer from such shocks as these. We learn that as early as a few years after 1795 it was discovered—though not acted upon—that good generals were more necessary than rank in the army. Miss Frampton's acknowledgment of this proves that in comparison with the rest of her set she was a fearless observer and an advanced and independent thinker. But the spectacle of the first gentleman in Europe, "in his own coach, drawn by six of the handsomest grey horses possible, most elegantly ornamented, so that nothing could be finer than his equipage," was not one to be resisted by a girl of sixteen, nor was the impression it made upon her ever subsequently effaced. We hear little from her that reinforces the unfavourable opinion that posterity has formed of George the Fourth, except that he once talked so much during divine service that a passage complimenting him on the discharge of his religious duties was scratched out of a sermon by the Bishop of Lincoln. His bow, we are again assured, was far more elegant than that of any other Prince of his time. Though he scandalized Lady Elizabeth Feilding by giving an actress precedence of a duchess, he regained her devotion by sending old Lady Charlotte Finch, who had been nearly burned in St. James's Palace, "a most beautiful letter, with an agate box of sedative pills to quiet her nerves after the fright." He took some trouble to procure for his daughter a trustworthy governess in the person of Mrs. Campbell, who seems to have been a sort of aristocratic Mrs. Gummidge. "Mrs. Campbell," says the Marchioness of Lansdowne, "is looking well for her, and if she would might be very happy; but she will think of every disadvantage and discomfort more than of the opposite side of the picture." One cannot help suspecting that the poor young Princess would have been content with a less respectable and more cheerful preceptress; but there is a gleam of something like a sense of moral responsibility in her father's conduct in the matter. Nor will any one think the worse of him for having had a miniature portrait of Mrs. Fitzherbert buried with him. In 1821, when he was no longer even a "fat Adonis of fifty," we get a glimpse of him in the following description by a man's hand:

> The King makes himself a strange figure by drawing in his great body with a broad belt, and by the close buttoning of a kind of uniform jacket more than a dress coat, and hiding the lower part of his face with a large black neckcloth, and then swelling out the upper part of his person with tags and embroidery and covering it with orders instead of the simple Star and Garter worn by his father; and yet for a man of near sixty he contrives to look young by the help of a wig without powder; and his air and manner are as graceful as they used to be.

There are many enthusiastic descriptions of the season of 1814, when the Allied Sovereigns were in London, and the head of cockneydom was so turned by perpetual pageantry that the tradesmen could not get their customers' orders executed, and the bankers complained that their clerks could not keep their books accurately, and that the acceptors of bills forgot to take them up. The hero of the hour was old Blucher, whose share next year in the victory of Waterloo has been rather resented by succeeding generations of Britons. The feeling just then towards Bonaparte finds expression in a letter from Lady Vernon:

> Was ever such a mean, despicable, as well as wicked wretch as this Bonaparte? I trust they will keep a sharp guard upon him. It is thought that his last wife will not be permitted (even if she were willing) to accompany him. He should have every species of humiliation and think himself well off that life is spared for repentance of his crimes.

Of the present reign Miss Frampton soon received a deplorable account. "I have amused myself," wrote her niece, Mrs. Mundy, "by drawing you a plan of the reception rooms, and shown where the Queen *stood* to eat her supper. She shocked me dreadfully, and horrifies

Grandmamma Ilchester, as there is not sufficient *state* in it?" At the coronation festivities hackney coach fares rose to "£8 or £12 each, double to foreigners." At the Queen's marriage, the Archbishop was so nervous that he nearly made Prince Albert put the ring on the right hand of the bride. He also shocked the Marchioness of Lansdowne by not Bowdlerizing the service, "which," she says, "is very disagreeable, and, when one looked at all the young things who were listening, most distressing. However, he mumbles a good deal." The littlenesses of which the book is compiled become still more little as it draws to a close.

Mary Frampton's style is invariably genteel, and generally free from the correctness of the professional writer. Thus she says of Lady Jersey: "Amongst other freaks she was a very fine lady, but in general respected my aunt." Mrs. Mundy has selected and arranged her curious medley of family letters so as to preserve the historical continuity of the journal, and has left nothing to be reasonably desired except an index, which would be a very acceptable addition to the fresh issues of the work which will probably be called for.

Editor's Notes

- Shaw read this book for review on 14 October 1885 and finished his review of it on the seventeenth (*Diary*, 118).
- Harriot Georgiana Mundy (?–1886). Her only claim to fame seems to have been that she was, in fact, the niece of Mary Frampton.
- Mary Frampton (1773–1846). She and her brother James (born 1769) were the only children of James Frampton, Esq., of Moreton in the county of Dorset, by his second wife Phillis, daughter and heiress of Samuel Byam of Antigua, and widow of Charles Wollaston, a scientist, whose death was occasioned by opening a mummy, he having previously by accident cut his finger. By him she had two children, Charlton Byam and Phillis Byam, and survived her husband (who died in 1784) by many years, dying in 1829 at the age of ninety-two. Mary Frampton died at Dorchester on 12 November 1846.
- A queue was a twist of hair, either natural or part of a wig, worn at the back of the head.
- Tufthunters are those who "meanly or obsequiously court the acquaintance of persons of rank or title" (*OED*); in other words toadies, or sycophants.
- Mrs. Gummidge is the widow of Mr. Peggoty's partner in Dickens's *David Copperfield*. After her husband's death, Mr. Peggoty offers her a home, and supports her for years. This kindness she acknowledges by sitting in the most comfortable fireside corner and complaining that she is a "lone, lorn creetur, and every think goes contrairy" with her.

▪ Mrs [Maria Anne] Fitzherbert (1756–1837), wife of George IV. Left a wealthy widow by her second husband, Thomas Fitzherbert, in 1781, she took up residence in Richmond, where she soon became the center of an admiring circle. In 1785 she first saw the Prince of Wales (b.1762), who fell in love with her at first sight, and, on one occasion, pretended to stab himself in despair. After his relentless pursuit, they were married in her drawing room, though the marriage was later declared invalid. She remained his mistress for some time, even after his legal marriage, and their friendship lasted until his death in 1830.

27 October 1885

THEREBY* [C156]

"THEREBY" hangs a tale. Two gentlemen pessimists, sitting with their wives and children in a pleasant garden, find themselves so exceedingly bored that they agree to toss up which shall murder the other, in order that the survivor may be diverted by a novel sensation. The children are sent into the house to fetch a pistol. On their return Papa D'Aubert, who has lost the toss, shoots Papa Noel, who dies exclaiming, "How do you like the new sensation?" This practical anticipation of the views of Hartmann and Schopenhauer sets up so strong a reaction in the children that they grow up with an intense conviction of the preciousness of life, and educate their own offspring to make the most of it while it lasts. They also form one of those atonement theories which occasionally puzzle the logician when he seeks relaxation in novel-reading. They become convinced that the evil done by the two annihilationists may be remedied by the intermarriage of their descendants. But these descendants have drifted out of one other's knowledge; and the blindfold matchmaking which results in their reciprocal discovery and happy union is the subject of "Fayr Madoc's" two volumes entitled "Thereby."

If we may conceive "Fayr Madoc" as asking, with some complacency, "How is that for an original plot?" we must admit that it is far

---

*"Thereby." By Fayr Madoc. Two vols. (London and Edinburgh: W. Blackwood and Sons. 1885.)

from commonplace, while in point of probability it compares favourably with the "Comedy of Errors" and "Frankenstein," both works of acknowledged merit. Unfortunately, its exposition is retarded by a mass of dialogue which is offered to the reader as the deliberate utterance of philosophers, sociologists, eminent physicians, and even bishops, but which is in fact a stream of impertinent chatter such as the most voluble sciolist would hesitate to undam even at a literary and scientific conversazione. "Fayr Madoc" should remember that as a stream cannot rise above its source, so a novelist cannot utter the thoughts of a bishop. Here is a sample of the conversation of Bishop Scroll, a very old, very wise, and very good prelate. "No, my boy, you don't," said the bishop; "you have misunderstood me entirely; I suggested to you to do an artistic thing; you find you can't accomplish my artistic end without employing inartistic means. Well and good. You must leave it alone. I resigned my bishopric for the same reason. I found the means by which I was expected to lead the world to righteousness were inartistic. I don't expect you to be less fastidious than I was." The eminent physician who is the hero of the tale, and who estimates that the villain, when "bleeding profusely from the femoral artery," would have died if he had been left without assistance for "another ten minutes," is to the eminent realities of Harley-street and Hanover-square much as Bishop Scroll is to the lords spiritual of the Upper House. The Radical ideal is expounded by a Mr. Item as an insanely crude State Socialism, and is confuted as "pauperizing" by the heroine, who has inherited immense wealth, and whose feeling towards less fortunate individuals is a survival of that which was common among the duller sort of Whig politicians in 1840 or thereabout. "Fayr Madoc's" programme, in short, is too ambitious. Were she another Goethe she would hardly stand acquitted of presumption. Being as yet only a clever smatterer—for she is at least guiltless of stupidity—her failure has been flagrant. In the scenes in which she is not out of her depth, there is some interest and more promise. When studying the mere commonplaces of society, however, she has omitted to notice that culture and unnecessary demonstrativeness tend to exclude one another. An excess of affectionate speeches, such as "You are very sweet, So-and-So, darling," does not usually characterize the public intercourse of cultivated men and women. Nowadays, even stage managers are becoming chary of terms of endearment.

Editor's Notes

- Shaw read *Thereby* on 2 October 1885, began his review the following day, and finished it on the third. We may presume he sent it to the *Gazette* at the same time, because he "corrected proof for *PMG*" on the seventh, but the review did not appear until twenty days later, after his review of *The Journal of Mary Frampton* on the twenty-first (*Diary*, 115–16).
- "Fayr Madoc" [pseudonym for Miss Maddock?] (n.d.), Welsh novelist. She also wrote *The Story of Melicent* (1883), *Margaret Jermine* (1886), and contributed short stories and verse to *Argosy, Belgravia,* and *London Society* magazines. In 1889 she visited the Royal Ophthalmic Hospital at Moorfields and published an account of her visit in *London Society* as an appeal for funds for the institution.
- Shaw refers to Arthur Schopenhauer (1788–1860), the pessimistic philosopher who regarded the world as a malignant illusion, and his disciple Karl Robert Eduard von Hartmann (1842–1906), for whom the "Unconscious" plays the role of Providence.

25 November 1885

MEMOIRS OF AN OLD-FASHIONED PHYSICIAN* [C170]

AN autobiography is usually begun with interest by writer and reader alike, and seldom finished by either. Few men care enough about their past to take the trouble of writing its history. Braggarts like Benvenuto Cellini, and morbidly introspective individuals like Rousseau, are the exceptions that prove the rule. Now, Sir Robert Christison was not in the least like Cellini or Rousseau; but it fell out in the fiftieth year of his professorship at Edinburgh University that he felt the need of a little change, and yet was so circumstanced that he could not get away from the town to the Highlands, his favourite place of recreation. So he sat down and began his autobiography. He chose that particular means of diversion partly because it refreshed his mind by taking him from the present into the past, and partly for an altruistic reason, which may be given in his own words:

---

*"The Life of Sir Robert Christison, Bart." Edited by his Sons. Vol. I., Autobiography. (London and Edinburgh: W. Blackwood and Sons, 1885.)

The time cannot be far off when the duty will be imposed on some kind friend of furnishing half a column of biography to the newspapers, and upon some president the labour of an obituary sketch for his address at the annual opening meeting of the Royal Society; and having myself felt the irksomeness of ferreting out sound information in the case of my departed friends in the like circumstances, it may be an act of mercy to furnish my future biographer with facts in my own case from the fountain-head.

He persevered in this laborious relaxation at intervals until he had completed an account of the first thirty-three years of his long life. The rest of the tale will be told in an as yet unpublished second volume by his journals and correspondence, arranged by other hands.

Christison was not at all a typical Scotchman. He performed his first successful elementary analysis on a Sunday, and actually went to the theatre (in Paris) to hear Georges and Talma on that day. He objected to logic and ethics, and could never be induced to admit that such distinctions as those made in the application of the patent laws between discoveries and inventions had any foundation in reason. He was only once tempted to take out a money-making patent, and upon that he turned his back for ever at a word from Sir Walter Scott. Though sufficiently tenacious of his own opinion—usually a sound one—he was not argumentative, and took his share of abuse and misrepresentation with a sympathetic equanimity which is the characteristic attribute of genuine natural superiority. Even when modern scientists rediscovered old discoveries of his, and blew the trumpet over them a little, he was not stung with jealousy or provoked to self-assertion, although he did not deny himself the pleasure of referring the discoverers, with a quiet chuckle, to some forgotten paper of his in which he had anticipated them. It would not be correct to say that he was no boaster. He has told us vaingloriously of his walking, his wrestling, his singing (he was a *basso profundo*), and of how, when he accidentally smashed a graduated glass in Robiquet's laboratory, he took a diamond and graduated a fresh one so neatly that Robiquet rejoiced in the destruction of the old one. Many readers will be left with the impression that these were the pet triumphs of a man who held his own with the lawyers as professor of medical jurisprudence, who gained a European reputation as a chemist and toxicologist by his treatise on poisons, who was a great authority in his time on diseases of the chest and kidneys, and who was president of the Royal

College of Physicians, the Royal Society of Edinburgh, and the British Association, not to lay stress on such honours as a baronetcy and the post of physician-in-ordinary to the Queen. All this he gained for himself. He was the son of a university professor, and does not seem to have had any greater advantages than other men of his standing.

Among the distinguished modern theorists whose views are antici-pated by the old Edinburgh physician must be placed M. Victorien Sardou. "One needs to look for the decline of the drama," says Christison, "only to the very late dinner hours." In his youth, he tells us, the usual family hour for dinner was four, and the company hour five; and he does not conceal his unfashionable opinion that the change has been for the worse. Our present dinner hour was at that time the chosen season of the resurrection man, a useful practitioner who should be carefully distinguished from the disreputable body-snatchers whose degeneration culminated in the unprofessional in-stincts of Burke and Hare, as shown by their resort to strangulation in order to create an artificial supply of subjects. The respectable resur-rection man trusted to the bounty of Nature for bodies. Though he nationalized the tenement of clay without compensation, he recog-nized the Henry Georgian distinction between that purely natural object and its shroud, which, as a product of human industry, he scrupulously replaced in the coffin. His method was calculated to ensure his own safety and to spare the feelings of the relatives of the deceased. With a wooden spatula, or "digger," he almost noiselessly uncovered the upper half of the coffin. He then slipped two broad iron hooks under the lid, and, pulling them up with ropes, broke a portion of it off, using sacking to deaden the crash. Through the opening thus made the "subject" was withdrawn and conveyed in a sack to the temple of anatomical science. The grave was carefully filled and its previous aspect restored; so that, as a rule, only the resurrectionist was any the wiser. Competition was the ruin of this as of other fine arts, and its history, until Burke and Hare discredited it, and Warbur-ton's Anatomy Act of 1834 extinguished it, was one of corruption and decay.

Christison's attempt to defend the old-fashioned treatment by bleed-ing, and yet to justify its disuse, is worth quoting. He says:

> For many years past blood-letting his been entirely given up in almost all these diseases, so that I question whether any man under forty-five could now perform what is really a rather nice operation to perform well. The present generation of practitio-

ners, indeed, have not only given it up, but are constantly railing at their precursors for their blindness and destructiveness in ever using it at all. My general answer is that acute local inflammations, during the first half of my life, were attended with a violence of arterial action unknown in the latter half, and that this is the simple reason why blood-letting was adopted in the early and abandoned in the later period. . . . All my professional brethren old enough to have seen both agree with me that for a long time past they have never met with such pulses, for force and hardness, in pneumonia, rheumatism, pleurisy, nephritis, &c., as they constantly encountered in their early days.

He adds that he never bled immoderately although he admits having taken ninety ounces of blood within thirteen hours from a negro who had violent pneumonia. The man of colour recovered, and seemed none the worse. Christison has something to say about hydrophobia, which M. Pasteur and a few energetic animals have lately made a question of the day; but he considered that enquiry into it had been pushed to its possible limits by Hertwig, of Berlin, in 1828. He has something to say, indeed, about a great number and variety of subjects; and his sketches and anecdotes of hospital and university life, and of a host of academic and medical heroes, from Dupuytren to Sir James Simpson, are all told good-naturedly, and with the technical parts translated carefully into the language of non-professional intercourse. The result is a lively narrative for the general reader, and some interesting material for the biographer and historian.

Editor's Notes

- The gap of almost a month between the previous review and this one is accounted for by the fact that Shaw wrote a review of Grant Allen's *Darwin* on 27/28 October 1885 that was rejected by Charles Morley, literary editor of the *Pall Mall Gazette*, on the ground that he felt compelled to print a review of the book submitted by a "distinguished contributor" (*Diary*, 120). Whether this was the only reason may be doubted: his editors later tampered with Shaw's reviews of Grant Allen's work [see page 454 below]. In view of Morley's excuse, however, it is interesting that during the writing of the review of *The Life of Sir Robert Christison, Bart.*, which Shaw began reading on 14 November and finished the following day, he actually sought a second opinion on the book from his medical friend James Kingston Barton (1854–1941), calling on him at 10 P.M. on 15 November "to ask him about it," but finding him out and leaving a note for him. Shaw completed his review on the 17 November (*Diary*, 124–25).

▪ [Sir] Robert Christison (1797–1882) was educated in medicine at the University of Edinburgh and at the Royal Infirmary in the same city, graduating in 1819. In 1820 he sailed for London and Paris to further his studies. He was inducted as Professor of Medical Jurisprudence at the University of Edinburgh in 1822. In 1827 he married a Miss Brown, and was also appointed one of the physicians of the Royal Infirmary. In 1832 he transferred his academic post to the Chair of Materia Medica, which he held until 1877, and he also became one of the University teachers of Clinical Medicine. His eminence was recognized by the Royal College of Physicians of Edinburgh, of which he was twice president. Besides contributing many papers to various scientific societies and journals, between 1832 and 1845 he brought out three editions of his *Treatise on Poisons*. His work on *Granular Degeneration of the Kidneys* came out in 1839, and the first edition of his *Dispensatory, or Commentary on the Pharmacopœia of Great Britain* in 1842. His wife died in 1849, leaving him three sons, who presumably collaborated in writing the "Life." Among many honors bestowed upon him was a baronetcy in 1871, and a LL.D. of the University of Edinburgh in the fiftieth year of his professorship.

▪ Benvenuto Cellini (1500–71), Italian sculptor, engraver, and goldsmith. He was at one time a pupil of Michaelangelo, and patronised by popes, the king of France and Cosimo de Medici. Shaw refers to his *Autobiography* (written between 1558 and 1562, though not published until the eighteenth century), which is a frank and exciting (though somewhat boastful) account of his adventurous life and a fascinating window on the Italian renaissance.

▪ Jean-Jacques Rousseau (1712–78), French philosopher and social and political theorist, whose political writings helped prepare the ideological background for the French Revolution, and whose educational theories led to a revolution of their own in methods of child care. Shaw refers, however, to his autobiographical work *Confessions* (1782, English translations 1783, 1790), which is a penetrating analysis of the emotional and moral conflicts of his own life.

▪ Mademoiselle Georges [Marguerite Josephine Weimer] (1787–1868) had her first stage role at the age of fifteen, as Clytemnestra in Racine's *Iphigénie en Aulide*. She was classically beautiful, and became Napoleon's mistress. She played at the Théâtre Français until 1808 when she left to join a Russian lover and act with the French company in St. Petersburg. In 1813 she returned to her old theater, but was too outspoken in favor of Bonaparte and was forced to leave France again in 1817. Later she played successfully the heroines of some of Victor Hugo's plays.

▪ François Joseph Talma (1763–1826), French actor with the Comédie Française who led a rebellion against the classic style of acting in 1787. At the time of the French Revolution, he and other young actors left the Comédie Française and formed the Théâtre de la République, which was reintegrated with the Comédie Française in 1799. Talma, who also enjoyed the patronage of Napoleon, looked for the humanity in the characters he portrayed, refusing to play the stereotypical king, father, or lover. Unfortunately, his humanity often expressed itself in violent transports of emotion. His Orestes was said to be like a madman in an insane asylum. However, in his *Life* Christison described him as a "true genius of the stage" (p. 220). Although every bit as great a Bonapartiste as Mlle Georges, Talma's public popularity was too great for the government to harass him in the same way.

- Almost certainly, Shaw used Christison's *Life* as a source for his own *The Doctor's Dilemma* (1911). Hints of Shaw's characters are to be found among the eccentric physicians and surgeons whom Christison met in his travels. In Paris, for example, we hear of Broussais, who "advocated the doctrine that most diseases owed their origin to inflammation somewhere, and were to be treated by blood-letting, especially by means of leeches used in handfuls" (p. 237). Surely in that sentence lies the seed that blossoms into Bloomfield–Bonnington in Shaw's play, who has a similar morbid preoccupation with blood poisoning. Christison himself can be seen as an interesting anticipation of Shaw's own "old-fashioned" physician, Dr. Paddy Cullen, in the following comment:

> Even when modern scientists rediscovered old discoveries of his [Christison's], and blew the trumpet over them a little, he was not stung with jealousy or provoked to self-assertion, although he did not deny himself the pleasure of referring the discoverers, with a quiet chuckle, to some forgotten paper of his in which he had anticipated them.

One hears in that Cullen's remark on the cyclic nature of medical fashion:

> I'm not belittling your discovery. Most discoveries are made regularly every fifteen years; and it's fully a hundred and fifty since yours was made last. That's something to be proud of.

Indeed, Shaw may have taken both the surname and the wit of his character from Christison's ill-fated friend William Cullen, who was "the wittiest man in conversation I have ever met" (p. 125), and who was the great-nephew of "our great Professor Cullen."

- Victorien Sardou (1831–1908), French dramatist, author of about seventy plays, including the well-known *Madame Sans-Gêne* (1893) and *Robespierre* (1899). He wrote *Fedora* (1882) and *La Tosca* (1887) for the French actress Sarah Bernhardt. Apart from admiring the "witty liveliness" of Sardou and de Najac's *Divorçons* (1880), which he saw adapted into *The Queen's Proctor* in 1896, Shaw consistently attacked what he called "Sardoodledom" and was derisive about the "mechanical dolls" of Sardou's "pièces bien faites." In 1895 he described Sardou's *Delia Harding* as "the worst play I ever saw," saying "Sardou's plan of playwriting is first to invent the action of his piece, and then to carefully keep it off the stage and have it announced merely by letters and telegrams." The suggestion in this book review is that both Christison and Sardou mistakenly attempt to account for the decline in drama by reference to external factors.

▪ William Burke and his mistress and William Hare and his wife (with the women acting as decoys) had contrived a scheme during the winter of 1827–28 for supplying the Edinburgh school of anatomy with bodies for dissection by murdering their lodgers. This they did by making them drunk and suffocating them, after which the bodies were delivered to the rooms of Dr. Knox, lecturer in anatomy, who was later stigmatized by Edinburgh society, had to leave the university, and eventually sank into destitution in London. Burke is said to have admitted to sixteen murders, and was hanged on 28 January 1829. Christison was instrumental in bringing him and his accomplices to justice.

▪ Warburton's Anatomy Act. The case of Burke and Hare brought to public attention the whole matter of the necessarily illegal manner of procuring cadavers for dissection in the medical schools: indeed, it became known as "Burking." Henry Warburton (1784–1858), radical politician representing the borough of Bridport in Dorset, championed the movement that led to the Anatomy Bill being put before the House of Commons. The bill, which became law in 1832, not 1834 as Shaw states, set about to prevent crime and promote science by suggesting sources of supply of bodies, the delivery of death certificates, and the appointment of inspectors to supervise the schools.

▪ Louis Pasteur (1822–95), French chemist and microbiologist. Now recognized as the founder of the microbiological sciences, Pasteur demonstrated that processes of fermentation and putrefaction in wine, milk, and other liquids are caused by microorganisms (or "germs") in the air to which the substances have been exposed, and are not self-generated by the substances themselves, as had previously been contended. This led Pasteur to an investigation into anthrax and rabies (or hydrophobia as it was originally called), and subsequently to the prevention of these and numerous other diseases in humans and animals. His researches also vindicated Jenner's work on vaccination, and were of great value to Lister in the development of antiseptic surgery. Notwithstanding this impressive record, Pasteur was much maligned in England in the 1880s, and Shaw, who had, after all, been raised in an atmosphere of medical scepticism, was among his attackers. What kept his scepticism alive, no doubt, was Shaw's acquaintanceship with Mrs. Annie Besant, whom he met for the first time at the Dialectical Society in 21 January 1885. On 4 March, Shaw "went to the Dialectical and denounced Pasteur" (*Diary*, 66). And later that year Shaw began contributing articles to Mrs. Besant's socialist journal *Our Corner* in which she seemed to be carrying on a personal vendetta against Louis Pasteur. Throughout the winter of 1885/6 she sniped derisively at him and his discoveries. In February 1886, hydrophobia, for which Pasteur had found a "cure," was said to have become "as common as measles" in New York; in March appeared a further attack on the "medical mania of inoculation"; and in April yet another jibe at Pasteur's

Salad for the Solitary and the Social

"supposed" discovery of a hydrophobia cure. In May of the same year, appeared an ironic comment on microbes in "Science Corner," the scientific column of Mrs. Besant's journal, in which she states "It has been found that a cubic metre of air from the centre of Paris contains no less than 9,850 microbes." Indeed, in spite of increasing evidence of his scientific success, enough of the derision remained in the air for Frances Cobbe to berate him in her tirade against vivisection *The Modern Rack* (1889) and for Ouida to attack Pasteur again in *The New Priesthood* (1893), both books which Shaw consulted when writing *The Philanderer* (1893). What immense point this gives to the fact that, in the first draft (subsequently discarded) of that play, the vivisectionist Dr. Paramore has a dog called "Pasteur"!

- Karl Heinrich Hertwig (1798–1881), German biologist. He made exhaustive inquiries into *Rabies canina* through experiment on and observation of animals.
- [Baron] Guillaume Dupuytren (1777–1835), French surgeon. From 1812 he was a professor of clinical surgery in Paris. He invented many surgical instruments.
- [Sir] James Young Simpson (1811–70), Scottish professor of midwifery at the University of Edinburgh during Christison's time there; a friend and at one time rival of Sir Robert Christison for principalship of the University—a position neither of them secured.

28 November 1885

SALAD FOR THE SOLITARY AND THE SOCIAL*
[C172]

IN estimating the value of such a work as this it must not be forgotten that though choice anecdotes, epitaphs, and comic songs about camomile tea (elucidative of "The Mysteries of Medicine") are not new, generations of men are. Every day the oldest story is poured for the first time into the youngest ears. Mr. Saunders only aspires to flavour and pour in. He is not a producer of stories, but a retail distributor; and he is justified in claiming that his function is as indispensable as that of the inventor or manufacturer, particularly as it includes the important work of selection and purification. Now,

*"Salad for the Solitary and the Social." By Frederick Saunders. (London: R. Bentley and Son. 1885.)

there are methods of purification which are not distinguishable in practice from adulteration. The addition of pure water to gin, for instance, renders it less noxious to the consumer, and benefits the distributor considerably. Hence the retailer is strongly urged, by considerations egoistic and altruistic, to purify his gin. A similar temptation besets the retailer of anecdote. Anecdote gains currency as a record of facts—as a piece of history. But mere records of fact do not always point a popular moral: nay, they often scandalize instead of edifying; and when this is the case, publishers will not issue popular editions of them with eulogistic prefaces. The anecdotic middleman is therefore moved by his tenderness for public morals and by his own temporal interests to judiciously alter and interpolate, just as the schoolmistress in "Edwin Drood" did when she read realistic novels aloud to the heroine. And it becomes all but his duty to deliberately select a notoriously incorrect version of an historic event when it seems to him to correctly represent what ought to have happened, no matter what some deplorable oversight in the direction of universal business may have allowed actually to occur. For example, it is evident that Voltaire, not having belonged to the Church of England, ought to have died in unspeakable mental torment. Such, accordingly, is the view taken by Mr. Saunders, who gives an impressive, if not absolutely authentic, account of the terrors of the deist philosopher's deathbed. Mr. Saunders has indeed a rare touch in depicting deathbeds. Many a tear will drop unbidden on the page containing the following account of Mozart's Requiem and death:

> He had been employed upon this exquisite piece (the Requiem) for several weeks. After giving it its last touch, and breathing into it that undying spirit of song which was to consecrate it through all times as his cygnean strain, he fell into a gentle and quiet slumber. At length the light footsteps of his daughter Emilie awoke him. "Come hither," said he, "my Emilie, my task is done; the Requiem—my Requiem—is finished."
>
> "Say not so, dear father," said the gentle girl, interrupting him, as tears—

But enough. Mozart had no daughter and never finished his requiem. "Emilie" is but a poetic vision of Mr. Saunders's. Still he has been careful not to misrepresent the number of females in the household of the illustrious composer of "Don Giovanni;" for in adding to him a daughter he has subtracted a wife. The narrative continues:

"Do not deceive yourself, my love," said the dying father; "this wasted form can never be restored by human aid. From heaven's mercy alone do I look for aid in this my dying hour. You spoke of refreshment, my Emilie; take these, my last notes, sit down by my piano here, sing them with the hymn of thy sainted mother; let me once more hear those tones which have been so long my solacement and delight."

It may seem unsympathetic to insist on the fact that Constance Mozart survived her husband many a long day, and gave a good deal of trouble about this same Requiem, which, being an elaborate composition for orchestra, chorus, and four solo singers, must have severely taxed Emilie's powers of playing at sight from a full score, as well as her vocal resources.

It may be said that Mozart's death, which was one of the most tragic events of the eighteenth century, deserved exceptionally poetic treatment. But Mr. Saunders is equally inspired by Beethoven, who died of dropsy during a thunderstorm, shaking his fist with undaunted crustiness at the lightning. Here is Mr. Saunders's description of the deaf tone poet's end: "He had been visibly declining, when suddenly he revived. A bright smile illumed his features as he softly murmured, 'I shall hear in heaven' (he was deaf), and then sang in a low but distinct voice one of his own beautiful German hymns." Here we have the central fact of Beethoven's death—which undoubtedly did take place—scrupulously retained; but all the incidents of it are idealized and sublimed by pure force of imagination. Mr. Saunders's descriptions are like the cemetery in which Keats was buried: they almost make us in love with death.

It would be easy to cull gem after gem from the five hundred odd pages of which this volume consists; but the limits of space forbid such an indulgence. It is a pity that Mr. Saunders has not supplemented his work with an index to facilitate reference to his stores of information, much of which it would be difficult to find elsewhere.

Editor's Notes

- Curiously, there is no reference in the *Diary* to the writing of this book review.
- Frederick Saunders (1807–1902), English librarian and author. He was

born in London, England, and went to the United States in 1837 to establish a branch of his father's (London) publishing house. In 1833 he married Ann Farr. He devoted his efforts, unsuccessfully, to securing an international copyright law from Congress. He became city editor of the *New York Evening Post,* and first assistant librarian (1859–76), and then librarian (1876–96) of the Astor Library. He was retired at his own request, but the trustees voted to continue his salary during his lifetime. He was the author of numerous compilations and balanced *Salad for the Solitary* (1852) with *Salad for the Social* (1856). (These were combined in one edition in America in 1872, and brought out in the popular edition reviewed above in London in 1885.) He also wrote *Festival of Song* (1866), *Evenings with the Sacred Poets* (1870), *A Festival of Art, Poetry, and Song* (1880), *Gems of Genius, and Poetry and Art* (1888), and *One Thousand Gems of Genius* (1889).

▪ The schoolmistress in *Edwin Drood* is Miss Twinkleton, who runs a boarding school for young ladies in Cloisterham. In chapter 22 she comes to London to complete Rosa Bud's education. The arrangement is not a success:

> Tired of working and conversing with Miss Twinkleton, she [Rosa] suggested working and reading: to which Miss Twinkleton readily assented, as an admirable reader, of tried powers. But Rosa soon made the discovery that Miss Twinkleton didn't read fairly. She cut the love-scenes, interpolated passages in praise of female celibacy, and was guilty of other glaring pious frauds.

▪ Either Shaw or his editor "corrected" rather freely the quotations from Frederick Saunders, who had a fondness for the parenthetic dash. In the original, for example, the phrase "cygnean strain" is in inverted commas; the sentence beginning "Come hither," said he, continues "my Emilie—my task is done—the Requiem—*my* Requiem—is finished." And the final sentence reads, "You spoke of refreshment my Emilie—take these, my last notes—sit down by my piano here—sing them with the hymn of thy sainted mother—let me once more hear . . ." etc.

▪ It was in fact Shelley who so described the cemetery where Keats was buried. The remark is quoted by Saunders on page 72 of his book.

▪ In the chapter entitled "The Mysteries of Medicine" with its eye upon the ludicrous aspects of the profession, Shaw may have found more material for his own assault upon doctors. Certainly the following two thoughts are sufficiently close to warrant speculation:

> Take up the first newspaper that comes to hand; look over the advertisements entitled Medical; is there not a panacea for every disability—consumption, dyspepsia, in short, everything that can make up the total of human wretchedness or human infirmity? How wonderful that death is still the great iconoclast, in spite of potions, ointments, and drops; in spite of pills that are infallible, in spite of philanthropists who

profess to eradicate all the "ills that flesh is heir to," and others that never existed. (*Salad for the Solitary and the Social*, 227)

SIR PATRICK: Ah, yes. It's very interesting. What is it the old cardinal says in Browning's play? "I have known four and twenty leaders of revolt." Well, Ive known over thirty men that found out how to cure consumption. Why do people go on dying of it, Colly? Devilment, I suppose. (Shaw, Bernard, *The Doctor's Dilemma* [London: Constable and Co., 1932], 88)

5 December 1885

*A STRANGE VOYAGE** [C177]

MR. CLARK RUSSELL's nautical novels are refreshingly briny and breezy results of the discovery of the picturesque. A very artful landsman, with the help of a gallery of flamboyant Turners and Admiral Smyth's "Sailors Word Book" might manufacture one ocean landscape and one squall that might pass for a genuine Clark Russell; but he would not return to the subject again and again with the inexhaustible zest of the author of "The Wreck of the *Grosvenor*," "A Sea Queen," and other novels in which ships, sails, seas, and skies are word-painted over and over again until the reader is fain to cry "Avast!" and to make all snug by the simple expedient of skipping when he sees another description coming. Like Mr. Pecksniff's articled pupils, who were condemned to draw Salisbury Cathedral from every possible point of view, Mr. Clark Russell presents his ship in all weathers, at all hours, and from all quarters of the horizon. He describes the *Silver Sea* in which "A Strange Voyage" was made, as she appeared from the shore in Plymouth Harbour, both at night and by day. Then he gets into a boat, and sketches her from the wavetops. Finally he goes aboard, and describes her from the deck; from the cabin; from foretop, maintop, and mizentop; in fog, storm, and calm; by moonlight and sunlight, temperate and tropical; in the Channel; in the Bay of Biscay-oh; in the trades; in the doldrums; in ballast and crank; afloat and aground; close hauled and running before a favour-

---

*"A Strange Voyage." By W. Clark Russell. 3 Vols. (London: Sampson Law and Co. 1885.)

able breeze; and in many other highly technical predicaments, which cannot be referred to here without misgiving as to the accuracy of the language employed. And in all these aspects the ship is refulgent with the splendid colours that make a sea voyage a wonderful panorama to people of Mr. Russell's way of thinking. Mr. Russell is a literary Turner in his fondness for effects of light and atmosphere. There is another aspect in which he resembles Turner. His landscapes are better than his figures.

The strange voyage is undertaken by a gouty gentleman in quest of health. A friend of his, a shipowner, lends him a ship, and accompanies him on his trip. The party consists of the invalid, his daughter, the shipowner, a colonel with his wife and daughter, and Mr. Clark Russell masquerading as Mr. Aubyn. Though their destination is the Cape, the men embark without a surgeon and the ladies without a maid. It would be hard to say which of these improbabilities is the harder to digest. The first startling incident that occurs is the rescue of a shipwrecked sailor who turns out to be a Finn. Now Finns are supposed to bring ill-luck on board ship. In nautical novels they invariably do so. This particular Finn is an unusually objectionable person. He corrupts the crew, throws the captain overboard, runs the ship aground, maroons the pleasure party on a reef off the Mexican coast, and makes off in a boat with their portable property. For the rest we refer our readers to the novel.

In telling this tale, Mr. Clark Russell has wasted his first volume in an attempt to interest the reader in the pleasure party by a deplorable comedy of manners, which is only successful from a realistic point of view inasmuch as it induces all the tedium of a real voyage. The shipowner and the colonel are bores; and superficial descriptions of bores are harder to bear than their originals in person. In short, the saloon of a passenger ship has not found its Molière or its Sheridan in Mr. Clark Russell; and his book only becomes interesting when, in the second volume, the adventures begin. Then it becomes not only interesting, but exciting: so much so that when the end of the third volume stops the way, the possibilities of the situation are not half exhausted, and the reader, with plenty of appetite left, vainly regrets all the space wasted at the commencement. The explanation suggested by the story itself is, that it was not exhaustively planned in advance, and that its details were invented from page to page. Intentions changed, forgotten, or found impracticable from bad economy of space, are traceable in many chapters. It is to be hoped that Mr. Clark Russell will not strand himself in this fashion when he embarks on his next novel. His sailing qualities are so excellent that his neglect to make the most of his three volumes of sea room is doubly aggravating.

Editor's Notes

- This review took longer than usual for Shaw to complete. Between bouts of debating, first with the Dialectical Society, then with the Fabians, he began reading the novel on 18 November and took it up again on the twentieth and read it for the next three days. On the twenty-fifth Shaw wrote part of the review, and on the twenty-seventh he finished and "sent off review of *Strange Voyage*" (*Diary*, 125–27).
- William Clark Russell (1844–1911), English novelist. He was in the British merchant navy from 1858 to 1866. Thereafter he wrote approximately sixty stories of sea adventures, of which the most important are *John Holdsworth, Chief Mate* (1875) and *The Wreck of the Grosvenor* (1877). Some of his contributions to *The Daily Telegraph* were republished in *My Watch Below* (1882) and *Round the Galley Fire* (1883). It is said that his writings led to improved conditions for merchant seamen. Later, Russell wrote biographies of the explorer William Dampier (1889) and the admirals Lord Nelson (1890) and Collingwood (1891).
- Joseph Mallord William Turner (1775–1851), English landscape painter, famous for the vibrance of his color and the power of his atmospheric effects, and for paintings like "Fishermen at Sea" (1796), "The Shipwreck" (1805), "The Fighting Temeraire" (1839), and "Peace—Burial at Sea" (1842), which depict the sea in its many moods.
- Admiral Smyth's *Sailor's Word Book* was compiled by Rear-Admiral William Henry Smyth, and was an alphabetical digest of nautical terms and archaisms of early voyagers. It appeared (revised for the press by Sir E. Belcher) in 1867.
- "Mr. Pecksniff's articled pupils" are victims of the cousin of Martin Chuzzlewit, in the Dickens novel of that name. Mr. Pecksniff is ostensibly an architect and land surveyor, though he has never designed or built anything. In fact, we are told, his professional engagements

> were almost, if not entirely, confined to the reception of pupils. . . . His genius lay in ensnaring parents and guardians, and pocketing premiums. A young gentleman's premium being paid . . . Mr. Pecksniff . . . turned him loose in a spacious room . . . where . . . he improved himself for three or five years, according to his articles, in making elevations of Salisbury Cathedral from every possible point of sight; and in constructing in the air a vast quantity of Castles, Houses of Parliament, and other Public Buildings.

30 December 1885

A NOVEL BY MR. JULIAN HAWTHORNE* [C182]

MR. JULIAN HAWTHORNE's latest novel, like most works of art produced during a period of transition, not only begins in one fashion and
ends in another, but preposterously exhibits the new fashion before
the old, instead of the old before the new. It is as if a publisher not
quite abreast of his time had commissioned Mr. James to write a
novel, and, finding the last chapter inconclusive and unsatisfactory,
had called in Miss Braddon to marry the lovers, kill the villain, and
wind up the business on the strictest principles of poetic justice. A
musician desirous of writing an overture illustrative of "Love—or a
Name" might hit it off by composing a prelude in the style of Wagner
with a coda in the style of Rossini.

The story opens in the Arcadia of modern noveldom, a New England village. In these outlands opportunities for persons of strong
predatory instincts are so limited, that the choicer spirits emigrate in
search of Tom Tiddler's ground. The average pressure of temptation is
low, consequently the average level of character is apparently high.
Contemplation of the village life is taken in doses by the American
novelist as a corrective to the pessimism induced by the spectacle of
rascality rampant in the great cities. Mr. Julian Hawthorne has only
two honest people in his narrative; and they both hail from the Arcadian village of Hickory. They are of course the hero and heroine. The
others are city bosses, prodigiously able as wirepullers, and genial as
private entertainers, but corrupt and indeed blackguard from the
point of view of the public moralist. Apparently no man in America
meddles with politics unless he has an axe to grind at them. Republican stinginess in what the Irishman who hired a bottomless sedan
chair called "honour and glory," would seem to have overreached itself
by leaving no inducement to legislators except money and the royalty
of the railway board. The sovereign people has got itself under the
thumb of the sovereign shareholder, who is after all, a doubtful improvement on George III.

When Warren Bell leaves Arcadia and goes "ambitioning" in New
York, he is a little sore and also a little relieved at having failed in his
wooing of Nell Anthony, who has refused him on suspicion of having

*"Love—or a Name." By Julian Hawthorne. One volume. (London: Chatto and Windus.
1885.)

proposed more in duty than in love. He falls into the hands of a diabolic Monte Cristo named Drayton, who has laid a plot to overthrow the Republic and become benevolent despot of the United States. According to this plan, a semblance of the usual Presidents and parties is to be maintained; but the presidents are to be deadheads, to be manipulated, with the parties, by the omnipotent Drayton, who is personally of a retiring disposition and does not wish his name to appear. Forseeing the need of a successor to himself, he selects Warren Bell, offering him a partnership in the scheme and the hand of his daughter Lizzie to boot. Warren, on patriotic grounds, accepts both; and he and Drayton set to work in the face of some opposition from Judge Muhlbach, the reactionist wirepuller. So far there is every promise of a capital story, with plenty of motive and plenty of human material. But all is prematurely and violently wrecked by Nell Anthony. She, too, comes up to New York from Arcadia; and full soon she sets things to rights. An attempt of Judge Muhlbach to obtain a heavy fine for a short lease of a rising town lot is penetrated and exposed by her with an economic insight so rare in one of her sex, years, and rustic breeding, that the defeated Judge offers her his hand, which she indignantly refuses. She then proceeds to the residence of Drayton, who, after a faint resistance, confesses his plot, merely pleading that his intentions were good and that he would have taken care of Warren Bell's interests if she had not interfered. The other characters are soon disposed of. Lizzie is run down by a fire engine and slain. Drayton obliterates the countenance of her perfidious lover with a cut glass decanter, and then shoots himself. Warren Bell courageously marries Nell and retires from public life. "Be he where he may," says the author, "there is reason to believe that she whom we have known as Nell Anthony is with him." This conclusion is cheerfully intended; but in view of Nell's uncommon strength of character, it has something of the minor cadence in it.

There is a highly civilized wit and wisdom about the telling of this story that makes the barbarism of its winding-up quite astonishing. All interest and belief in the narrative vanish at the first pistol shot. In their place comes a wondering demand as to what Mr. Julian Hawthorne has to do with gunpowder and fire engines and such transpontine stage properties. There are still people who like a book in which for three volumes hardhearted relatives and designing villains block the heroine's way to the altar only to be arbitrarily removed in the last chapter by battle, murder, or sudden death: the sympathetic reader breathing more and more freely as the slaughter proceeds, and obstacle after obstacle is removed (in the Invinciblist sense of that verb) from the path of true love. But these unsophisticated persons are the gluttons of fiction. Mr. Julian Hawthorne's work appeals to the epicures. To even moderately cultivated palates, the crudities of old-fashioned romance have by this time lost their relish. There is no longer any need for the novelist to tie a very complicated knot in his story; but if he does tie one, he must unravel it fairly and not cut it by a suicide and a fatal accident. That Alexandrine method is a rough-and-ready one, and has done hard service in its day; but just at present, it is, as Mr. Julian Hawthorne's compatriots would say, "played out."

Editor's Notes

▪ Shaw began reading this novel on Boxing Day, 1885, finished it on 27 December, and wrote his review on the twenty-eighth (*Diary*, 133–34).

▪ Julian Hawthorne (1846–1934), American author. He was the son of Nathaniel Hawthorne, the novelist, and brother of Rose Hawthorne Lathrop. He studied engineering at Harvard and later at Dresden, but did not graduate. In 1870 he married Mary Amelung. He was a hydrographic engineer (as was his hero Warren Bell of *Love—or a Name*), employed by the department of docks in New York from 1870 to 1872. Thereafter he devoted himself to authorship and journalism, becoming correspondent of the *New York Journal* in Cuba and elsewhere, and special commissioner of *Cosmopolitan Magazine* to India. He was also literary critic of the *Philadelphia North American* from 1901 to 1903. He resided in London for seven years, writing novels and contributing reviews to *The Spectator,* returning to the United States in 1882, where he remained until 1893, at which time he took his family (which now consisted of Mrs. Hawthorne and seven children) to Jamaica to farm. Among his publications are *Bressant* (1872), *Garth* (1875), *Mrs. Gainsborough's Diamonds* (1878), *Archibald Malmaison* (1879), *Ellice Quentin* (1880), *Prince Saroni's Wife* (1882), *Fortune's Fool* (1883), *Nathaniel Hawthorne and His Wife* (1885), *David Poindextre's Disappearance &c* (1888) [see page 427 below], *One of Those Coincidences, and Ten Other Stories* (1899), and *Hawthorne and His Circle* (1903). This last, a biographical tribute to his father, prompted the following comment from a reviewer in *The Nation:* "The son seems to have inherited from [Hawthorne] the habit of writing but not the art; certainly not *his* art" (vol. 77, no. 2003, 19 November 1903, 410–11).

▪ Henry James (1843–1916), American author. James's reputation was already well-established by his series of novels including *The American* (1877), *Daisy Miller* (1879), and *Portrait of a Lady* (1881). In the 1890s James wrote a number of plays. These last were not very successful; indeed, Shaw was almost alone when he praised *Guy Domville* for its "rare charm of speech" in *The Saturday Review* on 12 January 1895.

- Mary Elizabeth Braddon [Mrs. Maxwell] (1837–1915), English novelist [see pages 361 and 362 below].
- Tom Tiddler's ground was the name of a children's game in which one of the players is Tom Tiddler, his territory being marked by a line drawn across the ground. Over this the other players run, crying "Here we are on Tom Tiddler's ground, picking up gold and silver." They are chased by Tom Tiddler, and the player caught takes his place. Although Tom Tiddler's ground was used for any "debatable territory, a no-man's land between two states," it seemed to have a particular application to the United States. The following year, the novelist Florence Marryat called her account of a visit to North America *Tom Tiddler's Ground.*
- The Invincibles were members of an Irish assassination society, developing from the Fenians circa 1881/1882.

7 January 1886

THE TRUTH ABOUT SHAKSPEARE* [C187]

THE publication of the truth about anything or any one is attended with considerable risk in English society. We have agreed to keep up a national pretence that the black spots in human nature are white; and we enforce the convention by treating any person who even betrays his consciousness of them, much less ventures directly to call attention to them and suggest a purifying limewash, as a prurient person and an enemy of public morals. Bret Harte has given a delicate illustration of British polite taste in one of his condensed novels. "Once or twice," writes his Miss Mix, "a fearful yell rang through the house, or the rattling of chains, and curses uttered in a deep manly voice, broke upon the oppressive stillness. 'You don't hear anything, my dear, do you?' asked the housekeeper nervously. 'Nothing whatever,' I remarked calmly." There spoke the typical English lady, carrying out Mrs. General's great precept of never appearing conscious of anything that is not perfectly proper, placid, and pleasant, a precept that would be no worse than ridiculous if its systematic practice did not unfortunately deceive many innocent people into believing that there is no considerable evil in the world to be fought with, except the existence of a few criminals

---

*"Shakspeare's Sonnets." Facsimile in Photo-lithography of the first Quarto. With an introduction by Thomas Tyler, M.A. (London: C. Praetorius. 1885.)

whose repression may be left to the police. Now, there is a side of this convention which is relevant to Shakspeare's sonnets, because the sonnets are the autobiography of the greatest of Englishmen; and the convention rigorously exacts—under pretence of not speaking evilly of the dead—that biographers shall exhibit great men, not as they were, but as ideal figures in which the Village Blacksmith and Mr. Pecksniff are blended in proportions determined by the degree of sophistication suggested by the social circumstances of the hero subject. That the very worst sort of evil speaking, whether of the living or the dead, is the telling of lies about them, or that the very maddest presumption on the part of a biographer is the taking upon himself to decide how much of the truth is good for the rest of the world to know is not taken into account in judging biography, as Mr. Froude and others have recently been made to feel. The censors will tolerate no offence against hypocrisy, because when the matter is looked into our public decency is mainly public hypocrisy. Hence an offence against hypocrisy is an offence against decency, and is punishable as such.

It is to be hoped that Mr. Thomas Tyler duly weighed these consequences before he deliberately arranged his evidence against Shakspeare of an intrigue which could only have ensnared the Village Blacksmith in the wild days of his youth, and of which Mr. Pecksniff could not be suspected at any age or under any circumstances. If so, he need not be surprised to find himself presently denounced as "a literary ghoul" for disinterring and reconstructing the following piece of history. At the court of Queen Elizabeth there was a certain Mistress Mary Fitton, a maid of honour, young, beautiful (though not usually called so because it was bad policy to praise a dark woman at the court of a red-haired Queen), skilled in music, daring and adventurous, not strict in her behaviour, and, in short, as dangerous a woman as a poet could well find himself on the same planet with. Shakspeare, who was fourteen years her senior, met her and fell in love with her. He could not respect her, and could not respect himself as her lover; but he could not help himself for all that. His intellect was unclouded by her fascination: he saw through and through her; but his will was paralyzed. He succumbed; and took a strange revenge—on himself rather than on her—by the extraordinary sonnets he addressed to her, the first of which is numbered 127 in the first quarto. In them there is much affectionate flattery and good-humoured banter, chiefly at his own expense; but there is occasionally a fierce outburst of contempt and revulsion in which he mercilessly shows her that she has not conquered the higher part of his nature, or deceived him as to the real worth of her affection.

What Mistress Fitton thought of these struggles of her chained Titan, we have no means of knowing. But on Shakspeare's part it is evident that no such commotion could have been caused in his mind by a successful intrigue with a Court beauty had he been an habitually loose liver. He disregarded the claims of the wife from whom he was separated, and the husband—a mysterious Captain Lougher—whom Mistress Fitton had abandoned; but his scruples prove that he was no libertine. In the sequel, she deserted him for the handsome young Earl of Pembroke, his intimate friend, the "Mr. W. H." to whom the first series of sonnets—Nos. 1 to 126—are addressed. For the particulars and the evidence the reader must turn to the sonnets and to Mr. Tyler's introduction. It is sufficient to say here that Shakspeare's endurance of the injury was perfectly noble and free from vulgar malice or jealousy. For us, the fruit of the episode is probably the tragedy of "Antony and Cleopatra," of the heroine of which Mistress Fitton may be regarded as the model.

Mr. Tyler, the author of the introduction, is perhaps best known by his translation of Ecclesiastes; and it was perhaps in thinking his way through the Hebrew of Koheleth that he unintentionally trained himself to track the mind of Shakspeare through that pessimistic phase which recorded itself for the first time so startlingly in "Troilus and Cressida," and culminated in the group of tragedies of which "Hamlet" is the best known. In order to appreciate what Mr. Tyler has done for the interpretation of the sonnets, it is necessary, not only to read his unpretentious statement of the fruits of his study and research, but to have some knowledge of the dense obscurity in which he found the subject. The public had given up the sonnets as inexplicable, and refused to take any interest in the outrageous hypotheses which were from time to time put forward and gravely discussed. Puerile assumptions that all the personal allusions must be divided between Southampton and Queen Elizabeth, and ludicrous misconceptions arising from the notion that the first series was addressed to a woman, were the staple of sonnet criticism, and were only relieved by an occasional discovery like that of Professor Minto, who first identified the rival poet referred to in No. 86 as George Chapman. Mr. Tyler has changed all this obscurity to broad daylight. His penetration of the allusion to Essex's rebellion in Nos. 107 and 124 and to Southampton in No. 125 is a masterpiece of critical sagacity. The evidence as to the chronology of the sonnets is so far-fetched, and yet so closely brought home and so irresistible, as often to suggest, first, a wonder that none thought of it before, and then a greater wonder at the instinct which led Mr. Tyler to it in the dark. A little mist remains here and there; but part of it will be dispersed as the clues are followed further. The rest conceals nothing that greatly needs to be known.

The facsimile of the 1609 quarto, to which Mr. Tyler's introduction is prefixed, has been executed by Mr. C. Praetorius from the copy in the British Museum. It is published nominally by Mr. Praetorius, but really by Mr. Quaritch.

Editor's Notes

- Shaw's diary reports that on 3 January 1886, he "read Tyler's preface to the *Sonnets*," and the following day he "went off to Museum early, and wrote article for *PMG* on Shakspere's sonnets" (*Diary*, 137). One notes that his diary spelling of Shakespeare's name (like Tyler's) is "Shakspere," which differs slightly from the *Pall Mall Gazette's* (whose normal spelling was "Shakspeare") and from Shaw's own later spelling of it as "Shakespear." At this date, it seems, he took his cue from the New Shakspere Society [see below].
- Thomas Tyler (1826–1902), English scholar. He was a student of London University, graduating with a B.A. in classics in 1859 and an M.A. in 1871, obtaining prizes for Hebrew and New Testament Greek. He began biblical research, and in 1872 he joined the newly formed Society of Biblical Archæology. In 1874, he published *"Ecclesiastes," a Contribution to its Interpretation; with Introduction, Exegesis, and Translations with Notes*. He also lectured on Hittite antiquities at the British Museum, where he was a habitual frequenter of the Reading Room. There he made the acquaintance of Shaw in the early 1880s. Shaw attended lectures by Tyler, and with him was a member of the New Shakspere Society, founded by F. J. Furnivall in 1873. The New Shakspere Society was disbanded in 1894; but from 1874 to 1892 its *Transactions* represented some of the most important Shakespearean scholarship of the period; besides Furnivall and Tyler, other members were F. G. Fleay, James Spedding, Richard Simpson, J. K. Ingram, Stopford A. Brooke, [later Sir] Sidney L. Lee, William Poel, J. W. Hales, and W. A. Harrison, who gave a paper on "W. H. and Mary Fitton" on 12 February 1886. Two months before writing this review, Shaw had given over to Tyler the task of completing an index to the works of Thomas Lodge, which he had been compiling for the Hunterian Society. Later, in his play *The Dark Lady of the Sonnets* (1910), he was to utilize Tyler's thesis that the "dark lady" to whom many of the Sonnets appear to be addressed, was Mary Fitton (see below). In the Preface to this play, Shaw gives an account of his meeting with Tyler, and a humorous but kindly sketch of the latter's character.
- Francis Bret Harte (1836–1902), American fiction writer. As a young man he worked on various newspapers and periodicals in San Francisco, to which he contributed the short stories that made him famous, such as "The Luck of

Roaring Camp" (1868), "Tennessee's Partner," and "The Outcasts of Poker Flat" (both included in an 1870 collection). After 1885 Harte lived in England. Miss Mix appears in the "condensed novel" of that name, which is a parody of Charlotte Brontë's work, first published in 1871.
■ Mrs. General is the widow of forty-five in Dickens's *Little Dorrit*, whom Mr. Dorrit engages to "form the mind and manners" of his daughters. We are told that Mrs. General had no opinions:

> Her way of forming a mind was to prevent it from forming opinions. She had a little circular set of mental grooves, or rails, on which she started little trains of other people's opinions, which never overtook one another, and never got anywhere. Even her propriety could not dispute that there was impropriety in the world; but Mrs. General's way of getting rid of it was to put it out of sight and make believe that there was no such thing.

■ [Professor] William Minto (1845–93) [see pages 152–53 and 155–56 below].
■ George Chapman (?1559–1634), poet and playwright. Later Shaw was to speak of his "donnish insolence and perpetual thick-skinned swagger," and his "unique achievements in sublime balderdash" (See *Our Theatres in the Nineties* [London: Constable and Co., 1932], 3:317).
■ The Essex Rebellion took place on 8 February 1601. It was the Earl of Essex's bid for supreme power in Elizabethan England. Together with his followers, he marched on the Court, but was not popularly supported, and fled to Essex House, where he was arrested. The prime movers of the rebellion had all been executed by March 1601.
■ Shaw's seemingly uncritical acceptance of Tyler's theory (which is, however, certainly as reasonable as any of the more recent identifications of "the dark lady") may perhaps be accounted for by his warm feelings for the scholar, with whom he had clearly discussed it (his opinion on the authorship of a letter is cited by Tyler in his introduction to *The Sonnets*). Shaw abandoned Tyler's theory when a portrait of Mary Fitton came to light that indicated that she was not a dark lady but a fair one. Nevertheless, when he came to write *The Dark Lady of the Sonnets* in 1910 to raise funds for establishing a National Theatre as a memorial to Shakespeare, Shaw resurrected Tyler's notion, mainly because it presented the possibility of a "scene of jealousy between Queen Elizabeth and the Dark Lady at the expense of the unfortunate Bard." In the preface to that play, Shaw refers to his twenty-four-year old book review, which, he claimed, "let loose the Fitton theory in a wider circle of readers than the book could reach." His description in the review of Shakespeare's "affectionate flattery and good-humoured banter, chiefly at his own expense," and the occasional "fierce outburst of contempt and revulsion in which he mercilessly shows her that she has not conquered the higher part of his nature, or deceived him as to the real worth of her affection," are reinforced by his characterization of Shakespeare in the later playlet.

7 January 1886

*OAKS AND BIRCHES** [C188]

"Oaks and Birches" might have been called "Men and Women" or "Englishmen and Irishmen," by a more matter of fact writer than "Naseby." It is an earnest novel of the Kingsley school; and the author follows the practice of that eminent Christian Socialist in occasionally claiming indulgence for sins against art as a set off against his renunciation of the frivolities of ordinary romance. The hero of "Oaks and Birches" is an Irishman to whose genius and many winning personal qualities there is but one drawback. The heroine is an English lady whose excessive pride is nobly redeemed by her perfect truthfulness. Now it happens that the hero's solitary defect consists in his being an inveterate liar. Under these inauspicious circumstances they become engaged. She, believing him to be the soul of honour, is happy; but he knows that she has mistaken her man, and in his efforts to avoid being found out and abandoned, which mostly take the shape of solemn denials of patent facts, he of course precipitates the catastrophe he is sinning to avert. She breaks off the engagement, and is only induced to renew it and marry him by a masterpiece of mendacity on his part. He pretends to be converted to her religion, which he secretly scoffs at. Perfect domestic bliss follows until the Irishman, becoming somewhat blue-mouldy in his monotonous felicity, enlivens it by telling his wife how he has deceived her. She has a terrible struggle with her pride, but she subdues it and forgives him. He is so moved by her magnanimity that he becomes a genuine convert; and the book comes to an edifying conclusion as the regenerate Hibernian begins a new and, it is to be hoped, more truthful career. A novel of this kind, though an advance on the ordinary three volumes of pure silliness, does yet not quite satisfy the higher intelligence to which it appeals. To simplify the problem of life, and provide it with a mock solution, illustrated by a fictitious instance, is almost as futile as to ignore it altogether in the silly fashion. A husband full of doubts and a wife with a creed furnish material for an interesting story; but when the husband solves his doubts by adopting his wife's creed for no better reason

---

*"Oaks and Birches." By Naseby. Three vols. (London and Edinburgh: W. Blackwood and Sons. 1885.)

than that she does not abandon him and her child and home because he has told a lie for love of her, the conclusion, however orthodox, is hardly edifying. The sinner is safe within the pale of the Church, it is true; but he has climbed over the wall instead of coming in by the gate. One cannot help feeling that there was more stability in his honest doubt than there is in his sentimental faith, if faith it can be called.

Editor's Notes

- Shaw began reading this novel for review on 1 December 1885 and finished it the following day (*Diary*, 128). Owing to other commitments (chairing the Dialectical Society on the second and writing an article on oil painters for *The Dramatic Review*), he did not begin writing the review until the fourth, finishing it on the fifth.
- "Naseby" is a pseudonym for [Miss] Geraldine Penrose Fitzgerald (?1870–?1903). In addition to *Oaks and Birches* she also wrote *The Silver Whistle* and *Only Three Weeks* (1890). She also wrote under the pseudonym of Frances A. Gerard.
- The novels of the "Kingsley School" lived up to the label affixed to Charles Kingsley (1819–75) by the anonymous reviewer of *Tait's Edinburgh Magazine*, who, in 1858, coined the phrase "muscular Christianity" to describe what he perceived as a conjunction of religion and physical strength in Kingsley's novels, which do, indeed, contain sport and violence—even war in the case of *Hypatia* (1853), *Westward Ho!* (1855), and *Hereward the Wake* (1866).

15 January 1886

GROVE'S DICTIONARY OF MUSIC* [C189]

THIS work, the greatest of Sir George Grove's many services to music in England, is at last coming within measurable distance of the letter

---

*"A Dictionary of Music and Musicians." Edited by Sir George Grove, D.C.L. Part XXI (London: Macmillan and Co.)

Z. The last part issued begins with "verse" and ends with "Water-music." It therefore includes "Violin," "Vogler," and "Wagner"—that is to say, one technical subject of great importance, and two exceptionally interesting biographies. These last are as complete and as unstinted as might be expected from the editor's evident delight in the biographical department, in which he himself set an excellent example by his exhaustive monograph on Beethoven. The growth of Abt Vogler's reputation in this country since 1865 is not due to his music, which is never performed, but to the poem with his name which Mr. Browning published in that year. His history has hitherto been obscure, the best remembered fact about him being the sovereign contempt which he inspired in Mozart. Those who are interested in him can now, by turning to the Rev. J. H. Mee's article in the Dictionary, learn much more about the Abbé than Mr. Browning knew when he wrote "Dramatis Personae." The account of the Bayreuth master is from the pen of Mr. Edward Dannreuther, and extends over fifty-seven and a half columns. The author's intimacy with Wagner seems to have imposed a certain reserve on him: the personality of the great composer eludes us throughout the elaborate itinerary and list of compositions, writings, and performances. In this itinerary there is an omission on p. 353, where no mention is made of Wagner's departure from Paris in the spring of 1842. The reader is consequently puzzled by finding the composer making an excursion to the Bohemian hills, apparently from the French capital. The section devoted to Wagner's artistic theories is brief, and suggests that Mr. Dannreuther is either tired of explaining the subject, or sensible of the uselessness of second-hand expositions of it. The general effect of the biography is to leave the reader extremely curious to know more about its extraordinary hero, and Mr. Dannreuther is careful to give very full information as to the means of gratifying this curiosity as far as that can be done by the perusal of existing publications. Some very interesting passages from the composer's conversation are given. Little is said of the ignorant and foolish clamour which arose against his music here and elsewhere until the public shamed the hostile critics into observing at least the common decencies of discussion. One famous remark of Wagner's on the subject is, however, quoted. The poets, he said, thought highly of his music, and the musicians had some respect for him as a poet; but the professional critics would never countenance him in any capacity.

Editor's Notes

- Shaw read both this book and Johannes Carmen's *Worship Music* for review on 7 January 1886 and wrote reviews of them both the following day (*Diary,* 137–38). The *Pall Mall Gazette,* however, published only his review of Grove.
- [Sir] George Grove (1820–1900), English music critic. Born in Clapham, London, and educated at the local grammar school, Grove was originally apprenticed to a civil engineer, and worked as an engineer for several years. He was appointed secretary of the Society of Arts in 1849, and in 1852 became secretary of the Crystal Palace, the enormous glass and iron exhibition hall covering twenty-one acres, erected in Hyde Park for the Great Exhibition of the previous year. The Crystal Palace became famous for its concerts, and Grove wrote excellent critiques of the works performed there. He was editor of *Macmillan's Magazine* from 1868 to 1883, but is best known for having projected and edited the *Dictionary of Music and Musicians,* which was published from 1878 to 1889, of which the volume under review was part. Shaw himself bought the final volume of Grove's *Dictionary* (with Index) in 1890, cutting its leaves on 16 October that year. The work has been enlarged and revised several times since, and remains a standard reference in music. Grove was knighted in 1883, and appointed the first director of the Royal College of Music. Among his other publications is the monograph mentioned by Shaw, *Beethoven's Nine Symphonies* (1884).
- George Joseph [Abbé] Vogler (1749–1814), German musician and teacher. In Rome he was ordained a priest, and in 1775 returned to Mannheim, where he founded the first establishment of higher musical education in Germany. Although he composed operas, they were failures, and he was not celebrated as a composer, but as an organist and educator. His performing talents were greeted enthusiastically in London and Paris, and he assisted the foundation of conservatories in Stockholm, Prague, and Darmstadt, where he finally settled in 1807, including among his pupils Weber and Meyerbeer. Browning's poem (1864) is a twelve stanza meditation by Vogler, after improvising on the organ, on the impermanence of evil and the permanence of good, represented by music.
- Richard Wagner [see page 275 below]. Shaw's interest in Wagner began before he left Dublin and, in a sense, culminated in his famous critical essay "The Perfect Wagnerite" in 1898. Subsequent prefaces to that work, written in 1901, 1913, and 1922 reveal how rapidly the revolutionary of one age can become the reactionary of the next. By 1922 Shaw can write, "Musically, Wagner is now more old-fashioned than Handel or Bach, Mozart or Beethoven." Nevertheless, Shaw loved the music of Wagner all his life, though Wagner's influence on Shaw was philosophical rather than artistic—one notes in this review that he criticizes the section on Wagner's theories as "brief." In fact "The Perfect Wagnerite" reveals that Shaw's simultaneous study of Wagner and Marx in the British Museum in 1882 was not as surpris-

ing as his friend William Archer later implied. A reading of Shaw's "The Rhine Gold" in *The Perfect Wagnerite* also shows why the original title of Shaw's first finished play was to be *Rheingold;* and his original view of Wagner as a revolutionist in the same volume is perfectly in accord with his own Socialist views. However, when he came to shape his own plays into "recitatives, duets" etc., the operas cited as influential are *Il Trovatore* and *Don Giovanni* (See "Mr. Shaw on Mr. Shaw" in *Shaw on Theatre*, ed. E. J. West [McGibbon & Kee, 1958]), 186). Shaw also reviewed Wagner's book *On Conducting* [see pages 272–75 below].

▪ Edward George Dannreuther (1844–1905), German musicologist [see page 275 below].

18 January 1886
WHAT IS A GIRL TO DO? [C190]

"What is a Girl to Do?" By H. Sutherland Edwards. Three vols. (Chapman and Hall.) This knotty problem is becoming harder to solve as girls become more plentiful. Go on the stage; qualify as a hospital nurse; turn governess; try pianoforte playing or concert singing; marry! Mr. Sutherland Edwards's heroine does all these things; but her adventures throw little light on the question, because her circumstances and character are not common. She is beautiful, courageous, hard-headed, and as ignorant as every lady is expected to be of the abysses which yawn for those unfortunate ones who, deprived of their property by some unforeseen turn of the wheel, exchange the estate of lady or gentleman for that of unskilled labourer. So she innocently bears herself with unabated pride on the very brink of ruin and, with the luck of children, benighted travellers, and drunkards, makes her way safely through dangers not to be faced except unawares. Lilian West becomes an orphan in her early womanhood. As her patrimony is fraudulently appropriated by her wicked uncle, hard times seem to be in store for her; yet she refuses eligible suitors with a recklessness that drives her matron friends to accuse her of flying in the face of Providence. She is far too lucky and ladylike to be reduced to a last sixpence; but she soon finds herself reduced to her last £50 note. In this extremity, she proposes very innocently to work for a few hours every morning so as to gain the means of passing the afternoon in elegant leisure. Fortunately for her, her affairs come to a happy issue without disturbance to her illusions as to the conditions of proletarian existence in merrie England. But in the meantime she tries her hand at various occupations, chiefly artistic, by which she does not gain much except experience. Being a beautiful woman, she is pleasantly tyrannical in her prosperity. Being also a sensible one, she is not too thin-skinned in her adversity, which takes no graver form than insulting overtures from a Cossack colonel, and a few commonplace difficulties, in which she proves quite able to take care of herself. Mr. Sutherland Edwards, as an experienced musical critic, dramatist, war correspondent, and man of letters, is fully qualified to describe her efforts as pianist, prima donna, journalist, and Franco-Prussian ambulance nurse.

Editor's Notes

- Shaw's diary confusingly reports, "Read review of novel (*What is a Girl to Do?*) for *PMG*" on 1 December 1885 (*Diary*, 128). If by this he means he was reading his own review, then presumably he read the novel itself on one of the previous two days ("read a little for review . . . took the evening to myself reading for review"); but perhaps he meant to write "*Wrote* review of novel" on the first.
- H[enry] Sutherland Edwards (1829–1906), English author and minor illustrator. He was educated partly in London, partly in France. In 1856 he visited Russia and spent some time in Moscow. In the 1860s he was in Russia and Poland and Luxembourg as special correspondent of the London *Times,* and during the Franco-Prussian War was the *Times* correspondent with the German army. Later he was for a time editor of the comic paper *Pasquin* and in 1848 was engaged as a writer for *Punch*. For many years he was music critic for the *St. James's Gazette,* during which time Shaw wrote to him (on 6 September 1883) asking about the possibility of acquiring the post of music critic for the *Pall Mall Gazette*. He was a prolific and varied author. In addition to his periodical publications, he wrote translations, books of travel such as *The Russians at Home* (1861), plays (in collaboration with A. Mayhew) such as *The Goose with the Golden Eggs* and *The Four Cousins;* novels such as *The Three Louisas* (1866), *The Governor's Daughter* (1868), *Reuben Malachi* (1886), and *Dutiful Daughters* (1890); and books on music such as *The History of Opera from its Origin in Italy to the Present Time* (1862), *The Life of Rossini* (1869), *The Lyric Drama* (2 vols.) (1881), *Famous First Representations* (1886) [see pages 249–51], and *The Prima Donna* (2 vols.) (1888).

19 January 1886

MUSIC STUDY IN GERMANY* [C191]

IT is not surprising that this book, which appeared in Chicago in 1881, should have attracted the attention of Sir George Grove, to whose musicianly interest in it we are probably indebted for its republication on this side of the Atlantic by Messrs. Macmillan. It is a record of five and a half years spent in Berlin by an American girl studying pianoforte playing under the ill-starred Carl Tausig, under Kullak, Liszt and Deppe. Berlin between 1869 and 1875 was a lively place for a young musician. Miss Amy Fay dashed into her studies with great pluck and enthusiasm. Whether it was her nationality, her talent, her personal appearance, her character, or all four combined, that brought her so easily on good terms with her neighbours and her musical heroes, cannot, of course, be ascertained from her own letters. She was, at any rate, handy with her pen, and was no sooner settled in Europe than she began the correspondence with her relatives at home from which the volume under consideration was afterwards compiled. In America she had admired no one except Gottschalk; but in Berlin she began by shutting her ears and opening her mouth, thinking every goose a swan. She humbled herself like a saint by unceasing contemplation of her own imperfections. "My constant thought is," she writes, "when *will* my passages *pearl*? When will my touch be perfectly equal? When will my octaves be played from a lightly hung wrist? When will my thumb turn under and my fourth finger over without the slightest perceptible break?" These agonies of aspiration and despair, and the drudgery of finger exercises, were compensated by the ecstasy of find-ing in every concert-room a Walhalla, and in every virtuoso a divine hero—"a two-edged sword," as she says in one of her many outbursts about Liszt. Fellow students with wonderful eyes, destined to com-mand Europe by their genius, were as plentiful as blackberries in 1869. It is interesting to turn the leaves and see these exciting and delicious raptures going the way of all the illusions of youth as the young American devotee grows in years and wisdom. The two-edged swords become long-haired men playing Beethoven's Sonata in F mi-nor more or less badly. Girls who, in the refulgent sunset of youth,

*"Music Study in Germany." From the Home Correspondence of Amy Fay. (London: Macmillan and Co. 1886.)

seemed destined to be queens of musical Europe, reappear in the dawning of wisdom and womanhood as dowdy incipient governesses.

She began her studies under Tausig. When she first played to him "he kept calling out all through it in German. 'Terrible! Shocking! O Gott! O Gott!' " which naturally made poor Miss Fay cry, although she was resolved not to be beaten, and finished her piece with heroic cussedness before giving way. He was not a reassuring teacher. His pupils were "as thin as rails" with excessive study; and when he played a passage and bade them imitate him, it was as if he had required them "to copy a streak of forked lightning with the end of a wetted match." Presently, however, he tired of teaching, and abruptly abandoned his conservatory (conservatory here meaning a forcing-house for young pianists). Shortly afterwards all hope of his changing his mind was put out of the question by his death. So Miss Fay went to Kullak, who was much more amiable than Tausig, but who put her even more out of countenance by liberal displays of his own superiority as a pianist. With him, nevertheless, she remained until 1873, when she made a pilgrimage to Weimar, the shrine of Liszt, whose acquaintance she soon made. "He is just like a monarch," she wrote; "and no one dares speak to him until he addresses one first, which I think no fun." Liszt took a fancy to her, drew her out, encouraged her, let her play as she pleased, and made the best of it. The result was that when she returned to Berlin, Kullak, who before the Weimar trip had been "a great master, thoroughly capable of developing artistic talent to the utmost," appeared "so pedantic" that she found him intolerable after three or four lessons. Just then she met by chance Ludwig Deppe, who speedily convinced her that the four years she had spent paying gifted pianists to quarrel with her for not playing as well as they, were so much time wasted, and that she had better get taught to use her fingers forthwith. So she gave up Kullak and the concert at which she was about to appear as his pupil, and went to Deppe, who, to her great humiliation, set her to work on Czerny's "School of Velocity," which she had left behind her, as she thought, at school for ever.

She retained her faith in Deppe until her return to America in September 1875. The publication of her letters a few years later was quite justified by the lively sketches they contain of many famous musicians, besides the account of public feeling in Berlin during the war. Her judgements and criticisms, though surpassingly rash and unmeasured, are amusing, and often very happily expressed. The little sketches of Natalie Janotha, Herr Moskowski, and others whose fame has spread to London since Miss Fay was at Berlin, will be read here with special interest. Readers who are not musical will find some entertainment in the impression made by German etiquette on the free American girl, and will most likely agree with her that "the best plan is the old-fashioned American one—namely, give your children 'a stern sense of duty,' and then throw them on their own resources."

Editor's Notes

▪ Shaw began his review of this book on 14 January 1886 and finished it the following day (*Diary*, 139).

▪ Amy [Amelia Muller] Fay (1844–1928), American pianist. She was born in Bayou Goula, Louisiana, the third of six daughters and fifth of nine children of the Reverend Charles and Charlotte Emily [Hopkins] Fay. The Fays left Louisiana when Amy was four, returning north to St. Albans, Vermont, where she spent most of her childhood. She began to play the piano by ear and improvise when she was four. Her mother, also musical, taught her music, along with drawing and English composition, while her father taught her Latin, Greek, German, French, and mathematics. After 1862, Amy went to live in Cambridge with her sister (who was married to the Harvard philosopher Charles Peirce), studied piano with Professor John Knowles Paine of Harvard, and attended classes at the New England Conservatory given by Otto Dresel. At the age of twenty-five Amy decided to go to Berlin to study for a concert career with Carl Tausig, a pupil of Franz Liszt. During the six years (1869–75) that she spent in Germany, she wrote the detailed letters home that were eventually published in 1881 through the influence of Longfellow, who was a friend of the family. The book had twenty-one printings in America, was published in England, and translated into French and German. It is credited with having influenced hundreds of American music students, and encouraged many to seek a musical education in Germany, an influx that was at its height in 1891, when there were almost two thousand in Berlin alone. On her return from Germany, where she had performed in her first concert in Frankfurt in 1875, Miss Fay performed in New York, Chicago, Cambridge, and Boston, before settling in Chicago in 1878. She is said to have been the first pianist to play a full-length concerto at the Cambridge and Worcester Music Festivals. In Chicago she founded the Arts Concert Club. She also taught, among her pupils being the composer John Alden Carpenter. During the 1890s she moved to New York City, where she lived until the last eight years of her life. She was a familiar figure at concerts and recitals, and for twelve years was the president of the Women's Philharmonic Society in New York. She died of arteriosclerosis in a nursing home in Watertown, Massachusetts, at the age of eighty-three.

▪ Louis Moreau Gottschalk (1829–69), American pianist and composer. He studied music as a child in New Orleans, and then in Paris from 1842 to 1846, becoming the rage of the salons and winning praise from both Chopin and Berlioz. Thereafter he made successful tours through France, Spain, Switzerland, and the United States, playing and conducting his own compositions. He was extraordinarily popular, and continued touring until his death of yellow fever in Rio de Janeiro. He composed four operas and numerous orchestral pieces, but the majority of his compositions are for the piano, or piano with other instruments.

- Carl Tausig (1841–71) Polish pianist. Initially trained by his father (Aloys Tausig, a composer), he later studied with Liszt, whose style he emulated. He made his debut in 1858 at an orchestral concert conducted by Hans von Bülow in Berlin, where he settled in 1865. There he opened the Schule des Höheren Klavierspiels. He gave concerts throughout Germany and Russia. Shaw calls him "ill-starred" because he died in Leipzig of typhoid fever at the age of twenty-nine.

- Theodor Kullak (1818–82) German pianist and teacher. He was born in Krotoschin, and studied piano with local teachers. In 1837 at his father's request he went to Berlin to study medicine. He also studied music there with Dehn, before going to Vienna in 1842 to study with Czerny. On his return to Berlin in 1846, he became court pianist to the king of Prussia. In 1850 he founded a conservatory in Berlin with two other musicians, but the trio fell out, and in 1855 Kullak founded his own school, the Neue Akademie der Tonkunst, which became famous as Kullak's Academy. He published valuable teaching works and several albums of piano pieces.

- Ferenc ["Franz"] Liszt (1811–86), Austrian-born pianist and composer. Shaw, following Wagner, admired Liszt as a performer rather than a composer. He had reason to be grateful to Liszt for the latter's championing of Wagner, allowing his works to be performed at Weimar (where from 1848 to 1859 Liszt was musical director at the court of the Grand Duke) that were denied performance elsewhere. At the inauguration of the Bayreuth Theatre, Wagner paid him public homage. Miss Fay studied with Liszt at Weimar for five months in 1873, at which time he gave no "paid" lessons, but allowed those with sufficient talent to play to him. His class grew to about a dozen pupils; but he evidently was particularly pleased with Miss Fay, for in addition to hearing her play two or three times a week, he visited her and invited her to come to matinées that he gave and to concerts of his work in other cities. In his last years, however, Liszt retired more and more from public affairs. Three months after the above review was printed, Liszt made—as Shaw put it in *The Dramatic Review*—"his last pilgrimage . . . to the land of Purcell," and died in August of that year in Bayreuth.

- Ludwig Deppe (1828–90), German piano teacher and conductor. Born in Alverdissen, Lippe, he became a pupil of Marxsen at Hamburg and of Lobe at Leipzig. In 1857 he settled in Hamburg as a music teacher and founded a singing society, which he conducted until 1868. In 1874 he went to Berlin, and from 1886 to 1888 was court conductor. He also conducted the Silesian Music Festivals established by Count Hochberg in 1876. In addition to his teaching and conducting, he wrote a symphony and two overtures, *Zriny* and *Don Carlos*.

- Carl Czerny (1791–1857), Austrian pianist, composer, and teacher. Born in Vienna of Czech extraction, after receiving his early musical training from his father Wenzel Czerny, he had the privilege of studying for three years with Beethoven, with whom he became closely associated, and who entrusted him with the musical education of his favorite nephew. Many future piano virtuosos came to him for lessons, including Liszt (whom he taught without a fee), Thalberg, and Kullak. Although heavily committed to teaching, Czerny managed a prodigious output of compositions including piano studies (for which he became famous), concertos, string quartets, masses, and hymns.

- [Marie Cecilia] Natalie Janotha (1856–1932), Polish pianist, writer, and composer. She was born in Warsaw. Her father was a music teacher at the Moscow Institute of Music. She studied under Rudorff, Clara Schumann, Brahms, Princess Czartoryska, Franz Weber (piano), and Woldemar Bargiel (harmony.) She played at the court of William I when she was twelve years old, and later at Buckingham Palace for Queen Victoria and Princess Beatrix, for King Edward VII and Queen Alexandra, and for King George V. In 1885 she was appointed court pianist in Berlin. During a visit to London in 1916 she was deported because of her connections with the Kaiser, and she settled in the Hague. She was a prolific composer of piano and orchestral music, songs, and church music, and she authored several books on Chopin.
- Moritz Mos[z]kowski (1854–1925), Prussian/Polish pianist, teacher, and composer. He was born in Breslau (then part of Prussian Silesia), studied at the Dresden Conservatory, later at the Stern Conservatory, and at the Kullak Academy in Berlin. In the last-named academy he became a teacher. He gave his first public concert in Berlin in 1873, then played elsewhere in Germany and in Paris, establishing his reputation as a pianist as he went. In 1897 he settled in Paris. As a composer he exhibited a wide range of interest from full scale opera (*Boabdil der Maurenkonig,* 1892), through ballet, symphonic poems, concert waltzes, and études, to pieces for solo piano.

21 January 1886

SMALL TALK FOR SCOTCH HISTORIANS
[C192]

"THE LAIRD OF LAG"*

SIR ROBERT GRIERSON of Lag was one of those zealous champions of order who are always ready to serve a Government that has wicked

---

*"The Laird of Lag: A Life Sketch." By Lieut-Colonel Alexander Fergusson. (Edinburgh: David Douglas. 1886.)

work in hand. He helped Claverhouse to stamp the Whigs out of Galloway in the last years of the Stuart dynasty. Unlike Claverhouse, he was not above his work, which he seems to have thoroughly enjoyed. He was the chief of the tribunal by whose sentence the aged Margaret McLachlan and the young Margaret Wilson were fastened to stakes on Blednoch sands to be drowned by the rising tide of the Solway. Macaulay's description of the scene provoked an attempt to prove that it never really took place. But though the devil's advocate made out a tolerably plausible case, Lag's reputation is none the cleaner in his own country; and, indeed, he seems to have been one of those fine old country gentlemen in whose record a murder more or less makes little difference. Readers of Scott are familiar with him as Sir Robert Redgauntlet in "Wandering Willie's Tale," esteemed a masterpiece of narrative fiction by Mr. Ruskin. Colonel Fergusson has collected sundry scraps of information concerning Lag and strung them into a volume, which is readable for the light which it throws on the domestic manners of the time. He reprints "Wandering Willie's Tale" in full, and takes the astonishing liberty of "gratefully and affectionately inscribing" it to Mr. Ruskin. Colonel Fergusson's right to dedicate his own works to whom he pleases is undoubted, but he is not entitled to make dedications of the novels of Sir Walter Scott. The book is effectively printed and bound, with old-fashioned type, broad margins, gilt top, and silk ribbon to keep the reader's place when he nods. It has the further excellent merit of being composed of paper which, though substantial, is very light and dry.

"KAY'S EDINBURGH PORTRAITS"*

John Kay was an Edinburgh barber who at the age of forty-three beat his razor into an etching needle, and entered on a new career as caricaturist and printseller. He composed his pictures and designed his figures like a barber; but he drew faces like a realistic Fra Angelico. He caricatured nearly all the notable men who dwelt in or visited Edinburgh between 1780 and 1820; and the fidelity of his likenesses can still be verified by a glance at the faces of some of the living descendants of his subjects. His plates are etched in lines and dots: a few of them appear to have been rocked up here and there with a cradle. When they were first collected and published after his

*"Kay's Edinburgh Portraits." Popular Letterpress Edition. Two vols. (London: Hamilton, Adams, and Co.; Glasgow: Thomas Morison. Price 12s.)

death they were sufficiently large and numerous to fill two thick quartos, which, however, included a series of admirable biographic sketches by James Paterson, the antiquary. The work was necessarily expensive, and it did not reach the general public; although, as it was perhaps the most interesting of its kind in our literature, it speedily rose to a premium in the book market. The last edition from the original plates was published about eight years ago. Mr. Thomas Morison, of Glasgow, has now issued a popular edition containing reproductions of most of the prints on a reduced scale. In these the spirit and character of Kay's portraits are preserved; and even the delicacy of his touch is suggested with greater success than might have been expected. Such striking portraits as the arch-rogue Mackcouil's or that of Deacon Brodie, and such variously interesting ones as those of Adam Smith, Lord Monboddo, Dr. Graham of the Celestial Bed, Bruce the Abyssinian traveller, and Mrs. Siddons, are among those reproduced. The omission of one or two duplicates, and of the picture of Lunardi the aëronaut and others whose glory has passed away as completely as his, need not be regretted. The price of the two volumes, into which a prodigious quantity of letterpress has been packed, and in which there is nevertheless not a dull page, is twelve shillings.

Editor's Notes

- Shaw's diary for 29 December 1885, begins "Read *Laird of Lag* for review." The following day he writes, "Read *Kay's Edinburgh Portraits* and looked up art editions at Museum. Wrote reviews of it and the *Laird of Lag* in the evening and sent them off" (*Diary*, 134).
- [Colonel] Alexander Fergusson (1830–92), Scottish soldier and author. Born at Rotchell, Kirkcudbrightshire, Scotland, and educated at the Edinburgh Academy, he entered the military service of the East India Company in 1848, served through the Persian campaign (1856–57) and in the Indian Mutiny of 1857–59, and afterwards on the staff. He retired in 1869. In addition to the book reviewed above, he also wrote or edited *Life of the Honourable Henry Erskine, Lord-Advocate for Scotland: with Notices of certain of his Kinsfolk, and of his Time* (1882), *The Letters and Journals of Mrs. Margaret Calderwood of Polton, from England, Holland and the Low Countries in 1756* (1884), *Chronicles of the Cumming Club and Memories of Old Academy Days, 1841–1846* (1887), and *Major Fraser's Manuscript: his Adventures in Scotland and England; his Mission to and Travels in France; his*

Services in the Rebellion (and his Quarrels) with Simon Fraser, Lord Lovat, 1696–1737 (1888).

▪ [Sir] Robert Grierson (c. 1636–1733), the "Laird of Lag," was notorious as a magistrate, administering sharp and summary justice to the rebels who were fighting against the Episcopacy. His cruelty towards the Covenanters allegedly increased as time went on, and he became "invariably deaf to all entreaty on the part of the poor creatures for the briefest space of prayer before they were put to death" (p. 52). Shortly after the accession of James VII to the throne in 1685, Sir Robert had the baronetcy of Nova Scotia (and £200 a year) conferred upon him. Two months later occurred the terrible case of the "Wigtown Martyrs," as the two Margarets (mentioned above) are called. However, Sir Robert refused to conform to the new regime and accept William of Orange as his king, and in consequence he was imprisoned in Edinburgh in July 1689. He had hardly been released in 1693 when he was charged with "coining" false money. Finally, broken in health and seriously embarrassed in fortune, Sir Robert retired to Rockhall, the two-hundred-year-old family mansion. His first and third sons, William and Gilbert, both Jacobites, like their father, joined Lord Kenmure's rash expedition to England in 1715, were captured, and heavy fines were again levied on the Lag estates. A dispute between himself and his son clouded Grierson's final years, and he died on 31 December 1733.

▪ Margaret MacLachlan (or M'Lachlan) and Margaret Wilson, a maiden of eighteen, were victims of religious persecution in Wigtownshire in 1685. Allegedly they were offered their lives if they would abjure the cause of the Covenanters and attend Episcopal worship. They refused and were sentenced to be drowned. Whether, on 11 May 1685, they actually were staked to a spot where the Solway floods, and died martyrs' deaths, or not is still in dispute; but the legend and the few available facts strongly favor the circumstance.

▪ John Kay (1742–1826), Scottish artist and engraver. He was born near Dalkeith in Scotland, and suffered a discouraging childhood at the hands of an abusive uncle with whom he boarded after the death of his father. In spite of an early aptitude for drawing he was not encouraged to do this, nor to become a mason like his father; but at the age of thirteen he was apprenticed to a barber. In 1762 he married Lilly Steven who bore him ten children, all of whom died young, except his eldest son William. He purchased the freedom of the City of Edinburgh from the Society of Surgeon Barbers in 1771, and practiced there for several years. One of his influential customers was William Nisbet, who became a close friend, and on visits to Nisbet's house Kay again took up drawing. When his wife died in 1785, Kay dropped his old profession and became a full-time artist. He married again (Margaret Scott) in 1787, and until 1817 he was both artist and engraver. For nearly fifty years he drew anyone of fame or notoriety who visited Edinburgh, and maintained an independence from the sale of his prints from his shop on the south side of Parliament Square. He died in 1826 in his eighty-fourth year, his widow surviving him by nine years.

- Fra Angelico [original name Guido di Pietro] (c. 1387–1455), Italian painter and Dominican monk. His companions gave him the name "Angelico" partly because he painted religious subjects, and partly because of his personal piety. Shaw no doubt makes the comparison with Kay because Fra Angelico began his career as a painter of miniatures and an illuminator of devotional books, and because his later paintings are distinguished by the beauty of their facial expressions. In 1445 Angelico was summoned to Rome by Pope Eugenius IV to paint frescoes for the Chapel of the Sacrament in the Vatican. In 1449 he became prior of his old monastery in Fiesole. He died in the house of his order in Rome.

- James Paterson (1805–76), Scottish antiquary and author. He was the son of a farmer, who was first apprenticed to a printer, and in his thirteenth year began to contribute to Thomson's *Miscellany*. He worked on newspapers both in Scotland and Ireland. Returning to Edinburgh, he wrote the letterpress for Kay's book reviewed above, contributing the majority of the biographies. In 1839 he became editor of the Ayr *Observer*. Thereafter he was a diligent writer on Scottish national antiquities, family history, and biography. He wrote in a strongly descriptive style and was the author of about twenty books, all relating to Scottish affairs. Among the more notable of his publications were *The Contemporaries of Burns, and the more recent Poets of Ayrshire* (1840), *The History of the County of Ayr* (1847), *The Origin of the Scots and the Scottish Language* (1855), *Wallace and His Times* (1858), and *James the Fifth, or the Gudeman of Balengrich, his Poetry and Adventures* (1861).

- James Mackcoull (1763–1820), English pickpocket and bank robber. Mackcoull's greatest robbery was committed in 1807 when he robbed the Paisley Union Bank Office of £20,000. To save the life of one of the robbers who was taken, Mackcoull promised to restore the stolen money, but returned only a portion of the loot, at the same time giving evidence which ensured that the remaining bank robbers were transported to New South Wales. In 1812 Mackcoull was himself caught but again managed to bribe the bank with their own money to produce inadequate evidence of his guilt, and was freed. Finally in 1820 Mackcoull was tried for the robbery and sentenced to death, but became mentally unwell in prison and died in Edinburgh County Jail on 22 December 1820.

- William Brodie (?–1788), Scottish thief. Together with three other rogues, Smith, Ainslie, and Brown, he committed a series of robberies in Edinburgh in 1787. On 5 March, the following year, the same gang robbed the Excise Office, but Brown turned informer, and Brodie and his companion were taken, tried, and hanged. The play *Deacon Brodie* (1880) by R. L. Stevenson and W. E. Henley celebrates his exploits.

- Adam Smith (1723–90), Scottish philosopher and economist. His connections with Scotland were strong. Born in Kircaldy and educated first at the University of Glasgow, he was closely associated with the Scottish philosopher David Hume (1711–76), was appointed professor of logic and subsequently of moral philosophy at the University of Glasgow, and from 1766–76 lived in Kircaldy, while preparing his celebrated treatise on political economy *An Inquiry into the Nature and Causes of the Wealth of Nations* (1776) [see page 337 below].

- James Burnett [Lord Monboddo] (1714–99), Scottish judge. The eldest surviving son of James Burnett of Monboddo in the County of Kincardine, he was educated at Laurencekirk and King's College, Aberdeen, where he acquired a passion for ancient literature. After this he studied civil law for three years at Groningen. He graduated in 1737, and in 1767 was appointed a Lord of Session, and assumed the judicial name Monboddo. He was learned and well respected throughout his eighty-five years, though somewhat deaf and extremely eccentric. For many years he annually visited London, where, it is said, the King enjoyed his company greatly.
- James Graham (1745–94), Scottish physician. He studied medicine in Edinburgh, but perfected the art of quackery in America and, returning to London, set up the "Temple of Health"—a kind of *son et lumière* bridal chamber—designed to cure barrenness and promote matrimony. He lectured on sex education (which caused a minor scandal), and both preached and practised total abstinence from alcohol, while promoting vegetarianism, and earth bathing (burying his patients alive up to the neck for twelve hours). Later he began to suffer from religious mania, styling himself the Servant of the Lord, O.W.L. (Oh Wonderful Love) and attempting to begin a new chronology by dating his bills from the first month of the New Jerusalem Church. He died suddenly from the bursting of a blood vessel on 23 June 1794, leaving behind an assortment of publications on such topics as the "inadequate, ineffectual and absurd state" of surgical practice of the time, the duty of praying, the effects of simple earth, water, and air when applied to the human body, and how to live for many weeks, months, and even years without eating anything whatever.
- James Bruce (1730–94), "The Abyssinian Traveller." Explorer and author. Bruce's most famous exploit was the discovery of the source of the river Nile. After many perilous adventures, he returned in safety to Marseilles in March 1773 and was received with great consideration by the French Court. In England he had an audience with George III, to whom he presented the drawings of Palmyra, Baalbek, and other cities, as he had promised. His monumental work *Travels to Discover the Source of the Nile, in the Years 1768–69, 70–71, 72–73* in four large volumes, plus a volume of drawings, did not appear until 1790. The account of his adventures seemed to some critics extremely farfetched, and may have led to Rudolph Erich Raspe's *Baron Munchausen, Narrative of his Marvellous Travels*, published in 1785.
- Mrs. [Sarah Kemble] Siddons (1755–1831), English actress. Her reputation became so great that on her visit to Edinburgh (as part of a tour of Scotland and Ireland) in 1784, the rage for seeing her brought over two and a half thousand applications for only 630 places at the theater. In Scotland, where she was drawn by Kay, she played in Otway's *Venice Preserv'd* and Congreve's *The Mourning Bride*, among other plays; but she was best known to London and the world as the greatest Shakespearean tragic actress of her

day, particularly for her playing of Lady Macbeth. Her farewell appearance was in this role in 1812, by which time she had been the subject of works by painters better known than Kay, including both Reynolds and Gainsborough. In 1895 Shaw, who called her "Sarah the Respectable," mused, after attending an amateur performance put on for the Siddons Memorial Fund, "how much fresher [her memory] is . . . than those of many writers and painters of her day" (*Our Theatres in the Nineties* [London: Constable and Co., 1932], 1:130). Elsewhere, however, he speaks of the "picturesque plastique, and the impassioned declamation which one associates with the Siddons school" (ibid., 2:238).

▪ Vincenzo Lunardi (1759–1806), Italian balloonist. His fame, too, as an "aeronaut" had preceded him by the time he visited London and Edinburgh. On 5 October 1786, eighty thousand people gathered to watch him make his first Scottish balloon ascent from Heriot's Hospital Green in Edinburgh. A cannon was fired when the process of inflating the balloon began, and a huge cheer sounded as it took to the air. Lunardi traveled fifty miles before descending a mile west of Ceres, where he was greeted by a great crowd and the church bells ringing in his honor. In all he made five ascents from Scotland, on the last of which he came down in the sea and had to be rescued by a fishing boat. Lunardi greatly enjoyed the fame he received and apparently became rather arrogant. He was a man of volatile temperament, and was romantically attached to the young ladies of Scotland who, in turn, demonstrated their admiration for him by wearing what they called "Lunardi bonnets," which were for a time universally fashionable, consisting of gauze or thin muslin extended on wire, the top part representing the balloon. Lunardi died, it is said, "of a decline," whether in his reputation or his health is not clear; but he passed away in the convent of Barbadinus in Lisbon on 31 January 1806.

23 January 1886

A SCOTLAND YARD FOR SPECTRES* [C193]

THE Society for Psychical Research divides with the Browning Society the privilege of being the best ridiculed institution in London. Its members are conversationally known as "sikes," though *The* Sike is

---

*"Proceedings of the Society for Psychical Research." Part IX. (London: Trübner and Co. 1885. Price 4s.6d.)

not an individual, but the society. Sikes are sub-classed as soft-headed and hard-headed, each holding opposite views as to the object of their association. The soft-headed sike regards the society as an organization for the protection of imposters and the endowment of slate writers, and has subscribed his guinea on that understanding. The hard-headed sike is bent on a purely scientific investigation of phenomena alleged to be supernatural, and is by no means averse to the excitement of a little amateur detective work in hunting down roguish professional mediums. These hard-headed ones can both think and talk, and they naturally usurp the direction of the society, delivering all the lectures and publishing all the papers, whilst the emotional members can only sit in the bitter silence of outraged but inarticulate faith to hear their most cherished ghosts identified with rats and echoes, and their treasured letters from the other world shown to be in the handwriting of Mdme. Smith the medium. This is the more unbearable because in many respects the evidence adduced is necessarily one-sided. In the case of haunted houses, for instance, the soft-headed sike believes in the ghost, but is afraid to sleep in the house. His testimony is therefore set aside, while some gross materialist member of the committee, who believes nothing and would sleep anywhere, is allowed to give his prejudiced testimony uncontradicted. Besides, it is well-known that spirits only manifest themselves to sympathetic natures, so that the very failure of the hard-headed to attain to spirit-vision is in itself a proof of the soundness of the views held by the opposite party.

Perhaps the weightiest recommendation of the Psychical Society will be conveyed by the fact that out of 263 pages in the last published record of its proceedings, 200 are devoted to the exposure of an elaborate fraud. Four are occupied by the report of a committee concerning a gentleman whose left forearm became miraculously encircled by a metal ring, the conclusion being that "we" (the committee) "cannot infer that it is impossible that the ring should have come into the position in which we found it by known natural forces." The remaining fifty-nine are occupied by a paper by Messrs. Gurney and Myers on mesmerism and hypnotism; an account of some experiments on a confectioner in whose fingers anæsthesia was induced by mesmeric passes; and an elaborate report on "thought transference," in which it appears that the Vivisection Act has partly failed in its purpose, for on page 431 appears the cold-blooded note, "Back of neck pinched with scissors," an injury that cannot have been self-inflicted. The more zealous sikes, it appears, do not hesitate to submit to barbarous tortures in pursuit of the incipient science of telepathy. All the pin pricking, nose tweaking, ear nipping, and nostril tickling they endure are forgotten or forgiven when the exclamations, flinchings, and rueful rubbings of the blindfold medium prove that she too has telepathically shared their pangs. Mr. Guthrie actually took a mouthful of Worcester sauce as a test of taste transference; but the medium only observed placidly that she tasted "something sweet—also acid—a curious taste."

The most interesting part of the volume in question, and one that must be credited to the Psychic Society as a distinct public service, is the report of the committee appointed in May, 1884, to investigate the marvels testified to by the founders of the Theosophical Society. That body, it will be remembered, claimed the guardianship of certain mysterious Mahatmas of Thibet, who could project their "astral forms" to the remotest corners of the globe, and appear or deliver letters there to their friends and pupils. The latter were called chelas; and one of them, Mr. Damodar K. Mavalankar, had progressed so far as to be able to project himself; while another, Mdme. Blavatsky, could perform many amusing tricks with letters, cigarettes, and other light articles. They soon indoctrinated Colonel Olcott and Mr. Sinnett, who wrote English books about Theosophy. The bait of a new religion with plenty of miracles yet to come was greedily gorged; and all went well with the chelas until the General Theosophical Council expelled a certain couple named Coulomb, who immediately revenged themselves by publishing in an Indian paper some letters written by Mdme. Blavatsky, from which it appeared that the mysteries of the Mahatmas were of precisely the same nature as the mysteries of Messrs. Maskelyne and Cooke [sic]. Mdme. Blavatsky protested that the letters were forgeries. The hard-headed sikes sent out Mr. R. Hodgson to examine the manuscripts. The soft-headed ones denounced them for that deed as "ungentlemanly," pointing out that the Coulombs were "only servants." But Mr. Hodgson was, meanwhile, at work comparing handwritings, visiting the scenes of the alleged miracles, and examining the construction of "the shrine" at Adyar, into which the Mahatmas had been wont to project their letters. Its remarkable adaptation to miraculous purposes cannot fail to strike an attentive student of the accompanying plan: Mr. Hodgson's report could not be staved off by any device inventible by soft-headedness. It is upon that report mainly that the investigating committee based their conclusions, of which three may

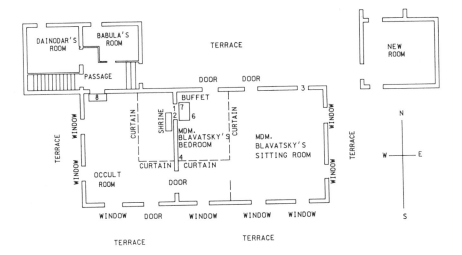

1. Thin wall substituted for original window.
2. Hole in wall behind the middle panel of Shrine.
3. Four-panelled boarding originally at back of recess immediately behind Shrine.
4. Bricked frame forming front of recess.
5. Aperture formed by removing bricks from one partition of the bricked frame.
6. Door of sideboard.
7. Hinged panel at back of sideboard.
8. Cupboard with secret double back opening into passage.

be quoted: 1."That there is a very strong general presumption that all the marvellous narratives put forward as evidence of the existence and occult power of the Mahatmas are to be explained as due either to deliberate deception carried out by or at the instigation of Madame Blavatsky, or to spontaneous illusion, or hallucination, or unconscious misrepresentation or invention on the part of the witnesses." 2."That after considering the evidence that Mr. Hodgson has laid before them as to Colonel Olcott's extraordinary credulity, and inaccuracy in observation and inference, they desire to disclaim any intention of imputing wilful deception to that gentleman." And 3. "That the committee regards Madame Blavatsky neither as the mouthpiece of hidden seers, nor as a mere vulgar adventuress. It thinks that she has achieved a title to permanent remembrance as one of the most accomplished, ingenious, and interesting imposters in history."

Editor's Notes

- Shaw's diary makes no reference to the dates on which he received this book, read it, or wrote the review.
- For an account of the Society for Psychical Research, see note on page 43 above.
- Frederic William Henry Myers (1843–1901), English scholar and member of the Society for Psychic Research. He was born in Keswick, where his father, the Rev. Frederic Myers, was a clergyman. At Cheltenham College, Frederic showed promise as a poet, a promise that grew when he went to Trinity College, Cambridge, in 1860. In his first year he won the University Poetry Prize with his poem "The Prince of Wales at the Tomb of Washington." Coached by Henry Sidgwick [see page 335 below], he became a Classical scholar, winning numerous prizes, including more for poetry. The last of these he resigned, however, following a charge of plagiarism. He graduated in 1864 and set out to travel in Greece and Asia Minor. At this stage in life he was a fervent Christian, a faith that by 1869 had dissolved into doubt. A friendship with Henry Sidgwick followed, and they were both members of the original committee that met to consider the possibility of founding a Society for Psychic Research. He was a school inspector of modest means in 1880 when he married, but he inherited wealth from his grandfather, who had been an industrialist. A great deal of this went towards subsidising the Society for Psychic Research on both sides of the Atlantic. Myers was also a prolific writer for the Society, to whose publications (according to Theodore Besterman's *F. W. H. Myers' Signed Contributions to the "Proceedings" and "Journal" of the Society for Psychic Research*) he contributed no less than eighty-seven items. In March 1898, he contracted pneumonia, which left him with permanent respiratory problems. After a further bout of illness, he and his wife traveled to the Riviera in 1900, and for further treatment to Rome, where he died on 17 January 1901.
- A chela (from the Hindi word for slave or servant) is, in esoteric Buddhism, a novice.
- John Nevil Maskelyne (1839–1917), English illusionist. He was born in Cheltenham, where, after starting life as a watchmaker, he made his first professional appearance. He and his partner Cook made a striking debut in 1865, declaring that they could reproduce by stage trickery all the psychic manifestations that the spiritualist brothers Davenport were claiming to be supernatural. He later performed at the Crystal Palace, at St. James's Hall, and at the Egyptian Hall, Piccadilly, where the partners stayed for thirty years. When Cook retired his place was taken by David Devant.
- Richard Hodgson (1855–1905), psychic researcher. He was born in Australia, where, from the University of Melbourne, he acquired a doctorate in law. His interest in philosophy and the sciences grew when he read a symposium on life after death in *The Nineteenth Century* for 1877. In 1878 he went to Cambridge to study Moral Sciences, where he came under the influence of Henry Sidgwick and joined the undergraduate society for psy-

chic research. He joined the Society for Psychic Research as soon as it was formed in 1882, and in 1884 had just obtained a position as a university extension lecturer when he was despatched to India, at Sidgwick's expense, to investigate the theosophical wonders allegedly taking place at Adyar— whither Madame Blavatsky had repaired a few years earlier. His report (included in the *Proceedings* reviewed by Shaw) accused her of wholesale fraud. In May 1888 he went to the United States where he assumed management of the American Society for Psychic Research. He died of a heart attack at the age of fifty.

▪ Elena Petrovna Blavatsky (1831–91), Russian founder of the Theosophical Society. She was born in Ekaterinoslav [now Dnepropetrovsk]. She traveled extensively and became interested in spiritism and the occult while visiting India and Tibet. With the American Theosophist Henry Steel Olcott (1832–1907), she founded the Theosophical Society in New York City in 1875 and established a branch of the organization in Bombay, India, in 1879. She won many followers throughout the world, until the report reviewed above of the Society for Psychical Research exposed her fraudulent practices. She wrote extensively on the esoteric doctrines of India, her principal books being *Isis Unveiled* (1877), *The Secret Doctrine* (1888), *Key to Theosophy* (1889), and *Voice of the Silence* (1889). For an account of her theosophical beliefs see the note above on page 51, and for Sinnett's book on her life see pages 231–33 below.

25 January 1886

OUIDA'S LATEST NOVEL* [C194]

"OTHMAR" is a sequel to "Princess Napraxine." Good news, this, for all who have not had enough of that gifted lady. And, indeed, when one considers Nadine Napraxine's celestial beauty, the Lubbockian extent of her reading, her exquisite taste in painting, her "profound and scientific knowledge of the tone art," her silvern speech adorned with choice expressions culled from the French language, her untold wealth, and her pedigree co-extensive with history, it is difficult to conceive that she could pall on any reasonable reader. And yet, such is the insatiable discontent of man, that he cavils even at this

*"Othmar." By Ouida. Three vols. (London: Chatto and Windus. 1885.)

phœnix—actually yawns and skips when the loftiest phases of her philosophy are in full exposition. The fact is that Nadine repeats herself to an extent surprising in a woman of her prodigious and mercilessly exercised power of analysing the smaller human weaknesses. And though she propounds problems of life and mind with a careless spontaneity that would have taken the late Mr. George Lewes's breath away, she does not do so, like him, with any intention of contributing to their solution, but rather as unanswerable conundrums—impassable obstacles that make no-thoroughfares of the courses of conversation, and confound her interlocutors. When she discusses art with a fashionable portrait painter, she silences him—shuts him up, in fact—by asking "Do you think Michel Angelo could have endured to dwell in Cromwell-road?" She then addresses the abashed hireling as "my poor court poodle," and leaves him to his reflections, which possibly turn on the manners of the aristocracy, and on whether Michel Angelo could have afforded to live in the Cromwell-road, even if he had made up his mind to endure the architecture there. On the whole, Nadine Napraxine hardly does herself justice in casual conversation, although even her husband (her second husband, to whom she has been married for several years) gives her plenty of opportunities. He is no commonplace paterfamilias. Where another man would have nothing more interesting to say than, "Naddy, dear; I shall want my breakfast early tomorrow morning," Othmar says, "Our minds are all finite, alas!" &c. The lamentable truth is that Nadine is an impostor whose conversational equipment is a precarious power of allusion gained by her from the references to art, letters, and philosophy, which she has come across in much desultory reading, chiefly of novels and periodicals. Her platitudes and impertinences might be pardoned to smart seventeen, or even to sweet and twenty; but in the mouth of a matron of thirty-two they are intolerable.

It must be admitted that the authoress, when she takes up the parable, delivers herself so much in the manner of her heroine as to suggest that the stream of Nadine's utterances "meanders level with its fount," as Robert Montgomery puts it; and that Ouida's attainments are only as genuine, and her culture and scholarship as profound and exact, as those of the Princess Napraxine. To prove her deficiency has been the easy task of many a swashing review. Probably no writer has ever been caught and exposed in the act of writing on subjects without knowing much about them so often as Ouida.

Into this "Othmar," for instance, she introduces an Anarchist, and quite wantonly mentions that "his prophet was Karl Marx," which is as sensible as it would have been to introduce an English Radical whose prophet was Lord Salisbury. Karl Marx might more easily have been left out. But the fatality which drives the burglar to sack a mansion and yet to leave behind him a footprint, or a bloodstain, or a visiting card of some sort for the police to find, pursues Ouida, and drives her to betray herself when she tries to invent observation and learning. The musicians discover that she does not know a fugue from a fandango; collectors wink at her extensive display of bric-à-brac; schoolboys laugh at her cricket matches; and murderers probably chuckle over her ideas of homicide. To which one may conceive her condescending to reply, "All very well, gentlemen; but when you have done pointing out my little technical errors, how will you proceed to account for my popularity?"

It can only be accounted for by the perfect sincerity of Ouida's view of the society she describes. She is true to herself and to the facts as she sees them. Though her share of the optimistic illusions of humanity tempt her from within, and Mrs. Grundy threaten her from without, she insists on the naked truth concerning the hordes of wealthy vagabonds who spend their lives unprofitably roving through Western Europe in pursuit of pleasure. She perceives that the society they form breeds monsters—that it is impervious to all healthy emotions and interests, and responsive only to coarse stimulation of its lower instincts. A noble nature, enlisted in it by the accident of birth, and rebelling against it, is a capital tragic theme. Graft some pure romance on this by providing a beautiful and heroic child of nature for the rebellious plutocrat to fall in love with; and eke out the whole by shoddy philosophical reflections and criticisms of imaginary works of art spuriously labelled with the names of real artists; add copious descriptions, repeated *ad libitum,* and you have the typical Ouida novel, diffuse, overloaded with worthless mock sociology, perceptibly tainted by a pervasion of the sexual impulses, egotistical and tiresome, and yet imaginative, full of vivid and glowing pictures, and not without a considerable moral stiffening of enthusiasm—half-reasoned but real—for truth and simplicity, and of protest against social evils which is not the less vehement because certain emotional and material aspects of it have a fascination which the writer has not wholly escaped.

Editor's Notes

▪ Shaw read part of this novel on 10 January 1886, continued it the following day, and finished it on the twelfth. He wrote the review on 13 January (*Diary*, 138–39).

▪ Ouida [Marie Louise de la Ramée] (1839–1908), English novelist. She was born at Bury St. Edmunds, the daughter of Louis Ramé, a teacher of French. Her pseudonym "Ouida" derived from her childish mispronunciation of her name Louise. Educated locally at first, she spent part of her childhood in Paris, where she early displayed an ability to write. She began contributing to *Bentley's Miscellany* in 1860. She wrote forty-five novels, most of which deal with fashionable life and exhibit a rebellion against the moral ideals displayed in much contemporary fiction. Among her better known works are *Under Two Flags* (1867), *Tricotrin* (1869), *Puck* (1870), *Folle Farine* (1871), *Two Little Wooden Shoes* (1874), *Moths* (1880), *A Village Commune* (1881), *In Maremma?* (1882), and *Bimbi, Stories for Children* (1882). At the height of her success, she moved to Florence, and then, in 1894, to Lucca, where she spent her last years in straitened circumstances, neglected by a reading public that had formerly made her famous. She died at Viareggio after a long illness, and was buried at Lucca. Notwithstanding its blemishes, Shaw seems to have appreciated her work. Its discussion of the "marriage question," may have furnished him with an idea or two on the subject in his early dramas. In his unfinished play *The Cassone* (1891), for example, Shaw's character Ashton, speaking of love, says

> this sort of vivisection is as villainous, perhaps as the other sort: at any rate there is a suspicious resemblance in the arguments by which they are justified. (B.M. MS 50595)

This figure may derive from Othmar's comment to his second wife Nadine:

> I wonder if you have any conception of what bitterly cruel things you say? . . . Or are the subjects of your vivisection too infinitesimally small in your eyes for you to remember their possible pain? (*Othmar* [London: Chatto and Windus. 1885], 2:10)

Shaw's debt to Ouida is particularly to be found in *The Philanderer* (1893). In that play the character of Julia Craven is based in part upon Shaw's practical experience of Jenny Patterson, one of his early lovers; but the underlying psychology of Julia Craven's actions may well have come from *Othmar*, which contains a "Court of Love," a sort of symposium of views on love and marriage. One of the cynical males in the Court of Love says:

> In woman, love may be defined to be the desire of annexation; and to consist chiefly in a passionate clinging to a sense of personal property in the creature loved. (*Othmar* [London: Chatto and Windus, 1885] 1:7)

This attitude is certainly exemplified by Julia Craven in *The Philanderer*. And one is reminded of her again when, during the long and penetrating amatory analysis that follows, a woman in the "Court" declares

> And I, from the feminine [point of view] classify it rather as a transition (regretted but inevitable) from amiable illusions and generous concessions to a wounded sense of offence and ingratitude. (Ibid., 12)

Moreover, Shaw was sufficiently in agreement with Ouida's views on vivisection as set forth in her stirring pamphlet on doctors, *The New Priesthood* (1893), to plunder it freely when writing *The Philanderer* in that year.

- [Sir] John Lubbock [First Baron Avebury] (1834–1913), naturalist, member of Parliament, and author. His avocation was natural science, and he pioneered studies of the life histories of insects; but he also wrote on an astonishingly wide series of subjects, from *The Origin of Civilization* (1870), *The Scenery of Switzerland* (1896), to *Marriage, Totemism and Religion* (1911). Among his most popular works were *The Pleasures of Life* (1887), and the list of the *Hundred Best Books* (1891).
- George Henry Lewes (1817–78), English writer and philosopher. He was sometime editor of the *Fortnightly Review*. In 1851 he made the acquaintance of George Eliot [Mary Ann Evans] and three years later formed a lifelong union with her. He also wrote on a variety of subjects, from Goethe to studies of animal life, but his most considerable work of some philosophical importance, and the one, no doubt, which Shaw was thinking of, was *Problems of Life and Mind* (1873–79).
- Robert Montgomery (1807–55), Scottish poet. The actual quotation, from *The Omnipresence of the Deity* (1830) reads:

> The soul aspiring pants its source to mount
> As streams meander level with their fount.

But Shaw may have remembered it from Macaulay's essay on *Robert Montgomery's Poems* (April 1830), where the simile was ridiculed as the "worst similitude in the world." Macaulay continued,

> In the first place, no stream meanders, or can possibly meander, level with its fount. In the next place, if streams did meander level with their founts, no two motions can be less like each other than that of meandering level and that of mounting upwards.

- Mrs. Grundy was the Victorian symbol of conventional propriety. She originated in Thomas Morton's successful comedy *Speed the Plough* (1798), where she is the neighbour (and obsession) of Dame Ashfield, who constantly wonders what Mrs. Grundy will think or say. Mrs. Grundy, however, never appears.

8 February 1886

CAGLIOSTRO REDIVIVUS* [C198]

No reader of Dumas *père* can have forgotten Joseph Balsamo, Count Cagliostro, who never aged, who could make gold out of cast horse shoes and whose casual remarks as to what he had recommended Titus to do at the siege of Jerusalem lit up his conversation with such piquant flashes of astonishment. About twelve years ago Mr. Bradlaugh, shaking the parish of St. Luke's with his eloquence, might have noted among his congregation at the Hall of Science a youth in whom the Great Cophta lived again. Cagliostro was greatly changed externally. He no longer talked of the philosopher's stone or the elixir of life. He had dropped the title of Count, and pretended to be nothing more than plain Willie Eglinton, a simple citizen of Islington. In 1874 he heard a debate at the Hall of Science between Dr. Sexton and Mr. G. W. Foote on the subject of spiritualism. His old weakness for astonishing people revived. He once more called spirits from the vasty deep; and they came at his command. They rapped; they turned the tables upside down; they wrote on slates; they carried letters from London to Calcutta in less time than the general post carries the mail from Kensington to Bayswater; they levitated him up and down stairs; they dropped heavy volumes on his crown and shot him, like another Zazel, headlong into the midst of his awestruck clients; they picked him up again and shook hands all round; they performed ravishingly on the musical box (an instrument in which he was himself unskilled); and they introduced him to the very best society—Royal as well as noble—in Europe. Mr. Gladstone spent a pleasant evening with him, and received supernatural counsel on a slate by his intervention. The Government, we are told, went so far as to offer him an appointment, which he declined.

Nevertheless, he was not happy. He broke away from spiritualism; became the Ross Publishing Company; and bartered all his money for a thorough conviction of the hazards of commercial partnerships. He again became, perforce, a spiritualist; but his sympathy with the worst form of human suffering led him presently to qualify himself as a dentist. Indeed, the position of professional go-between to two worlds

---

*"'Twixt Two Worlds: a Narrative of the Life and Work of William Eglinton." By John S. Farmer. (London: The Psychological Press. 1886.)

had been made irksome to him in many ways. The testimonial offered
on a post-card by Mr. Gladstone was disappointingly inconclusive.
The police, jealous of one whose sources of information enabled him
to put their mouchards to shame, persecuted the seer whenever he
quitted English soil. Scoffers, disguised as devotees, obtained admission to his séances and behaved like cuttlefishes, squirting ink over

the spirits, and then, when stains were found on his attire, aspersing the genuineness of his ghosts with an almost bestial obtuseness to the first condition of "materialization," which is, of course, that the medium lends his substance to the spirit, and so necessarily bears the marks of any outrage offered to it. Again and again William Eglinton was driven to exclaim that these sons of Zeruiah were too hard for him, and that he would lay down his spirit sceptre and take refuge in Paternoster-row, or at least deal only in such trances as are induced by the administration of nitrous oxide in the pursuit of painless tooth-extraction. But his destiny claimed him after each passing phase of discouragement, and he is still a "medium" and likely to remain one.

It is impossible to give details of the miracles which Mr. Eglinton has been performing in batches for some years past, at the average rate of 240 batches per annum. By the courtesy of the Psychological Press a spirit drawing is here reproduced as a specimen of the condition of amateur art in the other world. They may be compared, more or less to their advantage, with the works of William Blake; and it may be noted as a suggestive circumstance, that gentlemen of sensitive temperament, employed in the Foreign Office and other Departments of the public service, often become partially entranced in the afternoon, and almost unconsciously cover the national blotting pads with designs curiously similar to those of the spirits. Those who are anxious to hear more of Cagliostro in his latest incarnation cannot do better than consult Mr. J. S. Farmer's handsome quarto, with its etched portrait by M. Tissot of the famous medium in a moment of inspiration, and its vivid illustrations of appalling apparitions. There is, besides, quite a Court Directory of unimpeachable witnesses to the good faith of Mr. Eglinton, whose miracles are fully as well authenticated as miracles usually are. The tone of the book is decorous and at times fervently religious, as becomes an account of one whose mission it is to prove the immortality of the soul, and to place bereaved persons— for a trifling pecuniary consideration—in renewed intercourse with their deceased relatives.

Editor's Notes

▪ Shaw's diary reports that he "read *Life of Eglinton* for review" on 30 and 31 January 1886, began writing the review the same day, and finished and sent it off on 1 February (*Diary*, 142–43). The Latin title means "Cagliostro Restored to Life."

- John S[tephen] Farmer (1845?–1915?), English lexicographer. He edited numbers of early English dramatists, some of the "Tudor Facsimile Texts" editions of plays by Udall, Heywood, etc. He also wrote *Spiritualism as a New Basis of Belief* (1880), the second edition of which was entitled *A New Basis of Belief in Immortality.* In 1883 he published *How to investigate Spiritualism.* He is better known for compiling *Americanisms Old and New* (1889) and, with W. E. Henley [see pages 416–19 below], *Slang and its Analogues* (1890–1904).
- Alexandre Dumas *père* (1803–70), French novelist. Shaw is referring to *Joseph Balsamo; or Memoirs of a Physician,* one of Dumas's romances set in the years 1770–91. Balsamo is based upon a real figure, as many of Dumas's characters are. The actual Giuseppe Balsamo, known as Count Alessandro Cagliostro, was an Italian charlatan who went around Europe selling drugs and philters. Dumas, of course, magnified and dramatized his personality.
- Charles Bradlaugh (see pages 397–98 below). It had been more than twenty years since Bradlaugh's platform campaign for free thought won him a large following. In 1862 he became the proprietor of the *National Reformer.* He ran unsuccessfully for Parliament in 1868 and again in 1874, in which year on Sunday evenings at the Hall of Science he distributed certificates of admission to the National Secular Society. Here he met Mrs. Besant who describes his forensic skills:

> Eloquence, fire, sarcasm, pathos, passion, all in turn were bent against Christian superstition, till the great audience, carried away by the torrent of the orator's force, hung silent, breathing soft as he went on, till the silence that followed a magnificent peroration broke the spell, and a hurricane of cheers relieved the tension. (Besant, Annie, *Annie Besant: An Autobiography* [London: T. Fisher Unwin, 1908], 136)

For thirteen years their names were linked in connection with free thought and politics, until Mrs. Besant refused to follow Bradlaugh's opposition to Socialism. In 1880, Bradlaugh ran for Parliament a third time and was elected. However, he refused to swear the customary oath on the Bible before taking his seat, and thus initiated a controversy that lasted six years. In the General Election of 1885 he was returned again, and this time admitted to his seat. In the four and a half years he was a sitting member he concerned himself with matters of health and social welfare, particularly in India. His writings, apart from his *Autobiography* (1873), *The True Story of My Parliamentary Struggle* (1882), *Genesis: its Authorship and Authenticity* (1882), and *Rules, Customs and Procedures of the House of Commons* (1889), are mostly polemical pamphlets, some of which went into several editions.
- William Eglinton (1857–?), English medium. Born in Islington, he first heard of spiritualism in February 1874 at the debate mentioned above in the Hall of Science between Dr. Sexton and Mr. Foote. His father became a believer and formed a home circle. After initial scepticism William joined, and

soon became known as a powerful medium. He was besieged with so many requests for his services that he gave up his job in a printing firm to become a professional medium. The list of his marvels increased and many eminent men of the time attended his séances in which he levitated and produced materializations. The comment in the *Western Morning News* for 28 July 1876 gives a good impression of the effect of his powers on the general populace:

> If Mr. Eglinton is a conjuror he is undoubtedly one of the cleverest who ever lived. Maskelyne and Cook are not a patch upon Mr. Eglinton. The Egyptian Hall exposure of Spiritualism is mere child's play compared with what we witnessed.

Nevertheless, Eglinton's séances did produce allegations of fraud. During a séance in Owen Harris's house, Archdeacon Colley cut a piece of the robe and a piece of the beard off the materialized figure; and these pieces fitted exactly the muslin and beard which he found in Eglinton's portmanteau. Eglinton's visits abroad generally produced converts, but in 1882 he was accused of manufacturing a theosophic marvel with Madame Blavatsky, by appearing to send from his returning ship a letter which mysteriously appeared in Calcutta. In fact it was proved that he had left an identical letter with her, which she accordingly produced at the appointed time. This fraud is hardly mentioned in John S. Farmer's biography. After his return from India, he formed the Ross Publishing Company, but in August 1883 he broke with his partner and again became a professional medium, now, however, turning his attention to slate writing rather than materialization. In 1886 Henry Sidgwick's wife denounced Eglinton again as a conjuror, and this caused great division in the Society for Psychic Research, many members resigning over Eglinton's supposed psychographic feats.

- [Dr.] George Sexton (n.d.), English spiritualist and teacher. It was Robert Owen who directed his attention to spiritualism. At first sceptical, he became later one of its fiercest proponents. He gave many lectures in the 1870s, some of which were printed in pamphlet form. He also authored about a dozen books on theological and related topics.

- G[eorge] W[illiam] Foote (1850–1915), English secularist and lecturer. He was editor of the *Freethinker* and (after Bradlaugh) president of the National Secularist Society. Shaw attended a series of debates on Socialism between Mrs. Besant and Foote in the February of 1887, and later shared the stage with Foote to debate the Eight Hours Question in January 1891.

- When he turned playwright, Shaw continued to ridicule superstition:

> CLEOPATRA: Now let us call on the Nile all together. Perhaps he will rap on the table.
> CAESAR: What! Table rapping! Are such superstitions still believed in this year 707 of the Republic?
>
> *Caesar and Cleopatra*, Act IV

- Zazel [Rossa Matilda Richter] (?1860–?), English trapeze artist. She was the second daughter of Ernst and Susanna Richter of Dresden, but was born in Agnes Street, off the Waterloo Road, in London. She made her debut at the Raglan Music Hall in pantomime when she was five, and was subsequently engaged several times at Drury Lane. At the age of eleven she performed with M. Geary in the "leap for life." Her first trapeze engagement was at the Garrick Theatre, Whitechapel, under the name of "La Petite Lulu." She performed at Dublin, Marseilles, and Toulouse, where she was injured by falling from a trapeze, and was restored briefly to her father. Later, at Hamburg, she was exhibited in a high dive, and was regularly shot from a cannon by a man who called himself G. A. Farini (whose real name was Hunt). According to the journalist reporting on her appearance at the Westminster Aquarium in 1877,

> it should scarcely be necessary, we think, to draw the attention of those of our lady readers who have witnessed her matchless performance to the physical advantages of an athletic education such as Mr. Farini has imparted. Mr. Watts, R. A., pronounces Zazel's figure the most perfect he ever saw. H.R.H. the Prince of Wales has been twice to see Zazel, in whose praise it would be easy to write columns. (*The Illustrated Sporting and Dramatic News*, 26 May 1877)

It is clear from that and the accompanying illustrations that much of Zazel's appeal lay in the fact that, in order to fit into the cannon, she had to shed most of her Victorian clothing. She again met with a serious accident at the Aquarium, and again at Portsmouth, where the receiving net was rotten; and there was a move to have her performances stopped. (See *Truth: a Weekly Journal*, vol. 5, 22 May 1879.)

- "Sons of Zeruiah," a reference to 2 Samuel 19:22—

> And David said, "What have I to do with you, ye sons of Zeruiah, that ye should this day be adversaries unto me? Shall there any man be put to death this day in Israel? For do I not know that I am this day king over Israel?

- James Joseph Jacques Tissot (1836–1902), French painter, engraver, and enameler. He had a studio in London from about 1870 to 1880. Eglinton met him in Paris in 1885, and, in a materialization séance on 20 May, convinced him of spirit return. Tissot's mezzotint *Apparition Médianimique* was an idealized conception of his experience. He also traveled in Palestine in 1887 and made studies there for a set of three hundred watercolor paintings exhibited in 1894 under the title *Vie de Notre Seigneur Jesus Christ*.
- In his scrapbook, alongside the sentence beginning "They may be compared, more or less to their advantage, with the works of William Blake." Shaw, in the margin, had written in pencil: "there were 2 drawings originally, hence the bad grammar." He also added on the same occasion the comma after "public service."

13 February 1886

PRINCIPLES OF SINGING* [C201]

TREATISES on singing are eagerly purchased nowadays by great numbers of half-educated young people who are fond of theatre and of music and who are averse to the sordid ways of commerce, and to the severe intellectual efforts which alone can open the doors of the learned professions. Lazy and good-for-nothing individuals they are for the most part, with a sufficient turn for art to make them quite willing to become famous and well paid as great artists provided a royal road to that eminence be found for them; and they invariably feel that they have made a considerable advance when they have purchased a book on the subject of the art they happen to prefer. The demand thus created enables publishers to take up textbooks which would otherwise be unremunerative and so incidentally to place the counsels of experienced singers and teachers within reach of the few earnest students and inquirers who really profit by them. Mr. Albert Bach's book will of course not teach any one to sing, but it will convey much useful information, and some salutary warnings to any young vocalist who may consult it. Should another edition be called for, however, Mr. Bach will find some revision necessary. On page 92 we read of "the foundation of the opera under Peri Caccini Monteverde," as if these three men were one; while on the opposite leaf, Faustina, the wife of Hasse, is mentioned as if she were two persons. On page 119 in the diagram representing the strokes of the conductor's baton in triple time, the second beat is drawn to the left instead of to the right. On page 155 it is stated that "the tension of the lips reaches the highest degree" in forming the vowel *ee,* a sound with which the lips have nothing to do. On page 32 is a short paragraph to the effect that the timbre of wind instruments depends greatly on the materials of which they are made. Here Mr. Bach is in direct conflict with Mr. Blaikley, who, as a practical instrument maker, may be inferred to be better qualified to pronounce on the subject than a professor of singing. The assertion on page 166 that "in all voices the middle register is best," may be true in Edinburgh, where Mr. Bach practises, but it certainly does not hold good in England or in the countries whence

---

*"The Principles of Singing." By Albert B. Bach. (Edinburgh and London: W. Blackwood and Sons. 1885.)

our public singers come. Possibly Mr. Bach intended to convey that the middle register is best worth cultivating. Grave exception will be taken to the recommendation to persons conducting the studies of children "to endeavour to extend the natural limits of one register so as to make one or two of its notes reach into the adjoining register," a practice which should be strictly limited to the extension of a higher register downward. No fresh controversy is likely to arise over Mr. Bach's pages on the physiology of the vocal organs. He is evidently not fond of the laryngoscope, and has been content to take at second-hand from the best available sources his information on points extraneous to art. Appended to his book are about a hundred and twenty pages of exercises, of which those on the various intervals are likely to prove specially useful.

Editor's Notes

- Shaw read this book, the full title of which is *The Principles of Singing: A Practical Guide for Vocalists and Teachers, With Vocal Exercises*, at the British Museum on 23 January 1886, and wrote the review the following day (*Diary*, 141).
- Albert Bernhard Bach [family name Bak] (1844–1912), Hungarian baritone and author. He was born at Gyula and studied under Marchesi at the Vienna Conservatory in 1869–70, and later with Cunio, Weiss, and Gansbacher. He gave his first concert as a bass-baritone in Vienna. Later he studied at Milan (1876–77) under Lamperti, Ronconi, and Varesi, and sang at La Scala in 1877–78. He taught in Britain and Germany after 1886, and also sang there in oratorio and concert. In his recitals he always performed songs by Loewe (three volumes of whose ballades he edited, with English translations). He was a member of the Berlin Loewe-Verein. Shaw attended one of his recitals in June 1893. In addition to the book reviewed here, he wrote *Musical Education and Vocal Culture* (1880), *The Art Ballad: Loewe and Schubert* (1890), and he also published lectures on *Raphael, Mozart and the Renaissance* (1883).
- Jacopo Peri (1561–1633), Italian composer. He was maestro at the court of Ferdinando I and Cosimo II de'Medici, and from 1601 at the court of Ferrara. He composed the first opera *Dafne* (1597) and collaborated with Monteverdi, del Turco, and Gagliano.
- Giulio Caccini (c.1550–1618), Italian composer. He composed madrigals and sang to the accompaniment of the lute. He was called by Angelo Grillo "the father of a new style of music." He shares with Peri the honor of being one of the founders of opera, composed one of the very first (*Il rapimentop di Cefalo*), and indeed was the first to *publish* an operatic work.

- Claudio (Giovanni Antonio) Monteverdi (1567–1643), Italian composer. He began as a master of madrigals, and later established the foundations of modern opera, enlarging the orchestra and introducing new harmonies. He was a prolific composer, writing about a dozen operas, ballets, and a complete range of vocal music both sacred and secular.
- Faustina Hasse [née Bordoni] (c.1700–81), Italian mezzo-soprano. She made her debut in 1716 in Pollarolo's opera *Ariodante* and became an instant success. When she sang in Florence in 1722, a special medal was struck in her honor. Handel heard her in Vienna and engaged her for his operas in London, where she made her debut in 1726 to great acclaim. In 1730 she married the German composer Johann Adolf Hasse (1699–1783), and devoted her life to his success without, however, abandoning her own career.
- Subsequent editions of Bach's book corrected the comma faults on page 92, but retained the other passages to which Shaw objected.
- David James Blaikley (1846–1936), English acoustician. During his long career with the firm of Boosey and Hawkes as a designer of wind instruments, he became well known as an authority on woodwind and brass. He gave many papers to the Royal Musical Association on resonance, quality of tone in wind instruments, the velocity of sound in air, the trumpet scale, and the french horn. He also lectured to the Royal Society of Arts, the Royal Academy of Music, and the Royal College of Organists.

24 February 1886

MR. ROCKSTRO'S *HISTORY OF MUSIC** [C205]

THIS very compendious work begins with Hermes Trismegistus making a tortoise shell into a lyre on the banks of the Nile, and ends with M. Gounod's "Mors et Vita" and M. Massenet's "Manon." A history of all intervening music is condensed into five hundred pages of large and liberally leaded type. Within such limits the mere technical descriptions, with the necessary statement of dates, names, places, and compositions, crowd out the criticism. Not that Mr. Rockstro, whose imagination always kindles when music is his theme, has confined himself to a dry record of births, deaths, and opus numbers. On one page he writes from the fulness of his heart, as Berlioz wrote of Dalayrac. Over the leaf he recovers himself, and reassumes the historian and critic. But in this

*"A General History of Music." By W. S. Rockstro. (London: Sampson Low and Co. 1886.)

way discrepancies arise which might lead a reader previously ignorant of music to suppose that Méhul was a greater composer than Mozart, because Mr. Rockstro utters, in his gratitude to the composer of "Joseph," a eulogy that he feels would be superfluous and at best inadequate in the case of "Don Giovanni." There is no common measure in his criticisms: Raff gets as much praise as Beethoven. It would be unfair to say that all Mr. Rockstro's geese are swans; but some such inference might be drawn if his past services to the art had not established his right to a more favourable construction.

In a record which includes a work first heard at the Birmingham Festival in 1885, it is surprising to find no mention of the great Netherlander Pieter van Sweelinck, whose compositions were resuscitated for us with such striking effect at the very remarkable concerts of ancient Netherlandish music given at the Albert Hall last June, in connection with the Inventions Exhibition. Surely the statement that Orlandus Lassus was "the last great genius of the Netherlands" is a little hard on Sweelinck. A much more astonishing omission is that of Signor Verdi, whom Mr. Rockstro excuses himself from dealing with on the ground that "the tentative character of his later works is so self-evident, that all attempt to classify them, until the school shall have more fully developed its guiding principles would be both misleading and invidious." However this may be, a list of "the most important works given to the world since the middle of the nineteenth century" which contains Mdme. Sainton-Dolby's cantata "St. Dorothea," but not "Il Trovatore," is rather a curiosity of musical literature than a piece of history. And, though the English operas of Balfe, Wallace, Loder, Smart, and Hugo Pierson are duly recorded, there is not a word about the revival of comic opera in our own generation by Sir Arthur Sullivan and Mr. W. S. Gilbert.

The best illustrations in the volume are those borrowed from Sir George Grove's "Dictionary of Music and Musicians." The other portraits of the great composers are apparently taken from the photographs exhibited in most music shops. Any one who compares the brilliant *jeune premier* offered on page 277 as a representation of Mozart with a good engraving after the portrait by Tischhein, will see at once that the former is a libel that expresses nothing but the vulgar misconception of one of the most thoughtful of modern artists.

An appreciative notice of Wagner proves that Mr. Rockstro, though a veteran critic, is not behind his time. It is, however, as a book of reference that his history will chiefly be valued.

Editor's Notes

- On 12 February 1886, Shaw's diary records that he "read Rockstro's *History of Music* for review" and the following day that he "went to Museum and wrote review of Rockstro's *History of Music*" (*Diary*, 145–46). The full title of the work is *A General History of Music*.
- William Smyth Rockstro [real name Rackstraw] (1823–95), English music scholar. He was born at North Cheam, Surrey, and studied at the Leipzig Conservatory under Mendelssohn, Plaidy, and Hauptmann. When he returned to London, he became a teacher of piano and voice, actually conducting an English choir at the Inventions Exhibition concert mentioned by Shaw. He wrote a popular ballad entitled *Queen and Huntress*, published piano arrangements of various operas, and finally devoted himself to a study of church music, becoming an authority on plainsong. In 1876 he became a Roman Catholic. His other publications include *A History of Music for Young Students* (1879), *Practical Harmony* (1881), *The Rules of Counterpoint* (1882), *The Life of G. F. Handel* (1883), *Mendelssohn* (1884), (with Canon Scott Holland) *Jenny Lind the Artist* (1891), and (with Otto Goldschmidt) *Jenny Lind, Her Vocal Art and Culture* (1894).
- A legend ascribes the invention of the lyre to Hermes Trismegistus who, while wandering on the banks of the Nile, is said to have found an empty tortoise shell and to have used it as a framework for the first musical instrument ever constructed, fitting it with three cords formed from the dried tendons of the animal.
- Charles François Gounod (1818–93), French composer. He enjoyed great popularity in the Victorian period with light operas such as *Le Médecin Malgré Lui* (based on Moliere's comedy) (1858), and with serious ones such as *Faust* (1859). In all, he wrote twelve operas. He also composed several masses, motets, and hymns, a cantata, the famous *Ave Maria,* and the oratorios *La Redemption* (1882) and *Mors et Vita,* which was written for, and is the piece Shaw refers to as being first performed at, the Birmingham Festival in 1885. Speaking of its first London performance in the same year, Shaw said

> M. Gounod is . . . the romantically pious Frenchman whose adoration of the Virgin Mother is chivalrous, whose obedience to the Pope is filial, and whose homage to his God is that of a devoted royalist to his king. It follows that he is not a deep thinker. But his exquisite taste, his fastidious workmanship, and an earnestness that never fails him even in his most childish enterprises, make him the most enchanting of modern musicians within the limits of his domain of emotion and picturesque superstition. (Bernard Shaw, *How to Become a Musical Critic,* ed. Dan H. Laurence [London: Rupert Hart-Davis, 1960], 90)

- Jules Emile Frederic Massenet (1842–1912), French composer. He wrote oratorios, cantatas, instrumental pieces, and orchestral suites, one of which

(*Macbeth*) introduced his music to English audiences in 1878 and, according to Shaw, "established his reputation as one of the loudest of modern composers." He is best known for his operas, which include *Herodiade* (1881), *Manon* (1884), *Le Cid* (1885), *Werther* (1892), *Thais* (1894), and *Don Quichotte* (1910). *Manon* (based on the novel *Manon Lescaut* by French novelist Antoine François Prévost d'Exiles) was reviewed by Shaw in *The Dramatic Review* on 16 May 1885.

▪ Louis Hector Berlioz (1803–69), French composer. Shaw's reference, however, reminds us that Berlioz, like Shaw himself, was a brilliant music critic, writing from 1835 to 1863 in the periodical *Journal des Débats*.

▪ Nicolas [-Marie] D'Alayrac (1753–1809), French composer. He began with instrumental music; but after his first work for the theatre (a comic opera *L'Eclipse totale* first performed in Paris in 1782), he wrote over fifty-six operas and during the revolution he contributed to the music of the Republic by adapting old songs to patriotic words.

▪ Etienne Henri Méhul (1763–1817), French composer. According to Rockstro he was "remarkable for his inexhaustible vein of Melody, and for the beauty and dramatic power of his ever-varied instrumentation" (Rockstro, 299). In addition to his four symphonies, his works include the operas *Phrosine et Mélidore* (1794), *Euphosyne et Coradin* (1790), *Le Jeune Henri* (1797), *Uthal* (1806) and, perhaps his greatest work, *Joseph* (1807).

▪ Joseph Joachim Raff (1822–82), Swiss composer. He was born at Lachen near Zurich. Musically he was self-taught, but owed much to the help and influence of the composers Liszt, Hans von Bülow, and Mendelssohn, who became his friends. Shaw also describes him as imitating the aims and methods of Berlioz. He wrote three operas, *König Alfred* (1850), *Dame Kobold* (1870), and *Samson,* which he did not live to see performed. Perhaps his greater strength lay in symphonic composition: his eleven symphonies contain eloquent descriptive powers.

▪ Jan Pieterszoon Sweelinck (1562–1621), Dutch composer. He was also one of the great masters of the organ and a famous teacher, training the best German musicians of the day. Sweelinck's works for organ and keyboard have survived entirely in manuscript; but his vocal compositions were published between 1592 and 1619 in both the Netherlands and Germany. His enormous output includes French *chansons*, Italian madrigals, 153 *Psalms of David*, 37 motets, and numerous French and Italian rhymes and Latin canons. Shaw had attended the concert in question the previous July, and had contrasted the excellence of the Dutch double quartet with the poor performance of W. S. Rockstro's English choir, which also appeared. In his review Shaw was scathing about Rockstro's choir:

> Not since the days of Charles II, has England sustained a humiliation from the Dutch like that which has just befallen her at the Inventions Exhibition. . . . [Rockstro's choir] sang Allegri's famous *Miserere,* which is sung once a year (in Easter week) at the Sistine Chapel in Rome. If they sing it as Mr. Rockstro's choir sang it, once a

year is too often. Once a century is too often. . . . Most English ladies
and gentlemen can sing reasonably out of tune without perceptible
effort; but the extraordinary aptitude of Mr. Rockstro's vocalists for
this species of entertainment is far beyond anything usually available
even in private circles. (Bernard Shaw, *The Dramatic Review*, 18 July
1885, 1:398)

- Orlando di Lasso [Roland de Lattre, otherwise known as Roland de
Lassus] (c.1532–92), Franco-Flemish composer. He was born at Mons, but
since he traveled freely his name is known in the Italian variant Orlando di
Lasso, the Latin Orlandus Lassus, the French Orlande, and the German
Roland. In 1555 he published his *Primo Libro* (a collection of madrigals,
villanesche, chansons, and four-part songs). In 1556 Lassus was summoned
to Munich to become principal tenor in the choir of the Duke of Bavaria. In
1564, he was appointed ducal kapellmeister, a post he occupied until his
death, in spite of tempting offers from the French and Saxon courts.
- Giuseppe Verdi (1813–1901), Italian composer. This was indeed a significant omission from Rockstro's book: Verdi's operas, *Ernani, Attila, I Due
Foscari, Giovanna d'Arco, Alzira, Macbeth, Otello, Rigoletto, Il Trovatore, La
Traviata,* and the rest, were acclaimed throughout Europe; though Shaw,
who deplored the standards of English opera generally, claimed that

Verdi, by dint of his burning earnestness about the dramas he has
found music for, and for the relevance of every bar of his mature scores
to the dramatic situation, has also placed his best operas beyond the
reach of Covent Garden. (Shaw, Bernard, "Wagner in Bayreuth," in
The English Illustrated Magazine, reprinted in *How to Become a Musical Critic,* ed. Dan H. Laurence [London: Rupert Hart-Davis, 1960],
167)

Although no theorist like Wagner, Verdi, the other operatic "great" of the
nineteenth century, did advance the form, and shows some Wagnerian influence in *Aida* (1871), *Otello* (1887), and *Falstaff* (1893), in the increased
volume of sound and the refusal to divide his operas between arias and
recitatives.
- [Charlotte Helen] Sainton-Dolby [née Dolby] (1821–85), English singer
and composer. From 1832 she studied at the Royal Academy of Music, was
elected King's Scholar in 1837, remained at the Academy five years, and on
leaving was elected an honorary member. She made her first appearance as a
solo singer in 1842. In the winter of 1846–47 Mendelssohn, who had admired her singing in an oratorio at St. Paul's, obtained an engagement for her
at Leipzig, where she appeared with Jenny Lind, with great success. Mendelssohn dedicated his *Six Songs* (Op. 57) to her and wrote contralto arias in
Elijah for her voice. She also had successful concert tours in France and
Holland before, in 1860, she married M. Prosper Sainton, a violinist, and, ten
years later, retired from public life. In 1872, however, she opened her Vocal

Academy, and on her death the Royal Academy of Music founded a scholarship in her memory. In addition to the cantata *The Legend of St. Dorothea* (1876) to which Shaw and Rockstro refer, she wrote two other cantatas *The Story of the Faithful Soul* (1879), and *Florimel* (1885), as well as numerous songs and ballads.

- Michael William Balfe (1808–70), Irish composer. He was a prolific composer of light operas, his most popular being *The Bohemian Girl* (1843). In Shaw's *The Philanderer* (1893), when Julia and Charteris are interrupted in the middle of an angry row in Grace Tranfield's flat by the arrival of Julia's father and his friend Cuthbertson, Charteris stands as if singing, and Julia leaps to the piano and plays the symphony to "When Other Lips." This is Thaddeus's aria from *The Bohemian Girl*. Cuthbertson, fooled by the deception calls to them cheerily to continue.

> CHARTERIS: No, thank you. Miss Craven has just been taking me through an old song; and Ive had enough of it.

Balfe also wrote *The Daughter of Saint Mark* (1844), *The Enchantress* (1845), *The Maid of Honour* (1847) and *Satanella* (1858), in which his main claim to fame was his endeavor to bring closer to grand opera the form of English Ballad Opera by substituting music of a dramatic character for the dialogue.

- [William] Vincent Wallace (1812–65), Irish composer. He began his musical career in the band of the Theatre Royal, Dublin. At age twenty-two he made his debut as a composer, playing his violin concerto at the Dublin Anacreontic Society. In 1835 he emigrated to Tasmania, and thence to Sydney, Australia, where he gave numerous concerts. He traveled widely, performing in Chile, Lima, Jamaica, and Cuba before touring the United States. Leaving New York in 1844 he toured Germany and Holland before at last appearing in London in 1845. That year his successful opera *Maritana* was performed (running for over fifty nights). However, his next operatic effort, *Matilda of Hungary* (1847), was a failure. The last phase of Wallace's career began with the production of *Lurline* (1860), which was a success, though not on the scale of *Maritana*, containing, however—according to Rockstro—"some ingenious combinations of a very dramatic character" (Rockstro 439). Shaw had a soft spot for Wallace's music, with which he had been familiar from an early age.

- Edward James Loder (1813–65), English operatic composer. He was sent to Frankfurt in 1826 to study under Ferdinand Ries, whose unsuccessful English opera *The Sorceress* had been produced in London in 1831. When the English Opera House opened in 1834, Loder's opera *Nourjahad* was produced there and found favor with the critics. In 1846 his romantic opera based on a folktale, *The Night Dancers*, was a great success. In 1851, Loder became musical director of the Theatre Royal, Manchester; and his last and perhaps most important work, *Raymond and Agnes*, was performed there in 1855. Although musically an excellent piece, the performance was not a success, and shortly afterwards Loder was attacked by a brain disease that left him helpless. He died in poverty and isolation.

▪ Henry Smart (1813–79), English organist and composer. He was largely self-taught musically. From 1831 to 1836 he was organist at Blackburn parish church, where his first anthem was performed in 1835. The next year he settled in London as organist of St. Philip's Church, Regent Street, became critic for *The Atlas,* and a music teacher. He later became organist at two other churches in London; but soon after 1864 he became blind, and subsequent compositions had to be dictated. Among his works are operas and cantatas such as *Berta, or the Gnome of the Hartzberg* (1855), *The Bride of Dunkerron* (1864), and *King René's Daughter* (1871). He also wrote the oratorio *Jacob* (1873).

▪ Henry Hugo [Hugh] Pierson (1815–73), German composer of English origin. Educated at Harrow School, he was intended for the medical profession, but also studied music without the family's permission. While at Cambridge (between 1836 and 1839) he composed two sets of songs; he then lived in Germany where he studied with Rinck and Reisseger from 1839 to 1844, in which year he married and adopted the name of Edgar Mannsfeldt (from his wife's family). In about 1853 he settled on Henry Hugo Pierson as the final form of his name. He continued to compose, and his reputation grew with the production of the opera *Leila* (1848), which, for a time, was played annually on Goethe's birthday. Oratorios like *Jerusalem* (1852) and *Hezekiah* (1869) were not received so well in England, though his German reputation remained high after his death.

▪ The nine comic operas written to this date by [Sir] W. S. Gilbert (1836–1911) and [Sir] Arthur Sullivan (1842–1900) had made their names household words on both sides of the Atlantic, and certainly justified their inclusion in Rockstro's work. For ten years they had been delighting London audiences with such pieces as *Trial by Jury* (1875), *H.M.S. Pinafore* (1878), *The Pirates of Penzance* (1880), *Patience* (1881), and *Iolanthe* (1882); while *The Mikado,* which had opened the previous year (14 March 1885) and was still running, "was to be accounted the most valuable stage property in the world for the next seventy years" (Caryl Brahms, *Gilbert and Sullivan: Lost Chords and Discords* [Boston, Toronto: Little, Brown and Company, 1975], 140). Queen Victoria had requested the music, and Massenet had written to Sullivan congratulating a "Master." In fact Rockstro does not ignore the duo altogether, though he does not mention Gilbert by name. On page 452 of his book he gives a representative list of work currently in progress in England, and against Sullivan's name, in addition to his oratorios *The Light of the World, The Prodigal Son,* and *The Martyr of Antioch,* he lists "Numerous Comic Operettas; &c." A clue to his refusal to name Gilbert may lie in the phrase he uses to praise Balfe's substitution of music of a dramatic character "for the objectionable dialogue." More remarkable than Rockstro's omission of Gilbert and Sullivan is Shaw's inclusion of them. He was never very complimentary about Sullivan, speaking derisively of his "penn'orths of orchestral sugarstick" that sweetened Comyns Carr's *King Arthur* in 1895, and comparing the tired formula of literary romance with the predictable progressions in Sullivan's operas [see page 361 below]. He also became indignant when

Archer likened him technically to Gilbert [see, for example, Shaw's letter to Archer, 23 April 1894, in *Collected Letters 1874–1897*].

3 March 1886

JOHN HULLAH* [C208]

JOHN PYKE HULLAH was born in 1812; and it is but just two years since he died. The threescore years and ten which he fulfilled were as eventful musically as politically. In their first decade, Haydn and Mozart were the gods of modern music, and Beethoven an ignorant pretender, seeking to conceal the poverty of his ideas by presenting them in strange, uncouth forms, and making up for his lack of melody by over-charged instrumentation and abundance of discord. Soon Spohr was critically elected to the vacant post of greatest living composer of sacred and instrumental music. Mendelssohn succeeded him, with added glory, as the greatest of all composers, ancient or modern, and held that dignity until it could no longer be denied to Beethoven, who was posthumously installed as the Titan of music, his old distinction as the dunce being passed on to Schumann to keep warm for Wagner, who only recently shuffled it and his mortal coil off together at Venice. In the theatre, too, great reputations waxed and waned; much conservative criticism was set at nought; and much progressive enthusiasm dashed. The once universal Rossini, whose "Semiramide" appeared to our greener grandfathers a Ninevesque wonder, came at last to be no longer looked upon as a serious musician. Meyerbeer, the impressive, the original, the historical, the much imitated inimitable, is now only "the Jew that Wagner drew." Donizetti came and went with Bellini and others of less note. Yet there were new sensations in store. With the turn of the half-century came Verdi, vulgar and yet Victor Hugoesque, with his irresistible torrents of melody, a little muddy and mixed, but copious and impetuous enough to sweep away the critics who stooped for a spoonful to analyze. With him came Gounod, the French Mendelssohn of the stage. Their fame, also, is passing. Nowadays even the street pianists are ashamed to play "Ah, che la morte";

*"Life of John Hullah, LL.D." By his Wife. (London: Longmans and Co. 1886.)

and the composer of "Faust" is writing tediously beautiful oratorios, and adding descriptive "melodrame" to the Apocalypse. Still there was Goetz to come, with the greatest comic opera of the century, except "Die Meistersinger"; and there was the thirty-year-old novelty "Lohengrin." Meanwhile fashionable Italian opera decayed steadily, as those who could sing the music of Rossini and Bellini died and were replaced by others who could only horribly howl and scream the music of Verdi—a race happily unable to survive a year of Wagner, whose music is singable, but by no means howlable or screamable.

All this prolific period—from Weber to Bizet; from Beethoven to Wagner; from Rossini to Goetz; from Grisi, Rubini, and Tamburini to Materna, Unger, and Carl Hill—fell within Hullah's experience. How far he kept touch with it may be gathered from his *causeries* in the *Globe*, and from his lectures on the history of music; but certainly not from his biography, which, to tell the truth, deals far too much with events which, like Rogue Riderhood's imprisonment, "might have happened to any man." This, however, is not wholly the fault of the biographer. Nearly all of Hullah's history that concerns the world, besides what is recorded in the *causeries*, the lectures, and in his official reports as Inspector of Music, might be conveyed in a brief essay. He was an amiable man, fond of domesticity (he was twice married and had two families), fond of society, of reading, of writing, of talking, of singing, of sketching, of architecture, of music, and of travel. He had quite a mania for holiday trips, and never moved without luggage enough to embitter the autumn migrations of three ordinary men. A convivial trencherman and a late riser, he always lived as far beyond his income as his wife allowed him to; nor was he more provident in accepting work, which he undertook as it was offered, without the least reference to the limits of time and human endurance. His musical aims were wide and humanitarian. He saw that the people spent their leisure hours in dissipation mainly because they had no sufficiently attractive alternative; and he believed that music was such an alternative, and that it could successfully compete with beer and skittles. As to the method of teaching novices to read it, he insisted on the fixed *do* and the staff notation with the conviction of a man gifted with the power of recollecting the absolute pitch of musical sounds, and therefore insensible to the difficulties imputed by the tonic-sol-faists to his favourite Wilhem method. He seems to have regarded Curwen, Chevé, and all other inventors of movable *do* systems as quacks; yet he accepted their results without demur, and declared that teachers would teach best upon the systems in which they happened to believe and to which they were most accustomed. His main point was that the children should be taught to read music by one means or another; and no man did more than Hullah to convince a Philistine nation that it really was a point worth gaining.

In his last years he attempted an autobiography, and produced a few very readable chapters, which bring the narrative of his life past the year 1836, in which he composed music to "The Village Coquettes," by Charles Dickens. The work, which afterwards perished in a fire, was fairly successful. Nevertheless, he speaks of it slightingly, and adds: "With Mr. Dickens, I remained, till nearly the close of his life, on excellent terms. He had, like the majority of literary Englishmen of that day, no critical knowledge of music; but I fear he never quite forgave me for being mixed up with him in this matter." Nearly a quarter of a century elapsed between the point reached by the autobiography and the beginning of the period of which his biographer—the second Mrs. Hullah—writes from her personal experience. Here, accordingly, the book brightens; and frivolous details are admitted more easily. Pleasant as the writer's touch is, we feel that a little more of Hullah in his intercourse with Mark Pattison, F. D. Maurice, Dickens and others, and perhaps a little less of him in his packings and unpackings and Channel crossings, would have given us a deeper insight into the man. But as Mrs. Hullah could not accompany him on his inspecting circuit, she was not present at all the feasts of reason at which he was a guest. A supplement to her account from the hands of Lady Dilke and others of his hostesses would do much to complete it.

Hullah was a Liberal-Conservative in music, countenancing Schumann, but sticking at Wagner. In politics he was not so much a Conservative as a hater of Radicalism, which is the more noteworthy because his father, it appears, was something of a Jacobin. He inherited his musical talent from his mother.

Editor's Notes

- Shaw "began reading *Life of Hullah*" for review on 21 February 1886, continued the next day when his diary reports that he was "out of spirits," and finished on the twenty-third, but "instead of writing review wandered into reading the Dickens volumes of *Bentley's Miscellany*." He wrote and sent off the Hullah review the following day (*Diary*, 148).
- Frances (née Rosser) Hullah (n.d.), English artist and second wife of John Hullah. She was the only daughter of Hon. Lieutenant-Colonel G. F. Rosser.

She was a sculptor, and first met John Hullah in Edinburgh, where he visited her studio. (Later her sculpture "Italia" was placed in the sculpture room of the Royal Academy of Music.) They were married in December 1865 by the rector of Lincoln College, Oxford. A short honeymoon in Paris followed, after which Frances accompanied her husband to Edinburgh, where he conducted a concert for the Philosophical Society. In the summer of 1866 they took a trip through France, through Moret, Sens, Auxerre, Avalon, and Vezelay, sketching together. This was the first of several short holidays they enjoyed together on the Continent; but for the most part they traveled separately, and Frances was unable to accompany him on his annual journeys. To free the time for Frances both to accompany her husband and to take breaks from her family (usually by going to Lincoln College, Oxford, where Mark Pattison was rector), Frances's mother, Mrs. Rosser, used to take over the Hullah ménage. Although Frances Hullah's paper on "Needlework" (published in an 1878 book on pupil teachers' examination work) might not suggest it, she, like John Hullah, was a strong proponent of women's rights, and used her husband's name in canvassing to get women elected to the first London School Board in 1870. Frances became increasingly interested in the Women's Movement and held suffrage meetings in her house.

▪   John Pyke Hullah (1812–84), English composer and organist. He was a pupil of William Horsley. In 1833 he studied singing at the Royal Academy of Music. In 1836 he wrote an opera to a story by Charles Dickens *The Village Coquettes*, the manuscript of which was later unfortunately destroyed. The two operas that followed, *The Barber of Bassora* (1837), and *The Outpost* (1838), were not as successful as the first. In 1838 he married a Miss C. Foster who bore him five children. He became a church organist at Croydon, and made several trips to Paris where he became interested in the new system of vocal teaching established by Wilhem. He adapted it to suit English requirements, and in 1841 opened his Singing School for Schoolmasters at Exeter Hall. Encouraged by the success of this establishment, his wealthy friends helped him to build St. Martin's Hall for vocal performances by his students. The hall was opened in 1850, but ten years later it was destroyed by fire. From 1844 to 1874 Hullah taught singing at King's College, and later at Queen's College, and Bedford College, London; and he also conducted student concerts at the Royal Academy of Music. In 1862 his wife died. In 1865 he remarried [see above]. In 1872 he became an inspector of training schools. In 1876 he was awarded an honorary doctorate of Laws from the University of Edinburgh. Among his numerous publications are *A Grammar of Vocal Music* (1843), *A Grammar of Harmony* (1852), *The History of Modern Music* (1862), *The Third or Transition Period of Musical History* (1865), *The Cultivation of the Speaking Voice* (1870), and *Music in the House* (1877). He also wrote a number of popular songs, including *O that we two were Maying*, *The Storm* and *Three Fishers*.

▪   In the article in his scrapbook, Shaw scratched out "ir" in the word "their" in the second sentence, to make it begin: "In *the* first decade, Haydn and Mozart . . ." etc.

- Ludwig (Louis) Spohr (1784–1859), German violinist, composer, and conductor. Spohr's musical talent flourished early. At the age of five he began violin lessons; by the time he was fifteen he had already composed several violin pieces; and in 1802 Spohr accompanied the violinist Franz Eck on a tour of Russia, where he made the acquaintance of Clementi and John Field. In 1804 he made his first tour as a soloist, and the following year became concertmaster in the ducal orchestra at Gotha. In all he made six tours of England where his reputation as a virtuoso violinist was extremely high, and eventually he accepted the post of court kapellmeister in Kassel (originally offered to Weber), where he settled in 1822. He composed a prodigious amount of music, over half a dozen operas, several oratorios and cantatas, ten symphonies, fifteen violin concertos, quintets, quartets, and several overtures.
- Giacomo Meyerbeer [real name Jakob Liebmann Beer] (1791–1864), German operatic composer. He was born near Berlin, and his early studies were with Lauska and Clementi (piano) and Zelter and Anselm Weber (theory). In 1815 he went to Venice, where he wrote several operas in the Italian style. In 1834 he took up permanent residence in Paris, where his most successful opera to date *Les Huguenots* (with a libretto by Scribe) was first performed two years later. Shaw claimed that the part of Raoul in that opera "affords every possible opportunity to an artist, both vocally and histrionically." Meyerbeer's next two operas (also collaborations with Scribe), *Le Prophète* and *L'Africaine* established him as an operatic composer of the first rank. He helped Wagner financially, and conducted the latter's opera *Rienzi* in Berlin. Wagner repaid him with anti-semitic insults. While he was revising his opera *L'Africaine* in 1861, Scribe died. Three years later, while supervising the rehearsals of the opera, Meyerbeer himself died at the age of sixty-five.
- Gaetano Donizetti (1797–1848), Italian operatic composer. With Vincenzo Bellini (1801–35), whose most famous opera is perhaps *Norma* (1831), and Gioacchini Rossini (1792–1868) he makes up the brilliant trio of Italian operatic composers in the first half of the nineteenth century. From 1822 to 1829 Donizetti produced no fewer than twenty-three operas, including *Anna Bolena*, which established his reputation, *L'elisir d'amore* (Milan, 1832), *Lucrezia Borgia* (La Scala, Milan, 1833), and *Lucia di Lammermoor* (Naples, 1835).
- Victor-Marie Hugo (1802–85), French poet and novelist. The production of his drama *Hernani* (1830) was one of the chief events of the literary revolution that became the French Romantic Movement.
- Hermann Goetz (1840–76), German composer. He studied at the Stern Conservatory in Berlin from 1860 to 1863 with von Bülow in piano and Ulrich in composition. In 1863 he became organist at Winterthur in Switzerland, then lived in Zurich, giving private lessons and also conducting a singing society. He wrote a couple of operas, *Der Widerspenstigen Zähmung* [The Taming of the Shrew] (1874) and the unfinished *Francesca da Rimini* (the opera was in fact finished by Ernst Frank), a symphony, a string quartet, several pieces for piano, and a number of songs.

- Giulia Grisi (1811–69), Italian soprano. She made her first appearance at the age of seventeen as Emma in Rossini's *Zelmira* and caught the attention of Bellini, who wrote the part of Juliet for her in *I Capuleti ed i Montecchi* (1830). For two years she sang in Milan, and then in Paris in the title role of Rossini's *Semiramide*. She was enormously successful, and for the next sixteen years she sang at the Théâtre Italien. Her London debut was in Rossini's *La gazza ladra* in 1834, and for twenty-seven years she continued her annual visits to London. She appeared with Rubini, Tamburini, and Lablache in Bellini's *I Puritani* and other operas, and when the tenor Giovanni Mario replaced Rubini, she sang with (and eventually married) him. He was her second husband. She retired in 1861 and lived mostly in London.
- Giovanni Battista Rubini (1794–1854), Italian tenor. His debut was in Pavia in 1814, after which he sang for a time in Naples. In 1825 he was a huge success singing in Rossini's operas at the Théâtre Italien in Paris; and he was also so successful in the operas of Bellini and Donizetti that he is credited with increasing the fame of these two composers. He sang in Paris and London between 1831 and 1843, in which year he toured with Liszt through the Netherlands and Germany. He also was acclaimed in Russia. He paid a final visit to Russia in 1844, after which he settled on his estate near Bergamo, and spent his remaining years as a teacher.
- Antonio Tamburini (1800–76), Italian baritone. He first learned to play the horn (as a pupil of his father), then studied singing with Rossi and Asioli. His debut was at Cento in 1818, after which he sang all over Italy, his greatest triumph being in the operas of Bellini. From 1832 to 1841 he sang in a company that included Grisi, Rubini, Persiani, Viardot, and Lablache, at the Théâtre Italien in Paris, in alternate seasons appearing in London. Later he spent ten years in Russia, but in 1855 he retired to his estate near Paris.
- Amalie Materna (1844–1918), Austrian soprano. She was originally a church singer. After marrying the actor Karl Friedrich, she sang with him in light opera. She made her debut in Graz in 1865. In 1869 she sang at the Vienna Court Opera, and remained associated with them until 1894, when she became a member of Walter Damrosch's German opera company in New York. Wagner chose her for the role of Brünhilde in the first Bayreuth Festival of 1876. In 1877 she sang in London at a Wagner festival, directed by the composer, and later in the United States. In 1902 she returned to Vienna to open a singing studio.
- Georg Unger (1837–87), German tenor. Originally a student of theology, he made his operatic debut in Leipzig at the age of thirty. Hans Richter recommended him to Wagner for the role of Siegfried, the interpretation of which made him famous.
- Carl [Karl] Hill (1831–93), German baritone. Until 1868 he worked in the postal service; but for the next four years he sang in the Schwerin Court Theatre and in Leipzig and Cologne. In 1876 he sang the role of Alberich at Bayreuth. He died insane.
- Rogue Riderhood is the unsavory waterside character in Dickens's *Our Mutual Friend*, who, seeking the reward for a murder, implicates his partner,

Gaffer Hexam, the man who found the body. To do this he visits the lawyer Lightwood, who, taking his statement asks him about his own past:

"Ever in trouble?" said Eugene.
"Once." (Might happen to any man, Mr. Riderhood added incidentally.)

- John Curwen (1816–80), Congregational minister. He was a proponent of the tonic-sol-fa system, the basic idea of which originated with Sarah Glover, a Norwich schoolteacher, from whose book *A Scheme to Render Psalmody Congregational* Curwen took it. Although he devoted his life to perfecting her scheme, his motives were social rather than musical, and were designed to bring music within reach of the poorer classes generally.
- Emile Joseph Maurice Chevé (1804–64), French physician who abandoned his medical career to develop (with his wife and brother-in-law) a method of teaching sight singing based on that of Pierre Galin.
- Mark Pattison (1813–84), English author and rector of Lincoln College, Oxford. He was educated privately by his father (the rector of Hauxwell in Yorkshire) and at Oriel College, Oxford. Later he became a tutor at Lincoln College and, in 1861, rector. In the same year he married Emilia Frances Strong (afterwards Lady Dilke). Throughout his life he researched the lives of Casaubon and Scaliger, his biography of the former appearing in 1875, though his biography of the latter was never finished. He also wrote on Milton and Pope.
- [John] F[rederick] D[enison] Maurice (1805–72), English theologian. He was born in 1866, the son of a Unitarian minister, and entered Trinity College, Cambridge, in 1823, though at that time it was impossible for any who were not members of the established church to obtain a degree. He transferred to Trinity Hall, where he obtained a degree in law in 1827, after which he went to London and became a writer, producing a novel, *Eustace Conway: or the Brother and Sister* (1834), and editing the *London Literary Chronicle* and also, briefly, *The Athenæum*. Deciding to take Anglican orders, he entered Exeter College, Oxford, and obtained a degree in classics in 1831. He was ordained in 1834 and, after a short curacy in Warwickshire, became chaplain of Guy's Hospital, and a figure in the intellectual life of London. From 1839 to 1841 he edited *The Education Magazine*. In 1840 he was appointed professor of English history and literature at King's College, and obtained the chair in divinity in 1846. During this time in London, Maurice helped to found Queen's College (for the education of women) in 1848 and the Working Men's College in 1854, of which he was the first principal. His efforts at social reform led to the movement known as Christian Socialism, an aspect of which Shaw dramatised in *Candida* in the person of the Reverend James Mavor Morell (who actually has a copy of Maurice's *Theological Essays* on his bookshelf). Maurice's *Theological Essays* (1853), casting doubts upon eternal punishment, angered his superiors, and a committee of enquiry deprived him of his professorships. However, in 1866, Maurice was appointed professor of moral philosophy at Cambridge, and from 1870 to 1872 was incumbent of St. Edward's Church in that city.

9 April 1886

AN AUDACIOUS NOVEL* [C216]

THE title of this audacious novel greatly underestimates its contents. It is a romance of the entire cosmos. So far from confining herself to two worlds, the heroine positively apologizes, after a trip through myriads of solar systems, for having forgotten to visit the sun and the moon. She saw a little of Saturn, and stayed long enough in Venus to attract a crowd of Venusian boys and girls; but practically she paid little more attention to the familiar domain of the Astronomer Royal than a Cook's tourist does to the New River or Hoxton Church. It must be understood that the story is not a burlesque. It is the apocalypse of "Electric Christianity," a very complete exposition of which will be found in the fifth chapter of the second volume. With the subtleties of "the electric creed" it is perhaps better not to meddle here. To deal with them the critic should be a theologian and electrician—should combine in his single person the qualifications of a Newman and an Edison. And even with this equipment he might fail in his grapple with an author who expressly declares that "to achieve something that is above human comprehension: that is greatness."

On the lower plane of those who read romances for pastime the book will be hailed with gladness, if not with reverence. The author may be said to know approximately nothing of any art or science, yet in her mind there is no void; her reckless invention supplies her with physics, biology, music, painting—in short, with whatever she requires. Branches of knowledge are to her only branches of the tree of imagination, which flourishes greatly in her. It has enabled her to give us a painter who, after vainly seeking to rival Correggio as a colourist by using "expensive and highly guaranteed pigments," consults one Dr. Casimir Heliobas, a Chaldean gentleman resident in Paris, and is recommended by him to use luminous paint. The artist, wondering at himself for not having anticipated this simple and yet invaluable suggestion, loses no time in producing a series of radiant pictures, which leave Correggio's nowhere. Dr. Heliobas, it may be added, keeps a vegetable preparation of electricity in bottle, and by administering it to

---

*"A Romance of Two Worlds." By Marie Corelli. Two Vols. (London: Richard Bentley and Son. 1886.)

his sister preserves her beauty so perfectly that at thirty-eight she drives a Russian prince into singing—

> As the rocky-bound cave repulses a wave,
> So thy anger repulseth me.

Subsequently he endeavours to steal a kiss, and receives instead an electric shock that stretches him numb on the carpet. The heroine is an improvisatrice upon the pianoforte. She passes by the formal works of Beethoven and the other pen-and-ink composers, and only plays by ear what she hears aërial spirits singing around her—an explanation of her powers which recalls that of the boy who swallowed the musical box, and when questioned as to the source of his internal music replied that it must be the servant playing the harp in the cellar.

Besides the story and the electric creed, many pieces of practical information are given with a boldness which is either the outcome of perfect guilelessness or of unusual hardihood in the face of possible and probable imputation of interested motives. The merits of Messrs. Pleyel's pianofortes are urged upon the reader with an insistence which almost suggests that the young improvisatrice enjoys a commission on the sale of the instruments. The merits of Mr. Liberty as a provider of artistic costume are acknowledged in handsome terms; and Señor Sarasate will be flattered indeed if he ever reads the eulogies bestowed on him in pages which severely condemn Herr Joachim as coldly correct, Mr. Charles Hallé as icily null, and Miss Arabella Goddard as poor and mechanical. The dialogue sparkles with equally free literary criticism. Sometimes the Heliobastian discourses on electricity lull the reader into a vague forgetfulness that the book in hand is a novel, and not a pamphlet advertisement of the latest magnetic quackery. Then he is roused by such a statement as that "walking on the sea can be accomplished now by any one who has cultivated sufficient inner force." Rising incredulity is checked in this fashion. "Believe in anything or everything miraculous and glorious—the utmost reach of your faith can with difficulty grasp the majestic reality and perfection of everything you can see, desire, or imagine." Finally, one concludes that it will not do to take the author too seriously, and that so very lively and independent a romancer is to be congratulated on the scope which she has left for her imagination by an almost total abstinence from the stores of information and the aids to systematic study which are to be found in the works of her precursors in the fields of psychology. It is impossible for a sober critic to quite approve of her rush into print; but it may perhaps be admitted that "Marie Corelli" might do worse than rush again, so much less wearisome is she than many more exact philosophers.

Editor's Notes

▪ Shaw began reading *A Romance of Two Worlds* for review on 21 March 1886, read more of it the following day, and wrote the review on the twenty-third (*Diary*, 154).

▪ "Marie Corelli" [pseudonym for Mary MacKay] (1854–1924), English novelist. She studied music, but after a psychic experience became a novelist. *A Romance of Two Worlds* was her first novel, and in it she used her own experiences, writing about "spirit power and universal love." Shaw's encouraging advice that she "might do worse than rush again" was enthusiastically taken, since she wrote twenty-five equally imaginative novels, which reached a wide reading public and won her many admirers, including Gladstone and Oscar Wilde. Some of the most popular books were *Vendetta!* (1886) [see pages 188–91 below], *Thelma* (1887) [see pages 290–92 below], *Ardath: the Story of a Dead Self* (1889), *Barabbas: a Dream of the World's Tragedy* (1893), *The Sorrows of Satan* (1895), *The Mighty Atom* (1896), *Zisha: the Problem of a Wicked Soul* (1897), *The Master Christian* (1900), *Temporal Power* (1902), *The Young Diana: an Experience of the Future* (1918), and *The Secret Power* (1921).

▪ The New River was a channel "constructed" in the early years of the seventeenth century and opened in 1613, with the object of bringing water to Islington, London, from fresh springs over thirty-eight miles away at Chadwell and Amwell in Hertfordshire. This "river" rapidly became polluted, more so since it was accessible to a public that used it for swimming in summer, and at other times for the disposal of refuse. Although after 1852 filtration works were established at Stoke Newington and Hornsey, the place was still not pretty at the time of Shaw's writing.

▪ Hoxton Church, dedicated to St. John the Baptist, was erected in 1825–26, at which time Hoxton (part of the old borough of Shoreditch) was growing rapidly in population and losing its rural aspect. By 1886 it was one of the most distressing districts of London, where poverty and overcrowding made the borough of Shoreditch rank second among eastern area boroughs in the percentage of people living in poverty. In Shaw's *Candida* (1895), St. Dominic's parsonage, the home of James Mavor Morell, is situated at the edge of Victoria Park, whose sandpit is a "natural vermin preserve for all the petty fauna of Kingsland, Hackney, and Hoxton." Not surprisingly, a group of Communist Anarchists, The Hoxton Freedom Group, wishes Morell to address them. In the opening scene of *Pygmalion,* the Sarcastic Bystander with

his thick cockney accent is correctly identified by Professor Higgins as coming from Hoxton.
- Correggio [Antonio Allegri] (c.1489–1534), Italian painter. Born in and
named after his birthplace, Correggio, he was indeed seen as a colorist by the
nineteenth century. Ruskin's comment is worth quoting:

> Often in our English mornings, the rainclouds in the dawn form soft
> level fields, which melt imperceptibly into the blue. . . . No clouds form
> such skies, none are so tender, various, inimitable. Turner himself
> never caught them. Correggio, putting out his whole strength, could
> have painted them, no other man. (John Ruskin, *Modern Painters* (5
> vols.), vol. 5, *Of Leaf Beauty, Of Cloud Beauty, Of Ideas of Relation*
> [Boston and New York: Colonial Press Co., 1873], 182)

- Pleyel was a French firm of piano makers, founded in 1807 in Paris, by the
composer Ignace Pleyel. The firm quickly assimilated and improved upon the
best features of English piano making. Business increased so much that the
firm claimed 250 employees and an annual production of 1,000 pianos a year
in 1834. By the date of Shaw's review the annual output was 2500; so it is
unlikely that they required Marie Corelli's commercial.
- Arthur Lasenby Liberty came from a family of drapers in Buckinghamshire,
and worked initially for a firm that imported shawls from India. In 1875 he
opened his own shop in Regent Street, East India House, selling colored silks
from the East. By 1883 he had acquired two more shops in Regent Street, and
circumvented the jeweler's store between them by a humped double staircase
known as the Camel's Back. Liberty's exerted enormous influence upon late
nineteenth-century fashion. In 1881 Gilbert and Sullivan further enhanced
Liberty's fame by using their fabrics for the costumes in *Patience*. From 1884
to 1886 E. W. Godwin, the architect and designer, directed the costume department. He was responsible for introducing into women's clothes the soft draped
lines of the Pre-Raphaelite paintings. Among Liberty's famous customers were
Ruskin, Alma-Tadema, Burne Jones, Charles Keene, Rossetti, and Whistler.
- Pablo de Sarasate [Pablo Martin Meliton Sarasate y Navascuez] (1844–
1908), Spanish violinist. His playing was famous for its great tonal beauty
and perfection of technique, and he was a triumphant success on his many
tours of Europe, North and South America, South Africa, and the East. For
him Saint-Saens wrote his *Rondo capriccioso*, Lalo wrote *Symphonie espagn-
ole*, Bruch the *Schottische Fantasie*, and Mackenzie the *Pibroch Suite*.
Sarasate himself wrote a few works for violin and orchestra.
- Joseph Joachim (1831–1907), German violinist. He began to study the
violin at the age of five, and first played in public at the age of seven. His first
tour of England was in 1844, where his remarkable technique was much
admired. In 1868 he was appointed director of the Hochschule für Ausubende
Tonkust in Berlin, and soon became so famous as a teacher that violinists from
far and wide flocked to study with him. He did not relinquish his concert
career, visiting England every year from 1862, and receiving honorary degrees

from Oxford, Cambridge, and Glasgow. He was generally considered the great-est violinist of his day; and the Joachim Quartet, organized in 1869, was very celebrated in Europe. From 1882 to 1887 Joachim was one of the principal conductors of the Berlin Philharmonic Orchestra. He wrote numerous virtuoso pieces for the violin and orchestra, the best-known of which is probably his Concerto in D Minor (known as the *Hungarian Concerto*).

▪ [Sir] Charles Hallé [real name Carl Halle] (1819–1895), German pianist and conductor. After the 1848 Revolution, he emigrated to England, settling in Manchester where in 1858 he formed his own orchestra. This became famous as Charles Hallé's Orchestra, and he conducted it until his death. The Hallé Orchestra, as it became known, lasted for 125 years as one of the finest orchestras in Europe. Although based in Manchester, Hallé gave piano recit-als in London: in 1861, for example, he presented all of Beethoven's Piano Sonatas in six concerts. From 1873 to 1893 he conducted the Bristol Festi-vals, in 1883 he became conductor of the Liverpool Philharmonic Society (succeeding Max Bruch), and in 1893 he was appointed the first principal of the Royal Manchester College of Music. He was knighted in 1888.

▪ Arabella Goddard (1836–1922), English pianist. Born in France, she stud-ied with Kalkbrenner in Paris at the age of six, and made her first public performance in London at the age of fourteen in a Grand National Concert. She studied for three years with J. W. Davison, and married him in 1859; after which she made tours of Germany, Italy, the United States, Australia, and India. She also composed some piano pieces.

30 April 1886

TWO INSIDIOUS VOLUMES* [C222]

MR. S. LAING, on the most favourable diagnosis of such an alarming symptom as his novel, must be pronounced a sufferer from an acute attack of Barlowism. The mass of instruction which he has endeav-oured to convey in "A Sporting Quixote" is almost revolting. He is neither unconscious nor ashamed of this; for, in a prefatory note, he observes: "It may be doubted whether this little book deserves the name of a novel at all. Is 'Don Quixote' a novel, or 'Sartor Resartus'?" An affirmative answer to this question will not, however, cover Mr. Laing's case; for, though some novels may be didactic, it does not

---

*"A Sporting Quixote." By S. Laing. Two vols. (London: Chapman and Hall. 1886.)

follow that all didactic works are novels, even when their doctrine is presented in the form of conversations between imaginary persons. Joyce's "Scientific Dialogues" and Mrs. Markham's "History of England," improving as they are, are not novels; and the "Life of the Hon. Augustus Fitzmuddle" is more nearly akin to them than to "Don Quixote," although Mr. Laing falls as short of the impressive condescension of Mrs. Markham as of the insight of Cervantes. What excuse can be made for a novelist who places the marriage of his hero and heroine at the end of the first volume, and devotes the second to an account of their married life? It may be asked, why not? Is there not much post-nuptial novel material in domestic tragedies, jealousies, elopements, and divorces? Is not Othello married at the end of his first act? But Mr. Laing's couple do not quarrel. This is what they do. The wife suggests the purchase of some pictures. A little discussion on the subject of art arises thereupon; and she finally kisses her husband (an affable Earl) and says: "Let us think it over, and before we decide let us ask Mr. Jones, the great art critic down here for a day, and have a talk with him about pictures." Jones comes, and be-Barlows the reader during a whole chapter with his notions of art. Herr Professor Trubner Klatterer is then sent for to explain Wagner's music, and is triumphantly refuted by the Earl, who this time assumes the Barlovian magistracy himself, and vindicates the superiority of Rossini. Happening about this time to read Mr. Henry George, he becomes doubtful as to the justice of his manorial rights. In his perplexity he exclaims: "I'll tell you what we had better do. You know Mr. Herbert, who has written so many profound works on these subjects. Let us ask him down here, and see what he says to it." The sequel may be imagined.

But this is not the worst of it. Thirst for knowledge might overcome the reader's natural objection to stand being treated as if he were "little Frank" by Mr. Laing, if the qualifications of the teacher were beyond suspicion. But when it appears that the true moral of the story lies in the fact that Mr. Barlow has no special acquaintance with any of his subjects; that of music, painting, and economics he knows no more than all our little Franks may pick up in the course of their saunterings through life and letters, his homilies become exasperating. An omniscient Barlow is hard enough to bear, but a fallible Barlow is beyond all endurance. Besides, Mr. Laing's Barlowism is complicated by a resolution to take a cheerful view of everything, which, if the book be widely circulated will induce a pessimistic reaction. The Cheeryble twins in "Nicholas Nickleby" are not more insufferable than the optimistic sporting Quixote. Even Dickens found it necessary to atone for Cheeryble by giving us Mr. Bounderby, who may be regarded as the dual Cheeryble found out and shown up, as Flora Finching was the exposure of Dora Spenlow. Mr. Laing seems to have been inspired to create his Fitzmuddle by good-naturedly observing that a shy and awkward man may be a much better fellow than many of the smartest of those who ridicule him. But did he not know that we already have Tom Pinch and Dobbin to console us for our guilty consciousness of a share in their deficiencies, and even to persuade the clumsiest among us that it is positively virtuous to be a muff? And what honest muff will deny that, other things being equal, the readiest man deservedly bears the bell? On the whole Mr. Laing might well have spared us the life and adventures of the Earl of Muddleton. They contain too much matter which seems to have been printed on the assumption that what is not sufficiently considered for a volume of essays is good enough for a novel—a most pernicious extension of the principle that "ce qui est trop sot d'être dit, on le chante."

Editor's Notes

- Shaw's diary reveals that he "wrote part of review of *Modern Quixote* [*sic*]" on 24 March 1886, and that he finished it and sent it off the next day. It may have been the unnamed novel that he "finished reading" for review on 20 March (*Diary*, 154–55). The full title of the book is *A Sporting Quixote; or, The Life and Adventures of the Honble. Augustus Fitzmuddle*. Interestingly, having cut out and pasted the newspaper review in his scrapbook, Shaw, perhaps thinking of future publication, penciled through the heading *TWO INSIDIOUS NOVELS* and wrote an alternative title, *MR. BARLOW AGAIN*.
- S[amuel] Laing (1810–97), Scottish author and politician. He was born in Edinburgh, the son of Samuel Laing (1780–1868), the scholar who translated the *Heimskringla*. Samuel (junior) graduated at St. John's College, Cambridge, in 1832 and was called to the bar at Lincoln's Inn in 1840. He was chairman of the London and Brighton Railway Company from 1848 to 1855, and again in 1867. He was returned as a member of Parliament in 1852, and became Liberal member for Wick. He rose to become financial secretary to the Treasury in 1859, and finance minister in India from 1861 to 1863. Apart from the novel reviewed above, Samuel Laing wrote *India and China: England's Mission in the East* (1863), *Prehistoric Remains of Caithness* (1865), and *Modern Science and Modern Thought* (1885), which last was described by the *Academy* as "a popular handbook of Agnosticism," and *A Modern Zoroastrian* (1887).
- Mr. Barlow is the didactic tutor of the rich and unpleasant Tommy Merton

in Thomas Day's once popular *The History of Sandford and Merton* (3 vol., 1783–89).

▪ *Sartor Resartus: The Life and Opinions of Herr Teufelsdrökh* written by Carlyle, was originally published in *Fraser's Magazine* in 1833–34, and as a separate volume first in the United States in 1836, and in England two years later. It is in part a discourse on the philosophy of clothes based on the thoughts of an imaginary Professor Teufelsdrökh, and in part an autobiography of the latter.

▪ Joyce's *Scientific Dialogues* were written by Jeremiah Joyce (1764–1816), a Unitarian minister who published a number of sermons and educational works, of which his *Scientific Dialogues for the Young* was the most popular, six editions being published between 1846 and 1857.

▪ Mrs. Markham's *History of England* was written by Elizabeth Penrose (1780–1837). Sometime after marrying the Reverend John Penrose, she began to write histories for schools under the pseudonym "Mrs. Markham." Her *History of England* became a standard textbook, reaching in thirty-three years a sale of 88,000.

▪ The Cheeryble Twins in *Nicholas Nickleby* are two "sturdy old fellows," Ned and Charles, who find work for Nicholas and help him towards prosperity. Josiah Bounderby a banker and millowner of Coketown in Dickens's *Hard Times* who boasts of his humble beginnings, is, in his selfishness, certainly their antithesis. So, too, is Flora Finching, the first love of Arthur Clennam in *Little Dorrit*. A spoiled and demanding creature, after they part she marries Mr. Finching. Years later when Clennam meets her again, he is horrified to find her equally spoiled and demanding but lacking the earlier attractiveness he remembered. In *David Copperfield* the young hero falls in love with Dora Spenlow, the only daughter of his employer, and after the latter's sudden death, they marry; but she, although beautiful, is also selfish, and thoughtless, proves hopeless in domestic affairs, and dies after losing her baby.

▪ Tom Pinch is another Dickensian character, this time from *Martin Chuzzlewit*. He is the assistant to Mr. Pecksniff, in whom he has great faith. He is, however, disillusioned, realizing the hypocrisy of his employer.

▪ Captain (afterwards Colonel) Dobbin is from Thackeray's *Vanity Fair:* he is the honest and unselfish adorer of Amelia, who in turn dotes on the worthless George Osborne. It is Captain Dobbin who brings George to a realization of his own behavior. Both Tom Pinch and Captain Dobbin, then, are types of perhaps credulous but admirable honesty.

▪ "Bears the bell" is nineteenth century slang for "carries off the prize."

▪ "Ce qui est trop sot d'être dit, on le chante." Jack Tanner, in *Man and Superman* rebuking Enery Straker for whistling meaningfully at him, says:

Let me remind you that Voltaire said that what was too silly to be said could be sung.

STRAKER: It wasnt Voltaire: it was Bow Mar Shay.

TANNER: I stand corrected: Beaumarchais of course.

Man and Superman, Act II

14 May 1886

THE HISTORY OF A WEEK* [C228]

A WEEK is a short period for a history extending to nearly three hundred pages, and surveying mankind only from a Scotch country house to the neighbouring fishing village. Still, with a love affair; a ball; a carriage accident; a bedridden tippler engaged in constant whisky smuggling operations, in which his father plays the part of the preventive service; a haunted turret chamber; an incendiary fire; and a castle burned down with two people in it; the seven days do not hang too heavily on the reader's hands, while the style of the book, at once ornate and decorous, prevents undue excitement. There is a flavour—not unwelcome—of the Minerva Press in such passages as: "The hooting owl came and went from the window-ledge, and Madeline heeded it not. One thought, one great despair filled her soul—no room was left for lesser agonies. The golden chalice had already touched her lips; she had already tasted, and all life had been sweeter for that sip; and now, instead of the cup of joy, the draught of anguish: instead of fair visions, a frantic nightmare." This is much in the manner of Shelley's prose romance, "Zastrozzi," which is not generally classed among his masterpieces, being indeed a dreadful example of the long start Shelley's power of expression had of his power of invention. But the matter of "The History of a Week" must not be likened to that of "Zastrozzi." It is a comparatively rational little story, and Madeline, the heroine, is a lovable girl. The draught of anguish is nothing but a little misunderstanding brought about between her and her lover by mischievous cousin Tom; and the frantic nightmare is only her dread of seeing a ghost when she is locked up in the haunted chamber. As to the hooting owl coming and going from the window ledge, he gives Madeline a useful hint after all; for she presently goes from the window ledge herself, climbs down "the battlemented wall," and meets her lover, who accepts her explanations as to the misunderstanding, and marries her as soon as she recovers from the shock of finding, on her return, the castle burned to ashes, and cousin Tom done for, though

*"The History of a Week." By L. B. Walford. (W. Blackwood and Sons: Edinburgh and Lond. 1886.)

still lingering to declare handsomely that she is an angel, and to beg her forgiveness. And so the week ends happily for the good people, and edifyingly for the wicked. The book aims mainly at extracting the tear of sensibility; but there are a few shrewd bits of character in it, not unworthy the pen—so to speak—of a compatriot of the great Sir Walter.

Editor's Notes

- Before reviewing this book, Shaw read for review a novel by the American Frank R. Stockton, *The Late Mrs. Null* (23–25 April 1886) and on the twenty-sixth "wrote review of *Mrs. Null* and *History of a Week* for *PMG*" (*Diary*, 164). Shaw noted "This was inserted; but lost track of" in his list of books reviewed for 1886; but, as Stanley Weintraub informs us, Shaw was in error: the review was never published (*Diary*, 164–67).
- L[ucy] B[ethia] (née Colquhoun) Walford (1845–1915), Scottish author. She was born at Portobello, Scotland, the daughter of John Colquhoun (author of *The Moor and the Loch*) and granddaughter of Sir James Colquhoun, third Baronet, and of Janet, Lady Colquhoun. *The History of a Week* is set in Scotland, and the dialogue of its minor characters captures well the Scottish style of speech. In 1869 she married Alfred Sanders Walford of Cranbrook Hall, Ilford, Essex. In addition to contributing to *Blackwoods Magazine* and other periodicals, she wrote (among a score of other books) *The Merchant's Sermon, and other Stories* (1870), *Mr. Smith: a Part of his Life* (1874), *Pauline* (1877), *Troublesome Daughters* (1880), *Dick Netherby* (1881), *The Baby's Grandmother* (1884), *Cheerful Christianity: Brief Essays dealing with the Lesser Beauties and Blemishes of the Christian Life* (1886), *Her Great Idea, and other Stories* (1888), *One of Ourselves* (1900), *The Stay-at-Homes* (1903), *Lenore Stubbs* (1908), and *Recollections of a Scottish novelist* (1910).
- The Minerva Press was a publishing house in Leadenhall Street, London, which produced a series of extremely sentimental novels around the year 1800.
- *Zastrozzi* is a prose piece written while Shelley was still at Eton in 1810. It is full of Gothic horror and melodramatic utterance. In it, Zastrozzi, apparently helping Matilda di Laurentini to locate her lover Verezzi for altruistic reasons, is really seeking to torture and finally destroy him, motivated by revenge. The reader does not discover Zastrozzi's full motive until the end of the story, when he reveals that Verezzi seduced and spurned his mother, and that he is the bastard offspring. Captain Brassbound, wishing to revenge his mother, utters similarly melodramatic threats against Sir Howard Hallam in *Captain Brassbound's Conversion*.

29 May 1886

STANLEY JEVONS: HIS *LETTERS AND JOURNAL** [C231]

FOUR years ago, when the newspapers announced that Professor Jevons was drowned, the great world of outsiders understood little more than that some rather heterodox academic hero had been cut off before his time; while the comparatively few insiders—professors and students of logic and economics who had not reached the fossil stage before 1871—were greatly startled and distressed at the sudden end of the only man to whose future work they had been looking with anything like eager expectation. With the exception of the Conservative economists who believed that the last word worth listening to had been uttered by Cairnes, and the Socialists who believed that both the first and last word of the true gospel had been uttered by Karl Marx, all lovers of the dismal science were waiting hopefully for the great work on the subject which Jevons had in hand when he took that fatal dip at Galley Hill, which his heart, injured by overwork, proved too weak to withstand. The unfortunate incident stirred up the personal interest which his writings had already created in many who had never seen him; and there arose a demand for some further knowledge of him, which his widow, Mrs. Harriet Jevons, has at last met with a volume of selections from his letters and journal, connected by a few biographical notes so as to form a continuous record of his career.

William Stanley Jevons, born in 1835, was the son of a Liverpool ironmaster, and of Mary Anne Roscoe, a poetess, daughter of William Roscoe, the historian of Leo X. He was not one of those men of whom it can be said that he completed his education at any time or place; for his education was still proceeding when it was interrupted by his death. He matriculated at University College before he was nineteen, and went from the college to Sydney to work there for five years as assayer to the Mint. This appointment, with its considerable emoluments and prospects, he threw up a few years after his father's death in November, 1855, and returned to Gower-street to take his degree, and begin the world afresh. In 1860, having turned his atten-

*"Letters and Journal of W. Stanley Jevons." Edited by his Wife. One vol. (London: Macmillan and Co. 1886.)

tion to political economy, he wrote to his brother, "I have fortunately struck out what I have no doubt is the true theory of economy, so thorough-going and consistent that I cannot now read other books on the subject without indignation." The result was that when he presented himself next month, "confident of the first prize," for examination in political economy, the professors were apparently unable to read his answers without indignation; for he was placed third or fourth. So he laid his theory before the British Association at Cambridge in 1862; and it was received "without a word of interest or belief." But in 1863 Jevons made himself known by his demonstration of the fall in the value of gold. Persons unfamiliar with financial psychology will be at a loss to understand how such a theme could possibly excite sufficient interest to raise an unknown man into prominence as an economist. There are men of weight in Lombard-street to whom the idea of a fall in gold is inadmissible and intolerable. They repudiate it by instinct, and in the teeth of reason and experience, as a personal insult, much as Goldsmith passionately rejected the assurance that his upper jaw was fixed and his lower alone mobile. They rose in arms; everybody concerned took sides; the battle raged; and Jevons became famous.

In 1865 he distinguished himself anew; this time upon the still more prosaic theme of coal. As our mineral wealth gives us exactly the same advantage over other nations as the freeholder of a fertile farm has over the freeholder of a sterile one, enabling us, as it were, to exact rent from the rest of the world, Jevons ventured to regard our coal as the real basis of our commercial supremacy, and to prophesy that were it exhausted, and the mineral wealth of America brought to light, the sceptre would assuredly pass away from us to the other side of the Atlantic. And he proceeded to show, in cold blood, that such a result might be confidently expected in a century. This forecast was grievously offensive to those who saw in our commercial supremacy the natural and inalienable reward of an exceptionally noble national character. Mr. Gladstone, then Chancellor of the Exchequer, was impressed, and urged forward the work of extinguishing the National Debt as a preparatory measure; but many patriots vehemently declared that Jevons was an alarmist, a notoriety hunter, or a Laputan theorist, and that we had enough coal within our coasts to last until the day of judgment and to consume the globe afterwards. All this greatly increased Jevons's fame and stimulated him to fresh exploits, one of which, as if in defiance of the imputation of Laputanism, was the construction of a machine for performing operations in logic. His next remarkable work was the "Theory of Political Economy," published in 1871, in which he tore up the Ricardian articles of faith on the question of value, and substituted a theory of exchange which may be shortly called psycho-mathematic, inasmuch as it insisted on the fact that the utility of a commodity is not proportionate to its quantity, but diminishes as the possessor becomes satiated; that the problem of exchange is therefore one of quantities, not of commodities, but of utility; and that, as dealing with quantities, it should be treated mathematically. The metaphysicians and Millite Ricardian economists, especially those who could not manage the differential calculus, would have none of this. Their objections were put into shape by Cairnes, whereupon Jevons remarked, in a letter to Mr. G. H. Darwin "I much regret that Cairnes should have raised such absurd objections to the theory, proceeding entirely from misapprehension." That his theory was no mere crotchet of his own is proved by its independent discovery by Gossen in Germany, and M. Léon Walras in France. But that its acceptance involves the rejection of the Ricardian economics to which he opposed it, is by no means clear. He undoubtedly believed that he had knocked the bottom out of Ricardo's system; but Ricardians who do not altogether repudiate him will rather feel their position additionally fortified by his labour equation, which may be regarded as a restatement, in the manner of the new-fangled psycho-mathematician, of the theory of value advanced sixty years ago by the old-fashioned metaphysical stockbroker. Jevons's popularity and his unpopularity were analogous to those of a Broad Churchman. He shocked the evangelical economists (so to speak) by calling Ricardo, "An able but wrongheaded man," and Mill "his able but wrongheaded admirer," and by such statements as that Mill "never had any idea what capital was;" or that it was necessary "to pick up the fragments of a shattered science, and to start anew." On the other hand he was far too orthodox in his practical conclusions for those materialists of the science—the revolutionary socialists—who saw in him a mere "bourgeois economist," as their phrase goes. He does not seem to have had any suspicion that Mr. Hyndman and his friends made any economic pretensions at all; but it is remarkable that the most successful attack so far on the value theory of Karl Marx has come from Mr. Philip Wicksteed, a well-known Unitarian minister, who is an able follower of Jevons in economics.

Of what sort of a man Jevons was without and within, the portrait and letters in the volume just published by Messrs. Macmillan give a vivid impression. He had the power that goes to the making of all eminent men, of taking a deep interest in himself and yet of never gaining his own approbation easily. He acquired the habit of scribbling with facility, and contrived, though always a busy man, to write a good deal of introspective autobiography. In this way he formed his literary style, which, at its best, was clear, unaffected, and sympathetic, though it certainly was not luminous, suggestive, pithy, or artistically finished. He does not seem to have appreciated these qualities in others; for he describes "Wealth of Nations" as one of the driest books on political economy! Except for the few years he spent in Australia, where he lived like a hermit, his life was that of a student, professor, and learned-society man. He never lived the life or shared the sordid anxieties of the struggling millions whose business so interested him; and to this rather than to lack of sympathy must be ascribed the disappointing conventionality of some of his utterances on practical social and political questions, though his suggestions as to methods of studying them are always valuable. In his early years he was an uncompromising necessitarian and agnostic; but later on he became a Theist, and even a devout one. He seems to have had absolutely no vices: his faults were all negative. He was extraordinarily candid and sincere in his sayings and dealings, and altogether an interesting man, whose life is well worth the attention even of those who have no particular relish for the class of subjects which occupied him almost uninterruptedly from his boyhood to his untimely death.

Editor's Notes

- Shaw read this book for review on 13, 15, 18, and 19 May 1886, and wrote the review on the twentieth (*Diary*, 169–70).
- Harriet Ann Jevons [née Taylor] (1839–?). She was the third daughter (and second child of the second wife) of John Edward Taylor (1791–1844), founder and proprietor of *The Manchester Guardian* newspaper. Her mother, Harriet Boyce of Tiverton, had come to Taylor in 1835 as a governess for his children two years after his wife's death. She died in 1843, and her husband in 1844. On 19 December 1867 Harriet Ann married W. Stanley Jevons at the Unitarian Chapel at Altrincham near Manchester, after which she toured the southwest of England with him, the first of many such tours to Wales, Nor-

way, etc. These trips increasingly seemed to be in search of his health. Together they settled in Withington near Manchester, and Harriet did a great quantity of copying and arithmetical work for her husband. In 1875 she bore him a son (Herbert Stanley), who himself became an economist, and later two daughters, Harriet Winefrid [sic] (1877), and Lucy Cecilia (1880). After her husband's death, in addition to the book reviewed above, Harriet edited for the press his letters and others of his papers.

- Shaw's account of the life of William Stanley Jevons (1835–82), English economist and logician, is sufficiently accurate to make unnecessary a repetition of it here. Suffice it to say that Jevons introduced mathematical methods to economics, and was one of the first to use the concept of 'final' or 'marginal utility' (as opposed to the classical 'cost-of-production' theories). His work was enormously important to Shaw, who used it to refute parts of Marx's theory. As Holroyd says, "For Shaw, the substitution of Marx by Jevons was almost equivalent to the subsequent replacement of Darwin by Lamarck" (Michael Holroyd, *Bernard Shaw: Volume 1. 1856–1898. The Search for Love* [London: Chatto and Windus, 1988], 181). In addition to his *Theory of Political Economy* (1871), Jevons's *Principles of Economics* was published posthumously in 1905. A professorship in political economy was endowed in his memory at the University of Manchester.

- John Elliott Cairnes (1823–75), Irish economist. Educated at Trinity College, Dublin, he developed an interest in economics around the year 1854. Two years later he was appointed to the Whately Professorship of Political Economy, and in 1859 he was appointed professor of political economy and jurisprudence at Queen's College, Galway. At about this time he became a close friend of John Stuart Mill. In 1866 he became professor of political economy at University College, London, but resigned in 1872 for health reasons. His first work, *The Character and Logical Method of Political Economy* (1857), is regarded as the definitive statement of the English classical school of economics, stressing the deductive method of reasoning, the hypothetical nature of the discipline, and its independence from specific political or social systems. Although Cairnes tried later to improve on accepted classical theory, he had no sympathy with or understanding of Jevons's radical approach. Shaw was fully familiar with his subject and had written an article "The Jevonian Criticism of Marx," which had appeared in *To-Day,* January, 1885.

- John Stuart Mill (1806–73), Scottish political scientist. He is probably most famous for his "Essay on Liberty" (1859). In political economy he advocated policies he believed most consistent with individual liberty, believing that this could be threatened as much by social as by political tyranny. Paradoxically, in Parliament Mill was considered a Radical, because he supported public ownership of natural resources, equality for women, compulsory education, and birth control.

- Hermann Heinrich Gossen (1810–58), German writer on economics. His claim to fame is based on a single publication: in 1854 he published a book that develops a comprehensive theory of the hedonistic calculus. It postulates (as did Jevons) the principle of 'diminishing marginal utility'. His importance in the development of economic thought was not recognized until twenty years after his death, when Jevons and Walras, who had already published their own versions of the new theory of value, gave Gossen posthumous credit for his pioneering work.

- [Marie Esprit] Léon Walras (1834–1910), French economist. He was educated in Lausanne, Switzerland, where he first met Louis Ruchonet, who ten years later helped him to obtain the newly established chair in political economy at Lausanne. Once there he began to teach himself calculus, having been shown by Paul Piccard, a professor of mechanics, how to apply the technique of maximization to the theory of utility. Thus Walras developed independently his mathematical theory of marginal utility. He was chagrined to discover, on publishing his first paper on the subject, that Jevons had anticipated him, and his jealousy was only partly appeased by the later discovery that Gossen had anticipated them both, though Walras believed that his version of the theory was more rigorous and elegant than those of the other two. His most significant publication is probably *Elements d'économie politique pure* (written between 1874 and 1877). Walras retired from teaching in 1892, but continued to write, refining the theory of capital and money. His posthumous reputation was very great.

- Philip Wicksteed (1844–1927), English economist. Wicksteed took Jevons's notion of 'final degree of utility' (which was his way of describing the idea that the more we have of something, the less is the value of an additional unit of it), and renamed it 'marginal utility'. He then developed the theory applying it to the pricing of labor and capital, and this, his integration of the theories of the value of goods and of resources, he set out in *An Essay on the Co-ordination of the Laws of Distribution* (1894). Wicksteed's background as a Unitarian minister was perhaps responsible for the humanitarian feelings he brought to the science of economics, and he was much involved with the Fabians, who utilized his economic expertise.

16 June 1886

MR. LAURENCE OLIPHANT'S NEW NOVEL*
[C235]

MR. LAURENCE OLIPHANT has had a call from the occult world. The theosophic recrudescence of spiritualism has made no more distin-

---

*"Masollam: a Problem of the Period." By Laurence Oliphant. Three vols. (London and Edinburgh: W. Blackwood and Sons. 1886.)

guished convert since it won over M. Tissot, one of the most successful of whose recent beginnings in the art of mezzotinting represents a "materialization," and may be taken (perhaps unwarrantably) along with his etched portrait of the gifted Mr. William Eglinton, as an artistic confession of the modern form of belief in ghosts. Comparing the mezzotint with the novel, one cannot help voting the graphic method of propagating the oldest of new gospels superior to the literary in point of vivacity and brevity. A three-volume novelful of spiritualism, however brilliantly handled, is too much. It is true that Mr. Oliphant is careful to declare that his spiritualism is not the vulgar table-rapping and slate-writing of commerce; and the disclaimer is a significant expression of the dislike of the company he finds himself in; but his fanciful modern witchcraft is essentially the same as the commoner sort in its errors of reasoning; its desperate assumption of a high tone with the scepticism of science; its pretence of being a brand new result of "the extraordinary increase of acute nervous sensibility characteristic of the present generation," contradicting its claim to an Oriental origin of remote antiquity; its sham piety; its miracles, kneelings, trances and vigils; and its priestesses in Eastern costumes, wearing jewels of unearthly lustre and prodigious size, and carrying the inevitable "small phial" from which to pour "a few drops of a liquid with a strong aromatic odour." Surely all this hocus-pocus is familiar to Mr. Laurence Oliphant! Surely he must know that it is no more "a problem of the period" than quackery, credulity, and bad logic are. At what period were not its votaries "collecting funds" for the regeneration of the world and the travelling expenses of some arch-quack or other? At what period has it ever made good its pretensions?

To deal with an irresponsible romancer thus hardheadedly may seem like breaking a butterfly on a wheel. But the introduction of quack theosophy into works of art raises the whole question of the morality of fiction. It will be remembered that when William Blake, on his return from a walk taken by him at a tender age, informed his father that he had seen, among other objects of interest, a tree laden with golden fruit; the view taken by the parent Blake was that the young poet was telling a lie. A similar view of the inventions of novelists was common until comparatively recent times among men who professed to enjoy solid parts and sound understanding; and there is obviously much to be said in support of it. A person who describes events that never happened and persons that never existed is generally classed as a liar—possibly a genial and entertaining liar, but still a liar. And what is the business of a novelist if not to describe events that never happened and to repeat conversations that never took place. Dickens, for example, not only did both, but actually held up one of his fictitious characters to reprobation and ridicule for following his example. If his reproach to Mrs. Gamp that there was "no sich a person" as Mrs. Harris be a valid one, does it not equally condemn himself, seeing that, as a matter of fact, there was no such a person as Mrs. Gamp? A distinction cannot be made between the two cases on any other ground than that Mrs. Gamp was true as a type if not as an individual, as a composite photograph is true; whereas Mrs. Harris, with her morbidly sympathetic temperament, her exaggerated maternal instinct, amd her heroine-worship of the monthly nurse, was nonrepresentative, impossible, dishonestly intended, and in effect a piece of false evidence brought forward by the most interested party to support an inaccurate theory of Mrs. Gamp's moral character. Now, when Mr. Laurence Oliphant invents scenes and characters which, if typical and possible, would go to prove that there is something more in spiritualistic theosophy than there was in the quackery of Cagliostro, the question whether he is in the position of Dickens towards Mrs. Gamp, or in that of Mrs. Gamp towards Mrs. Harris cannot be stifled. It seems to have grown on him as he wrote; for in the first half of his second volume he has unexpectedly interpolated an address to the reader, partly apologetic, partly defiant; ingenious, but not, on the whole, satisfactory. The present generation may, as Mr. Oliphant pleads, have produced several such persons as his Masollams; but those of whom authentic records are accessible have succumbed either to the police, the Society of Psychical Research, or the tests devised by private scepticism. And the "extraordinary increase of acute nervous sensibility," though it has certainly extended our powers of self-deception, has by no means established telepathy on the scale in use among the Masollam mystics.

Apart from the cleverly furbished pleas for fanciful psychics as conceivably realizable in the infinite possibilities of the future, Mr. Oliphant's novel contains nothing worse than a plot of that old-fashioned and happily obsolescent pattern in which everybody turns out to be somebody else's long lost child, parent, or other blood relation. In other respects the book sustains the author's reputation. Its manners and morals are those, not of noveldom, but of real intercourse among cultivated people abreast of civilization. The spreading cry for a purer social life and a loftier morality is audible throughout: the fashionable ideal being dismissed with outspoken contempt. One of the best and freshest strokes is the development of refinement of perception and nobility of character in Florence Hartwright, a young lady who is introduced with a very objectionable crust of vulgarity and frivolity. This, being happily a social and not a natural product, is completely dissipated by a change of moral atmosphere. A novelist of no more than ordinary depth would have treated it as a radical defect.

Editor's Notes

▪ Shaw received this book (which he called *The Masollams*) for review on 11 June 1886, read it on the thirteenth and fourteenth, on the last date also writing the review and sending it off (*Diary*, 226, 176).

▪ Laurence Oliphant (1829–88), South African novelist and travel writer. He had an erratic early education in England, afterwards joining his family in Ceylon, where his father was chief justice. Instead of going to a university, he became his father's secretary; but at nineteen he began those wanderings which continued all his life. He traveled widely, in India, Russia, the United States, and Canada, often in war zones, and his life was frequently in danger. He supposedly plotted with Garibaldi, was secretary to Lord Elgin in Washington, Canada, China, and India, where the Mutiny was at its height. He was the *Times* correspondent during the Polish insurrection of 1863 and saw the war in Schleswig-Holstein the following year. In 1865 he returned to England and obtained a seat in Parliament, but was dissatisfied with his progress there, and so resigned to become a full-time writer. He had already written *A Journey to Khatmandu* (1852), *The Russian Shores of the Black Sea* (1853–54), *A Narrative of the Earl of Elgin's Mission to China 1857–9* (1859). His satirical novel *Piccadilly* (1870) was well-received, but increasingly, Oliphant had come under the influence of the American "prophet" Thomas Lake Harris, whose Brotherhood of New Life in New York State he joined, and to whom he surrendered all his and his wife's property. When he became disenchanted with Harris in 1881, he recovered some of his lands by law. Subsequently Oliphant and his wife formed a community for Jewish immigrants in Palestine. There he wrote his second novel *Altiora Peto* (1883), and *Sympneumata* (1885), allegedly dictated by his wife while she was possessed by a spirit. He also wrote *Episodes in a Life of Adventure* (1887) [see pages 299–301 below]. Finally, Oliphant considered his writing merely a medium for spiritualism. He died suddenly during a return visit to England.

▪ Mrs. Gamp, the fat old midwife and nurse in *Martin Chuzzlewit*, who always carries a loosely rolled umbrella and has an imaginary friend she calls Mrs. Harris. It is Mrs. Prig, her nursing partner, who utters the "memorable and tremendous words, 'I don't believe there's no sich a person!' "—a declaration that causes the two friends to part.

28 June 1886

TWO CLEVER NOVELS* [C238]

THERE are bold spirits who declare that were a foreign foe to take advantage of the facilities for destroying our fleet afforded by our naval administration, the yachtsmen of England would by themselves enable us to brave the battle and the breeze for another thousand years. In a like sanguine mood, it might occur to a student of letters that were our legislative bodies, temporal and spiritual, to be dynamited out of existence as a practical protest against the deferring of Home Rule, their shattered ranks could be efficiently recruited by novelists. Then might we expect a congenial settlement of all conceivable social problems, carried out with an easy discursiveness, a lightness of legislative touch, and a halo of romance which would make politics extremely interesting, and have a more or less elevating effect on everything, except, perhaps, Consols. It is true that a congenial settlement of a social problem is not quite the same thing as a scientific solution; and that such settlements, in third volumes of novels, involve arbitrary combinations of massacre with matrimony which would be open to objection from a constitutional point of view if frequently resorted to by a Fiction Cabinet. But it may be doubted whether, on the whole, this method would prove more wasteful of human life and happiness than the accepted one; whereas its advantages, in point of picturesqueness, are obvious.

These remarks are not intended to lead up to anything in particular concerning "Court Royal," the latest novel by the author of "Mehalah." It is merely hoped that their impressiveness may convince him that he is now in more serious hands than those of the critic (mentioned in the preface) who said to him, apropos of "John Herring," "We critics have no time to dive for purpose: we skim for story." The author thereupon concluded that "a purpose, a moral, must not be sunk in the depths like a pearl; but tossed up on the margin as the amber, conspicuous to the first passer-by." Now, in the amber of "Court Royal" there is a fly. The moral of the passing away of the feudal order

---

*"Court Royal." By the Author of "Mehalah." Three vols. (London: Smith, Elder, and Co. 1886.)

"The Crack of Doom." By William Minto. Three vols. (London and Edinburgh: W. Blackwood and Sons. 1886.)

is vitiated by the fact that in the instance given it passes away, not from any inevitable element of decay inherent in or peculiar to itself, but simply because its representatives live beyond their income—a failing which is a general characteristic of humanity, flourishing with equal vigour among the aristocracy, the plutocracy, the professions, and the proletariat. The Duke of Kingsbridge inherits expensive traditions and a relatively moderate income. He maintains the traditions and is sold up. This is hardly solemn enough for such a comment as "Quod antiquatur et senescit—prope interitum est." The case is not a typical one of the British aristocracy succumbing to economic necessity or an iron law of social development, but simply one of a particular Duke succumbing to his own extravagance and want of common sense.

Readers who imitate the featly alliterative critic of "John Herring," and "skim for story," will find "Court Royal" an amusing book, in spite of—sometimes even because of—its reckless violations of ordinary verisimilitude in detail. Perhaps the School Board has wrought greater changes than we have yet realized; but it is hard to believe in a little "slavey," drudging miserably in the kitchen of an exceptionally sordid Jewish pawnbroker, addressing her master in these well-chosen terms: "My hands are wet: I cannot take the paper without reducing it to pulp. Read me what you want to know: I can listen and scour the saucepan." This is but a mild example of the petty incongruities which make "Court Royal" too unbelievable a book to "dive for purpose" in, although the characters, relatively to one another, are drawn and grouped with considerable insight and felicity. Besides, the picture of aristocratic life is an ideal one; and the ideal is false. In actual life, imbecility and vulgarity are never so far asunder as they are made to appear in the house of Kingsbridge. Family traditions do not ennoble ignoble temperaments. An example of a cognate amiable illusion will be found on the sixty-sixth page of the third volume, where there is a rhapsody about "the perfect English lady," which nobody outside the Primrose League is likely to take at the author's valuation.

Mr. William Minto's "Crack of Doom" is made of very solid materials throughout, though they are heaped together to little purpose. Interest is at once roused by a hero who "did everything on principle, or at least found a principle for everything that suited his inclination"; but he does not fulfil the promise of his introduction until, at the climax of a flirtation, he snatches a kiss from fair Fanny Douglas, who becomes serious and tells him that he "must not make a habit of that." He is so ill-advised as to ask her why not, whereupon, " 'I am sure I have no objection, dearest,' Fanny said, as, after gazing tenderly at him for an instant, she threw herself into his arms." From this parlous trap he escapes subsequently without much trouble, at the cost of a relapse into insignificance so far as the reader is concerned. Fanny is much more to the point, clever, capable, egotistical, jealous, jolly, and odious—a typical intellectual and artistic female rowdy. Among the men, Tom Brockley, alias Count Ramassy, an impostor by constitution, is made interesting in a fresh and thoroughly rational way as a case of mental disease, showing itself at first by such commonplace symptoms as a little apparently harmless lying, and ending fatally. The freshness and variety of the company in the book are due to unprejudiced study of human action and motive from actual life: its weakness to the absence of any general conclusions arising from such study. The escape from the monotony of mere romance is delightful; but the indifferentism and want of grip and purpose, though eminently characteristic of the nineteenth century brilliant writer without illusions, are relaxing, and indispose one for the trouble of following the story, which turns upon the threatened destruction of the earth by collision with a comet.

Editor's Notes

- Shaw read *Court Royal* for review on 3 June 1886 (and perhaps thereafter), and *The Crack of Doom* on 11, 16, 17, and 18 June. He wrote the review of both novels on 21 June, sending it off the following day (*Diary*, 174–78, 226).
- Sabine Baring-Gould (1834–1924), English novelist, essayist, and miscellaneous writer. He was born in Exeter, the eldest son of the squire of the three thousand acres of Lew-Trenchard, in North Devon. He took both his B.A. and M.A. from Clare College, Cambridge. In 1864 he was ordained and became a curate at Horbury, Yorkshire. Here he fell in love with his future wife (a mill-hand), paid for her education at York, and married her in 1868. Two years previously he had become vicar at Dalton, Yorkshire, and in 1872 rector at East Merton, Essex. In 1872, on the death of his father, he inherited Lew-Trenchard, to which he retired for the remainder of his life. The family estate had the living in its gift, the post held by his uncle; and, when the latter died in 1881, Baring-Gould became the vicar there, serving until his death. He was also the local justice of the peace, and has been called the last "squarson"—a word coined from the combination of "squire" and "parson." He was a voluminous writer, producing a formidable list of works on subjects mythological, theological, and topographical, as well as about a score of fic-

tional works, among the better known of which are *Mehalah* (1880), *John Herring* (1883), *Red Spider* (1887), *Eve* (1888) [see pages 450–51 below], *The Pennycomequicks* (1889), *Urith* (1890), *Mrs. Curnenven* (1893), *Cheap Jack Zita* (1893), *The Queen of Love* (1894), *The Crock of Gold* (1899), *The Frobishers* (1901), and *Chris of All Sorts* (1903). He also wrote church songs, including the words to "Onward Christian Soldiers"—set to music by Arthur Sullivan.

- The vexed question of Home Rule for Ireland had culminated in this very year in the first Home Rule Bill introduced by Gladstone, which proposed to abolish Irish representation at Westminster, providing instead for the creation of a legislative assembly in Dublin, which was to have control of taxation (except of customs and excise), but was forbidden to legislate on any matter relating to the Crown, defense or foreign relations! The bill divided the Liberal party: many of Gladstone's Cabinet deserted him (including Lord Hartington, Sir Henry James, Mr. Bright, and Mr. Chamberlain), and in consequence, when the bill failed, it precipitated a general election, which proved how unpopular the legislation had been.

- Consols: an abbreviation of *consolidated annuities,* that is, the government securities of Great Britain. The *Oxford English Dictionary* credits the *Pall Mall Gazette* with introducing the phrases "consol-holder" and "consol market" in February 1885.

- "Quod antiquatur et senescit—prope interitum est" (That which decayeth and waxeth old is ready to vanish away.) This is the motto of the Kingsbridge family in *Court Royal,* whose fable is essentially an anticipation of Chekhov's *The Cherry Orchard,* the decay and collapse of an ancient family, symbolized by the loss of their house. In Baring-Gould's story the melodramatic money-lender Lazarus substitutes for the self-made serf Lopakhin of Chekhov's play.

A significant image from *Court Royal* may have lingered in Shaw's mind: speaking of the apathy of the Duke of Kingsbridge in the face of the family's imminent destruction, young Beavis Worthivale says:

> "He must be taken out of his apathy."
> "I do not believe it is possible."
> "Then everything remains *in statu quo*—captain, pilot, crew, all must have their sleep out whilst the vessel fills. It is cruel to wake them. They need repose. It is impossible to rouse some, they sleep so sound. All at once the ship gives a lurch, and the waves engulf her, as all wake up, and rub their eyes, and ask where they are?"
>
> *Court Royal,* 70

The image and its referend are remarkably similar to Shaw's in *Man and Superman* (1901–3) when Don Juan asks the Devil:

> Does a ship sail to its destination no better than a log drifts nowhither? The philosopher is Nature's pilot. And there you have our difference: to be in hell is to drift: to be in heaven is to steer.

THE DEVIL: On the rocks, most likely.
DON JUAN: Pooh! which ship goes oftenest on the rocks or to the bottom? the drifting ship or the ship with a pilot on board?

This metaphor was to be further actualized in *Heartbreak House,* written some thirty years later.

- The School Boards were created by Gladstone's Liberal government of 1870 (in Forster's Education Act) in answer to social pressure that had been building up during the 1860s. Under the provisions of the Act people were elected locally onto these boards, which had the power to establish schools under their own management, and this was the beginning of the present organized system of national education in England. Unfortunately, the voluntary schools were disqualified from receiving any aid from the rates, and so a dual system of education came into being, with the voluntary schools trying to improve their own standards to keep up with the Board schools. Hence Shaw's comment. He uses the singular because for the whole of London there was only *one* School Board (as there was in each town). School Boards were destoyed by Balfour's conservative government in 1902.

- The Primrose League was an organization for disseminating Conservative principles among the British people. It obtained its name from the favorite flower of Lord Beaconsfield, a wreath of primroses having been sent by Queen Victoria to be placed upon his coffin. On the day of the unveiling of Lord Beaconsfield's statue, all the Conservative members present were decorated with a primrose. The first meeting of the League (which was modeled somewhat upon the Orange Society in Ireland) took place in the Carleton Club; then a small office was taken in Essex Street, Strand, but the League soon outgrew its quarters. Ladies were included from the beginning, but eventually developed their own distinctive Council. The League's motto, "Imperium et Libertas," its seal of three primroses, and its badge, a monogram containing the letters PL surrounded by primroses, soon became well known, as its numbers grew enormously from 957 in 1884 to 2,053,019 in 1910.

- [Professor] William Minto (1845–93), Scottish author. Born at Alford, Aberdeenshire, he took his M.A. degree at the University of Aberdeen, with honors, and won the Scottish University Ferguson Scholarship. He entered Merton College, Oxford, in 1866, but left the next year without taking his degree. For some years he acted as assistant to Professor Bain of Aberdeen. In 1873 he settled in London. He was a contributor to the *Examiner* and was appointed editor in 1874, a post he held for four years. Afterwards he was on the literary staffs of the *Daily News* and the *Pall Mall Gazette.* In 1880, William Minto was appointed professor of English in Aberdeen. He wrote a number of books, among the best known being *Manual of English Prose Literature, Biographical and Critical* (1872), *Characteristics of English Poets from Chaucer to Shirley* (1874), and *Defoe* [in the "English Men of Letters" series] (1879); *The Mediation of Ralph Hardelot* (1888) and *Was She Good or Bad?* (1889), which were both romances, like *The Crack of Doom;*

and several literary biographies in *The Encyclopædia Britannica*. He also contributed to magazines, including the *Fortnightly Review* and the *Nineteenth Century*. Minto's heroine, Miss Douglas, is a figure that might have especially appealed to Shaw, who was shortly going to create a gallery of strong heroines, beginning with Vivie Warren: Miss Douglas is described as "emphatically a strong-minded woman" who "refused to stay under the same roof with her parents; . . . set up a studio and a small establishment in company with her stockbroking brother in Bloomsbury. Here she painted, smoked cigarettes . . ." (p. 94).

5 July 1886

MEMOIRS OF A FAMOUS FIDDLER* [C241]

WE have at last an English memoir of Ole Bull, not before it was urgently needed. For, it being nearly a quarter of a century since the great Norwegian violinist played publicly in the United Kingdom, it had come about that while young America knew Ole Bull as well as we know Joachim and Sarasate, young England very commonly supposed him to be an octogenarian negro. That we failed to attach him to us as a yearly visitor was rather our misfortune than our fault. It is true that he was intrigued against and cheated here; but there was nothing peculiar to us in that. Bull invariably assumed his fellowmen to be honest until he found out the contrary: and it is due to the alert commercial spirit of Europe and America to say that, to his cost, he almost invariably did find out the contrary. In whatever quarter of the globe he sojourned he found the general public ready to heap gold upon him, and the particular man of business equally ready to relieve him of it. In America a hasty speculator, who had just made a large haul in this way, was foolish enough to attempt to take off by poison the goose that laid the golden eggs. On another occasion a ruder pioneer of civilization, coveting a diamond which sparkled in the magic fiddle bow, approached the player, knife in hand, with a view to its extraction. But Ole Bull, like Sinfiotli, instinctively saw death in the cup, and refused to drink, whilst the unfortunate pio-

---

*"Ole Bull." A Memoir by Sara C. Bull. (London: Fisher Unwin. 1886.)

neer with the bowie knife took nothing by his enterprise except a rough estimate of how much nerve and muscle go to the making of a Norseman who can play the violin in four-part harmony. Ole Bull's gain, on the whole, greatly exceeded his loss. Wherever he went he soon found himself the focus of all the hero worship in the place. He knew everybody worth knowing; he never was sea-sick; and he never grew stout. His strength, courage, and skill did not wane as his popularity grew. Though he ventured to start a colony in America, and was even rash enough to attempt the foundation of a national theatre in his own country, he died a rich man with fair estates. Illnesses, brought on by overwork and misadventures in the course of his travelling, occurred sufficiently often to impress upon him the value of his happier hours. Litigation and the demoralizing worry of being cheated he probably brought upon himself by his unbusinesslike habits; but as these meant nothing more than a natural repugnance to treat men as knaves by tying himself and them down with stamp and signature in the strong bonds of the law (which is the essence of businesslikeness), perhaps he gained as much as he lost even on this point. For, gold magnet as he was, even he found men honest occasionally. On the whole, there is reason to believe that though he suffered, like all great artists, from the hucksterdom of his environment, he yet succeeded in doing it more good than it did him harm. Genius was not in him a disease: he enjoyed robust moral as well as physical health, and, indeed, illustrated in his person the interdependence of the two.

As a violinist, he was of no school, and somewhat of Paganini's sort. His beginnings scandalized the orthodox disciples of Lafont, Rode, and Baillot; and, though he subsequently assimilated the essence of the Italian classical tradition, he became famous, not as an interpreter of the great composers, but as the utterer of a poetic inspiration which he claimed to have had direct from the mountains of Norway. He played his own music; but he had the power of making all genuinely popular music his own. Wherever he went, he found either folk songs, which he immediately regenerated for the people so that they no longer sounded hackneyed; or else, for audiences too highly civilized or sophisticated to be won over in this way, he played his own Norse music, and brought the foreigners under the spell it had laid on himself. His physical aptitude for his instrument enabled him to acquire a prodigious command of it; and in displaying his power in all its phases and in all its exuberance he did not escape the reproach of charlatanism. But he must have been far more than a charlatan to have conquered the world as he did, and to have gained the respect of so many artists who thoroughly knew the value of a player's work. His appreciation of, and capacity for music of the highest class is proved by his successful devotion to the music of Mozart, which, whilst it makes extraordinary demands on an artist's sensibility, affords no cover for his shortcomings. Besides his mastery of the manipulative difficulties of violin-playing, Ole Bull knew well the shades of tone and expression of which the alternative resources of the four strings afford such rich variety, and which only a born fiddler can exhaustively learn and use.

Mrs. Sara Bull's memoir of her gifted husband is for the most part an itinerary, enlivened with anecdotes and favourable newspaper criticisms. As her personal knowledge of him dates only from the year 1868, its advantages hardly counterbalance the partiality entailed by close and affectionate friendship. In truth the Ole Bull described in her pages is no real man, but an ideal Norse hero—a Berserk or Viking, with a dash of Orpheus and the Pied Piper—a product, not of nature, but of nineteenth-century imaginative literature. A widow's biography of her husband has necessarily something of the defect and excess of an epitaph: it omits faults, and records common instincts as special virtues. But a widow who regards her husband as the embodiment of a poetic ideal which grew up in the course of her reading and day-dreaming before she knew him must be even less than ordinarily trustworthy as a critical biographer. That Ole Bull was thus idealized by his second wife is much to his credit; but he must surely have had a failing or two. One would like to hear the devil's advocate before pronouncing a verdict.

The anecdotes concerning Ole Bull are very like the anecdotes about Paganini, Liszt, and the rest of the great *virtuosi*. It is inspiriting to learn that he did not need police protection against canine pets, though his kicking the Princess Damerond's snappish doggie into the chandelier is not so suggestive of tenderness towards animals as the mode of his touching reconciliation with the Danish poet Ohlenschläger, who narrates it as follows:

> When he at one time, on board the steamer, had caused my displeasure by a too severe criticism of the Swedes, and I had taken my seat on a bench, he came leaping towards me on his hands and feet, and barked at me like a dog. This was a no less original than amiable manner of bringing about a reconciliation.

On a Mississippi steamer he astonished a rowdy who was shocked at his unnatural objection to whisky by performing upon him the feat known to British wrestlers as "the flying mare." When the rowdy came to, he offered his bowie knife as a tribute to the strongest fiddler he had ever seen.

Fiddle-fanciers will find much to interest them both in the memoir and appendix. Ole Bull was a fancier as well as a player, and, like Paganini never used a Stradivarius, preferring the purer, if less even, tone of the masterpieces of Amati and Guarnerius. Eventually he used almost exclusively a violin by Gaspar da Salo, whom he believed to be identical with Gaspar Duiffoprugcar, a lute-maker patronized by Francis I. His instrument must therefore have been the oldest of its kind in use. His bow was a heavy one, exceeding the customary length by two inches.

Editor's Notes

▪ The note in Shaw's diary on 22 June 1886, "continued reading Ole Bull's life for review," suggests an earlier date for beginning the book; but though he received it on 20 June, there is no earlier reference. Certainly he "finished reading Ole Bull" on 24 June and wrote his review the following day, correcting the proofs on the second of July (*Diary*, 178–79, 181).

▪ Sara Chapman Bull [née Thorp] (1850–1911), Ole Bull's second wife. She was the only daughter of the Honorable Joseph G. Thorp, a wealthy lumberman and Wisconsin state senator, and Amelia Chapman Thorp, who had moved from Oxford, New York, to Eau Claire, Wisconsin, to open a lumber business. Extremely fond of music (she had designed the family's grand piano), she was swept off her feet by the violinist Ole Bull when he stayed as a guest at the Thorp mansion in 1870, although he was by that time sixty years old, and she only twenty. Her brother Joseph Jr. married the youngest daughter of the poet Longfellow, and her mother was anxious for her daughter to make an artistic match. Her father was opposed to the marriage, but her mother overrode his objections and, with her daughter and Ole Bull, embarked for England on the steamship *Russia* in April 1870. In June they traveled to Christiana where Ole Bull and Sara were quietly married. They returned to the United States in September, where they were remarried in style in Madison, Wisconsin. The marriage has been described as decidedly a misalliance, and seems to have suffered from the disparity between Sara's social conventionality and Bull's bohemianism. It also suffered from Amelia Chapman Thorp, who, having stagemanaged the wedding, seemed determined to conduct the marriage. This led to the unhappy necessity of Sara having to choose between her mother and her husband. Finally, it seems, after a two-year separation, she opted in favor of her husband, and their remaining domestic years were spent in peace. She bore him one daughter, Sara Olea (born in 1871); she frequently accompanied her husband on the piano; and she translated into English the novels of the Norwegian writer Jonas Lie. After her husband's death, Björnstjerne Björnson, the Norwegian poet, accompanied Sara back to the United States, where he was her guest in Cambridge, Massachusetts. Here she became a well-known figure in the ensuing years, conducting "conferences" and discussions with the brightest minds in American society. She also visited London and met Annie Besant and W. T. Stead.

- Ole Bull [Bornemann] (1810–80), Norwegian violinist and composer. Born in Bergen, he was the eldest of ten children. Both his parents were musical and, with his uncles, performed family quartets, so that from a very early age Ole became familiar with the quartets of Krummer, Haydn, Mozart, and Beethoven. Also, while still a boy, he began to study the nature and construction of the violin. At the age of nine he played first violin in the local orchestra when his father (a noted amateur actor) was performing on stage. In 1822, Lundholm, a Swedish violinist, settled in Bergen and gave Ole Bull instruction, prophesying a great future for the boy. In 1828 he went to attend the university in Christiana [Oslo], his father intending him to study theology; but he failed the entrance examination. He was appointed director of the Philharmonic and Dramatic Societies. Determined to succeed in music, he took a trip to Kassel to visit Louis Spohr, whose playing in a quartet was so different from his that Ole Bull almost abandoned music altogether. However, in 1831, on the proceeds of money made in concerts in Trondheim and Bergen, he went to Paris, intending to take lessons with Baillot. He ran out of funds, and, while destitute, met the lady who was to become his first wife, Alexandrine Félicie Villeminot, an orphan. Fortunately, Ole Bull was sustained by the generosity of friends back in Christiana, until he made the acquaintance of the Duke of Montebello (Marshal Ney's son), and in April 1832 gave his first concert under the Duke's patronage, sharing the platform with Chopin, Ernst, et al. From then on he enjoyed enormous success. He became a friend of Chopin (and George Sand); he gave concerts in Switzerland and Italy (where he furthered his violin studies), and made a great success in Bologna, substituting at the last moment for de Beriot. Here he composed his *Concerto in A*. He was also a huge success in Rome in 1835, where he played his *Polacca Guerriera,* in which he fingered four distinct parts at once on the violin, a feat which caused amazement, and even led to accusations of trickery. In fact he whittled the bridge of his instrument almost to the level of the fingerboard. In 1836 he played for the first time in London: another triumph. In the summer of that year he married and brought his bride to England, where in 16 months he gave no less than 274 concerts. He made the acquaintance of Paganini in Paris, and then toured Germany, Russia, and Finland before returning to Christiana. He saw little of his family: his first child was left with an uncle while he toured, and his second was born while Ole Bull was on tour. He played in Salzburg for the Mozart Fund (with Mozart's wife present at the performance). Mozart, he later declared, was his favorite composer. In 1840 he made the acquaintance of Liszt, with whom he played a good deal. He visited the United States for the first time in 1843, giving concerts in all the major centers, both north and south from 1843 to 1845, receiving many honors. In 1847 he "conquered" Algiers and Spain, and in the 1850s played a return engagement in the United States. In 1861–62 he played forty-six concerts in England, Scotland, and Ireland, during which absence his wife died. From 1863 to 1867 he toured Germany, Poland, and Russia, and then in 1867 paid his third visit to the United States, where, in the winter of 1868 he met the author of the book reviewed above, who was to become his second wife. He married her in 1870, and thereafter divided his time between Europe and America. He met Longfellow, who describes him at length in *Tales of a Wayside Inn*. He arrived home in Norway for the last time in 1880, a sick man, and died at Lyso. Edvard Grieg played at his funeral; and afterwards his body was removed to Bergen, where Björnstjerne Björnson delivered a eulogy. Ole Bull's compositions were mostly of a sentimental nature, with titles such as *La preghiera d'una madre* and *Variazioni di bravura*. They are rarely played today. Ten months after this review was published, Shaw visited his friend William Archer's house to hear Alexander Bull (Ole Bull's son) play. Shaw's diary reports "He played a Guarnerius and got tremendous tone from it. An uncultivated musician, but a born player" (*Diary*, 269).

▪ Sinfiotli is a character in William Morris's *Sigurd the Volsung and the Fall of the Niblungs* (1876), the son of Sigmund and Signy. He aids his parents in their revenge upon Siggeir, the evil King of the Goths. Siggeir is burned in his palace, but Sinfiotli is poisoned.

▪ Niccolò Paganini (1782–1840), Italian violin virtuoso and composer. An infant prodigy, at eight composing a sonata for the violin, he appeared before the public when he was eleven. From 1795 he studied with Ghiretti and began to compose seriously. He possessed remarkable technique and great showmanship. He reached Berlin in 1829, Paris in 1831, in which year he also conquered London and made a fortune. He spent the winter of 1833–34 in Paris, and then retired to his villa in Parma. He often visited Paris (meeting Ole Bull there in 1836). Two years later he wintered in Paris, but became ill and went in search of sun and fresh air to Nice, where he died.

▪ Charles-Philippe Lafont (1781–1839), French violinist and composer. He studied in Paris with Kreuzer and Rode, becoming the latter's successor at the Russian court in St. Petersburg in 1808. He returned to Paris in 1815 as solo violinist to Louis XVIII. In Milan the following year he engaged in a violin-playing duel with Paganini, which the latter won. Lafont was killed in a carriage accident in southern France. He composed two comic operas, seven violin concertos, numerous fantasias and variations for violin, and about two hundred *romances* for voice.

▪ [Jacques-] Pierre [Joseph] Rode (1774–1830), French violinist and composer. He was taught by Fauvel and Viotti, and with the latter made his debut in Paris, at the Théâtre Feydeau in 1790. After touring the Netherlands and Germany and visiting London, he was appointed professor of violin at the newly opened Paris Conservatory in 1795. In 1800 he was court violinist to Napoleon, and from 1803 to 1808 was in Russia, where he became first violinist at the court of Alexander I. Boccherini wrote concertos for him, and

Beethoven wrote for him the G *Major Sonata* (Op. 96), performed by Rode in Vienna on 29 December 1812. In 1814 he married in Berlin, then retired to Bordeaux. He wrote thirteen violin concertos, twenty-four caprices, twelve études, and three books of violin duets.

- Pierre-Marie-François de Sales Baillot (1771–1842), French violinist and composer. At the age of nine he became a pupil of the violinist Sainte-Marie, and later studied under Pollani in Italy. Returning to Paris in 1791 he met Viotti who obtained for him a position in the orchestra of the Théâtre Feydeau. In 1795 he became teacher of violin at the Paris Conservatory, but continued to study composition with Cherubini, Reicha, and Catel. In 1802 he joined Napoleon's instrumental ensemble and toured Russia. He also gave concerts in Paris, Belgium, the Netherlands, and England. In 1821 he became first violinist at the Paris Opera. Among other works he wrote nine violin concertos and three string quartets.
- It must have pleased Shaw that Ole Bull's favorite composer was Wolfgang Amadeus Mozart (1756–91). In addition to being a perfect Wagnerite, Shaw was a staunch defender of Mozart, who, in spite of the fact that the first Salzburg Mozart Festival took place in 1856, was not much in vogue in England in the later nineteenth century. As A. Hyatt King points out

> By the 1870's the attraction of Mozart's instrumental music, restricted as it was in performance, seems to have begun to fade everywhere before the mounting popularity of Beethoven, Mendelssohn, Chopin, Schumann, and Brahms. (A. Hyatt King, *Mozart in Retrospect Studies in Criticism and Bibliography* (Oxford University Press, 1970), 26)

- A Berserk was "a wild Norse warrior of great strength and ferocious courage, who fought on the battlefield with a frenzied fury known as the 'berserker rage' " (*OED*).
- Adam Oehlenschläger (1779–1850), Danish poet. He was the first of the Danish Romantics (the Romantic movement had come to Denmark via Germany) who, having rediscovered Scandinavian mythology, tried to reproduce the meters of Danish and Norse heroic poetry. In his early years he exhibited a fire of inspiration, which dulled rather as he grew older.
- Antonio Stradivari [Stradivarius] (1644?–1737), Italian violin maker. Perhaps the greatest of violin makers, he was a pupil of Niccolo Amati (1596–1684), himself the most illustrious of the famous Amati family of violin makers; while [Bartolomeo] Giuseppe Antonio Guarnerius [known as Giuseppe del Gesu from the initials IHS often appearing on his labels] (1698–1744) was likewise the most celebrated of the famous Guarneri family of violin makers in Cremona.
- Gasparo da Salo [family name Bertolotti] (1540–1609) was an Italian instrument maker, born in Polpenazzi, but baptised in Salo. He is less known for his violins than for his viols, viole da gamba, and contrabass viols. He is not the same person as the Bavarian instrument maker Gaspar Duiffoprugcar [or Tieffenbrucker] (1514–71), who for some time was credited with being

the first maker of violins, a claim rejected by Vidal in *Les Instruments à archet*.

■ Francis I (1494–1547), king of France, son of Charles of Angoulême and Louise of Savoy. He was born in Cognac, and succeeded his father-in-law Louis XII in 1515. However musical he may have been himself, his reign was not very harmonious: his fear of Lutheranism and Calvinism led to repressive policies that culminated in the massacre of Vaudois (1545), and the rivalry, begun with Charles V, between France and the Austro-Spanish Hapsburgs was to last until 1756.

■ Since Shaw did not receive *Ole Bull: A Memoir* until 20 June, it is unlikely that his reaction to a street incident on the twelfth was inspired by Ole Bull's performance of the "flying mare;" but there is sufficient similarity in the wording of the diary entry to suggest Shaw's reason for selecting as praiseworthy this aspect of Ole Bull's character:

> In Wigmore [Street] we saw a young rough beating a girl and I disturbed myself for the rest of the evening by flying at him. (*Diary*, 176)

26 July 1886

A BOOK FOR ORATORS AND SINGERS* [C243]

THOUGH there must by this time be in existence almost as many handbooks for singers and speakers as a fast reader could skip through in a lifetime or so, publishers still find them safe investments. Young people who are born into that fringe of the musical and theatrical professions from which we draw our great stock of deadheads are generally much at a loss when the question of earning a living comes home to them. They find, to their surprise, that they can neither read nor write the various languages in which they have so often chattered to the musical foreigner. Their knowledge of the ways of mummers and minstrels will no more pass with managers and impresarios as artistic skill and culture than a sexton's opportunities of helping the beneficed clergy into their surplices would recommend him to a bishop as preacher or theologian: yet they do not

---

*"Hygiene of the Vocal Organs." By Morell Mackenzie, M.D. (London: Macmillan and Co. 1886.)

recognize their unfitness for an engagement, as a sexton, to do him justice, recognizes his unfitness for ordination. Their ineptly stagy manners and appearance, like their morals, are the impress of an environment of bismuth and rouge, overcoats with Astrakan collars, moustaches, sham concerts for the benefit of sham singers out of engagement, and an atmosphere which creates an unquenchable craving for admission without payment to all sorts of public entertainments, especially to the Opera. An engagement at £200 a night at Covent Garden usually strikes them as a peculiarly eligible means of subsistence; and their parents, eager to have a prima donna in the family to exploit all to themselves, encourage the project while there is a spark of life in it. Unsuspicious of their own futility, they have some distorted ideas of practice, but none of study. They are always in search of a method—especially the old Italian one of Porpora; and they will even pay cash for a handbook of singing, a set of unintelligible photographs of the larynx, or an ammoniaphone from which to suck a ready-made compass of three octaves with the usual fortune attached. They are not damped even by the reflection that if prima donnas could be made on these terms the supply among the Western nations would exceed the demand by several millions, and the market value of an Elsa or Valentine sink to eighteen shillings a week exclusive of expenses. Mdme. Patti can build castles because, besides the wages of a highly skilled workwoman, she enjoys the rent of her monopoly of a highly popular form of ability. If every one with a musical turn could do as much as she after a course of complimentary tickets and a few whiffs from the ammoniaphone, there would be no more castles for poor Mdme Patti: she would at once be reduced to the needy ranks of unskilled labour.

It may seem unjust to Dr. Morell Mackenzie to harp in this place on a parasitic class to which his book is not specially addressed. But he has himself created the association by a certain facetiousness and quotativeness that would vanish from his mind in the presence of an audience upon whose scientific and artistic culture he could rely. There is hardly a chapter in which he does not seem to be making allowances, with good-humoured contempt, for the untrained reason of vulgar readers in one sentence, and in the next writing down to their level with a sort of jocoseness permissible at a musical-at-home, but decidedly not good enough for a carefully weighed treatise. It is ill to be dull even when correct; excellent to be lively, witty, and vernacular as well as correct; but intolerable to be chatty and trivial in manner merely to reconcile slovenly people to the correctness and authority of your matter. Dr. Morell Mackenzie's backsliding in this direction would not be worth insisting on but for the importance of his book, which is the most interesting English record of laryngoscopic investigation since Mdme. Seiler's. He recognizes two vocal registers, which he calls long reed and short reed respectively, asserting that in chest voice "the pitch is raised by means of increasing tension and lengthening of the cords," whilst in head voice the same result is brought about "by gradual shortening of the vibrating reed." He does not regard the closure of the cartilaginous ends of the cords as a change of register, because the reed still lengthens as the pitch rises. It is when "stop closure" of the ligamentous glottis takes place, and the reed begins to shorten with the ascent of the voice, that he admits a change of register. He has discovered eminent singers, tenor and soprano, singing throughout the whole compass in the long reed register, although the quality of tone seemed unmistakably that proper to the short reed, the laryngoscope thus ruthlessly discrediting judgment by ear. His table of fifty voices examined by him is full of curious points; and his remarks on the difficulty of learning to manipulate the laryngoscope and read the image aright, carrying all the authority of his exceptionally extensive practice with the apparatus, are very suggestive as to the contradictory observations of previous investigators. His general hints to singers and speakers are practicable: he does not irritate the reader by prescribing habits, clothes, diet, and hours that would cut an artist off from human society under existing arrangements. There is the inevitable warning against tight lacing, high heels, open mouths, sudden changes of temperature, and excesses of all kinds, which will probably prove just as effectual as previous admonitions to the same effect. With respect to what is called "breaking" of the voice in adolescence, he points out that only about seventeen per cent. of boys' voices actually crack; and he declares his ignorance of any reason for disusing the voice during the change that would not justify disuse of the limbs during the growth of the long bones of one's skeleton.

Dr. Mackenzie is perhaps the greatest living authority on such matters and, notwithstanding the defects of style which we have pointed out, this volume deserves to be widely read as a most authoritative treatise on a subject in which we are all of us interested.

Editor's Notes

- Shaw read this book on 15 July 1886, began his review the next day, and finished it on the nineteenth. He revised it and sent it in on the twenty-first (*Diary*, 185–86).
- [Sir] Morell Mackenzie (1837–92), English physician. He was born at Leytonstone, Essex, the son of Stephen Mackenzie, a surgeon, and educated at the London Hospital, and in Paris, Vienna, and Pesth, where he learned the use of the newly invented laryngoscope under J. N. Czermak. He returned to London in 1862, where he worked again at the London Hospital and took his degree in medicine. The following year he won the Jacksonian Prize at the Royal College of Surgeons with his essay on "The Pathology of the Larynx," after which he became a specialist in diseases of the throat. In 1863 the foundation of the Throat Hospital (in King Street, Golden Square) was largely owing to him, and through his work there and at the London Hospital (where he served from 1866 to 1873) he became recognized throughout Europe as a leading authority, and established a wide practice. Interesting, in view of Shaw's censure of Morell Mackenzie's "good-humoured contempt" for the reader, is the fact that only a year after this review was printed (in May 1887), the doctor suffered a much greater rebuke to his pride. He was specially summoned to attend the crown prince of Germany (later Emperor Frederick III), who was suffering from a disease of the throat. The German physicians, in attendance since March, had diagnosed his condition as cancer of the throat; but Morell Mackenzie (basing his opinion on a microscopic examination of a portion of throat tissue) disagreed, insisting that the disease was not demonstrably cancerous, and that therefore the surgery planned for 21 May 1887 was unnecessary. The matter was as political as it was medical, because should the ailment prove fatal, according to the family law of the Hohenzollerns, the prince should renounce his succession to the German throne. Indeed, some of the German doctors were suspected of making a "political" diagnosis. Morell Mackenzie, however, was believed, and the crown prince went with him to London for treatment, and was present at the Jubilee celebrations in June. For his services Morell Mackenzie was knighted in September 1887 and decorated with the Grand Cross of the Hohenzollern Order. In November, however, the German doctors were again called in, because it turned out that the disease really was cancer. Indeed, the prince became emperor on 9 March 1888 and died on the fifth of June. Mackenzie claimed that the condition had become malignant *since* his first examination, as a consequence of the treatment by the German doctors, and this precipitated a quarrel between Morell Mackenzie and the German medical world. An account of the illness was published there; Morell Mackenzie replied to it in a work entitled *The Fatal Illness of Frederick the Noble* (1888), and was censured for this by the Royal College of Surgeons. The remainder of his life was uneventful.

    Interestingly, in his scrapbook of press cuttings where Shaw kept this review, he had omitted the final paragraph.

- Astrakan (more properly Astrakhan) is "the skin of stillborn or very young lambs from Astrakhan in Russia, the wool of which resembles fur" (*OED*).
- Nicola Antonio Porpora (1686–1768), Italian composer and singing teacher. Although he composed forty-four operas, eleven oratorios and many masses and motets, he gained an enormous reputation as a singing teacher, dividing his time between Naples and Venice, and numbering among his pupils Farinelli, Caffarelli, Umberti (who out of respect for his teacher called himself "Porporino"), Salimbeni, and Metastasio.
- The "ammoniaphone" was Dr. Carter Moffat's invention: it was a tube containing a strip of cotton soaked with a combination of peroxide of hydrogen and ammonia, the vapor of which was inhaled through a small mouthpiece. By inhaling the vapor, it was alleged, the natural voice would be "transformed, so that the harsh sputterings and cacklings of our Northern throats should become softened to the melodious cadence of Italian utterance" (Mackenzie 155). Mackenzie is scornful of the device, humorously suggesting that in the same manner the fire of Italian eyes might just as well be "brought hither by some chemical Prometheus, and infused into our colder orbs"!
- Elsa is the soprano heroine of Wagner's *Lohengrin,* and "Valentine" is presumably a misprint for "Valentin" the baritone brother of Marguerite in Gounod's *Faust.*
- Adelina [Adela Juana Maria] Patti (1843–1919), Spanish-born coloratura soprano. She was of Italian parents who moved to the United States before she was ten, and from 1851 to 1855 she sang at many concerts there. Her first formal debut in New York was in 1859 as Lucia; and her first appearance in London was two years later at Covent Garden. In 1877 she sang for the first time at La Scala, Milan, where she did indeed receive the "wages of a highly skilled workwoman": she appeared nine times that year at La Scala, and four times in Venice at a fee of 8,000 fr. (£320) for each performance (see *The Theatre,* 30 October 1877, 217). She retired from the stage in 1895, but continued to appear from time to time, finally giving an official "farewell concert" at the Albert Hall in London in 1906. Shaw had attended a previous "farewell concert" of Patti's: the one she gave before she left England for a South American tour in 1889. In all he wrote six notices of her, praising the "wonderful even soundness of the middle of her voice, its beauty and delicacy of surface, and her exquisite touch and diction" (Bernard Shaw, *The World,* 30 May 1894).
- Emma Seiler (1821–66), American teacher of singing and student of voice production. Born and raised in Europe [Germany, Austria, Switzerland], she came to the United States and settled in Philadelphia. In 1858 she studied the action of the larynx in voice production by means of a laryngeal mirror, and wrote several books on the subject, including *The Voice in Singing* (1861) [translated from the German by W. H. Furness in 1881], which edition is cited by Morell Mackenzie. Emma's more famous son Carl Seiler (1849–1905), much influenced by his mother, studied medicine at the University of Pennsylvania, and immediately after his graduation devoted himself to laryngology, becoming first a fellow of the American Laryngological Association in 1879, and its vice president in 1882.

28 July 1886

A HANDBOOK OF HUMAN ERROR* [C244]

OF the many correctives which physicians have administered to diseased mankind since the human constitution first began to develop its
remarkable power of getting out of order, few can have been harder to
swallow than the essays with which Dr. Maudsley treats the optimistic illusions of human vanity. Like an accomplished metropolitan consultant, he gives us his opinion with most persuasive grace, never
forgetting his business, but not failing to relieve the strain on our
attention by an elegant discursiveness, borrowing apt illustrations
from the joyous arts, and softening the impossibility of holding out
any hope of recovery by adroit belittlements of his own skill and fore-
sight, and cheering reminders that among the infinite possibilities of
nature even a scientific basis for optimism may be awaiting discovery.
But for all that, he makes us feel that we are doomed. Our illusions
wither at his words; he kindles a fire among our gods; our castles in
the air dislimn as he breathes upon them; and the millennial golden
city which we were looking forward to, and perhaps helping to build,
reveals itself through his field glass as a valley of dry bones. Among
the egotistical vanities which he describes with so much charm, we
recognize, to our utter confusion, the high estimate of our own resolute altruism, the faith in our mission, and the sanguine reliance on
our wonderful luck which have disguised so many humiliating truths
from us. Worst of all, when he has filled us with sorrow and left us no
comfort but the reflection that we are at least filled with wisdom, he
confesses to us that disillusionment means stagnation and death—
that he has morally murdered us in robbing us of the dreams which
are the food of our souls.

   Now, a doctor who can do all this in a perfectly polished and pleasant
manner must be admitted to possess exceptional culture and adroitness. Immense, indeed, need be the tact of one who, when we make
that momentous first appeal of "Doctor: let me know the worst," dares
to take us at our word—a sufficiently disconcerting proceeding even in
trivial cases, but doubly dreadful when the disease in which he is a
specialist is one which he deems incurable, and of which he sees malig-

---

*"Natural Causes and Supernatural Seemings." By Henry Maudsley, M.D., LL.D. (Lon-
don: Kegan Paul, Trench, and Co. 1886.)

nant symptoms in every descendant of Adam. Yet, shrink from his remorseless prescience as we may, we can no more resist calling him in than we can resist reading the ghost stories that send us quaking to our beds. Pessimists are, after all, often wonderfully pleasant fellows in their way of putting unpleasant things. The Dance of Death is not so gladdening as a novel by Miss Rhoda Broughton; yet Holbein imparted a fascination to his skeletons which has already lasted some three centuries longer than the utmost vogue one would care to predict for Joan or Nancy. Ecclesiastes is not an encouraging page of the Scripture; nevertheless, the most optimistic passages of the New Testament are not more familiar in our mouths than Koheleth's melancholy apostrophes to the futility of our lives. Shakspere and Swift are popular favourites, though their philosophy is the philosophy of despair. Is it then matter for wonder that Dr. Maudsley is one of the most agreeable of our essayists, although his mission is to tell us that Nature returns the same answer to the skilled questioning of modern science as she did to Koheleth, Hamlet and Gulliver? Behind and before us is the blind cave of eternal night, from which we had much better never have issued, since we have gained nothing but an oppressive consciousness that it is waiting to swallow us up again, all to no discoverable purpose. Our progress is from nothing to nothing; and we are making as much fuss about it as if it were from nothing to everything. Naturally this does not content us. We turn to the men who have an intuition of a nobler answer—nobler we call it and feel it to be, because it is more flattering to us. And when Dr. Maudsley comes down upon us with an irrefutable demonstration that our optimistic intuitions are indistinguishable from the illusions of epilepsy, hysteria, and even ordinary unreasonableness, we kick against the tyranny of reason as becomes free Britons, and fight as living men with overpowering instincts of self-preservation against a pessimism whose logical outcome is suicide.

But is pessimism, after all, as depressing a philosophy as might be expected? At Dr. Maudsley's grave declaration that "to the race as to the individual, wisdom cannot fail to bring disillusion, and increase of knowledge to be increase of sorrow," the average man certainly cannot help feeling what America calls "kinder solemn." Again, hear the final verdict:

> Were it not for the persistence of the ideal in the human heart, and for the redeeming instances of the few noble lives which it inspires and sacrifices, the faithful study of human history would be calculated to demoralize human nature. The student could hardly help rising from it with the deeply imbued convic-

tion that, whatever man has been, it would have been something better not to have been; and that, whatever he may be destined to become at his best, it were something better not to be at the cost of what he has been, is still, and must continue to be in the long and painful process of becoming it.

In the very saving clause at the beginning of this there is a sharper sting than in the conclusion; for though it is admitted that heroes have existed who were not epileptic egotists, we are reminded in the same breath that they have been treated all the worse on that account. Dr. Maudsley, in fact, confirms and gives a more decorous form to the opinion of the King of Brobdingnag, who described our history as "only a heap of conspiracies, rebellions, murders, massacres, revolutions, banishments, the very worst effects that avarice, faction, hypocrisy, perfidiousness, cruelty, rage, madness, hatred, envy, lust, malice, and ambition could produce." Now, granting that this is the fulness of wisdom—and such a view of it is really frightfully plausible—is it also the fulness of sorrow? Dr. Maudsley returns a melancholy affirmative; but in doing so he lapses into dogmatism: for the facts do not verify his inference.

Editor's Notes

- Shaw began reading this book for review on 25 May 1886, but must have put it aside; for he reported it afresh on 5 July, continued reading it on the sixth, and wrote the review on 7 and 8 July, sending it in on the ninth (*Diary*, 171, 182, 183, 226).
- Henry Maudsley (1835–1918), English physician and psychiatrist. He was born near Settle in Yorkshire, and educated at Giggleswick School, privately, and at University College, London, where he qualified as a physician in 1857. Soon afterwards he devoted himself to the study of mental disorders. He was the medical superintendent of Manchester Royal Lunatic Hospital from 1859 to 1862, a physician at West London Hospital, Hammersmith, from 1864 to 1874, and from 1869 to 1879 professor of medical jurisprudence at University College, London. He wrote a number of books that influenced deeply psychiatric thought, among them *Responsibility in Mental Disease* (1874), *The Physiology of Mind* (1876), *The Pathology of Mind* (1879), *Body and Will* (1883), *Life in Mind and Conduct* (1902). *Heredity, Variation and Genius* (1908), and *Organic to Human, Psychological and Sociological* (1917). He also donated a large sum of money for the creation of a psychiatric hospital, which was named in his honor and opened after his death. His later writings, prepared after his retirement at Bushey, expressed his materialist philosophy.

- Hans Holbein the Younger (1497–1543), German painter and master designer of woodcut illustrations. He added his contribution to the medieval notion of the "dance of death" that levels all classes, by painting a series of small genre scenes (*Imagines mortis* 1523–26) in which a sardonic Death suddenly confronts his victims in their daily occupations: the pope in conclave, the emperor in his court, the mason on his scaffold, and the farmer behind his plow.
- Rhoda Broughton (1840–1920), English novelist. She began her literary career in 1867 by publishing two novels that enjoyed a *succès de scandale*, thought daring at the time because of the passionate emotions of their characters: *Cometh Up As a Flower* and *Not Wisely but Too Well*. From this point on she published on the average one novel every two years. The two to which Shaw refers, *Nancy* and *Joan*, were published in 1873 and 1876 respectively.
- Shaw was fond of referring to Koheleth [or Qoheleth: a Hebrew term probably meaning "The Assembly-speaker," hence "The Preacher"], the author of *Ecclesiastes*, the basic theme of which is the ultimate futility of a life based upon earthly ambitions and desires. The Devil in *Man and Superman* speaks of the world as "an infinite comedy of illusion," and of "the profound truth of my friend Koheleth, that there is nothing new under the sun."
- In spite, or perhaps because, of its pessimistic outlook, Maudsley's book was popular, running to three editions. Shaw may have remembered it—or consulted it again—when he was writing *Saint Joan;* for Maudsley's book has two chapters on hallucinations and illusions, in which among many other examples, he praises the great work done by Joan of Arc while under the influence of hallucination, saying: "Nevertheless the feeling and aim were not hallucination, nor was the mighty work which came of it" (Maudsley, 210). In the same way, Shaw in "Joan's Voices and Visions" in the preface to his play accepts the hallucination for the sake of the result. Elsewhere, Shaw's uneasy acquiescence with Maudsley's materialism—which, in its gloom sounds almost like the "Absurdist" philosophy as expounded by Beckett, et al.—suggests that he is tiring of slum clearance, and is ready for the architectural planning of the Life Force. This is quickened by his review of Samuel Butler's *Luck, or Cunning?* [see pages 277–79 below].

31 July 1886

PRINCIPLES OF EXPRESSION IN PIANOFORTE PLAYING [C245]

"Principles of Expression in Pianoforte Playing" (W. Reeves) Professor A. Christiani, of New York, has, in a copiously illustrated 300 page quarto, formulated what he has to teach on the subject of pianoforte playing. When a musician is intelligent enough to feel the need of arranging his knowledge, he is commonly astonished at the ease with which he can introduce order into chaos by adopting a few rough categories. Unsuspected analogies and logical links come to light at every step of his work. No one having suggested them to him he is apt to conclude that they have never occurred to anybody before. Hence it is rare to meet with a handbook by a trainer of artists without an exordium in which the writer's crude stumblings on the metaphysics and psychology of his subject are announced in good faith as epoch-making developments of speculation and research. Mr. Christiani has not quite escaped this pitfall; but the practical part of his book is none the worse in consequence. His protest against Schumann's perplexing trick of writing whole movements with the bar divisions and time signature proper to some quite different rhythm is likely to raise some controversy among those who persist in believing—as Schumann presumably did—that a commonplace theme will sound odd to the audience because its notation looks odd to the player. The point can be tested experimentally by playing from Schumann's notation and Mr. Christiani's alteration of it successively, and challenging the hearer to distinguish them by the effect on the ear alone. In dealing with phrasing, accent, pauses, and retardations of speed, Mr. Christiani indicates very clearly the artistic treatment which he approves of. Of the merits of his favourite style the reader must judge for himself. "De gustibus non est disputandum."

Editor's Notes

- Shaw had received this book for review as early as 29 May 1886, when he lent it to his friend Laura Warley. She had presumably returned it by 20 July, on which date Shaw wrote his review, revising and sending it together with his review of Morell Mackenzie's book on the twenty-first (*Diary*, 172, 186).
- Adolf Friedrich Christiani (1836–85), German pianist. He was born in Kassel. From Germany he went to London in 1855, and afterwards to the United States where he taught in Poughkeepsie, Pittsburgh, Cincinatti, and, in 1877, New York. In 1880 he became director of a music school in Elizabeth, New Jersey. His book was published in the United States, Germany, and England.
- Shaw's comment on Christiani's assumption that his "method" was an "epoch-making development of speculation and research," reminds one of the

old musician in *Caesar and Cleopatra* who is asked by Cleopatra whether he can teach her the harp:

> MUSICIAN: Assuredly I and no-one else can teach the queen. Have I not discovered the lost method of the ancient Egyptians, who could make a pyramid tremble by touching a bass string? All the other teachers are quacks: I have exposed them repeatedly.
>
> *Caesar and Cleopatra*, Act IV

■ "De gustibus non est disputandum." (There is no disputing about tastes.)

7 August 1886

SOME MISCELLANEOUS LITERATURE* [C248]

A TRIP FROM BEIRUT TO THE BALKANS

IN this latest record of Dr. Field's travels, he plays the part of the chatty clerical tourist from Beirut to Varna, where the Bulgarian soil makes a historian of him, eliciting a few excellent chapters descriptive of the massacres, the Russian crusade, and the driving of the Sick Man to the verge of the Bosphorous, across which Dr. Field would have rejoiced to see him swept finally into Asia. A clear and unembarrassed description, from an American point of view, of the conditions which produced that pregnant war, will compensate the reader for wading through several preceding chapters of tourist's bookmaking. (Always assuming, that is, that the reader is sternly intolerant of bookmaking, a seductive art which Dr. Field well understands.) The reflections which occur to a clergyman on tour with several other clergymen naturally smack occasionally of the cloth. Glimpses of the coast of Asia Minor, with Patmos and Scio, for instance, give rise to invidious comparisons between St. Paul and Alexander the Great, St. John

---

*"The Greek Islands and Turkey After the War." By Henry M. Field, D.D. (London: Sampson Low and Co. 1886.)

"Next Door." By Clara Louisa [sic] Burnham. One vol. (Edinburgh: David Douglas. 1886.)

"Melita." By Louise M. Richter. 1 vol. (London: T. Fisher Unwin. 1886.)

and Homer, culminating in a sentence which should be noted by the New Shakspere Society as probably unique in its complex erroneousness. "It is said," says Dr. Field, "that Homer was blind; but so was King Lear when on the cliffs of Dover he listened and said, 'Hark! do you hear the sea?' " Once or twice, in a transport of reassuring affability, the author has expanded his columns with such superfluous information as that though the Romans rifled Rhodes of its statues, "yet the island itself remains"; or that, "strange as the Turk is, and unlike as he is to an Englishman or a Frenchman, yet he is an inhabitant of the same planet." Also it must be said that the time has come when even a tourist should be able to pass a graveyard without saying— much less writing—"After life's fitful fever they sleep well." Apart from such amiable vagaries of the pen, there is nothing to complain of in Dr. Field's book. It is illustrated by a couple of useful maps, and may be safely recommended to those who desire an easy introduction to the geography and recent history of the Balkan peninsular.

"Next Door"

"Next Door" is as harmless as a novel can conceivably be. There is no villainy, no squalid poverty, no deep suffering nor high achievement; nothing but Aunt Ann with her pet cat, her pleasantly ladylike nieces, and the pleasantly gentlemanlike swains who marry them. How to make from these mild materials a neither dull nor priggish book is a secret upon the possession of which the author may be unreservedly congratulated.

"Melita"

Madame Richter, in attempting to tell a Turkish love story in English, has been embarrassed by a language with which she is evidently not familiar. At times her ineptitudes give the book an air of being an unconscionably long hack-translation of the argument of an opera libretto. The taste of the narration, like the English, is Oriental. We are told that "the eye is lost in following the glories of the Golden Horn"; also that "Melita's slender figure was lost in red satin cushions placed for her"; that "Adilé Hanum's rosy lips did not despise the cigarette," &c. Amid many loving but careless allusions to the fine arts, we find a Turkish gentleman who plays Arabian tunes on a modern West European pianoforte; a lady who, sitting in her boudoir in a cashmere dress, is said to look "more than ever like the Venus of Milo"; and a famous poem of Goethe's attributed to Schubert, probably because he composed music to it. Mdme. Richter need not be surprised if the cumulative effect of these petty thoughtlessnesses should make her critics forgetful of the success with which she has achieved her object of giving us a glimpse of Turkish society and domesticity as they are known to a lady who spent "the golden days" of her life on the shores of the Sea of Marmora.

Editor's Notes

- Shaw received *The Greek Islands and Turkey After the War* on 13 July 1886, and read it for review on the twenty-seventh. It was presumably one of the "4 reviews" he wrote for the *PMG* two days later; for his diary records that he sent it off on that date. *Next Door* Shaw had received on 20 June 1886, and, since he dispatched his review on 29 July, we must again presume it to have been one of the "4 reviews" he wrote on that day. *Melita* he had received on 13 July 1886. He read it for review on the twenty-sixth, and dispatched it with the others on the twenty-ninth (*Diary*, 187, 188, 226).
- Henry M[artyn] Field (1822–1907), American author and clergyman. He was born in Stockbridge, Massachusetts, the brother of Cyrus Field; graduated from Williams College in 1838, and was pastor of a Presbyterian Church in St. Louis, Missouri, from 1842 to 1847; then, after spending three years in Europe, he became pastor of a Congregational Church in West Springfield, Massachusetts, from 1850 to 1854. From that year until 1898 he was editor (and for many years sole proprietor) of *The Evangelist,* a New York periodical devoted to the Presbyterian Church. He wrote a series of travel books that proved enormously popular. His first two, *From the Lakes of Killarney to the Golden Horn* (1876) and *From Egypt to Japan* (1877), passed through more than twenty editions! In addition to books about travel, he also wrote *The Irish Confederates and the Rebellion of 1798* (1850), *The History of the Atlantic Telegraph* (1866), *On the Desert* (1883), *Among the Holy Hills* (1884), *Faith or Agnosticism? the Field-Ingersoll Discussion* (1888), *Old Spain and New Spain* (1888), and *The Life of David Dudley Field* (1898). He spent the last years of his life in retirement in Stockbridge, Massachusetts.
- "The Sick Man" [of Europe] was the diplomatic appellation and popular nickname for the Ottoman Empire.
- In Shakespeare's play it is, of course, the Duke of Gloucester who is blinded and his son Edgar who asks him the question, "Hark! do you hear the sea?"
- "After life's fitful fever they sleep well." This "adaptation" of Lady Macbeth's comment on Duncan, "After life's fitful fever he sleeps well," Shaw used for comic effect nineteen years later in his one act play for barns and

booths, *Passion, Poison, and Petrifaction,* where Lady Magnesia Fitztol-lemache also misquotes Lady Macbeth shortly after three people have been struck by lightning and killed in her bed-sitting-room.

- Perhaps Shaw himself enjoyed this "easy introduction to the . . . recent history of the Balkan Peninsular," for although Field's book deals with a conflict earlier than the one depicted in Shaw's play *Arms and the Man* (1894), Shaw might well have consulted the detailed colored maps of the region it contains, and also might have remembered Field's account of the Russian soldier Skobeleff while developing the character of Sergius Saranoff:

> No figure in modern military history is more striking than that of Skobeleff, always in the advance, seeming to court death by his con-spicuous figure, as he always went into battle wearing a white uniform and mounted on a white horse, as if to offer himself as a mark for the enemy, yet by this very recklessness giving an example of courage which electrified his soldiers, and made them follow him in the deadly breach. Nearly all his staff were killed, yet he escaped unhurt. (Field, 201)

- Clara Louise Burnham [née Root] (1854–1927), American author. She was born in Newton, Massachusetts, the daughter of Mary O. Woodman, a musician, and George Frederick Root, the composer and publisher. He wrote numerous popular songs, (including *The Battlecry of Freedom* and *Tramp, tramp, tramp*) and several cantatas for which Clara Louise wrote the words. When she was nine, the family moved to Chicago, where she attended public and private schools and studied music, which she intended to make her profession. Before she was twenty she married a lawyer, Walter Burnham, and soon afterwards began to write. Her first accepted work was a poem published in *Wide Awake* and a novel *No Gentlemen* (1881). A sampling of her many novels would include *A Sane Lunatic* (1882), *Dearly Bought* (1884), *Young Maids and Old* (1889), *The Mistress of Beech Knoll* (1890), *Miss Bagg's Secretary* (1892), *Dr. Latimer* (1893), *Sweet Clover* (1894), and *The Wise Woman* (1895). From 1902 onward she became interested in Chris-tian Science, and her later novels reveal this: such works as *The Leaven of Love* (1908), *The Inner Flame* (1912), *The Right Track* (1914), *Instead of the Thorn* (1916), *In Apple-Blossom Time* (1919), and *The Lavarons* (1925). She also continued to contribute stories and poems to *Wide Awake, St. Nicholas* and *The Youth's Companion.* Shortly before she died, she visited Hollywood, where she sold the motion picture rights of *The Lavarons.*

- [Mrs] Louise [Luise] M[arie] Richter [née Schwaab] (1852–1938), Ger-man author and art critic. Born at Brusa in Asia Minor, where her father had founded a silk industry, she went to England as a young girl in the company of her sister, later the wife of the orientalist, Dr. G. W. Leitner. At that time her ambition was to follow a musical career, for she had a fine voice; but in London she met and, in 1878, married Dr. Jean Paul Richter, an art historian, by whom she had two sons and two daughters. Together they traveled through Italy, where she learned much about art. Shaw's comment on her poor English in *Melita* must have been particularly galling, but it does not seem to have been deterring, since she translated Giovanni Morelli's *Italian Masters in German Galleries* into English in 1883, and was to translate Hermann Knackfuss's *Rubens* in 1904. She also wrote *Chantilly in History and Art* (1913) and *Algeria and its Centenary* (1930) and contributed to the *Burlington Magazine, Connoisseur,* and the *Gazette des Beaux-Arts.* She divided her time between Italy and London, where she had many musical, artistic, and literary friends; and for the last seven years of her life she lived in Lugano, where her husband predeceased her by only four months.

▪ No doubt Shaw's continuing interest in "the marriage question" to be explored in *The Philanderer, Candida, You Never Can Tell, Misalliance, Getting Married, Fanny's First Play,* etc., was further stimulated by reading *Melita,* which depicts the harem (in which the Turkish women are "caged up birds") as the edifice of man's distrust and jealousy and women's subjection and degradation.

9 August 1886

A ROMANCE BY MR. RICHARD DOWLING*
[C249]

WHEN writers of fiction label their books romances, they cut from beneath the critic's feet the slippery foothold of realism which, as against novelists who neglect that precaution, he secures by desperately pretending that their works are "criticisms of life." It is a shabby advantage to take; for when the taker, like Mr. Richard Dowling, is reasonably cautious in his grammar, and does not expose himself by romantic excursions into the French language, it renders him quite invulnerable, except to general accusations of dulness and other matters of mere taste. Not that "Fatal Bonds" is dull: it is only disastrous, as a romance needs must be. And yet it seems hard that the heroine, an interesting and good-looking young woman, should be married over and over again; pitched from a bridge by the hardness of one husband, fished from under a barge by the heroism of

*"Fatal Bonds." A Romance. By Richard Dowling. 3 vols. (London: Ward and Downey. 1886.)

another, and brought round in a hospital only to creep away to a desolate tower and stab herself, which final catastrophe could not have occurred but for her unaccountable habit of carrying a dagger. Then there is her friend, Nanette Jaussin, a charming little woman, who disappears from the story without a word of explanation, as if the only characters worth our curiosity were the bigamists, stabbers, and suicides. The fact that Nanette, though an innocent creature, is nevertheless the most interesting person in the book, will, it is to be hoped, be so impressed from all quarters upon Mr. Dowling that he may have no excuse in future for mistrusting his power to interest readers without the tiresome crimes that keep the shadow of the police-court over all his narrative, and leave no means of disembarrassing the righteous in the third volume save indiscriminate slaughter of the wicked. Even in the realm of the shilling shocker these manners and morals are passing away. The romancer, like the torpedo, is exhausting himself and benumbing his victims by much shocking; and the day is at hand when the humblest reader, ere he yields his shilling, will require some subtler stimulus than felony complicated with philandering. For what are the dilemmas of the criminal classes to us, whose consciences are bowed down with offences of which the laws know nothing, nor we the laws? We want our own troubles—our problems of life and mind—suggestively restated, if not solved for us. Which of us is married to a bigamous Frenchwoman, madly fond of us, and given to showing it by daggering? Not one in fifty, let us hope: perhaps even a smaller proportion. Our wives are straitly married to us; and therein, it may be, lies much of our trouble. They are not madly fond of us; and therein too is trouble and consolation mingled. As for weapons, they speak daggers, but use none. It would be, to say the least, more sympathetic in Mr. Dowling to typify in his pages those ills we have than fly to others that we know of but care nothing about.

However, since Mr. Dowling prefers romance, let him have the credit of romancing with some success. Although we are aware in our hearts that his tale is all make-believe, and that his mysterious ways will prove no-thoroughfares in the last two chapters, yet he compels us to follow his words with fearful expectancy of some impossible final satisfying sensation. We are disappointed, of course, as we deserve to be; but the hope, while it lasted, shortened a tedious hour or so without unduly straining our intelligence.

Editor's Notes

- Shaw received *Fatal Bonds* for review on 31 July 1886, read it on 1 August, began the review on the third, finished and revised it the following day, and sent it in on the fourth (*Diary*, 189, 227).
- Richard Dowling (1846–98), Irish journalist, humorist, and novelist. He was born at Clonmel, and educated at St. Munchin's College, Limerick. In 1870 he moved to Dublin, where he wrote for *The Nation, Ireland's Eye*, and edited a comic paper *Zozimus*. In 1874 he moved to London (two years before Shaw), and was initially connected with *The Hornet* (famous for Shaw's first journalistic efforts). In fact Shaw spoke familiarly of him when he met him at the house of Oscar Wilde on 14 September 1886 (*Diary*, 198). Dowling appears to have been almost as prolific a journalist as Shaw at this point, contributing to *The Illustrated Sporting News, Cornhill, Belgravia*, and *The Dramatic Review*. He also edited his own comic paper, *Yorick*. In addition to collections of stories, like *On the Embankment* (1884) and *While London Sleeps* (1895), he wrote over a score of novels, including *The Mystery of Killard* (1879), *The Sport of Fate* (1880), *The Weird Sisters* (1880), *Under Saint Paul's* (1880), *The Duke's Sweetheart* (1881), *The Last Call* (1884), *The Hidden Flame* (1885), *Miracle Gold* (1888), *An Isle of Surrey* (1889), and *Old Corcoran's Money* (1897).
- Although Julia Craven in Shaw's *The Philanderer* (1893) was based in part upon Jenny Patterson, one wonders whether Shaw also remembered the fiercely melodramatic Louise in *Fatal Bonds*. He seems to have been impressed, favorably or otherwise, with the desperate return of Louise to her phlegmatic and callously indifferent English husband, with her threats to stab him, and with her actually throwing herself off a bridge in a suicide bid; for Julia Craven's stormy scene with Charteris in Grace Tranfield's flat contains all of these elements, including the threat (but not the actuality) of throwing herself out of a window.

20 August 1886

A BRACE OF NOVELS* [C250]

"IN A SILVER SEA"

MR. FARJEON, apparently disgusted with the artificialities of civilization, and perhaps impatient of the complexity which it introduces into

---

*"In a Silver Sea." By B. L. Farjeon. Three vols. (London: Ward and Downey. 1886.)
"Alicia Tennant." By Frances Mary Peard. Two vols. (London: Richard Bentley and Son. 1886.)

the affairs of noveldom, has taken refuge in Arcadia, which he calls in his latest romance the Silver Isle. In this favourite old spot the soil is of equal fertility throughout, and the population never increases. So much, at least, may be deduced from the perfect economic equilibrium of the place, and the millennial tranquillity of society there. No stray autumnal literary man descends on its shores, nor is any column set up in a London paper to commemorate his visit, pay his expenses, and bring a host of seasiders down by the next steamer. The art of letting lodgings is unknown to the inhabitants: they mistrust strangers, and, though too amiable to be pointedly rude to them when they arrive, dwell in the course of conversation rather on the facilities for departure by the next tide than on matters connected with rest and refreshment. These hints seldom fail to take effect; and the isle remains a peaceful if somewhat dull retreat for the world-worn wanderers of Mr. Farjeon's tale. Old friends, indeed, are all these wanderers. As the unbidden tear flows for the fiftieth time over their crosses and bereavements, the weeper pauses to wonder that man is still unhardened to sorrows that he has witnessed in imagination over and over since he began to read romances. There is the long-lost child, the long-lost sister, the trusting maiden, the smiling seducer, the cynical wordling, the honest and opportune rescuer whose roof is ready to shelter the betrayed, the recluse expiating a dreadful crime, the herculean dwarf whose misshapen shoulders heave with the throes of a noble heart, the angel child with golden curls whom alone of all mankind he softens to, the madwoman who flits about the graves in the ghostly moonlight, the hidden hoard of gold which provides virtue with unlimited cash at a critical moment, the diary which explains everything, the duel which avenges everybody, the storm and fatal accident which clear the inconvenient people out of the way, the restoration of the long-lost ones, and the final epithalamium and chime of wedding bells. Just the thing, as Lincoln said, for the people who like that sort of thing. But not by any means the thing with which serious criticism has now anything to do. Mr. Farjeon, by his plot, left himself just one chance of being original. He might have attacked the subtle problem of what society would be like in an island where the economic conditions which are the matrices of our own social institutions were in abeyance. He has not troubled himself to do so. His Silver Islanders are ordinary, unsophisticated people, without money worries or fashionable habits. As philosophical concepts they are less advanced than Swift's Houyhnhnms, between whom and the conventional New England villagers of American fiction they are a cross. Considering that Swift wrote in bitterness and darkness a century and a half ago, when all the sociology outside the Bible was half superstition and half chaos, Mr. Farjeon, having left on his ideal community no marks of what we have learned in the interim, can hardly complain if he finds the popularity of his book, in spite of the philosophic vein of some of its dialogue, confined to districts where literary tastes are primitive, and the University Extension not yet popular.

"ALICIA TENNANT"

"Alicia Tennant," though of feminine origin, enforces the masculine moral that the first and hardest duty to perform well is one's duty to oneself. Cowardice and weakness are so apt to masquerade as self-sacrifice and consideration for others, and women so prone to abet the deception, that it is a relief to find a woman dealing a blow at it. Alicia Tennant's aunt is one of those master spirits who appoint themselves the task of laying down programmes for other people and "bossing them through." Poor Alicia is bossed with the tenderest solicitude through the programme laid down for her; but it unluckily happens to be a misfit, and Alicia is bossed into her grave in consequence. The main item in the programme is marriage with Mr. Lynne, an estimable gentleman of steady habits and considerable means. Alicia finds Major Saunderson, "a tall, soldierly looking man, with a keen eye and a long, closely fitting nose," more to her taste. No such subtlety as the attraction of a closely-fitting nose is needed to explain the preference; for Mr. Lynne is a prig, or person stuffed with unassimilated knowledge, chiefly about the ancient Etruscans. Alicia does not like the match, but, having acquired the habit of allowing her aunt to think for her, she lumps it, as the nursery locution runs, much as Captain Bunsby lumped his nuptials with Mrs. MacStinger. The Major then forsakes the pleasures of society, and exposes his closely fitting nose to the spearmen of the Soudan, who, however, fail to dislodge it. How he travels in Italy; how the cholera seizes him there; how Alicia's honeymoon trip leads her to the hotel where he lies; how she loses her self-control, and tells poor Mr. Lynne why; how the Major recovers, and runs the quarantine blockade; and how Alicia returns home to die, not of a broken heart (for men have died and worms eaten 'em; but not for love), but of want of interest in a life which she is not allowed to boss for herself: all this, and much more concerning a cousin Geoffrey and his adventures at the East-end, may be learned in detail by perusal of the two volumes. Alicia's submission to the marriage is just a little weakened—and that quite unnecessarily—by the accident that clinches Aunt Eleanor's victory; but as our toleration of the heroine's want of backbone is just saved by it, it may be that its introduction was well advised.

Editor's Notes

- Shaw began reading *In a Silver Sea* for review on 27 April 1886, but did not finish reading it until 24 May. Another month went by before he wrote the review on 29 June, on which date he also sent it to the *PMG* (*Diary*, 164, 171, 180, 226). When he began reading *Alicia Tennant* is not recorded (it could have been the book he "read a little for review" on 4 June (*Diary*, 174]); but on the eighth he reports that he "finished reading *Alicia Tennant* for review," and he wrote and dispatched his article on the twenty-ninth (*Diary*, 175, 180, 226).
- B[enjamin] L[eopold] Farjeon (1838–1903), English novelist. He was the second son of Jacob Farjeon, a merchant, born in London and educated at a private Jewish school until, when he was fourteen, he entered the office of the *Nonconformist* newspaper. Three years later, after a religious argument with his parents, he embarked for Australia, traveling steerage. During the voyage, however, he produced some editions of a ship's newspaper (*The Ocean Record*) and was consequently given decent quarters. After gold prospecting in Victoria and New Zealand, he settled in Dunedin as a journalist, helping to manage and finally part owning the colony's first daily paper, established by Julius Vogel in 1861. He also wrote a novel, a play, and several burlesques and stories. These last brought an appreciative letter from Charles Dickens, on the strength of which Farjeon travelled to England in 1868. For the next thirty-five years he wrote novels, among the most popular being *Grif* (1870), *Blade o' Grass* (1871), *Joshua Marvel* (1872), *London's Heart* (1873), and *The Duchess of Rosemary Lane* (1876). As time went on, he turned from the Dickensian treatment of humble life and began writing the sort of mystery novels that Wilkie Collins was to make famous. Such novels as *Great Porter Square* (1884) and *The Mystery of Mr. Felix* (1890) are good examples of this genre. In 1877, he married Margaret Jefferson, daughter of the American actor, who bore him four sons and one daughter. His daughter, Eleanor, herself became a well-known writer of children's literature and collaborated with her brother Herbert in plays. Two other children, Joseph Jefferson and Harry, also distinguished themselves, the first as a playwright and the other as a composer and music critic.
- Lincoln's judgment on a book, recorded in G. W. E. Russell's *Collections and Recollections* (1898), was "People who like this sort of thing will find this the sort of thing they like."
- Swift's Houyhnhnms are the talking horses in *Gulliver's Travels* whose gentle, idealistic view of life is contrasted sharply with that of the Yahoos.
- In the *Pall Mall Gazette*, the phrase "Philosophic vein" was misprinted "philosophic *view*" and Shaw corrected it on his copy, just as he later altered

the punctuation in the sentence about Alicia returning home to die not of a broken heart, "but of want of interest in a life which she is not allowed to boss for herself. All this, and much more . . . ," by changing the period after "herself" to a colon.

- The University Extension, a system whereby university instruction was carried on outside the walls of the institution to the benefit of all classes of society, was new in Shaw's day. Cambridge University began the idea in 1866, and the London University Extension Society was founded ten years later, with Oxford following suit in 1885.
- Frances Mary Peard (1835–1923), English novelist. She was the daughter of Captain George Peard, R.N. She traveled widely and spent some time in India, experiences which she used in such novels as *The Ring from Jaipur* (1904). She wrote a great many novels, among them *One Year; or a Story of Three Houses* (1869), *The Rose Garden* (1872), *Near Neighbours* (1885), *Madame's Grand-daughter* (1887), *His Cousin Betty* (1888), *Tales of the South of France* (1892), *An Interloper* (1894), *Jacob and the Raven* (1896), and *The Flying Months* (1909). She also wrote several boys' books, such as *Scapegrace Dick* (1886), *The Blue Dragon* (1889), and *The Abbot's Bridge* (1891). In her later years she was an invalid, and towards the end of her life practically blind as the result of an acute form of rheumatism.
- In Shaw's sentence "Cowardice and weakness are so apt to masquerade as self-sacrifice and consideration for others . . ." we hear the beginning of a notion that Shaw was to develop in numerous plays, including *The Devil's Disciple* (1897) and *The Shewing-up of Blanco Posnet* (1909).
- Captain Jack Bunsby in Dickens's *Dombey and Son* is master of a vessel called "The Cautious Clara," and a warm friend of Captain Cuttle, who, notwithstanding his independence, is finally captured and married, perforce, by his landlady, Mrs. MacStinger.
- Rosalind's comment to the love-sick Orlando in *As You Like It* is, "But these are all lies; men have died from time to time, and worms have eaten them, but not for love."

2 September 1886

MR. NORRIS'S FRIEND JIM* [C252]

As a purveyor of light literature warranted not to cause mental indigestion or remorse for time misspent, Mr. Norris takes the cake—if that

*"My Friend Jim." By W. E. Norris. Two vols. (London and New York: Macmillan and Co. 1886.)

expression, picked up "by ear," as the musicians say, is a proper one. Readers who, after repeated misadventures in choosing books at Mudie's, have come to regard novelists as uncultivated persons crudely airing their illusions, may confidently except him as one who, if he does not exactly know the world (who does?), knows fully as much of it as a gentleman has any business with. Familiar, but by no means vulgar, he puts on no company manners with you—has none, in fact; but, as if he liked and knew you quite well enough to be at ease in your society, tells you his story in one of the most amusing of narrative styles. And this not only because he values your applause. No: he studies your comfort too, by being unobtrusively concise, polite, and accurate. His humour is of fine flavour, and highly civilized: whilst you are his guest you are never expected to laugh at horseplay, or to join in ridiculing age or natural infirmity. It would be impertinent to compliment him on his ability to write a novel: that much is expected from everybody nowadays; but his retention in his literary capacity of the good humour and good manners of decent social intercourse is too rare an excellence to pass without a word of grateful recognition.

"My friend Jim" is one of those persons who would be entirely lovable were it quite certain that their softness of heart is not really an affection rather of the head. When a man resolutely refuses to think evil of his friends, he may be too noble to conceive other men base; but he may also be merely shrinking from unpleasantness—shutting his eyes for the sake of a quiet life. It is extremely convenient to pretend to be imposed on. We—even the hardest of us—do it every day. We accept excuses that we do not believe: we shake hands cordially with people who deserve to be cut, and congratulate them on achievements for which we would kick them were we strong enough: we allow ourselves to be fleeced of small sums by undeserving beggars who pretend to be only borrowers: we laugh genially at conversation that disgusts us: in sum, we walk through society assiduously holding our candle to the devil, that he may save us from minor rows, and keep us on good terms with everybody. Now, this purely propitiatory amiability is not, to say the least, a heroic quality; and though, for Mr. Norris's sake, one would wish to take as favourable a view as possible of his friend, Jim's claims to any loftier variety of altruism are by no means clearly made out. Maynard, who tells his story, evidently thinks him a good-natured ass, although he now and then helps up the hero theory of him by a little special pleading. The point, however, is of little importance in comparison with that raised by the relations between

Mr. Norris, Maynard, and the public. Mr. Norris, being the real author of the tale, is responsible for the soundness of its sociology and the salubrity of its moral. What right has he, then, to put up this man of straw, Maynard, as spokesman, and make him answerable for the bias given to the reader by the manner of telling the tale? Maynard expresses opinions which many will hold damnable: he describes an ordained clergyman as "an old donkey," and approves of duelling. Arraign Mr. Norris for these heresies, and he can reply that he is no more bound to Maynard's views than Shakspeare was to Iago's. Such virtual doing away with the author is carrying fiction too far, and is, besides, flatly retrograde to the spirit of the age, which considers the author much more important than his work. What person of any fashion, for instance, does not know and care much more about Mr. Ruskin than about his books? Perhaps Mr. Norris deems this state of things unhealthy, and hides himself behind Maynard out of mere modesty. But such a consideration cannot override the supreme importance of having some responsible person to hang in case of national disaster traceable to the teaching of the volume.

Unhappily, the levity with which too many readers take their fiction renders it possible—probable even—that Maynard, in spite of his false position, may be accepted without any very general or strenuous protest. Certainly, he tells the tale uncommonly well; and we can even believe of him, what we can so seldom believe of the inevitable literary man in a novel, that his contributions would be found acceptable by a real editor; for he is an amusing dog, with no more of the prig and the trifler in him than is necessary to account for so brilliant a writer confining himself to articles and reviews instead of becoming the Molière of his age. The heroine is a most refreshingly bad one. Not that she is a felon, or that she comes very terribly to grief from the stroke of poetical justice in the last chapter—for Mr. Norris is never so disgracefully at a loss as to have to trade on our love of the police news; nor has he so low an opinion of us as to invent dire punishments to deter us from following the example of his wicked characters. Lady Bracknell has not a gleam of virtue nor a stroke of ill-luck throughout. It is true that she loses both her little boy and her husband; but she does without the one very cheerfully, and replaces the other to considerable advantage: besides, she is not the woman to complain of bereavements in any case. The boy's deathbed is capitally described. Jefferies, if he were alive, would not weep so very copiously over it as over the death of Paul Dombey; but many who protest against the pathos of "Dombey and Son" as egotistical, unphilosophic and suburban, will spare a tear for poor little Lord Sunning without feeling compromised. Some readers take a good deal of harrowing before they cry; and on such Mr. Norris's quiet realism will perhaps be thrown away; but the rest will finish the scene with a strong sense of having actually witnessed it. One barbarism mars the end of the tale. A whole railway train is wrecked to get rid of Lord Bracknell. This is burning down the house to roast the pig. Why should a number of innocent passengers be maimed, slain, or delayed in their travels merely to kill a man who might have been removed without any such sacrifice of life or rolling-stock? Could he not have been run over, or struck by lightning, or rent by an unmuzzled dog? As an ample set-off to this solitary blemish may be taken the brevity of the book, which, though it contains as much matter as two ordinary novels, is contained in a pair of convenient and pleasantly printed volumes. Their mere aspect is enough to tempt a busy man to neglect his affairs and spend an afternoon in the No-man's land of fiction.

Editor's Notes

- Shaw received this novel on 27 August 1886, read the book the next day, began his review on the twenty-ninth, continued it on the thirtieth, and finished and sent it off on the thirty-first (*Diary*, 194–95, 227).
- William E[dward] Norris (1847–1925), English novelist. He was born in London, the son of Sir William Norris, the chief justice of Ceylon, was educated at Eton (from 1860 to 1864), entered the Inner Temple in 1871 (in which year he also married Frances Isobel Ballenden), and was called to the bar in 1874, but never practiced. Encouraged by Leslie Stephen (Virginia Woolf's father), at that time editor of *Cornhill Magazine*, to try writing a novel, his first effort was called *Heaps of Money* (1877). Subsequently he produced over a score of novels, many of which first appeared in the *Temple Bar* and *Cornhill* magazines, including *Mademoiselle de Mersac* (1880), *No New Thing* (1883), *Major and Minor* (1887) [see pages 340–42 below], *The Rogue* (1888), *The Countess Radna* (1893), *The Despotic Lady* (1895), *Clarissa Furiosa* (1897), *Giles Ingleby* (1899), *The Flower of the Flock* (1900), *Nature's Comedian* (1904), *Not Guilty* (1910) and *Trevalion* published in the year of his death. He resided in Torquay. His wife predeceased him in 1881.
- "takes the cake" This is the first recorded instance of this phrase (*OED*).
- Charles Edward Mudie (1818–90), founder of a circulating library, whose name became a household word among the Victorian public. With its guinea subscription for new books, "Mudie's" helped foster the vogue of the three-volume novel. Mudie had been a stationer and bookseller in Southampton

Row, London, and started to lend books in 1842. This was so successful a venture that ten years later he moved his "Select Library" into the big store-house that became such a familiar landmark in New Oxford Street. In 1860 these premises were enlarged, and different branches established, and in 1864, "Mudie's" became a limited company. Its fortunes declined, however, and it finally closed its doors in the summer of 1937. Aware of the narcotic effect of its romances on the Victorian public, Shaw once solemnly declared, "The most dangerous public house in London is at the Corner of Oxford St, and is kept by a gentleman named Mudie."

▪ Lady Bracknell has nothing but the name in common with Oscar Wilde's famous creation.

▪ "Jefferies". In spite of the spelling, Shaw must be referring to the response to Paul Dombey's death of Francis [Lord] Jeffrey (1773–1850), founder of the *Edinburgh Review*, who was also Dickens's old friend and critic, and who corresponded regularly with him while he was writing his novels, recording his feelings and opinions. After the episode containing the death of Paul Dombey, Dickens reports

> I have had a tremendous outpouring from Jeffrey about the last part, which he thinks the best thing past, present, or to come. (John Forster, *The Life of Charles Dickens* (London: Chapman and Hall, 1912), 372)

▪ The death of little Paul Dombey, Mr. Dombey's son and heir, is described at length in chapter 16 of Dickens's novel. Of this event Anna Marsh-Caldwell (1798–1874), the novelist, said that "it threw a whole nation into mourning." (See *The Oxford Illustrated Dickens* [Oxford University Press, 1947].)

11 September 1886

*VENDETTA!** [C254]

LAST spring there appeared in these columns a notice of an audacious novel entitled "A Romance of Two Worlds." The writer of that notice, a gentleman of whose judgment the present reviewer entertains a favourable opinion, declared in conclusion, "It is impossible for a sober critic to quite approve of the author's rush into print; but it may

---

*"Vendetta!" By Marie Corelli. Three vols. (London: Richard Bentley and Son. 1886.)

perhaps be admitted that 'Marie Corelli' might do worse than rush again, so much less wearisome is she than many more exact philosophers." "Marie Corelli" has accordingly rushed again, quite as impetuously as before, and with the advantage of the experience gained in her former attempt. The impression then made by her vivid imagination, her extraordinary ardour, and her facility in description and declamation, is confirmed and reinforced by a most prodigal display of them all in her new work. Its plot, though extremely sensational, contains no surprises for the reader, whose interest depends rather on a clear prevision of what is coming. Therefore a sketch of it will in no way discount the effect of "Vendetta" on those who may read it hereafter. Count Fabio Romani tells us how he died of cholera at Naples in 1882; how he was buried; how he revived, burst his coffin, found a vast treasure concealed in his family vault, and disinterred himself and it; how he went home to find his widow in the arms of his bosom friend, not for the first time; and how, seized with a diabolical jealousy, he planned and carried out a revenge in which the most merciful incidents were the murders which completed it. Count Fabio is a gentleman as the devil is said to be one: his appetite for evil is so intense that vulgar vices and littlenesses are tasteless to him. He has a conscience too: for its sake he assumes death to be the just punishment of adultery, and so persuades himself that he is but a sword in the hand of God. Thus, in order that the murder he desires to commit may pass for an execution, he becomes, by his own appointment, legislator, judge, prosecutor, jury, witness, counsel on both sides, and hangman. Unfair as the trial is, there is no doubt as to the guilt of the culprit. She is by nature incapable of being a respectable woman and honest wife. What should be done with such a person? "She must die; else she'll betray more men," says Othello. "Ce n'est pas la femme, ce n'est même pas une femme; elle n'est pas dans la conception divine, elle est purement animale; c'est la guenon du pays de Nod, c'est la femelle de Caïn; tue-la," says M. Alexandre Dumas. Count Fabio agrees, but goes further. As his daughter is in heaven, he insists that his wife shall go elsewhere; and as to the method of killing her, he describes as "the best" that which "shall inflict the longest, the cruellest agony upon those by whom honour is wronged." His contempt for the British divorce court may be imagined. Our simple rule of not marrying such women, or, if we marry them unawares, untying the knot and quitting them, seems as sordid to him as his wounded vanity and lust for vengeance seem puerile to us. His opinions will nevertheless find friends in England. We have always with us men and women who, born after their due time, clamour to have the clock put back, and would, if they might have their way, reinstate flogging, duelling, confiscation of the property of wives, and a dozen other barbarisms which the rest of us have outgrown. These belated people gain for a time the support of enthusiastic young geniuses overtaking them on the way to maturity. It is possible that the author of "Vendetta" may be such a passer-by; for we are not told whether Count Fabio is offered as an example or as a warning. If the former, then the book must be intended to do for London what "L'Homme-Femme" was intended to do for Paris. In that case, nothing that is said here in recognition of Marie Corelli's success as a romancer must be taken as implying the smallest concession to the "tue-la" doctrine. If we cannot let the loose woman severely alone—if we must make a heroine of her, let us confine her to farcical comedy as the form of art that flatters her least. Her pet notion that the vulgarity of her emotional instability is redeemed by some sort of tragic interest, is only nourished by the Fabio Romani regimen of pistols and daggers. The prosaic methods of Sir James Hannen are far healthier for her and for us.

To compare Marie Corelli to Ouida may seem an equivocal compliment; but the association is inevitable, so much alike are they in many striking points. There is more freshness and fire in the younger writer; her men are far manlier and her women more real; she is guiltless of Ouida's terrible repetitions; and her culture is not wholly fictitious. But the resemblance is strong for all that. In the Corelli as in the Ouida novel we find an almost rancorous insistence on the corruption of modern society; a taste for artificial splendour indoors and for blue skies or moonlit seas without (drop scenery, in short): romantic Southern servants, peasants, or sailors whose impossible little conversations serve for padding; and a partial view of character, resulting from a keen insight into the erotic impulses without sufficient observation or study of the rest of life. The author of "Vendetta" appears to have some advantage of the author of "Tricotrin" both in intelligence and conscientiousness; but her probation is not yet ended. Her imagination, if scientifically trained, will make her: if let run wild, it will mar her. The latter course is the easier, and probably the more lucrative. It is the path of inspiration, which is popularly supposed to be the breath of genius. But Marie Corelli's renunciation in her new work of the supernatural quackery which disqualified "A Romance of Two Worlds", raises some hope that she is becoming aware that inspiration is never right save by an improbable accident; and that genius consists chiefly of the power of detecting inspiration's errors, although much current novel-writing is nothing more than recording them in black and white.

One detail in Count Fabio's narrative needs transposition. When he issues from his tomb, he disguises himself as a coral-fisher before returning home. But the motive for his disguise does not exist until he arrives there and discovers his wife's treachery. If a report that Mr. Gladstone had lost his coat while bathing in the Tegernsee, and had thereupon hurried to a slop-shop and purchased a coal-heaver's costume to return home in, were to appear in tomorrow's newspaper, we should be either incredulous or alarmed for the great statesman's sanity. Count Fabio is represented as acting no less unreasonably without a word of explanation. It is a small improbability among many great ones; but it sticks in the throat for all that. The consumer of fiction, though not a very dainty feeder, strains at the gnat in spite of the complaisance with which he bolts the camel.

Editor's Notes

- *Vendetta!* was received for review on 27 August 1886. Shaw began reading it on 5 September, finished it the next day, and immediately began his review. He continued writing it on the eighth, and finished and dispatched it on the ninth. (*Diary*, 227, 196).
- Shaw's quotation does not do justice to Dumas's comment, which is not only the climax of a 177 page essay, but is final advice from father to son after no less than nine conditional clauses, which, if not bringing the view of women to an enlightened stage, at least modify the savagery of the thought, thus:

> And now if you have been deceived by appearances or double-dealing, in spite of precautions, inquiries, knowledge of men and of things, virtue, patience and kindness; if you have married a creature unworthy of you; if, after having vainly tried to make of her the spouse that she ought to be, you have been unable to save her by motherhood—that earthly redemption of her sex; if, no longer wishing to listen to you as husband, father, friend, nor master, not only does she abandon your children, but from just anybody, gives birth to other children who will continue her accursed race in the world; if nothing is able to prevent her prostituting your name with her body; if she hinders you in your human activity and your divine function; if the very same law which gives itself the right to bind refuses to unbind, declaring itself powerless, then declare yourself personally—in the name of your Master, the judge and the executioner of this creature. *She is not a genuine woman; she is not a woman at all; she has no place in the divine*

conception: she is purely animal; she is the she-monkey from the land of Nod; Cain's female. Kill her. (Alexandre Dumas *fils*, *Homme-Femme: réponse à M. Henri D'Ideville*, dixième édition [Paris 1872], 175–76)

The translation is mine, as are the italics, which represent the portion quoted by Shaw.]

• Sir James [Baron] Hannen (1821–94), English judge. He was widely respected as a clear and accurate thinker, and had a meteoric career. In one year, 1868, he was appointed a judge of the Court of Queen's Bench, made sergeant-at-law, and knighted. In 1872 he was made judge of the Court of Probate and the Divorce Court, and also a member of the Privy Council. In 1875 he became president of the Probate, Divorce, and Admiralty division of the high court. A year after Shaw's review Hannen was selected by the government to act as president of the Special Commission to enquire into the charges brought by the *Times* against Charles Stewart Parnell and other Irish nationalists.

• At Tegernsee was the beautiful Bavarian home of Lady Acton's sister, Baroness Arco. Gladstone would go there when he wished to recover from the stress of parliamentary life, to climb the surrounding hills, or to row across the lake with Lord and Lady Acton. After the rejection of his Irish Home Rule policy in the summer of 1886, Gladstone resigned, and made his way to Tegernsee and its therapeutic quiet. He was still there at the time of the above review.

• "slop-shop": "slop" is an outer garment, or loose jacket or tunic; more often used in the plural, it refers to ready-made, cheap, or inferior clothes generally supplied to sailors from ship's stores (*OED*).

• Marie Corelli took the lucrative course: *Vendetta!* alone had run to thirty-nine editions by 1925. It may have provided Shaw with some thoughts about cholera and the medical profession, which he used in *The Philanderer* and *The Doctor's Dilemma*.

15 September 1886

A BOOK ON IRELAND AND IMPERIAL FEDERATION* [C255]

A CALM, orderly, and impartial review of the Irish question being at this moment impossible, a spirited plea for Home Rule by an excited

---

*"The Making of the Irish Nation." By J. A. Partridge. (London: Fisher Unwin. 1886.)

but competent advocate is perhaps the next most instructive document available. This Mr. Partridge gives us in a volume of which the cover—more than three-fourths green and less than one-fourth orange—indicates the bias of its contents. In point of arrangement and literary finish his work bears marks of premature delivery, for which Mr. Fisher Unwin, the publisher, is probably responsible. History, having broken from her old stately march to take a short breather after Lord Randolph Churchill, would not wait for Mr. Unwin; and Mr. Unwin dared not wait for the author's finishing touches. This, though but a surmise, uninformed by private knowledge, shall be Mr. Partridge's excuse here for having set down events in the order in which they were shaken out of his sheaf of memoranda rather than in that of their occurrence, and for his occasional substitution of passionate rhetoric for carefully reasoned composition. His own eloquence is supported by vehement repetitions of the utterances of Grattan, O'Connell, and many minor orators. If the reader be not convinced, he will at least be most strenuously persuaded.

Mr. Partridge is an advocate of Imperial Federation. As much, however, may be said of many persons with whom he would certainly not shake hands; for there are two distinct varieties of English Imperialism. The appetite for new markets abroad, cheap native labour, and official appointments, civil and military, in newly annexed districts (cleared by the machine gun), has been dubbed "Imperial Instinct" by Lord Salisbury who carries on his late leader's business of phrase-making much as Wordsworth's son was supposed by the peasants of the Lake country to carry on the business of poem-making. Gentlemen rich in this instinct, and impatient to be rich in solider metal, are at present rallying to the standard of Imperial Federation, and keeping away many honest people who suspect any cause, however worthy, that brings them into bad company. Then there is your philosophic Imperialist, who recognizes that Federation is a step higher in social organization, and that we must inevitably and quite desirably come to it unless we are content to go backward. Of the same stamp, but a lazier thinker, is the poet who longs for "the Parliament of Nations, the Federation of the World." Mr. Partridge is not an annexationist: he is philosophic and poetic. He insists very strongly that an empire must be a federation of nations, each subject only to the whole empire, and not to the nucleus or strongest member of it. Thus he is at once Irish Nationalist and British Imperialist, claiming for Ireland absolute political independence of England, whilst admitting and advocating her subjection to the Empire of Great Britain, Ireland, Canada, Australia, and the colonies. He suggests, too, that the Imperial Senate might fill in the public eye the blank to be left by the abolition of the House of Lords. The rest of his book is historical. It tells the story of the 1783-1801 College-green Parliament; describes in the spirit of Fox, Grattan, and Mr. Gladstone the provoked rebellion and purchased Union; deals at some length with O'Connell's agitation; mentions Isaac Butt; and, after a rapid survey of recent history under Mr. Parnell's dictatorship, leaves the sympathetic reader on the brink of the future, with his soul in arms and eager for the fray.

The unpolicied reviewer, writing without editorial responsibility, may perhaps be permitted to opine that neither history from the Nationalist nor sociology from the Imperialist point of view will assuage Ireland's longing for separation. History so written is a sensational tale of an atrocious wrong done by England: sociology so considered is a plea for leaving matters as they are until the Imperial project is ripe for execution. The one makes the Irishman grind his teeth and hide a pike under his straw mattress: the other tempts Englishmen to postpone a question that will not wait. Why does not some Democratic Internationalist declare the fact, unseen by the indignant Nationalist and overlooked by the future-dreaming Imperialist, that the people of England have done the people of Ireland no wrong whatever? What voice in the councils of the younger Pitt had the English yoke-fellows of the '98 rebels? What were the sufferings against which the Irish then rose compared with those which led to the first abortive Factory Act of 1802? Surely the English people, in factory, mine, and sweater's workshop, had reason to envy the Irish peasant, who at the worst starved on the open hillside instead of rotting in a fœtid tenement rookery. Irish landlords may have shown themselves "vultures with bowels of iron"; but are there not extant in factory inspectors' reports, Royal Commissioners' reports, philanthropic protests, "Bitter Cries," and utterances of our Shaftesburies and Oastlers (not to mention Mrs. Reaney), records of rapacious and cruel English capitalists whose little fingers were thicker than the loins of the real masters of Ireland? Allusions to these matters are suppressed in polite society; and they are consequently seldom made except by the orators of the street corner; but when book after book from the press, and speech after speech from the platform, lay upon all England the odium of misdeeds that no Irishman can contemplate without intense bitterness—that too many cannot think of without bloodthirsty rage—it is surely expedient to point out to that most distressful country that she has borne no more than her share of the growing pains of human society, and that the mass of the English people are not only guiltless of her wrongs, but have themselves borne a heavier yoke.

In short, the main fault in Mr. Partridge's book is in this sentence quoted from p. xxi of the preface:

> Politics based on property and things are used for property and things, and that is what we have been doing in Ireland— farming out law, land, religion, and nation on behalf of property and pretences, and against the national manhood and life.

The inference from the words "in Ireland" is that we have not been doing all this elsewhere. Yet there is not a civilized country in the world of which it is not equally true. Remind the Irish of that, and perhaps they will be patient with Sir Redvers and Lord Randolph yet a little while.

Editor's Notes

- Shaw received Partridge's book on 27 August 1886, began reading it on the thirty-first, was still reading it on 2 September, and finished it on the third. He wrote his review on the fourth and sent it off the next day (*Diary*, 195, 227). That he may have consulted it again when he was writing *John Bull's Other Island* (1904) is possible, since Larry Doyle's arguments recapitulate the subject matter and, more interestingly, the tone of Partridge. However, there was much publicity for the outrages perpetrated upon the Irish in 1886: Wilfred Blunt's account of the "rack-renting" of a mountain, and the eviction of a tenant who owed less than a hundred pounds is a striking example, which Shaw must have read (see the *Pall Mall Gazette*, 5 April 1886).

- J[ohn] A[rthur] Partridge (n.d.), English political author. He also wrote *The False Nation and its Bases; or, Why the South can't Stand* (1863), *The Making of the American Nation; or, The Rise and Decline of Oligarchy in the West* (1866), *Democracy: its Factors and Conditions* (1866), *From Feudal to Federal; or, Free Church, Free School, the completed bases of equality; with some of its results in State-Constitution and Empire, etc.* (1872), *Citizenship vs. Secularists and Sacerdotalists in the Matter of National Teaching, by a Birmingham Liberal* (1873), *The Policy of England in relation to India and the East* (1877), and *Confederation and Home Rule* (1890).

- [Lord] Randolph Henry Spencer Churchill (1849–95), English politician. During his early years in Parliament, he traveled to Ireland (where his father, the Duke of Marlborough, was Lord-Lieutenant), and thence derived his special interest in the affairs of that country. He attacked the alliance between Gladstone and the "Parnellites" in 1883/4; and he took a prominent part in the heated debate on the Home Rule Bill (which he called a "desperate and insane measure"), which (as Shaw indicates) dominated the spring and summer of 1886, seeking to unite those who were opposed to it. In the ensuing general election, which defeated Gladstone and brought Salisbury back as prime minister, on 22 July 1886, he was reelected, and accepted the second place in the ministry, the chancellorship of the Exchequer and the leadership of the House of Commons. At the opening of Parliament on 19 August he made a detailed statement of ministerial policy, particularly with regard to Ireland. However, he resigned the chancellorship four months later, over a dispute, and thereafter his political energy declined. He was again reelected in the general election of 1892, but he suffered from a form of gradual paralysis, and, although a favorite among the Conservatives, in the session of 1894 his few attempts to speak in the House of Commons were failures, and he died in the first month of the new year.

- Henry Grattan (1746–1820), Irish politician. Born in Dublin and educated there at Trinity College, in 1767 he proceeded to the Middle Temple in London, but was less interested in law than in debates in the House of Commons. In 1772 he was called to the Irish Bar, and in 1775 he entered the Irish parliament. He conducted a popular campaign for legislative independence from Britain, and when the Rockingham Ministry collapsed in 1782, the Irish parliament voted Grattan £50,000. However, "Grattan's Parliament" as it was called, did not live up to its aspirations, although Grattan himself devoted his time to the reform of abuses; and eventually it was supplanted by the movement of the United Irishmen. Although a Protestant, Grattan spent his later life campaigning for Catholic emancipation.

- Daniel O'Connell (1775–1847), Irish political leader. He was born in County Kerry and educated at St. Omer and Douai, and Lincoln's Inn. He was called to the Irish bar in 1798. He was a leader in the fight for Catholic emancipation, ironically, since when he was elected M.P. for Clare in 1828, he was prevented, as a Catholic, from taking his seat. He was elected again in 1830, by which time the Catholic Emancipation Act had passed, and thereafter devoted his political energy to repealing the Union. He was called "The Liberator," and spearheaded the agitation movement, until Wellington poured 35,000 troops into Ireland; and, early in 1844, O'Connell was imprisoned and fined for a conspiracy to raise sedition. The House of Lords set aside the verdict, but he had languished in jail for fourteen weeks. The potato famine followed, and a fight with the Young Ireland party, which was impatient of his tactics, and finally his health broke. He left Ireland for Rome in January 1847, and died at Genoa.

- Lord [Robert Arthur Talbot Gascoyne, 3rd Marquis of] Salisbury (1830–1903), English politician. Following the collapse of Gladstone's brief administration in 1886, he again became prime minister, and again, for the last time, in 1895. Following a series of international incidents, which on more than one occasion nearly led to war, he resigned the foreign secretaryship in 1900 and, although he remained at the head of the government during the Boer

War (1899–1902), he retired from public life in the July of that year, dying a year later.

- Shaw misquotes line 128 from Tennyson's poem *Locksley Hall* (1842):

In the Parliament of man, the Federation of the world.

Ironically, the same poet this very year had just published a sequel entitled *Locksley Hall Sixty Years After* (advertised, incidentally, in the *Pall Mall Gazette* on 16 December), composed in the same rhythm, but containing the rather more pessimistic observation,

Chaos, Cosmos! Cosmos, Chaos! who can tell how all will end?

- Charles James Fox (1749–1806), English politician. His oratorical "style" was revealed when Pitt came to power, and the long contest between the two men began. Fox fought Pitt over the regency, the trial of Warren Hastings, and the French Revolution.
- Isaac Butt (1813–79), Irish politician. He was the first advocate of "Home Rule," born in County Donegal, educated at Raphoe and Trinity College, Dublin. He was a scholar, edited the *Dublin University Magazine* from 1834 to 1838, and was chairman of political economy from 1836 to 1841. He was called to the Irish Bar in 1838, and at first opposed O'Connell; but from 1852 to 1865 he defended the Fenian prisoners in the state trials, and in 1871 he was elected to lead the Home Rule party in the House of Commons.
- Charles Stewart Parnell (1846–91), Irish politician. Together with eighty-six supporters, Parnell had thrown in his lot with the Liberals to bring about the fall of Salisbury's government in 1886; but on the collapse of Gladstone's government (when the Home Rule Bill was defeated) he resigned from Parliament. At this point scandals began to hound the Irish leader. He was suspected of having approved of the "Phoenix Park Murders" (of Lord Frederick and permanent under-secretary Thomas Henry Burke on 16 May 1881), and his appearance as corespondent in the Captain O'Shea divorce case led to Gladstone's demand that Parnell retire as leader of the Irish members. This and the condemnation of his behavior by the Church decimated his support, and probably hastened his sudden death at Brighton, five months after marrying Mrs. O'Shea. Predictably, Shaw took Parnell's side in the matter of the divorce scandal, writing a letter to *The Star* on 20 November 1890, and blaming the law

that tied the husband and wife together and forced Mr. Parnell to play the part of the clandestine intriguer, instead of enabling them to dissolve the marriage, by mutual consent, without disgrace to either party.

Later, Shaw was to make that divorce law the subject of his own attack in *Getting Married* (1908).

▪ Shaw's contention that the English have treated their own people worse than they have treated the Irish finds indignant voice again in the character of Hodson, Broadbent's cockney valet in *John Bull's Other Island* (1904):

> You Awrish people are too well off: thets wots the metter with you. [*With sudden passion*] You talk of your rotten little fawm cause you mide it by chackin a few stones dahn a ill! Well, wot prawce maw grenfawther, Oi should lawk to knaow, that fitted ap a fust clawss shop and built ap a fust clawss dripery business in Landon by sixty years work, and then was chacked aht of it on is ed at the end of is lease withaht a penny for his goodwill. You talk of evictions! you that cawnt be moved until youve ran ap ighteen months rent. Oi once ran ap four weeks in Lembeth wen Oi was aht of a job in winter. They took the door off its inges and the winder aht of its sashes on me, an gev maw wawf pnoomownia. Oi'm a widower nah.
>
> *John Bull's Other Island*, Act 3

▪ "The Bitter Cry" reference is to a pamphlet entitled *The Bitter Cry of Outcast London, An Inquiry into the Condition of the Abject Poor* (1883). This publication, compiled by A. Mearns and other Congregational ministers, presented cases of almost unbelievably squalid housing conditions in London, and in the words of the *Annual Register* "startled the most careless" [see page 4 above].

▪ Anthony Ashley Cooper, 7th Earl of Shaftesbury (1801–85), English politician. He was born in London and educated at Harrow and Christ Church, Oxford. He entered Parliament in 1826 and succeeded to the peerage in 1851. He was the leader of the factory reform movement in 1832, steering the Factory Acts of 1847 and 1850 through the House and the acts that regulated conditions in coal mines and provided lodging-houses for the poor in 1851. His Coal Mines Act (1842) prohibited underground employment of women and children under thirteen. In addition to the above he was chairman of the Ragged Schools Union for forty years, helped Florence Nightingale in her attempts to improve army welfare, and took an active interest in missionary work, and the mentally handicapped.

▪ Richard Oastler (1789–1861), English reformer. He was an advocate of the ten-hour working day and the factory laws.

▪ Mrs. G. S. [Isabel Edis] Reaney (1847–?), English philanthropist and author. From an early age she interested herself in religious and social endeavors. The wife of the Rev. G. S. Reaney, at one time pastor of the Stepney Meeting Congregational Church, and later of a church in Manchester, she produced a quantity of narrative tracts on everyday duties and temperance, such as *Waking and Working; or from Girlhood to Womanhood* (1874), *Our Homes. A series of small books on Christian temperance* (1881), and *How to help; pen and pencil sketches of the East End* (1888). Shaw went to a lecture on "Church Reform," given by her husband on 9 December 1886.

▪ Sir Redvers Henry Buller (1839–1908), English general. He was seconded for civil employment in August of 1886 and, by order of the Salisbury administration, which thought that a "fresh, vigorous mind, accustomed to strict discipline" would be helpful, proceeded to Ireland to restore law and order in County Kerry. He succeeded so well that in November he was made undersecretary for Ireland, and called to the Irish Privy Council. He did not, however, like the task, sympathizing with the oppressed Irish peasantry to the point where he was frequently at odds with the government. Accordingly, on 15 October 1887 he returned to military duty as quartermaster-general. In October 1899 he embarked for South Africa, to command the British forces in the Boer War. After a series of defeats, he was replaced as commander-in-chief, though he remained to fight throughout the war. Unfortunately, his subsequent career was again clouded after an indiscreet speech at a public luncheon at the Queen's Hall, Westminster, a few years later, and Buller was removed from command, though he remained on the active list for five years more.

18 September 1886

A NEW NOVEL BY MR. WILKIE COLLINS*
[C256]

Is it too much to hope that Mr. Wilkie Collins may be remembered as the last really able novelist who shackled and crippled his genius, and worried his admirers almost into giving up reading him, by systematically cumbering his stories with what are called "plots"? The perverse ingenuity with which he devises these Procrustean scaffolds cannot excuse the cruelty with which he stretches or chops the children of his imagination to fit them. The proper framework for a book is its own natural skeleton: if it be born without one, then let it perish as a shapeless abortion: no external apparatus of splints and crutches will make it presentable. Shakspeare has set us a bad example in this matter. He unfortunately suffered himself to be persuaded by custom and prejudice that plots were necessary; and as he was far too great a man to be capable of inventing them, he stole them. His sin soon found him out. The stolen plots forced him to deform his plays by uncharacteristic actions, inconsistencies, anachronisms, digressions,

*"The Evil Genius." By Wilkie Collins. Three vols. (London: Chatto and Windus. 1886.)

wordy trivialities, impertinent messengers, tedious journeys, and uninteresting letters, to which, after all, nobody attended; for we find the
bard, by the mouth of Hamlet, complaining that the clowns made the
pit laugh whilst the serious actors were wearying it by "some necessary question of the play." Would we had such clowns now! Shakspeare was not wiser than the whole world. His irritation at having
taken a great deal of trouble for nothing was quite natural: but the pit
and the clowns were right and he was wrong. The wise readers skip
all explanations in novels: the wise playgoer, during the exposition of
the drama, sleeps if alone, or, if companioned, discusses Home Rule.
It is a mistake to suppose that the public cannot accept a situation
without knowing exactly what has led to it. The flâneurs who stop to
witness a street fight do not find the spectacle a whit less enjoyable
and instructive because they do not happen to know the antecedents
of the combatants or the particulars of their feud. The fight's the
thing.

Mr. Wilkie Collins's plots, unlike Shakspeare's, are honestly come
by. He makes them for himself with travail and heavy sorrow, hardly
disguising his sense of the respect and gratitude we owe him in return. To so conscientious a workman no honest person will deny respect. But gratitude is out of the question: enough that we try to
forgive him! Perhaps Mr. Wilkie Collins innocently believes that it is
in average human nature to like his cryptograms, his deciphering
experts, his lawyers, his letters, his extracts from diaries, his agony-
column advertisements, his detectives, his telegrams, and his complicated railway and hotel arrangements. If so, he errs: these things are
only tolerable for the sake of the stories they all but strangle. In "The
Evil Genius" we have hardly one volume of human life and character
to two volumes of plot. We bear with this because we cannot help
ourselves, just as we submit to take our milk two-thirds water. Would
the milkman but leave us the milk and water in separate jugs, we
should willingly pay the same price and throw the water away. Fain
would we take in Mr. Wilkie Collins's plot and his story in separate
covers; but, like the milkman, he insists on mixing them and then
denying our analysis.

"The Evil Genius" begins well with an amusing jury discussing a
criminal case, and with the most entertaining loves of Mrs. Wester-
field and James Beljames. The story of the neglected child who escapes from drudgery in a sordid school to happiness in a refined
home, and then is driven by her unlucky star to wreck that home, is
full of interest. The two scenes which form the dramatic climax of this

part of the narrative are especially effective. But the plot soon begins to close in and crush the life out of the book. A marionette lawyer enters; and Mr. Wilkie Collins strives desperately to make him seem alive. Characteristics supposed to be inherited from a French ancestry are tacked on to him. His appetite for truffles is enlarged upon. His mechanical plottering is relieved at five-minute intervals by a jerk at the wires, which makes the poor puppet start spasmodically. In vain! there is no life in his gambols: he is only there to advise every one to carry on the plot, and to supply missing links by letters to his wife such as no male creature ever yet did or will write. He is clumsily abetted by a certain Captain Bennydeck (there is but one novelist alive who could have perpetrated such a name), a sanctimonious bore, who makes an infirm bid for the dignity of hero late in the book, and is eventually, like a virtuous but ineffectual politician, kicked upstairs into the odour of philanthropy, and left with an off chance of marrying the disgraced governess. The mother-in-law, Mrs. Presty, though she too is used chiefly to engineer the plot, has some independent merits. The child Kitty is delightful: the brightest pages in the book are those which record her doings and sayings. The dialogue, as usual in a Wilkie Collins novel, is sometimes natural and expressive; sometimes a mere string of terse statements, having no purpose except to advance or to explain the plot incubus, and no humanity or interest except as examples of the author's mannerisms. On the whole, novels are like other works of art: uninteresting just so far as they are machine made.

Editor's Notes

- Shaw himself was unsure of the date on which he received Collins's novel for review (his diary says "11/9?"); but he read it on 13 September 1886, began his review the next day, and finished it on the fifteenth when, his diary records, he "worked slowly and with difficulty." On this day he sent it to the *PMG* (*Diary*, 197–98, 227).
- William Wilkie Collins (1824–89), English novelist. He was born in London, the son of a well-known painter, William Collins (1788–1847). He was educated partly at Highbury, but spent three years (from 1836 to 1839) with his parents in Italy. Intended for the Church, he declined the vocation, spent four years with a firm of tea importers, and began studying for the bar. The death of his father relieved him of this necessity, and he decided to live on his mother's income until he could support himself by his writing. His first book

was a life of his father (1848). His first novel *Antonina, or the Fall of Rome* (1850) was modeled after the fashion of Walter Scott's successful historical novels of thirty years previously. *Basil* (1852) was his second novel. He never married but lived with two women companions, the first of whom was Caroline Graves, whose daughter by a previous marriage Collins adopted. Later, when Caroline married a plumber, Collins acquired a second female companion, Martha Rudd, who had three children by him. Two or three years later, Caroline returned and lived with him until he died. He contributed to Dickens's paper *Household Words* and became friends with Dickens, who enjoyed his easygoing company. He and Dickens collaborated on a book about a tour to the north of England together; a novel by Collins, *The Dead Secret* (1857), was serialized in *Household Words*, and they were constant visitors in one another's homes, though, for reasons of propriety, Mrs. Dickens never visited the Collins ménage. *The Woman in White* (1860), originally serialized in Dickens's second magazine *All the Year Round* made him famous. Thereafter came *No Name* (1862), *Armadale* (1866), *The Moonstone* (1868), and *The New Magdalen* (1873). In all Collins wrote about twenty novels and collections of fiction.

▪ Shaw abominated the mechanical contrivance of the "plot" in Victorian fiction and drama; by which he seems to have meant "contrived or constructed stories in which characterization is subordinated to the events of the fable." But in view of the use of stretched coincidence and sudden discovery in his own plays, whether it be Sir Howard Hallam meeting both the man he sentenced to prison and the son of the woman he "wronged" in *Captain Brassbound's Conversion*, Mendoza meeting by chance the brother of the woman he loves in *Man and Superman*, the convenient discovery that Cusins is a foundling in *Major Barbara*, or the absurd coincidence in *Heartbreak House*, where the burglar who just happens to break into Captain Shotover's house turns out to be his old bosun, it is clear that Shaw's dislike of "plots" did not extend to the use of unlikely or forced events for comic purposes. On a deeper, more symbolic, level he seems not to have been aware that the strength of some fictions lies in their instructive use of the fable itself.

23 September 1886

THE REYNOLDS OF THE NORTH* [C257]

MR. RAEBURN ANDREW has had to make bricks with very little straw in compiling a biography of his great-grandfather, "the Reynolds of

---

*"Life of Sir Henry Raeburn." By William Raeburn Andrew. (London: W. H. Allen and Co. 1886.)

the North." Raeburn came from the hands of nature a ready-made portrait painter. He took his place at the head of his profession without a struggle; married a rich widow, who seems to have been a very good wife to him; and thereafter occupied a distinguished position in Edinburgh society until his death. It was his happiness to leave no history except the catalogue of his works. Probably so able a man could have told something worth knowing about his development as an artist and his experiences as he viewed them from the inside. From the outside, however, they were conventional, and there is no more to be learned about him now than is set forth in this modest and business-like memoir, which can be read easily at a single sitting. As an artist he is not likely to be forgotten in these islands while his Scotch sitters, from Sir Walter Scott downward, are remembered. Some of them will be remembered for his sake, and remembered more favourably in point of personal dignity than they perhaps deserve; for Raeburn never allowed his patrons to look mean on canvas. That was at least one reason for his great popularity as a portrait painter. He was a quick workman. An exhibition of his pictures was held at Edinburgh in 1876, and, though it was necessarily incomplete, the catalogue gives particulars of 325 works from his hand.

Editor's Notes

- Shaw received this book for review on 13 July 1886. He read it on the twenty-sixth, and presumably it was the fourth of the reviews he wrote and sent in on the twenty-ninth (*Diary*, 187–88, 227).
- William Raeburn [St. Clair] Andrew (1853–1914), English lawyer and author. The younger son of Sir William Patrick Andrew, C.I.E., the geographer and author of *India and her Neighbours*, *Our Scientific Frontier* and other works, he was educated at Harrow and Exeter College, Oxford, and called to the bar in 1878. He was well known as a conveyancer and equity draftsman; and in addition to writing the book reviewed above, he collaborated with another Oxford lawyer, Charles Augustus Vansittart Conybeare, on *The Married Women's Property Act, 1882: together with the Acts of 1870 and 1874* (1882). However, he was best known as the author of the above, the first important biography of his great-grandfather, which went to two editions.
- Sir Henry Raeburn (1756–1823), Scottish portrait painter. Born in Edinburgh, he was trained as a jeweler, but began to paint in oils at an early age. He was largely self-taught, but soon acquired a local reputation and commissions. In 1780 he married Anne Leslie, a widow of independent means. In 1785 he went to Rome for two years, but his visit to Italy does not seem to

have affected his painting style. His first London exhibition was in 1793 at the Shakespeare Gallery in Pall Mall. He established a practice at his studio in York Place, Edinburgh. In 1812 he became president of the Society of Artists of Edinburgh, and was subsequently elected to the Royal Academy. In 1815 he became a full academician, and in 1822, when George IV was on a visit to Edinburgh, he was knighted. The nickname "The Reynolds of the North" is objected to by art historian Kenneth Garlick: "[It] is misleading as his work has neither the intellectual content nor the variety of Reynolds; but it has virility, purpose, and a very considerable sympathy with and understanding of character."

5 October 1886

IDEAL LONDON* [C259]

"IN December, 1883, Mr. William Westgarth offered the Society of Arts a sum of £1,200 to be awarded in prizes for essays on the best means for providing dwellings for the London poor, and on the reconstruction of central London." The only possible comment on this first sentence of Mr. Trueman Wood's preface to the Westgarth essays is, "Why did I not know of this delightful offer?" For what inexpensive pleasure can be greater than that of strolling through London of an evening, and reconstructing it in imagination? Just think of it! To begin with, you make a fine straight boulevard from your house (or perhaps your lodging) to your office, and establish a commodious omnibus service along it. Abolishing St. Pancras, Victoria, Waterloo, and the rest, you bring all the great railways to a common terminus within five minutes' walk of your door. Then, your own modest needs being satisfied, you indulge in architectural meditation, fancy free. You burst the bonds and bars of the Duke of Bedford; you make Notting-hill low and exalt Maida-vale by carting the one into the other; you make Southwark Bridge a less formidable obstacle to traffic than Primrose-hill; you extend the Embankment from Blackfriars to the Tower, as an eligible nocturnal promenade from which to commit holders of portable property to the deep; you rescue the unfortunate

---

*"Essays on the Street Realignment, Reconstruction, and Sanitation of Central London, and on the Rehousing of the Poorer Classes." (London: G. Bell and Sons. 1886.)

persons who, having at one time or another ventured into the laby-
rinth between Bond-street and Park-lane, are still wandering, lost in
Mayfair; you turn the mountainous tract south of Pentonville into a
deer forest for urban sportsmen; you lead stray churches from the
middle of the Strand into the courtyard of Somerset House; you build
an underground London in the bowels of the metropolis, and an overhead London piercing the fog curtain above on viaducts, with another
and another atop of these, until you have piled us up, six cities deep,
to Alpine altitudes with a different climate at each level. Sanitary
arrangements amid which disease cannot exist; smokeless fires that
will gently lull us to permanent repose with carbonic oxide; spotless
statues and shirt-fronts; common kitchens in all the squares; phalanstères, familistères, reading rooms, museums, baths, gymnasia, laun-
dries, and open spaces, with all such items as water, fuel, gas, and oil,
guaranteed not to cost more than a farthing for sixteen hours—all
these will ensue spontaneously from your arrangements. For purposes
of transit you will devise a system of pneumatic tubes, through which
passengers, previously treated by experienced dentists with nitrous
oxide, can be blown from Kensington to Mile-end in a breath; or, as an
ingenious gentleman at the Colonial Office has already suggested,
endless bands might be let into the pavement and kept in perpetual
motion by steam drums at each street corner. Upon these the pedes-
trian might step and be borne away to his destination, where he would
simply spring aside to the stationary part of the pavement, leaving the
long line of tradesmen's boys, solicitors, statesmen, and who not,
mass and class, streaming by on the bosom of the band. What a
London that would be! It would cost nothing either: the unearned
increment would pay for all, and return a huge profit besides.

And to think that for merely pointing out how it might be done, one
could have got £1,200 from Mr. Westgarth in December 1883! It is
now nearly December, 1886; and the £1,200 is awarded, and perhaps
spent. As the young ladies in "Patience" say, "such an opportunity will
not occur again." The published essays by Mr. William Woodward, Mr.
Henry Hewitt Bridgman, and Mr. J. Corbett fall short of the above
programme in comprehensiveness and audacity of the scientific imagination; and this is a fault in them which their comparative feasible-
ness does not compensate; for of what use is it to be practical in
planning improvements which are not in the least likely to be carried
out? The three essays certainly contain some interesting suggestions
and criticisms from the point of view of the architect; but they are, in
sum, and setting aside a few more or less Utopian maps and plans,

only an expression of opinion to the effect that some new thorough-fares would quicken the circulation of London, and that the very poor might well be less disgracefully housed than at present. Which is undeniable, but not worth twelve hundred pounds. The problem, un-fortunately, is not one of realignment and patent dwellings. It is one of the development of individual greed into civic spirit; of the extension of the *laissez-faire* principle to public as well as private enterprise; of bringing all the citizens to a common date in civilization instead of maintaining a savage class, a mediæval class, a renaissance class, and an Augustan class, with a few nineteenth-century superior persons to fix high-water mark, all jostling one another in the same streets, so that we never know where we are, or whether, on any advanced measure, the tenth century will not be too strong for us. In the mean-time we must be content with the new streets through St. Giles's, and the periodical washing of the Albert Memorial. Perhaps, too, the Metro-politan and District Companies, instead of delighting to bark and bite, may take counsel together, abolish their absurd ticket offices, and replace them by automatic turnstiles which will allow whoever drops a penny into a slit, to go wherever on the circle his business and desire may point him. To accommodate people who prefer first-class travel-ling, a Pullman car might be attached to each train, with a conductor, or another automatic turnstile, to take the extra fare. For of all our elaborate arrangements for wasting the time of a community acutely conscious that time is money, none are more unphilosophical than our costly weighing and measuring and ticketing of the individual require-ments of four millions of people, instead of providing for the average need without regard to peculiarities which, in such a mass, are as broad as they are long. Such wasteful methods, it is safe to predict, will never be altered until London belongs to, and is governed by, the people who use it.

Editor's Notes

- Shaw did not indicate in his diary when he received this book for review, but he began reading it on 30 July 1886, not finishing it, however, until 20 September. On the twenty-first he began writing the review, which he fin-ished on the twenty-second, sending it to the *PMG* the following day (*Diary*, 188, 199, 200, 226). A month later, on 16 November 1886, a letter to Shaw from H. S. Foxwell (mainly about land nationalization) suggests that he had been moved by this review:

I know you cannot make genius run in grooves, that every man has his own mission: but I often wish your great literary power could be exerted in the advocacy of what seems to me practical and real—if humble reform.

One wonders to what extent such encouragement prompted thoughts in Shaw towards resuming his first play, which dealt with slum-landlordism, and which had been abandoned two years previously.

▪ William Westgarth (1815–89), Australian colonist and politician. He was born in Edinburgh, and educated at Newcastle-on-Tyne, and at Leith and Edinburgh, but he left school early to enter the office of George Young & Co., Australian merchants. In 1840 he decided to emigrate to Port Phillip (now Victoria), where, in Melbourne, he began business as a general merchant and importer. He showed such an active interest in the colony that in 1850 he was elected member for Melbourne in the legislature of New South Wales, and he was at the same time elected first president of the Melbourne chamber of commerce. He was active in promoting numerous proposals for the social advancement of the colony, including that of a uniform tariff of import duties for all Australasian colonies. In the early 1850s he visited England, and in 1857 returned there to stay, founding the firm of Westgarth & Co., colonial brokers, agents and financiers, and becoming a leading authority on Australian loans on the London market. In July 1881 he was instrumental in founding the London chamber of commerce; and, about the time of "The Bitter Cry," he interested himself in the housing of the poor, and in the "sanitation and reconstruction" of central London, on which he himself wrote an essay in 1884. Through the Society of Arts he offered a series of prizes for the best practical essays on these two subjects. He retired from business in 1888 and revisited Melbourne to be present at the Centennial Exhibition, where he was warmly received. He returned to London in November, 1888, and died suddenly there a year later.

▪ The Society of Arts (since 1909 known as the Royal Society of Arts) was founded in 1847 under the presidency of the prince consort. The International Exhibition of 1851 was an outgrowth of smaller exhibitions sponsored by this Society, to which was added an East Indian section in 1869, and Foreign, Colonial, and Chemical sections in 1874.

▪ "Bursting the bonds and bars of the Duke of Bedford" refers to the fact that the earls and dukes of Bedford owned large sections of metropolitan real estate, principally Covent Garden and Bloomsbury, where many of the streets bear Russell family names, or titles and names from their family estates.

▪ Phalanstères were (according to Fourier's scheme for the reorganization of society) buildings occupied by a phalanx or socialistic community, hence such a community, numbering about 1800 people; and familistères were the abode of a group of people living together as one family.

▪ What the young ladies in Patience actually say is "Such an opportunity may not occur again;" but only after Bunthorne has said it first: which is appropriate, since the opportunity in question is to win him in a raffle!

• The three prize-winning essayists were William Woodward, an associate of the Royal Institute of British Architects, and president of the Association of Sanitary Engineers; Henry Hewitt Bridgman, Fellow of the Royal Institute of British Architects and surveyor, who two years earlier had collaborated with John J. Cayley in a scheme for a central wholesale fish market for London; and Joseph Corbett, a Manchester sanitation engineer, whose essay was the result of "nearly thirty years' observation and practical connection with the housing of the poorer classes."

• The "new streets through St. Giles's" refers to the series of London street improvements effected in the middle to late 1880s, from the enlarging of Piccadilly Circus to the completion of Shaftesbury Avenue in 1886, and the construction of the Charing Cross Road from Charing Cross to Tottenham Court Road, a project which was in progress when Shaw wrote the above review (see G. L. Gomme, *London in the Reign of Victoria (1837–1897)* [London: Blackie and Son, 1898], 162). In fact, Charing Cross Road, connecting Trafalgar Square with Oxford Street, was opened by the Duke of Cambridge four months later, on 26 February 1887.

• Both "The Metropolitan and District Companies" owned stretches of the underground railway system, now subsumed under London Transport.

12 November 1886

A VOLUME ON VOICE TRAINING* [C265]

OF this little "Book for Everybody" the author hopefully says: "It will be useful to the general public. It will serve to brighten and sharpen articulation, and render conversation more intelligible." And no doubt it will, if its precepts be discreetly followed; for it is not a bad book of its kind, in spite of such funny sentences as, "The word horse calls up into the presence-chamber of the mind a certain animal with four legs and without feathers:" or: "The student may think out for himself the colour he would like to give to the several phrases in Ex. 6. There is no better practice than applying the colour of anger"—a recommendation which suggests that at Brigstock, of which Mr. Sandlands is vicar, the parishioners are accustomed to energetic and even comminatory sermons. In the same vein are many misleading exhortations to "tease

---

*"How to develop General Vocal Power." By J. P. Sandlands, M.A. (London: Sampson Low and Co. 1886.)

it out," to "strive after power," and the like. The singers and speakers who "strive after power" are those who never get it. They do, as Talma said, "ce que font tous les jeunes acteurs." One is afraid to think of what the Rev. Mr. Sandlands would say to Talma's calm estimate of "at least twenty years" as the necessary apprenticeship for a man who would move assemblies. Another of the vicar's questionable bits of advice is to read at the pitch of "F in the bass," and to persevere at it in spite of difficulty. This is, in another form, the old pet precept of second-rate teachers to "get it from the chest." What would Charles Mathews, whose voice never aged, and who gave the widest of berths to F in the bass, have said to it? And what would our curates, with their "clergyman's sore throat," brought on by persisting in what Artemus Ward called "a sollum vois," say to it? "F," Mr. Sandlands assures us, "is the foundation tone; and the student must get it. It is as necessary for good speaking as a good foundation is for a building that is meant to be permanent." This means simply that Mr. Sandlands has a bass voice; that its normal pitch in speaking is F; and that he therefore concludes that all other men have bass voices with the same normal pitch, or, if they have not, that they ought to be made have them [*sic*]. Imagine the effect of a sepulchral course of lessons in the key of F on Mr. Hare, Mr. Grossmith, Mr. Penley, Mr. Giddens, Mr. George Barrett, or Signor Salvini! These so-called "foundation tones" vary with each individual: Del Sarte's favourite one was B flat, which was at least less likely to be generally mischievous than F. Then, as to speaking with gutta-percha balls in the mouth [a practice not unknown among schoolboys], we are told that Demosthenes used pebbles; so doubtless there is something to be gained by the exercise, though it is hard to see exactly what. The stress laid by Mr. Sandlands upon the importance of seeing in the mind's eye what one speaks about, shows that he possesses the faculty which Mr. Galton has named "visualization," and that he supposes everyone else to possess it too, which is by no means the case. Besides, speakers are not always engaged in describing material objects. So much for Mr. Sandlands' errors, which are those of robust innocence and impatience rather than of pretence and quackery—the usual failings of the voice-trainer. As a set-off against them may be taken his ingenious and useful exercises, of which two specimens may be quoted: "The soldiers steer the boat. The soldier's tear fell on the page." Here the point is of course not the sensibility of the literary soldier, but the difficulty of differentiating "soldiers steer" from "soldier's tear." Again, "Violins and violoncellos vigorously vamped with very versatile voices vociferating various strains very vehemently vexes Valentine's violent valet," is good practice. So is, "The zealot Zephaniah rode a zebra zigzag up Zaboim." On the other hand it is nothing short of a duty to protest against the student saying in "full voice"—or indeed, in any voice whatever—

Not a drum was heard, not a funeral note.

An excellent feature in the book is the condemnation of the rule that, if the consonants are watched, the vowels will take care of themselves. An Englishman who can pronounce *do, re, mi, fa* decently is a *rara avis*.

Editor's Notes

• Shaw received this book, whose full title is *How to Develop General Vocal Power and Cure Stammering and Defective Speech,* on 15 October 1886, and, though it is not named, it was presumably one of the books he read for review on the twenty-third, and his article one of the "batch of reviews" he wrote on the twenty-fifth, because he sent it to the *PMG* on the twenty-sixth (*Diary,* 207, 227).

• J[ohn] P[oole] Sandlands (1838–1915), English clergyman and author. His schooling was at Lichfield College (which he entered in 1864), and Trinity College, Dublin, where he obtained a B.A. in 1870 and an M.A. in 1873. He was curate of St. Luke's, Hanley, from 1866 to 1869, and of Brigstock, Northamptonshire, from 1869 to 1873, in which year, on 17 September he became vicar. According to *The Kettering Leader* of 5 February 1915, Brigstock vicarage developed into a kind of sanatorium during Sandlands's incumbency, to which patients came from all over the world. He was an authority on voice production, and was visited by eminent men for treatment, including cabinet ministers, church dignitaries, and stage celebrities. He was the author of numerous works on speech, health and related subjects, including *The Voice and Public Speaking, A Book for all who Read and Speak in Public* (1879)—this ran to at least three editions—*How to be well, or the principles of health* (1896), *Natural Food* (1902), *"Science in the daily meal" criticised; or Plasmon confounded* (1903), *Corpulence. A Case and Cure; or Why grow Fat?* (1903), *Quacks and What they Do. By one of them* (1904), *Health; a royal road to it* (1909), and *Consumption. An appeal to common sense* (1910). From 1905 he was the editor of *Health and Beauty.* He was in advance of his time in advocating what would now be known as "a healthy diet," although he disbelieved in the existence of germs (which he called microbes). Part of his treatment was to advise patients never to take any medicine. He said "I do not heal disease—I introduce health into the system." Like Shaw, he was a vegetarian, a nonsmoker, and a total abstainer. He believed that the cause of disease was "unwholesome food," and that cancer could be cured by eating only natural food (fruit, nuts, etc.). He was very much against *white* bread. He was a notable eccentric, and is still remembered in Brigstock Village by two roads named after him: Sandlands Avenue and Sandlands Close. His own death occurred at the age of seventy-seven when he fell down the stairs in the vicarage.

• Charles [James] Mathews (1803–78), English comic actor. He was the son of Charles Mathews (1776–1835), another comic actor famous on both sides of the Atlantic. In 1838 he married Madame Vestris. It was said of him that his "enunciation was a marvel of incisive and elegant precision, effected with perfect ease, and often with extreme velocity."

• [Sir] John [Fairs] Hare (1844–1921), English comic actor and manager. He was born at Giggleswick, in Yorkshire, and made his debut as Lord Ptarmigant in T. W. Robertson's *Society* at the Prince of Wales. Here he played in several other plays of Robertson's from 1865 to 1874, was co-manager of the Court Theatre from 1874 to 1879, and joint manager (with the Kendals) of the St. James's Theatre from 1879 to 1888 (where on 8 March 1886, Shaw had seen him in *Antoinette Rigaud*), and the Garrick Theatre from 1889 to 1895. He was knighted in 1907. On 4 October 1887, a year after writing the above book review, Shaw transcribed the completed two acts of his first, as yet unfinished, dramatic effort, *Rheingold* (later to be retitled *Widowers' Houses*); and on 4 October he gave it to his collaborator, William Archer, with an accompanying letter in which he fancifully casts it with the foremost actors and actresses of his time. John Hare he casts as Sartorius (see *Collected Letters 1874–1897*, 175–76).

• George Grossmith (1847–1912), English comic actor and entertainer. In 1875, while playing in the chorus of Gilbert and Sullivan's *Trial by Jury*, he was introduced to the composer of the piece, Arthur Sullivan, who became friendly with him, and two years later offered him the comic lead (John Wellington Wells) in *The Sorcerer*. Thereafter he played the comic lead in all the Gilbert and Sullivan operas until 1889; and, as such, required remarkable diction to cope with Gilbert's "patter songs." With his brother Weedon he wrote *The Diary of a Nobody* (1892), a comic classic, first published in *Punch*.

• W. S. Penley (1851–1912), English actor and manager. He was born at St. Peter's, near Margate, the son of a schoolmaster, and educated at Westminster School. In his youth he was a chorister at the Chapel Royal, Savoy, and at Westminster Abbey. He was also for a time a clerk in a drapery business. His first appearance on the professional stage was at the Court Theatre in 1871, as Tim in *My Wife's Second Floor*. In March 1875 he appeared as the Foreman in Gilbert and Sullivan's *Trial by Jury*, and subsequently toured in the same company's *H.M.S. Pinafore*. In May 1884 he took over from Beerbohm Tree the role of the Rev. Robert Spalding in *The Private Secretary* at the Globe Theatre, a part with which he was associated for many years. In 1892 he produced *Charley's Aunt* (in Bury St. Edmunds), appearing himself as

Lord Fancourt Babberley. This play became enormously popular, was produced at the Royalty and the Globe Theatres in London, and ran for 1,466 successive performances. Penley retired from the stage in 1901.

- George Giddens (1845–1920), English actor. He was born at Bedfont, Middlesex, the son of a farmer, and was originally a clerk in a solicitor's office before making his stage debut in November 1865 at the Theatre Royal, Edinburgh, as Kelly in *Arrah-Na-Pogue*. He spent the next six years in provincial theaters, and in 1871 accompanied Charles Wyndham to the United States, appearing with him in such plays as *Caste* and *London Assurance*. He traveled around the United States and also Australia before making his first appearance on the London stage in 1878, in Charles Wyndham's *The Idol*. He remained under Wyndham's management for the next twelve years (except when he briefly became himself lessee of the Novelty Theatre in 1888). In 1893 he paid his second visit to America; in 1906–7 he toured the United States a third time, and again in 1910 returned to the New York stage, remaining in America for some years. He joined Annie Russell's company at the Thirty-ninth Street Theatre in New York in November 1912. In 1915 at the Park Theatre, New York, he played in three Shaw plays, portraying William in *You Never Can Tell,* Major Petkoff in *Arms and the Man,* and Mr. Burgess in *Candida.*

- George Barrett (1849–94), English actor. He made his debut at the Theatre Royal, Durham, in 1866, in *The Woman in Red*, and had acted widely in the provinces before his first appearance in London in 1872 in Robertson's *Progress*. After visiting India (supporting C. J. Mathews), he returned to London, appearing at the Criterion, Folly and Globe Theatres in the 1870s. Shaw had last seen him on 18 February 1886, playing Tribulation Tizack in the first performance of Henry Arthur Jones's *The Lord Harry* at the Princess's Theatre. This was, in fact, one of a series of originally conceived parts in the first performances of Jones's plays presented at the Princess's Theatre, which at that time was managed by his brother, Wilson Barrett. Later that year he was to tour in America as part of his brother's company. In the letter to Archer mentioned above, Shaw casts George Barrett as Lickcheese.

- Tommasso Salvini (1830–1915), Italian actor. He was born in Milan and fought in the revolutionary war of 1848. As an actor he first became known as a member of Ristori's company. He appeared in Racine's plays in Paris, and in Shakespeare's in London, scoring great successes with the roles of Othello and Hamlet. Although he was successful in comic roles (particularly in the comedies of Goldoni), he is remembered primarily as a tragedian. He retired from the stage in 1884.

- François Delsarte (1811–71), French singer, actor, and voice teacher. He espoused the notion of "applied aesthetics." Three months before (on 31 July 1886) Shaw had attended a lecture at Drury Lane on Delsarte given by one of the latter's disciples, Edmund Russell, and written a long notice of it for Mrs. Besant's magazine *Our Corner*. In this he reveals that he had learned about del Sarte (as he spells him) from a German ex-opera singer, who had known Delsarte and believed him to be an artist of extraordinarily subtle perception and noble taste; a faultless teacher of elocution, deportment and gesture; and a philosophic student as well as a practical master of his profession. Whether del Sarte was actually all this or not, I, of course cannot say. (Shaw, Bernard, *Our Corner,* September 1886, 181)

- Demosthenes (c.383–322 B.C.), Athenian orator. His fame was acquired through his eloquent orations designed to alert his countrymen to the danger of the subjugation of Greece by Philip of Macedon (orations which gave rise to the word *philippic*).

16 November 1886

THE YEAR OF JUBILEE* [C266]

Vivat Victoria! cries Mr. A. H. Wall, on the title page of his "book for the Royal Jubilee of 1886–87." Hooray! responds the loyal reader. But if the vivat were at the end of the book instead of at the beginning, the response would be neither so prompt nor so hearty. Fifty years even of a bad queen's reign would make a longish chronicle; and the history of a good Queen, such as ours, needs still more careful handling. The truth is that queens, like other people, can be too good for the sympathies of their finite fellow-creatures. A few faults are indispensable to a really popular monarch. One would rather be Edward the Confessor than Charles II, or George IV, it is true; but if the choice lay between St. Louis and Henri Quatre, the leaning to Virtue's side would be less certain. And if the Royal Jubilee is to be a success, the sooner some competent cynic writes a book about Her Majesty's shortcomings the better. With her merits we are familiar, and may expect to be more so before the last Jubilee bookmaker has given the throne a final coat of whitewash. We know that she has been of all wives the best, of all mothers the fondest, of all widows the most faithful. We have often seen her, despite her lofty station, moved by famines, colliery explosions, shipwrecks, and railway accidents; thereby teaching us that a heart beats in her Royal breast as in the humblest of her subjects. She has

---

*"Fifty Years of a Good Queen's Reign." By A. H. Wall. (London: Ward and Downey. 1886.)

proved that she can, when she chooses, put off her state and play the pianoforte, write books, and illustrate them like any common lady novelist. We all remember how she repealed the corn laws, invented the steam locomotive, and introduced railways; devised the penny post, developed telegraphy, and laid the Atlantic cable; how she captured Coomassie and Alexandria, regenerated art by the pre-Raphaelite movement, speculated in Suez Canal stock, extended the franchise, founded the Primrose League, became Empress of India, and, in short, went through such a programme as no previous potentate ever dreamed of. What we need now is a book entitled "Queen Victoria: by a Personal acquaintance who dislikes her." Not, observe, by a rebel or republican, who would feel bound to disparage her as a Fenian feels bound to deny musical merit to the National Anthem, or as a good secularist will stick to it that Tom Paine was a better writer than John Bunyan. The proper person for the work would be some politically indifferent devil's advocate who considers the Queen an over-rated woman, and who would take a conscientious delight in disparaging her.

Such a book, one would think, could not greatly scandalize the nineteenth century. The world is growing out of loyalty. A good deal of the extra mouth honour that will presently be paid to the throne will be pure hypocrisy, at which the incorrigibly polite people will keep the abjectly venal people in countenance. Yet there must be much genuine superstitious loyalty still among us. That the Queen, if no longer actually hedged with divinity, is yet more than merely human in the eyes of many of us, is made plain by the sacredness which trivial things assume when touched by a Royal hand. What is more *banal* than a pair of boots? What more uninteresting than an umbrella? But the Queen's boots! are they *banal*? the Queen's umbrella! what would you not give for the reversion of it? When a tornado devastates an American province it is chronicled in a quarter of a column. Yet were a gust of wind to blow off our Sovereign's head-gear tomorrow, "The Queen's Bonnet" would crowd Bulgaria out of the papers. Clearly, the ideal of Royalty is still with us; and it is as the impersonatrix of that ideal that the Queen is worshipped by us. This feeling is the real support of thrones. The nation does not always think much of the King; and the King very frequently has the lowest opinion of the nation; but while both believe in Royalty the people will maintain the throne, and the King, instead of saying, "By your leave, my lords and gentlemen, I prefer to give up my part in this farce, and retire into private life on my savings," will put on his regal finery and set about his duties with an air of conviction that will awe Tom, Dick, and 'Arry in spite of themselves.

Mr. Wall has, of course, not ventured to treat his subject quite sympathetically and sensibly. Any such profane course would have cut off prospects of publication. But he has not played the toady. While recording the virtues of his Queen with benevolent enthusiasm, he has managed to convey good humouredly that her education was a little old-fashioned, and that her force of character has often enabled her to hold out against the more modern requirements of perfect altruism—in brief, that her Majesty is a little obstinate and a little clannish, like most ladies whose conceptions of duty were formed when George III was king. To her resolute conscientiousness within the limits of that conception he does full justice. His style is persuasive, genial, slipshod, and so prosy that he has had to leave the last twenty years untouched in consequence of having recklessly used up his allotted space over the first three decades of the half century he undertook to chronicle. The reader, however, will not complain: he will, to tell the truth, have had enough of it; for even the most easygoing author may congratulate himself if the satiety produced by a thirty years' chronicle of Court life does not turn into active resentment. Mr. Wall, who has been painter and actor as well as author, has something interesting to say about the stage and studio as they were a couple of generations ago. In writing of the Queen, he is, like the King of Bohemia in "Hernani," apt to be familiar. "Her plump litttle Majesty," and "her modest little Majesty," are hardly respectful phrases; and "shy little Victoria" is downrightly audacious. On page 137 he claims cousinship with the Queen by calling her his father's pretty little niece. It is, however, possible that the possessive pronoun refers to George IV, who is mentioned in the same chapter. The following anecdote of the Duke of Cambridge is hardly credible. "In 1850, when returning from the deathbed of her uncle, the Duke of Cambridge, a tall man, of gentlemanly appearance, struck at her Majesty's face with his stick, crushing her bonnet, and wounding and bruising her face." Surely our Commander-in-Chief was never so ungallant. Besides, though his appearance is gentlemanly, he is not exceptionally tall. King Leopold's account of the Prince Consort's reason, or rather excuse, for marrying also strikes one oddly. "He considers that troubles are inseparable from all human positions, and that therefore, if one must be subject to plagues and annoyances, it is better to be so for some great or worthy object than for trifles and miseries."

Space forbids more than one other quotation, which needs no further preface than an assurance that the punctuation—notes of admiration and all—is Mr. Wall's own. "The Duke of Kent was taken seriously ill.

In vain his physicians prescribed calomel! and James's powder! in vain they extracted from his veins one hundred and twenty ounces of blood, and regretted that he had not bled more freely! Two days after he was dead."

Editor's Notes

- Shaw received this book, whose full title is *Fifty Years of a Good Queen's Reign. A book for the Royal Jubiliee of 1886–87*, on 27 August 1886. On 16 September he began reading it, and continued the following day. His diary notes that he was still reading it on 23, 24, 25, and 26 September, and that he finished it on 8 October. Finally he wrote his review and dispatched it to the *PMG* on 14 October (*Diary*, 198, 200, 203, 205, 227).
- A[lfred] H[enry] Wall (1828–1906), English painter, photographer, and author. He was born in London. His early youth was spoiled by an "unsympathetic stepfather," causing him to run away from home. He first joined one of the earliest daguerrotypists, and then joined Macready's acting company as a "super". In 1850, he and a partner went into business in Cheapside, London, as miniature painters and daguerrotypists. In 1851, he was assistant to a photographer working near the Great Exhibition and later opened a studio in the Strand as a miniaturist and portrait painter. This failed. In 1852 he married, and set out with his wife as a touring portrait painter, using the name R. A. Seymour. This was a successful venture; but the early death of his wife sent him back to the stage. He edited *The Illustrated Photographer* (for Hazel Watson and Viney) from 1868 to 1870, was a contributor to *The British Journal*, founded the South London Photographic Society, and was one of the founders (and a most active member) of the Solar Club. The later years of his life were spent as curator of the Shakespeare Memorial Library, Stratford-on-Avon. In addition to the book reviewed above, Alfred Wall also wrote *A Manual of Artistic Colouring as Applied to Photographs: a practical guide to artists and photographers. Containing clear, simple, and complete instructions for colouring photographs on glass, paper, ivory and canvas* (1861), *Shakespeare's Face; a monologue on the various portraits of Shakespeare in comparison with the death mask now preserved as Shakespeare's in the Grand ducal museum of Darmstadt* (1890), [with Andrew A. Anderson] *A Romance of N'Shabe* (1891) [being a record of "startling adventures in South Central Africa"], *Artistic landscape Photography; a series of chapters on the practical and theoretical principles of pictorial composition* (1896), *The Fall of Constantinople. A Romance* (1897), and *Bookshelves and books. Giving Instructions for the planning and making of bookshelves, for the collection, classifying, indexing, arranging and cataloguing of books. With designs and diagrams of shelves* (1902).
- St. Louis [Louis IX] (1214–70), the ascetic, stern, and just King of France

who was canonized in 1297 is contrasted with Henri IV (1553–1610), who was equally successful politically, but whose private life was scandalous enough to earn him the nickname of *le Vert-Gallant*.

- Queen Victoria was an inveterate diarist and sketcher. She went public with both in her book *Leaves from the Journal of Our Life in the Highlands* (1868). The book sold twenty thousand copies at once, and ran to several editions. It was followed in 1883 by *More Leaves*.

- Shaw's sarcasm is directed as much against Wall's book as against the Queen: *Fifty Years*, etc. does indeed have chapters entitled, for example, "The Penny Post" in which the coincidence of the latter's inception falling in the same year as Queen Victoria's coronation has led the author rather recklessly to add it to the list of her contributions to the world.

- Coomassie [or Kumasi] was the city in what is now central Ghana, the capital of the Ashanti kingdom until 1874, when it was captured by the British who opened new trade routes that diminished its importance; Alexandria (Egypt's chief seaport) was the scene of a major riot in 1882 in which four hundred European residents were massacred. England used this as an excuse to occupy all of Egypt and administer it as a colony.

- Thomas Paine (1737–1809), English-born political leader, who became famous in America with the publication of *Common Sense* (1776), which urged immediate and complete independence. During the war that followed, he issued a series of pamphlets entitled *The Crisis* (1776–83) to encourage the Americans. He returned to Europe and supported the French revolution by writing *The Rights of Man* (1791–92), was condemned in England for treason, and entered politics in France, where he was sent to prison! Here he began his great deistic work *The Age of Reason* (1794–96). He spent his declining years in America embittered by controversy and poverty.

- The word *banal* is no doubt italicized because it was a neologism, scarcely three years old.

- It would certainly have taken a great deal to "crowd Bulgaria" out of the newspapers in 1886. Ten years previously, the Bulgarian uprising (a reaction in part against the centuries-old domination by Turks and Greeks, and against the settlement by the Turkish government of Tartars and Circassians on land taken without compensation from Bulgarian peasants), was so ferociously put down (fifteen thousand persons were massacred, and fifty-eight villages and five monasteries destroyed in the district of Philippopolis alone) that it led to international outrage. Gladstone denounced the atrocities in a pamphlet, and even Queen Victoria, usually contemptuous of his opinions, confided to her journal her horror of the Turkish atrocities. Finally Servia declared war, and was joined by two thousand Bulgarian volunteers. In 1877 Russia joined in against the Turks, and the victorious advance of the Russian army to Constantinople was followed by the Treaty of San Stefano, which realised to the full the aspirations of the Bulgarian people. However, in 1879 a Russian proposal was adopted that elected as the first king of Bulgaria Prince Alexander—a nephew of Czar Alexander II. Immediately a struggle broke out against both Russian involvement in Bulgarian affairs and the autocracy of this young ruler, who, unable to reconcile the warring factions, assumed absolute authority in 1881. He was assisted by the Russian general Ernroth, who saw to it that the prince was invested with absolute power for seven years. Unfortunately for Russian hopes, the prince began to feel sympathy for the Bulgarian nationals still under Turkish rule, and sought to unify his country. On 18 September 1885, the "Kazioni" or treasure-seekers, a party desirous of bringing about Bulgarian independence, seized the governor-general of the Philippopolis district and proclaimed union with Bulgaria. The revolution took place without bloodshed, and Prince Alexander entered Philippopolis to great cheering. At this point Servia, hoping to profit by the difficulties of neighboring Bulgaria, suddenly declared war. Simultaneously, Russia withdrew all the Russian officers from the Bulgarian army, leaving them only subalterns. However, contrary to expectations, the Bulgarians successfully resisted the Servian invasion, and achieved brilliant victories at Slivnitza and Tsaribrod late in November, 1885. This period of Bulgarian history is dealt with by Shaw in *Arms and the Man* (1894). However, the victories, which made the prince a national hero in Bulgaria, only intensified the Russian desire to remove him, which was managed by a conspiracy in the summer of 1886. The conspiracy was denounced, and the prince was returned, but he had decided to resign his crown into the hands of Russia. Two months before this review was written he announced his abdication, and left Bulgaria. At the time of this review, Stamboloff, who had filled the vacancy created by the prince, was fending off attempts to throw his country into anarchy, and the progress of events there was eagerly read about by readers of the *Pall Mall Gazette*.

▪ The elector, king of Bohemia, announces political victory to Don Carlos in *Hernani* (1830) by Victor Hugo.

24 November 1886

A SCIENCE OF GHOSTS* [C269]

THIS formidable array of ghost stories, collected, arranged, and commented on by Messrs. Gurney, Myers, and Podmore, somehow reminds one of those "several manuscript confessions upon which Mr. Wemmick set particular value as being, to use his own words, 'every

---

*"Phantasms of the Living." By Edmund Gurney, M.A., Frederic W. H. Myers, M.A., and Frank Podmore, M.A. Two vols. (London: Trübner and Co. 1886.)

one of 'em lies, sir.' " It is useless to mince matters in dealing with ghost stories—the existence of a liar is more probable than the existence of a ghost. "One of the advantages of personal inquiry," says Mr. Myers, in his introduction, "is the security gained by it as to the *bona fides* of the witnesses concerned. They have practically placed themselves on their honour; nor need we doubt that the experiences have been, as a rule, recounted in all sincerity." It is unpleasant but necessary to rejoin that the custom of accepting as conclusive the solemn statements of persons of good repute concerning events that are known to be natural does not hold when marvels are in question. There is a point at which it is easier to impute deliberate falsehood to a Washington or a Bayard than to believe them. The most intelligent man may be misled by hallucination: the wisest may suddenly go mad: the best may sin against strict veracity. Such aberrations are more probable than the appearance of a man miles away from where he lies dying. As to ordinary witnesses, the great majority are so ignorantly convinced that seeing is believing, so little aware that the evidence of their senses requires highly skilled interpretation before it can exert weight in the balance of science, that they are the last persons who can be depended upon to give a trustworthy account of what has actually passed in their presence. In saying, therefore, that it yet remains to be seen whether the toughest contents of these two well filled volumes are true, no accusation of intentional falsehood against the deponents is implied. That some of them have said the thing that is not is extremely likely; that they knew they were doing so does not necessarily or even probably follow.

These considerations have hitherto frightened away from "psychical research" almost all who were adequately qualified for it. Indeed, as the very love of the marvellous which makes the subject irresistibly attractive to certain temperaments indicates a lack of the scientific spirit in which it should be studied, adequately qualified men would perhaps not often be found working at it even if there were nothing to frighten them away. On other accounts, too, the work cannot be very pleasant. Invitations to the public to tell ghost stories at once bring the investigator into contact with a host of witnesses of whom the most eager, the most communicative, and the most officious are obscurely epileptic or hysterical persons, incorrigibly conceited and mendacious. Even when the investigator has become expert enough to decide very easily in nine cases out of ten whether his informants are intellectually honest or not, still the tenth case is likely to depend on the credit of a witness who is imaginative and obviously strongly addicted to the miraculous, but whose intelligence and sincerity make it difficult to reject his story, which is likely to be the best told of the ten. In the face of all these difficulties, the three authors have acquitted themselves admirably. Mr Myers's introduction and Mr. Gurney's commentary confirm the impression, which no guest of the Psychical Society has ever failed to receive, that they are extremely superior men. "How poor, how fragmentary," exclaims Mr. Myers, "were Aristotle's fancies compared with our conception, thus gained, of cosmic unity! our vibrant message from Sirius and Orion by the heraldry of the kindred flame! . . . The insentient has awoke, we know not how, into sentiency; the sentient into the fuller consciousness of human minds." Fine as all this is, Mr. Myers, unexhausted, goes on to talk about the microcosm and the macrocosm in a way that really does one good to read. Mr. Gurney follows with more sobriety, but not less ability; and Mr. Podmore, like a subtle essence, so pervades the whole that, to quote the preface, "his name could not possibly have been omitted from the title-page."

The main contention of the book, foreshadowed by the title, is startlingly contrary to all received ideas of the supernatural. Every Englishman believes that he is entitled to a ghost after death to compensate him for the loss of his body, and to enable him to haunt anybody that may have murdered or otherwise ill-used him in the days when he was solid. But our authors contend that a dead man can have no ghost. It is during life that we have the power of "appearing" to our friends; and a plain necessity for fresh legislation arises from the fact that although no privacy can hide us from them if we really make up our minds to haunt them, they have no defence or legal remedy against such incorporeal trespass, except the power of exerting their will so as to detain and converse with our ghosts—a process which gives our bodily selves a bad headache. As to those whose wills are weak, we can simply frighten them out of their wits when we please. We can not only make them see things, we can make them feel, taste, and smell them; write down what we are thinking of; and in fact induce sensations in them as a current in one telegraph wire induces a current in another. Fortunately we can only do this while we are alive and ought to be more usefully employed. Macbeth's strong opinion that when "the brains were out the man would die, and there an end" was well founded; and his vision of Banquo but an hallucination.

For innumerable instances of the exercise of these weird powers, reference must be made to the volumes themselves. Their thousand pages of marvels will save the nervous, the lonely, and the sleepless from tedium during the long winter nights. Those who have no nerves will find interest in cases like that of Miss Drasey, who, we are told, in a footnote to page 110, vol.i., "fainted away, and nearly dropped some dishes she had in her hands." This way of putting it hardly does justice to the uncommon presence of mind of a lady who remembered, even in a swoon, what was due to her fragile charge.

It would be unfair to conclude a notice of Messrs. Myers, Gurney, and Podmore's work without an acknowledgment of public indebtedness to them for useful and arduous work diligently and ably done. Human nature being frail, the critical eye cannot be prevented from twinkling occasionally as it travels over their pages; but the reader must not infer therefrom any intention to disparage a valuable and interesting contribution to the elucidation of a branch of science which scientific men have hitherto carefully let alone.

Editor's Notes

- Shaw received *Phantasms of the Living* for review on 2 November 1886. On the eleventh he began his review of it, "and unfortunately got *Great Expectations* at the Museum to quote from with the result that I wasted nearly all day reading it" (*Diary*, 212). On the thirteenth he finished his review and sent it to the *Pall Mall Gazette* (*Diary*, 212–13, 216, 227).

- Edmund Gurney (1847–88), English scientist and essayist. He was the son of a clergyman, educated privately and at Trinity College, Cambridge, which he entered in 1866 as a minor scholar in classics. Initially, however, his ambitions were musical. In 1872 he was elected to a Trinity Fellowship, and devoted himself to music study under John Farmer. His dialectical skills, wit, and charm made him prominent among the younger men of Trinity. George Eliot, who met Gurney at Cambridge in 1873 was so taken by his good looks that for several days she could think of nothing else, and she afterwards "discovered that his mind was as beautiful as his face" (O. Browning, *Life of George Eliot* [London: 1890], 116). Indeed, she is said to have founded the character of Daniel Deronda in part on Edmund Gurney. Notwithstanding the charm he exercised upon others, he developed a strain of melancholy in his own character that led to bouts of depression; a condition which was reinforced in 1875 when three of his sisters were drowned in a boating accident on the Nile. In that year he moved to London, and in 1877 he met and married Kate Sibley, and embarked on a course of medical studies at University College, London. In 1880 he obtained his second M.B. Unfortunately, when he began the clinical part of his training at St. George's Hospital, his inability to endure the sights and sounds of the "dressing room," as it was called, put paid to his prospects of a medical career. He then turned to law, but lost interest and did not graduate. In 1880, combining his musical and medical knowledge, he published *The Power of Sound*. He became a member of "The Scratch Eight," a philosophical discussion group, and contributed papers to *Mind* and other journals. Several of the essays were collected in the first volume of *Tertium Quid* (1887). His own religious doubts and his intense interest in human suffering caused Gurney to give his support in 1882 to the Society for Psychic Research, of which he became first honorary secretary. Together with Myers and Podmore [see below], he was made responsible for *Phantasms of the Living*, the great majority of whose thirteen hundred pages were written by Gurney. The book finally appeared in October 1886, and prompted this and the next review by Shaw. In December 1887, Shaw reviewed *Tertium Quid* [see pages 369–72 below]. Less than a year later, alone in a Brighton Hotel, Edmund Gurney died, apparently of an overdose of chloroform.

- Frank Podmore (1855–1910), English writer. The son of a clergyman, he studied classics and natural science at Oxford, but became a civil servant working in the General Post Office in London. In his youth a Spiritualist, he joined the Society for Psychic Research in 1882. Two years later, he was a founding member of the Fabian Society (which he named), and was on its executive for some years, coauthoring with Webb the Fabian tract *Government Organisation of Unemployed Labour*. However, he became more closely connected with Myers and Gurney while the S.P.R.'s enormous project *Phantasms of the Living* was being collated and seen through the press, and his interest seems to have swung increasingly back to the Society for Psychic Research, of which he became honorary secretary (from 1888 to 1896) after Gurney's death. Nevertheless, he does not seem to have been on intimate terms with the leading lights of the group. Whereas Myers wrote the introduction to *Phantasms of the Living*, and Gurney wrote the body of the book, Podmore seems to have been simply an investigator of a large number of cases. As such he seems to have become an increasingly sceptical observer. In addition to his part in the above project, Podmore wrote several other books, including *Apparitions and Thought-Transference* (1894), *Modern Spiritualism* (1902), *The Newer Spiritualism* (1910), and *Robert Owen* (1923). His death in 1910 looked suspiciously like suicide.

- Mr. (John) Wemmick is Mr. Jaggers's confidential clerk in *Great Expectations*, a dry man, rather short in stature with a square, wooden face. His features seem to have been imperfectly chipped out with a dull-edged chisel. He is a kindly man at heart, and has a pleasant home at Walworth, where he devotes himself to the comfort of his venerable father, and "brushes the Newgate cobwebs away" in many delightful ways, perhaps the most important of them being the transformation of Miss Skiffins into Mrs. Wemmick.

- George Washington's talent for truth telling is well known; the Bayard in question, however, is less likely to be that other American statesman, James Asheton Bayard (1767–1815), than the French knight Seigneur Pierre du Terrail Bayard (1473–1524), known in legend as the "chevalier sans peur et sans reproche."

- The *Macbeth* quotation is from Act III, Scene 4, and reads in full:

the time has been,
That, when the brains were out, the man would die,
And there an end.

16 December 1886

SOME OF MR. GURNEY'S GHOST STORIES
[C274]

MR. EDMUND GURNEY'S remonstrance concerning the doubt expressed in our review of "Phantasms of the Living" as to the truth of the curious stories contained in that book, induces us to place a few of them before our readers, who can judge for themselves of the weight of the corroboration upon which Mr. Gurney relies:

> Mr. Edmund Gurney gently remonstrates with the reviewer of "Phantasms of the Living," who somewhat bluntly suggested that the accounts contained in that book were perhaps simply false, and omitted to mention that many of them are so far corroborated that they are proved to refer to events, such as deaths, accidents, &c., which have actually occurred, and that their falsehood involves the hypothesis not of a single liar, but a conspiracy of liars in each case. In Mr. Gurney's own words, some of the cases "admit of no doubt except on the hypothesis of a widespread and deliberate plot to deceive." Now, the cases taken by themselves, do not require a hypothesis of "widespread" plots; for some of the most conclusive cases rest on the statement of two persons closely related to one another. And as it is a common saying that if a man will but assert boldly that he has done a thing, some bystander is sure to declare that he saw him do it, the testimony of two witnesses to an event of a marvellous character, though mightier than that of one, is so far as we yet know more likely to be false than a ghost story is to be true. By "widespread," then, Mr. Gurney must mean that the several stories are so like one another that the narrators must have conspired to tell the same sort of tale, in order to bolster up the theory of telepathy. This is as much to say that men must concert mea-

sures if they would prevent themselves from producing original fiction. But the reviewer—being a reviewer—knows better. That the stories collected by Mr. Gurney are alike in pattern proves only that the narrators' brains are alike in pattern, and by no means that the narratives are true. The absence of a widespread plot being then insufficient corroboration, what remains? Readers can judge for themselves by the appended specimens. The procedure, it will be seen, has been something like this:—Mr. Gurney invites the public to send him ghost stories. Mr. A. B. responds to the effect that at five o'clock he saw his brother's ghost and mentioned it to his wife, and that at ten o'clock news of his brother's death came. It is then Mr. Gurney's painful duty to write to Mrs. A. B., virtually to the effect that unless she is prepared to say that she heard her husband's favourite ghost story for the first time before ten o'clock, his veracity will be gravely called in question. Would not any wife, short of a perfect Jeanie Deans, under such pressure remember what would save her husband's credit rather than what actually happened? A brother, a servant, a debtor, or an obliging friend might feel the same pressure, and yield the same sort of corroboration. It is something; but not enough to exclude the vulgar hypothesis of simple falsehood.

This is the worst the reviewer has to say. Ungracious as it is, it had to be said; for Mr. Gurney's intellectual honesty and the judgement with which he has handled his material left nothing unsettled except the credit of the witnesses. By his ability and thoroughness he forced back his critic to that one point, and it is but natural for the critic to hold by it as long as it is tenable. His pertinacity is thus an indirect compliment to Mr. Gurney and his collaborators.

"NEVER MIND WHETHER THE STORIES ARE TRUE: LET'S HEAR THEM."

And now, as there is no affecting to ignore the public cry of "Never mind whether the stories are true or not: let's hear some of them," we will comply, under the following reservations.

We shall not quote the narratives verbatim, and we shall select neither the most amusing nor the most sensational stories, but those which are, to our mind, most satisfactorily corroborated. Let us begin with a dream.

A Prophetic Dream

Case 23, vol. I., p. 199.—Mr. Fred Featherdale, a gentleman of a sceptical turn, residing in France, says: "On the night of Thursday, the 25th March, 1880, I dreamed that I was lying on my sofa, reading. On looking up I saw distinctly my brother sitting on the chair before me. I spoke to him; but he simply bent his head in reply, rose, and left the room. When I woke I found myself standing with one foot on the ground by my bedside and the other on the bed, trying to speak and to pronounce my brother's name. . . . My sense of impending evil was so strong that I at once made a note in my memorandum book of this appearance, and added the words, 'God forbid!'. . . . Three days afterwards I received the news that my brother died on the 25th of March, 1880, at 8:30 P.M., from terrible injuries received in a fall while hunting with the Blackmore Vale hounds." Corroboration: The memorandum book with the entry; the announcement of the death in the *Times*, besides an account of it in the *Essex Independent;* and a letter from a French Prince who recollects having heard the story from Mr. Featherdale on the 4th of April, 1880, but was not surprised, because such things had happened in his own family. Here the apparition occurred some hours after the death. According to Mr. Gurney's theory, the impression must have been made by the deceased gentleman during his lifetime; but his brother, who was preoccupied in reading at the time, did not become distinctly conscious of it until he retired to rest.

Ghostly Visitors

Case 26, vol. I., p. 207. Mr. Stepping, a retired farmer, was "perfectly wide awake" at about two o'clock in the morning on the 21st October, 1881, when he saw a cousin of his, usually called Robinson Crusoe, enter, contemplate himself in the mirror, and vanish on being spoken to. Four days later, news came that Robinson Crusoe had died at the hour of his appearance. Corroboration: A declaration by three witnesses that they are "positive of hearing Mr. Stepping one day say that he saw the apparition of Robinson Crusoe during the previous night (that is to say, before the news of the death had arrived.)"

Case 28, vol. I., p. 210.—A. B. C., sitting one evening with his wife at home, suddenly saw his dear friend Y. Z. standing before him. Y. Z. "looked with a fixed regard, and then passed away." A. B. C.'s hair stood on end, and he quoted Job. He then asked his wife the hour, and she replied that it was twelve minutes to nine, upon which he told her that Y. Z. was dead. Next day news came that Y. Z. had been found dead from rupture of the aorta at nine on the previous evening. Corroboration: The announcement of the death at the given date in the *Times;* a letter from Mrs. A. B. C. confirming the question and statement as to the hour and the ghost; and a letter from Y. Z.'s brother to the effect that when he was about to break the news to A. B. C. the latter forestalled him by saying, "Your brother is dead."

A GHOST IN GREY TWEED

Case 175, p. 443.—At about seven o'clock in the morning, on the 2nd of December, 1883, Mr. Crowder dreamed that Mr. Witchet was lying beside him on the coverlet of the bed, dressed in grey tweed. Mr. Crowder presently awoke, but he still saw Mr. Witchet, who, however, presently disappeared. Mr. Crowder, much concerned, mentioned the matter that day to Mr. Yeansly. Subsequently news came that Mr. Witchet had died about six hours after his appearance in Mr. Crowder's bed. Corroboration: Announcement in the *Darlington and Stockton Times* of the death of Mr. Witchet on the date given; and a letter from Mr. Yeansly stating that Mr. Crowder did indeed describe the apparition to him before the news of the death came.

A GHOST FROM THE CRIMEAN WAR

Case 210, vol. I., p. 556.—Captain Shooter, when a boy, was spending his holidays in Midlothian. His brother Oliver, then on active service before Sebastopol, wrote home in low spirits, whereupon, says Captain Shooter, "I said in answer that he was to cheer up, but that if anything did happen to him, he must let me know by appearing in my room, where we had often as boys together sat at night and indulged in a surreptitious pipe and chat." Subsequently Oliver Shooter was killed by a shot through the temple at the storming of the Redan; and on the same night [8th September, 1855] his brother, suddenly awaking, saw him kneeling in a phosphorescent light, with a wound in his temple, looking "lovingly, imploringly, and sadly" at him. The boy eventually shut his eyes and "walked through it" out of the room . . . and he was rebuked next morning by his father for telling "such nonsense." Corroboration: The date of the Redan action and the list of the slain in the *Gazette;* and a letter from Captain Shooter's sister describing the incident as told by him on the 8th of September, before the news arrived. It will be seen that there is a discrepancy of a day in the date here. A Major B. is also said to have been in the house at the time; but Mr. Gurney does not mention whether any attempt was made to obtain his testimony.

THE GHOST OF A VOICE, OR THE VOICE OF A GHOST?

Case 272, vol. ii., p. 107.—"About midday of the 24th July, 1875, I was in the baths at Llandudno, when I suddenly and distinctly heard my boy's voice calling loudly and in an agonized tone, though I believed him to be, as indeed he was, at the other side of the Orme's Head, three or four miles away. The boy was killed at that very time by a fall from the rocks." Corroboration: An account of the incident in the *Stockport Advertiser,* which gives the date as the 26th; a letter from the narrator's wife, stating that her husband told her the story before their boy was missed; and the testimony of a Southport gentleman, who heard it the day after the funeral.

Editor's Notes

- The curious typesetting of the above looks almost as if it was to be printed as a letter to the editor.
- Edmund Gurney's "remonstrance" took the form of a letter to the *Pall Mall Gazette* dated 7 December 1886. It reads as follows:

"THE SCIENCE OF GHOSTS"

To the EDITOR *of the* PALL MALL GAZETTE.
  SIR,—May I point out to the writer of the friendly notice of "Phantasms of the Living," which you published the other day, that he has overlooked a most important feature in the evidence for telepathy— namely, the large number of cases in which the percipient's experi-

ence was recorded or described by him before the fact of the corresponding event at a distance was known? Your reviewer's contention appears to be that no amount of evidence that A's senses received a vivid impression of B's presence, at the time that B unexpectedly died, could be conclusive, because the "evidence of the senses" cannot be trusted, and the best of men are subject to hallucinations and mistakes. Now this mistrust of the evidence of the senses would be quite in place if the question were whether what A thought he perceived was really there; but it is not in place when the question is simply what he thought he perceived. In other words, we may grant—and in the book I have not only granted but persistently urged—that A's experience is an hallucination; but it clearly does not follow that his report that he has experienced it is a mistake.

Put in a nutshell, the matter stands thus. Hallucinations of the senses of a marked sort are things which, though they occur to only a small minority of persons, still do occur occasionally to persons in apparently sound bodily and mental health. If, therefore, somebody of good character and intelligence reports one day, as a singular and surprising incident, that he has seemed to see the absent B in his room, the supposition that he is consciously or unconsciously inventing would be as unreasonable as if he reported any other experience which occurs to only a small minority of persons—for example, that he had been overturned in a cab. And if the supposition that he is inventing would be unreasonable on the day that he makes the statement, it cannot become reasonable next day merely because the news arrives that B died at that time. And if such cases have occurred too often for it to be possible to regard the coincidences as accidental, then we are driven to conclude that A's experience was in some way due to B's condition, or, more technically, that the hallucination or phantasm was of telepathic origin. Now, I submit that there is a sufficient basis for this conclusion in the cases of the above type cited in "Phantasms of the Living"—cases where the fact that A's record or mention of his unusual experience preceded the news of the corresponding event admits [sic] of no doubt except on the hypothesis (which I understand your reviewer to repudiate) of a widespread and deliberate plot to deceive. But these best-substantiated cases by no means exhaust the cumulative argument for telepathy, for if once they are admitted it becomes unreasonable to regard as inventions all the first-hand reports of similar occurrences where the percipient's experience did not happen to be instantly recorded or described, since there is nothing in the unexpected news of a friend's death specially calculated to make a person imagine that he had had a novel and startling experience a short time before. Still, whatever the strength of the cumulative argument may be, it can be, and ought to be, made yet stronger; and I take this opportunity of begging any of your readers who may know of cases which they believe to be authentic to communicate with me. Any conditions which they may attach to their communications will of course be observed.—I am, Sir, your obedient servant.

14, Dean's-yard, S. W., Dec. 5   EDMUND GURNEY.

- Jeanie Deans is the heroine of Scott's *Heart of Midlothian* (1818), devoted to her half sister, Effie, but even more devoted to the truth; for she refuses to give the false evidence which would have secured an acquittal for Effie, who was charged with child murder.

21 December 1886

OXFORD MEMORIES [C275]

"Oxford Memories." By the Rev. James Pycroft, B.A. Two vols. (Bentley and Son.) Mr. Pycroft's reminiscences of Oxford date from the thirties. Of the surface aspects of University life in those days he has nothing new to tell; and beneath the surface he, for lack of insight (except into cricket), could not see. His moral, admirable, if somewhat trite, is that the student should read diligently and avoid debt. His stories are the ordinary collegiate stories, nothing if not facetiously told. The effect of such facetiousness in print has been sufficiently tested in "The Adventures of Mr. Verdant Green," admirers of which will doubtless be glad to give "Oxford Memories" a place among their serious books. Mr. Pycroft's chapters on cricket are as interesting as his writings on this his special subject usually are; and he makes some sensible remarks concerning the value of a university training and the pecuniary equipment needed by a student.

Editor's Notes

- Shaw received Pycroft's *Oxford Memories* on 24 September 1886, and dispatched his review of it on 26 October. Presumably, therefore, it was one of the "batch of reviews" that he had polished off the previous day (*Diary*, 227).
- James Pycroft (1813–95), English author and clergyman. He was born in Wiltshire, matriculated from Trinity College, Oxford, on 25 May 1831 and graduated with a B.A. in 1836, in which year, he claimed, he and Bishop Ryle

instituted the Oxford and Cambridge cricket match. Upon his graduation he became a student of Lincoln's Inn, but in 1840 abandoned the study of law and was ordained in the Church of England. He became second master of the collegiate school at Leicester for five years, during which time he married. After being curate of Chardstock, Dorset, for a year, he was perpetual curate of St. Mary Magdalen, Barnstaple, from 1845 to 1856, when he resigned from clerical duties and devoted himself to literature and cricket. He certainly was an enthusiastic cricketer, becoming a member of the Lansdowne Club, though his strength lay less in his athletic ability and more in his knowledge of the rules and finer points of the game. In 1859 he published a religious novel *Twenty Years in the Church: An Autobiography* (which ran to four editions), followed by its sequel *Elkerton Rectory* (1860). Other books by him are *Principles of Scientific Batting* (1835), *On School Education, designed to assist Parents in choosing and co-operating with Instructors for their sons* (1843), *Greek Grammar Practice* (1844), *The Collegian's Guide, or Recollections of College Days. Setting forth the Advantages and Temptations of a University Education* (1845), *Four Lectures on the Advantages of a Classical Education as an Auxiliary to a Commercial Education* (1847), *The Cricket Field, or the History and Science of Cricket* (1851), *Agony Point; or the Groans of Gentility* (1861), *The Cricket Tutor* (1862), *Dragon's Teeth: a Novel* (1863); and *Cricketana* (1865). Pycroft died of influenza in Brighton.

• *The Adventures of Mr. Verdant Green* (1853–57) by Cuthbert Bede, B.A., a facetious (and very popular) account of Oxford life, was written by Edward Bradley (1827–89), the first of the more than twenty books by this English author and clergyman, born at Kidderminster and educated at the University of Durham.

29 December 1886

FIFTY-FIVE GUINEAS REWARD [C277]

"Fifty-five Guineas Reward." By Fred C. Milford. (Field and Tuer.) This latest enterprise of Messrs. Field and Tuer is what it is the fashion at present to call a "shocker." The author, Mr. F. C. Milford, has disregarded the rule that an impossible but probable incident is more credible than a possible but improbable one. He tells of a careless gentleman who slays his cousin in the presence of a phonograph, which, revolving by clockwork, registers the altercation between the murderer and his victim, the stroke of the razor, the "gurgle," and some other circumstances which fix the guilt for a time on an innocent man. The story is written solely to turn this conceit to account, and has no other merit than that of serving its purpose.

Editor's Notes

- Shaw's diary records a question mark over when he received this book, though it may have been on 11 September 1886. However, he was "reading 55 *Guineas Reward* for review" on 19 October, and again the review appears to be one of the "batch" he wrote on 25 October. He sent it to the *PMG* on the twenty-sixth (*Diary*, 206, 227).
- Frederick C[] Milford (n.d.), English novelist. He also wrote *Lost! a Day* (1886), *In Crime's Disguise. A novel* (1890), and *What Became of Him?* (1897).

6 January 1887

A LIFE OF MADAME BLAVATSKY* [C279]

WHEN Mr. Sinnett undertook to compile a memoir of Mdme. Blavatsky, he set himself a difficult and delicate task. Only such faith as his could achieve a reverent and sincere account of a lady at whose "first command and look there came rushing to her through the air her tobacco pouch, her box of matches, her pocket handkerchief, or anything she asked"—who by a look can root a flimsy card-table to the floor, so that athletes tug at it in vain until she unexpectedly releases it—who, as a child, made herself "the terror of the domestic circle" by her invariably fulfilled prophecies of misfortune, accident, or death—who by merely placing her hand for less than a minute on a piece of paper, can produce portraits having "all the essential qualities which distinguish portraits by Titian, Masaccio, and Raphael,"—who can by a wave of her hand make the air harmonious with "arpeggios of invisible chords,"—who, above all, is under the spiritual guidance of a guru. [This is not the place to explain what a guru is; but it may interest

---

*"Incidents in the Life of Madme. Blavatsky." Compiled and edited by A.P. Sinnett. (London: George Redway.)

theosophists to know that as long ago as 1850 there was published in
the thirteenth chapter of the adventures of David Copperfield a description of a marine store dealer at Chatham whose usual mode of address
was, "Oh, my eyes and limbs! oh, my lungs and liver! oh, goroo, goroo!"
And we are told that "he was well known in the neighbourhood, and
enjoyed the reputation of having sold himself to the devil."] People who
have not yet "emerged from the bog of mere mystic incredulity" are apt
to say unpleasant things about such a career, however "substantiated
by a multiplicity of guarantees." Unpleasant things have in fact been
said; and Mr. Sinnett is moved in his preface to call those who say them

"laughing jackasses." A committee of the Society for Psychical Research, on the strength of a report from an investigator who actually "attempted the investigation of occult mysteries by the methods of a Scotland-yard detective," went so far as to compliment Mdme. Blavatsky on being one of the most accomplished imposters in history. Mr. Sinnett, however, offers on all the disputed points explanations which will be perfectly satisfactory to those who do not agree with the committee of the Psychical Society, which, he adds, "has stultified its own name by investigating an episode in her career as if psychical developments were so much ironmongery."

The "outline" of Mdme. Blavatsky's life extends from 1831, when she was "ushered into the world amid coffins and desolation," to the recent period when she founded the Theosophical Society in "a modest flat of seven or eight rooms in West Forty-seventh-street, New York," and subsequently scandalized the English colony in India by wearing a red flannel dressing-gown; smoking innumerable cigars; and swearing like a trooper—habits which are described with all possible frankness by Mr. Sinnett. "Her occult gifts," he tells us, "have not included the power of forecasting the vicissitudes of her own career," and her powers of memory are almost equally narrow; for she not only forgot the situation and lost the title deeds of the American property in which she invested one of her fortunes, but when questioned as to previous visits to London she has had to reply that, "as to names and numbers, you might as well ask me to tell you what was the number of the house you lived in in your last incarnation." This is the more to be regretted, as that portion of her career which Mdme. Blavatsky does not accurately remember is much more wonderful, wild, and romantic than the years since 1870, concerning which there is some evidence obtainable. It may, however, be taken as proved that Mdme. Blavatsky is an extraordinary woman, and that her Theosophy is a considerable advance upon spiritism, or spiritualism, or spookism, or kikimoreyism, as the "medium" cultus may, it appears, be indifferently called.

Mr. Sinnett's memoir is fluently written, and is free from unsympathetic scepticism. It is illustrated by a copy in photogravure of Herr Schmiechen's portrait of Madame Blavatsky, reproduced above. Theosophists will find both edification and interest in the book; and the general student of science will profit more or less by having his attention called to "the law of forced post-mortem assimilation," and the statement that "there is no such thing as the law of gravitation as it is generally understood."

Editor's Notes

■ Shaw received *Incidents in the Life of Madame Blavatsky* for review with two other books on 23 November 1886. His diary reports on 15 December that he was "reading *Life of Mme. Blavatsky*" and, two days later on the seventeenth, that he "wrote review of Mme. Blavatsky's *Life* and sent it off" (*Diary*, 221, 227).

■ A[lfred] P[ercy] Sinnett (1840–1921), English journalist and author. Educated at London University School, he became assistant subeditor of the *Globe* in 1859, and afterwards subeditor and leader writer on various London newspapers. In 1865 he was appointed editor of the *Hong Kong Daily Press*. Three years later he returned to London. In 1871 he went to India as editor of the *Pioneer*, Allahabad, and became interested in the theosophical movement, becoming a member of the Society in 1879. In 1881 he wrote *The Occult World*. In 1882 he returned to England where he became president of the London chapter of the Theosophical Society. In 1883 he wrote *Esoteric Buddhism*, and this was followed by two novels based on occult ideas, *Karma* (1885), and *United* (1886). In the same year he published *The "Occult World Phenomena," and the Society for Psychical Research: with a Protest by Madame Blavatsky*. He also wrote *The Growth of the Soul* (1896), edited a monthly review entitled *Broad Views* (1904–7), and wrote a play *Married by Degrees*, which was produced in 1911.

■ Helena Petrovna Blavatsky (1831–91), Russian founder of the Theosophical Society. Two years later Shaw was to receive from *The Star* newspaper two volumes of Mdme. Blavatsky's *The Secret Doctrine* for review. Stanley Weintraub recounts how,

> Uninterested, Shaw sent it to Annie Besant. The bible of Theosophy converted Mrs. Besant and changed her life. She would spend her later years in India, and die there as a great lady, having achieved a sort of Eastern sainthood. (*Diary*, 455)

Annie Besant makes the more extravagant claim that W. T. Stead himself gave into her hands

> two large volumes. "Can you review these? My young men fight shy of them, but you are quite mad enough on these subjects to make something of them." I took the books; they were the two volumes of "The Secret Doctrine," written by H.P. Blavatsky. (Annie Besant, *An Autobiography* [London: T. Fisher Unwin, 1893; second edition 1894], 340)

■ Masaccio [Tomasso Guidi] (1401–?28), Italian painter. He was a pioneer of Italian renaissance painting and influenced such masters as Michelangelo and Raphael.

■ Dickens's description of this particular marine store dealer is not flattering:

He was a dreadful old man to look at, in a filthy flannel waistcoat, and smelling terribly of rum.

- The term *kikimoreyism,* according to Partridge's *Dictionary of Slang and Unconventional English* (London: Routledge and Kegan Paul, 8th ed., 1984), 645, means "swank," "side," or "pose," (clearly not what Shaw means by it). Partridge cites J. Manchon's *Le Slang: lexique de l'anglais familier et vulgaire* (Paris: Payot, 1923), 172, in which it is defined as "de la pose; de la *gomme, viz.,* pretentiousness or 'showing off' "; whereas Shaw, in using it as a synonym for Spiritualism, seems rather to mean pretense, "phoniness," or sham.

11 January 1887

SOMETHING LIKE A HISTORY OF MUSIC*
[C280]

HAS the reader ever wiled away a few hours with a popular history of music—one of those innocent compilations which rattle one along from Tubal Cain's time to yesterday, when poetry and music, having coyly approached one another in Beethoven's Choral Symphony, at last rapturously embraced in "Tristan und Isolde," or, if you prefer a more whistlable instance, "Trial by Jury"? How learned we used to think the historian when he told us of how Hucbald discovered the delightful art of writing in consecutive fifths, often since independently struck out by amateur composers who never heard of Hucbald! What a capital story that was about Porpora keeping Caffarelli at a single sheet of exercises for six years, and then, when the pupil, as pupils will, ventured to ask for a song, saying to him, "Go, young man: you are now the greatest singer in the world"! What desperate hashes of biography, anecdote, and criticism answered for the history of modern music from Bach to Goetz! How the dark ages of the art were stumbled through on outrageous assumptions that there could not possibly have been more music then in the world than in the surviving treatises of the pedants! How ignominiously the Greeks were dismissed with the remark that they knew nothing of harmony! and oh, how all the newest composers used

*"A History of Music." By J. F. Rowbotham. 3 vols. (London: Trübner and Co.)

to catch it at the end! These books made, and still make, merry times for students who are not too desirous to learn anything important, as well as for the cultured art worshippers who feel extremely musical when reading about the great composers, and extremely sleepy while listening to great compositions.

Mr. Rowbotham's history is of a different sort. It will be to English what Ambros's "Geschichte der Musik" is to German, and Gevaert's "Histoire et Théorie de la Musique de l'Antiquité" to French readers. Mr. Rowbotham goes beyond these authors in claiming that it is possible, "by a certain divine intuition, to penetrate the secrets of ancient nations, which else must have remained unknown to us." Whether his intuitive account of the birth and growth of music is true history, will not be easily settled. It is a work of the reconstructive imagination; and all that can be confidently said is that it is plausible, fascinating, and supported with remarkable ingenuity, learning, and research, taking us back into ages which have left no records, and tracing the development of prehistoric music through a drum stage, a pipe stage, and a lyre stage, "which," says Mr. Rowbotham, "are, it seems to me, to the musician what the Theological, Metaphysical, and Positive stages are to the Comtist, or the Stone, Bronze, and Iron ages to the archæologist." Now, the reconstructive imagination, indispensable as it is to the historian, is apt to get itself out of dark places by the help of pure invention. Hence the extraordinary boldness with which Mr. Rowbotham exercises it is anything but reassuring. He gives nearly all his conjectures as authentic history, and offers his descriptions with the confidence of an eye-witness. He criticises the orchestras of the builders of the Pyramids as confidently as the musical critic of this journal criticises the last Saturday afternoon performance at the Crystal Palace. He helps us to a knowledge of the Greek theatre by the methods of the descriptive reporter and interviewer, and tells us about Sappho just as Mr. William Archer tells us about Mrs. Kendal. Yet it is hard to catch him speaking without warrant. Every detail is an inference, sometimes far fetched, but always conceivably right, from some hieroglyph or old instrument, or traveller's tale, or poem, or passage from ancient literature or extant document of one kind or another.

There is less room for doubt in the analytic part of Mr. Rowbotham's work. His discovery of fugue subjects and answers in Pindar may seem supersubtle; but the lines at least can be referred to for confirmation, although unhappily the Greeks had no phonograph to transmit

Pindar's delivery to us on a tinfoil cylinder. Nevertheless Mr. Row-botham is quite satisfied that he knows how Pindar pronounced and scanned. He gives "analytic programmes" of the Odes, and restores the lyre accompaniments according to rule. He finds in the strophe, antistrophe, and epode of Stesichorus the three divisions of the modern sonata movement: the strophe corresponding to the themes, the epode to the free fantasia, and the antistrophe to the repetition of the themes. He attributes the fact that Haydn, whom we fondly call the father of the sonata, put the epode between the strophe and the antistrophe instead of after them, to the divorce of music from dancing. His account of the evolution of rhythm, and of how poetry was danced into lines and melody into strains, is interesting, and fairly conclusive; and his view of the growth of the scale, though there is a missing link or two in the argument, is likely to serve us until some future writer improves on it. Comic songsters will be glad to learn that mankind has always sung in the key of G; but we are told nothing as to the pitch of this G.

Mr. Rowbotham's style is one that challenges special attention. In the second volume, which is entirely devoted to Greek music, he becomes saturated with Hellenism, and not only begins all his sentences with "And," as Edgar Poe did in his more affectedly written tales, but actually ventures on such constructions as "a voluntary omission for the purpose of producing a pleasing effect on the ear, which how it did so we cannot now judge." This sort of English is pardonable in a Greek or in Mrs. Gamp, but not in an historian whose native tongue is English. The effect of the "which" is only laughable; but the superfluous "ands" are more serious: they disturb, irritate, and finally infuriate the reader. On the characteristically rare occasions when an opinion is advanced doubtfully, Mr. Rowbotham's form is "the present writer seems to think," or "I seem to imagine." In point of grammar, the following sentence leaves something to be desired: "And how does Pindar play with it, and makes offers at it, as in the second line of the strophe!" The use of "bid" and "forbid" for "bade" and "forbade," is not even good Greek. However, as Mr. Rowbotham says, "to mince with exceptions is to miss the joy of generalization;" and it is joyfully and generally true that he writes well, even when he writes not quite soberly. Fine writing indeed he frankly goes in for; and it does not misbecome him as it would a less imaginative author. When he follows music into the domain of morals he begins to deal in epigram, telling us that "credulity is the flower of love, but scepticism is the offspring of hate," and that "imitation is a distrust of oneself, and a desire to be like other people. And it is Hesitation incarnate, and Cowardice transfigured."

The third volume of the history is as yet only promised. When it comes, readers of the first and second are not likely to leave it uncut.

Editor's Notes

- Shaw received *A History of Music* for review as far back as 31 July 1886. More than two months passed before his *Diary* for 24 October reveals that he "read Rowbotham's *History of Music* for review in the train" (on his way to and from a lecture he gave at Croydon). He was still reading it on 15 November, but was interrupted by the arrival of some Socialist friends. For the following nine days he was "still reading Rowbotham," and he finally began writing his review on 3 December. He finished this on the seventh, on which day, presumably, he dispatched it to the *PMG*. The summary of books for review in his diary erroneously records that he sent it off on 7 November (*Diary*, 207, 213, 218, 219, 227).
- [Reverend] J[ohn] F[rederick] Rowbotham (1854–1925), English music historian and poet. He was educated at the Edinburgh Academy, Rossall, and Balliol College, Oxford, where he took a 1st Class in classical moderations. He traveled for some years in Spain, Italy, Austria, Germany, and France, collecting information for his history of music, before being ordained in 1891. In 1892 he became vicar of Ratley, in 1895 rector of Huntley, in 1896 British Chaplain of Buda-Pesth and Hungary, and the following year vicar of Abbotsley. His final post was as vicar of Sutton Cheney in 1916. In addition to the above work (which was his first book), he founded and edited *The Bard* (1910), and also wrote *The Death of Roland, an Epic Poem* (1888), *The Human Epic* (1890), *A Short History of Music* (1891), *The Private Life of the Great Composers* (1892), *The History of the Troubadours and the Courts of Love* (1895), *The God Horus, a novel of Ancient Egypt* (1898), *The Epic of London* (1908), *The Epic of God and the Devil* (1911), *The Epic of the Swiss Lake Dwellers* (1913), *The Epic of the Empire* (1914), *The Epic of Semiramis, Queen of Babylon* (1920), and *The Epic of the Globe* (1921).
- Tubal-cain (as distinct from Cain the Biblical nomad and first murderer) is mentioned in Genesis as the "instructor" of every artificer in brass and iron. It was Jubal, his half brother who was the "father of all such as handle the harp and organ" (Genesis 4:21–22).
- *Trial by Jury* (1875) was Gilbert and Sullivan's second operetta.
- Hucbald [c.840–930], Flemish monk and musical theorist, credited with writing among other works *Musica enchiriadis*, which contains the first account of polyphonic music. However, W. Muhlmann, in *Die 'Alia Musica'* (Leipzig, 1914) established that Hucbald was not the author.

- Nicola Antonio Porpora (see page 168 above). This Italian composer and singing teacher from 1711 to 1725 was maestro di capella to Philip, landgrave of Hesse-Darmstadt. He acquired a tremendous reputation as a singing teacher in both Naples and Venice, numbering among his pupils the famous castrati Farinelli, Cafarelli [see below], Uberti, and Salimbeni. In all he composed forty-four operas, eleven oratorios, numerous masses and motets and a great deal of instrumental music.
- Cafarelli [Gaetano Majorano] (1710–83), Italian artificial soprano ("castrato"). He was a poor peasant boy who possessed a beautiful voice, discovered by a musician (Domenico Cafarelli) whose name he adopted in gratitude. He studied for five years with Porpora, who did indeed predict a brilliant future for him. His debut in Rome in 1724 was triumphant, and he later sang in London, Paris, and Vienna. He retired from the opera in 1756 and bought a dukedom with the fortune he had amassed during his career.
- August Wilhelm Ambros (1816–76), German lawyer and musical historiographer. He was appointed public prosecutor in Prague in 1850, but continued to devote his efforts to publishing books on music. The work mentioned by Shaw, *Geschichte der Musik* (commissioned by the publisher Leuckart in 1860), was his major contribution, for which he carried out research in the libraries of Munich, Vienna, and several Italian cities, but which remained unfinished in its fourth volume at the time of his death, and was completed by others.
- François Auguste Gevaert (1828–1908), Belgian composer and musicologist. His numerous scholarly writings on music are considered more important than his compositions (which, however, included twelve operas and three cantatas). Beside the one mentioned by Shaw, *Histoire et théorie de la musique de l'antiquité*, which was published in two volumes (1875 and 1881), perhaps his most monumental work was *La Melopée antique dans l'église latine* (1895).
- Comtists were followers of Auguste Comte (1798–1857), French philosopher and chief exponent of the positivist philosophy, which excludes metaphysics and revealed religion, substituting the religion of humanity and sociological ethics, based on history and designed for the improvement of the human race.
- Sappho, Greek lyric poetess, born in the middle of the seventh century B.C. in Lesbos, which she allegedly left for political reasons, ending her days in Sicily. The theme of her poems is love.
- William Archer (1856–1924), Scottish dramatic critic and author. Born at Perth, he was educated at Edinburgh University where he trained as a barrister, though he never practiced. While still at college, Archer became a salaried leader writer for the *Edinburgh Evening News*, and when, after a world tour, he settled in London in 1878, he began as dramatic critic on the *London Figaro* for three years, before going on to be a critic for the *World, Nation, Tribune, Morning Leader,* and *Manchester Guardian* newspapers. His translation of Ibsen's *The Pillars of Society* was the first of Ibsen's plays to be produced in London (in 1880), and a decade later he published his transla-

tion of all of Ibsen's prose dramas, followed by the complete works in 1906–7. When he first met Shaw is unclear: Shaw himself, in his preface to Archer's *Three Plays* (1927) mentions that it was "some forty-five years ago," which would make it 1882, a date confirmed, but not authenticated, by St. John Ervine, who claims that the meeting was in the winter of 1882/3 (*Bernard Shaw: His Life, Work, and Friends* [London: Constable, 1956], 112). The year 1883 is favored by Michael Holroyd (*Bernard Shaw*, vol. 1, *The Search for Love* [London: Chatto and Windus, 1988], 134), while Stanley Weintraub prefers 1884 (*Bernard Shaw: The Diaries, 1885–1897* (Pennsylvania and London: The Pennsylvania State University Press, 1986], 53). At all events, Archer it was who became Shaw's mentor, guide and friend while the latter was "deviling in London" [see above, Introduction]. Archer wrote numerous books about the drama, perhaps the best-known being *Masks or Faces?* (1888) and *Play-making* (1912). He also edited the works of Congreve, and wrote four plays, the most successful of which was *The Green Goddess* (1923).

▪ Mrs. Madge Kendal, stage name of Margaret Brunton Grimston, née Margaret Shafto Robertson (1849–1935), English actress. She was born in Lincolnshire, the sister of the dramatist Tom Robertson (1829–71), and displayed an early talent for the stage, appearing in Shakespearean roles even in her teens. By the 1870s she was the leading lady at the Haymarket Theatre. In 1869 she married the actor William Hunter Kendal [properly Grimston] (1843–1917), with whom she appeared in numerous (particularly Shakespearean) productions. She was created Dame of the British Empire in 1926.

▪ Pindar (c.522–442 B.C.), Greek lyric poet. He was employed by many winners of the Games to celebrate their victories. Although he wrote many kinds of verse, the only surviving poems of his are the ones for which he has been justly celebrated, namely his *Epicinia,* or triumphal odes, which exercised great influence on subsequent poets.

2 February 1887

*FROM MOZART TO MARIO** [C284]

READERS of the *World* will pounce avidly on these two volumes, in which their musical guide, philosopher, and friend, the unique

---

*"From Mozart to Mario." By Louis Engel. Two vols. (London: Richard Bentley and Son. 1886)

"L. E.," gives them his "Reminiscences of Half a Century," comprised, with characteristic indifference to ordinary computation, between the years 1756 and 1886. Dr. Engel is really an extraordinary man. His rapid surveys of the composers of any age leave an impression that there is not a composer of eminence among his contemporaries who has not confessed his influence; nor a European potentate who has not button holed him for half an hour's pleasant chat and wise counsel. Popes and cardinals have conferred with him at the Vatican; and he has been a spiritual father—sometimes "worse than two fathers," as the American humourist puts it—to all the queens of song in Christendom. The extent of his stock of second-hand epigrams (all the good ones are second-hand by this time) is only less remarkable than the capriciousness with which he ascribes them to the first historical or unhistorical personage who happens to occur to him as his pen runs on. Appreciating the ways of professional musicians as one who has worked and played with them without catching their illusions or losing touch with the unprofessional and unmusical world, he has learned to temper his partialities with a cynicism which is far more effective in the orbit of Mr. Yates's journal than a comprehensive philosophy could be. For he has partialities, and strong ones. He is a partisan of Madame Patti against Madame Nilsson; of Meyerbeer against Wagner; and of Rossini against the verdict of posterity: always writing hard at the Opposition save when, in short-lived moments of patriarchal calm, he rises above mundane strife, and, Jacob-like, gives to Tweedledee all that is left after the blessing previously accorded to Tweedledum. In explaining the intentions of a composer, he fortifies himself impregnably by the *ipse dixit* of the Master, just as Dr. Furnivall, by a simple citation of what Mr. Browning told him, or what Shelley told his father, dumbfounders all rival commentators on these poets. Popular ignorance of the subject which he treats places the public at his mercy. In a land where the majority of educated ladies and gentlemen will tell you with half-concealed pride that they don't know one note from another—where they are awed by such mystic words as "subdominant" and "diminished seventh," as Whitefield's disciple was awed by "Mesopotamia," a man as accomplished as Dr. Engel is more than a critic: he is an oracle.

   The book now in hand is introduced in a preface as "a child sent forth with its father's best wishes." Says "L. E." modestly, "Maybe its babbling will amuse; it has learned, if that be any recommendation, to speak the truth." Unfortunately for this position, the truth, in criticism, is a matter of opinion; and the child's opinions, like those of other clever children, are old-fashioned. A nurseling that has nothing better to tell us about Wagner at this time of day than that he "wrote music without melody"; wickedly drank his coffee from a golden cup; and showed the "blackest ingratitude to Meyerbeer," should be sent to bed until it submits to acknowledge its past errors. Yet its little heart is in the right place, for it assures us that "there is no mother who would not willingly give her all for her child, be she high or low born, from the lamented Princess Alice down to the poorest woman." A beautiful doctrine; but one has to be a child indeed to believe it and deliberately set it down nowadays. Very babyish, too, is the long inventory of Mdme. Patti's jewellery, and the apparent confusion of her wreaths, her rings, her bracelets, her hairpins, her fans, and her combs with her vocal and artistic accomplishments. The innocence of childhood peeps out funnily in the statement that Mdme. Nilsson "was born a little tow-headed girl." Among ineptitudes of another sort is a translation of *glissando* as a "sliding scale"; but one has to be both pianist and trade-unionist to catch the full flavour of its exquisite absurdity. A more commonplace blunder is the Englishing of "la propriété" as "possession," of course with reference to poor Proudhon, who no more "went so far as to say that possession is theft" than any Briton goes so far as to speak of his hat or stick as his estate. Even when on its own ground as a musical prodigy, the child makes a slip or two. When it declares that in the Nibelungen Ring the singers "have intervals to sing which it does not matter a bit whether they sing as they are written or not, for false they are at any rate," it is either talking nonsense or playing—not elegantly—upon words. To say that "just as Beethoven created the power of the orchestra in the concert-room, so Meyerbeer established it in the theatre," is to ignore Mozart and Weber. Even from the point of view of the mid-century Parisian, which "L. E." has never quite forgotten, it ignores Gluck.

Of Dr. Engel's two volumes generally, it need only be said that they have the merits and defects of the weekly articles which have made him known as a writer. Quaintly written, chatty, discursive, first-personal, and occasionally also pointedly third-personal, they are the fruit of native shrewdness, long intercourse with musicians, and desultory reading. Favourites are idolized, foes unsparingly pilloried, friends and heroes unconsciously belittled as they appear reflected in the mind of the musical man about town, which is the character frankly adopted by Dr. Engel for his purpose. The book is not, on the whole, edifying; but it is amusing, and contains scraps of information which musical biographers will find worth referring to.

Editor's Notes

- Shaw received this book on 23 November 1886, read it for review on 8 December, wrote his review the following day, and corrected it and dispatched it on the tenth (*Diary,* 219, 227).
- Louis Engel (n.d.), Shaw's predecessor as music critic on *The World.* In 1890, owing to an indiscretion, Engel hurriedly left the country, and Archer suggested Shaw as his replacement. As Shaw put it

> Edmund Yates . . . discovered that his musical feuilletonist was in trouble through an affair of gallantry that made the Continent more desirable as a residence than London. (Bernard Shaw, Letter to Frank Harris, 15 January 1917, *Bernard Shaw, Collected Letters 1911–1925,* ed. Dan H. Laurence [London: Max Reinhardt, 1985], 453)

In addition to the book reviewed above, Engel also wrote *From Handel to Hallé, Biographical Sketches* (1890).
- *The World* was edited by Edmund Yates. Shaw at this time was its art critic (from 1886 to 1889), and became Engel's successor as music critic in May 1890.
- In his scrapbook Shaw had underlined a *PMG* typographical error, "composer" (l.6) to indicate the omission of the "s."
- In referring to the American humorist who claimed to be "worse than two fathers" Shaw incidentally reveals the source of one of his own witticisms. In *Pygmalion* Liza Doolittle, complaining of Higgins's behavior toward her, says

> One would think you was my father.
> HIGGINS: If I decide to teach you, I'll be worse than two fathers to you.

- Kristina Nilsson (1843–1921), Swedish soprano. She studied in Paris, where she made her debut as Violetta in *La Traviata* in 1864. She had successful tours in London and other continental cities, and in America. She revisited America in 1883, in which year she made her debut on the opening night of the Metropolitan Opera House, singing Marguerite in *Faust.*
- "Jacob-like." Shaw means, of course, Isaac-like; for it was Jacob, who disguising himself like his brother Esau, received from his blind father Isaac his brother's blessing, leaving Esau to plead with his father for what blessing he had left (Genesis 27).
- Dr. [Frederick James] Furnivall (1825–1910), English philologist. Born at Egham, Surrey, he was educated at London and Cambridge, studied law, and

was called to the bar in 1849. He was a member of the Philological Society from 1847 to 1910, was its secretary from 1862 until his death, and in 1861 undertook editorship of the society's proposed English dictionary, which became the *Oxford English Dictionary*. He also became interested (through F. D. Maurice) in Christian Socialism and in social reform generally, met Ruskin in 1849, and helped to found the Working Men's College in London. He was a prodigious founder of societies: he formed the Early English Text Society (1864) (he edited numerous early English texts and ballads), the Chaucer Society (1868) (he also edited the works of Chaucer), the New Shakspere Society (1873) (he wrote the introduction to the "Leopold" Shakespeare), the Wycliffe Society (1881), the Browning Society (1881), and the Shelley Society (1886). Shaw too was a member of the New Shakspeare, Browning, and Shelley Societies. In a letter to Archibald Henderson, 3 January 1905, Shaw spoke of his reviewing days:

> I had quiet literary offnights at the New Shakespear Society under F. J. Furnival [sic], and breezy literary offnights at the Browning Society, to which I was elected by mistake, though I stood by the mistake willingly enough. The papers thought that the Browning Society was an assemblage of longhaired aesthetes: in truth it was a conventicle where pious ladies disputed about religion with Furnival, and Gonner and I (Gonner is now a professor of political economy in Liverpool) egged them on. When Furnival founded the Shelley Society I of course joined that; and we pulled off a great performance of The Cenci before we succumbed to our heavy printers' bills. (Bernard Shaw, *Collected Letters 1898–1910*, ed. Dan H. Laurence [New York: Dodd, Mead & Company, 1972], 487)

▪ The actor David Garrick (1717–79) related of the great preacher George Whitefield (1714–70) that "he could make men either laugh or cry by pronouncing the word 'Mesopotamia.' "
▪ The "lamented Princess Alice" was Alice Maud Mary, Grand Duchess of Hesse-Darmstadt (1843–78), second daughter and third child of Queen Victoria. No doubt she was "lamented" not only because she was popular and her death fairly recent, but also because her life had been somewhat tragic. The preparations for her marriage to Prince Louis of Hesse were interrupted by the sudden death of her father, the Prince Consort, whom she had nursed during his fatal illness; and her own death was from diphtheria contracted by nursing one of her own sick children.
▪ Christoph Willibald (Ritter von) Gluck (1714–87), German composer. Educated at Kamnitz and Prague, he went to Vienna in 1736, and was chamber musician to Prince Lobkowitz. In 1737 he went to Milan, where he became a student of Sammartini. Four years later he began to write successful operas; in 1745 he visited London, and the following year appeared with Handel at a public concert. He married in 1750 and settled in Vienna.

▪ Shaw in his scrapbook has indicated an omission after the word "Gluck," between the last paragraph and its predecessor, and written in shorthand the word "Omission."

3 February 1887

A SON OF HAGAR* [C286]

MR. HALL CAINE has written a preface to say that he wrote this novel on purpose; and now it is time to remonstrate. A guild must be formed—a guild of nineteenth century authors, with their imaginations out of long-clothes and fairly grown and educated—all sworn to write henceforth according to the following rules: 1. That the fictitious persons in their books shall not belong to the criminal classes. 2. That their property, parentage, and family relationships shall remain unchanged and unquestioned throughout the story. 3. That no two of them shall resemble each other sufficiently to make a mistake of identity possible. 4. That they shall have lucid and fairly cheerful intervals at least once in every five chapters. 5. That their actions and circumstances, though not necessarily possible, shall always be moderately probable. 6. That they shall bear their disappointments in love with reasonable fortitude, and find something else to talk and think about after the lapse of a week. 7. That none of them shall spend more than a sovereign upon letters, telegrams, advertisements, and railway journeys during one book. 8. That the heroine shall not be subject to fainting fits. 9. That if the hero be incurably addicted to using his hands when irritated, he shall be thrashed by the villain in a fair stand-up fight at least once in the third volume. 10. That persons whom the author does not know how to dispose of otherwise, shall be got rid of without railway accidents, colliery disasters, or cataclysms involving the destruction of many innocent persons. 11. That the deceased persons shall not leave ghosts or wills, or exact solemn oaths from the survivors; and that if they know any important secret they shall out with it at once to save trouble. 12. That nobody, living or

*"A Son of Hagar." By Hall Caine. Three vols. (London: Chatto and Windus. 1887).

dead, shall be capable of inventing, cribbing, or deciphering a crypto-
gram. 13. That all marriages shall be legal, and not solemnized in
Scotland. 14. That books shall not be written at all except under
irresistible provocation. 15. That the author shall not seek to mislead,
baffle, or excite the reader by the use of plots, or any cognate artifices,
but that a straightforward understanding shall be maintained between the two at every step of the narrative. 16. And finally, that the
story shall exist for the sake of the characters, and not the characters
for the sake of the story.

Under these conditions a civilized school of novel and drama might
be formed, and the lives of reviewers almost indefinitely prolonged.
But what would become of Mr. Hall Caine is not so clear. What excuse
would he have for his two heroes, one exactly like the other, although
they are not even twins, only half-brothers? How about his villains
with visions imprinted in features of fire in their brains and burning
there like molten lead? Would not the reviewer, smarting under
former injuries, mockingly exclaim, "Where be your certificates of
birth now, your Scotch marriages, your foundlings, your mistaken
identities, that were wont to set the countryside in a maze?" These
things are called by Mr. Hall Caine "the sheer humanities" [see preface: "This novel relies, I trust, on the sheer humanities alone"]; but
the phrase is hardly a happy one, except it be meant cynically.

So much by way of solemn protest against the sheer humanities.
Better swallow them now, and describe enough of "A Son of Hagar" to
enable any experienced novel-reader to guess the rest. Mrs. Ritson,
the wife of a Cumberland dalesman, has three sons—one illegitimate,
another legitimate, but not distinguishable from his half-brother in
outward seeming, and the third a thoughtful and cultivated person.
The illegitimate son has been lost in his childhood, and the others
know nothing of him. Hugh, the cultivated brother, becomes jealous
of Paul, and goes to work to ruin him. The lost brother, who has a
defective sense of proportion, wrecks a train in order to pick the pockets of the distracted passengers. Hugh contrives that Paul shall be
sent to penal servitude for the offence. After a while he grows tired of
his melodramatic villainy, which is indeed as dull and troublesome as
the most rigid virtue could be, and explains matters to the authorities.
He then dies, apparently by the mere exercise of his volition; and Paul
lives happily ever afterwards, while the unlucky Ishmael takes his
place at Portland. The story is full of plot and passion; the persons
concerned are never at ease and seldom in safety; nearly everything

takes place at night; and except for a little cockfighting and wrestling there is nothing but worry for every one concerned. This is just what many people like, and, though it would be useless and unfair not to admit that it produces in others an exasperation which has perhaps slightly biassed the judgment expressed in these lines, it will be understood that what are here feelingly disparaged as faults may from another point of view be regarded as delightfully exciting qualities. Mr. Hall Caine has imagination. Now there are two sorts of imagination: the imagination that imagines all things, and the conscientious imagination which submits to verification or strict deduction. Mr. Hall Caine's is of the former kind. His chief redeeming quality is earnestness. His intense grip of his story keeps it together in spite of its congenital unsoundness and extreme old age.

Editor's Notes

- Shaw received this book on 19 January, began reading it for review the following day, and it took him three days. On the twenty-fourth, he wrote the review and sent to off (*Diary,* 235, 329).
- In his scrapbook, Shaw altered in ink the opening sentence of this review to read as follows:

> MR. HALL CAINE, in a preface, says that he wrote this novel on purpose; and now it is time to remonstrate.

He also changed the third to last sentence, correcting it in shorthand, to read:

> Mr. Hall Caine has imagination, of which there are two sorts: the imagination that imagines all things, and the conscientious imagination which submits to verification or strict deduction.

- [Sir Thomas Henry] Hall Caine (1853–1931), English novelist. He left school at the age of fourteen to become apprenticed to a Liverpool architect, but three years later abandoned the project because of ill health and returned to his birthplace, the Isle of Man, and for a year he was schoolmaster at Kirk Maughold Head. Returning to Liverpool he contributed articles to *The Builder* and *Building News,* which brought him to the attention of Ruskin. He also joined the "Notes and Queries" Society, and made many other useful friendships in the late 1870s, most notably that of Dante Gabriel Rossetti, who, after Hall Caine's lecture on the poet in 1879, invited him to stay in his home. Rossetti died in 1882, in which year Hall Caine married. There were two sons of the union. He then worked for a while on the staff of the *Liverpool Mercury*, in which his first novel, *The Shadow of a Crime*, was serialized in 1885. Two years later, when he had settled in the Isle of Wight, his novel *The Deemster* (set in the Isle of Man) was enormously popular, and thereafter he produced a score of novels, which were translated into many languages, one of which, *The Eternal City* (1901), sold over a million copies, and several of which, including *The Manxman* (1894), were adapted to the stage. Shaw reviewed this last in *The Saturday Review* on 23 November 1895, pretending that he had never heard of Hall Caine, ridiculing the play, and saying

> Even when I put my personal distaste for The Manxman as far as possible on one side, I cannot persuade myself that it is likely to live very long. (Bernard Shaw, *Our Theatres in the Nineties* [London: Constable and Co., 1932), 1:252)

A year later, to his surprise, he was called upon to review a revival of the same play, this time declaring

> I do not see why Mr. Hall Caine should not write excellent dramas if he would give up wallowing in second-hand literary pathos, and realize the value of actual life. (Ibid. 2:265)

In 1892–93 Hall Caine visited Poland and the frontier towns of Russia (at the request of the Russo-Jewish Committee) to investigate the facts of the Jewish persecutions, and in 1895 he went to Canada to negotiate important changes in Canadian copyright laws. From 1901 to 1908, he was a member of the Manx House of Keys. Notwithstanding Shaw's view of Caine the writer, on 11 October 1909 a pamphlet by Shaw (*The Critics of the White Prophet*) was issued to the press defending Hall Caine's recently published novel *The White Prophet,* which had been severely criticized—according to Shaw because it dealt heavily with British policies in Egypt. Thus, he defended the novel more on political than artistic grounds, claiming that "Egypt is a leading case on which we shall have to fight the whole question of coercive Imperialism versus federated Commonwealths" (Letter to Gilbert Murray, 29 August 1909, *Collected Letters (1898–1910)*, 865). In World War I, Hall Caine devoted his energies to Allied propaganda. He was knighted in 1918 and made a Companion of Honour in 1922.

▪ The old chestnut of the illegality of marriages solemnized in Scotland had long been subject for comedy. It is, for example, the hinge of the plot in W. S. Gilbert's *Engaged* (1877).

▪ Ishmael was Abraham's illegitimate son, born of Hagar the Egyptian, expelled with his mother for mocking Sarah (Genesis 21).

▪ The Isle of Portland—more properly a peninsular—on the coast of Dorsetshire, England, contained a convict prison with accommodation for about fifteen hundred prisoners in Shaw's day. The shores of Portland are wild and rugged, and the place inaccessible from the sea.

28 February 1887

FIRST NIGHTS AT SECOND HAND* [C291]

MR. SUTHERLAND EDWARDS is, better than most men, in a position to make a considerable contribution to the history of the stage during as much of the latter half of the present century as any one is yet in a position to speak of with confidence. His experience as a "first nighter" has been great. He was not an absolute novice when he produced his "History of the Opera" in 1862; and since then there have been many "famous first representations." With some of these, notably the popular successes of Verdi, Gounod, Bizet, and Thomas, he has already dealt. But there remained the production of the "Niblung's Ring" and "Parsifal," at Bayreuth; Goetz's "Taming of the Shrew"; the commotion about Wagner when "Lohengrin" was produced in London, and popularly supposed to be an audacious novelty (it was twenty-eight years old in 1875); the earlier attempt (1870) with "The Flying Dutchman" at Drury Lane, when Mdme. Ilma di Murska and Mr. Santley sang in it, and its great popular success in English at the Lyceum six years afterwards; the second night of the Poet Laureate's "Promise of May" at the Globe with the famous oration of the Marquess of Queensberry; the production of "The Cup" by Mr. Irving; the appearance of the Saxe-Meiningen Court Company at Drury Lane; the first night of Signor Salvini's Othello; Messrs. Booth and Irving in the same play; and the birth of Gilbert-Sullivan comic opera on the first night of "Trial by Jury." All or most of these Mr. Sutherland Edwards could probably have chronicled with the authority of an eye-witness. Instead, he has given us descriptions of fifteen performances, nearly all of which took place before his own first night in his cradle. The result is a book which had better be avoided by those who are tired of Mr. Samuel Pepys's adventures with Nell Gwynne; who have already learned that "The Beggar's Opera" made Gay rich and Rich gay; who are satisfied that Handel's "Messiah" was first performed in Fishamble-street, Dublin; who have read Otto Jahn's "Life of Mozart"; and who know all about "Hernani," Théophile Gautier's red waistcoat, and Mdlle. Mars's not wholly unreasonable objection to calling her stage lover "her lion."

*"Famous First Representations." By H. Sutherland Edwards. (London: Chapman and Hall.)

Of course there are growing millions who have yet to learn these things, and to such Mr. Sutherland Edwards may be recommended for his light and unaffected style, his inexhaustible stock of more or less stale tit-bits for use as padding when he is gravelled for lack of matter, and his sense of the vanity of all criticism that requires mental effort to follow. As a musical critic he is conservative in principle, Italian and frivolous in taste. He began well as a faithful admirer of Mozart; but then the composer of "Don Giovanni" and "Die Zauberflöte" was a man of great range: you may delight in him for a knack that he shared with Offenbach, or admire him reverently for qualities that class him with Molière and Goethe, Praxiteles and Raphael. Not that Mr. Sutherland Edwards is deaf to all the notes in Mozart's compass except those within the Offenbach register. Though we may suspect at times that "Il Barbiere" is his favourite opera, we cannot suppose that he considers it as great a work as "Le Nozze di Figaro," or, to put it generally, that he stops short of perceiving that Mozart's capacity at least exceeded that of Rossini, Donizetti, or Signor Verdi. But this is almost as mild a critical achievement as the discovery that Mr. Swinburne is not, on the whole, so great as Shakspere, or that Miss Braddon's novels are of cheaper quality than Scott's. The two really crucial tests which the musical experts of this century have undergone have been the successive developments of the art by Beethoven and Wagner. Mr. Sutherland Edwards escaped the first; for by the time he took up the pen it was obvious to much less keen intellects than his that it was all up with the old estimate of Beethoven as an obstreperous madman who had attempted to conceal lack of melody by excess of discord. But the fashion of abusing Wagner on exactly the same grounds and in practically identical terms had just set in; and Mr. Sutherland Edwards's great chance as a critic was that of being beforehand with us in appreciating "the music of the future." The question for him and his generation was not of the relation of "Il Barbiere" to "Le Nozze," but of "Die Meistersinger" to "Il Barbiere." It was a severe but not unfair examination test; and Mr. Sutherland Edwards was plucked in the good company of Hector Berlioz and others who should have known better. His utmost concession was a relenting towards Meyerbeer, of whose works he has given some appreciative descriptions, which are very different in tone from his earlier allusions to that unaccountably striking composer. Now, to praise Meyerbeer is, in a manner, to affront Wagner, who hated the musical ways of the curiously gifted Jew. Mr. Sutherland Edwards would not have Wagner at any price; and the honesty of his opinion is proved by the courage with which he sticks to it now that he no longer has even the largest mob on his side.

Editor's Notes

- Shaw received this book on 6 October 1886, "finished reading it" on the thirteenth, and "finished and sent off review" on the twenty-first (*Diary*, 204, 206, 227). The four-month delay in its publication is unaccountable.
- H. Sutherland Edwards [see page 89 above].
- Arthur Goring Thomas (1850–92), English composer. He was a pupil of Emile Durand in Paris, and of Arthur Sullivan and Ebenezer Prout at the Royal Academy of Music in London. He later studied orchestration with Max Bruch in Berlin. His operas include *The Light of the Harem* (1879), *Esmeralda* (1883), *Nadezhda* (1885), and *The Golden Web* (posthumously performed in 1893). He also composed minor religious music.
- Ilma di Murska (1836–89), Croation soprano. She made her debut in Florence in 1862. Following a European tour, she was engaged at the Vienna Opera. Her first appearance in London was as Lucia in 1865, and she returned to favorable audience response, toured America and Australia between 1873 and 1876, and was again in London in 1879. She suffered, however, a turbulent private life (being married three times) and finally poisoned herself in a fit of depression.
- [Sir] Charles Santley (1834–1922), English baritone. He studied in Italy and London, and made his professional debut as Adam in Haydn's *Creation* in 1857. His operatic debut was in the same year in *La Traviata* (in Italy), followed two years later by his debut at Covent Garden in *Dinorah*. In 1875 he joined the Carl Rosa Company and toured with it, visiting America and Australia. In August, 1877, "ghost-writing" in *The Hornet,* Shaw described him as "the best baritone singer with whom the London public is familiar," and went on to praise him for retaining his English name. Ten years later he was made a Commander of the Order of St. Gregory by the Pope, and in 1907 he was knighted. He also wrote songs under the pseudonym Ralph Betterton, a volume of reminiscences and two books on the art of singing, *The Singing Master* (1900) and *The Art of Singing and Vocal Declamation* (1900).
- An uproar occurred on the second night of Tennyson's *The Promise of May* at the Globe Theatre on 11 November 1882. The play was perceived as an attack on Socialism, and since many early Socialists were also agnostics, it was believed by some to be an attack on free thought. Accordingly, the Marquis of Queensberry arose from his seat to protest in the name of free thought against "Mr. Tennyson's abominable caricature." Later he wrote to the editor of the *Daily News* to defend his action, saying

We Secularists and other bodies of Freethinkers are fighting now tooth and nail to be recognized as a body of people who have a religion and who have a faith. . . . What did I care about my missing my play? I wished to draw public attention and get my protest properly reported in the daily papers.

- Tennyson's tragedy *The Cup* was first performed at the Lyceum Theatre on 3 January 1881, where it ran for over 130 nights. It was a huge success, and scenically both authentic and beautiful. (See Ellen Terry, *The Story of My Life* [London: Hutchinson & Co., 1908], 213–15.)
- When he became Duke of Saxe-Meiningen in 1866, George II used all the resources at his command to reform the stage and create a theatre of the actual, the observable. His remarkable acting company, the Meininger, toured Europe from 1874 to 1890. In 1881 they appeared at Drury Lane, performing Wallenstein's *Lager*, Goethe's *Iphigenia,* and Wolff's *Preciosa*. In fact the press's favorable comments were made mainly on the costumes, the plays, the acting, and the scenery being regarded as below London standards. (See Steven DeHart, *The Meininger Theater 1776–1926* [Ann Arbor, Michigan: UMI Research Press, 1981].)
- Salvini appeared as Othello on 1 April 1875, at Drury Lane.
- Though his Othello was the subject of critical controversy, Iago was considered one of Henry Irving's finest creations. On 2 May 1881 at the Princess's Theatre, he appeared in the part for the first time to the Othello of Edwin Booth (1833–93), and the Desdemona of Ellen Terry. Up to June fifteenth of that year, Booth and Irving alternated the roles of Othello and Iago.
- Gilbert and Sullivan's *Trial by Jury,* as has been stated, was not their first collaboration, but their second, the first being *Thespis, or the Gods Grown Old,* which was performed in 1871. However, to *Trial by Jury* belongs the distinction of inaugurating the D'Oyly Carte Opera Company, which was to create the remaining twelve operas of the duo.
- John Rich (?1682–1761), manager of the Lincoln's Inn Fields Theatre, which first produced John Gay's *Beggars Opera* (1728) after it had been turned down by Colley Cibber for Drury Lane. Gay's letter to Swift of 20 March 1728, in which he says

I have got by all this success between seven & eight hundred pounds, and Rich, (deducting the whole charges of the House) hath clear'd already near four thousand pounds

suggests in the words of C.F. Burgess that the "traditional *bon mot* that *The Beggar's Opera* made 'Gay rich and Rich gay' [was] more poetry than truth" (*The Letters of John Gay,* ed. C.F. Burgess [Oxford: The Clarendon Press, 1966], 72).

- Victor Hugo's *Hernani* was revolutionary, introducing sonority and flexibility into verse, which had for generations been rigid. The battle that was fought over its first performance took place on 23 February 1830, and was allegedly led by Théophile Gautier (1811–72), who rallied the "troops" behind the flag of his rose-red waistcoat.

- Mademoiselle Mars [Anne Françoise Boutet Monvel] (1779–1847) was a leading French actress at the Comédie Française. She created the role of Doña Sol in *Hernani;* and when Victor Hugo refused to change the line *Vous êtes mon lion superbe et généreux*, Mlle Mars herself altered it to *Vous êtes mon seigneur superbe et généreux.*

- Sir Walter Scott (1771–1832), Scottish novelist and poet. Shaw's thorough familiarity with the more than thirty Waverley Novels (written between the years 1814 and 1832) is evidenced by his frequent references to them.

25 March 1887

(from) LITERARY AND ART NOTES, etc.* [C297]

Novelists beware! A parallel case to that of Duverdy *v.* Zola is afoot in London. A Novel entitled "Dr. Phillips: A Maida Vale Idyll," by "Frank Danby," has offended the Jewish interest in that quarter. Somebody who perceives in one of the characters a caricature of himself threatens an injunction against Messrs. Vizetelly and Mr. Mudie. The author has retained Messrs. Lewis and Lewis (of all people, considering the ethnological peculiarity of the grievance), and is probably rejoicing in the prospect of a capital advertisement.

Editor's Notes

- This brief note (part of an assortment of separate paragraphs of literary gossip) seems to have been the result of a chance meeting. On 24 March 1887, William Archer being ill with German measles, Shaw deputized for him at the Gaiety Theatre to review H. M. Paull's comedy *The Great Felicidad* for *The Manchester Guardian*. While there he met Augustus Moore, the younger brother of novelist George Moore, who walked with him after the show to Mudie's library, where he introduced Shaw to Julia Frankau. On the same day his diary records "sent off notes to *Manchester Guardian* and a note to *PMG* about the precedence given Mrs. Frankau's book" (*Diary*, 254). On 13

*"Dr. Phillips: A Maida Vale Idyll." By "Frank Danby." (London: Vizetelly. 1887.)

April, immediately following Shaw's review of Beatty-Kingston's *Music and Manners,* another of the *Gazette's* reviewers wrote a disapproving notice of *Dr. Phillips* saying "There are Jews and Jews, and even of the *Juif sensuel moyen* Mr. Danby's portrait is too aggressively unsympathetic."

• "Frank Danby" [real name Julia Frankau, née Davis] (1863–1916), Anglo-Irish novelist. Born in Dublin, she married at nineteen a wealthy merchant, Arthur Frankau (who died in 1904: the eldest of their children, Gilbert Frankau, became a novelist in his own right). She wrote journalism while still in her teens, and then published the book reviewed above, which was a great success. Two or three years later, she began to study old engravings, and produced three books on them, *Eighteenth Century Colour Prints* (1900), *The Life of John Raphael Smith* (1902), and *The Lives of James and John William Ward* (1904). Subsequently, she returned to fiction, her best known novels being *Pigs in Clover* (1903), which, like *Dr. Phillips,* enjoyed a *succès de scandale,* in this case because it lampooned a living person, and *A Babe in Bohemia* (1889), *The Heart of a Child* (1908), *An Incompleat Etonian* (1909), *Joseph in Jeopardy* (1912), and *Full Swing* (1914).

30 March 1887

A NEW NOVEL BY BERTHA THOMAS* [C298]

EDMUND SPARKLER'S ideal woman, "well-educated, and with no non-sense about her," has not yet been realized among lady novelists. They have gained the education (some of them); but they have not shaken off the nonsense. Perfect novel-writing requires nerve. Your pet characters have to be disappointed, disilluded, and bereaved without chloroform; and if they don't like it they must lump it. Your villains, sneaks, and selfish coquettes must have justice and even some sympathy: you ought to deal with them humbly, as George Eliot sometimes could, in the spirit of that prosperous Alderman who said, as he saw a wretch dragged to Tyburn, "But for the grace of God, there go I." In spite of these excellent precepts, when a woman who is not a George Eliot writes a novel, she knows no truth in maltreating her wicked puppets; and she will do anything to make her favourites happy. She will bring them wonderful strokes of luck to atone for their disappoint-

---

*"Elizabeth's Fortune." By Bertha Thomas. Three vols. (London: Richard Bentley and Son. 1887).

ments, and sweeter illusions to replace those which have been dispelled. As to bereavements, she thinks nothing of raising the dead in the last chapter, and restoring lost darlings to their young widows, without the least regard to the wasted sympathies of the reader, or to difficulties connected with the devolution of property which make such events excessively inconvenient. It is to this extremity of sentimental self-indulgence that the author of "Elizabeth's Fortune" has fallen. She had not the heart to do it. And yet how had she the heart to do it—to wreck a delightful novel, a model novel, a novel with no nonsense about it save this one luckless eruption that lays waste all the rest? But let the circumstances speak for themselves.

Elizabeth Adams is an orange seller in Bloomsbury. In telling her own story, she is hampered, like all fictitious autobiographers, by the necessity of explaining that she is beautiful and good without knowing it. She is promoted to the post of slavey in a parson's household. The parson's son comes home, and proposes, by letter, in these idiomatic terms, using his boots as a post office: "If you're game, so am I; and let's go along and get married before the world's a week older." Elizabeth cleans the boots, and makes them the vehicle of the following discreet reply: "The displeasure of your family, which you regard so lightly, would yet have been a dark spot on our felicity, which might have poisoned the stream at its source could I have requited your sentiments." Elizabeth gives warning, and casts herself on the world, which, agreeing with the parson's son as to her attractive appearance, makes room for her as a walking lady on the boards of a metropolitan theatre. She would have preferred Lady Macbeth; but experience has cured her of any genteel propensity to quarrel with her bread and butter. She takes what the gods offer, and eventually they offer her leading business. Thus far the story is a capital one—no mad bulls, no rescues, no murders, no suspense, no paragons, no demi-devils, nothing but life, truth, and humour. The reader, delighted with the author, declares her unsurpassed in her art. Suddenly a Mr. James Romney comes into the narrative and suspicion awakens. Elizabeth becomes grossly partial: she overrates the fellow monstrously. Not that there is anything against him: he behaves very creditably; but there is really nothing uncommon in him. However, Elizabeth, who has twice his brains, marries him; leaves the stage; and settles down as a poor officer's wife in a town which has a cathedral and a garrison. Two children are born; and then her James goes to India and joins an expedition which is presently killed and buried by an avalanche. His death is not perhaps an absolutely certain thing; but by this time the author has so gained upon the reader that the possibility of her taking advantage of this loophole to go back on him at the last moment suggests itself only to be disdainfully rejected.

The situation of the widow is interesting. As the mother of an English officer's sons, she is loth to go back to the stage. But she can do nothing except act; and there is upon her the tremendous economic pressure that forces us to do what we can do in this world, instead of what we would like to do. There are certain relations with the other persons of the story which heighten the interest of the problem. How is it solved? It is not solved at all: it is disarranged, spoiled, unmade, undone. The native servant enters, speechless with emotion. The widow stares wildly at him, an impossible hope maddening her. A manly hand, brown with the suns of Ind, puts aside the *portière*. And the reader, with frenzied, unprintable exclamations against the weakness and perfidy of novel-writing woman, dashes the third volume into the fireplace. No need for his wife [who thinks the end charming] to rescue it in order to make sure that James Romney has come back. The avalanche, the widowhood, the problem—all sacrificed to please puling girl readers, who know nothing of life, and would suspend the Bank Charter for six months for the sake of a happy upshot to a romance.

It remains to admit, as cordially as such a disappointment allows, that had the intrusive James been kept under the snow, this notice must have been monotonously eulogistic. The acuteness and delicacy of the character sketching, the subtlety of the strokes of humour, the catholic good nature, the observant avoidance of the vulgarities of unaided and uncorrected imagination—all these are manna in the desert of fiction. As to the style, it is so pleasant that one never thinks about it until pulled up by this odd instance of a negative that tempts you to condemn it as redundant: "That, of course, no more than whether I could play the fiddle, I could not tell till I tried."

Editor's Notes

- Shaw's diary records that he received this book on 11 February 1887, on which day he began reading it for review; he continued on the thirteenth and finished the following day. On 15 February he sent the review to the *Pall Mall Gazette* (*Diary*, 341, 329).
- Bertha Thomas (n.d.), English novelist. The daughter of Canon Thomas, vicar of All-Hallows, Barking, and granddaughter of Archbishop Sumner. She wrote numerous other books, among them *Proud Maisie* (1877), *Cressida*

(1878), *The Violin-Player* (1880), *In a Cathedral City* (1882), *George Sand* [in the "Eminent Women" series] (1883), *Ichabod: a Portrait* (1885), *The House on the Scar: a Tale of South Devon* (1890), *Camera Lucida; or, Strange Passages in common life* (1897), *The Lucky Sister, a Fairy Play* (1900) and *Picture Tales from Welsh Hills* (1912). She also contributed short fiction to *Fraser's Magazine*.

- Edmund Sparkler, in Dickens's *Little Dorrit*, is the son of Mrs. Merdle by her first husband. Before he marries Fanny Dorrit, Dickens tell us that he is

> monomaniacal in offering marriage to all manner of undesirable young ladies, and in remarking of every successive young lady to whom he tendered a matrimonial proposal, that she was a "doosed fine gal—well educated too—with no biggodd nonsense about her."

- It was John Bradford (1510?–1558), who said, on seeing the procession of condemned criminals, "But for the grace of God there goes John Bradford."
- Perhaps Shaw *did* remember the better part of this story: in *Pygmalion* (1912), Shaw's heroine (possessing the same name as Bertha Thomas's), though selling flowers in Covent Garden rather than oranges in Bloomsbury, also "invades" the home of someone of a higher social standing, and also is called upon to "act" the part of a Duchess. Freddie Eynsford-Hill, however, is hardly James Romney!

6 April 1887

*THE WORLD BELOW** [C302]

TIME was when a book with such a title as Mrs. Whishaw gives her newest novel would have suggested a journey in the footsteps of Dante or of the author of "Vathek." Nowadays every one will guess rightly that the world below is the parish of St. George's-in-the-East, the inferno to which, as we cannot help uncomfortably thinking at times, mere ill luck may send our favourite child any of these days. It is the home of persons of no more than ordinary ability who have neither property nor influential friends; and its seventh-circle yawns for those who have had both and lost them. From Mrs. Whishaw's

---

*"The World Below," By E. M. Abdy-Williams (Mrs. Bernhard Whishaw) Three vols. (London: Swan Sonnenschein and Co. 1887.)

dedication it appears that she has dwelt in this doleful place; and although she lived there "for fun," as the children say, which is a very different thing from having to stay there whether you like it or not, her testimony, as that of a sympathetic eye-witness with experience of a better life, is as good as any we are like to get under existing conditions. The story, however, does not all pass in the world below. Nor does it introduce us to much middle-class society, perhaps because ugly respectability is no relief to squalid poverty, and Mrs. Whishaw has therefore been tempted to refresh her imagination by pictures of rich, beautiful and unphilistine people, mostly fond of string quartets. That the rarest of these favoured ones falls into the abyss, and finds herself working for her living in Nightingale-lane (which, by the bye, is not half a bad place as lanes go in the neighbourhood of the Mint), need hardly be said; nor will the old novelistic hand be surprised to hear that she, after learning enough of the condition of the poor to reconcile her to a university-settlement sort of socialism, marries a baronet of that persuasion. But instead of conventionally returning to Mayfair and finishing in great splendour as Lady Bountiful, she remains a poor woman; her husband throws his title after his lost inheritance; and the end of the story leaves them as an honest working couple among the people whose cause they have made their own.

If all the chapters were worthy of the last one the book might be commended without reserve. Unfortunately they are not so. Mrs. Whishaw, by the terms of her dedication, shows that she is conscious of having missed the qualities which great energy and diligence alone can give to literary work. No one will refuse her on this score the indulgence for which she pleads on the ground of ill-health. Few readers, indeed, will perceive that it was called for. But there is less excuse for the compromise attempted between the old-fashioned romance and the modern study in sociology. Mrs. Whishaw begins as if bent on the latter. Then, with a sudden and quite needless misgiving that the reader is falling asleep, she hastily shakes him up with an oubliette in a ruined castle, and a murderous lunatic proceeding to fling down a young girl, who is rescued, of course, in the nick of time by her devoted lover, inspired by novelistic providence to look in just then. At which innocent device for plunging him into breathless suspense the reader can but laugh good-naturedly. Later on, Mrs. Whishaw, again suspecting him of nodding, sends a child down a seething mill-race; knocks its brave boy rescuer on the head; and brings its mother with sorrow to the grave: the whole being pure interlude, thrown in, as the elder Mozart put it, to tickle the long ears. But why not leave the long ears to be catered for by the purveyors of penny novelettes? Mrs. Whishaw underrates both her own powers and her reader's good sense by letting her grip of reality slip in such a fashion whenever she fancies herself gravelled for lack of matter.

Editor's Notes

- Shaw received *The World Below* on 19 January 1887, began reading it for review on 26 January, and was still reading it the next day, but did not finish writing the review until 1 February, on which day he sent it off (*Diary*, 236, 238, 329).
- E[llen] M[ary] Abdy-Williams [Mrs. Bernhard Whishaw] (1857–1914), English author. In addition to the above (her most famous) book, Mrs. Whishaw wrote *Two Ifs: a Novel* (1884), *For his Friend* (1885), and *Forewarned* (1885). Shaw knew her personally from Fabian Society meetings; and two years before, when he was engaged in a payment dispute with Swan Sonnenschein over his short story "The Miraculous Revenge," to be published in *Time* magazine, Miss Abdy-Williams, at that time editor of the journal, accidentally exacerbated the dispute by casually asking Shaw at a Fabian Society meeting to review Michael Davitt's book on economics for *Time*. This he did, but again received no payment for the work, Miss Abdy-Williams informing him that she understood that the Davitt review was to be paid for by a copy of the book in question. Shaw accepted this, though without his customary geniality, and later received a cheque from Miss Abdy-Williams for £1, which he kept.
- *Vathek, An Arabian Tale* (1786) was written by William Beckford (1759–1844). Its story of a man who sells himself to Eblis (the Devil) for a sight of the treasures of the pre-Adamite sultans is thought to reflect the spiritual pilgrimage of its author.
- Shaw himself was an interested researcher in the area of slum housing and the working conditions of the poor. As a matter of fact his last novel and his first play both concerned the former, and his third play the latter.

7 April 1887

MR. WILLIAM BLACK'S NEW NOVEL* [C304]

Sabina Zembra! How much sweeter it sounds than Maria Parkinson, or Daisy Cooper, or any other name from the roll-call of a real ladies'

---

*"Sabina Zembra." By William Black. Three vols. (London: Macmillan and Co. 1887)

school! It cannot be denied that when Mr. Black requires a name, a landscape, a studio or other convenience for his novels, he treats himself and his readers to a pretty one. In the story of which Sabina Zembra is the heroine, it does not get dark of evenings; but "the velvet-footed night comes stealthily over the land." The moon is no common white article with a man in it, but a golden one dwelling afar in a sky of pale rose-purple. And is not this a charming notion for a ball? "From the hall upwards and onwards there was no decoration but roses. Ropes of roses adorned the staircase; festoons of roses hung above the doors; masses of roses gave colour to the pale-gold ballroom; and on the supper table lay a bed of roses from end to end." Was a "ghost-white alabaster swan" needed to enhance such a scene? Perhaps not; but Mr. Black gives away such luxuries with both hands, and does not count their cost, which, after all, is to him no more than a few pennyworths of ink. What their cost may be to society if it goes too far in trying to live up to Mr. Black's novels evidently gives him no concern. Like Mr. Luke Fildes, who tells us that painting flower-girls as they don't exist is pleasanter than painting "casuals" as they do, Mr. Black smooths life and art for himself by making the best of the freaks of Dives; dealing gently with his failings; trying to correct his taste and soften his manners; and giving him a hint or two for his next season's at-homes. Why not? If there is anything wrong—and the affair looks a little queer from Lazarus's point of view—it is the business of the citizen and statesman to set it right, not the novelist's. Pretty sunsets, rose decorated balls, and rich people with lovely daughters whose names suggest some delightful specific for making the hair glossy and luxuriant, are at least pleasant. Then, since a novel's function is to please, why not make them a prominent feature of one's novels?

There is, however, one disadvantage—if it may be considered one—incurred by the author-voluptuary. The critics cannot take his work so seriously as that of the writer who faces disheartening facts of all sorts, and denies himself the consolations of romance, in the acceptance of his duty to make his work scientifically sound as well as entertaining. And entertainment is not exactly the same thing as flattery. A novelist, before striving to please, should bethink him that there are masses of readers who will not be pleased by anything sincere. Happily, these find a dreadful joy in being lectured, bullied, satirized, terrified, and—at need—flatly insulted. The pessimists have ever been the heroes of literature; and damnation has made more preachers popular than salvation. It pays to denounce society. Therefore the authors who encourage it instead do so under no sort of compulsion. Mr. Black might let fly at the West-end and its rose-decorated balls with Mr. Ruskin before him as an example of how safely and popularly that may be done nowadays. If he refrains, and even throws his weight into the opposite scale, it is because he is an imaginative Sybarite, whose ideals are sensuous rather than moral, and whose kindly disposition and refined tastes incline him to stifle the scientific instinct.

Let us then relax the scientific attitude, and humour our Sybarite by supposing that Kensington is Arcadia; that a polish of fine art covers all the sins of Dives, and that the ardours of generosity and affection are best exhibited in the lavishing of costly presents by people who have more money than they know what to do with. This gives us the environment of Sabina Zembra, who is beautiful and pre-eminently bland. A celebrated epitaph has taught us to expect that a lady who is bland shall also be passionate and deeply religious; but on these qualities Mr. Black does not insist: the blandness is what he harps on. Sabina is philanthropic and irresistibly loveable. Lindsay, a painter with a snug property, adores her. He is supplanted by no less a person than a gentleman jockey, Fred Foster, whose perfect health, perfect immorality, and perfect selfishness make him so exceptionally cheerful and thickskinned that he seems good humour incarnate. Him she marries, her Arcadian training having predisposed her to look leniently on gambling as a means of livelihood. Of course, she is dragged through the mud as far as a good woman can be, the moment his luck deserts him; but at this point he becomes so unpleasant that he acts as a crumpled rose-leaf in the bed of the Sybarite, who accordingly banishes him for many chapters from the story, and, on his reappearance, delicately slays him. Sabina's blandness, temporarily disturbed by the misdeeds of the unfortunate jock, returns; and Lindsay, who has won her esteem by sheer expenditure, and her pity by a cataract which, when its purpose is served, is neatly removed by a distinguished oculist, leads her to the altar.

It is a thin story; but it is told with a pleasant grace and shrewdness that well becomes a novelist equipped with all the culture of the drawing-room. Such culture, at its best—and Mr. Black has it at its best—is not to be despised. In the narrative of the courtship between the abnormally altruistic woman and the abnormally selfish betting man, there is a touch of genius—fragile and very self-indulgent genius, but still genius. It is only a touch: Mr. Black is far too fond of his dreams, his roses, his artistic furniture, and his millinery, to have any stomach for the struggle with real life in which the fictionist's crown has to be sought to-day.

Editor's Notes

■ Shaw received *Sabina Zembra* for review on 2 April 1887, began reading it the same day, and finished and sent it off on the third (*Diary*, 256, 257, 329). Even by Shaw's standards this was quick; and the review does bear some marks of haste, particularly in the punctuation.

■ William Black (1841–98), Scottish novelist. Black was educated at private schools and the School of Art in Glasgow; but he felt that he was a failure as a landscape painter, and, forced to make a living on the death of his father in 1855, he turned to writing. He began as a journalist, but wrote his first novel *James Merle* (a failure) in 1864. He then went to London where he made the friendship of the poet Robert Buchanan, and joined the staff of the *Morning Star*. In 1865 he married, but his wife died the following year, leaving him a son, who, in turn, died five years later. For a time he wrote for *The Star*, and also edited the *London Review*. In 1870 he became assistant editor of the *Daily News*, but soon was able to support himself and his new wife (whom he married in 1874) by writing novels. Among his many successful stories are *Love or Marriage* (1860), *The Monarch of Mincing-Lane* (1871), *Green Pastures and Piccadilly* (1877), *The Pupil of Arelius* (1881), *Yolande* (1883), *The Wise Woman of Inverness* (1885), *The Strange Adventures of a House Boat* (1888) [see page 420 below], *The Penance of John Logan* (1889), *Donald Ross of Heimra* (1891), and *Wild Eelin* (1898).

■ [Sir Samuel] Luke Fildes (1844–1927), English painter of genre and portraits and book illustrator. Shaw's comment ironically reflects the change that had come over Fildes's work. Many of his early black and white drawings— especially those he did for *The Graphic*—were stark with social realism: pictures of the poor and destitute. Some, like "Applicants for Admission to a Casual Ward" were turned into large oil paintings which increased his fame. However, after 1872 he took to painting fashionable subjects, finally being commissioned to paint numerous state portraits (of King Edward VII and Queen Alexandra, for example), and he was knighted in 1906.

■ The parable of Dives (the rich man) and Lazarus (the poor one) is in Luke 16.

■ John Ruskin (1819–1900) English writer, art-critic and reformer. Shaw in "The Impossibilities of Anarchism," praises Ruskin for seeing

> the whole imposture [the State] through and through in spite of its familiarity, of the illusions created by its temporal power, its riches, its splendor, its prestige, its intense respectability, its unremitting piety,

and its high moral pretension. (*Fabian Tract No. 45* [London, 1893], 26)

There is perhaps a gentle irony in Shaw's citing Ruskin as an example of how safely and popularly [attacking the West-end] may be done "nowadays;" for nine years previously James Whistler had won a libel action against Ruskin for condemning his painting "A Falling Rocket," for which, however, he was awarded only a farthing damages, the expenses of the trial forcing him into bankruptcy.

• The epitaph to which Shaw refers is undoubtedly that of Lady O'Looney, in Pewsey churchyard, which reads:

> Bland, Passionate, and Deeply Religious; also
> she painted in Water Colours, and sent several
> Pictures to the Exhibition. She was the first
> cousin to Lady Jones; and of such is the Kingdom of Heaven.

13 April 1887

TWO BOOKS FOR MUSICAL PEOPLE* [C306]

Mr. Beatty-Kingston, though he lacks that perfection of ignorance which enables many of our novelists to impart unearthly vocal accomplishments to their heroes and heroines, is yet not too deep in music to gossip with people who like to sport on the surface. He knows a good deal about executants, composers, and compositions; and he spreads out his information before you without insisting on co-ordinating it into some brain-breaking synthesis of *Tonempfindung;* just as he knows much of men and affairs, but is happily free from theories of human nature or politics. He admires music of all sorts, and instead of rancorously insisting on proving that the composers whose music does not happen to please him are so many incarnate principles of social decay, he saves his temper for judicious expenditure on ill-ventilated opera houses with uncomfortable stalls. His estimate of

---

*"Music and Manners." By W. Beatty-Kingston. Two vols. (London: Chapman and Hall, 1887.)
"Studies of Great Composers." By C. Hubert H. Parry, Mus. Doc. One vol. (London: Routledge and Sons, 1887.)

Gounod's "Faust" as "the noblest opera of modern times" may be a weakness; but it is an amiable and a popular one; and, after all, he does not make any pretence of being ready to go to the stake for it: perhaps he would say as much another evening for "Tristan" or "Traviata." A writer who describes an ellipse as "an oblong circle" must not be taken *au pied de la lettre*. On the whole, the musical public will find that Mr. Beatty-Kingston, as a pleasant gossip, nobly upholds the reputation of the Imperial Order of the Medjidieh, the Royal Orders of the Redeemer, Star of Roumania, Crown of Roumania and Takovia of Servia, the Imperial Order of Francis Joseph, and of the I. R. Austrian Order of Merit of the First Class, &c., with all of which he has, as we gather from the title-page, been variegated.

The decorators have not gone to work in this hearty fashion on Mr. C. Hubert H. Parry, who is only a doctor of music. He has composed sonatas, string trios, and a setting of Shelley's "Prometheus Unbound"; and as he is nevertheless evidently not in want of food and leisure, it may safely be inferred that he is a gentleman of independent means; for to the unpropertied musician who would express himself in the classic forms nowadays, society offers its pet incentive to honourable industry—certain ruin. Mr. Parry is a thoughtful writer, not pretentious, heavy, nor given to unprovoked metaphysics, but a library friend for all those to whom music is something more than a mere peptic to help away the dulness of after-dinner. Many a Philistine would be surprised, if not disgusted, at the number of perfectly serious people who owe all the happy and wholesome part of their experience to music. To these music does not mean the sum of the public performances they have witnessed. In the concert room and salon there are amateurs; there is the woeful fact that no earthly music is ever perfectly in tune; there is bad ventilation, fatigue, an unmusical neighbour in the throes of boredom, an uninteresting number in the programme, and a dozen other flies in the ointment. It is when, tired of work and of the world, the musician gets to his own pianoforte, that he has hours which all the desperate execrations of the people in the next house cannot interrupt or embitter. Less serenely lofty, but perhaps more agreeable to the other citizens, are the musical reveries into which the amateur falls when walking on his business through the town. His music then disturbs no one; and his involuntary gestures are rather attractive than otherwise to observant street boys.

One cannot help liking those modern enthusiasts in whom no doubt has ever arisen that music gained by the turn given to it by

Beethoven, the first great composer who deliberately introduced the baser elements of popularity into the symphony. To Mr. Parry, at least, it has never occurred that Haydn, shaking his head over Beethoven's early work, may have done so with prescience of the obscene musical orgies which are familiar to us, and which affect even their professed admirers exactly as brandy affects intemperate people. Beethoven was riotous because he liked excitement, and never could see why he should not indulge his humour. The experiment succeeded because the public liked excitement too; and consequently many pages of demoralizing mœnad music, fruit of the misdirected ambition and aborted genius of Berlioz, Raff, Liszt, and others of less note, are now figuring at their true level as plagiarisms in the scores of our comic operas. Wagner, who has been blamed for much of this, really rescued music from it. It is true that the Tannhäuser ballet music is a flagrant example of it; but then the Tannhäuser ballet music was an abomination expressly put forth as such—as a thing intolerable for any length of time by any man with a possibility of salvation left in him.

However, Mr. Parry was right not to mar his study of Beethoven by cavilling at the faults of his hero's qualities. Of his chapters on Bach and Wagner, it is high praise to say that they are adequate, whilst those on Weber and Mendelssohn are written with fine tact and just appreciation. The Schubert article is one of the best of its kind that has been written. Mr. Parry writes kindly and generously, even of Haydn and Mozart—no favourites with his school; and one cannot doubt that he is quite sincere when he writes that Mozart was indifferent to the quality of the librettos he set, mad as the statement appears to any one who has more than a superficial acquaintance with Mozart's operas. There is only one merely conventional remark in the book. It is to the effect that all Berlioz's orchestral effects were sure to sound as he intended. No one can possibly tell whether they did or not; and it is certain that many of them sound very differently at different performances. But this little carelessness is a very small blemish on a very pleasant book.

Editor's Notes

- Shaw had received *Studies of Great Composers* on 5 November 1886, and his diary records that he was reading it on 10 and 11 January 1887. Thereafter it is not mentioned until he writes the review, which seems to have been stimulated by receiving *Music and Manners* on 22 February 1887. This book he read on the twenty-fourth. On the twenty-sixth he "wrote review of Kingston's *Music and Manners* and Parry's *Great Composers*. Stayed in the Museum until 20 and when I got home sat up until 1 to finish and send off review" (*Diary*, 227, 232–33, 245–46, 329).

- W[illiam] Beatty Kingston (1837–1900), English journalist, poet, and composer. After spending his early years in the consular service, he became special correspondent for the *Daily Telegraph* in Berlin, Vienna, and other continential cities. He was present in campaigns of the Austro-Prussian, Franco-German, and Russo-Turkish wars, and went on confidential missions to Egypt, Turkey, Rumania, and Russia. From 1879 he was on the editorial staff of the *Daily Telegraph* and contributed verses to *Punch* from 1883 to 1887, many of which were republished in *My Hansom Lays* (1889). He also contributed articles to *The Lute* and other musical journals, and composed some piano pieces. In addition to *Music and Manners*, he wrote *The Battle of Berlin* (1871), *William I: German Emperor and King of Prussia* (1883), *Monarchs I have Met* (1887), *A Wanderer's Notes* (1888), and other books. He died on board the steamer "Albatross" on his way from Bordeaux to England.

- *Tonempfindung*, literally "sound-impression."

- [Sir] C[harles] Hubert H[astings] Parry (1848–1918), English composer, scholar, and teacher. Having obtained his Bachelor of Music degree while still at Eton (where he worked with George Elvey of St. George's Chapel, Windsor), he studied composition with Henry Hugo Pierson at Exeter College, Oxford, took his B.A. in 1870, and went to work for Lloyd's shipping register, while continuing his music study with Edward Dannreuther [see page 275 below]. The latter introduced him to the music of Wagner, whose influence is found in Parry's early compositions. Although he began publishing songs in the 1860s, it was not until the 1880s that he began to be well known, when his *Piano Concerto in F#* was performed by Dannreuther at the Crystal Palace, and a cantata, *Scenes from Prometheus Unbound* was played at the Gloucester Festival. Parry is known for his songs (both sacred and secular) and piano music rather than for his longer vocal works, or for chamber or orchestral music (though he did compose ten oratorios, a number of trios and motets, and four symphonies). His contribution to English music was not confined to composition: he wrote for Grove's *Dictionary*, and joined the staff of the new Royal College of Music, of which he became director in 1894. In 1900 he succeeded Stainer as professor of music at Oxford, but resigned the chair eight years later. In 1894 Shaw reviewed and declared his indebtedness to Parry's *The Art of Music*, a book in which the Darwinian concept of evolution was applied to the art of music. Parry also wrote *The Music of the Seventeenth Century* (1902) and *Johann Sebastian Bach: the Story of the Development of a Great Personality* (1909).

15 April 1887

*WELLERISMS** [C308]

(By the Rev. C. W. Stiggins, Junr., of Box Hill)

In detaching the utterances of the elder and younger Weller from the attractive framework in which Dickens presented them, the authors of this little book have rendered a service to English morality. That two men, illiterate, intolerant, sensual, ribald, and unseemly, should be idolized in the nineteenth century merely because their solutions of the most pressing problems of life were so inadequate as to be irresistibly ludicrous, is a strong argument against the modern fashion of encouraging from the pulpit the national habit of novel reading. The old but unreverend Anthony Weller, who, though well-to-do in his station, drove his son into the streets to shift for himself when very young; who, though himself so gross a feeder and tippler that he was called "Corpulence" in his own family, yet sneered at women for drinking tea, and brutally assaulted the guest who trespassed on his hospitality for a glass of pine-apple rum; who, whilst cowering before the woman who craved some better spiritual food than perpetual Wellerisms, forced a bout at fisticuffs upon a man greatly inferior to him in weight, and rendered incapable of self-defence by the machinations of two confederates who drove coaches to Oxford, and were experts in all disgraceful practices ["two friends o' mine as works the Oxford road, and is up to all kinds o' games"—see page 77]; who never attended a place of worship or [assuming him to have been an Agnostic] a scientific lecture—this unnatural father and ignorant and greedy scoffer, coward, and bully has outlived the toleration which his absurdity and the low ethical standard of his day gained him for a time.

Of Samuel Weller it need only be said that he was his father's son. He had the gutter point of honour—to have a humiliating repartee for all comers, the pothouse accomplishment of skill and readiness as a pugilist, and the true outcast-class instinct to resist officers of the law and prevaricate in the witness-box [see The Queen *v.* Pickwick and Tupman, Bardell *v.* Pickwick, and the disgraceful Boldwig affair]. His fidelity to his master is accounted for by the fact that he could not have changed his place except for a worse one. That he had no real

*" 'Wellerisms' from 'Pickwick' and 'Master Humphrey's Clock,' " By C. F. Rideal and Charles Kent. (London: George Redway.)

faith in Mr. Pickwick is shown by his evil construction of the mistake about the bedroom in the Ipswich hotel, and his instantaneous conviction of the justice of Mrs. Bardell's case, which he nevertheless did not hesitate to damage in court to the utmost of his power [see pages 19, 35, 84, &c.] Of honesty he seems to have had no conception; for he admits without apparent shame that when he wanted anything he asked for it in a respectful and obliging manner; but, if refused, took it, lest he should be led to do anything wrong through not having it— an explanation which proves that he was conscious of a murderous disposition in himself. In certain matters he was truthful: his disregard of the feelings of others and his indifference to their opinion of him led him to be frank on occasions when a more sensitive man would have been reticent; but as to his allegations concerning the young nobleman and the parlour door, the gentleman in difficulties, the parrot, the soldier whose evidence Mr. Justice Stareleigh properly declined to admit, the gentleman on the right side of the garden wall, the Lord Mayor and the Chief Secretary of State, the King dissolving the Parliament, the peer who obtained a pension, and other persons far outside the sphere of a valet who had graduated as a waggoner's boy, no one who has critically examined these will hesitate to reject them as fictions. They are probably not even original: a retentive memory, and the narrator's inordinate love of displaying his sharpness before an audience, sufficiently account for their introduction. There is absolutely no historical authority for the saying attributed to Richard III [page 42]. Even that "extensive and peculiar knowledge of London" which has been so much insisted on by Wellerolators shrinks on examination to a chance acquaintance with a peculiarity in one of the tables in a certain public-house. Of the treasure-houses of science and art in the metropolis, its temples, and its hallowed relics, he knew nothing. He was, in fact, at best a liar, a thief, a ruffian, and an ignoramus: and the sooner the foolish fashion of admiring him is dropped, the better for the tone of English society.

The Wellers were probably not indigenous Londoners. Comparative philology suggests rather a German Jewish origin for the family. [See p. 80, "Put it down a we, my lord," and other locutions of the same kind.]

Editor's Notes

▪ Shaw received this book on 23 November 1886, and wrote the review on 27 December, on which day he sent if off (*Diary*, 224, 227). This is the first instance in the book reviews of Shaw adopting a persona. The one chosen is particularly appropriate: it provides a most humorous view of the Wellers to see them through the eyes of the "son" of the intemperate and hypocritical evangelist who was addicted to pineapple rum (he was the "guest" who was "brutally assaulted"). The Reverend Stiggins Sr. was always surrounded by women (among them Mrs. Weller), and frequented the "Marquis of Granby" at Dorking, whence he was finally ejected by Tony Weller, and his head ducked in the horse trough outside!

- C[harles] F[rederick] Rideal (1858–?), English journalist and author. Educated in Lancashire, he studied medicine, and although he abandoned it owing to ill health, when he became a journalist (and an editor of *Life, London,* and *Magazine and Book Review*), he remained interested, establishing and editing *The Nursing Record* and *The Medical Review* and becoming involved in the foundation of the British Nurses' Association for enrolling hospital-trained nurses. He also founded the Medical Defense Union. He wrote at length and lectured widely on Charles Dickens. In 1887 he was elected Fellow of the Royal Society of Literature. With Mrs. K. St. Hill he edited the *Palmist and Chirological Review* from 1892, and under the pseudonym Freeman Morris he coauthored a number of plays, including *Cassock and Crown, Little Nell, Our Girls,* and *Lady Betty's Bracelet.* He also wrote *People We Meet* (1888) and *Young Ladies of Today* (1891). That Rideal was hurt by, and completely misunderstood the irony of, Shaw's review of the above book is clear from his introduction to its second edition, in which he praises the press reception of its first, claiming that there were but two exceptions, the *Pall Mall Gazette* and the *Athenæum:*

> The first named periodical, in one of its hyper-hysterical moments—it was thus very much troubled in those days—issued a fervent diatribe against the Wellers, and placing them in its journalistic pillory, called them a "deceitful, drunken, lying pair," with various other elegant allusions of an equally complimentary kind.

- Charles Kent (1823–1902), English poet, biographer, and journalist. In 1853 he married Ann Young, the eldest daughter of Murdo Young, owner of the *Sun* newspaper, of which, from 1845 to 1870, Kent became editor. He was called to the bar of the Middle Temple in 1859. From 1874 to 1881 he was editor of the *Weekly Register.* Kent was a prolific author and editor, some of the more notable of his works being *The Vision of Cagliostro* (1847), *Aletheia, or the Doom of Mythology* (1850), *The Derby Ministry, A Series of Cabinet Pictures* [under the pseudonym Mark Rochester] (1858), *Dreamland, or Poets in their Haunts* (1862), the *Gladstone Government* [by "A Templar"] (1869), *Kent's Poems, 1st Collected Edition* (1870), *Father Prout* (1881), *Wit and Wisdom of Lord Lytton* (1883), and *The Humour and Pathos of Charles Dickens* (1884). He was also a contributor to the *Dictionary of National Biography, Encyclopædia Britannica, Blackwood's Magazine, Household Words,* and *All the Year Round.*

■ Weller's comment on Richard III is "Business first, pleasure arterwards, as
King Richard the Third said when he stabbed the t'other king in the tower,
afore he smothered the babbies."

5 May 1887

THE COPPER QUEEN* [C315]

IT is not within the province of this review to inquire into the feelings
of Mr. H. A. Jones on seeing his Silver King trumped by a Copper
Queen. Miss Blanche Roosevelt, whose hand has dealt him this
stroke, is, it is said, that very Signora Rosavella who, some seasons
ago, sang with an ample but unruly voice at the Italian opera in this
town. It may therefore be concluded that the unruliness got the worse
of the amplitude, and that Miss Tucker—for such was the open secret
of her real name—has relinquished her prospects as a personally
attractive but vocally inefficient *prima donna* to become the most
recklessly entertaining lady novelist at present before the public.

It is difficult to describe "The Copper Queen." To praise it would
be treason to Literature: to condemn it would belie the sensation of
reading it. For pure folly, its description of the Princess of Wales at a
ball in Buckingham Palace, could hardly be surpassed. The heroine
"knew that she" [the Princess] "was a woman and mother, yet could
much easier [*sic*] fancy her a vestal kneeling at some shrine. . . . No
other woman in England could touch her for the way she puts on
her clothes." For flippant brutality, it would be hard to match the
description of a trial for murder as "the most interesting affair since
Washington interviewed that cherry tree, or Wilkes Booth immortalized a family of hitherto only passable comedians by his Good Friday
impromptu in Ford's old Baltimore Theatre." Of unscrupulous sarcasm a completer specimen could not be desired than the following
conclusion of a striking description of the great fire of Chicago. "The
calamity had indeed been terrible; but the ruin to the city, the national and individual loss, was nothing compared to the personal

---

*"The Copper Queen." By Blanche Roosevelt. Three volumes. (London: Ward and
Downey).

satisfaction felt by every human being in the town when it was realized beyond a doubt that the greatest fire the world had ever known had taken place in Chicago." And for bad taste, the remark that prima donnas "all begin by singing 'Traviata' at Covent Garden and end by acting it in the Haymarket" is astonishing even from the cynical villain in whose mouth it is placed. This villain, by the by, himself begins by being "transported for criminal complication in a murder," and ends by dying "of his first violent and sustained effort at telling the truth." The hero is an English gentleman. How English Miss Roosevelt has succeeded in making him appear, may be gathered from his exclamation: "Me a farmer! Oh bother it! why can't I have everything I want in this world anyway?"

Without admitting that any qualities can excuse faults like these, it is but just to add that the book has a certain irreverent shrewdness, humour, and candour which make its undeniable rowdiness captivating. The dialogue, well salted with American smartness, is vivacious and realistic even in situations such as most commonly induce artificial speechifaction. The sketches of plutocratic society, in spite of exaggeration and hoydenish ridicule, are irresistibly convincing. The extremely incorrect style is also extremely graphic. The judgments, ignorant and rash as many of them are, evidently come from an acute and impressionable writer who has been about in the world, and has seen the outside of life in a variety of phases. If there is as yet no deep insight to character, there is at least a shrewd sense of difference in personality; for all the persons in the story are sharply distinguished from one another. And there are points at which Miss Roosevelt shows a sincerity, good nature, right feeling, and even common sense, which, with some earnest cultivation, might be trusted not to abandon her so often and so suddenly as they do at present. To advise her to write another book would be to assume an unbearable responsibility; but there is at least nothing of bitterness in the reflection that she is very likely to persevere in her latest profession without the slightest regard to anybody's advice.

Editor's Notes

- Shaw received this book on 26 November 1886, read it for review on 16 April 1887, and wrote and dispatched his review on twenty-five (*Diary*, 227, 260, 262).

▪ Blanche Roosevelt [née Tucker] (n.d.), American author and singer. Educated in Virginia, she made her first appearance in opera at Covent Garden, London, in *La Traviata* on 23 April 1876. Thenceforth she sang in light opera, achieving a success in the first production of Gilbert and Sullivan's *The Pirates of Penzance* at the Fifth Avenue Theatre, New York. She abandoned the stage and took to literature, her most popular books being on musical subjects, and became the correspondent and friend of Browning, Lord Lytton, and Longfellow. In addition to the book reviewed above, she wrote *The Home Life of Henry W. Longfellow* (1882), *Marked 'In Haste': a Story of To-Day* (1883), *Stage Struck; or, She Would be an Opera Singer* (1884), *The Life and Reminiscences of Gustav Doré* [for which she received a decoration from the French academy] (1885), *Verdi, Milan and Othello* [which made her name known in Europe as an author] (1887), *Hazel Fane and Elizabeth of Roumania* (1891), and *Familiar Faces* (1895).

▪ Henry Arthur Jones (1851–1929), English dramatist. Four years earlier, in 1882, *The Silver King*, which he wrote in collaboration with Henry Herman, was his first great success. In all he wrote some sixty plays, many of which, like *Saints and Sinners* (1884), *The Middleman* (1889), *The Case of Rebellious Susan* (1894), *Michael and his Lost Angel* (1896), and *The Liars* (1897), were performed by the leading actors of the day and were extremely popular. In the eighties he gained a reputation for being avant-garde, and his plays were frequently praised by Shaw who was present at the first nights of many of them. He thought sufficiently highly of Jones's craft in this year (1887) to suggest to Archer that their own unfinished collaborative effort (subsequently entitled *Widowers' Houses*) should be given to H. A. Jones, who might borrow a notion from it for a drama touching socialism (*Diary*, 228). Shaw had met Jones personally for the first time on 4 May 1885, and thereafter a friendship developed which lasted until the first World War, when it crumbled. Jones's anger at Shaw was exacerbated by the removal of his still successfully running play *The Lie* (1922) from the New Theatre to make way for Shaw's *Saint Joan* in 1924.

28 May 1887

WAGNER ON ORCHESTRAL CONDUCTING*
[C319]

WHEN this little work was published at Leipzig in 1869, it was not worth any publisher's while to have it translated into English. To the

---

*"On Conducting." By Richard Wagner. Translated by Edward Dannreuther. (London: W. Reeves.) 1887

few who had then heard of him here, Wagner was known as a pretentious and quarrelsome person who persisted, on principle, in writing ugly music in spite of repeated failure, and who had been dropped by the Philharmonic Society (admittedly the greatest authority on music in the world) after a couple of trials as conductor. Times have changed now with a vengeance. No other music than his can be depended on to draw large audiences to orchestral concerts; the intensity of Beethoven's popularity is waning as that of the newer tone poet's waxes; and selections and arrangements from his operas take precedence of symphonies and concertos in programmes that are nothing if not classical. And this concise treatise of his on orchestral conducting will be sought for to-day as a monograph, unique of its kind, by the greatest composer, conductor, and critic of our own time.

It is perhaps as well to explain that "Ueber das Dirigiren" is not an academic text-book of time-beating. It does not offer diagrams supposed to be traced by a bâton indicating four in a bar, six in a bar, &c.; nor advice as to how to manage the three simultaneous dances in "Don Giovanni." Nor does it contain the slightest recognition of that adroitness in driving inefficient orchestras through scratch performances which many professional musicians, and even some critics, regard as the first and last qualification of a conductor. "The whole truth of the matter is," says Wagner, "that in a proper performance the conductor's part is to give always the proper tempo." His insistence on this may do us some service; for we suffer much from conductors who can do everybody else's business in the orchestra so well—even to counting their rests for them, and showing them how to finger difficult passages—that no one dares to hint that their own special function of choosing the proper tempo is never successfully discharged when really great work is in hand. The illustrations given from the "Freischütz" overture, the Eroica, C minor, and choral symphonies, and Mozart's symphony in E flat will come home to all loving students of these works. It is as true here as in Germany that, "if music depended on our conductors, it would have perished long ago." How well, too, we have reason to groan with Wagner at the habitual opera mutilation which provoked such a passage as "Cut! Cut!—this is the *ultima ratio* of our conductors: the pleasant and never-failing means of accommodating to their own incompetence the artistic tasks which they find impossible." Again—"They have no notion that, with even the most insignificant opera, a comparatively satisfactory effect on educated minds can be secured by correctness and completeness in performance." Does Mr. Carl Rosa agree here; and if so, would it be too much to ask him to give us "Lohengrin," if not complete, at least without such butcherly cuts as that sometimes made in the instrumental prelude to the second act? Much that Wagner has said about famous orchestras trading on the departed excellence they were wrought up to by some deceased or seceded conductor, might have been written of the Covent Garden orchestra when, though some of its nightly performances would have disgraced a circus, it was still generally spoken and even written of, as the first orchestra in England, merely because it had been so under the direction of Costa, who had then returned to the rival house, and had of course taken the orchestral supremacy with him. To this day there are people who talk of the Covent Garden orchestra as if there were in the neighbouring cabbages a musical magic of which nothing could rob a band in Bow-street.

The disappointing impressions which Wagner complains of having received from public performances of classical music in his earliest youth were common and indeed inevitable experiences in London before he brought Herr Richter to conduct his festivals at the Albert Hall. The new conductor certainly had his work cut out for him. He had to reveal Wagner; to save Beethoven from vulgarization; and to restore Mozart, whose music was almost extinct. For when Herr Richter first conducted the great Symphony in E flat here, concert goers had fallen into the habit of expecting nothing from Mozart but a certain vapid liveliness—the English phase of that "Mattigkeit der Mozartschen Kantilene" which so astonished Wagner when he, too, began to suffer from incompetent conductors. That such a difference could have been made by merely changing the man who noiselessly waved the stick has puzzled many people and reduced them either to incredulity or to irrelevant statements—offered with an explanatory air—as to Herr Richter's extraordinary memory and his practical acquaintance with the art of playing the horn. Those who desire some more intelligent account of what constitutes a good conductor will find it in this book, which will, it is to be hoped, be read or re-read by the expert as well as by the general reader and the student. Mr. August Manns, for example, might take, as to the slow movement of the Ninth Symphony, a hint from Wagner which would come as an impertinence from any ordinary critic. And Sir Arthur Sullivan might find something to interest him in the trenchant passages in which Wagner points out that the modern Mendelssohnian "culture," with all its refinement, its elegance, its reticence, and its "chastity," is far too negative to equip a conductor for a struggle with Bach or Beethoven.

Mr. Edward Dannreuther is not responsible for the wording of all the passages quoted above. His version of them, though adequate when taken with the context, happened to be inconvenient for quotation. The variations are therefore by no means offered as improvements. Mr. Dannreuther has done his manuscript very conscientiously, and with an evident sense of its being well worth doing for its own sake. The acknowledgment must, however, be strictly limited to the manuscript. "Procrustus" and "ultimo ratio" are only mild examples of the results of careless proof correction, undiscovered even by the compiler of the list of errata, which is itself an inexcusable adjunct to a book of one hundred and twenty-two pages.

Editor's Notes

- Shaw received this book on 13 April 1887, on which day he began reading it. He began his review on the eighteenth, but "found that I could not work." On the nineteenth his diary again reports that he was "reviewing Wagner's *Ueber das Dirigiren*," and the following day he finished and sent it off (*Diary*, 259, 260, 261, 329).
- Wilhelm Richard Wagner (1813–83), German composer, musical theorist, and originator of the music drama. Shaw never ceased to let his critics know that he had recognized Wagner's genius before many others. Dan Laurence reminds us that, even as Shaw was praising Wagner as a great musician, profound thinker, and moralist, Ruskin

> was proclaiming that "of all the affected, sapless, soulless, beginningless, endless, topless, bottomless, topsiturviest, scrannelpipiest, tongs and boniest doggrel of sounds I ever endured the deadliness of, that eternity of nothing [*Die Meistersinger*] was the deadliest." (Bernard Shaw, *How to Become a Musical Critic*, ed. with an introduction by Dan H. Laurence [London: Rupert Hart-Davis, 1960], xix.)

- Edward Dannreuther (1844–1905), German pianist and music scholar. Born in Strasbourg, he went with his parents at the age of five to Cincinnati, where he studied with F. L. Ritter. Later he was to visit the United States several times. From 1859 to 1863 he studied at the Leipzig Conservatory with Richter, Moscheles, and Hauptmann. He made his debut in London in 1863, and subsequently introduced into England the piano concertos of Liszt, Grieg, and Tschaikowsky. In 1872 he founded the London Wagner Society, whose concerts he then conducted for two years. In 1895 he became a professor at the Royal Academy of Music. He also wrote numerous articles, particularly on Richard Wagner.
- Carl Rosa [Karl Rose] (1842–89), German-born opera impresario. Born in Hamburg, at the age of twelve he was touring Germany, England, and Denmark as a violin virtuoso. He furthered his studies in Leipzig and Paris before

becoming concertmaster at Hamburg from 1863 to 1865. He gave concerts in England and the United States. In 1867 he married the singer Euphrosyne Parepa. Together they organized an English opera company, which toured the United States until 1871, when it returned to London. His wife died in 1874, after which he formed the Carl Rosa Opera Company, which was an important part of English cultural life for many years.

▪ [Sir] Michael [properly Michele] Costa (1806–84), Italian composer and conductor of Spanish parentage. He was born in Naples, studying first with his grandfather, then his father, both composers, afterwards at the Naples Conservatory. The four operas he wrote during this time, all performed in Naples, were well received. His introduction to England was, however, unfortunate: at the Birmingham Music Festival, because he was thought too young, he was forbidden to conduct Zingarelli's *Super Flumina Babilonis* (although it was at the composer's request that he had come to conduct it). For his fee he was forced to sing a tenor part in the piece, which he did indifferently. Notwithstanding this inauspicious debut, he decided to stay in England, and in 1830 was engaged as *maestro al cembalo* at the King's Theatre, London. In 1832 he became music director; in 1833 music director and conductor. His three ballets performed during this period were also well received, *Kenilworth* (1831), *Une Heure à Naples* (1832), and *Sir Huon* (1833). He also produced two operas in London, a revision of an earlier work *Malvina*, called *Malek Adel* in 1837, and *Don Carlos* in 1844. In 1846 he became conductor of the Philharmonic and of the Royal Italian Opera; from 1849 he was the regular conductor of the Birmingham, and also the Handel Festivals. In 1869 he was knighted, and was appointed "director of the music, composer and conductor" at Her Majesty's Opera, Haymarket, from 1871 until 1881. Shaw thought highly enough of him to say in 1922

> Since Sir Michael Costa no conductor has been able to give such an air to a concert as Eugene Goossens. (Bernard Shaw, Letter to Harriet Cohen, 1 April 1922, *Bernard Shaw Collected Letters, 1911–1925,* ed. by Dan H. Laurence [London: Max Reinhardt, 1985], 767)

▪ Hans Richter (1843–1916), German conductor. Born in Hungary, he studied in Vienna the violin and the French horn, and for four years was a horn player in a Viennese orchestra. He met Wagner at Triebschen in 1866, and this revolutionized his career; he became one of Wagner's favorite conductors, and frequently prepared rehearsals of the latter's operas. Wagner chose him to conduct the entire *Ring des Nibelungen* at the Bayreuth Festival in 1876. Accompanying Wagner to London in 1877, he conducted several Wagner Festival concerts at the Royal Albert Hall, and in May 1879 this became an annual event known as "The Orchestral Festival Concerts," and later simply as the "Richter Concerts," which he continued to conduct until 1897. In that year he became conductor of Manchester's Hallé Orchestra. He also regularly conducted at the Birmingham Festival, and the Wagner Operas at

Covent Garden. He gave his farewell concert with the Manchester Symphony Orchestra in 1911.

- "Mattigkeit der Mozartschen Kantilene," literally the "weariness with Mozartian cantilena (or melody)."
- [Sir] August Manns (1825–1907), German-English bandmaster and conductor. Born near Stettin, he learned to play violin, clarinet, and flute, and after conducting several bands in Germany, went to London in 1854, became conductor at the Crystal Palace, and began the famous series of Saturday Concerts there, which he conducted for forty-five seasons, until 1901. He became a celebrated figure in London, and was knighted in 1903.
- [Sir] Arthur Sullivan [see page 124 above], whose knighthood was exactly four years old, was, in addition to being a composer, a popular conductor. He conducted the Leeds Festival for twenty years.

31 May 1887

DARWIN DENOUNCED* [C320]

WE are such an inveterately idolatrous people that it would perhaps be well for us if we could go back frankly to the cultus of the graven image, and leave our great men unworshipped. It would take the conceit out of them and do the graven images no harm. Better to adore in silence the brazen effigy in Parliament-square, as do the Primrose Leaguers, than to falsify and pervert, and exaggerate, and gloze, and special-plead in defence of our favourite geniuses, or in impeachment of those of our neighbours. We are overburdened with gods and sects: our Walhalla is as disorderly as the Church of the Holy Sepulchre, in which Moslem soldiers keep the Christian worshippers from coming to blows with one another, would be without the soldiers. We are Gladstonians, Wagnerians, Pasteurians, Burne-Jonesians, Browningites, Marxites, Darwinians, or else we belong to the simply heathen majority.

In "Luck, or Cunning?" we read of "greater nonsense than it would be prudent even for him [Darwin] to write"; of the years that it will take "to get evolution out of the mess in which Mr. Darwin left it"; of a work [Lamarck's "Philosophie Zoologique"] which, though weighted

*"Luck, or Cunning?" By Samuel Butler. "Op.8." One volume. (London: Trübner and Co. 1887.)

with "defects, shortcomings, and mistakes," is yet "an incomparably sounder work than the 'Origin of Species' "; of how Mr. Darwin first grossly misrepresented Buffon and then told him to go away; of a suave but "singularly fraudulent passage" as to Robert Chambers; all capped by two declarations at which Mr. Grant Allen will hardly refrain from rending his clothes. "For myself," says Mr. Butler, "I know not which most to wonder at—the meanness of the writer himself, or the greatness of the service that, in spite of that meanness, he unquestionably rendered." And, again, "I know no more pitiable figure in either literature or science." After this, it is not surprising to learn that Mr. Butler has been "very angrily attacked," and that he has, "as a matter of business," made himself "as unpleasant as he could in his rejoinders."

The usual etiquette of scientific controversy is to shake hands fulsomely with your adversary for at least fifteen minutes, and then seize the first opportunity of hitting him below the belt, taking care to wrangle over his complaint of unfair treatment with the utmost acrimony and ill humour. Mr. Butler omits the handshaking, and falls to fairly intended blows at once, choosing to be frankly unamiable rather than hypocritically considerate. The question at issue is—granted the survival of the fittest, were the survivors made fit by mere luck, or did they fit themselves by cunning? Mr. Butler is for cunning; and he will have it that Darwin was all for luck. The quarrel is a pretty one; for if you decide in favour of cunning, the Darwinian will reply that it was a great piece of luck in the survivor to have that cunning; whereas, if you back luck, the Lamarck-Butlerian will urge that the survivor must have had the cunning to turn his luck to account. Now, evidently the essence of pure luck is that it brings more than average good fortune without the exercise of more than average ability. Luck is luck only in so far as it is independent of cunning. Otherwise luck and cunning are convertible terms, in which case the dispute is about words, not about ideas. This is not Mr. Butler's view. He admits pure luck as a factor in evolution, but denies its sufficiency as an explanation of all the phenomena, and insists that organisms that have the luck to be cunning make further luck for themselves by the deliberate exercise of that cunning, and so introduce design into the universe—not design as we used to conceive it, all-foreseeing from the first, but "a piecemeal, *solvitur ambulando* design," which, as it becomes more self-conscious and intelligent, tends to supplant natural selection by functional modification. Darwin, says Mr. Butler, sought to eliminate design and functional modification wholly from evolution. Lamarck thought functional modification more important than natural selection. Ergo, Lamarck was a greater philosopher, if not a greater naturalist, than Darwin; and the incense we burn at the shrine of Darwin is stolen from the temple of Lamarck. The controversy is one of those in which the last word is everything.

It is not expedient to discuss here the main point raised by Mr. Butler, particularly as he is evidently quite capable of writing another book on the scientific attainments of the *Pall Mall Gazette,* if provoked by contradiction. Let it suffice to acknowledge his skilful terseness and exactness of expression, his frank disdain of affected suavity or imperturbability, his apparently but not really paradoxical humour, his racy epigrams, and the geniality of his protest against "a purely automatic conception of the universe as of something that will work if a penny be dropped into the box." Ordinarily, a man who should write a book to complain that previous works of his had been overlooked, slighted, or borrowed from without acknowledgment, would be coughed down, or even, when he went on to denounce Darwin as mean and Goethe as a writer of "dull diseased trash" ["Wilhelm Meister"] hooted down. The fact that Mr. Butler has succeeded in doing this, and yet securing not only a hearing, but considerable attention and interest, is a conclusive proof of the exceptional ability with which he has stated his case.

Editor's Notes

- Shaw received *Luck, or Cunning?* for review on 10 December 1886. On 25 January 1887, his diary reports that he is reading the book at the British Museum. It seems to have been slow going. On 28 February Shaw "spent the afternoon in the Museum trying to read [Samuel Butler's] *Luck, or Cunning?* but was much interrupted," The following day he is reading the book again, and on 2 March he "walked in Hyde Park reading *Luck, or Cunning?*" On 5 March he went again to the British Museum, where he "finished reading" Butler's book. On the seventh he wrote his review, which he finished and sent off the following day (*Diary,* 227, 236, 246, 247, 248). This was something of a milestone in Shaw's philosophical pilgrimage [see Introduction, page 5]. The discovery of the date of this review puts to rest the critical vagueness of those like R. E. Burton *Bernard Shaw: the man and the mask* (1916) who, in describing Blanche Sartorius in *Widowers' Houses* as a "rather unlovely exemplar of the life-force," (p. 45) fails to take account of the fact that Shaw had created Blanche three years before he reviewed Butler's book.

- Samuel Butler (1835–1902), English philosophical author. Born in Bingham, near Nottingham, at the age of eight he was taken to Italy. In 1848 he was sent to Shrewsbury public school, where, when he was thirteen, he became enamoured of the music of Handel. Italy and Handel were the two loves of his life. Graduating from St. John's College, Cambridge, in 1858, he affronted his family's hopes that he would proceed to ordination in the Church of England (like his father), by proposing to study art. This resulted in his being banished to New Zealand, and early in 1860 he became a sheep-farmer on Canterbury Island. He was a highly successful farmer, doubling his capital investment in less than five years, and, returning to London, he settled down to painting, writing, and music. Though considering himself a painter, he began to weave certain articles and sketches into a sustained satirical narrative that was published anonymously at his own expense, entitled *Erewhon: or Over the Range* (1872). This account of the discovery of a country wherein manners are the opposite of those in England, where poverty and ill health are crimes, and where theft results in hospital treatment, achieved wide acclaim. In 1873, he published a rationalist satire on religion *The Fair Haven* [under the pseudonym of John Pickard Owen], and the same year began his novel *The Way of All Flesh*. His interest in the theory of evolution (which had germinated in New Zealand, where he first read Darwin), resulted in a series of books on the subject, including *Life and Habit* (1877), *Evolution, Old and New* (1879), *Unconscious Memory* (1880), and the one reviewed above, whose full title is *Luck, or Cunning as the Main Means of Organic Modification?* Butler's love of Italy resulted in books like *Alps and Sanctuaries of Piedmont and the Canton Ticino* (1881), and *Ex Voto: An Account of the Sacro Monte or New Jerusalem at Varallo-Sesia* (1888). His love of Handel resulted in several musical compositions (composed jointly with Festing Jones) including *Gavottes, Minuets, Fugues* (1885), and a burlesque oratorio *Narcissus* (1888). The following year, Shaw was introduced to Butler, "talked about music," and played "some of his music for him" (*Diary,* 559). In his last years Butler was concerned with mysteries surrounding Homer (in March, 1893, Shaw chaired his lecture entitled "Was *The Odyssey* written by a Woman?" and in April attended his lecture on "*The Odyssey* and the Woman Question" [*Diary,* 913, 926]), and Shakespeare's *Sonnets;* but the last book published in his lifetime was *Erewhon Revisited* (1901), showing how a religious cult can grow from a supposed miracle.

▪ Shaw's word "Marxite" commonly coexisted with its more modern-sounding counterpart "Marxist," which finally supplanted it c.1914.

▪ At the end of the first paragraph, Shaw, in his scrapbook, indicates an omission from his text.

▪ Jean Baptiste [Chevalier de] Lamarck (1744–1829), French biologist and botanist, some of whose notions of "creative evolution" where "needs create new organs" Shaw was to develop into his own philosophy, expounded in so many of his later works, notably *Man and Superman* (1905) and *Back to Methuselah* (1922). In fact, Darwin borrowed from Lamarck the theory of the transmissibility of acquired characteristics; but otherwise their evolutionary views were incompatible.

▪ Georges Louis Leclerc Buffon (1707–88), French naturalist, whose *His-*

toire Naturelle in thirty-six volumes (1749–88) was a pioneer work which dealt, among other things, with the origin of the earth.
- Robert Chambers (1802–71), English publisher, who, apart from establishing *Chambers's Journal* in 1832, also wrote about the evolution of the species in his book *Vestiges of Creation* (1844).
- Grant Allen [see pages 410–11 below].
- "Solvitur ambulando," [the problem] "is solved by walking"—practical experiment.
- At the end of the third paragraph, Shaw again in his scrapbook indicates a material omission.
- *Wilhelm Meisters Lehrjahre* (Wilhelm Meister's Apprenticeship) (1796), and *Wilhelm Meisters Wanderjahre* (Wilhelm Meister's Travels) (1821–29) by Johann Wolfgang von Goethe (1749–1832) are romantically written bildungsromane, including educational and sociological reflections.
- At the end of the review, Shaw, in his book of clippings, wrote in shorthand "This is most annoyingly mutilated."

9 June 1887

AN AUTOBIOGRAPHY FROM THE KITCHEN*
[C324]

By an English Mistress

IN this book a domestic servant has so far forgotten herself as to write descriptions of the family life she has been permitted to share, and she has unfortunately prevailed upon a man of letters to assist her in publishing them. Of the society in which Mr. Sims moves I, of course, know nothing. I am told by the young gentlemen with whom my daughters bring me in contact that he is a well-known man, that he is connected with the theatre, that he is a contributor to papers which appear on Sunday, that the information concerning his domestic affairs contained in his own writings is not considered trustworthy, and that his real name is not Sims but Dagonet. Such general statements as to a public man are not sufficiently precise to warrant me in

*"Mary Jane's Memoirs." Compiled from her original M.S. by George R. Sims. (London: Chatto and Windus. 1887.)

criticising his fitness for a literary task of peculiar delicacy; but I may at least say, while making every allowance for the influence of circumstances upon character, that I hardly think any one will recognize in Mr. Sims exactly the adviser for a girl like Mary Jane Buffham, who was, I believe, by nature an industrious and respectable housemaid. Unhappily she was egotistical and indiscreet, and not honest enough to perceive that in sitting up at night to write her memoirs she was misappropriating time purchased by her employers; making use of family matters which in no sense belonged to her; and wasting not only gas and coals, but also the health and strength needed for the efficient discharge of her duties. When she brought her manuscript to Mr. Sims, he seems to have seen nothing reprehensible in it except its untidiness. It was his plain duty to have detained the manuscript and sent it to the various persons whom it concerned, partly as a warning to them to be careful of taking their servants too far into their confidence, partly that they might have the satisfaction of perfect certainty as to its destruction. Instead of this, he thoughtlessly praised the work, encouraged Buffham, and published her disclosures with her photograph as a frontispiece. From his conduct when she called on him—which she would hardly have ventured to do if on previous occasions he had kept her at a proper distance—we may learn, I think, something as to the man himself. On hearing her knock, he opened the door in person, a thing which no gentleman should ever do. I had rather give the sequel in Mr. Sims's own words:

> I found myself face to face with a neatly dressed young woman of about eight-and-twenty, whom I at once recognized as a girl who had been in the service of a member of my family for a short time. "I beg your pardon, Sir, for calling," said the girl, colouring up to the eyes. "I beg your pardon; but—er—could I speak to you for a moment alone?" There was nobody else on the doorstep; but I understood what the girl meant. She wished our conversation to be less public. "Certainly," I replied; "come into my study."

I do not for a moment suggest that Mr. Sims meant any harm; but the request was improper, and the compliance reckless beyond all excuse.

It is difficult to criticise Buffham's narrative without widening the effect of her breach of confidence by further publicity. It is due to her to say that she was unfortunate at first in her choice of situations, falling, as she did, into the houses of dipsomaniacs, common lunatics, and, on one occasion, into that of an author. Not that I am so prejudiced nor so old-fashioned as to believe that professional authors are necessarily inferior to persons in the steadier and more reputable walks of life; but it is a matter of common report that their habits are unsuited to the strict household order which trains good servants, and Buffham's misplaced literary ambition might never have overcome her had she been fortunate enough to escape such influences. Apart from her scribbling propensities she seems—naturally giving a favourable account of herself—to have been a sober young woman, and as industrious as persons of her class ever are. Her faults were curiosity, indiscretion, occasional untruthfulness, and want of reticence with policemen and other persons with whom her duties made her acquainted. Since the mischief done by the publication of her memoirs is now irrevocable, ladies may be recommended to read them for the sake of the light they throw upon the feelings and habits of the kitchen class. I am not sure that they will not soon be out of date; housemaids of Buffham's type are certainly less common than they were within my recollection; but for the present her views are, in the main, fairly representative.

Mr. Sims (*soi-disant*) has not seen fit to chasten or correct the poor girl's phraseology; and I must add that his own style might with advantage be made somewhat less familiar.

Editor's Notes

- Shaw received this book on 28 May 1887. On the thirty-first, his diary records that he was reading it for review, while preparing drafts for the Fabian Basis Committee. On the morning of 6 June, Shaw "began review of *Mary Jane's Memoirs*. Could not work very well—restless." On the seventh he finished "review of Sims' book and sent it off" (*Diary*, 273, 274, 275, 330). This is the second instance of Shaw assuming a persona ("An English Mistress") to write a review. No doubt it reflects the fact that his sensibilities were more creative than critical in the eleven days in question (he was engaged at the same time in writing his final, unfinished, novel), which might also account for his listlessness and frustration recorded in the diary in these days. It is also a further step on Shaw's road towards becoming a dramatist. One remembers that his very first play contained a maidservant (Annie), added to the manuscript in 1892, and that he elsewhere deprecated the efforts of other dramatists (and actresses) to produce one. (See *Our Theatres in the Nineties*, 3:195–96.)
- George R[obert] Sims (1847–1922), English author. He wrote long fiction such as *Three Brass Balls* [a novel] (1882), poetry, like *The Lifeboat, and other Poems* (1883), a great deal of short fiction, like *The Ring o' Bells, and*

other Tales (1886), and plays like *Two Little Vagabonds* [with Arthur Shirley] (1896), which Shaw reviewed fairly kindly, saying "Mr. Sims is a humorist, and has some genuine faculty as a storyteller" (*Our Theatres in the Nineties* [London: Constable and Co., 1932], 2:207). Shaw's remark in the review of *Mary Jane's Memoirs* that the author's "real name is not Sims but Dagonet" is a reference to *The Dagonet Ballads* (1881), chiefly reprinted from *The Referee* to which, in 1888, were added *The Dagonet Reciter and Reader; being readings and recitations in prose and verse selected from his own works by G. R. Sims.* Later still he would write *Dagonet Abroad: a record of personal adventure* (1895). He dabbled in comic opera, too, writing *Little Christopher Columbus,* a burlesque opera (1893), a musical comedy in two acts *Skipped by the Light of the Moon* (1897) (also reviewed, and dismissed by Shaw in twelve lines), *The Dandy Fifth. An English military comic opera* (1901), and translating Szel's three act operetta *The King of Sharpers* in 1912. That he remained unchastened by Shaw's review is clear from his publication the following year of a sequel to the book reviewed above, *Mary Jane Married: Tales of a Village Inn* (1888).

▪ Shaw's shorthand marginal comment in his scrapbook, beside the sentence beginning "Not that I am so prejudiced . . . " indicates that the *Pall Mall Gazette* had "omitted part."

25 June 1887

POETS' CORNER* [C328]

THE modest author of "Law Lyrics" does not disclose his name. He is a follower of Robert Burns, and finds in the court and in the Temple an inspiration which the great Scotch poet found in the fields of Ayrshire. He rhymes with remarkable spirit and freedom, making his verse ring with such happy echoes as "chancellor" and "answer for," "interlocu-

---

*"Law Lyrics." Second Edition. (Paisley and London: A. Gardner. 1887.)
"A Lawyer's Leisure." By James Williams. (London: Kegan Paul, Trench, and Co. 1887.)
"Isaure" and other Poems. By W. Stewart Ross. (London: W. Stewart and Co. 1887.)
"Reciting and Reading: Studies of Poems." By Edwin Drew. (London: Wyman and Sons. 1887.)
"How he Died," and other Poems. By John Farrell. (Sydney: Turner and Henderson. 1887.)
"Verona," and other Poems. By L. Ormiston Chant. (London: David Stott. 1887.)
"A Trilogy of the Life to Come," and other Poems. By Robert Brown Jun. (London: D. Nutt, 1887.)
"The Sad Story of John Dalrymple." By D. Paterson. (Glasgow: Gillespie Brothers. 1887.)

tor," and "shock you for," "judges go" and "grudges so," &c. Should a blackbird come across the little volume, he will be pleased to find himself described as "the coal black singer of the crocus bill."

Mr. James Williams puts himself out of court by confessing that his harmless and sometimes graceful lines are the outcome of "A Lawyer's Leisure." Valuable verse is the outcome of a poet's hard work and not of anybody's leisure—even a lawyer's.

"Isaure, and other Poems," are inspired by an imagination so vivid and strenuous, and so unrestrained by common intelligence, that they are really not safe to read suddenly or in large instalments. Here is the cry of the jilted lover in "Mabel":

> More love in my little finger,
>   More brain in my topmost hair,
> Than blessed the *tout ensemble*
> Of Lord Fitzdoodle's heir.
>
> And I was so near to the winning,
>   Till came the auriferous spell,
> And the foot of the mamma sent me spinning
> From the apex of heaven to hell.

This, however, gives no idea of the extraordinary impetuosity of Mr. Stewart Ross's versification or his singular choice of words. "Black was the sea and gurly, beneath the rolling stars," almost suggests Mr. Lewis Carroll. The following, from "Leonore: a Lay of Dipsomania," somehow strikes the reader specially:

> "Blue devils and insane," they said;
> And men for me a jacket made
>   And built a padded room.
>
> It holds me not, nor earth nor air,
> For, gods and demons, I am there!
>   There! by that open tomb.

Mr. Edwin Drew introduces his little book of poems and sketches with the remark that "here and there, perhaps, you may come across a gleam of intelligence." This is certainly modest; and it must be acknowledged, in justice to Mr. Drew, that such gleams do actually occur more than once in his pages. He writes with a consistent purpose, mentioning his name and address frequently for the sake of elocutionists who may desire to seek instruction from him or recite his verses. His skill as a critic may be estimated by his judgment of Macaulay. "Lord Macaulay was a man whom I have always regarded with profound admiration. He expressed some extraordinary opinions on men and manners." "Composers," says Mr. Drew again, "occasionally favour me by asking me to write lines for them. When I am asked I never can. If I ever have a thought worth attention it is when I am not thinking." In view of this explanation, it may be said that these studies are evidently the result of hard and persistent thinking on Mr. Drew's part. His poems include "The Dumb Countess" and "Blood-tub Bill"; and the opening stanza of the latter is a fair sample of what Mr. Drew's muse can do:

> If ever villany proclaimed
> Itself on any face
> It was on his, and virtue seemed
> Without the smallest trace.

> A robber and a murderer
> The horrid Blood-tub Bill,
> Who seemed to walk God's earth that he
> Might work the devil's will.

Take an imaginative bushranger; fire his ambition with a copy of the works of Bret Harte; tone him up [or down, according to your point of view] with a stray volume of Mr. Robert Browning; polish him in the school of James Thompson [sic]; and Mr. John Farrell, of Sydney, will have a rival. He handles his lines with some rough force, occasionally showing both humour and eloquence; but the morality of his tales smacks of that taste for indignation meetings and lynching so strongly developed in our pioneers of civilization. It springs, no doubt, from a hatred of evil; but the love of good which might be expected at the root of it is frequently obscured by an addiction to whisky drinking, summary pistolling, profanity, and horseplay; and it suggests the reflection that where Justice is least popular she finds most bloodhounds to help her when she goes a-hunting. Irrational ethics and somewhat sanguinary sentimentality apart, Mr. Farrell's undeniably striking work has considerable interest and merit.

A lady so altruistic, so enthusiastic, so facile in utterance, and so sensitive as Mrs. Ormiston Chant naturally writes poems. In doing so she shows her faults and her qualities with a rapt unconsciousness. At her worst, she is excessively sentimental, and sometimes writes very bad verse. At her best she is, to use a phrase of her own, "trembling with music," intensely earnest, and happily and nobly inspired. Some of the shorter poems, such as "Finding Love," are memorable expressions of some of the most deeply felt truths of common experience.

Mr. Robert Brown is a learned man and an inveterate rhymester, full of scholarly conceits and glittering fancies; but he is only a poet insofar as all men, like Silas Wegg, drop into poetry occasionally. When he "sat beside the margin of the gently swelling deep ere yet the brightest star of heaven had passed the western steep," he moralized thus:

> Q.—What is Eternity? A.—Myself. Q.—What am I? A.—Progress.
>   Then
> Eternity is but the change upon immortal men.
> Perfection is a flight of steps half-hidden by God's throne,
> Yet all His myriad creatures forever climb thereon.

Mr. Brown ought to know that he cannot preserve the reverence of the reader's imagination while presenting it with such a slippery image as that of a throne on a flight of steps. No man who has ever helped to get a cottage pianoforte upstairs can read such a line in the spirit of the author. In the "Trilogy of the Life to Come" there are some attractive passages; but the reader is too often tripped up by perversely ingenious rhymes, or by such cockneyisms as—

> Our fragile nature, overcome with awe,
> Fell at his feet, and I beheld no more.

"John Dalrymple," having many obvious rhymes, is a good name for the hero of a satiric narrative in as much of the metre and manner of Don Juan as Mr. Paterson can attain to. Mr. Paterson is, it appears, a man of business to whom the depression of trade has given a leisure which he makes elegant by essays in verse. They show some wit; but they are difficult of scansion. For example—

> Look at Russia now! Look at Afghanistan!
> That even got the back up of old Gladstone—

is surely a little infelicitous. Nor in the following couplet does the force of the political criticism quite conceal the imperfection of the rhyme:

"The Grand Old Man! You mean the Grand Old Ass!"
His guest retorted. Rennie stared aghast.

Editor's Notes

▪ According to the checklist he kept in his diary, Shaw received this batch of books on 6 May 1887 and appears to have dispatched the Drew review on the ninth, and the rest on the nineteenth; but the diary entries for those dates reveal no mention of any of these books by name (*Diary*, 330).

▪ The anonymous author of *Law Lyrics*, the first edition of which had appeared in 1885, was the Scottish poet Robert Bird (1854–?), who also wrote *The Falls of Clyde, and other Poems* (1888), and *More Law Lyrics* (1898). Bird's amusingly forced rhymes ("chancellor" and "answer for," "interlocutor," and "shock you for," "judges go" and "grudges so") should have made Shaw blush at the remembrance of his own past attempts at poetry, still to be seen in his notebook diary for 1873, with their Gilbertian attempts to rhyme "dangerous" with "pain'd yer us," and "enchantment" with "my aunt meant."

▪ James Williams (1851–1911), English lawyer and writer. He was educated at Oxford, where he eventually became a Fellow of Lincoln College and All Souls Reader in Roman Law. He was called to the bar in 1875, became a justice of the peace in Flintshire, and high sheriff there from 1906–7. He received an honorary doctorate from Yale, and published over one hundred articles in successive editions of *The Encyclopædia Britannica*, and in *Law Magazine and Review*. He wrote other books of verse: *Simple Stories of London* (1890), *Ethandune* (1892), *Briefless Ballads* (1895), *Ventures in Verse* (1898), *The Oxford Year* (1901), *Thomas of Kempen* (1909), etc.

▪ W[illiam] Stewart Ross [also known by the pseudonym *Saladin*] (1844–1906), Scottish author. He was a prominent agnostic, and editor of the *Agnostic Journal*. In addition to the book reviewed above, he wrote a number of poems and works on agnosticism, among them *Lays of Romance and Chivalry* (1881), *Did Jesus Christ Rise from the Dead?* (1886), *God and His Book* (1887), *Woman: Her Glory, Her Shame, and Her God* (2 vols.) (1888), *Why I am an Agnostic* (1888), *Roses and Rue* (1890), *The Whirlwind Sown and Reaped* (1891), *The Bottomless Pit* (1894), *The Holy Lance* (1898), *The Book of Virgins* (1900), and *The Man she Loved* (1904).

▪ Edwin Drew (n.d.), English elocutionist and author. He also wrote *Fiction, Fun, and Fancy* (1877), *How to Recite: being Studies of Poems, with Fresh Readings and Articles connected with Elocution* (1886), *Elocutionary Studies: with New Readings and Recitals* (1888), *Speech Studies: with Fresh Readings Recitations, Anecdotes,&c.* (1888), and *The Chief Incidents of the "Titanic" Wreck* (1912). He collaborated with John Green on a series of penny-lantern readings, wrote poems on Dickens and Tennyson, and an appreciation of Henry Irving, besides editing *The Actor and Elocutionist*.

▪ John Farrell (1851–1904), Australian journalist and poet. Born in Buenos Aires, of Irish parents and brought to Australia in 1852, he left school early (on his mother's death) and worked on his father's farm until 1870, at which time he took a position in a brewery. After two years he left, and for another two years went gold mining and tree felling. In 1875, he was offered another post as a brewer; the following year he married, and settled in Albury in 1878, where his literary career really began. He contributed humorous verse to *The Albury Banner* and *Border Post*, wrote an ode for the Melbourne Exhibition in 1879, and regular poems for a Sydney newspaper called *The Bulletin*. However, he still depended financially upon the brewing industry until 1887, at which point he bought a newspaper *The Lithgow Enterprise*. This, although a popular newspaper, failed in a year owing to Farrell's unbusinesslike practices, and he then became editor of *The Australian Standard*, and for a time of the (Sydney) *Daily Telegraph*. In addition to the book reviewed above (the first one to take his name outside Australia), Farrell wrote *Ephemera: An Iliad of Albury* (1878), *Two stories: a fragmentary poem* (1882), *Australia to England* (1897), and *My sundowner, and other poems* [ed. and with a memoir by Bertram Stevens] (1904). Shaw's future dramatic efforts are signalled in his comment on John Farrell's work. His own play *The Shewing-Up of Blanco Posnet* (1911), though set in America rather than Australia, was to present "that taste for indignation meetings and lynching so strongly developed in our pioneers of civilization." The addiction to whisky drinking is illustrated in Shaw's character Elder Daniels, threats of summary pistoling, profanity, and horseplay abound; Shaw's play, like Farrell's poem, concerns a ride for life on a horse, and does indeed suggest the reflection that "where Justice is least popular she finds most bloodhounds to help her when she goes a-hunting."

▪ L[aura] Ormiston Chant [née Dibbin] (1848–1923), English (nondenominational) preacher, lecturer, composer, and writer. She was privately educated, and then taught in schools, nursed in hospitals, and became assistant manager of a private lunatic asylum. After her marriage she was an enthusiastic reformer, advocating women's suffrage, temperance, purity, and Liberal politics, and became a public lecturer on literary and social subjects. She received a medal from the King of Greece for taking nurses out to Crete and the Greek frontier. In addition to the book of poems reviewed above, Mrs. Chant wrote a novel *Sellcuts' Manager* (1899), short stories, and numerous pamphlets on temperance, poor-law politics, and purity. She also composed songs and hymns. Shaw met her personally two years later, when she addressed the Shelley Society.

▪ Robert Brown [Jr.] (1844–?), English lawyer, politician, and author. Educated at Cheltenham College, and by avocation an archaeologist and antiquarian, he was an enthusiastic student of Greek mythology, a member of the Society of Biblical Archaeology, and a Fellow of the Society of Antiquaries. He was a Liberal in politics, and was returned for North Lincolnshire in the election of April 1880. He was friendly with Gladstone, and corresponded with him, mainly on antiquarian and linguistic matters. In addition to the above book, he wrote numerous volumes on mythology, linguistics, and astronomy, including *Poseidon: A Link between Semite, Hamite, and Aryan; being an Attempt to trace the Cultus of the God to its Sources* (1872), *The Great Dionysiack Myth,* [Two volumes] (1877–78), *Language and Theories of its Origin* (1881), *The Unicorn: a Mythological Investigation* (1881), *The Law of Kosmic Order: an Investigation of the Physical Aspect of Time* (1882), *Eridanus: River and Constellation: a Story of the Archaic Southern Asterisms* (1883), *The Myth of Kirke: including the Visit of Odysseus to the Shades: an Homerick Study* (1883), [Translation] *The Phainomena or "Heavenly Display" of Aratos: Done into English Verse* (1885).

▪ D[] Paterson (n.d.), this unidentified (possibly Scottish) author seems to have produced only the above book. In view of its satirical, not to say libelous, content, the name may be a pseudonym.

▪ Silas Wegg is the balladmonger (who also keeps a fruit stall) in Dickens's *Our Mutual Friend.* He undertakes to read to Mr. Boffin for half a crown a week. If he is to read poetry, it would be more expensive, he says, for he should have to be paid for its weakening effect upon the mind. Boffin replies that he wasn't thinking of poetry, except in so far as this:

> "If you was to happen now and then to feel yourself in the mind to tip me and Mrs. Boffin one of your ballads, why then we should drop into poetry." (Book I, chapter 7)

▪ Thomas Babington [First Baron] Macaulay (1800–1859), essayist and politician.

29 June 1887

OUIDA'S SUCCESSOR* [C329]

MARIE CORELLI, imagining a new heaven and a new earth, and throwing them passionately in the teeth of an obstinate reality that will not conform to them, must greatly stir the hearts and fire the fancies of her younger readers. Her latest heroine, "Thelma," comes from the land of the midnight sun. Thelma's father, a worthy descendant of the sea kings, repudiates modern civilization and worships Odin. A baronet arrives in a steam yacht; marries the Norse maiden; and bears her off to "the land of Mockery," known to cab men as the four mile

---

*"Thelma." By Marie Corelli. Three vols. (London: Bentley and Son. 1887.)

radius. The point of the story lies in the intense superiority of Thelma to the frivolous units of London society. Now, far be it from any reasonable critic to justify the West-end ways which Thelma found so weary, or to exalt that race-in-the-wrong-direction after Pleasure which ends in a pessimistic conviction that Pleasure is a mirage, and life not worth living. But the ground of Thelma's alleged superiority to her London circle turns out to be her barbarous superstitions, ignorance, and prejudice. London wives shocked her. "Her character," we are told, "moulded on grand and simple lines of duty, saw the laws of Nature in their true light, and accepted them without question. It seemed to her quite clear that man was the superior, woman the inferior, creature; and she could not understand the possibility of any wife not rendering instant and implicit obedience to her husband, even in trifles." Let us, for the sake of illustration, apply these grand and simple lines of duty to a particular case. Man is superior to woman; therefore any man is superior to any woman; therefore Mr. E. M. Langworthy is superior to Florence Nightingale, Mrs. Josephine Butler, the Queen, or any other female; therefore his wife is bound to render him instant and implicit obedience even in trifles. Thelma's pity for the fine ladies who knew better than this, was no more grand or dutiful than is the pity which Mr. Cody's Indians possibly feel for us when we go to Earl's Court to wonder at them.

Thelma, disgusted at finding men of science "trying to upset each other's theories," attributed this necessary incident of progress and research to "mean jealousies" and "miserable heartburnings." She also "invited two lady authoresses of note to meet at one of her at-homes; welcomed both the masculine-looking ladies with a radiant smile; and introduced them, saying gently" (and, it must be added, most impertinently), " 'You will be pleased to know each other.' " As it happened, they were not pleased; and Thelma's "simple Norse beliefs in the purity and gentleness of womanhood were startled and outraged," as they were later on by "the platform women, unnatural products of an unnatural age." How if the "platform women" were to retort by inviting the "Mudie women" to meet their audiences face to face, and submit their criticisms of society to the prompt and stern discipline of public discussion? If Marie Corelli may write her opinions, why may not other women speak theirs?

These indignant misunderstandings, which prompted the vile phrase "a society novel" on the title-page of "Thelma," need not, however, be taken too seriously. Their ignorance, their audacity, even the groundless assumption of superiority in them, are so amusingly sincere and well intended that they are never insufferable. Their author evidently feels that she is fearlessly fighting the good fight; and though she has the vaguest notions of what the good fight is about, and is youthfully deficient in charity and spiritual modesty, most of her blows fall on people who, for one misdeed or another, deserve them. As a romancer, she lacks nothing but originality; and she fails in that because she is more learned in operas, poems, and tales than in the realities of the living world, for which she has far too little sympathy. Her maiden in white, singing at the spinning-wheel, is borrowed from M. Gounod; and her Odin worshipper meeting the Walkyrie comes from the "Nibelungen Lied," and was probably impressed on her by the scene between Siegmund and Brynhild in Wagner's "Die Walküre." Still, these things are not tiresome as stale denunciations of society papers and footmen's calves are. And it must be acknowledged that she transfigures even her own shortcomings by the glamour of her ardent and vivid imagination, recklessly furnishing her air castles with all that is costly, magnificent, and voluptuous; peopling them with heroes, vikings, and sun maidens; surrounding them with landscapes of tropical glow or Alpine majesty; suffusing them with the warmth and radiance of splendid days; hiding them in the gloom and terror of dreadful nights; and, in short, playing prodigal in that No Man's Land of luxuries for which there is nothing to pay, of poignant griefs that do not hurt, thrilling joys that do not satisfy, virtuous aspirations that do not ennoble, and fierce crusades that leave evil none the weaker, but rather the more prosperous for the advertisement.

Editor's Notes

- Shaw's diary records a doubt as to when he received *Thelma* for review ["?/ 6/-]; but he was reading the novel on 18 June 1887, and began the review itself on the twenty-second, "but did not get on very well with it." The following day he "finished review of *Thelma* with difficulty," and his diary records that he dispatched it the same day (*Diary*, 278–79, 330).
- Marie Corelli [see page 134 above].
- The story of the "Langworthy Marriage" would have been well known to readers of newspapers in 1887. E[dward] M[artin] Langworthy (?1847–?), English barrister-at-law and wealthy playboy, was educated at Eton, Oxford, and the Inner Temple, where he was called to the bar in 1878. He did not,

however, practice law, but with an inheritance (from his father's cotton fortune) bought grain, rice, sugar, and tobacco plantations in the Argentine, in the colony known as the "Langworthy Grant," which consisted of thirty-two square leagues in the north of Toscas where lived and worked 250 families. It also boasted a town hall, a church, a schoolhouse, a sugar factory, sawmill, and tramway. At Curmalan, he also owned a seventy-thousand-acre personal estate on which his mansion "Bella Vista" was erected, and a 235 ton steam yacht, "The Meteor" in which he spent the majority of his time cruising. His first wife (the sister of the Earl of Limerick) died, and he was about thirty-five when, in February 1881, he met in Paris Mildred Sabine Palliser Long, an educated middle-class Irish school-teacher, convalescing after a skating accident. They became engaged the following year and, because of his mother's objection to Mildred Long as a daughter-in-law, were married secretly at Caen by a Catholic priest in September 1882. Since Mildred was not a Catholic, and worried about the Latin ceremony, they were again secretly married in Antwerp in January 1883, this time by an American Presbyterian minister. In that year, too, Mildred became pregnant, at which point her husband's demeanor changed. She was kept prisoner on the yacht, tortured, beaten, starved, force-fed morphia dosed with mercury and Angostura bitters (in an attempt to induce a miscarriage), and finally abandoned in Buenos Aires in March 1883 with the announcement that the two marriages had been fakes, and that therefore she was not legally his wife. Her efforts, on her return to England, to establish the legality of her marriage were met with contemptuous silence. In August 1883 the child was born. Again she tried through law for child support. High-handed, arrogant threats followed, from both Langworthy and his lawyers. His daughter was referred to as "the alleged child." Lying affidavits were sworn; and even when these were contradicted in court by the testimony of the Presbyterian minister, Langworthy still refused to pay alimony, and four years were spent in legal fencing (disputes over Langworthy's domicile, whether or not his wife had "deserted" him, the legality of the marriages), until Mrs. Langworthy was destitute, and unable to find employment because of the scandal. The courts finally agreed that the two marriages, although solemnized by religious ceremony, had not been legally registered in the countries where they took place; and Mrs. Langworthy became, therefore, an "unmarried mother," and was forced to sue her husband for "breach of promise"! Langworthy refused to return to England, and his mother (who was busy transferring his money and property from England to the Agentine) refused to attend the court on his behalf, claiming ill health. Finally, in the spring of 1887, Mrs. Langworthy turned in desperation to the *Pall Mall Gazette;* and in consequence the "Langworthy Marriage" became another of Stead's crusades: the *Pall Mall Gazette* devoted part of its first and all of its second pages to the affair for twenty straight days in April and May 1887, and published a seventy-page "special," (no. 35, *The Langworthy Marriage; or, a Millionaire's Shame)* in the same year. It also established and solicited contributions for the "Langworthy Defence

Fund," to defray Mrs. Langworthy's legal expenses. As a direct consequence of Stead's crusade, questions about false statements made by Langworthy to defeat his wife's application for alimony were asked in the House of Commons, the courts renewed the quest for justice, and after five years a financial settlement was reached, including an annuity for the child (Gladys Elizabeth), and an apology from Langworthy himself on 10 August 1887. Nevertheless, as the *Birmingham Times* put it,

> if only a fraction of what has been admitted by his own counsel be true, Mr. Edward Martin Langworthy is a disgrace to his country and his sex.

▪ Mrs. Josephine [Elizabeth] Butler [née Grey] (1828–1906), English philanthropist and women's activist. She was educated in Newcastle, and from an early age concerned herself with the "double standard" by which men and women were judged. In 1852 she married George Butler (1819–90), a scholar of Cambridge and Oxford, who took holy orders and became first vice-principal of Cheltenham College, and then principal of Liverpool College. It was in Liverpool that Josephine Butler began her work among the poorest of women, visiting hospitals, quays, and oakum sheds. She and her husband bought properties that became hospitals for incurables; she campaigned for equality of educational advantages for women, and formed the North of England Council for the Higher Education of Women. Her fierce crusade against the state regulation of prostitution (which had begun in France, spread through the Continent, and was being proposed for England by 1864) took her all over the country, mustering support to defeat the proposed bill and also to crush the Contagious Diseases Act currently in force, which allowed the forcible examination of women suspected of carrying venereal disease. Finally, due to her efforts, the proposed legislation was withdrawn. Thereafter she took her crusade to Europe (from 1873 to 1875) with some success. Finally, in England, as a result of her efforts, the Contagious Diseases Act was repealed in 1886. She was also a tireless advocate of women's suffrage. Among her many publications were pamphlets such as *The Education and Employment of Women* (1868) and *The Revival and Extension of the Abolitionist Cause* (1887), biographies like *Catherine of Siena* (1878), and *Jean Frederic Oberlin* (1882), and journals she herself edited, such as *The Dawn* (1888) and *The Storm-Bell* (1898–1900).

▪ The Wild West Show of William "Buffalo Bill" Cody (1846–1917), organized in 1883, regularly visited Earl's Court, in London. The *Pall Mall Gazette* praised its "wonderful feats of shooting and riding" on 10 May 1887, and reported that Mr. Gladstone had "conferred with Red Shirt in his wigwam." On 6 September 1892, Shaw went with Florence Farr to see the show (*Diary*, 850–51).

▪ The Leipzig-published two-volume 1887 Tauchnitz edition of *Thelma, A Norwegian Princess* is subtitled merely *A Novel*.

14 July 1887

IN FIVE ACTS AND IN BLANK VERSE* [C334]

THIS is the sort of thing we have all done. We hardly know what blank verse is; and of the nature of an "act" we are utterly ignorant: yet we do it to give expression to the Shakspere in us. Nobody reads it when it is done—not even the reviewer who makes merry over it: there is always enough in the first page he chances on to inspire as many gibes as we are worth. No matter: gibe as he may, he has done it himself. In his bureau, pushed to the back of the drawer, over littered and dusty, is his Cromwell, or Raleigh, or Caractacus, or Timour, "an historical tragedy, in five acts and in blank verse." If it was not published, that proves only that the author was poor. Had he possessed the needful spare cash, some bookseller of the High-street, Oxford, would have been the richer and the British Museum catalogue the longer for him. The present writer was poor, and gave in before the third act was finished. What is he that he should sit in judgment on others? Yet there were some fine lines in it—finer than any he has since reviewed.

What is blank verse?

Esther; Place a light in my uncle's study.

Is that blank verse? The author of "Wiclif" says it is. But, "be it not said, thought, understood"; for no actor that ever mouthed could make blank verse of it. It should run—

Esther; A light place in mine uncle's study.

Or, better still, to save the ambiguity and lack of distinction—

Yare, yare, good Esther;
Pour thou the petrol oil: snip thou the wick:
Light up the study.

*"King James the First: an Historical Tragedy." By David Graham. (London: Macmillan and Co. 1887.)
"Wiclif: an Historical Drama." (London: Kegan Paul. 1887.)
"The Love Affair." By W. W. Aldred. (London: G. Redway. 1887.)

This at least cannot be mistaken for sane prose. Mr. David Graham, the author of "King James the First, an Historical, &c.," understands the matter better than the author of "Wiclif." He featly turns the phrase "Italian minuet" into blank verse, thus—

Aminuet
Straight from the sunny land of Italy.

This is the true blank manner. Mr. Graham's characters even laugh in blank verse:

Queen: And the tenth General Council would break up
          With—No decision come to. Ha! ha!
Abbott: Ha! ha! ha!

Here the measured cachinnation preserves the stately march of tragedy. There is one dangerous line in "King James the First"; and that, significantly enough, adorns a scene in which the author soars into prose. The King, early in the third act, says:

This is of interest: go on.

In actual performance that line might bring down the house, very much as it was brought down by Kemble's delivery of—

And when this solemn mockery is o'er—

in Ireland's "Vortigern," which, by-the-by, was really not a bad historical tragedy as such works go. "Vortigern" was a well-intended blend of what most people like in "Macbeth" and Cibber's "Richard III." Should any of our popular plagiarists need a benefit Mr. Irving might find a worse play to revive for the occasion.

The Elizabethan lymph does not seem to have taken satisfactorily with the author of "Wiclif." The late R. H. Horne would have thought him a poor creature. His metaphors lack immensity; and his language is too little magniloquent. A successor of Chapman and Marlowe cannot afford to play the gentle student, avoid hyperbole, and treat history in the modern sociological spirit. Nor must he so delude himself as to hope that moderate prose, cut into lengths, will pass as even Byronic blank verse. The following is a sample of "Wiclif":

Yet had I wished a little more of life,
A little longer still to ply the oar,
To carry still yet further [*still yet further is really too bad*] on her
    way
The ship we sail by. We shall sleep at last
Beneath the bunkers when our work is done,
And go unconsciously to our longed haven.

Now, in cold blood, was this worth doing? Is the thought beyond the
capacity of a well-educated poodle? Is the expression specially apt,
harmonious, forcible, suggestive, or in any way interesting? Is the
metaphor not fitted to Tom Tug rather than to Wiclif? Were bunkers
known years before steam navigation? and are dead shipmen buried in
them? Is the power to write such lines any excuse for the error of
thinking them worth writing? Above all, does the consciousness of
having written an historical tragedy compensate one for the publisher's
bill, and the unpleasantness of being publicly asked such questions as
the foregoing?

Mr. W. W. Aldred, in his "Drama of an Ancient Democracy," has lain
low for his reviewers in a singular fashion. We have all heard of the
gentlemen who send rolls of blank paper to theatrical managers, and
receive them again with neat notes to the effect that "their play" has
been read attentively, but is not suitable for presentation on the
boards. Mr. Aldred, having so poor an opinion of human nature as to
suspect that reviewers, lost to all professional honour, criticise dramas
in blank verse without having anxiously scrutinized every line, has
laid a trap. On page 176, in the middle of the fifth act, the scene being
ancient Rome, the time 82 B.C., and the personages Sulla, Pompey,
Cæsar, Cato, &c., he has interpolated, without connection, warning,
or explanation, a ballad, as follows:

POMPEIUS: Ah, do not jest, Tullius. I am too anxious in mind to laugh
    with you.

BALLAD.

The last shots are growing more distant,
    Hushed is the cannon's roar,
And he lies with his soldiers around him,
    All silent for evermore. &c., &c., &c.

In the flush of triumph at having escaped this ambush, one may
magnanimously admit that there are gleams of nature, of wit, of obser-

vation, and even of verse, in "The Love Affair." The style is free from mere verbiage and line padding; and it changes with freedom from the old and stately to the modern and familiar. For example—

> Oh, now methinks the Fates look at the clock
> And wait the hour which is to change the world—

is Marlovian. But the following smacks of our own time:

CENTURION (to soldiers): Halt! Shoulder arms! Fall out!
SPY: You understand?
CENTURION: No; I'm damned if I do. But I will carry out the orders. Fall in! Dress your ranks! Left wheel! Quick march!

Editor's Notes

- Shaw received these books on 6 May 1887. On 11, 13, and 14 June, his diary records that he was "reading plays for review;" on the fifteenth that he was "reading for review," and on the sixteenth that he "continued review of plays, but could not finish it as I could not find one of the books—must have forgotten it somewhere." On 18 June he reports "finished review of plays." His checklist records that he sent them off the following day. On this day, after speaking in Regent's Park, Shaw was walking home when "an inquiring young stranger walked with me to Fitzroy St. where I called at the Blacks to get a date for my review of *A Love Affair*" (*Diary*, 276, 277, 278, 330).
- David Graham (1854–?), Scottish author. Born in Falkirk, he was educated there, and at St. Andrews University. Later he took law at Edinburgh. He also wrote *Robert de Bruce: an Historical Play* [verse] (1884), *Rizzio; an historical tragedy* (1898), *Pompilia: a play* [based on Browning's *The Ring and the Book*] (1928), and *Darnley* (1900).
- Charles E[dward] Sayle (1864–1924), English author. *Wiclif* was his only dramatic work. Indeed, apart from a book of poems entitled *Bertha. A Story of Love* (1885) the bulk of Sayle's writing was of a bibliographic or antiquarian nature. He wrote *Early English Printed Books in the* [Cambridge] *University Library (1475 to 1640)* (1900–1907), *Initial Letters in early English printed books* (1904), *Annals of Cambridge University Library, 1278–1900* (1916), *Bibliotheca loquitur. Random notes on the library of St. John's College, Cambridge University* (n.d.), *Catalogue of the early printed books bequeathed to the* (Fitzwilliam] *museum by Frank McClean, M.A.,F.R.S.* (1916), etc. He also edited a number of books.
- W[ ] W[ ] Aldred (n.d.), unidentified author. He also wrote *The Lost Cause. A story of the last rebellion in Poland* (1881).

- William Henry Ireland (1777–1835), forger of Shakespearean manuscripts. Having access to Elizabethan parchments in the lawyer's chambers
where he was employed, in 1794–95 he forged a number of Shakespearean
documents including the plays *Vortigern and Rowena* and *Henry II,* which
deceived many experts. Sheridan produced *Vortigern* (unsuccessfully) at
Drury Lane in 1796. Ireland finally confessed his fraud.
- R[ichard] H[enry, or Hengist] Horne (1803–84), English playwright and
poet. Shaw refers to his tragedies, *Cosmo de' Medici* and *The Death of Marlowe* (1837), *Gregory VII* (1840), and *Judas Iscariot* (1848), which, like
many other poets of the time, he wrote in imitation of the great Elizabethans.
His were at least spirited and grand in tone. His epic *Orion* (1843) was
acclaimed widely; but the bulk of his poetry was poor. From 1852 to 1869 he
went to Australia as commissioner for crown lands, and in 1874 he received a
civil list pension. He had much correspondence with Elizabeth Barrett Browning and published two volumes of her letters to him.
- Both George Chapman (1559?–1634?) and Christopher Marlowe (1564–
93) were known for their flamboyant verse style.
- Shaw certainly had produced his own quota of bad blank verse. He seems
to be referring here to his unfinished "Passion Play" (1878), which collapsed
in the second scene of its second act; but he was not yet finished with the
form, which he returned to in the dramatization of his own novel *Cashel
Byron's Profession,* called *The Admirable Bashville; or Constancy Unre-
warded* (1901), *Cymbeline Refinished* (1937), and the last play he wrote, a
year before his death, the puppet play *Shakes versus Shav* (1949). His
guarded praise for Aldred's work, which "smacks of our own time" was to bear
fruit in Shaw's own Roman plays; his Centurion in *Androcles and the Lion*
(1912), for example, managing to retain his Roman character while conveying the modern sound in his parade ground commands.

15 July 1887

A RUNAWAY FROM CIVILIZATION* [C336]

MR. LAURENCE OLIPHANT is a many-sided man. To be precise, he is
four-sided, as a square man ought to be; and one of his complaints is
that he could find nothing but round holes in English society, wherefore he dwells in the East, and holds communion with spirits. That is
one of his sides—belief in the supernatural, vehemently denying that

---

*"Episodes in a Life of Adventure; or, Moss from a Rolling Stone." By Laurence Oliphant.
(London and Edinburgh: Blackwood and Sons. 1887.)

it is superstition, of course, and repudiating all kin to vulgar mysticism and marvel-hunting, but denying and repudiating in vain. On his second side he is a diplomatist, with something of the literary qualities and faults of the dispatch writer, and an official contempt for popular notions of foreign policy. Again, he is a special correspondent, restless, adventurous, not too careful of the morrow, and sufficiently interested in his own experiences to offer them as a contribution to history. Fourthly, he is a novelist, in extenuation of which he may plead, like the wife beater in the Wellerist fable, that, after all, it is an amiable weakness. In the latest record of his travels we find only the diplomatist and the special correspondent: fiction is absent (unless we are much taken in); and superstition is content with a modest page or two of self-assertion.

Beginning with a description of the overland route to India forty-six years ago, Mr. Oliphant tells us what he saw of the Italian revolution of 1848, of Lord Elgin's diplomacy in the United States, of the helpless retreat and decay of the red men before the white in Canada, of the Crimean War, of filibustering in Central America, of Calcutta during the Mutiny, and China during the war of 1857–9, of Garibaldi, of Japan before Anglomania smote it, of the Polish insurrection of 1863, and of the war in Schleswig-Holstein. From all these he has learned, like the Pirate of Penzance, that "if you come to sheer respectability, there can be no doubt in the mind of any one who has tried both, that the life of a filibuster is infinitely superior in its aims and methods to that of a politician." And he doubts "whether any more healthy or innocent form of enjoyment exists than the chase in wild tropical mountains of the grand animals with which they abound." Another of his opinions is that the Chagres river is tolerably certain to prevent M. de Lesseps from finishing the Panama canal. Among minor matters, he tells us how he discovered that Mrs. Jordan's maiden name was Thimbleby; and he estimates half an hour's unforced march in Tsusima as, "at least three miles," which suggests that the soil of Japan is exceptionally favourable to pedestrianism.

Mr. Oliphant turned his back on English political life just before the Reform Bill of 1867 took effect, and politics became something more than the retailing of Palmerstonian anecdotes and Foreign Office rumours. He had been concerned with Sir A. Borthwick in a sixpenny paper called the *Owl*. It had made a hit by publishing foreign telegrams and private letters which, though on the face of them outrageous fabrications, showed that the paper was mysteriously well informed as to what it was joking about. A comparison of the *Owl* with the successful journals of to-day shows how quickly a democratic suffrage is teaching us that statecraft begins at home. That lesson Mr. Oliphant has missed by deliberately backing out of English life to nurse his superstition in a comparatively barbarous country, whence he now informs us that the majority of us "continue to think the world a very good world as it is, and that the invention of new machines and explosives for the destruction of their fellow men is a perfectly sane and even laudable pursuit." This is all Mr. Oliphant knows about the twenty years which began with the Education Act; witnessed a course of Irish legislation that would have seemed madly revolutionary to the *Owl;* and so awakened the public conscience that, whatever Mr. Oliphant's supernatural advisers or Foreign Office correspondents may assure him to the contrary, the shallow optimists and Palmerstonian Jingoes whom he supposes to constitute "a majority of his fellow men" do not at present represent even the members of the Primrose League, much less the people of England. Mr. Oliphant says that when he looked back on the period of his life described in his book, it appeared to him "distinctly an insane period." He can hardly expect us to believe that he mended matters in this respect when, by his flight to the East, he made himself dependent for his knowledge of the condition of his countrymen on diplomatic straight tips and on newspapers which were in a conspiracy of silence as to the most vital social questions. Nor has our study of such novels as "The Masollams"[*sic*] in the very least disposed us to imitate him in searching for a political philosopher's stone in "magnetism, hypnotism, and spiritualism." Such suspicious matters should be investigated, not in the East, which being the land of wonders, affords special facilities for imposture, but here, under the eye of the Psychical Society, which has published more researches in five years than Mr. Oliphant has in twenty, with results which justify us in positively refusing to attach any importance to his hints at a possible regeneration of the human race by a revival of faith in ghost stories. His novels, his travels, his sporting adventures, his delightful sketches of the convents of Moldavia with their armies of crinolined nuns reddening his scalp with their kisses (it was only their mode of saluting a stranger), will always be welcome; but since he has run away into the desert from the battle of public life in England, we must with all possible good nature decline his services as pioneer, guide, counsellor, critic, soothsayer, or even purveyor of the sort of information that enabled him to boast of the *Owl* as "the only instance of a paper which paid all its expenses by the sale of its first number."

Editor's Notes

- Shaw received this book for review on 25 June 1887 and read it on 27, 29, and 30 June and 1 July. On the fourth of that month he is "writing review of Oliphant's book," and on the fifth he "finished and sent off review of Oliphant" (*Diary*, 280–82, 330).
- Laurence Oliphant [see page 150 above].
- In *The Pirates of Penzance* (1880), it is The Pirate King who says:

  I don't think much of our profession, but contrasted with respectability, it is comparatively honest.

- [Vicomte] M. [Ferdinand Marie] de Lesseps (1805–1904), French diplomat and engineer, and builder of the Suez Canal, headed the French organization, the Panama Canal Company, which began in 1880 the construction of a canal across the Isthmus of Panama. Oliphant's prophecy was partly right, though it was not the Chagres river which was the culprit: after eight years of vainly trying to push a sea-level canal across the Isthmus, the Panama Canal Company went bankrupt in 1889. In 1905 the Isthmian Canal Commission decided to build a canal with, instead of a seal-level channel, locks that lower ships to Pacific tidewater level.
- Sir A[lgernon] Borthwick [first Baron Glenesk] (1830–1908), English journalist and editor. Educated in Paris and London, in 1850 he was sent to Paris as foreign correspondent of his father's newspaper the *Morning Post*. On his father's death in 1852 he became editor, and subsequently owner of this newspaper. It was in 1864 that he joined Evelyn Ashley, Lord Wharncliffe, and J. S. Wortley in producing the periodical called *The Owl*, which lived for only six years, finishing in 1870 when Borthwick had insufficient leisure to produce it. In that year he married and later had two daughters and a son. After 1872, Borthwick devoted less time to his newspaper and more to public life. He was returned as Conservative candidate for South Kensington in 1885 and again in 1892.

19 July 1887

MR. GEORGE MOORE'S NEW NOVEL* [C338]

IT is customary to say of such books as Mr. George Moore's that they are not *virginibus puerisque*. Yet the lasses and lads are the very

---

*"A Mere Accident." By George Moore. (London: Vizetelly and Co. 1887.)

people who read them—if they ever do read them—without being any the worse. Those who have been allowed the run of the library in their childhood know by experience that in young hands "Tom Jones" is as innocent as "The Pilgrim's Progress," and that "Mademoiselle de Maupin" is unreadably dull to little bookworms whose choice of literature is still subject to the parental censorship. As to people old enough to insist on choosing for themselves, they are under no compulsion to read Mr. Moore's novels; and as his licence is now notorious, and his method not in the least insidious, it is only necessary, each time he publishes a book, to indicate plainly how far he has gone in it. Our readers can then decide for themselves whether the book is to be widely read or not; for Mr. Moore's existence as a novelist depends wholly on the general reader and not on the particular reviewer.

The "mere accident" which gives the novel now in question its name is this. A young lady, a clergyman's daughter, about to be happily married, is overtaken on a lonely road by a tramp and outraged. Next day she goes mad, throws herself from a window, and dies. In describing this "realistically," Mr. Moore has not done his worst: by making the victim insensible, he has contrived to avoid the most painful moment of his narrative. From his point of view this is perhaps a sacrifice of principle—a flinching from his duty. From the point of view of the British public, it will be welcomed as a commendable reticence that might have been carried further, even to the point of not writing the book. For there is no moral. The incident is described for its own sake. It has no consequences or antecedents to recommend it; and unless Mr. Moore wished to bring home to us in a startling way the danger of allowing young ladies to go out without an escort, he must stoop to be classed with the vulgar novelists who depend for their effects on the mere sensation stirred up by any appalling crime or abnormal occurrence. In their school, the taste of the sensationalist author determines the particular crime selected; and Mr. Moore's ready preference for a rape is explained by the opportunity it affords him for one of his favourite sham clinical lectures on morbid sexual conditions. Let it be freely admitted that these discourses would, if truly realistic, have a scientific value sufficient to fortify Mr. Moore against prudish criticism. But as they are realistic only as symptoms of the condition of Mr. Moore's own imagination, which hardly deserves a set of volumes all to itself, they have no more claim on our forbearance than the gratuitously romantic passages in a shilling shocker. The objection, in fact, to Mr. Moore, is not that he is realistic, but that he is a romancer who, in order that he may take liberties, persuades himself that he is a pathologist. Now, whilst there are people who like to take liberties, and other people who like to submit to them, they will be taken, and, within the due limits of personal freedom, must not be interfered with; but pray let us have no hypocritical pretence that they are disinterested researchers in psychology or sociology. They are not even an acceptable protest against the evil of obscurantism; for their effect is really to reinforce it. The remedy for obscurantism is responsible scientific instruction, and not licentious fiction.

The workmanship of "A Mere Accident" can be most conveniently considered by calling a truce—a temporary truce—with Mr. Moore on the subject of his moral accountability. It has been often urged upon him that "fine writing" is his weak point. He evidently thinks it just the reverse; and he is right. To appeal to the intelligence, and lead it to convictions which become a permanent spring of emotion, is all very well for writers who can do it; but Mr. Moore's business is to strike the fancy and rouse the imagination with pictures and rhythms. Accordingly he first "gets up" the needful Sussex scenery as if he were commissioned to write a guide book, and then he describes it thus:

> The country is as flat as a smooth sea. Chanctonbury Ring stands up like a mighty cliff on a northern shore: its crown of trees is grim. The abrupt ascents of Toddington Mount bear away to the left, and tide-like the fields flow up into the great gulf between.

That is not the landscape style of Bunyan, or Cobbett, or George Borrow; but it is the style of styles to serve Mr. Moore's turn; and he sticks to it wisely, and does it well. But when, inspired by Mr. Walter Pater, he applies the same method to mediæval Latin, and pours out the result in twenty-page doses, the critic, detecting "cram," winks, and—unless he skips—even sleeps. Nor, despite his interest in the doctrine of heredity, is he disposed to admit the term "psychical investigation" as appropriate to a long explanation of the hero's temperament, in which "direct mingling of perfect health with spinal weakness had germinated into a marked yearning for the heroic ages—for the supernatural as contrasted with the meanness of the routine of existence." Pretentious fustian of this kind abounds in the book; but the persons of the story are none the less shrewdly sketched; for Mr. Moore, within his range, is no bad observer. It is a range peopled by drunkards and vagabonds, by the "average sensual man," the half educated, the morbidly adolescent, the provincial and ignorant gentry—in short the unfit and inadequate for all noble parts in life. Among them there is not stuff enough to make a successful costermonger. Since they have their place among the many failures of our civilization, they must have their limner and chronicler. Only, one would fain meet some handsome and wholesome fellow-creature among them, if only as a standard to measure the shortcoming of the others. Here is Mr. Moore's own description of his hero:

> To the superficial, therefore, John Norton will appear but the incarnation of egotism and priggishness; but those who see deeper will have recognized that he is one who has suffered bitterly, as bitterly as the outcast who lies dead in his rags beneath the light of the policeman's lantern.

A couple of hundred pages or so of pseudo-psychologocial analysis of this gentleman's emotions will reconcile most readers to his sufferings. As to the young lady with "the delicate plenitudes of the bent neck bound with white cambric," in the author's most characteristic style, it need only be said that what there is natural of her is evidently drawn from an Irish model, and that it is not her fault that Mr. Moore did not find a better use for her.

Editor's Notes

- Shaw received Moore's novel on 7 July 1887, on which day he began reading it for review. The following day he finished reading it and began writing the review. He finished this on 9 July, and despatched it on the tenth. (*Diary*, 282–83, 330).
- George Augustus Moore (1852–1933), Irish novelist. His formal education had been slight by the time he set out for Paris in 1873, determined to become an artist. His failure in this medium turned him to writing, and in 1880 he was in London, struggling to make a living by his pen. His first novel *A Modern Lover* (1883), though crudely written, was noticed. It was followed by *A Mummer's Wife* (owing something to Zola and Flaubert), which was in advance of its time as a realistic novel. His reputation, which had increased with the publication of *A Drama in Muslin* (1886) and *Confessions of a Young Man* (1888), reached its peak in 1894 with the appearance of *Esther Waters*. Feeling that his art had reached a barren plateau at the turn of the century, he was persuaded by W. B. Yeats and Edward Martyn to return to Ireland, where he spent the next ten years of his life. The richness of his Irish associations led to a volume of Irish stories *The Untilled Field* (1903), a short novel *The*

Lake (1905), and his three autobiographical volumes *Hail and Farewell: Ave, Salve* and *Vale* (1911, 1912, and 1914). In 1911 he settled again in London, producing more short stories, *In Single Strictness* (1922), and *Celibate Lives* (1927), a play *The Apostle* (1911), and more novels *The Brook Kerith* (1916), *A Story-Teller's Holiday* (1918), *Heloise and Abelard* (1921), among others. Shaw, who had met him for the first time on 14 November 1885, recorded their infrequent meetings in his diary, but the two men, in spite of their common heritage and ambition, apparently never became close friends.

▪ *Mademoiselle de Maupin* (1835) is a novel by Théophile Gautier, which scandalized the public of its day. It concerns a young poet who finds the embodiment of love in Théodore, a young squire who comes riding out of the wood, and who turns out to be Mademoiselle de Maupin. The work is long, and the allegory rather confusing but the book is full of sensuous description, and its preface one of the first manifestos of "Art for Art's Sake."

▪ George Borrow (1803–81), English novelist who wrote of gypsies, and whose novels like *Lavengro* (1851) and *The Romany Rye* (1857), are permeated with the spirit of "the wind on the heath."

▪ Walter Horatio Pater (1839–94), English critic and Fellow of Brasenose College, Oxford, whose works, like the prose romance *Marius the Epicurean* (1885), are exquisitely styled with vivid imagery.

▪ The last sentence in Shaw's review angered Moore, who wrote to the *Pall Mall Gazette* the following day. His letter was published as follows:

"INTENSELY VIRGINAL" INDEED

To the EDITOR *of the* PALL MALL GAZETTE.

SIR,—I have never before broken silence to contradict a critic; the occasions are rare when an author may, with propriety, intervene. But surely this is one, for in the concluding lines of his article on my book, "A Mere Accident," your critic says: "It need only be said that what there is natural of her (Kitty Hare) is evidently drawn from an Irish model, and it is not her fault if Mr. Moore did not find a better use for her." So plain a statement calls for contradiction; a number of your readers may not understand it as a mere surmise; a gratuitous personality used with no worse intention, probably, than as a means of winding up the article in an effective manner. Your critic's opinion concerning the nationality of Kitty Hare can serve no purpose except to set my relatives, friends, and acquaintances in Ireland by the ears, and engender much mischievous speculation. I will therefore ask you to allow me to contradict your critic on the point flatly; and to enforce belief in my veracity I will say that Kitty Hare is no more than a rapid impression of an English girl seen once in an English drawing-room. I was struck by an extreme girlishness, by an intensely virginal air. An idea was thus created, and I strove to convey in "A Mere Accident" this idea of extreme girlishness, of perfect and adorable virginity.—Yours very truly,

The Green, Southwick, July 21.   GEORGE MOORE.

20 July 1887

LORD LYTTON'S LATEST* [C339]

ONE can hardly say of this volume, in its own words:

> Unlearn'd the listener and untaught the lay;
> But blithe were both in their instinctive way.

Lord Lytton's lay is the cynical lay, the pessimistic lay, the lay of the man who has gone young into modern culture with hope and enthusiasm, and come out middle-aged without them. Nothing less blithe in its instinctive way can be imagined. But what is Lord Lytton to do? If he cannot see beyond our present arrangements, then certainly the only alternative to Panglossian folly is pessimism; for we may as well admit handsomely that it would puzzle the most ingenious devil to contrive as much evil as we blunder into year after year with the best intentions. Under these depressing circumstances, only five courses have been found for the serious poet. 1. He may turn optimistic humbug, and versify the thing that is not. 2. He may, piercing the illusions which make the present order seem eternal, show the world its great future. Shelley did this; but it must be remembered, as a set-off, that he displeased Mr. Matthew Arnold. 3. He may turn his back petulantly on his contemporaries and dwell in King Arthur's court, with Lancelot and Guinevere and other picturesque phantoms. Lord Tennyson and Mr. William Morris indulged their imaginations thus; but that was before the idle singer of an empty day had gone into the subject of "surplus value," and founded the Socialist League. 4. He may brood bitterly on fate, sneer cynically at man, and sweeten the mixture with a tale of burning love. This is the Byronic manner. 5. Or he may sing with all his might in praise of anything that comes handy—revolution, coercion, Garibaldi, the Jubilee, Venus, or the Church of England— producing the effect of a series of new departures in politics, religion, and morals; and affording those who all along declared that there was more sound than sincerity in his pæans the innocent luxury of saying, "I told you so." There remains the recondite inconsistency of Mr.

---

*"After Paradise; or, Legends of Exile. With other Poems." By Robert, Earl of Lytton [Owen Meredith]. (London: David Stott. 1887.)

Browning, but, except to him, it is not worth its trouble, though it has incidentally saved English verse from utter emasculation.

It is not easy to assign Lord Lytton his class; for he is eclectic even to the point of taking his goods, as freely as Molière, Handel, or anybody, where he finds them. But since he has lost his illusions, and has neither belief that human society ever was, nor hope that it ever will be, otherwise than he has known it; and since, too, he only sings of life with relish when woman is his theme, he may be fairly described a Byronic-fabulist. His verse is Byronic too: he does not string words together in the spirit of a jeweller, but gives measure and music to human speech. There is no doubt that if he had anything really valuable to say he would say it very well.

In his latest volume he explains fancifully how matters went with Adam and Eve after their expulsion from Eden. The angel creates the past and future by summarily cutting eternity into halves with his flaming sword. Adam forgets the past; but Eve remembers; and many things about her daughters are prettily but unscientifically referred to this circumstance. Later on, the beasts leave Paradise in search of Adam, and bring him gifts from Eden. The ass, however, proposes to give a share only of his gift, which is Benevolence. Adam, in his greed, divides unfairly, and takes the greater part of Benevolence, leaving the less to the ass. Now, according to Lord Lytton, Benevolence = Stupidity + Patience; and Stupidity is the larger of the two. Hence man took stupidity, and left the ass patience. Here the quality of the pessimism is rather poor; but doubtless Lord Lytton has done his best, and no man can do more. The Byronic formula is fulfilled in the remarks made by the serpent to Eve:

> Behold, then, in thyself the primal source
> Of Human Progress, and its latest force!
> For, since from thee shall thy fair daughters, Eve,
> A subtler sex than all thy sons receive,
> Their beauty shall complete what thine began,
> Thou crown'd Queen Mother of the Queens of Man!

Editor's Notes

- Shaw received this book on 14 July 1887, on which day his diary records that he was also reading it for review. The following day Shaw is "writing review of Lytton's poems. Got on very badly with it." On the sixteenth he "finished and sent off review of Lytton" (*Diary*, 285, 331).

▪ Lord Lytton [pseud. "Owen Meredith." Edward Robert Bulwer, First Earl of Lytton] (1831–91), English statesman and poet. Educated at Harrow, he was sent to Washington to serve as an unpaid attaché to his uncle, Sir Henry Bulwer, who was then minister to the United States. With him he traveled to Florence in 1852. In Italy he made the acquaintance of the Brownings, and in 1855 published his first volume of poems, *Clytemnestra,* under the pseudonym "Owen Meredith," a name he continued to use until 1866, when George Meredith, the novelist, complained. In 1854 he was sent to Paris, and in 1856 to the Hague; and in 1858, a collection of lyrics entitled *The Wanderer* was published. The following year he was appointed second secretary to the embassy in Vienna, where he finished a novel in verse, *Lucile.* In 1864 he married. He contributed to journals such as *All the Year Round* and *Blackwoods,* published more verse, and in 1875, after a number of diplomatic positions in Europe, he became Viceroy of India. His viceroyalty was eventful, including, as it did, the Afghan War, the famine relief, and the proclamation of Queen Victoria as Empress of India. Lord Lytton returned to England in 1880, and settled down with his family at Knebworth, dividing his time between writing and the House of Lords. He wrote his father's biography (1883), *Glenaveril* [a long narrative poem] (1885), and *King Poppy* (1892). In 1887 he accepted the post of British ambassador to Paris (a fact to which Shaw alludes in his book review of 26 March 1888), where he died at the age of sixty.

▪ Dr. Pangloss (in Voltaire's *Candide*) is the optimistic philosopher who, in spite of a series of harrowing adventures including an unsuccessful hanging by the Inquisition, believes that all is for the best in this best of all possible worlds.

▪ Shaw's active membership at this date of the Browning Society, the New Shakspere Society, and the Shelley Society reveals his considered interest in the social role of the poet. The previous April at a Shelley Society meeting Shaw had argued in favor of a poem "taking the nature of a political treatise."

▪ When Shaw began to write his "Metabiological Pentateuch," *Back to Methuselah,* in 1918 he (perhaps coincidentally) captured a similar tone to Lytton, familiar and modern-sounding; but his work was forward-looking, not imbued with nostalgia for a lost innocence. In Lytton's poem Adam significantly has revelations of his past:

> He knew not whence they came,
> Nor was it in his power to reinvoke
> Their coming: but at time thro' all his frame
> He felt them, like an inward voice that spoke
> Of things which have on earth no utter'd name . . .
> *After Paradise* (*The Legend of Poetry*), p. 25

Shaw's Adam, too, hears voices, but they speak of the future:

ADAM: There is a voice in the garden that tells me things.
EVE: The garden is full of voices sometimes. They put all sorts of thoughts into my head.
ADAM: To me there is only one voice. It is very low; but it is so near that it is like a whisper from myself.

Back to Methuselah, Act I

26 July 1887

MR. PROCTOR'S *CHANCE AND LUCK** [C343]

BY AN INVETERATE GAMBLER

SPEAKING as a man who, with a fair experience of different plans to kill time like a gentleman, had rather gamble than do anything else, I must say that this book of Mr. Proctor's is a curious attempt to induce me, and those who think with me, to change our habits. It seems to us a book that would set an archbishop gambling. It has set me doing what, gambler as I am, I never did before: I mean tossing with myself, and by myself. Not that I have abandoned myself to it, like Mr. Proctor, Buffon, Professor De Morgan, and other scientific gentlemen, who think nothing of a couple of thousand ventures; but I confess I did my hundred and fifty straight off the moment Mr. Proctor's book put me up to it. The first fifty tosses gave exactly the scientific result, twenty-five heads and twenty-five tails; and I will take three to one against Mr. Proctor's getting that result the first time *he* tries. Out of the next fifty, I got the same result from the first forty (twenty heads and twenty tails); but then, by an extraordinary run of luck, I tossed heads ten times running; and I will make a sporting reduction on the scientifically moral odds against Mr. Proctor tossing heads ten times running in the first hundred tries. Solitary tossing is much better than playing patience. It is easier, and yet more scientific, particularly when you have read about it.

Now, the fact is that nobody except a gambler can write a satisfactory book about gambling. It is like a man with no ear trying to write a

---

*"Chance and Luck." By Richard A. Proctor. (London: Longmans and Co. 1887.)

book about music. That is where Steinmetz scores off Mr. Proctor in spite of the mathematics. Just listen to this, for instance:

> The idea to be controverted is: that if a gambler plays long enough there must come a time when his gains and his losses are exactly balanced. Of course, if this were true, it would be a very strong argument against gambling; for what but loss of time can be the result of following a course which must inevitably lead you, if you go on long enough, to the place from which you started?

Imagine a man—a man clever enough to write in the Encyclopædia Britannica—calling play "loss of time"! Is the pleasure of playing—the excitement—"the dreadful uncertainty," as the boy says of the fireworks in Mr. Pinero's comedy—nothing but loss of time? A blind man in a picture-gallery might lecture an art critic much as Mr. Proctor lectures me. If in the course of a year I win fifty thousand pounds and lose fifty thousand, have I not had a year's delicious excitement for nothing?—not to mention the occupation, which saves my faculties from decaying and myself from deteriorating morally, as idle men always do. And if I lose a thousand more than I gain, can Mr. Proctor show me where I can get a cheaper thousand pounds' worth of enjoyment? I say nothing about winning, because Mr. Proctor says that is impossible. I have done it though, all the same.

But Mr. Proctor himself, with all his science, argues to win, and shifts from black to red just as he wants to prove a point one way or the other. First he tries to show that there is no such thing as luck. Start tossing, he says, and you will find that heads will turn up as often as tails if only you go on long enough. This is just what I always tell a greenhorn when he flinches: only go on long enough and you are sure to get your money back. But when Mr. Proctor comes to deal with the doctrine of "the maturity of the chances," he tries to back out of his mathematical certainties. If the mathematics mean anything at all, they mean that there is a strong probability that out of a given number of tosses about half will be heads and half tails (as actually happened with me when I tried a minute ago). Now if I begin a set of a hundred tosses, and there is such a run on heads that when I get to fifty I have tossed tails only ten times and heads forty, then I say it is four to one that the next toss will be a tail instead of a head. "Oh, no," says Mr. Proctor, "because, for all you know, the mathematical chances may not be established in the second fifty any more than in the first, or, for the matter of that, in the thousandth." Then I say there's luck in it. "Oh, no," says my philosopher again, "because if you only go on long enough—say to a million tosses—the result will for a certainty correspond to the mathematical chances." "Very good, then," I reply: "all that that amounts to is that the result of a million tosses is a certainty, but the result of a smaller number depends on luck." In future, when I toss, I shall bar going on to a million, if the shortness of life doesn't bar it for me. That will keep the luck alive. But for my part, who am no mathematician, but a plain, honest sportsman, may I perish if I see why the mathematical chances should come right in a million tosses any more than in two!

But Mr. Proctor himself has proved to me that runs of luck which I should have thought impossible are certain to occur, and always do occur: that, in fact, the only luck in it is who they occur to. Further, he proves that they are as likely to occur to me as to anyone else, though, so as to discourage me [but a child could see through his little ways], he puts it that anyone else is as likely to win as I. Just so; and that's their inducement to play with me: to that I owe the blessed fact that I am able to gamble at all. Besides, as Mr. Proctor shows, if the event were a moral for me [sic], I should be a rascal to bet on it. Uncertainty is what makes a bet fair. And when Mr. Proctor says (p. 100) that "it is absolutely certain that no such thing as *luck which may be depended upon* exists," he admits that there is such a thing as luck. For luck which could be depended on wouldn't be luck at all. You don't call loaded dice lucky, although they are to be depended on if you have the proper knack of throwing them.

When Mr. Proctor leaves his calculations and begins to preach, he goes out of my line rather. When he says that "the object of all gambling transactions is to win without the trouble of earning," I refer him to his own proofs that gambling is a losing business pecuniarily speaking, and so must be followed for sheer disinterested love of sport. And when he says that "the gambler is blameworthy, since his desire is to obtain the property of another without giving an equivalent," I only think how precious little—if he will excuse my saying so—he must know of the world. What does any gentleman of property do for his living? I should like to ask. What equivalent does a landlord, or the mortgagee who has bought part of his rights, give to the tenant-farmer for the rent and interest they take from him? What equivalent do our shareholders and fundholders give to the people who do the work? To read Mr. Proctor you might think that the only difference between an English capitalist and an Irish landlord was that one pays Paul by robbing Peter, and Peter by robbing Paul, whereas the Irish squire robs Peter and Paul straight out without any hocus-pocus. That is what you come to by talking about "giving an equivalent" and setting up to be better than other people. I say that I live as other gentlemen do; and the equivalent I give is my equal risk of losing, and my services as layer or taker of the odds.

All the same, I think Mr. Proctor's book is a very useful one; and I freely confess that I have gambled more upon a principle, as it were, since I have read it. He is quite right about martingales. They are not worth the trouble; and I have always found at the tables that it pays better to go it blind.

Editor's Notes

- Shaw received this book, whose full title is *Chance and Luck: a Discussion of the Laws of Luck, Coincidences, Wagers, Lotteries, and the Fallacies of Gambling; with notes on Poker and Martingales* on 25 June 1887. His diary does not record when he began reading it, but on 29 July he "finished reading Proctor's *Luck and Chance* for review." The following day he began writing his review, which he finished and sent off on the twenty-second (*Diary*, 286, 330).

- Richard A[nthony] Proctor (1837–88), American astronomer and mathematician. Born in England, and educated at King's College, London, and at St. John's College, Cambridge, his interest in mathematics led him to study astronomy, on which subject he became the most prolific popular writer of his day. His theory of the solar corona (advanced in 1869) has now been generally accepted; he was active in the "transit-of-Venus" expeditions (1874 and 1882), and disputed with the astronomer-royal as to the best methods of observation. In 1866 he was elected a Fellow of the Royal Astronomical Society, and in 1873 he was made an honorary Fellow of King's College, London. From 1873 to 1879 he lectured in the United States, Australia, and New Zealand. On his second visit to the United States in 1884, he settled in St. Joseph, Missouri, and became an American citizen. His early works include *Saturn and its System* (1865), *Gnomonic Star Atlas* (1866), *Half-Hours with the Telescope* (1868), *Half-Hours with the Stars* (1869), *Other Worlds than Ours* (1870), *Light Science for Leisure Hours* (1871), *Border Land of Science* (1873), *Transits of Venus—Past, Present, and Future* (1874), and *Myths and Marvels of Astronomy* (1877). Among his later works are *First Steps in Geometry* (1887), *Easy Lessons in the Differential Calculus* (1887), and his last book, *Old and New Astronomy*, issued at the time of his death. He also contributed articles on astronomy to the *Encyclopædia Britannica* and the *American Cyclopædia*.

- Professor [Augustus] De Morgan (1806–71), English mathematician and logician. He was professor at University College, London, from 1828 to 1831, and from 1836 to 1866. He published the *Essay on Probabilities* (1838), *Formal Logic* (1847), *Trigonometry and Double Algebra* (1849), and treatises on calculus. He was one of the independent discoverers of the principle of quantification of the predicate; and in a series of memoirs on the syllogism published from 1850 to 1863, among other things he developed a new system of nomenclature for the expression of logic, gave his name to "De Morgan's Theorem," and advocated decimal coinage. His son, William Frend de Morgan (1839–1917) became an artist and novelist.
- [Charles Proteus] Steinmetz [originally Karl August Rudolf] (1865–1923), American electrical engineer. He was born in Breslau, Germany, but was forced to leave that country because of a socialist editorial he wrote in 1888 for a Breslau newspaper. The following year he settled in the United States, becoming in 1893 a consultant for General Electric (Schenectady, New York), and in 1902 a professor at Union College. His contributions to the field of electrical engineering include the calculation of alternating current phenomena, and the development of lightning arresters for high-power transmission cables. He was a great inventor, patenting over one hundred inventions, many of them improvements to generators and motors. He also wrote several books on engineering mathematics and radiation.
- The Pinero play in question is *The Schoolmistress*, which Shaw had been to see at the Court Theatre exactly a year before (on 21 July 1886). A servant in the girls' school, Tyler is described as "an unhealthy-looking youth, wearing a page's jacket." He carries fireworks on his person.

> TYLER: (*regarding them fondly*) Fireworks is my only disserpation. There aint much danger unless anybody lunges at me. (*producing some dirty crackers from his trousers pockets, and regarding them with gloomy relish*) Friction is the risk I run.
> JANE: (*palpitating*) Oh, don't, Tyler! How can you 'ave such a 'ankering?
> TYLER: (*intensely*) It's more than a 'ankering. I love to 'oard 'em and meller 'em. Today they're damp—tomorrow they're dry. And when the time comes for to let them off—
> JANE: Then they don't go off—
> TYLER: (*putting the fireworks away*) P'raps not—and it's their 'orrible uncertainty wot I crave after.

As a matter of fact they do go off, causing a fire that demolishes Volumnia College.
- On 27 August 1887, the *Pall Mall Gazette* published the following response to Shaw's review by the author of the book. Its length and the distance it had to travel are indications of Shaw's impact as a reviewer, even at this date:

NOTE ON LUCK AND GAMBLING

By Mr. Richard A. Proctor

I should be dull indeed if I did not recognize in "An Inveterate Gambler's" notice of my little book "Chance and Luck" (*Pall Mall Gazette* for July 26) as much kindness as fun. To use his own expression, and in as kindly a sense, "a child could see through his little ways." Yet "still I am not happy" till I have set right a point of two.

First, let me sketch a little gambling scene, which I recall somewhat vividly because the circumstances were unusual. Chief among the *dramatis personae* were the late Henri Ketten, eminent pianist, and a German professor about to take up his residence on a small island of the Pacific for philosophic purposes. The minor personages were Captain Cargill of the good ship *Australasia,* a boat's crew, three or four whist players (including myself—and a wretched whist player I was in those days), and a few islanders in incomplete attire and canoes. The scene may be regarded as divided between the *Australasia* and the Pacific Ocean; time, May, 1880. The following conversation took place:

> Philosophic German: Goot-bye, my frents; I go to be consumed by cannibals in the interests off my pelovt science.
>
> Omnes (except Ketten): Good-bye, old boy! And good luck!
>
> Myself: Don't forget Sydney Smith's advice—if they eat you, be sure to disagree with them.
>
> P. G.: Aha! Sydney Smid said well! He was what you call one fonny fellow. I will follow his advice. (P. G. *descends half-way down the side ladder.*)
>
> H. Ketten: Stay, Herr G.: you forget something.
>
> P. G.: Vas is das?
>
> H. Ketten: There is your little vist balance—five pounds eleven!
>
> P. G. (*proceeds—still on the side ropes—to extract the requisite amount of coin*) : I had, as you say, forgotten. (*Hands up the money, Ketten's length of limb enabling him to reach down some five feet.*) Already, you see, gentlemen, the cannibals have begun upon me. (*Descends sadly; then glances round at the islanders.*) On the whole, I prefer my unclothed cannibals.

It is in that part of the gambler's business which M. Ketten here unflinchingly performed that I am alone wanting. "An Inveterate Gambler" quite mistakes when he supposes I have no sympathy with gamblers, no sense of the enjoyment they find in running risks. Judging myself, as from without, I suppose few men have ever had a much keener taste of running chance risks than I have had. I may even say that the zeal with which I have urged the true philosophy in such matters, though it may have been in great part due to love for the mathematical relations involved, has chiefly had its origin in the constant occasion I have found through life to oppose, in such matters, reason to inherited instincts. But I should never, I think, have grumbled much, even if I had yielded to the temptation to run the risk of losing; for the simple reason that I could never pocket winnings with a comfortable conscience or other than a shamed face; and no one who is troubled with this weakness can ever become a Steinmetz or a Garcia. One tires of paying over losses and omitting to collect winnings.

I must remark, however, that I have nowhere suggested that gambling is criminal. It is admitted by all, because it has repeatedly been shown by experience that gambling is demoralizing. (I doubt if "An Inveterate Gambler" has gambled much for such sums as he could ill afford to lose, because he is obviously a good fellow, and no one who gambles much for such sums ever remains a good fellow long.) It is only going a little beyond the demonstrated fact that gambling is demoralizing to maintain that it is essentially immoral—for all who thoughtfully weigh its true nature. But what is immoral is not necessarily criminal, though what is criminal is necessarily immoral. It is hardly necessary to add that what "An Inveterate Gambler" says on this point is all in favour of my position, and cannot really have been intended otherwise.

But my chief point in writing is to show (though I fancy "An Inveterate Gambler" sees it well enough) that it is the gambler with his belief in "being in the vein" and in the "maturity of the chances" who really tries to be on both sides of the fence, not the student of probabilities who shows that both ideas are wrong. I am in the vein, or lucky, says the gambler, and he goes on playing, believing that his luck can be depended on. "An Inveterate Gambler" is quite mistaken in saying that "luck which could be depended on would not be luck at all:" it is essential to a true belief in luck that it should be regarded as something to be counted on; and this is the only form of faith in luck which is worth the trouble of controverting. The gambler who thus goes on because he trusts in his luck either finds his faith confirmed by the event or he does not. If he does, he points out that *there* is an illustration of the advantage of playing on when "in the vein." If he does not, and the luck turns, he points out that *there* is an example of the "maturity of the chances"; his vein had run out. Whatever the event, one or other of his superstitions is confirmed.

But it may be said that this is equally true of the scientific objections to these two ideas or superstitions. Whatever the event, one or other of the ideas rejected by science must be disproved; what then can be the value of the disproof? The answer is that science attaches no value whatsoever to such disproof. Science maintains, on perfectly distinct and independent grounds, and proves by experiment (as in coin tossing), that the run of past events (depending on pure chance) cannot influence in any way events of the same kind still in the future. The actual events may be indifferent, or a continuance of the preceding run, or may run the other way. We cannot guess what they will be, nor can their nature, let it be what it will, prove of itself anything either for or against the superstitions of the "vein" and the "maturity." Of one thing only we may feel tolerably sure: these events will confirm the gambler in one or other of his superstitions—in the "vein" fancy if they run well for him, and in the "maturity" notion if they run adversely.

As an example, take "An Inveterate Gambler's" idea that if in fifty tossings of a coin there have been forty heads and but ten tails, the odds are four to one that the next toss will be a tail. Of course this is wrong; the chances for head and for tail are even for that as for every other toss. The wrong idea in this case is the "maturity" notion. A gambling bystander watching the tossing might prefer the "vein" fancy; and a Steinmetz who had been actually tossing, winning when "head" appeared, would assuredly think he was "in the vein," and to such a tune that the odds were probably four to one in favour of his getting another "head" at the tossing. The science of probabilities comes in and explains, what ought to be obvious, that the next tossing is quite independent of all the past ones, and that the betting should be even on "head" and on "tail." But Buffon and the other fellows who tried the experiment of tossing a coin many thousand times proved this experimentally. For in all those multitudinous trials it was found that there was not the slightest trace of a tendency towards "head" after runs of "tails," or *vice versa*. There were many sequences of even ten or twelve "heads," yet following these "head" came as often as "tail."

It cannot be too often pointed out that the tendency to numerical equality of results, when the chances for one or other of two possible events are even, is not a tendency to minuteness of absolute difference, but to minuteness of relative difference. "An Inveterate Gambler" cannot for the life of him see, he tells us, why the mathematical chances should come right in a million tosses any more than in two. He is right enough if he imagines the mathematical chances point to absolute equality. In a million tossings, the event actually most probable among many millions of millions of millions of possible events (the actual number is two raised to the power of one million, a number containing 301,031 digits, which I would rather not calculate) is that there should be 500,000 heads and 500,000 tails. Yet this chance, though the largest, is largest among a number of chances which are exceedingly minute. The odds are many thousands to one against absolute equality. But they are also many thousands to one against numbers of heads or tails so disproportioned as 500,500 to 499,500. Now, in tossing a coin only four times there are sixteen possible events, and in six of these the heads equal the tails; so that there is a fair chance of actual equality. On the other hand, in the remaining ten cases the disproportion is as great as, or greater than, three to one; and in two cases out of the sixteen all four tossings are the same, so that the odds are only seven to one against even this result. I hope, then, that "An Inveterate Gambler" will no longer feel that he need: "perish if he can see" that the number of trials makes no difference in such cases.

As for the thought that gamblers, even though not absolutely inveterate, should be led to drop gambling because of anything urged in my little book, the preface showed I had no such hope. But it is as well the weaklings should be shown what odds they fight against. And there are many on the border line who may be saved.

St. Joseph, Mo., Aug. 10   RICHARD A. PROCTOR

25 August 1887

THE LATE PHILIP BOURKE MARSTON
SENTIMENTALIZED BY A FRIEND* [C348]

THIS collection of novelettes is not a happy memorial of the late Philip Bourke Marston. Perhaps happy is not exactly the word for any possible memorial of the man; for he was so unlucky that no one thought of blaming him for being in a measure beaten by his ill luck. He was a poet; he was blind; he was sensitive; he was weak; he was poor; and, instead of the intellectual training which enabled Milton and Henry Fawcett to see their way through the world without eyes, he had only that knowledge of fiction and poetry which, to uneducated people, looks like education, but which can only lead those who rely upon it into dangers and humiliations from which Philistine ignorance enjoys a square-toed freedom. As if all this were not misfortune enough for Marston, he was thrown by his father's circumstances into a literary and artistic set which had its imagination immensely stimulated by the sensational spectacle of a blind poet. To them the episode of his engagement to Miss Nesbit and her untimely death was a treasure-trove. They pounced on it and embellished it with harrowing details, until the story in its final form would not have seemed out of place in a

---

*"For a Song's Sake: and other Stories." By Philip Bourke Marston. With a Memoir by William Sharp. (London: Walter Scott. 1887.)

novel by Hugh Conway. Thenceforth nobody appears to have taken Marston seriously. He was Philip the unfortunate, Philip the bereaved, Philip the baffled in strife against the implacable grudge of the gods; in short, a realization, long sought, of the hero of innumerable bad novels. The number of men who can resist the temptation to play up to humbug of this flattering sort when it is once set afoot about them is not large; and that "poor Philip" was not one of them is abundantly shown in the memoir prefixed to this volume by his friend Mr. William Sharp—a memoir which may be taken as a fair sample of the nauseous nonsense that helped to make Marston the wreck he at last became. Here is a passage:

> When the ceremony [Dante Rossetti's funeral] was over, Marston whispered to me that he could not rejoin our friends just then; as we went along the cliffs and over the wide reaches of the shore, speaking no word. As we returned, he suddenly stopped, and with eager emphasis begged me to grant him one desire of his. I soon discovered that his desire was that I should see little of him henceforth; for, as he bitterly explained, "every friend whom I love seems to be brought within the influence of my unhappy fate." When, later on, I became dangerously ill, poor Philip sent me a letter full of remorse and sorrow. He had heard that I could not recover, and he believed that I had succumbed to the malign fate which pursued him and his. Looking through the letters which he at different times addressed to me, I find that note of apprehension ever recurring; and I believe the same would be found by his few really intimate friends.

If so, then the more shame for his few really intimate friends for encouraging him therein. If Mr. William Sharp cannot see that the above passage, instead of producing the effect of the speech of Mary Queen of Scots over the dying Douglas in Scott's "Abbot," only exhibits "poor Philip" as a maudlin egotist who was so untrained in the use of his brain as to fall into one of the commonest and crudest—but that it sounds harsh just now one might say the vainest and silliest—forms of logical error; then Mr. Sharp's readiness to write memoirs is a terror added to death. No doubt he was sincerely anxious to set off his friend's failings to the best literary advantage; but it would have been kinder to admit frankly that though Philip undeniably was maudlin sometimes, he was so for unromantic reasons that have prevailed with many another poet and good fellow. Mr. Sharp could then have claimed, with some chance of gaining attention, that when Marston was quite himself, and with people who dealt honestly and sensibly with him, he was incapable of affecting to believe that his existence had anything more to do with the fate of Miss Nesbit, Oliver Madox Brown, James Thomson, and Rossetti, than with that of the dozens of his friends who did not die, or who even, like Mr. Sharp himself, happily recovered on the very brink of fulfilling the Marstonic legend. If the blind poet ever finds a biographer whose personal knowledge is informed by a deeper insight into the sources of human happiness than can be gained by the study of sentimental fiction, it is not unlikely that those whose feelings Mr. Sharp has harrowed may be told bluntly that it is extremely doubtful whether the restoration of Marston's sight or the preservation of Miss Nesbit's life would have much bettered his lot. It would be easy to name poets who were not blind, who married the women they loved, who sustained no exceptional bereavement, and of whom it may be said as truly as of him that upon them "unmerciful disaster followed fast and followed faster, till their songs one burden bore." The fact is that Philip's blindness was like other people's blindness—a cruel inconvenience which he put up with because he had to, and because he was used to it. Precious as eyesight is, yet without it a man with a hard head, a strong soul, good company, and a sound training, might see a sweetheart and a few well loved friends go the way of all flesh, and yet laugh at Mr. Sharp's lugubrious sallies about "the long toil, the abiding pain, the infinite weariness," and the "Philip Marston, unhappy, often lonely, smitten cruelly by adverse fate, and dwelling continually in blank and terrible darkness."

The prose tales of which, besides Mr. Sharp's essay, this memorial volume consists, are not to be compared to Marston's best poetry. His delicate touch and sad strain are in them all; but their matter is monotonous: they run too repeatedly on an unconvincing story-book sort of love and brokenheartedness; on rain, storm, and the fall of the leaf; on drawing-room songs; and on attacks of consumption. They belong to the school that provoked the realistic reaction—the school of writers who, knowing nothing of the world, set to work to manufacture artificial joys and sorrows for the delectation of readers who knew less. Marston had some of the fine qualities that can give even this sort of work a charm; and he put bits of himself into it that were interesting. It helped to boil the pot and its day, and it may carry the holiday-maker through a tedious autumn railway journey for a season or two yet; but it must soon sink into oblivion; and one or two of "poor Philip's" flintier acquaintances will perhaps be glad to think that it is tied fast about the neck of Mr. Sharp's memoir, and will sink that too. Meanwhile, will not some publishing firm give the blind poet's fame a fair chance by collecting and reprinting his verses in a single volume? If it has been worth while to do this with his worst work, surely it is worth while to do it with his best.

Editor's Notes

- Shaw received this book on 25 June 1887, and his diary records that he was reading "Marston's stories for review" on 21 August. The next day he "wrote, finished and sent off review of Marston memorial volume" (*Diary*, 293).
- Philip Bourke Marston (1850–87), English poet. He was born in London, and since he was allegedly descended from John Marston, the Elizabethan dramatist, and his father was John Westland Marston, the dramatist (and a member of the Dickens circle), he was brought up in a literary atmosphere. However, he suffered the partial loss of his eyesight at the age of three, and for most of his life he was blind. Unquestionably his love of poetry was nurtured during his growing years by the guests in his father's house, who included Dickens, Browning, Tennyson, Rossetti, William Morris, and Swinburne. Shortly after his mother's death he fell in love with Mary Nesbit. His first book *Song-Tide and Other Poems* (1871) reflects his devotion to his fiancée, but in the very year of its publication Mary Nesbit died, the first of a series of personal losses that led to Marston's frequently depressed state. Oliver Madox Brown (the writer) died in 1874, Marston's sister Cicely (his traveling companion and amanuensis) in 1878, his second sister Eleanor in 1879, her husband, (the poet) Arthur O'Shaughnessy in 1881, and the poets Rossetti and James Thomson in 1882. His book *All in All* appeared in 1874, and *Wind Voices* in 1883. By the fall of that year, however, his own health was failing. Shaw had met Marston at Edward Aveling's on 6 March 1885 (*Diary*, 67), and may have noted Marston's drinking habits then, though his diary simply records the meeting without comment. In 1886 Marston suffered an attack of "brain fever," and the following January he suffered a paralytic stroke. He died on 14 February 1887.
- William Sharp ["Fiona Macleod"] (1855–1905), Scottish poet and critic. Born in Paisley, near Glasgow, he was educated at Glasgow Academy and the University of Glasgow, but did not take a degree. His early years were beset with hardship, including an abortive attempt at law, a trip to Australia, failure as a bank clerk, the collapse of a more congenial job in an art gallery, and two years with no employment whatever. In 1882, however, he was commis-

sioned by Macmillan to write a biographical memoir of the poet Dante Gabriel Rossetti (whose friendship he had enjoyed in the latter's declining years). This started him on a career of published authorship, and the friendship of many of the literati of the day. He first met Marston in 1880 through the intermediary of Rossetti and became a close friend. In 1882 his own first volume of poems was published, and the following year he obtained steady employment as art critic for the *Glasgow Herald,* for which he traveled on the European continent. In October 1884 he married his cousin, Elizabeth Sharp [see page 352 below], and his writing increased. He wrote for the *Academy, The Examiner,* and the *Athenæum,* edited *Sonnets of this Century* (1884), and wrote a novel *The Sport of Chance* (1887). In this year, too, he succeeded Eric Robertson as editor of *Young Folks' Paper,* for which he also wrote several stories. His second volume of poems in 1884, and *Romantic Ballads and Poems of Phantasy* (1888), together with his books on Shelley and Heine, brought him to the notice of the literary world on both sides of the Atlantic (he traveled more than once to the United States and Canada). But it was when he secretly assumed the pseudonym "Fiona Macleod" in 1894 that his work drew its most favorable critical attention. In fact, the creation of the female persona was much more than the adoption of a name: it was a kind of *alter ego* that released in him a different set of poetic visions. He maintained the reputation of William Sharp concurrently by publishing novels like *Wives in Exile* (1896) and *Silence Farm* (1897). Throughout his life he had battled failing health, and his death at the age of fifty occasioned little surprise among those who knew him.

▪ Henry Fawcett (1833–84), English economist. Graduating from Cambridge in 1856, he studied law at Lincoln's Inn, but was forced to rest because of weakness in the eyes. Ironically, while he was recuperating at his home, he was blinded by his own father in a shooting accident. Notwithstanding this tragedy, Fawcett refused to despair and returned to Cambridge where, by using readers, he studied political economy. He became professor of political economy at Cambridge from 1863 until his death. In 1865 he was elected to Parliament as a Liberal, and, although ineligible through blindness for a cabinet post, finally served as postmaster general in 1880. In 1867 he married Millicent Garrett, herself a remarkable woman, who later was a moving force in women's suffrage. Fawcett's writings include *Manual of Political Economy* (1863), *The Economic Position of the British Labourer* (1865), *Pauperism: Its Causes and Remedies* (1871), and *Speeches on Some Current Political Questions* (1873). His health failed in 1882, through diphtheria and typhoid. On his death a scholarship for blind students was established at Cambridge in his memory.

▪ "Hugh Conway" [pseudonym of Frederick John Fargus] (1847–85), English novelist. Sent at age thirteen to the school frigate *Conway* (a training ship for the Royal Navy), he was not allowed to join the navy when he graduated, but, after more schooling, in 1868 he succeeded to his father's auctioneering business, which he somehow managed to combine with literature (adopting as his pseudonym the name of the ship in which he spent his happiest days). The supernatural was the basis of his fiction, which gave rise to the term "shilling shocker." His novel *Called Back* (1883) was an enormous success, being translated into several languages, and made into a play by "Conway" himself, and *Dark Days* (1884) was almost as popular. Conway's own life was tragically short: ordered to the Riviera to quell the symptoms of tuberculosis he contracted typhoid and died at Monte Carlo at the age of thirty-seven.

- In Scott's *The Abbot*, a sequel to *The Monastery* (1820), Mary Queen of Scots says "God help me, I ruin every one whom I approach." One of these is George Douglas, whose death on the battlefield is an affecting climax to Scott's novel:

> "Look—look at him well," said the Queen, "thus it has been with all who loved Mary Stewart!—The royalty of Francis, the wit of Chastelar, the power and gallantry of the gay Gordon, the melody of Rizzio, the portly form and youthful grace of Darnley, the bold address and courtly manners of Bothwell—and now the deep-devoted passion of the noble Douglas—nought could save them—they looked on the wretched Mary, and to have loved her was crime enough to deserve an early death! No sooner had the victims formed a kind thought of me, than the poisoned cup, the axe and block, the dagger, the mine, were ready to punish them for casting away affection on such a wretch as I am!—Importune me not—I will fly no farther—I can die but once, and I will die here!"
>
> While she spoke her eyes fell fast on the face of the dying man, who continued to fix his eyes on her with an eagerness of passion, which death itself could hardly subdue.—"Mourn not for me," he said faintly, "but care for your own safety—I die in mine armour as a Douglas should, and I die pitied by Mary Stewart!"
>
> *The Abott*, Chapter 37

- Perhaps not surprisingly, Shaw's review provoked an angry letter to the *Pall Mall Gazette*, which was published on 29 August:

ANOTHER OF PHILIP BOURKE MARSTON'S FRIENDS

To the EDITOR *of the* PALL MALL GAZETTE

SIR,—As a friend of the late Philip Marston, I cannot allow your article of the 25th to pass without some protest. I am not concerned with your opinion of Mr. Sharp's memoir, nor of the stories themselves; and I certainly shall not be guilty of the absurdity of appealing to your reviewer's sense of good taste. But in the name of common decency, and for the sake of many relatives and friends to whom it will give the bitterest pain, I protest against this brutal, wanton, and cowardly personal attack upon a dead man. One of Philip Marston's strongest characteristics, as all his friends can testify, was his delight in other men's work and his desire to help them in it, if help was needed; and that he should be branded as a "maudlin egotist" because your reviewer has a grudge against Mr. Sharp is a disgrace to journalism.—

I am, Sir, yours &c.   H. E. CLARKE
10, *Benson-road, Forest-hill, August 26.*

- The author of the above letter was Herbert Clarke, who five years before had discovered the dying poet James Thomson (1834–82) at the house of Philip Marston, and had with some difficulty arranged for him to be hospitalized.
- Shaw's diary reveals that on 26 August, he "wrote reply to a furious letter written to the *PMG* about my article on P. B. Marston." This [C349] was published the same day, and reads as follows:

Readers who may have forgotten or skipped the review referred to by Mr. Clarke will be surprised to hear that it was a protest against Mr. William Sharp's exhibition of Philip Bourke Marston as a maudlin egotist, who affected to believe that the death of Dante Rossetti and others was due to a mysterious fate that overtook all whom he loved. No reference whatever was made to his personal good nature and interest in other men's work. Will Mr. Clarke kindly rub his eyes and read the review again, if his feelings will permit him? I am quite aware that I might have made my work easier, and gratified many private persons, by endorsing the sentiments of Mr. Sharp. That, however, would have been log-rolling, not criticism. I can understand, too, that from the log-roller's point of view a favourable criticism is "a very nice notice," and an unfavourable one "a personal attack." But why a friend of Marston's should stigmatize as "brutal, wanton, and cowardly" an attempt to defend his manliness is inexplicable on the hypothesis that the friend is a reasonable being. I take it that Mr. Clarke, being a little upset by the novelty and unexpectedness of a sensible word about Philip Marston, is for the moment, not quite reasonable.—*The Writer of the Review.*

Years later, Shaw complained to Archibald Henderson:

people have a strong feeling that if a man has lost his hearing or sight bravely in a noble cause, the world is thereby bound in decency to assume for ever after that he had the eye of an eagle and the ear of a hare. I have never belittled misfortune in that way. Long ago when [name crossed out], a blind poet, (on second thoughts I scratch out his forgotten name) died, and certain maudlin speeches of his were repeated in print as expressions of the pathos of his darkened existence, I said, also in print (*Pall Mall Gazette,* 25 August 1887), that he always said these things when he was drunk, and the fact that he was blind may have added to the pity of them, but did not give them any sort of validity. (*Collected Letters 1898–1910*, ed. by Dan H. Laurence [New York: Dodd, Mead & Company, 1972], 483)

6 September 1887

SPIRITUALISM EXTRAORDINARY!* [C353]

By a Firm Believer

THE Society for Psychical Research has been at it again. It was founded, whatever it may pretend to the contrary in its prospectus, to prove the existence of ghosts and all sorts of supernatural phenomena. It got no end of guineas on that understanding. Yet it does nothing all the time but knock the supernatural to pieces. When Mdme. Blavatsky came a few years ago, with her bright army of gurus, theosophists, and chelas, to rescue us from the sordid realities of nineteenth century materialism, we were pleased, stimulated, interested, and morally regenerated. Nobody asked the Psychical Society to interfere. But they did, and spoiled the fun, too, in no time. Actually sent a man named Hodgson—a man who called himself a gentleman—who reckoned up Mdme. Blavatsky as if he were a detective and she a common card-cutter and fortune-teller. He found out a lot of things which he might as well have kept to himself; and the end was that Mdme. Blavatsky was exposed by the very society that might have been expected to shield her.

But one favourite of the unseen world was left to us. If we wanted a message from a deceased relative, or a hint, written by shadowy hands, as to the final mystery of existence, we could still buy a threepenny slate; bring it to William Eglinton; and there we were. You might wash that slate, and tie it up, and screw it down, and never take your one eye off it and your other off William Eglinton: you might grab it tight with your right hand and him with your left: you might keep your questions unuttered in the most secret recesses of your soul: yet

*"Proceedings of the Society for Psychical Research." Part XI. May, 1887. 4s. (London: Trübner and Co.)
  "Spirit Workers in the Home Circle." By Morell Theobald, F.C.A. (London: T. Fisher Unwin. 1887.)

when you untied and unscrewed the slate you would find your answer, or your loved and lost one's message, written there in her own
writing and in any coloured chalk you liked to name. He laughed at
the Psychical Society, did Mr. Eglinton. He admitted—for a more
candid man never breathed—that when it came to downright "materializations," with the spirits of the departed walking about the room
and playing on the musical box, he preferred a special class of audience. But he would slate-write before anybody. Psychography, he
called it. Mr. Hodgson was welcome to search the rooms and set the
servants talking as much as he pleased: he would go away as wise as
he came. It was of no use: the Psychical Society were shut up at last;
and they knew it.

Nobody would believe the mean thing the Psychical went and did
under these circumstances. Hodgson was in it, of course; but they got
another man, named Davey, who, no doubt, dropped the suffix Jones
in order to hide the real nature of his powers. He started slate writing
under the name of Clifford (and I need not remind your readers of a
celebrated line about a certain place being full of such Cliffords). This
man, it is plain, entered into an unholy covenant with those malignant
occult beings whose animosity Mr. Eglinton has gained by his consistent choice of the highest spiritual companionship. Seconded from
below, Davey set to work to do everything Mr. Eglinton had done: that
is, everything that was marvellous in it to vulgar observers. He did not
get the beautiful consoling messages, the high aspirations, the quietly
fervid blessings that have made Mr. Eglinton's sitters so happy and
hopeful; but, of course, he got the writing in the coloured chalks on
the washed, tied, screwed, jealously-watched slates; and all the
merely extraordinary stuff, such as answering hidden questions, quoting lines from books that had been secretly selected from the shelves
by the sitters and other things which are on the face of them utterly
impossible except by supernatural aid. And now he has the audacity to
turn round and declare that he is only a conjuror, and that therefore
poor Mr. Eglinton may be a conjuror too!

But to show how much too clever he has been, it is only necessary
to say that he has to deny the accounts of his own witnesses. Their
descriptions of what they saw prove the impossibility of any merely
human agency having been at work. And their sincerity is obvious. All
the thanks they have had from Mr. Davey is his assurance to the
public that they are not to be depended on—that they transposed the
order of the events they witnessed, mentioned precautions that they
did not take, omitted precautions that they did take, and, above all,

that they repeatedly declared that they never took their eyes off the slates, when as a matter of fact (according to Mr. Davey) they lost sight of them for considerable periods. The inference is obvious. The evidence for Mr. Davey's miracles is as striking as that for Mr. Eglinton's. But Mr. Davey's miracles were conjuror's tricks. Ergo, Mr. Eglinton's miracles may also be conjuring tricks. This may be convincing to materialists, who deem that anything is more probable than that Mr. Davey should be in league with the powers of Darkness. But to us, who already know that Mr. Eglinton is in league with the powers of Light, such an unholy compact is far more credible than that a number of respectable ladies and gentlemen should, even at the instigation of the man who blasted the career of Mdme. Blavatsky, wilfully bear false testimony. Of course, Mr. Davey tries to explain that they only made mistakes, and were not wilfully untruthful; but if people cannot be trusted to believe their own eyes, then there is an end of trusting to direct evidence at all. The discrepancies between accounts of the same *séance* by persons who thought spirits were at work, and by others who had been told that it was conjuring, only show to my mind how much mischief is done by false pretences.

Mr. Morell Theobald's "Spirit Workers in the Home Circle" is a welcome relief from the Psychical Society's volume, with its record of Mr. Davey's pretended trickery, and of the hypnotic suggestions of Mr. Gurney, who might take a lesson from Mr. Eglinton and "suggest" some nobler ideas to his poor subjects than dog-fights and balloon ascents. Mr. Morell Theobald tells us with touching directness how his family life has been passed in the sweetest communion with spirits, who not only write messages on the ceilings, but helpfully light the fires, boil the kettles, and make the tea in the mornings. Nothing can be more conclusive than the way in which he deals with the objection that these employments are too trivial for the dignity of spiritual activity.

> Lighting a fire is not always a simple act. It may assume a transcendent and mystic import if it enters into organic relation with the education and discipline of a human life. The words themselves—light, fire—need only to be spoken with a pause of reverent contemplation, and the spirit is lifted into holy worship or kindled into poetic ecstasy.

How different from the cold, sceptical, unsympathetic carping and logic chopping of Mr. Hodgson, Mrs. Sidgwick, Mr. Davey, and other

Pyschical Researchers! They shall not take our Eglinton from us as they took our Blavatsky.

I am sorry that I cannot dwell at greater length on the 300 pages in which Mr. Morell Theobald gives example after example of the intimate and familiar intercourse which he has enjoyed for years with the guardian spirits of his hearth. In reading them one feels how intensely interesting it would be to know some of the members of his household, were it even but a discharged housemaid. Some of the numerous facsimiles of spirit writing might have been reproduced here were they not too human and real—even to an occasional slip in the spelling—to greatly impress the ordinary reader. I will conclude with a little incident which might touch even Mr. Hodgson, so unforced is its simple domestic pathos:

> After breakfast, while M. was in another room, she heard the knife machine going in the kitchen where no one was; for the boy who cleans the knives was out; and on my daughter going in she found all the knives which we used for breakfast cleaned and put on the table. In the afternoon the kettle was again filled by our little invisible friends and put to boil, and while both were sitting in the room the teapot was half filled with boiling water and the tea made.

Mr. Fisher Unwin, the publisher, is entitled to the thanks of all for bringing out this most remarkable book.

Editor's Notes

- Shaw received Morell Theobald's book on 25 June 1887, and the Proceedings of the Psychical Society on 21 July; yet he did not begin the reviewing process until 18 August. This was an extremely busy time for Shaw: from 12 July to 16 August the bulk of his critical energy was devoted to an enormous review of Marx's *Das Kapital* for *The National Reformer* (although during that time period he managed to write the reviews of Lytton and Proctor printed above). He also wrote a tale "The Truth about Don Giovanni"; and this outburst of creative writing may have suggested the form of Proctor's review and this one: the personae chosen have distinct voices, and Shaw seems to obtain as much fun out of "characterizing" his "reviewers" as he does out of their comments. That this conscious irony was gravely misunderstood by some of his readers is apparent from the response of the journal *Light* reprinted below. On 17 July, the day after he finished the Marx review, Shaw began reading the Psychical Society *Proceedings*, continued the next day, and on the nineteenth "began review of Psychic books." There is no specific reference to Morell Theobald's book, but one assumes he read it after the *Proceedings*. On 20 July, Shaw "finished and sent off review" (*Diary*, 292–93, 330, 331).

• Morell Theobald (1828–1908), English spiritualist. He came from a family that believed it had psychic gifts (both his grandfather and his father saw spirits), and his acquaintanceship with similar families (the Howitts and the Everitts) initiated him into writing-mediumship in 1855. The loss of three of their six children seems to have deepened the Theobald family's faith in spiritual phenomena, and a book written by his sister *Heaven Opened; or Messages for the Bereaved from their Little Ones* (1870) details experiences of table rapping, furniture movement, and the "control" of living children by the deceased ones. In 1882 the family cook, Mary, was discovered to have clairvoyant powers, and the following year the events occurred that Shaw somewhat sarcastically refers to. In 1884 Theobald's first book appeared, *Spiritualism at Home*. Theobald underwent tests by the Society of Psychical Research in 1886, in which he undertook to reveal the contents of sealed envelopes. After the successful completion of the test, humiliation followed when it was stated by the Society that the envelopes had been opened and gummed up again. Theobald's attribution of this unfortunate circumstance to the work of mischievous spirits is echoed by Shaw's parodic assertion above that Mr. [S. J.] Davey was assisted by wicked powers.

• In nautical slang (dating from the eighteenth century) Davy Jones is the spirit of the sea, or the sailors' devil. Hence Davy Jones's Locker, which is the ocean.

• Shaw seems to be referring to one of the Lord Cliffords of Shakespeare's *Henry VI* trilogy: Lord Clifford who slaughters the young Earl of Rutland is bloodthirsty enough to be in hell; but there is no line about hell being full of Cliffords.

• Part XI of the *Proceedings of the Society for Psychical Research* consisted of the Opening Address (given by Professor Balfour Stewart, F.R.S.), and papers given at the Twenty-fourth General Meeting by Edmund Gurney, Anton Schmoll, Professor Carvill Lewis, M.A., F.G.S., Richard Hodgson, S.J. Davey, and W. H. Myers.

• This review prompted an attack on the *Pall Mall Gazette* by the spiritualist journal *Light* on 17 September 1887, which begins as follows:

The fact that the *Pall Mall* of the 6th contains a flippant article on Spiritualism has caused us to receive a number of copies, and to devote some attention to this specimen of the newest journalism.

Since the article is a lengthy attack on the complete contents and philosophy of the newspaper, it is not appropriate to reproduce it in its entirety. The paragraphs that refer specifically to Shaw's review follow:

Then comes our article on "Spiritualism Extraordinary." It would be impossible, in any space at our command, or with any regard for the forbearance of our readers, to give a fair idea of the flippant vulgarity, stupidity, and general 'Arryism of this most offensive article. The material on which it professes to be founded is Part XI of the *Proceedings* of the Society for Psychical Research, and Mr Theobald's *Spirit Workers in the Home Circle*. And the column and a-half that somebody has been allowed to write on these publications is, we should think, unique in journalism. "The Society for Psychical Research has been at it again. It was founded, whatever it may pretend to the contrary in its prospectus, to prove the existence of ghosts and all sorts of supernatural phenomena. Yet it does nothing all the time but knock the supernatural to pieces." What chaste and delightful language; what a pure and perfect style! Then we have an allusion, displaying true knowledge, to Mdme. Blavatsky, "with her bright army of gurus, Theosophists, and chelas," and afterwards this delicious bit, which, it should be explained, is fun, pure childish merriment:

"Nobody asked the Psychical Society to interfere. But they did, and spoiled the fun, too, in no time. Actually sent a man named Hodgson—a man who called himself a gentleman—who reckoned up Mdme. Blavatsky as if he were a detective and she a common card-cutter and fortune-teller. He found out a lot of things which he might as well have kept to himself; and the end was that Mdme. Blavatsky was exposed by the very society that might have been expected to shield her."

Is it necessary to quote more trash of such a nature, or to spend any pains in noticing it? We have, of course, Mr. Eglinton, and equally of course now, Mr. Davey, who is replacing Mr. Maskelyne in the part that he once played—a kind of Egyptian Hall understudy—and last we get some occult references to Mr. M. Theobald's book, references so occult as to be unintelligible. The reviewer realises "how intensely interesting it would be to know some of the members of his household, *were it even a discharged housemaid.*" There comes in the touch of nature, and we know where we are, and the sort of person we have to deal with.

The article concludes:

And this is the stuff which the *Pall Mall* treats at length, and advertises with all its adjuncts of "Glory Hole" sensationalism, while it jeers and sneers at the beliefs, held on evidence enough to establish any fact, of men of trained scientific intellect, of unquestioned probity, of prominent social position, of established life-long reputation.

Could the newest journalism more conspicuously write itself down for what it is?

26 September 1887

PROFESSOR SIDGWICK AND MR. BELFORT BAX* [C356]

SURELY the world has not hitherto produced two contemporary philosophers less alike in temperament than Professor Sidgwick and Mr. Belfort Bax. Just as no man was ever so wise as Lord Eldon looked, so no man was ever so impartial as Professor Sidgwick makes himself appear. In ethics, economics, politics, or what department you please, he makes it his business to set up a fence exactly between progress and reaction, and sit upon it with a passionless academic placidity that carries much authority, but that is inexpressibly aggravating at times. For no matter what field you are in, you are an extreme person compared with the man on the fence. The temptation to pull him on to your side and welcome him as an ally, or to push him off to the other and let him be prosecuted as a trespasser, is strong. For example, you are an uncompromising advocate of *laisser faire;* and you claim the support of Professor Sidgwick as an orthodox economist. Undoubtedly he agrees with you; but he also points out certain exceptions to the application of the principle, which, as they can be stretched so as to cover the whole sphere of human conduct, leave you in doubt as to whether he is not a rabid Socialist after all. Again, you are an enthusiastic member of the Cobden Club, and would fain overwhelm the Fair Trader with the authority of an economist of the Professor's eminence. But he, while fully alive to the considerations which weighed with the classic economists and their pupil Cobden, yet mentions, for completeness' sake, the possibility of protection proving advantageous under certain circumstances, which a malignant protectionist might venture to assert were the very circumstances of England at this present hour. Even at the Psychical Society, nobody knows, or ever will know, whether Professor Sidgwick believes in ghosts or not, though

---

*"Outlines of the History of Ethics. For English Readers." By Henry Sidgwick. (London: Macmillan and Co. 1886.)

"A Handbook of the History of Philosophy." By Ernest Belfort Bax. Philosophical Library. (London: G. Bell and Sons. 1886.)

"An Inquiry into the Nature and Causes of the Wealth of Nations." By Adam Smith, LL.D With an Introduction by E. Belfort Bax. Two vols. Bohn's Standard Library. (London: G. Bell and Sons. 1887.)

he has these many years been investigating them with an impartiality which even they must find somewhat unsubstantial.

Now, Mr. Belfort Bax's worst enemies cannot accuse him of impartiality. Let Professor Sidgwick plant his fence where he will, you shall
not catch Mr. Belfort Bax astride of it. Seek the spot most extrava-
gantly and conspicuously remote from it; and there you will find him
waving a flag red enough to incarnadine the multitudinous seas. It
was Mr. Bax who recently startled readers of the *Pall Mall Gazette* by
the suggestion that Lipski's confession of murder was extracted by
the fear of torture. It was he who declared shortly before that, in an
astonishing contribution to the woman question, that men are systematically sacrificed, in police-courts and elsewhere, to a sentimental
leaning towards the side of the softer sex; and that man is really the
more delicate and fragile organism of the two, as was proved by the
case of a lady who, having fallen 245 feet, "experienced but slight
constitutional disturbance"—a "record" in toughness which man is
certainly not likely soon to beat. It is Mr. Bax again who has advanced
the startling proposition in applied ethics that it is, though illegal, not
immoral to travel by rail without a ticket, since a railway company
admittedly represents nothing but capital, without body to be kicked
or soul to be damned and therefore also without personality to which
individual man can conceivably have duties. And Mr. Bax's chief historical contribution has been a monograph on Marat, quite unanswer-
ably exhibiting that clamourer for other people's heads as the most
sympathetic of the French revolutionists. When Mr. Hyndman, at the
banquet given by our native Socialists to a delegation of French work-
men at the Holborn Restaurant proudly cited Mr. William Morris as
the sort of poet, and Mr. Walter Crane as the sort of artist Socialism
could boast of, it was to Mr. Bax that he pointed as a specimen philosopher and metaphysician. And though the record of Mr. Bax's exploits
may suggest, at the first blush, that he is qualified to write a handbook
of perverseness rather than of philosophy, his special department is
indeed the ultimate problem of what in us is conscious of our consciousness. The putting forward of seeming blasphemies about railway tickets, and the metaphysical spiflication of rash members of the
bourgeoisie who zealously hurry, horror-stricken, to denounce and
confute him, are but his disportings for the entertainment of members
of the Socialist League who like to see that capitalistic institutions will
not stand really learned (because mostly incomprehensible) criticism.
It was to Mr. Bax the translator of Kant's "Prolegomena" for the Bohn
Library, and not to Mr. Bax the enemy of civilization, that Messrs. Bell

turned when they required a manual of the history of philosophy to replace that of Tenneman, of whose book their new historian remarks that had he merely attempted to bring it up to date it would have resembled that relic of the Thirty Years' War respecting which we are told that "the head, neck, legs and body have been renewed: all the rest is the real horse." And since, in this country, academic tradition stamps all philosophers as economists *ex officio,* Messrs Bell, when they wanted an editor for a reprint of Adam Smith's "Wealth of Nations," applied, as a matter course, to their philosopher. It was natural; but, to some of the venerable Whig economists, Adam Smith edited by a Socialist pupil of Marx must be as startling as would be Butler's "Analogy" edited by Mr. Bradlaugh.

Professor Sidgwick, in expanding his article in the Encyclopædia Britannica into "Outlines of the History of Ethics," has had a more specialized task than Mr. Bax, inasmuch as he has dealt with a department only of philosophy, and that, too, as far as the modern part is concerned, with reference chiefly to what he calls "English Ethics." It is not an exciting work; but it is calm, moderate, provokingly impartial and, within its express limits, what reviewers call thorough, meaning, not that any mortal history ever was exhaustive, but that the author apparently knows as much as or more than his critic. Mr. Bax, by compressing into 400 pages a history of philosophy from Thales to Mr. Herbert Spencer, has executed a very arduous commission, and at certain points an unavoidably dull one, since there was, between the crises of the various schools, so much futile thinking to be chronicled. He has, however, proved himself the very man for the work. His historical sense never fails; he never loses his grip of his dialectical method; and he shows a remarkable faculty for seizing the distinctive views of thinkers of different schools, and expressing them almost vividly, in spite of their abstractness and of the fact that pure philosophy can hardly be said to have a language. His introductory and concluding chapters are made fascinating by his note of faith in the future of man, and helpful by the keen intelligence with which he presents the problem of philosophy proper quite disentangled from the sciences with which it is popularly either confounded or placed in antagonism.

Mr. Bax's excursion into economics as an editor of Adam Smith falls far short of the level attained by him in his History of Philosophy. It is pleasant to have "Wealth of Nations" in two excellently printed volumes of the Bohn Library, cheaper than the Clarendon Press edition by Mr. Thorold Rogers, and more readable than the Edinburgh reprint from the battered plates of the old McCulloch edition, with Professor Shield Nicholson's notes and preface. But Mr. Bax writes without the practical information of the one annotator, or the special economic training of the other; and he all but hints that such information is impertinent and such training superfluous. He presently, however, makes himself an example of the need of at least the latter; for his pointed historical sketch of political economy is spoiled at the end by a perverse misapprehension of the work of his contemporaries, notably Jevons, whose revival of purely scientific economics, and establishment of the law of the variation of utility, make it absurd to class him with those professors of Manchester factory apologetics whose doctrinairism Karl Marx dubbed "the vulgar economy." Mr. Bax seems to be exasperated by Jevons's mathematical method, and to rely absolutely on the theories of Marx, whose conclusions he sums up in six propositions, not one of which, probably, would be assented to by any skilled economist in Europe, socialist or other. In fact, he has been unfair to Marx as he has been to Jevons, dwelling on the weak points in both and ignoring their real contributions to the development of economic science. The value of Mr. Bax's historic sense and intelligent method appears in one or two of the scanty notes; but on the whole it cannot be said that he has made the most of such an enviable opportunity as a great classic like Adam Smith presents to an editor.

Editor's Notes

▪ Shaw received Sidgwick's book on 13 July 1886, but did not start reading it for review until 21 November that year. There is no reference to his receipt of the Bax volumes. On 28 November, he "read Sidgwick's *Ethics* on the train" on his way to Leicester to lecture on "Socialism and Malthusianism." On 13 December, he "read Sidgwick's *Ethics* in the afternoon. Bax at Museum. He came to tea here." Shaw then seems to have laid Sidgwick's book aside for almost nine months. His diary for 18 December 1886 contains the sentence "began reading Bax's *History of Philosophy.*" He continued reading Bax's book for the next two days; and on the thirtieth he reports "still reading Bax, *Philosophy of History*" [sic]. On 2 February 1887, Shaw read "a little of Bax's philosophy," and again on the fifth, the seventh, and the ninth. On 14 March, he again takes up the book, and for the next two days he reads it. Thereafter it is not mentioned until 23 August 1887, when again he reads Bax for three days, reporting on the twenty-fifth: "Finished Bax's book. He came to the Museum in the afternoon. Got his edition of Adam Smith from him to read the preface." On 8 September 1887, he "read Prefaces to *Adam*

Smith and other economic documents at the Museum." The following day finds him "working at review of Bax, Sidgwick, etc." and on the tenth he is "still at review, chiefly reading for it." On the eleventh, he "finished and sent off review of Bax and Sidgwick" (*Diary*, 215, 217, 220–22, 226, 239, 240, 251, 252, 293, 294, 297, 298). According to St. John Ervine, it was the length of time between the receipt of Sidgwick's book and the writing of the review that cost Shaw his job on the *Pall Mall Gazette!* He claims that Shaw did not feel competent to criticize Sidgwick's work until he had read about a dozen volumes, ranging from "Thales to George Henry Lewes."

> A year later, the review had not yet been written, and the publishers complained to the editor who, therefore, ceased to send Shaw any more books. (St. John Ervine, *Bernard Shaw: His Life, Work and Friends* [London: Constable and Co., 1956], 184)

While this is not true (Shaw reviews books published in 1888), it is a fact that he does not list any further books from the *Pall Mall Gazette* after December 1887.

- Henry Sidgwick (1838–1900), English philosopher. Born in Yorkshire, he was educated at Rugby and Trinity College, Cambridge, where he was made fellow and assistant tutor in 1859. In 1875 he was made prelector of moral and political philosophy at Trinity, and Knightsbridge Professor of Moral Philosophy in 1883. Sidgwick's most important philosophical work relates to ethics, in particular his *Methods of Ethics* (1874). In this work his doctrine "combines an intuitional notion of duty . . . with an empirical discovery of the nature of goodness." Another of his interests was the higher education of women. In 1876 he married Eleanor Balfour (sister of Arthur), and she became the first president of Newnham, the Cambridge women's college. His other chief pursuit, the investigation of psychic phenomena is described above on pages 43 and 104. Apart from the work reviewed above, his other works include *Ethics of Conformity and Subscription* (1871), *Principles of Political Economy* (1883), *The Scope and Method of Economic Science* (1885), and *Elements of Politics* (1891).
- Ernest Belfort Bax (1854–1926), English philosophical author and lawyer. Educated privately in London and in Germany, he studied music (theory and composition), and philosophy, primarily the German movement from Kant to Hegel. While in Germany he acted as a foreign correspondent from 1880 to 1881. On his return to England, he was one of the founders of the English Socialist movement. Bax was a prolific writer: apart from the books reviewed above, his publications include *Jean-Paul Marat* (1878), *Kant's Prolegomena etc., with Biography and Introduction* (1882), *Religion of Socialism* (1886), *Ethics of Socialism* (1889), *The French Revolution* (1890), *The Problem of Reality* (1898), *German Society at the Close of the Middle Ages* (1894), *Outspoken Essays on Social Subjects* (1897), *The Peasants' War in Germany* (1899), *Rise and Fall of the Anabaptists* (1908), *The Last Episode of the French Revolution* (1911), *German Culture, Past and Present*

(1915), and *The Real, the Rational and the Alogical* (1920). He also edited the journals *Time* and *To-Day* (with James Leigh Joynes [see page 407 below], and Hubert Bland), the last of which publications serialized two of Shaw's novels, *An Unsocial Socialist,* between March and December 1884, and *Cashel Byron's Profession,* between April 1885 and March 1886. In fact Bax and Shaw were close friends in the middle and late eighties, Shaw either meeting Bax at the British Museum and taking him home to tea, playing piano duets with him, or visiting his house in Croydon. Bax was Shaw's predecessor as musical critic of *The Star,* writing under the pseudonym "Musigena;" and it was Bax who invited Shaw to fill in for him while he was on vacation, which he did until Bax resigned in February 1889, at which point Shaw, under the more famous pseudonym "Corno di Bassetto," took over.

▪ To Charles James Fox (1749–1806) is attributed the quotation, "No man could be so wise as *Thurlow* looked," the Thurlow in question being Edward [1st Baron] Thurlow, who was Lord High Chancellor from 1778 to 1792. This is quoted in Campbell's *Lives of the Lord Chancellors* (1846), 5:661. Shaw's substitution of Lord Eldon—presumably the one appointed Lord High Chancellor in 1801—is an interesting variation.

▪ [Israel] Lipski [real name Lobulsk] (1865–87), Russo-Polish immigrant stick maker. Born in Warsaw, he was indicted for the murder of Miriam Angel, who, with her husband, shared his Whitechapel house, on 28 June 1887. Allegedly, he knocked her senseless and poured nitric acid down her throat, choking her, afterwards taking some of the acid himself in an apparently failed suicide attempt. His defense was that two other men had killed Mrs. Angel, and then tried to kill him. The presiding judge was Mr. Justice Stephen [see page 403 below]. The trial began on 29 July, and was concluded on the thirtieth. Lipski was found guilty, and condemned to death. Doubts about Lipski's guilt surfaced during the trial, and unaccountable disparities of fact led the press to mount a campaign to save him. *The Rock, The Daily News, The Daily Chronicle, The Morning Advertiser, The Tablet, The Methodist Times, The Jewish World,* and *The Jewish Chronicle* all ran editorials pleading with increasing urgency for the "new evidence" to be examined, and for Lipski's reprieve. No newspaper, however, ran a more powerful campaign than the *Pall Mall Gazette,* which aimed its shafts squarely at Home Secretary Henry Matthews [see page 403 below], and finally published a penny pamphlet entitled *Shall We Hang Lipski? or the Mysterious Murder of Miriam Angel.* The pleas reached a pitch of hysteria by 20 August. Charges of obstruction were made against the Whitechapel police, questions were asked in the House of Commons, one of the jurors from the trial wrote a desperate appeal to the *Pall Mall Gazette,* and a petition with five hundred names was presented to the Home Office. Still Home Secretary Matthews refused to grant a reprieve. Finally, on the eve of his execution, Lipski confessed his guilt. For a moment, the press, embarrassed by this *volte face,* tried to play down their earlier efforts, claiming that all they had called for had been the truth, which was now clear. But the day after Lipski's execution, the *Pall Mall Gazette* published an article (originally published in *The Commonweal*), written by William Morris and Belfort Bax. This pointed to even more glaring disparities in the confession than there had been at the original trial. They asked

> Who knows what kind of cajolery, or even threats, might not have been employed, since the occasion was so urgent, and so much was at stake?

And, reminding the readers that the condemned man was from Russian Poland, where a confession of guilt is necessary before a condemned criminal can be executed, and that there torture is admitted to be used on occasion to extract such a confession, wondered whether Lipski

> might have had a confused idea that the same thing might happen here, and seeing his case was hopeless, and that he had to die, submitted to what he might think was a general formula for the sake of dying without unnecessary worry. ((W.) Morris, and (E.B.) Bax, "Is Lipski's Confession Genuine?" *Pall Mall Gazette*, 23 August 1887)

▪ Jean Paul Marat (1743–93), French revolutionary, whose journalistic attacks on the assembly, Louis XVI, and his ministers possibly precipitated the bloody massacres of 2–7 September 1792.
▪ Walter Crane (1845–1915), English painter and illustrator. As a painter, he is classified with the Pre-Raphaelites. He was, however, primarily an illustrator, and with William Morris is considered to be a leader in the "Romantic movement" in decorative art. He illustrated numerous books, his most famous being Spenser's *Faerie Queene* in the years 1894 to 1896. He was also an author of books on aesthetics, an influential teacher of art (he was director of three schools, including the Royal College of Art in South Kensington). He was indeed an active Socialist, contributing political cartoons to socialist journals and founding the Art Workers' Guild.
▪ Wilhelm Gottlieb Tenneman's (1761–1819) *Manual of the History of Philosophy* (1798–1819) was translated into English by the Rev. Arthur Johnson in 1832, and revised and enlarged by J. R. Morrell in several subsequent editions.
▪ Smith's *Inquiry into the Wealth of Nations* [for Adam Smith see page 98 above], the first comprehensive treatment of political economy, sets out the doctrine that the labor of the nation (and not land, as the French physiocrats claimed) is the source of its means of life. Shaw wrote a note for the *Commonweal Calendar* on the anniversary of Smith's death in June 1888, in which he found the treatise not "old-fashioned."
▪ [Joseph] Butler (1692–1752) was successively Bishop of Bristol and of Durham. His monumental work *The Analogy of Religion, natural and Revealed, to the Constitution and Course of Nature* was first published in 1736. It went through innumerable editions, and was systematically analyzed and argued over by generations of theologians.
▪ Thales, one of the "Seven Wise Men" who flourished in Greece in the sixth

century B.C., was the first to acknowledge that myths could not satisfy man's curiosity about the origin of the world.

- Herbert Spencer (1820–1903), English social philosopher. Born in Derby and mainly self-educated, he became (like Shaw) a believer in Lamarck's theory of creative evolution. In 1851 *Social Statics* stressed the necessity for individual freedom and the importance of science. *Principles of Psychology* (1855) expounded the doctrine that all organic matter originates in a unified state and that individual characteristics emerge through evolution. His comprehensive system of philosophy was likewise based upon evolution and sought to integrate all existing fields of knowledge. In 1860 he wrote a prospectus of this system called *A System of Synthetic Philosophy*.

28 September 1887

A COUPLE OF NOVELS [C357]

"Fifine." By Alfred T. Story. Two vols. (London: G. Redway. 1887.) "Memoirs of Jeremy Diddler the Younger." Two vols. (London: Sampson Low and Co. 1887.) Mr. Alfred Story's "Fifine" is apparently the result of an attempt to write a novel in the style of Hans Andersen. It is to be hoped that it will effectually discourage him from repeating the experiment. The goody-goody Claus Bromm is a bore; the baddy-baddy Goldwhistle is no less a bore; and all the rest are milksops, except Zerafine, who is not interesting. Even the dog is an impossible nuisance; and the storks might have their necks wrung without a protest from the reader. Mr. Story has so far the advantage of the average novelist that he evidently knows something of serious literature; and he has a certain turn for mildly humorous philosophizing; but he has turned both to but childish account in writing "Fifine." He rides his knowledge of German as a hobby beyond all patience; and on the whole, though he has carried out his whim of painting a German interior in minute domestic detail, he has not succeeded in making it entertaining.

The author of "The New Democracy" has been more fortunate in choosing a subject than in treating it. Evolution has already differentiated the Jeremy Diddler of to-day from the Diddlers known to our forebears, and his portrait would therefore be something more than a repaint of his father's. But that portrait has yet to be done, in spite of these two volumes which give us nothing but a Pecksniff about town, described in the laboriously satiric style of Albert Smith, Cockton, and the obsolete funny men of the Boz period. The assumption that Jeremy is unconscious of his own meanness is doubtless true to nature; but it is made to appear insincere and absurd by the author's failure to catch the point of view from which selfishness becomes invisible to itself. Jeremy is made to tell his experience, not as it appeared to him, but as it would have been described by a sarcastic observer. Hence the book cannot be accepted as a very rich or subtle piece of humour; but it is amusing in its way, and will kill an idle hour as well as most novels.

Editor's Notes

- Shaw received Story's novel on 11 February 1887, and *Memoirs of Jeremy Diddler the Younger* on 28 May, but did not begin a review of the first until 14 May, and the second until the thirtieth of the same month. Both reviews were dispatched on 24 August. It is, perhaps, interesting to note that the day he began reading *Fifine,* Shaw also began writing a new novel himself—his last (unfinished) one (*Diary,* 269, 273, 329, 330).
- Alfred T[homas] Story (1842–1934), English writer. Born in Yorkshire, he was educated first in Manchester, then in Germany and Geneva. He was twice married, by his first wife having four sons and three daughters. He was also a prolific author on a wide variety of topics. Among his publications are *A Book of Vagrom Men and Vagrant Thoughts* (1889), *The Old Corner Shop* (1890), *The Life of John Linnell* (1892), *William Blake: His Life, Genius and Character* (1893), *The Building of the Empire* (1898), *The Martyrdom of Labour* (1899), *Master and Slave* (1901), *The Story of Wireless Telegraphy* (1904), *How to make a Man* (1907), *American Shrines in England* (1908), *The Sculptor's Model, and other Poems* (1914), *Songs of a New Age* (1918), and *The Trumpeter of the Dawn, and other Poems* (1923).
- The author of *The Memoirs of Jeremy Diddler the Younger* is unknown. She or he was also the author of the novel *The New Democracy; a fragment of Caucasian history* (London: Sampson Low, Marston, Searle and Rivington), 1885, and of *Shooting Niagara* (n.d.).
- Jeremy Diddler was the chief character in James Kenney's farce *Raising the Wind* (1803). His principal method of "raising the wind" is by borrowing small sums which he never pays back—a practice that probably gave rise to the verb "to diddle" meaning to cheat, or victimize.
- Albert [Richard] Smith (1816–60) was a writer of burlesques and panto-

mimes, and Henry Cockton (1807–53) was a comic novelist, both popular at the time when Dickens was contributing to the *Morning Chronicle* under the pseudonym of "Boz."

29 September 1887

REALISM, REAL AND UNREAL* [C358]

Were Mr. Norris, without further explanation, set down here as a realistic novelist, misunderstanding would inevitably ensue. Mr. George Moore might amazedly demand why Mr. Norris was classed with him; and it is not impossible that Mr. Norris might second him very strongly in the inquiry. The Real has always been a hard bird to catch. Plato did not succeed in getting it under his hat until he had divested it of everything that is real to the realists of noveldom today: these gentlemen are not Platonic realists. They do not seem to have got much further than an opinion that the romance of the drawing-room is less real than the romance of the kitchen, the romance of the kitchen than that of the slum, that of the slum than that of the sewer, and, generally, that reality is always in inverse proportion to self-control, education, health, and decency. For this discouraging view M. Zola and his "tail"—which seems to grow, by-the-by, faster than he can bite it off—are less to blame than society, in which, quite unquestionably, conditions discreditable to civilization make up the greater part of our national life. Nor is there any form of toleration of evil more contemptible than the "good taste" which pretends not to know this, and strives to boycott those who refuse to join the conspiracy of silence. Whilst the slums exist and the sewers are out of order, it is better to force them on the attention even of the polite classes than to engage in the manufacture of eau-de-cologne for sprinkling purposes, and sedulously ignore, like Mrs. General, everything that is not perfectly proper, placid, and pleasant. But it must not, in the heat of the reaction against Mrs. General, be

---

*"Major and Minor." By W. E. Norris. Three vols. (London: Richard Bentley and Son. 1887.)

forgotten that the proper, the placid, and the pleasant, even when quantitatively less than the improper, the hysterical, and the noisome, are quite as real. And when the separate question as to which is fitter for the three-volume treatment arises, it is to be considered that no born romancer can help imparting a certain attraction, morbid or healthy, to his subject matter; and that when he treats of the improper, the hysterical, and the noisome, he must, whether he will or no, clothe them with the fascinations of his art. If, for example, he takes a culpable prostitute for his heroine, he makes a heroine of a culpable prostitute; and no mechanical heaping of infamy and disease upon her in the third volume will quite despoil her of that glamour. And as to the prostitute whom it is inhuman to call culpable—the woman who can only save herself and her family from starvation by eking out her miserable wage by prostitution—it is not clear that she can be helped by serving her up as a new sensation for the novel-reading classes. The corruption of society today is caused by evils which can be remedied only by the aspiration of the masses towards better things, and not by the shrinking of the classes from horrors known to them only by clever descriptions. Besides, one cannot help suspecting that those who shrink do not read, and that the rest dreadfully enjoy, the paper sensation. When, on any definite issue, the apathy or selfishness of the classes stands in the way of a needed reform, then have at their consciences by all means, without the very slightest regard for their "delicacy." But to persist in showing the classes repulsive pictures of evils which they are powerless to abolish, without ever striving to show the masses the better conditions which they have the power to make real as soon as they have the will, is shallow policy put forward as an excuse for coarse art.

So much for the present concerning the realistic school to which Mr. Norris does not belong. There is a naturalist school to which he does belong; and its founder was Anthony Trollope. Society has not yet forgiven that excellent novelist for having worked so many hours a day, like a carpenter or tailor, instead of periodically going mad with inspiration and hewing Barchester Towers at one frenzied stroke out of chaos, that being notoriously the only genuine artistic method. Yet, if we except the giants of the craft, he is entitled to rank among English writers as the first sincerely naturalistic novelist of our day. He delivered us from the marvels, senseless accidents, and cat's-cradle plots of old romance, and gave us, to the best of his ability, a faithful picture of the daily life of the upper and middle classes. If any contemptuously exclaim here, "Aha! The upper and middle classes! Why did not the snob give us the daily life of the slum and the gutter, on which all society rests to-day?" the answer is simple and convincing. He, as an honest realist, only told what he knew; and, being a middle-class man, he did not and could not know the daily life of the slum and gutter. And it must be added, at the risk of giving a violent shock to literary slummers, that every middle-class novelist who professes to arrive at his descriptions of that daily life by the inductive or Zolaistic method, is to that extent a flagrant humbug, although he may, through the ignorance of his readers, be as safe from exposure as an East-end dog-stealer would be if he undertook the fashionable intelligence for a paper circulating exclusively in Bethnal-green.

Mr. Norris is by no means Anthony Trollope over again, though he exploits the same region, and produces good work rapidly enough to suggest that he, too, must turn out so much manuscript per hour, rain or shine. But, standing on Trollope's shoulders and belonging to a later generation, he is droller and brighter than Trollope; he knows the time of day in the political and social movement better; and he can, on emergency, go deeper into human motive, though it is hardly fair to say that his average profundity is greater. In "Major and Minor" he has taken the world easily. Major and Minor are brothers, who, since one is virtuous and the other rascally, would in an ordinary novel run a heavy risk of being very much underdone and overdone respectively. Mr. Norris has done both to a turn, never overstepping the modesty of nature in his treatment of them except for a moment in the third volume, where he has indulged himself with a superfluous blackening of the villain's eye, very much as Dickens, in one of the most ridiculous moments of his immaturity, set the elder Chuzzlewit belabouring Mr. Pecksniff with a nobby stick. In the first volume, too, there is a chapter or so of unpleasant suspense for the reader. When the father of the brothers disinherits the elder; settles the estate on the younger; and then relents, it becomes evident to experienced readers that he must die before he carries out his intention of revoking the will. A horrible curiosity as to how Mr. Norris is going to polish off this hale old man takes possession of the imagination, and is so demoralizing that one is fain to say, as Macbeth did in a similar mental attitude, that "'twere well it were done quickly." Mr. Norris finally does the deed with a chunk of old red sandstone, but contrives to avoid suspicion of plagiarism from a well-known passage in Bret Harte. On the whole, the worst that can be said of "Major and Minor" is that it might have been better in two volumes only, like "My Friend Jim." But it is an amusing and sensible novel: and its realism is perfectly sincere and in no way offensive.

Editor's Notes

- Shaw received *Major and Minor* for review on 17 September 1887, on which day his diary records that he also began reading it. He was still reading it the next day, and finished it on the nineteenth. On 20 September, he wrote the review, and corrected and dispatched it on the twenty-first (*Diary*, 299, 300, 331).
- W. E. Norris [see page 187 above].
- Emile Zola (1840–1902), French novelist. In the 1880s Zola was accepted by the literary establishment as the "apostle of Realism," producing the same conflict of opinion among his critics as Ibsen. He was not, however, accepted by the government of the day, as the Parliamentary debate in May 1888 reveals. [See above, Introduction, pages 9–10.]
- Shaw's corrective approach to the prostitute "whom it is inhuman to call culpable" was to blossom six years later in *Mrs Warren's Profession*. Clearly in this play Shaw is concerned with both social and dramatic reform; for what was true of the novel was also true of the play. One of the abuses of Ibsenism in England had been the romantic treatment of "the woman with a past" by dramatists conditioned by Victorian stage conventions.
- A week after writing this review, Shaw gave William Archer (his dramatic collaborator) a transcript of the first two acts of their play "Rheingold"—later to be known as *Widowers' Houses*. The covering letter reveals Shaw's interest in "realism" at this time: he objects to Archer's "long-lost old woman" who, if introduced, will destroy the *realism* of the thing; Shaw's genius, he claims, has brought Archer's romantic notion into contact with *real* life; and the title of the play "Rheingold" is to be dispensed with on the grounds that it is romantic, whereas Shaw's play is *realism*.

8 October 1887

AN AUTHOR'S ALMSGIVING IN KIND [C361]

"Voluntaries." For an East London Hospital. By various hands. (London: D. Stott.) This very presentable volume of 200 pages is from the pens of twenty different authors. Their contributions are undeniably good works, inasmuch as they have been presented to the Hospital for Children at Shadwell. Doubtless the book was a tempting opening for the rejected manuscripts of early days; but it does not seem to have been abused in that way. Lord Lytton sends a characteristic effusion beginning, "How fleas are put to death we all know well." One of the best poems in Mr. Stevenson's "Underwoods" has a place; and the Bishop of Bedford, in a moving sonnet, describes how, when he was "weary with the strife and din" and wanted to "flee from out the fray" into some rural home, a little stranger child came to him, climbed upon his apron and comforted him. The happy sketch of Miss Mulligan in Miss Mabel Robinson's "Lady Land Leaguer" is the freshest of the prose. The most melancholy page is the record of the weights of 250 patients at the children's hospital. The contrast of the weights as they are with the weights as they ought to be is appalling.

Editor's Notes

- Shaw received this book on 25 June 1887 (the month it was published), and the above was, no doubt, one of the "three minor reviews" that he wrote and sent off on 24 August (*Diary*, 294, 330).
- Short biographies of the twenty contributors, the titles and a brief description of their "voluntaries" for this volume follow, in their order of presentation:

> Mrs. Heckford (n.d.), wife of Dr. Nathaniel Heckford (1842–71), who founded the East London Hospital for Children at his own cost in a warehouse at Ratcliff Cross in 1868. Her contribution was therefore "The Story of the East London Hospital for Children." Her account is largely a tribute to this remarkable man who set aside the possibility of advancement in his profession to take care of the sick in one of the poorest quarters of London.
>
> Andrew Lang (1844–1912), English journalist and author. Educated at St. Andrews and Oxford, he was elected to a Fellowship at Merton College, but chose instead to be a London journalist. He was a prolific author, writing on Scottish history, folk-lore, and fairy tales and publishing a prose translation of Homer. He also produced a quantity of poetry, which, after the ill-received *Helen of Troy* (1882), became increasingly lightweight and belletristic. To the above volume he contributed "Ballade of the Dream," a poem lamenting the loss of a dream on waking.
>
> May Kendall (1861–1943), English author. She also wrote *That*

Very Mab in collaboration with Andrew Lang (1885), and four novels, *From a Garret* (1887), *Dreams to Sell* (1887), *Such is Life* (1889), and *White Poppies* (1893). Her contribution to this volume was "The Boy who Followed the Sunset," a symbolic, rather opaque, tale of a boy's quest.

Walter [Herries] Pollock (1850–1926), English author and journalist. He was educated at Eton and Cambridge, graduating from Trinity College in 1871. He was called to the bar in 1874, and was first assistant editor, and then (in 1883) editor of the *Saturday Review,* which he left in 1894. He also wrote literary critical works, including *The Modern French Theatre* (1878), and *Jane Austen, her Contemporaries and Herself* (1899), dramas like *The Charm and Other Drawing-Room Plays* [with Sir Walter Besant] (1896), stories such as *Hay Fever* [with Guy Cameron Pollock] (1905), and poetry such as *Sealed Orders and Other Poems* (1907). His contribution to *Voluntaries* was "Knurr and Spell" a long short story (in nine "chapters"), a sort of whimsical exchange between two friends.

T[homas] Ashe (1836–89), educated at Cambridge, his *Sorrows of Hypsipyle* (1866) suggested a promise he was unable to fulfil. His contribution to *Voluntaries* was "A Machine Hand," subtitled "(London E.C.)": a short poem about the death of a young milliner.

E[llen] M[ary] Abdy-Williams (Mrs. Bernard Whishaw) [see page 259 above]. Her contribution was "The Chippendale Chair," a three-stanza poem about a lady and her two suitors, the last of whom, offering love instead of wealth, is allowed to share the "chippendale chair" with her.

J[ohn] L[awrence] Toole (1830–1906), English actor, and theater manager. Although essentially an actor of farce "unequalled in the expression of comic bewilderment," he was capable of pathos in parts like Caleb Plummer in Boucicault's adaptation of Dickens's *Cricket on the Hearth* (1862), and Michael Garner in H. J. Byron's *Dearer than Life* (1868). His contribution to *Voluntaries* was itself a farcical little story: "How I Paid Half-a-Crown to See 'Trying a Magistrate,' " a prose description of Toole, unrecognized by the box-office lady, trying to obtain admission to see his own recitation for charity!

[Dr.] Thomas Gordon Hake (1809–94), English physician and poet. He was a close friend of the poet D. G. Rossetti. Between 1870 and 1880 he published *Madeline, Parables and Tales, New Symbols, Legends of the Morrow,* and *Maiden Ecstasy.* To this book he contributed "Queen Victoria's Day. A Jubilee Ode," a sonorous and lengthy poem, in various metrical forms, ending with a "Grand Chorus," in praise of Queen Victoria.

C[harles] Cheston (n.d.), English author. He graduated with an M.A., from Merton College, Oxford, in 1864. He wrote a travel book *Greece in 1887* (1887), which was translated into French and Greek. At this time he was chairman of the Board of Management of the East

London Children's Hospital, and his wife was the promoter of the book *Voluntaries*. His offering for it was "The Two Cots," a longish poem in rhymed iambics, beginning with a description of the treatment given a sick rich man's child in contrast to that given to a sick poor man's child, culminating in a pæon of praise for mothers, whose self-sacrifice "amid this money-cursèd age" gives a hope of heaven.

Lord Lytton [see page 309 above] contributed "A Vicious Circle," another longish poem in rhymed iambics, describing how—through the intermediary of a flea (Tom Puce)—blood passes from a doctor to his mistress, through a chain of noblemen, women and animals, and finally back to the doctor's wife.

Mrs. Lucy W[illiam] K[ingdon] Clifford [née Lane] (?–1929), English author. Born in Barbados, British West Indies, she married in 1875 William Kingdon Clifford (1845–79), a rising young intellectual, later professor of applied mathematics at University College, London, and settled in St. John's Wood. To their home came many of the literary and scientific notables of the day, including Huxley and Tyndall. For her husband's health they traveled to the Mediterranean in 1878. The following year, however, he died in Madeira. After his death Mrs. Clifford became an author, writing such works as *The Dingy House at Kensington* (1881), *Anyhow Stories, Moral and Otherwise* (1882), *Very Short Stories and Verses for Children* (1886), *Love Letters of a Worldly Woman* (1891), *A Wild Proxy* (1894), *The Modern Way* (1906), and *Sir George's Objection* (1910). Her contribution to the above volume was "The Last Scene of the Play," a slow-moving story about a man who has murdered his first wife explaining to his second his plan to shoot himself rather than be taken. In the event she keeps the forces of law at bay until he has done so.

[Henry] Austin Dobson (1840–1921), English poet. Educated in France (his grandmother was French), at sixteen he became a clerk on the Board of Trade, where he remained until 1901. His retirement was occupied chiefly with critical and biographical work, his most prolific poetic period being from 1864 to 1885. His submission to *Voluntaries* was "To the Mammoth Tortoise of the Mascarene Islands," the most incongruous offering in the book: a poem in four short stanzas in praise of giant tortoises.

W[illiam] E[rnest] Henley [see pages 418–19 below]. His contribution was "Hospital Sketches," thirteen brief poems, all written from the standpoint of a hospital patient from "First Impressions" to "Discharged."

F[rances] Mabel Robinson (n.d.), English author. She was the sister of the poet Mrs. Agnes Mary Frances Darmesteter [née Robinson], their father being the archdiaconal architect for Coventry. She wrote translations from the French and fiction, like *Mr. Butler's Ward* (1885), *Disenchantment: an Everyday Story* (1886), *The Plan of Campaign; a story of the fortunes of war* (1888), *A Woman of the World; an every-day story* (1890), *Hovendon V.C., the Destiny of a Man of Action* (1891), and *Chimæra: a novel* (1895). She also wrote *Irish History for English Readers from the Earliest Times to the Close of the Year 1885* under the pseudonym William Stephenson Gregg (1886). It was clearly material from this last that inspired her offering for *Voluntaries*, which was "A Lady Land Leaguer," a short story about Miss Mulligan, who distributed "Land League" checks to the evicted Irish, and her stormy relationship (ending in marriage) with Callaghan, the man who wrote the checks and did the accounts.

[Rt. Rev. William Walsham How, D.D.] The Bishop of Bedford (1823–97), English churchman. Educated at Shrewsbury and Oxford, he was rector of Whittington from 1851 to 1879, at which point he was offered the living of St. Andrew's Undershaft in the City of London (it is from a foundling in this parish that the family in Shaw's *Major Barbara* was descended). He thus became the Bishop Suffragan of East London with the title of Bishop of Bedford—a title he disliked as meaningless (though it had to be used to conform to the list of bishops in an Act dating from the time of Henry VIII). He was soon a familiar figure in the streets of the East End, and revolutionized the diocese, establishing the East London Church Fund [see page 459 below] to provide money for clergy and missions, crossing all barriers (even on one occasion preaching to the Salvation Army). He turned down the bishopric of Manchester to continue his work in the East End, and at the time of the publication of *Voluntaries* in 1887 he was a patron of the East London Hospital for Children, and his wife was on the General Committee. However, she had died a month before Shaw's review came out, and Bishop How had a disagreement with the new Bishop of London who thought How was spending too much time in the East End, and in consequence in 1888 he was transferred and became the first Bishop of Wakefield. He published numerous sermons and biblical commentaries, besides hymns and poems. His contribution to *Voluntaries* was a short poem, "A Comforter," about a child comforting him when he was in distress.

Clement [William] Scott (1841–1904), English critic and poet. He was born in London, son of the Rev. William Scott, educated at Marlborough College, and became a clerk at the War Office in 1860. He contributed to various London newspapers, and, on retiring from the Civil Service in 1879, joined the staff of the *Daily Telegraph* as drama critic. In 1880 he also became editor of *Theatre*. He himself adapted French plays for the London theaters, and wrote several books of verse, including *Lays of a Londoner* (1882), *Poppy-Land Papers: descriptive of scenery on the East Coast* (1885), and *Lays and Lyrics* (1888). Scott, who was implacably opposed to the new drama in general and to Ibsen in particular, and who had a highly sentimental view of women, was to be satirized by Shaw as Cuthbertson in *The Philanderer* (1893). His contribution to *Voluntaries* was, predictably, "A Woman's Song," a three-stanza poem dated 30 April 1887 in praise of Woman, who took her Song "to Beauty's side," "along the street," and finally "to those who rest/Safe in the clasp of Nature's breast."

A[lfred[Egmont Hake (n.d.), son of Thomas Gordon Hake [see page 345 above]. He wrote *Free Trade in Capital* (1891), and invented a new system of banking. His "contribution" to the book was simply to make available "Three Unpublished Letters of General Gordon," which were both printed and presented in facsimile. Since his father had written a life of the general, one might suppose that the letters were left over from that project.

Arthur Gaye(1845/6–). Little known English author. He was educated at Oriel College, Oxford, and contributed widely to periodicals. His contribution to *Voluntaries* was "On the Shelf," the life story told in the first person of an old book.

R[obert] L[ouis] Stevenson (1850–94), Scottish author. His reputation had been assured since 1885 with the publication of *The Strange Case of Dr. Jekyll and Mr. Hyde*. In 1884 he had accepted a commission from the *Pall Mall Gazette* for a "crawler"—a thriller for the Christmas season. After trying "Markheim" (later published in the collection called *The Merry Men*), which was deemed too short, he finally submitted "The Body-Snatcher," which was a great success. In this same year (1887) Archer had sent Stevenson Shaw's novel *Cashel Byron's Profession,* which Stevenson had described as being "full of promise." At the time of this review Stevenson had been in America for a month. His contribution to *Voluntaries* was from *Underwoods*, which had been published a few weeks previously: "Ad Matrem," another tribute to a Mother in eight stanzas.

Edward Rose (1849–1904), English dramatist, and critic for the *Times*. He collaborated in burlesques and wrote mostly light comedies. His adaptation (from Anthony Hope's novel) of *The Prisoner of Zenda* in 1896 revived a fashion for swashbuckling plays (he later collaborated with Hope in another work) and Shaw, although disliking the piece, said that it brought into action "Mr. Rose's best qualities as a dramatist: his humor, his intelligence in the more generous issues of human feeling, and his insight . . ." (*Our Theatres in the Nineties* [London: Constable and Company Ltd., 1932], 2:10). However, Rose's attempt some months later to capitalize on the new vogue by adapting Stanley Weyman's novel *Under the Red Robe*, changed Shaw's "personal regard for Mr. Rose . . . into malevolent exasperation." Shaw's personal regard for Rose may have begun almost a year before writing the *Pall Mall Gazette* review (on 6 November 1886), when Shaw had played the part of Chubb Dumbleton in a matinée performance of Rose's play *Odd! to say the least of it*. Two days later he received a letter from Rose thanking him for playing the part. Rose's contribution to *Voluntaries* was "The Singer," a sentimental poem about a dying child, who is also, apparently, a singer.

12 October 1887

SOME BOOKS ABOUT MUSIC* [C362]

THE only disappointing feature of the third volume of Mr. Rowbotham's work is the word Finis at the end. It would be unreasonable
to complain of it, since, when the historian of music has faithfully
guided us through the dark ages, showing us how the recitations of
the early Christians became Gregorian chants, or picked up a pagan
grace or two and became Ambrosian hymns; when he has traced the
grafting of the peasant's dance and the vagabond's ballad, and the
influence of Arabian science and subtlety; when he has followed the
tedious evolution of the art of writing music to its final employment in
replacing improvised descants by preconcerted harmony, then only a
word or two more is needed to show the fugue form in embryo in the
popular forms of the Middle Ages: the rest, as far as Western Europe is
concerned, is plain sailing to all who have a fair knowledge of living
music, from the compositions of the great Netherlanders and Pal-
estrina to Mr. Cowen's last cantata. Still, his company through the
unknown land was so interesting that the denial of an expected stroll
through the familiar fields with him is disappointing. His vivid descriptive criticisms of Terpander, Sappho, St. Ambrose and Notker make
one long to verify the soundness of his taste by hearing him on Bach,
Haydn, Mozart, Beethoven, and Wagner, about whom we have our
own opinion to compare with his. Besides, Western Europe is not the
world; and Mr. Rowbotham is just the man to tell us all about the
music of those nations whose strains are never heard at the Crystal
Palace on Saturdays. So it is to be hoped that he will reconsider his
Finis, and go on whilst there is any ground left for him to cover.
Meanwhile, one or two points in which the history as it stands is
deficient had better be mentioned.

   First, there are no dates. The student has to keep his reckoning by
repeated references to biographical dictionaries and bald chronolo-
gies, just as he has to peep into bakers' shops for the hour when his

---

*"A History of Music." By John Frederick Rowbotham. Vol. III (London: Trübner and Co.
1887.)
   "Studies in Musical History." By Louis S. Davis. (New York and London: G. P. Putnam's
Sons. 1887.)
   "The Great Composers." By George T. Ferris. Edited by Mrs. William Sharp. (London: W.
Scott. 1887.)

watch is in pawn. Then there is no sharp line between fable and history, conjecture and record, deduction and guess, so that though Mr. Rowbotham's remark that "to controvert the givings out of tradition is but an unamiable thing to do, and of inconsiderable importance in the due conception of history" may be true, it is not reassuring. The historical method is strictly applied throughout; but experience has proved by this time that the historical method is quite as likely to lead to pure romance as the *a priori* method to hypothetic and unreal conclusions; and if Mr. Rowbotham can defy us to prove that any of his pages are not history we can no less confidently defy him to prove that some of them are not romance. Further, his free use of the ordinary notation for describing divisions of the scale in various systems, and for writing ancient or foreign melodies and harmonies, is not accompanied by any warning to the modern reader—who is apt to run to his pianoforte or organ to try the effect—that the tuning of our keyed instruments in equal temperament is a new and not altogether happy device, and that the absolute pitches of the Greek modes can only be guessed on the assumption that the cultivation of the voice in Greece had much the same results as among us, which is, to say the least, a discouraging view of Greek art. The next edition of the work will give Mr. Rowbotham an opportunity of remedying such of these omissions as he has not made on principle. In the meantime he may congratulate himself on having produced the foremost work of its kind in the contemporary English literature of music.

Mr. Louis Davis, an American musician, has nothing new to say, nor does he say the old things with any literary skill; but the great heart of the world (as he is quite capable of calling it in one of his grandioso passages) will surely go out to him for saying, "We have all reason to thank the Lord that so few men and women are able to sing; or, whether they can or not, that so few do sing." Equally true, though less profound, is the remark that "without the ear the organ would have never existed; without the continuance of the ear it would immediately cease to exist." "This," adds Mr. Davis gravely, "is a glimpse into a field into which, at some future day, I hope to enter more fully." Gentlemen who write indignant letters to the papers about church bells will appreciate his statement that "the fact is, the bell is not in sympathy with the age; but with the Church it is different." His sense of the power of music to express ratiocinative processes may be gathered from his exclamation: "Among great thoughts, what is there more similar than a Bach fugue and an essay by Mill?" But when the seeker for biographical information concerning William the Silent is referred to Beethoven's "Eroica" Symphony in preference to Motley's "Dutch Republic," one feels that it is time to dismiss Mr. Davis as too rash a guide for the old-world student, however eagerly the new may have received him.

Another American writer upon music, Mr. George T. Ferris, has been chosen by Mrs. William Sharp to enrich the "Camelot Classic" series with sketches of the great composers. Whether he is responsible for the orthographic peculiarities of the volume, or whether they have been touched in by an editor or printer, is not clear; but such names as Massinet (Massenet), Bonacini (Buononcini), Metastasia (Metastasio), and Les Trojans (Les Troyens) flourish abundantly through the pages. Giving Mr. Ferris the benefit of the doubt as to inaccuracies of spelling, pass we on to his inaccuracies of statement. He calls Allegri's Miserere "Allegri's great mass"; he says that the mysterious stranger who ordered Mozart's Requiem was Count Walseck (Walsegg) in person; he repeats the hackneyed and absurd statement that the overture to Don Juan was composed as well as written down in six hours; he ascribes the failure of the "conflagration" in Berlioz's "Sardanapalus," caused by a mistake in the orchestra, to the effect of the music; and he describes the score of Donizetti's "Lucia" as "strongly flavoured by Scottish sympathy and minstrelsy." Sometimes he is inaccurate as if accuracy were not worth the trouble: sometimes as if the truth were not romantic enough for his pages. He is a capricious critic, now severely noting "scientific faults" in "La Sonnambula" and undramatic treatment in Donizetti's "Lucrezia," and anon easily declaring Gounod's "Faust" the greatest of modern operas, or quoting without protest the claim of a French critic for superior "insight into the spiritual significance of Goethe's drama" on the part of Berlioz. With the calmness of one who utters a truism, he begins a sentence with the words, "However deficient Wagner's skill in writing for the human voice." Some of his enthusiasms are not unwelcome as echoes of a bygone time, when "Semiramide" and "William Tell" seemed the grandest of operas; when Meyerbeer was daring, original, and new; when the hero-worship of opera singers was as fashionable in Mayfair as it now is in Maida-vale; when there was no such person as Goetz; and when Wagner was known chiefly as the arranger of the pianoforte score of Donizetti's "Favorita." If the Camelot Classics are intended to "strike a chord," as Mr. Guppy said, in the breast of the old fogey, then no doubt Mr. Ferris was well chosen for the musical part of the task. Young students desirous of being abreast of their time may confidently be recommended to seek fresher counsel.

Editor's Notes

- Shaw's review of the first two volumes of *A History of Music* had appeared on 11 January 1887 [see pages 235–38 above]. On 7 July 1887 Shaw received the final volume of Rowbotham's work, which he began reading for review on 15 September. The next day he began reading Ferris's book, which, with Louis Davis's book, he had received on 6 May 1887. On 22 September, Shaw's diary again records that he is "reading Rowbotham's *History of Music*," and again the following day. On the twenty-eighth we read, "finished reading *History of Music*," and on the twenty-ninth, "began review of musical books." Finally, on 5 October, Shaw reports "finished and sent off reviews of musical books" (*Diary*, 299, 300, 301, 304, 330).

- [Rev] John Frederick Rowbotham (1859–1925) [see page 238 above].

- Louis S. Davis (n.d.), American musician and writer.

- George T[itus] Ferris (1840–?), American author. He also wrote *The Great German Composers* (1879), *The Great Italian and French Composers* (1879), *Great Singers: Faustina Bordoni to Henrietta Sontag* (1880), *Great Singers (second series): Malibran to Titiens* (1881), and *Great Violinists and Pianists* (1881).

- Mrs. [Elizabeth Amelia] William Sharp [née Sharp](n.d.), Scottish author. In October 1884 she married her cousin William Sharp, whom she had first met when he was eight years old. Their engagement lasted nine years. They traveled a great deal after their marriage, sometimes separately. After 1890, they traveled almost continuously. Like many wives of the period, she subordinated her own talents to those of her husband, and in the frequent moves (made to accommodate his uncertain health) she generally carried the burden of household duties. After a trip to Rome in 1892, her own health cracked under the strain, and the Sharps went to North Africa hoping that a change of climate would help them both. Nevertheless, Elizabeth Sharp maintained her interest in music (in 1892 traveling to Bayreuth to hear Wagner, rather than accompanying her husband to Scotland), played the piano, contributed to periodicals under the pseudonym "Elspeth H. Barzin," edited some volumes of verse, and collaborated with her husband in the production of a book called *Lyra Celtica*.

- [Sir Frederic Hymen] Cowen (1852–1935), English composer. Born in Kingston, Jamaica, his musical precocity caused his parents to bring him to London at the age of four. He later studied at Leipzig and Berlin, and succeeded Sullivan as the conductor of the Philharmonic Society of London from 1888 to 1892, and again from 1900 to 1907. He also conducted the Liverpool Harmonic for seventeen years, received an honorary doctorate of music from

Edinburgh, and was knighted in 1911. He composed six symphonies, four operas and as many oratorios, his most successful being *The Veil* (1910), and cantatas, besides numerous piano pieces and songs.

- Terpander, the father of Greek classical music and lyric poetry, was born on the island of Lesbos, c. 675 B.C., and was supposedly the inventor of the seven-string (which replaced the four-string) lyre.
- St. Ambrose (c. 340–97), French saint. Born at Trèves, he became a celebrated bishop of Milan, one of the Fathers of the Church. He developed the use of music in church services, restoring its ancient melodies, and founding the "Ambrosian chant" (as opposed to the Gregorian chant introduced two centuries later by Pope Gregory the Great). He also composed hymns, and—according to one tradition—the "Te Deum."
- Notker (?840–912), Swiss monk. He was called "Balbulus" (the stammerer), and is best known for his sacred music, particularly his hymns and sequences. He was beatified in 1512.
- [John Lothrop] Motley (1814–77), American historian. Born in Dorchester, Massachusetts, he was educated at Harvard, whence he graduated in 1831. Ten years later he became secretary to the U.S. legation at St. Petersburg. From 1861 to 1870 he was successively U.S. minister to Austria and Great Britain. From 1847 he interested himself in Dutch history and published *The Rise of the Dutch Republic* in 1856. It deals at length with William (1533–84), surnamed the Silent, Prince of Orange and Count of Nassau, who sacrificed himself to rescue the Netherlands from the tyranny of Spain and to help found the Dutch republic. Motley also published *The History of the United Netherlands* in four volumes and *The Life and Death of John of Barneveld* (1874).
- *Semiramide* (1823) the opera in two acts by Rossini, is based on Voltaire's tragedy about the Queen of Babylon [see page 125 above].
- Mr. Guppy is the lawyer's clerk in *Bleak House* who conceives a passion for Esther Summerson and makes her a ridiculous proposal of marriage. She refuses him, and, thereafter, when he is reminded of her he becomes upset, repeating "there *are* chords in the human mind . . ."

18 October 1887

WANTED, AN ENGLISH JOURNAL OF ECONOMICS! [C365]

WANTED, an English magazine for amateurs of Political Economy! Twenty years ago there were practically no such persons, and consequently no such magazine could have supported itself. The great impulse of the "Smithianismus" was exhausted, as was to be expected in its ninetieth year, with Carlyle showing how much easier and more popular it was to vilify than to understand it. But there have been new impulses since then—Karl Marx, with his claim for the economic soundness of Socialism in 1867, Stanley Jevons, with his successful rehabilitation and completion of the old supply-and-demand theory of value in 1871, and Mr. Henry George with his revolutionary Ricardianism ten years later; so that the dismal science is now on its legs again: amateurs abound even at the street corners. Accordingly, from America comes the first volume of the *Quarterly Journal of Economics*, published for Harvard University by Mr. G. H. Ellis, at 141, Franklin-street, Boston, with type and paper unexceptionable, price moderate (2 dols. a year), invaluable quarterly bibliographies of contemporary publications, and articles and discussions by Professor Marshall, General Walker, and others: notably an account of the Knights of Labour, by Colonel Carroll D. Wright, a historical sketch of Law's system, by Mr. McFarland Davis, and some interesting articles on the railway system, all tending in the direction of their transfer to the State. There is something, but happily not too much, about the silver question. Pending an English enterprise of this nature and equally well carried out, economists here, amateur and professional, will find the Harvard journal useful.

Editor's Notes

▪ This could have been one of the "three minor reviews" that Shaw wrote and sent off on 24 August 1887 (*Diary*, 294, 330). His diary entry for 13 September records that he called "at Co-op Bookbinders, Bury St., for *Quarterly Journal of Economics* 4/2." Since he paid (four shillings and two pence) for this journal to be bound, it is clear that Shaw subscribed to the periodical, which is mentioned on future occasions in the diary (pp. 298–99, 320, 346, 435, and 436). There is no reference in the diary to when he first received the journal, nor when he wrote the review.

▪ The list of writers and their contributions in this edition includes Richard Aldrich ("Some Objections to Profit-Sharing"); F. Coggeshall ("The Arithmetic, Geometric, and Harmonic Means"); Uriel H. Crocker ("General Overproduction"); Edward Cummings ("Action under the Labor Arbitration Acts"); Andrew McFarland Davis ("An Historical Study of Law's System"); Charles F. Dunbar ("The Reaction in Political Economy" and "Deposits as Currency");

Franklin H. Giddings ("The Theory of Profit-Sharing"); Arthur T. Hadley ("Private Monopolies and Public Rights"); Albert Bushnell Hart ("The Disposition of our Public Lands"); S. Dana Horton ("Silver before Congress in 1886"); J. Laurence Laughlin ("Gold and Prices since 1873" and "Marshall's Theory of Value and Distribution"); S. M. Macvane ("General Overproduction" and "Analysis of Cost of Production"); Arthur Mangin ("Letter from Paris"); Alfred Marshall ("On the Theory of Value" and "The Theory of Business Profits"); Erwin Nasse ("The Economic Movement in Germany" [*letter*]); Simon Sterne ("Some Curious Phases of the Railway Question in Europe"); F. W. Taussig ("The South-western Strike of 1886"); Francis A. Walker ("The Source of Business Profits"); H. M. Williams ("Legislation for Labor Arbitration"); and Carroll D. Wright ("An Historical Sketch of the Knights of Labor").

12 November 1887

MR. BESANT'S LITERARY PARADISE* [C372]

From a Socialist's Point of View

THOUGH the paper entitled "The Security of Literary Property," lately read by Mr. Walter Besant at the conference of authors, soon became notorious, and has now been republished in book form, no protest has yet been recorded against the extraordinarily covetous scheme for the exploitation of all English-speaking peoples sketched therein as "a beautiful dream." Since I, as well as Mr. Besant, am a sufferer from that strange brain disease which drives its victims to write long stories that are not true, and to delight in them more than in any other literature, I cannot claim to be exempt from the egotism and rapacity which I detest in other fictionists; but when it is gravely proposed that I shall strive for a legal monopoly of the symptoms of my brain disease as against four hundred millions of people in order that I may become a plutocrat in whose presence a Vanderbilt might feel the sting of

---

*"The Grievances between Authors and Publishers." With Papers read by Mr. Besant. &c. (Field and Tuer. 1887. 2s.)

envious poverty, even I cannot quite stomach all that such an ambition implies.

Let me recall the incidents of the "beautiful dream." First, copyright, of course—property—monopoly—extending over half the world, or, if English becomes, as some hope, the language of all mankind—the future Volapuk—over all the earth. But, at the very least, copyright against 200 millions in North America, 50 millions in these islands, 100 millions in Australia, 30 in New Zealand, and 30 here and there elsewhere. Total: 410 millions of people able to read English. The Society of Authors, with a central office in Chicago or London, publishing all copyright books at the highest price that can be screwed out of the 400 millions by threat of literary starvation. The whole rent of the monopoly going to the authors. Hear Mr. Besant, ecstatic in the contemplation of this Midas's Utopia:

> Think what that would be, even now, for a successful author! Think what it will be in the future, when international copyright has been granted by the only nation in the world which now refuses it! Think what it will be when these millions upon millions of the English-speaking race are all educated, all reading, all demanding new books! In these happy days, with such a society at work, to be an author will mean being a member of a profession whose prizes are beyond the hopes of the merchant or speculator. No owner of a silver mine was ever half so rich as will be the man who thus becomes the favourite of the world: no fairy gift in the history of fairies will come anywhere near the gift of writing so as to delight the world. Well: you can make that vision become true, &c., &c. It is a beautiful dream—a dream of the future; but not of the far distant future—after my time, but in the time of my children perhaps, and my grandchildren certainly.

I venture to say that however beautiful it may seem to Mr. Besant and those who applauded him, it is at bottom as unworthy a plot to get an unfairly large return for a day's work as any wheat ring, cotton corner, or railway combination known in Wall-street or Capel-court. If this is the true literary spirit, then every honest man will share the bias which, as Mr. Hollingshead told the Conference, judges display against authors when they attempt to establish doubtful copyrights by process of law. Is the Society of Authors really composed of people who throb with "the hopes of the speculator," and whose ambition is to rival "the owner of a silver mine"? A speculator is a gambler: a gambler is essentially a thief, since his object is to get wealth otherwise than by honest work. Or if the authors are indeed so base, does Mr. Besant really believe that in the time of his grandchildren one man will be allowed to hold a silver mine, or any other natural store of wealth against the rest of mankind? Mr. Besant may regard this as mere cavilling, and may be willing to mend his illustration; but his first choice betrays, beyond all retractation, his belief that to literary men, as to gamblers and monopolists, the Beautiful means the prospect of doing very little for other people, and making them do a great deal for you.

Just at present an author has absolutely no special grievance worthy a moment's attention from the public at large. If he has exceptional ability to write desirable books, he can, by paying sufficient attention to his own business, exact the full rent of that ability during his lifetime, whereas a new machine is made common property as soon as the inventor has made enough out of his patent to recoup him for the actual work his machine cost him. If the author's ability is not exceptional, he drudges for just enough pay to keep him going, while his employer the publisher, his employer's landlord, and the capitalist from whom his employer has borrowed capital, divide between them what his share of the work fetches in the market, less his pittance as aforesaid. But every other propertyless worker of no more than average skill in the kingdom is in the same plight. It is open to the author to complain of this at Willis's Rooms if he thinks that will do him any good. It is also open to him to stand in with the fourteen million workers in the country who are suffering in the same way; to see how hideously worse off many of them are than he; and to help them raise themselves and raise him too from that dependent condition. But it is not decently open to him to aspire to the power to do unto others that which he now complains of others doing to him. Besides, he never could attain it, international copyright or no international copyright, so long as his ability was not exceptional. Competition would soon bring him to the old level; and the "beautiful dream" would only be realized by the favoured few who can produce books of a scarce or unique congeniality to book buyers. The remuneration of the literary work that one educated person can do as well as another after due apprenticeship, must fall, not rise, with the spread of education from which Mr. Besant hopes so much.

If the Associated Authors were likely to be at all influenced by my opinion, I should exhort them to this effect: 1. As to legislative interference on your behalf, I advise you to stand aside and hold your tongues until millions of other workers, whose needs are far more pressing, and whose utility is far less questionable than yours, are served. 2. Do not fancy yourselves a trade union. The distinctive principle of a trade union is that the members shall not underbid one another for employment, but that all shall stand or fall together. There is no reason to suppose that the literary profession is as yet sufficiently elevated morally to make trades unionism possible in it. 3. Try co-operative publishing; and back it up with all the log-rolling and boycotting power at your command.

To the Legislature on the other hand, I should say, with the modesty of a born writer, 1. Don't waste your time on the authors whilst there is so much more important work undone in other directions. If you are assailed by a literary gentleman who is disconsolate because Mrs. Henry Wood got none of the profits of the stage right of "East Lynne," send him for a walk through Bethnal-green, and then ask him whether the nation has time to waste just now in securing half as much again to novelists who are already getting the labour cost of their manuscripts repaid fivefold. 2. When you have got Bethnal-green and other places of the kind swept and garnished, and can spare a few hours for the authors, set to work at once to cut down their copyrights. Let every international extension of copyright be accompanied by a reduction in its duration, which, like that of a patent, should always be adjusted so as to enable the author to get a fair return for his labour in inventing and writing the book, and not a penny more. By the time that a public of 400 millions becomes available, copyright in works of fiction must be utterly abolished, and a cumulative income tax imposed on authors whose advance sheets bring them an abnormal return. Dictionaries, encyclopædias, constitutional histories, and the like, might still require protection: if so, they could have it. A sufficient guide for all cases would be found in the principle that an author is entitled in equity to just what his work costs him. Every measure that cuts down or raises his gain to this is a step in the right direction. The sooner he is wakened from his "beautiful dream" that he is a whit more respectable or deserving than any other useful worker in the community, the better for himself and his neighbours.

G. Bernard Shaw.

Editor's Notes

- There is no indication in Shaw's diary as to when he received the above book. However, his entry for 23 March 1887 reads, "wrote article on Besant's paper read at the Society of Authors and sent it to *PMG*" (*Diary*, 254). This is the only signed book review Shaw wrote for the *Pall Mall Gazette*.
- [Sir] Walter Besant (1836–1901), English novelist. He was born in Portsea and educated at home, at King's College, London, and at Christ's College, Cambridge, whence he graduated in 1859. For two years he tried journalism in London, and was an instructor in mathematics at Leamington College until, in 1861, he accepted the senior professorship at the Royal College, Mauritius. He spent his vacations studying French and writing essays. Consequently, when because of ill health he was forced to refuse the rectorship of the Royal College and return to London, he was able to write a successful book *Studies in Early French Poetry* (1868) that enabled him to continue his studies in French literature. In 1874 he married and had two daughters and two sons. He was a seminal influence in several societies, founding the Rabelais Club in 1879, acting as secretary to the Palestine Exploration Fund from 1868 to 1886, and being the moving spirit behind the Society of Authors, founded in 1884 to improve copyright laws, and to protect authors from exploitation by publishers. He addressed this subject in *The Pen and the Book* (1898). As a contributor to *Once a Week*, Besant made the acquaintance of its editor, James Rice, with whom he collaborated on a novel, *Ready-Money Mortiboy* (1872), which was so successful that the two collaborated on eleven more novels until, in 1881, illness prevented Rice from continuing. Besant continued writing novels alone, producing about thirty in the next twenty years. He also produced a few collaborative dramatic efforts, and historical works. His chief social interest lay in the city of London, for whose poor he founded a "People's Palace," which contained schools, a gymnasium, library, etc., and upon a survey of which he was engaged at the time of his death.
- [John] Hollingshead (1827–1904), English journalist and theater manager. He was the first manager of the Gaiety Theatre (from 1866 to 1888), where he not only produced burlesques and operas, but also the first Ibsen play in England, *The Pillars of Society* (1880).
- Volapuk was an artificial language, chiefly made up of scraps of European languages, invented in 1879 by a German priest, Johann M. Schleyer, as a means of international communication.
- Capel-court, named after the Capel family, who owned a house on the site in the sixteenth century, at this date led to the London Stock Exchange.
- Willis's Rooms, the fashionable restaurant in King Street, St. James's. It had degenerated into an auctioneer's salesroom before it was destroyed by bombs in 1941.
- Mrs. Henry Wood [see page 402 below].

23 November 1887

OLD STORIES IN NEW NOVELS* [C375]

NOTABLE among the latent talents developed daily by the curiosity of children stands fiction, or the art of entertaining lying. The father who, requested by his boy to explain a locomotive engine or the phenomenon of the tides, concentrates the life work of Stephenson and Newton into one frantic moment, and produces an accurate explanation, red hot, of matters which he never suspected himself of understanding, might well engage our admiration if he were germane to the triplet of novels now in hand. But as he has clearly nothing to do with them, he must give place for the present to the predicament of his wife when she is met in the nursery with the demand, "Tell us a story." Now, although it is quite true that everybody writes novels in these days, it is also undeniable that there are several million nobodies of mothers who never made the slightest attempt of that sort in their lives. Them, consequently, the voice of the nursery finds unprepared. Under these circumstances there is nothing for it—short of changing the subject to games, toys, sweets, and the like—but either to rebuke the craving for fiction as sinful, or to exhume from the memory the remains of Little Red Riding Hood. If the effort be well received, story-telling will become an institution in the family. Presently it will be found that the one thing that will not succeed there is what critics call originality. The little human animal listens without much interest until it hears a story that pleases it, and ever thereafter it only desires to hear that story over and over again, told in exactly the same way. When it grows up, its culture may be wide and its taste exalted, yet when it wants to be amused you find it reading its Shakspere or its Dickens for the hundredth time; prowling in the National Gallery before the pictures it has seen oftenest; or listening to the "Messiah" or "Don Giovanni," or Beethoven in C Minor, as if these were the latest fashions in music. Or if, as a typical Briton, it "does not understand classical music," and only knows Shakspere as the author of "Hamlet" and "The School for Scandal," it may still read an amazing quantity of

---

*"Like and Unlike." By the Author of "Lady Audley's Secret." (London: S. Blackett. 1887.)

"Old Blazer's Hero." By D. Christie Murray. (London: Chatto and Windus. 1887.)

"The Fiddler of Lugau." By the Author of "The Atelier du Lys." (London: Hatchards. 1887.)

novels with great delight and excitement, provided only that they are each its favourite story over and over again, with the same characters, the same incidents, the same scenery, the same names, and the same words. You are half disposed to admit the identity of the characters, incidents, and scenery; but you doubt the identity of the words. Well, here is a new novel by Miss Braddon. There is not a phrase in it that is not as familiar as the progressions in Sir Arthur Sullivan's comic operas. And the names? Listen!—Adrian Belfield, Lucy Freemantle, Mrs. Leo Baddely, Dolly Toffstaff, Reginald Rockstone. Dares any man pretend that he cannot tell without opening the book which is the hero, which the sweet young English maiden, which the fast married woman of fashion, which the unmarried dasher of the same species, and which the mild and scholarly clergyman?

Somehow, nobody does this sort of thing better than Miss Braddon. The oftener we read her favourite story the more it interests us. The touch of time mellows but does not wither that dear old murder: the splendid, jealous, wicked woman is as inexhaustible as Cleopatra: the mystery that by this time surely cannot mystify any properly sophisticated modern baby thrills us as it did long ago before all the town found out "Lady Audley's Secret." The formula is so simple and so congenial to the romantic instinct that it is impossible not to be pleased and interested. And withal, Miss Braddon knows her world so well, and, whilst allowing it its little comforts in the way of fiction, takes such a sensible view of it on the whole, that even the sternest art missionary may pray that when she next doth tell her tale may he be there to read.

Mr. D. Christie Murray has taken his work very easily in "Old Blazer's Hero." The three illustrations have cost Mr. A. McCormick much more elbow grease than there are any marks of in the 300 well spread pages of letterpress. The plot is of the simplest. The heroine marries a good-for-naught. All the male characters thereupon take to drink: the good-for-naught from taste, Old Blazer's hero from disappointment, and the rest from sympathy with Old Blazer's hero. On the death of the good-for-naught, the hero marries the heroine, and, with his following, forswears the ardent bowl. The curtain falls on the reign of bliss and total abstinence in Old Blazer. Smaller beer Mr. Murray could hardly have drawn for us.

"The Fiddler of Lugau" is another good old-fashioned story, with a dash of musical interest in it. The fiddler labours under the disadvantage, common to most fiddlers, of being an extremely indifferent performer on the violin. He has, for his time (*circa* 1810) very advanced notions of instrumentation, writing "chromatic passages for the horns," and proposing to write for one bassoon and three trumpets in four part harmony; for, he says, "thus we shall obtain complete chords." These niceties will be lost on the ordinary reader; but the initiated will not be surprised to learn that the Fiddler of Lugau had no great success as a composer. The quaintness of his social position and surroundings in the old German town is presented with considerable skill and insight; and the old story, finishing duly with a married hero and a slain villain, is retold with more freshness than might have been expected. Mr. Ralston's drawings, without possessing extraordinary merit, are not, like most illustrations, a hindrance to both author and reader.

Editor's Notes

- Shaw received *Old Blazer's Hero* on 23 September, *The Fiddler of Lugau* on 5 October, and *Like and Unlike* on 11 October 1887. On 19 October, his diary reports him reading *The Fiddler of Lugau* "for review," a task he completed the following day. Two days later he is "reading novels for review," and on the twenty-third "reading a novel of Miss Braddon's for review." The twenty-fourth again finds him "reading novel for review," and the following day he reports "finished reading novels for review." On 26 October he is "writing review of Miss Braddon, etc." and the following day he "finished review and sent it off" (*Diary*, 307, 308, 309, 331).

- Mary Elizabeth Braddon [Mrs. Maxwell] (1837–1915), English novelist. She was born in London and educated entirely at home, but her training was thorough. She became famous on the publication of *Lady Audley's Secret*, which first appeared in *The Sixpenny Magazine* and was issued separately in 1862. She also wrote plays and journalism (for *Punch* and *The World*), and herself edited magazines, including *Temple Bar* and *Belgravia*. However, she is best remembered for her more than eighty novels, two of which, the one reviewed here and *The Fatal Three* [see page 422 below] Shaw reviewed.

- D[avid] Christie Murray (1847–1907), English novelist and journalist. He attended private schools in Staffordshire, where he was born, but at the age of twelve began work in his father's printing shop. His first regular literary work was reporting police-court cases for the *Birmingham Morning News*. In 1865 he went to London where, after working in a printing works, and enlisting as a private in the Royal Irish Dragoon Guards (from which his discharge was purchased by a kindly great-aunt), he became a parliamentary reporter for the *Daily News*, and, from 1879 until his death, writer of at least a novel a year. He married twice (1871 and 1879), and had a son and a daughter. He was a great traveler, and was absent from London for long periods: from 1881 to 1886 he lived mainly in Belgium and France, and later for a time in North Wales. He also was successful as a traveling lecturer, touring Australia and New Zealand, Canada, and the United States. From 1898 onward he devoted much energetic writing to support Zola's case for Captain Dreyfus, the French officer wrongfully condemned for espionage.

■ Margaret Roberts (1833–1919), Welsh novelist. Educated privately, she lived much in Italy, France, and Germany. Indeed, her first novel, *Mademoiselle Mori* (1860), was first written in Italian. Most of her approximately forty books were first published anonymously. They include *Denise* (1863), *Madame Fontenoy* (1864), *Women of the Last Days in Old France* (1872), *Friends in Fur and Feathers* (1875), *The Atelier du Lys; or, An Art Student in the Reign of Terror* (1876), *Fair Else, Duke Ulrich and other Tales* (1877), *France* (1881), *Grammar of the French Language* (1882), *In The Olden Time: a Tale of the Peasant War in Germany* (1883), *Miss Jean's Niece* (1884), *Hester's Venture* (1886), *A Little Step-Daughter* (1887), and *Under a Cloud* (1888).

29 November 1887

BOOKS FOR CHRISTMAS—II.

A Batch of Books for Boys [C377]

THE cheapness of paper this year is reflected in a greater quantity of Christmas books than ever. Mr. G. A. Henty alone has five more or less bulky volumes—all published by Messrs Blackie—with which to perplex the intending purchaser. If the sale of Mr. Henty's works is not individually great, it will be because he is his own enemy. First, there is "Orange and Green," a story of the battle of the Boyne; second "Bonnie Prince Charlie," which introduces us to the author of the last attempt to regain the throne of England for the Stuarts, and takes us through Fontenoy and Culloden; third, "For the Temple," a vivid picture of the efforts of the Jews to stay the advance of the Romans; fourth, "In the Reign of Terror," which Mr. Henty has no difficulty, of course, in turning to admirable account; and fifth, "Sturdy and Strong," which he has apparently produced in order to show that he can still give us interesting stories of ordinary, as well as of extraordinary, trials and adventures. These works are admirable in many ways. Their wealth of incident and the intimate knowledge with universal history which Mr. Henty displays are equally noteworthy. Of the five, "Bonnie Prince Charlie" is the most intensely thrilling. It has a good plot, excellently unravelled. "Orange and Green," though it shows less constructive skill, is also a capital story, and if parents are anxious to make their sons Home Rulers they cannot do better than place this account of some of the earlier struggles between Ireland and England in their hands. But how would Mr. Henty like to have to parse such sentences as the following before a critical audience: "When each had finished their portion;" "Never even in the height of the feudal system were the mass of the English people more enslaved as have been the peasants of France;" "How can I tell you are not thieves who seek to ransack the house, and that your warrant is a pretence?" "I am quite sure you would be as quick and ready as me in most circumstances." Mr. Henty is not the only writer in the department of history, and those who read his "Bonnie Prince Charlie" and "Orange and Green" should also read the quieter but none the less valuable story of events more or less connected with those of which Mr. Henty writes by Mrs. Emma Marshall, called "Dame Alicia Chamberlayne" (Seeley and Co.). Mr. Henty's and Mrs. Marshall's works are almost equally good for boys and girls, and the stirring incident of the former's will be wholesomely seasoned by the more domestic treatment of the latter's. "Dame Alicia Chamberlayne" is a story of Cromwell's time, with the siege of Gloucester for its central situation, and is really the autobiography of the dame, which Mrs. Marshall has been so fortunate as to secure. "Aboard the *Atlanta*" by Mr. Henry Frith (Blackie), is concerned partially with the American civil war, and conveys an excellent idea of the manner in which certain "privateers" ran the blockade of Charleston and other ports. It is the old, old story of the boy who runs away from school and undergoes adventures of all degrees of pleasantness and unpleasantness in consequence. Mr. Frith knows how to tell a story with humour and spirit. While Mr. Frith deals with America's greatest struggle, Captain Percy-Groves in "The War of the Axe" (Blackie), takes his readers, not for the first time, through one of England's little wars in South Africa. Shipwrecks, fights with leopards, conflicts with Kaffirs, and wonderful escapes, make up the volume, which is written in Captain Groves's usual dashing style. As their titles imply, "Chivalric Days," by Mr. E. S. Brooks (Blackie), and "Stories of Old Renown," by Mr. Ascott R. Hope, are far removed from the times treated by Mr. Frith and Captain Groves. The two works are similar in all respects. Both are composed of stories of "the days of old, when knights were bold," both have a smattering of superstition, and both are gathered from what Mr. Brooks would call "the mists that obscure the history" of various countries. Both are "written up to date" with freshness and vigour, and will supply boys with many a half-hour's revel in the courtesies and the cruelties, the courage and the chivalry, of the olden time. There is only one criticism to be made on either. In "Stories of Old Renown" Mr. Hope describes Guy of Warwick as unhorsed, and fighting the dragon with his sword after he has been thrown and has lost his spear. Mr. Gordon Browne's illustration shows Guy on horseback fighting with the sword. Which is right?

From stories of history, we come to those of general adventures. Mr. R. M. Ballantyne adds to his long list of boys' books only one, and a first-class one it is. Madagascar is a suggestive field, and in "The Fugitives; or the Tyrant Queen of Madagascar" (Nesbit), Mr. Ballantyne makes the most of his materials. Like all Mr. Ballantyne's books, there is a good deal more in this than mere description of hair-breadth escapes. It is an animated picture of life in Madagascar under the cruel and Christian-hating Queen Ranavalona. Dr. Gordon Stables is well-known as a trustworthy boys' author. "Harry Milvaine" (Nesbit) is a story of a Highland lad who has adventures with a bull, goes seal-fishing, returns home, goes South, fights slave dhows, and gets taken prisoner. The narrative is generally correct in point of grammar, but we may tell Mrs. Milvaine through Dr. Stables that governesses undertake to teach children, and not to "learn" them. A second work by Dr. Stables is "In the Land of the Great Snow-bear" (Sunday School Union). The idea of the young laird falling in love in Iceland, and overcoming at last his mother's aristocratic scruples against his union with Meta, interwoven as it is with stirring scenes of Arctic life, forms the groundwork of a far from commonplace story. "Winning his Laurels" by Mr. F. M. Holmes (Nesbit), is an ordinary school story, not uninteresting, but a little prone to didacticism. It might have been called "How to be a Gentleman." "The Lads of Lurda," [sic] by Mrs. Jessie M. E. Saxby (Nesbit), is a collection of stories of very meagre merit. Shetland cannot fail to be interesting, however poorly its attractions are availed of. The author has not made the most of them, nor worked up the situations as they might be worked up. The dedication to her son revelling in the freedom of the "prairie wild" is the best thing in the volume.

Editor's Notes

• Shaw's diary gives no indication when he received or read the above books, but on 17 November 1887, he was "writing an article on 'Books for Children' for the *PMG*." This, however, was a longer piece entitled "The Best Books for Children." It appears that the editors reduced his work to the above paragraphs—which is no doubt why Shaw omitted the review from his scrapbook of press cuttings. The remainder of the article has been published (with an introduction by Ray Bradbury) in *Shaw: The Annual of Bernard Shaw Studies. Volume Nine. Shaw Offstage. The Nondramatic Writings,* ed. Fred D. Crawford (University Park and London: Pennsylvania State University Press, 1989), 23–28.

• G[eorge] A[lfred] Henty (1832–1902), English novelist and writer for boys. He was born at Trumpington in Cambridgeshire, and educated at Westminster school and Caius College, Cambridge. He went out to the Crimea in the Purveyor's Department of the Army, but was invalided home. Subsequently he served with the Italian Legion. From 1866 he was special correspondent for *The Standard* in various wars, including the Austro-Italian, Franco-Prussian, and the Turco-Serbian, experiences he was to turn to account when he began writing for boys. His first adventure story for boys, *Out of the Pampas,* appeared in 1868. He was a prolific writer, frequently turning out three books a year, and writing about one hundred in all: among his best-known works are *The Young Franc-Tireurs* (1871), *Winning His Spurs* (1882), *Facing Death* (1882), and *The Lion of St. Marks* (1888). In 1880 he succeeded W. H. G. Kingston as editor of *Union Jack,* a journal for boys.

• [Mrs.] Emma Marshall [née Martin] (1832–99), English novelist. She was born in Norfolk into a family of bankers, and in 1854 married Hugh Marshall, a director of the West of England Bank, and they had five sons. They numbered the Arnolds and the Kingsleys among their friends, and Longfellow among their correspondents. In 1878 her husband's bank failed, leaving them with heavy financial liabilities. Accordingly, Emma became the chief wage earner, and over the next twenty years she wrote nearly two hundred books. They were very popular; so much so that, at the time of the above review, the returns from her literary work were between £300 and £500 per year. She specialized in historical romances, often with a clerical setting, such as *Under Salisbury Spire* (1869) and *Life's Aftermath* (1876). Shaw knew Mrs. Marshall since they were both members of the Zetetical Society; his diary records a meeting with her at the Royal Historical Society in April of 1887.

• Henry Frith (1840–?), Irish children's writer. Born in Dublin, he was educated at Cheltenham College and Trinity College, which he entered with the intention of becoming a civil engineer. However, he received an appointment in the War Office, where he stayed until 1875, when he retired on a pension, and thenceforth devoted his time to writing. In addition to the above book, whose complete title is *Aboard the "Atlanta;" the Story of a*

Truant, he managed a prodigious outpouring of children's stories and translations from the French and German, including works by Madame Colomb, Alexandre Dumas, Philippe Daryl, J. Girardin, Jules Verne, P. Villars, and J. R. Wyss, and many other works including *My Wife's Relations; or, Passages in the Life of a Young Runaway Couple* (1877), *Little Valentine, and other Tales* (1878), *Schoolboys All the World Over* (1880), *Jack o' Lanthorn: a Tale of Adventure* (1883), *For Queen and King; or, the Loyal 'Prentice* (1885), and *The "Saucy May," or, the Adventures of a Stowaway* (1888). He also contributed to the *Boys' Own Paper*, collaborated with Edward Heron-Allen in a book on chiromancy, with W. H. G. Kingston on *Notable Voyagers* and *Great African Travellers*, and wrote a biography of the Seventh Earl of Shaftesbury.

- Captain [John] Percy Groves (n.d.), English children's writer. He served as a captain in the 27th Inniskillings Regiment, from which experience he drew most of the material for his stories. In addition to the above book, whose full title is *The War of the Axe; or, Adventures in South Africa*, Groves wrote many other books with military themes, among them *From Cadet to Captain* (1883), *A Soldier Born; or the Adventures of a Subaltern of the Ninety-Fifth in the Crimea and Indian Mutiny* (1885), *Reefer and Rifleman; a Tale of the Two Services* (1886), *The Duke's Own; or, the Adventures of Peter Daly* (1887), *Anchor and Laurel: a Tale of the Royal Marines* (1888), and *The Sixty-Sixth Berkshire Regiment a Brief History of its Services, 1758–1881* (1888).

- E[lbridge] S[treeter] Brooks (1846–1902), American author. He was born in Lowell, Massachusetts, son of a Unitarian minister, who held charges in three cities, including New York, where Elbridge attended the Free Academy. He left, however, in his junior year, and became a clerk for a publishing firm. In 1870 he married, and had two daughters, one of whom became a writer. In 1879 he joined the staff of the *Publisher's Weekly*. From 1883 to 1885 he was dramatic critic and literary editor of the Brooklyn *Daily Times*, and in 1884 he also became associate editor of the children's magazine *St. Nicholas*. Finally, in 1887, he moved to Somerville, Massachusetts, to become editor of D. Lothrop and Co., a position he maintained for the rest of his life. In addition to the book reviewed above, whose full title is *Chivalric Days, and the Boys and Girls who Helped to Make Them*, Brooks wrote in all over forty books for children, with such titles as *Historic Boys: their Endeavors, their Achievements, and their Times* (1885), *In Leisler's Times: an Historical Story of Knickerbocker New York* (1886), *Historic Girls, Stories of Girls &c.* (1887), and *The Story of the American Sailor in Active Service on Merchant-Vessel and Man-of-War* (1888). He also wrote *The Life Work of Elbridge Gerry Brooks* (1881), *Century Book for Young Americans* (1894), and the *True Story of the United States* (1897). From 1891 to 1893 he was editor of *Wide Awake*.

- Ascott R[obert] Hope [Moncrieff] (1846–1927), Scottish author. Born in Edinburgh, he was educated privately there, and in England. He did some work towards the Scottish bar, but "penned a stanza" etc., at an early stage, served some time as a school teacher, and eventually became a prolific writer, producing some two hundred volumes of fiction, history, schoolbooks, and guidebooks. Among his children's fiction, his better-loved works include *The Men of the Backwoods; true stories and sketches of the Indians and the Indian Fighters* (1880), *Stories of Old Renown; tales of knights and heroes* (1883) [reviewed above], *The Hermit's Apprentice* (1886), *Hero and Heroine; the story of a first year at school* (1898), and *Round the World* (1905).

- R[obert] M[ichael] Ballantyne (1825–94), Scottish author of children's fiction. Born in Edinburgh, at the age of sixteen he went to Canada where he worked as a clerk for the Hudson Bay Company for six years, his experiences there serving as excellent material for later stories. For seven years thereafter he worked for the publishing firm of Thomas Constable in Edinburgh. In 1856 he wrote his first book, *The Young Fur Traders*, which was an instant success, and in less than forty years he had produced over eighty books, frequently traveling abroad to gather material. It is said that he visited Algiers before writing *The Pirate City* (1875), went to sea for two weeks to write *The Young Trawler* (1884), and lived in a lighthouse before writing the book of that name. He was also an accomplished artist, and sometimes illustrated his own work. Among his more famous stories are *Ungava: a Tale of Eskimo Land* (1857), *The Coral Island* (1857), *The World of Ice* (1859), and *The Dog Crusoe* (1860). He died in Rome.

- [Dr William] Gordon Stables (1840–1910), Scottish physician and author. Born in Banffshire, he graduated in medicine at the University of Aberdeen, served in the navy from 1863 to 1871, and for another two years in the merchant service. Finally he was invalided out with half-pay. About 1875 he settled down to a career of writing. Stables was a prolific author, producing about four books a year for thirty years. He lived in a caravan and toured the countryside, writing as he went. In addition to those reviewed above, Stables wrote several books about domestic pets, such as *Cats: their Points, Classification, Ailments, and Remedies* (1874–77), *Friends in Fur: True Tales of Cat Life* (1877), and *Practical Kennel Guide: Rearing and Breeding Dogs* (1877), and a great many adventure stories, among them *Jungle, Peak, and Plain: a Boy's Book of Adventure* (1877), *The Cruise of the "Snow Bird:" a Story of Arctic Adventure* (1882), (this was his first serial for the *Boys' Own Paper* where it appeared in 1880), *O'er Many Lands, On Many Seas* (1884), *The Cruise of the Land Yacht "Wanderer;" or, Thirteen Hundred Miles in my Caravan* (1886), and *Wild Life in the Land of the Giants: a Tale of Two Brothers* (1888).

- F[rederic] M[orell] Holmes (n.d.), English author. In addition to an abundance of children's stories, such as the one Shaw reviewed (whose full title was *Winning his Laurels; or, the Boys of St. Raglan's*), and others even more didactic (e.g. *Danger Signals: Volumes of Temperance Tales* (1881)), he also produced the occasional adult book, such as *Exeter Hall and its Associations* (1881), and *The History of the Irish Land League, impartially reviewed* (1882).

• Mrs. Jessie M[argaret] E[dmondston] Saxby [née Edmonston] (1842–?), Scottish author. Born at Halligarth in the Shetland Isles, the daughter of a medical doctor, Laurence Edmondston, she was educated privately, and began writing while yet a child. In 1859 she married Henry Linkmyer Saxby, M.D. Her son C. F. Argyll Saxby became a children's writer himself. In addition to the above novel (whose correct title is *The Lads of Lunda*), she wrote upwards of thirty books, most of them dealing with Shetland Isles folklore, nature notes, tales of adventure in the Shetlands, and the modern life of the islands, where she made her home. She also contributed to numerous periodicals, such as *Scotsman, Leisure Hours, The Antiquary, Chambers's Journal, Boys' Own Paper, Girls' Own Paper, Dundee People's Friend, British Weekly,* and *The Queen.*

2 December 1887

TERTIUM QUIDDITIES* [C380]

IN these "chapters on various disputed questions," Mr. Edmund Gurney, by endeavouring to coax the disputants into the more considerate and reasonable position occupied by himself, has tried to reconcile his inbred politeness with his propensity to chop logic. "The truer view," he says, "seems to me" [note the polite horror of dogmatism in the phrase] "to depend on taking a standpoint, or in recognizing facts and principles other than those which partisans have usually recognized or taken. And this truer view—if such it be—is not one that would extenuate differences or induce lions to lie down with lambs, or generally tend towards compromise in the ordinary sense: its immediate tendency, on the contrary, is rather to make each of the duels triangular. In short, it is a *tertium quid.*" But here Mr. Gurney has confused two very different models of duel; for a triangular duel is one in which A fires at B, B at C, and C at A; whereas in the *tertium quid* duel, B, with a pistol in each hand, fires simultaneously at A and C, whilst they both let fly at him. It is really far more modest and less dangerous to call out one man at a time. To drop the metaphor, surely Mr. Gurney can see that however he may shrink from asserting that

*"Tertium Quid." By Edmund Gurney. Two vols. (London: Kegan Paul and Co. 1887.)

his opinion is sounder than A's, and again that it is sounder than B's, he does not improve his position by declaring that he knows better than either of them. It is this very *tertium quiddity* of transcendent impartiality and freedom from partisanship that stamps Mr. Gurney as the suave superior person, just as his psychical colleague, Mr. Myers, is the bumptious superior person of modern magazine-articledom. Mr. Myers is probably incurable; but Mr. Gurney impresses one agreeably as the last person likely to maintain such an attitude when once he has been made conscious of its effect.

The subjects dealt with in the two volumes under notice include music, vivisection, psychical research, ethics, poetry, and natural religion. In the chapter on the Utilitarian Ought, and the cognate parts of the other essays, Mr. Gurney seems occasionally disabled by the popular "greatest number" conception of happiness as something varying directly with the number of persons experiencing it, and therefore measurable by the population. Now the greatest happiness in the world is clearly no greater than that of the happiest individual alive: the greatest misery no worse than that of the most unfortunate wretch. Suppose happiness be regarded as cumulative—that the happiness or hunger of two persons be counted as double that of one: then, if we express the pain of a fleabite as -1, and that of acute toothache as -500, it follows that 501 fleabites, suffered by 501 separate individuals, is a greater evil than the acute toothache of one person; and that one person ought, if the alternative presented itself, to suffer acute toothache to save 501 of his neighbours from one fleabite apiece—a proposition which only a fiend would maintain.

Something of the same confusion has crept into the chapters on vivisection. Mr. Gurney's view is that when the specific suffering inflicted on an animal by a vivisection is outweighed by the abstract suffering saved to human beings, the vivisection is justified. But as vivisection is experimental, it is not always or even often certain that the result of an operation will save any suffering at all. And if the suffering saved is calculated by placing a positive sign before each quantity saved to an individual, and then adding them up, it is hard to say what vivisection would be too diabolically cruel and frivolous to claim justification. The question is really one of the acknowledgment of a moral relation between man and beast. Deny such relation, and men may clearly be as cruel to animals as they please. Admit it, and you still have a right to make a horse work for its living, but not to inflict upon it tortures which no reasonable man would or ought to submit to.

Mr. Gurney's chapter on Poetry is not unlike an old-fashioned essay on the existence of the soul. It goes to show that poetry is distinguished by "an essence of beauty that cannot be proved or discussed in terms of reason"—something, in short, that Mr. Gurney has not been able to put his finger on. But at any rate he shows that Mr. Austin and Mr. Arnold have been no more successful than he. On much the same lines, when dealing with "The Psychology of Music," he contends that music has a soul which eludes the scalpels of Mr. Sully and Professor Stumpf.

Over Wagner and "Wagnerism," Mr. Gurney, as usual, comes heavily to grief. He does not like Wagner's music; and he is bent on proving up to the hilt that he *ought* not to like it. It is the last weakness of the individual artistic mind to believe that art work which displeases it is bad work. Mr. Gurney goes with melancholy diligence through the rigmarole that has done duty in successive generations against Handel, against Mozart, and against Beethoven. And just as the anti-Beethovenists used honourably to offer the devil his due by admitting the prettiness of the Septet, and lamenting that the Ninth Symphony was not like it, so Mr. Gurney magnanimously speaks of the "haunting delight of the March in 'Tannhäuser' "! After seventy pages which have absolutely no relevance to Wagner except on the assumption that his music is formless and lacks "the two dimensions of melody," Mr. Gurney has to admit that it fulfills all the conditions that he has been able to lay down, but that "the shapes are shapeless—are inartistic, fortuitous, and unarresting"—in short that they do not please Mr. Gurney, which he might have told us in less than twenty thousand words.

For his appeal entitled "A Permanent Band for the East-end," many less entertaining mistakes than his polemic against Wagner may be forgiven him. As he truly says, music is "the unique means for fighting the public-houses." He wants £100,000 to establish an orchestra under cover in the East-end; and he has no hope of getting it. His "fifty good second-class players" would not be enough: the day for really efficient orchestras less than a hundred strong is gone by. On the other hand, the players need by no means be second class: there would be no difficulty in getting a hundred comparatively unknown men in London who, after playing daily together for a few years under a good conductor, would be better than any "first rate" in

England. The real difficulty would be to get the good conductor; for unless he were of the best the money might be worse than wasted. (One orchestra, by the by, would not be enough; but it would create an effective demand for others.) And then, how to exclude the West-end people if the orchestra became fashionable, and they began to crowd out and shame out their poorer townspeople! As the dangers of the scheme crowd upon the mind, the hundred thousand pound harmony in the clouds dislimns and disperses; but it still seems hard that the poor cannot hear a decent band occasionally, to keep them out of mischief. There is Toynbee Hall, for instance! Could not the haloed young gentlemen of that settlement, in gratitude for what they have learned from the people they went East to teach, study the trombone, and turn out of a night in Commercial-street to show their skill?

It would be ungrateful to conclude without acknowledging that these essays, though sometimes abortive, are never dull or unsuggestive. For the little personal confession at the end of "The Psychology of Music" Mr. Gurney may count for the sympathy of many faithful lovers of that art who are in the same predicament as himself.

Editor's Notes

- Shaw's diary indicates uncertainty as to when he received this book (5/11?); but he was reading it for review on 6 November 1887, and again on the ninth and tenth. His deliberations were interrupted by "Bloody Sunday" (13 November) in which the mass meeting called in support of Free Speech in Trafalgar Square was broken up by mounted police. Shaw, who had escaped in the confusion, spent the fourteenth and fifteenth writing about the affair to the *Pall Mall Gazette* [see page 403 below]. On the sixteenth he was again "reading Gurney for review," and on the seventeenth he wrote the review, which he finished and sent off the next day (*Diary*, 312–16, 332).
- Edmund Gurney [see pages 221–22 above].
- [Alfred] Austin (1835–1913), English poet, fiction writer, and political journalist. Although he published over twenty volumes of verse during the next half century, the quality is very poor. His attacks on Tennyson, Browning, and Whitman only made their author ridiculous, and his appointment as Poet Laureate in 1896 (which was probably political) was greeted with derision. From 1883 to 1895 he edited the *National Review.*
- Matthew Arnold (1822–88), English poet and critic. The bulk of his prose works appeared after 1860, including *The Study of Poetry* (1880), which was

originally the general introduction to *The English Poets,* edited by T. H. Ward, in which Arnold develops fully his statement that "poetry is a criticism of life."
- James Sully (1842–1923), English psychologist and philosopher. He was a professor at University College, London, and wrote *Sensation and Intuition* (1874). He also wrote reviews in *Mind,* in volume 6 of which he published a critique of Gurney's *The Power of Sound.*
- Professor C[arl] Stumpf (1848–1936), German musicologist. He was professor at Würzburg, and later a pedagogue at Prague, Halle, and Munich. In 1893 he went to Berlin and founded the Psychological Institute. He wrote *Musikpsychologie in England* (Leipzig, 1885) and *Tonpsychologie* (2 vols; 1883, 1890). Gurney's chapter "The Psychology of Music" is entirely taken up with defending his book *The Power of Sound* against the above critics.
- Toynbee Hall, in Commercial Street, was the Universities' Settlement in East London, named after the social philosopher Arnold Toynbee. Canon Barnett was its founder [see pages 454–58 below], and it opened its doors on Christmas Eve, 1884, offering programs of educational and social activities.

5 December 1887

A NOVELIST BORN, BUT NOT YET MADE*
[C381]

In the days of "The Colleen Bawn" Mr. Dion Boucicault used to enchant us by a ballad concerning a gentleman who, without displaying either conspicuous virtue or even ordinary good sense, won all hearts by the irresistible plea that "old Ireland was his country, and his name it was Molloy." It is difficult to avoid a rush to the conclusion that the author of "A Modern Magician" is heir as well as namesake to Mr. Boucicault's hero. As a story teller he is the Bobadil of fashionable mysticism: as a literary workman he is a pretentious bungler: his syntax is inconceivable, his dialogue impossible, his style a desperately careful expression of desperately slovenly thinking, his notions of practical affairs absurd, and his conception of science and philosophy a superstitious guess: yet he has an indescribable flourish, a dash

---

*"A Modern Magician." By J. Fitzgerald Molloy. Three vols. (London: Ward and Downey. 1887.)

of half-ridiculous poetry, a pathetic irresponsibility, a captivating gleam of Irish imagination, and, above all, an unsuspicious good-nature, that compel a humane public to read his books rather than mortify him by a neglect which he has done nothing malicious to deserve. And, indeed, the reading is not unpleasant, except to the tender-hearted reviewer, who finds forced upon him at every page the barbarous duty of convicting Mr. Fitzgerald Molloy of some solecism which would irretrievably damn a literary workman merely born in England and named Smith or Jackson.

Here is an example of the syntax that has served Mr. Molloy in six fairly successful books. "It had been better if you accepted her invitation, because it will be uncertain when I get back." As this occurs in a dialogue, its inaccuracy might be forgiven if it were colloquial. But Mr. Molloy scorns the colloquial: his most acute attacks of literary form have prostrated him in mid-dialogue. Thus, his heroine, instead of saying to her husband, "You were right in what you thought about me," declaims, "The conclusions you drew regarding me were just." A detective, after the usual murder in the third volume, wants to say, "We found out who he was by his papers," but cannot get any nearer to it than, "His watch, ring, purse, and papers were found on the body: the latter led to the discovery of his identity." A husband says to his wife, "The law shall enforce you to live with me"; and a young wife conversing familiarly with her aunt says, "He may have wed me because of some passing fancy," as calmly as if such speeches were human. Not until the aunt presently observes that "when two persons don't agree, one always believes the other doesn't understand," can the reader recover some opinion of Mr. Molloy's shrewdness.

The above are examples of bungling, which is much more disgraceful to a man of letters than mere blundering. But Mr. Molloy blunders too: he speaks of "mutual kinsmanship"; writes "sunk" for "sank"; and repeatedly puts his adjectives at the beginning of the sentence and then makes his nominative an accusative. When he at last induces his grammar to go smoothly, he gets into trouble with the police, sending his hero to Scotland-yard to give notice of his wife's elopement, and subsequently allowing him the privilege of being bailed out as a matter of course on a charge of murder.

Mr. Molloy frequently puts off the story teller and assumes the sage. Here are a few samples of his weightier utterances: "Until a foretold event is accomplished it is not a fact." "A king in his palace may be as miserable as a beggar in his hovel." "From whence [sic] have men started, and to where [sic] do they tend?" "Few men and women with sacred fire in their hearts make loyal and loving spouses. Wherefore this should be, God knows." The following is a graceful version of the proverb about leading a horse to the water. "Others may carry grapes to our lips: we alone can taste of them." On the whole, the equine illustration, if the less elegant, is the better, since horses not only may be but customarily are led to the water, whereas it is etiquette for "others" to allow us to help ourselves instead of carrying grapes to our lips. One more example of Mr. Molloy's philosophic style. When his hero falls in love, we are told that "the influence of the feminine on the male, exemplified in all the kingdoms of nature, finding utmost expression in humanity, was here perceptible."

It only remains to draw the unexpected conclusion that a man may be a tolerable novelist without knowing how to write. Shocking as some of the above samples of Mr. Molloy's workmanship may be to experts, the people whom he calls "the bran-brained crowd" will find "A Modern Magician" quite readable. There are shrewd bits, imaginative bits, naïvely absurd bits, and yards of outrageous fustian about "earth shaking on her axis convulsed by fear," and "confusion of sounds as of wailing infants strangled at birth"; but there is hardly any of the flat, commonplace, correct padding that kills the ordinary three-volume novel. Mr. Molloy has the natural gift in style—a good ear: what he lacks is intellectual training, address, and comprehension of society, as distinguished from familiarity with "at-homes." His imagination, though it has apparently made him the dupe of the shallow imposters whose exposure and disgrace is the chief amusement of the Society for Psychical Research, has also enabled him to transfigure Wimbledon Common into something like the Wolfschlucht in "Der Freischütz." After all, one must be a born romancer to place an incantation scene on the lines of "Macbeth" and Bulwer Lytton's "Strange Story," at Wimbledon. Even foggy London is represented as a mist peopled with phantoms; and Mr. Molloy's grave statement that "few Londoners have ever seen the City by night" would not be absurd if he had added "as I see it in my mind's eye"; which is no doubt what he meant.

Mr. Fitzgerald Molloy is a writer born, not made. Will he kindly take the trouble to get made before he again challenges criticism from the literary point of view?

Editor's Notes

▪ Shaw received this book on 25 October 1887. On 19 November, his diary records him reading it for review, and finishing it on the twentieth. On the twenty-first he was "writing review of Molloy's novel;" he was still "working at" the review again the next day, and on the twenty-third he "finished and sent off review of Molloy" (*Diary*, 317–18, 331).

▪ [Joseph] Fitzgerald Molloy (1859–1908), Irish poet and novelist. He was born at New Ross, County Wexford. He left Ireland at the age of twenty and for a time was private secretary to S. C. Hall and Sir C. G. Duffy. He spent four years in the London office of the agent-general for New Zealand. Shaw was well-acquainted with him, on numerous occasions visiting his house, at which gatherings of literati occurred. Oscar Wilde was also a frequent visitor in the 1880s. In addition to the novel reviewed above, Molloy wrote about a score of books, including *Songs of Passion and Pain* [under the pseudonym "Ernest Wilding"] (1881), *Court Life Below Stairs, or London Under the First Georges* (1882), *Court Life Below Stairs, or London Under the Last Georges* (1883), *The Life and Adventures of Peg Woffington* (1884), *Royalty Restored* (1885), *Famous Plays* (1886), *The Life and Adventures of Edmund Kean* (1888), *The Most Gorgeous Lady Blessington* (1896), *The Romance of the Irish Stage* (1897), *The Sailor King, William IV, His Court and His Subjects* (1903), *The Russian Court in the Eighteenth Century* (1905), and *Sir Joshua and His Circle* (1906).

▪ Dion[ysius] George Boucicault (1822–90), Irish dramatist and actor. From 1870 he lived mainly in the United States. He wrote or adapted from the French about 150 plays, the most successful being *The Corsican Brothers* (1882), and *The Colleen Bawn* [an Anglo-Irish title meaning "The Fair Girl"] (1860), based on a novel *The Collegians* by Gerald Griffin. Shaw's review of this play in *The Saturday Review* for 1 February 1896, in which he accuses Boucicault of "blarneying the British public," contains the seeds from which his own drama *John Bull's Other Island* will grow eight years later.

▪ Captain Bobadill is a character in Ben Jonson's *Every Man in his Humour* (1598). He is an soldier, vain, boastful, cowardly, yet preserving gravity and decorum.

▪ The "Wolfschlucht", or "Wolf's Glen," in Carl Maria von Weber's *Der Freischütz* (literally *The Free-Shooter,* one who shoots with magic bullets), is the haunt of Samiel the wild huntsman (otherwise the Devil), where the seven magic bullets are molded.

▪ Bulwer Lytton's *Strange Story* (1862) concerns a materialistic medical man, who, having exposed and indirectly brought to ruin and death a rival physician (a believer in "mesmerism" and "somnambular clairvoyance"), finds himself through remarkable circumstances coming to believe in occult powers. Lytton's success in persuading the reader of the reality of the occult derives paradoxically from our identification with the solid common sense and scepticism of his principal character.

27 December 1887

SOME SMALL POETRY OF 1887* [C385]

ENGLAND is famous among nations for her poetry. Here are twenty-two volumes of it. Heigho! First, seven Jubilee poets, knowing nothing, or thereabouts, of the history of the reign, the geography of the Empire, or the personal characteristics of our Royal family, yet loyally ready, like Mr. Wemmick's witnesses (or Mr. Poland's) to "swear, in a general way, to anything" courtly on these subjects, Jubilee, Liberty, Hail to Thee, Queen of the Sea, and so on. Also, in bolder, less fastidiously correct rhyme, "From age to age, from clime to clime, Rings out the song that is divine;" and, "As o'er the blue dark heaving main, Our sailors true shall bless thy name." Mr. Winscombe, a Unionist, varies his blank verse by a dashing slap at "the brainless logic of the massive brain" of Mr. Gladstone. Dr. Goodchild prefaces his third series of "Somnia Medici" with the remark, founded apparently on Ussher's chronology, that "there be fifty brother eras in the story of mankind"—

But of all the fifty brothers in the long historic list
One shall live beyond the others as the Nineteenth after Christ.

*"V.R. and I., 1837–1887, Jubilee Odes," by G. Gravener Shrewsbury (Harrison and Sons); "A Song of Love and Liberty, or Fifty Golden Years," by G. H. Addy (Field and Tuer); "A Song of Jubilee and other Poems," Mrs. R. S. de Courcy Laffan (Kegan Paul); "Westminster, Past and Present," J. Cave Winscombe (W. H. Allen and Co.); "Somnia Medici" (third series), John A. Goodchild (Kegan Paul); "Albynne, a Dramatic Medley," by Esca (W. H. Beer and Co.); "Minora Carmina," by C.C.R. (Swan Sonnenschein); "Actæon," by M. B. Williams (The Author, at 15, Bernard-street, W. C., 1887); "The Modern Faustus," an Agnostic Allegory (London Literary Society, 1887); "Edward the Black Prince," by Douglas Sladen (Griffith and Farran, 1887); "Legends and Records of the Church and the Empire," by Aubrey de Vere (Kegan Paul and Co., 1887); "The Cid Ballads," translated by the late James Young Gibson, 2 vols. (Kegan Paul and Co.); "The Castle of Knaresburgh," by Richard Abbay, M.A., F.R.A.S. (Kegan Paul and Co.); "The Poems of Giacomo Leopardi," translated by Frederick Townsend (New York and London: G. P. Putnam's Sons, 1887); "Somnia," by G. Gladstone Turner (Longmans and Co., 1887); "Sketches in Song," by G. Lansing Raymond (New York and London: G. P. Putnam's Sons); "Lower Merion Lilies and other Poems," by Margaret B. Harvey (Philadelphia: Lippincott Company); "Echoes of the Anvil," by William Wilson (Edinburgh and Glasgow: J. Menzies and Co., 1886); "Three Little Emigrants," by Sarah M. B. Piatt (Elliot Stock); "Lays of the Seaside," by Aliph Cheem (Army and Navy Stores); "Who wrote Shakspere?" by William Henderson (David Stott); "Victorian Hymns: English Sacred Songs of Fifty Years (Kegan Paul and Co.)

"My mind," says "Esca," in "Albynne," a dramatic medley, "is all a blank except in one thing; and would that were a blank!" If the one thing is blank verse, then, in all sincerity, would it were! C. C. R's "trivial verses" are no more than they profess to be; but they jingle prettily, and the Jubilee is kept within the bounds of a single page.

"Actæon," by M. B. Williams, has that in it which gives the critic pause. M. B. Williams, who is evidently in his nonage, has read Shelley's "Alastor" and been hard hit by it; and has unsophisticatedly handed his poem in manuscript to a printer and received it back in the shape of a little book without a publisher's name, bearing heavy marks of the free hand allowed by the author to the compositor. Young gentlemen who do this sort of thing are not lightly to be encouraged; and perhaps Mr. Williams has already found out that "Actæon" is an immature effort. But it certainly reads as if the author had material for poetry somewhere about him.

"The Modern Faustus, an Agnostic Allegory," is no improvement on the established Faustuses, being so extremely agnostic that no one will be the wiser for reading it. The labour of finding this out is enlivened by some passable verse, and an amusing doggerel lecture on evolution. Less abstract but more readable is Mr. Douglas B. W. Sladen's "Edward the Black Prince," a successful modern example of the old-fashioned stage "history" in blank verse. Mr. Aubrey de Vere's "Legends and Records of the Church and the Empire" will, even to those who cannot accept the author's philosophy of history, be acceptable as old stories of saints and martyrs finely told in verse of considerable beauty. Old stories of another sort are to hand in the Cid Ballads, translated by the late James Young Gibson, with whom the lays of Spanish chivalry were a hobby. His two volumes are capital reading for boys. Fully-grown minds are also, alas! no more able to stand the Cid nowadays than Darwin could stand Shakspeare. Young readers will also enjoy Mr. Richard Abbay's "Castle of Knaresburgh," a metrical account of the relief of York by Prince Rupert, and the battle of Marston Moor. In style it is a frankly slavish imitation of Scott, as "The White Mare of Whitestonecliff," which follows it, is of Ingoldsby Barham.

Leopardi, who died fifty years ago at the age of thirty-nine, was too weak a man to make the sort of reputation that passes frontiers. He was romantically patriotic; and his own circumstances and those of Italy were unhappy enough to tune his harp to notes of woe. The graceful translation of his poems made by Mr. Frederick Townsend of New York will serve English readers who may be curious as to the nature and limits of Leopardi's genius. Mr. G. Gladstone Turner shows some boldness in calling his little volumes of verse by such titles as "Errata," and "Somnia;" but his confidence shall not be abused here by remarks to the effect that his books are aptly named. The only poem in "Somnia" which seems to have had its impulse from real life is "Society," in which Mr. Turner expresses an opinion that if Divorce Court circles do not mend their morals somebody will have to be lynched. Mr. Lansing Raymond, an American writer, is more alert than Mr. Turner: he looks about him and rhymes on this or that more or less happily and by no means profoundly. From the West, too, hails Margaret B. Harvey, author of "Lower Merion Lilies" and other poems. In them there is the unmistakable music and feeling of genuine poetry, with that pleasant strain of the best side of Puritanism, characteristic of the women poets of America.

Mr. William Wilson, professional blacksmith and amateur poet, may safely challenge the whole Savile Club to knock off occasional verses that ring like his or have as much stuff in them. The illustrations to his volume, by Thomas Wilson, are of considerable merit. Of quite different texture are the "child's world ballads" of Sarah M. B. Piatt, of whom the *St. James's Gazette* once neatly confessed that it found "that Mrs. Piatt's Muse is the Muse of the American girl." Aliph Cheem's "Lays of the Seaside" are grown-up-and-not-too-intelligent-child's-world ballads. They are comic enough to set an indulgent messroom in a roar, and to stir up all the latent malice in the critic to whom they are seriously submitted. Mr. William Henderson, in his "Who Wrote Shakspere?" also seems bent on mild jocularity.

Finally, the subject of the Jubilee is brought back by Messrs Kegan Paul's volume, bound in plain white buckram with gold lettering, entitled "Victorian Hymns," and containing some of the most sincere expressions of pious mood from Matthew Arnold, Alfred Tennyson, Anne Brontë [sic], Christina Rossetti, and Adelaide Proctor, besides the expected selection from Keble, Bonar, Faber, and other hymn writers. The gems of the collection are Tennyson's "Strong Son of God, immortal Love;" Christina Rossetti's exquisite "I would have gone: God bade me stay" from "Goblin Market;" and Anne Brontë's [sic] "My God, O let me call Thee mine," with its touching third verse,

I cannot say my faith is strong
I dare not hope my love is great,
But strength and love to Thee belong,
O do not leave me desolate!

Editor's Notes

■ Shaw received this collection of "small poetry" on 7 July 1887. His diary for 28 November reports that he "began review of 22 minor poets for *PMG*." On 10 December, he "continued review of 22 minor poets;" and on the thirteenth he "finished and sent off" the review (*Diary*, 319, 322–23, 330–31).

■ G[eorge] Gravener Shrewsbury (n.d.), unidentified author. He seems to have written just this one book.

■ G[] H[] Addy (n.d.), unidentified author.

■ Mrs. R[obert] S[tuart] de Courcy [Bertha Jane] Laffan [née Grundy] (?– 1912), English novelist and poet. Born in Cheshire, she lived in New Brunswick from 1867 to 1871 with her first husband (Surgeon-General Dr. Andrew Leith-Adams). She wrote the poem ("A Friend Across the Sea") read by Henry Irving at the opening of the fountain presented to the town of Stratford-on-Avon. Her first novel, *Winstowe,* came out in 1877, followed by one or two a year for the next six years. In 1883 she married the Reverend Robert Stuart de Courcy Laffan, who, two years later, became headmaster of King Edward's school, Stratford-on-Avon. From 1878 she was a journalist on the staff of *All the Year Round,* and continued to publish mostly novels, among them *Louis Draycott* (1891), *Bonnie Kate* (1892), *The Peyton Romance* (1894), *The Old Pastures* (1895), *Accessory After the Fact* (1898), *The Vicar of Dale End* (1906), and *Dreams made Verity* (1910). She also wrote several plays, songs, and other books of poetry.

■ J[ohn] Cave Winscombe (n.d.), unidentified author. In addition to the above book, he wrote *Isoe, and other Poems* (1871), *Waves and Caves and other Poems* (1873), *Camden and other Poems* (1876), and *Wild Oats* (1879), under the pseudonym "Cave Winscom", and *"Resurgam" and Lyrics* (1898). He also wrote under the pseudonym "John Cave."

■ [Dr.] John A[rthur] Goodchild (1851–?), Scottish poet, mystic, and antiquarian. He became first a correspondent and then a friend of William Sharp [see pages 321–22 above], with whom he traveled in Scotland in 1904. The book reviewed here was part of three series: *Somnia Medici* (1884–87.) He also wrote *Chats at St. Ampelio* (1888), *A Fairy Godfather* (a tale) (1890), a verse drama *The Two Thrones* (1895), and *The Light of the West* (1898).

■ "Esca" (n.d.), pseudonym for unidentified poet.

■ C. C. R. (n.d.), pseudonym for C. C. Rhys, English writer. He also wrote *Up for the Season, and other Songs of Society* (1889), which was a second edition of *Minora Carmina,* and *Country House Sketches* (1891).

■ M[] B[] Williams (n.d.), unidentified poet.

■ Douglas Sladen [Brooke Wheelton] (1856–1947), English writer, educated at Cheltenham and Oxford, where he took a first-class degree in history. Later he was the first to hold the chair in history at the University of Sydney. In addition to editing *Who's Who* from 1897 to 1899 and *The Green Book* from 1910 to 1911, he was a prolific author, writing over forty books on a wide variety of subjects, including Australian poets (he was instrumental in having a bust of Adam Lindsay Gordon placed in Westminster Abbey), American poets, and reminiscences of travel.

- Aubrey [Thomas] de Vere (1814–1902), Irish poet, essayist, and critic. He was privately educated in Ireland and entered Trinity College, Dublin, in 1832. When he left Trinity in 1838, he devoted himself to study and travel, a visit to Oxford leading to his lifelong friendships with J. H. (Cardinal) Newman and (Sir) Henry Taylor, and a visit to Cambridge introducing him to Tennyson, Monckton Milnes, and Spedding. In London in 1841 he met Wordsworth, with whom he became close friends. In 1846 he returned to Ireland on the death of his father and worked on relief committees attempting to alleviate the suffering from the famine. In 1851, at Avignon, probably under the influence of Newman, de Vere became a Catholic. In 1854, when Newman was appointed head of the new Dublin University, de Vere was given the Chair of Social and Political Sciences, which he held until Newman's retirement in 1858. He died unmarried. De Vere was a prolific writer, producing twelve volumes of poetry before his *Poetical Works* in three volumes were published between 1884 and 1889. He also wrote prose works on the Irish Question and other matters and many critical essays, which were collected into three volumes from 1887 to 1889.
- Richard Harris Barham (1788–1845) in the last part of his life wrote the popular *Ingoldsby Legends*—a comic treatment of medieval legend.
- Giacomo Leopardi (1798–1837), Italian poet. He wrote patriotic odes and thirty or forty short poems and the collection of essays and dialogues, *Le Operette morali* (1827).
- James Young Gibson (1826–86), Scottish translator. Born and educated in Edinburgh and at the University of Halle, in 1854 he was ordained a minister of the United Presbyterian Church, but four years later was compelled to resign his charge owing to ill health. He spent the remainder of his life in study and travel, chiefly in the East, Italy, and Spain. In addition to the Cid Ballads reviewed above, he translated poems and a tragedy by Cervantes.
- [The Reverend] Richard Abbay (1844–1924) was educated in York and at Oxford, became a lecturer and demonstrator at King's College, London, in 1868, and a Fellow of Wadham College, Oxford, in 1869. The following year he was a member of the Eclipse expedition to Southern Spain, and in 1871 he went to India, where from 1872 to 1874 he was rector of Kandyan Province. In 1874 he joined the French Transit of Venus expedition to New Caledonia. In 1878 he returned to England and became rector of Little Bromley in Essex. In 1880 he became rector of Earl Soham in the neighbouring county of Suffolk; and in the same year he married, a union that produced two sons and three daughters. He remained at Earl Soham until his retirement in 1912. In addition to the civil war tale in verse reviewed above, and another volume of verse entitled *Life, a Mode of Motion* (1919), he published papers in the journals of the Royal Astronomical, Geological, Physical, and Linnæan Societies.
- Frederick Townsend (n.d.), unidentified American translator.
- G[eorge] Gladstone Turner (n.d.), English poet. He also wrote *Hypermnestra, a Græco-Egyptian myth* [in verse] and *Errata* [poems] (1886).
- G[eorge] Lansing Raymond (1839–1929), American educator, poet, and critic. Born in Chicago, he was educated at Williams College and Princeton Theological Seminary, from which he graduated in 1865. He studied art in

Europe for three years. After four years as a Presbyterian pastor, he returned to Williams College in 1874 as a professor of English literature, aesthetics, oratory, and elocution. He was a highly successful instructor, and in 1880 assumed the Chair of Oratory and Aesthetics at Princeton, which he held for twenty-five years. From 1905 to 1912, he taught aesthetics at George Washington Unversity. In addition to the book of poems reviewed above, Raymond wrote a novel, *Modern Fishers of Men* (1879), a few plays, some textbooks (including *The Orator's Manual* (1870) which became a standard text), and a great deal of verse.

- Margaret B[oyle] Harvey (?–1912), American poet.
- William Wilson (1830–?), Scottish blacksmith and poet. He was born at Burntisland. His father was a "clever sailor" and "nothing ever came wrong to his hand." His mother was a resourceful woman, frequently supporting her five children singlehanded, when his father was at sea. He was educated at Mount Pleasant School until he was thirteen, when he crossed the Firth in a small boat and became apprenticed to a blacksmith in Edinburgh, where he remained for seven years. The next seven years he spent in the heart of Buckinghamshire, where he was a leading engine smith with the London and North Western Railway Company. The Buckinghamshire countryside inspired him to write poetry, and his reciting and literary prowess soon won him a wide circle of friends. In 1857 he moved to the south downs in the employ of the London and South Coast Railway Company. One of his poems (circulating in manuscript) was intercepted and published by the editor of the *Brighton Observer.* While in Sussex he also befriended and came to the financial aid of another artisan poet, the Lancashire weaver John Critchley Prince. More of his work was published in journals in Dundee and Edinburgh, to which city he returned in 1863. For the next twenty-two years he was employed by the North British Rubber Company, in Castle Mills, as a foreman engine smith. In addition to writing poetry, he spent his spare time fighting social and political battles for the betterment of his fellow workers.
- Sarah M[organ] B[ryan] Piatt [née Bryan] (1836–1919), American poet. Born in Lexington, Kentucky, she was educated at Henry Female College, New Castle, Kentucky. She began to write when still young, her first poem being published in a Texas newspaper, *The Galveston News.* Subsequent work was published in the *Louisville Journal* and the *New York Ledger,* which ensured her popularity throughout the United States by 1860. The following year she married John James Piatt, another poet; in fact, she collaborated with him on two books of poetry, *The Nests at Washington* (1864) and *The Children Out-of-Doors* (1885). She had seven children, and for several years resided in Washington, D.C., where her husband worked in the Treasury Department. In 1882, however, they moved to Ireland, where John Piatt served as United States consul at Cork until 1893. During this time they made the acquaintance of numerous poets and authors, including Lady Wilde [see pages 427 and 429 below], Edmund Gosse, Austin Dobson, Edward Dowden and Katharine Tynan. Sarah Piatt was a prolific writer, producing seventeen books of poetry, among her best, perhaps, being her work in Ireland, including *An Irish Wild-Flower* (1891) and *Pictures, Portraits,*

and People in Ireland (1893). Her collected poems were printed in 1894. In their final years the Piatts were beset with financial problems, and received help from the Authors' Club Fund. John Piatt died in 1917, and Sarah two years later.

- Aliph Cheem [Captain Walter Yeldham] (1837–?). Educated at King's College, London, and Gonville and Caius, Cambridge, he obtained his law degree in 1860, was admitted to the Inner Temple, but not called to the bar. In 1861 he joined the army as a lieutenant in the 18th Hussars, went to India, became a captain in 1868, and retired in 1877. In addition to the book reviewed above, he wrote *Lays of Ind* (1871), and *Basil Ormond and Christabel's Love* (1878).
- William Henderson (1831–91), Scottish printer and poet. He was born in Biggar, Lanarckshire, and became a compositor with T. & A. Constable of Edinburgh. Later he worked as a type music printer with Novello, Ewer, and Company in London. He went into partnership with J. C. Rait and also with M. Spalding as type music printers in 1861, and they acquired a worldwide reputation. In addition to the book reviewed above, he also wrote *The Cedars: a Poem* (1872), and was a composer of some ability.
- Anne Brontë (1820–49), English poet and novelist, sister of Charlotte and Emily, coauthored with them *Poems by Currer, Ellis, and Acton Bell* (1846).
- Adelaide Anne Proctor (1825–64), English poet, daughter of B. W Proctor (songwriter and dramatist), was the author of *Legends and Lyrics* (1858–61) (including "A Lost Chord,"), *A Chaplet of Verses* (1862), and *The Message* (1892).
- The three celebrated writers of sacred verse are [John] Keble (1792–1866), whose poetical work is contained in the *Christian Year* (1827), and after whom Keble College, Oxford, was named in 1870; [Frederick William] Faber (1814–63), English clergyman who converted to Roman Catholicism, and was a founder of the London Oratory; and [Dr. Horatius] Bonar (1808–89), Scottish clergyman and hymnwriter, who wrote, among others, "I Heard the Voice of Jesus Say" and "Thy Way, not Mine, O Lord."

7 January 1888

MR. MARION CRAWFORD'S NEW NOVEL*
[C387]

MR. MARION CRAWFORD, with an exceptionally intelligent sense of character, and no lack of the minor gifts of a well-graced novelist,

*"Paul Patoff," By F. Marion Crawford. Three vols. (London: Macmillan and Co. 1887.)

seems nevertheless to have partly disabled himself by excessive indulgence in the modern vulgarity of travelling. Not that there is any insuperable objection to a writer of fiction passing through his years of wandering. Cervantes, Milton, Goethe and Goldsmith, who travelled, did as well according to their capacities as the many great ones who, like Shakspere and Bunyan, stayed at home. But in their day books of travel were finished art products, made by men of letters like Defoe from raw material accumulated by travellers. They still give us the model for fictitious travels; and none of the artistic writers of the present century, from Edgar Poe to Mr. R. L. Stevenson, have been able to improve upon it. Meanwhile, however, a new department of literature has grown from the development of steam locomotion, postage, telegraphy, and journalism. Instead of the traveller who was no literary artist, and the literary artist who had never travelled, we now have the special correspondent, who flies through continents and writes as he flies. His business is eternal description, without ulterior motives, of costumes, vehicles, shops, climates, travelling inconveniences, and all the impertinences of life, with now and then a coronation, battle, or other sensation scene. All this makes readable copy, but is in no sense fiction (although the special correspondent may occasionally draw a farther-shooting long bow than his ancestor did at Cressy). Still, since it is amusing and often curious, it can very easily be used as padding for three volume novels. But such use of it is flat adulteration. You pay your money for so much solid manufactured fiction; and you get an article which is half or two-thirds flimsy special correspondence.

This is the main objection to Mr. Marion Crawford's "Paul Patoff." Descriptions of shopping and sightseeing in Constantinople and of hotel life in the Black Forest are all very well in their way; but they are not what Mr. Marion Crawford professes to supply, and indeed does supply in exceptional quality when, for very shame, he has to cease descriptive small talk about his fashionable vagabondage, and set to work at his story. Paul Patoff is a Russian diplomatist, with a stately mother and a handsome brother. The mother has neglected Paul and spoiled Alexander. Paul being a man of strong parts, the natural result is that he does not like either of them, and carves his own fortune successfully without their help. The result of that again is that Madame Patoff, waxing jealous for her pet son as his inferiority tells upon his career, begins to hate Paul and eventually becomes his mortal enemy. All this would be natural and inevitable enough in real life; but in noveldom, where family feeling is exemplary, and stately mothers play sedulously up to the ideal "*ma mère*" of the sentimental Frenchman, it marks the work of an acute and candid observer of men. Unfortunately, Mr. Crawford does not, in "Paul Patoff" apply any constructive process to his observations. He shelters himself behind the fictitious personality of one Paul Griggs, a shrewd middle-aged bachelor who has looked about him and knows the ways of his set, which he supposes to be the ways of the world, but who has nothing in the shape of principle except the class traditions of the period when onehalf the world did not consider it genteel to know or care how the other half lived—the sort of man who is a poetic Republican of independent means in his youth, and who later on becomes a strenuous Churchman out of sheer practical Atheism, and a worshipping believer in the myth of the fine old English gentleman out of sheer practical cynicism. Through just such a melancholy incarnation of the *Saturday Review* does Mr. Marion Crawford speak in those chapters of "Paul Patoff" that are not mere copy from "our special at Constantinople"; and the delicacies and insights of the real novelist get confused with the superstitions of the fictitious narrator in a way that makes it difficult to pronounce confidently upon the intentions and merits of either. All that can be confidently said is that the narrative is interesting, and the characters finely touched. At the end, when the heroine is at a loss which brother to choose, her mind is made up for her by the hackneyed expedient of an adventure which gives Paul an opportunity of conspicuously outdoing his brother in physical courage; and one cannot help feeling that the settlement, however satisfactory, might have been more subtly contrived. For the rest, the book suggests that if Mr. Paul Griggs were out of the way, Mr. Marion Crawford might take a higher place among contemporary writers of fiction.

Editor's Notes

- Shaw received Crawford's novel for review on 29 November 1887, on which date he began reading it for review. On 1 December he was still reading the novel, and again on the third and fourth. On the fifth he reports "Trying, unsuccessfully, to review Crawford's novel;" and the following day "Still could not get on with the review of *Paul Patoff*." On 7 December he was "writing review of *P. Patoff*," and he finished and sent it off the next day. He corrected the proof of his article on 6 January 1888 (*Diary*, 320–21, 332, 335).

- F[rancis] Marion Crawford (1854–1909), American novelist. He was born in Italy of American parents, and after the death of his father his mother remarried. His education took place partly in America at St. Paul's School in Concord, Massachusetts, and at Harvard, but mainly in Europe, at Trinity College, Cambridge, the University of Heidelberg, and the University of Rome. Although never relinquishing his American citizenship, he was intensely cosmopolitan, and even spent some time in India (from 1879 to 1881 editing a newspaper in Allahabad). He returned to the United States and continued his journalism career in Boston and New York. His first novel, *Mr. Isaacs,* was published in 1882, and in the following year he moved to Italy, where he lived for the rest of his life (though he generally spent the winter months in New York). In 1884 at Constantinople, Crawford married the daughter of a Civil War general, and they had two sons and two daughters. His books were popular from the first, and his need for funds to support his rather extravagant lifestyle necessitated the production of about two novels a year. The following is a selection of his works: *Dr. Claudius* (1884), *Zoroaster* (1885), *A Tale of a Lonely Parish* (1886), *With the Immortals* (1888), *A Cigarette Maker's Romance* (1890), *Don Orsino* (1892), *Katharine Lauderdale* (1894), *A Rose of Yesterday* (1897), *In the Palace of the King* (1900), *Man Overboard* (1903), *Whoever shall Offend* (1904), *Fair Margaret* (1905), *The Little City of Hope* (1907), *The White Sister* (1909), and *Wandering Ghosts* (1911). Crawford also wrote some travel books, a biography of Pope Leo XIII, and a play, *Francesca da Rimini* (1902).
- The "travelling authors" are Miguel de Cervantes (1547–1616), who lost his left hand at the Battle of Lepanto and spent years as a prisoner in Algiers; John Milton (1608–74), who traveled for two years from 1637 to 1639 (chiefly in Italy), as did Johann Wolfgang von Goethe (1749–1832) when he wearied of the life of the Weimar Court in 1786 and felt the need of new perspectives; and Oliver Goldsmith (1728–74), who, in his early years, wandered throughout Europe supporting himself by playing the flute and begging.

12 January 1888

MR. PAYN'S ROBINSONIAD* [C389]

PALMERSTON'S experience in foreign affairs led him to the conclusion that the greatest enemy to knowledge is the man who has lived there for twenty years and speaks the language like a native. Some years

---

*"A Prince of the Blood." By James Payn. Three vols. (London: Ward and Downey. 1888.)

ago Mr. Payn illustrated this by writing in London a novel half about England and half about China, whither he had never been. The result was that the Chinese part was intensely convincing and actual, whereas no human being now remembers the shadowy romancing about the neighbourhood of the author's ain fireside. The fact is, China is conceivable by persons who have never seen it; but London, when you have once seen it, is inconceivable, and the more you have seen of it the less you can believe in it. Shelley, whose brain was big enough to take a great deal of it in, described Hell as "a city much like London." Dickens, who knew London, depicted it as full of strange monsters, Merdles, Veneerings, Finches of the Grove, Barnacles, Marshalseas indigenous to the Borough but cropping up sporadically among the monuments of Rome and Venice: all dreadfully answering to things that we know to be there, and yet cannot believe in without confusion and terror. How pleasant it is to shrink back to the genial Thackeray, who knew comparatively nothing about London, but just saw the fun of the little sets of ideas current in Russell and Bryanston-squares, Pall-mall, Fleet-street, and the art academies in Newman-street. One can believe in his London because he had never really seen it any more than Mr. Payn ever saw China. Still, Thackeray did see his three streets and his couple of squares; and if Mr. Payn never was in China, he might have been, and he can hardly have helped meeting people who were. To obtain complete and undeniable illusion in a story, it must be told of some place which nobody has seen, or ever will see. Hence that supreme achievement of fiction, the desert island. We cannot believe in Major Pendennis as we believe in Robinson Crusoe, in Morgan as in Friday, much less in a social anomaly like St. James's-street as in that island near the mouth of the Caribbean sea, which has been idiotically identified with Juan Fernandez—as if even in a novel a ship could jump across a whole continent.

Such are the considerations which (as far as one can gather) have led Mr. Payn to write a novel about a desert island. "A Prince of the Blood" is slighter than "Robinson Crusoe," lighter than "Foul Play," and decidedly more amusing and less Pecksniffian than "The Swiss Family Robinson." None of the time-honoured ingredients are missing: there are storms, shipwrecks, rafts, gunpowder, natives, blow-pipes and "woorali," mutinous Bill Atkinses, and everything complete. A pleasing-painful variation, characteristic of our day, is the moral inferiority of the British castaways to the virtuous natives of the island. It is Gulliver and the King of Brobdingnag over again, only less so. There is a certain point, by the by, on which Mr. Payn might take a hint from Swift. A woman who devotes her life to the memory of the dead, as Mr. Payn's bereaved heroines—following a distinguished example—are apt to do, is only cultivating a particularly unsocial form of self-indulgence, which should be remorselessly discouraged, as it was among the Houyhnhyms [sic].

The verisimilitude of the narrative is occasionally disturbed by the author's feelings getting so far the better of his literary tact as to make him represent a skipper as saying, "Madam: you do me wrong," and a very ordinary English lady as suddenly breaking out with a passage from the Book of Ruth, which has by this time been vulgarized by excessive exploitation for the purposes of sentimental romance and drawing-room music. Mention of music suggests the further criticism that a tribe of islanders who, though their music sounds barbarous and discordant to English ears, go into raptures over a Scotch song sung by a midshipman, is rather a rash invention. Whenever the intervals of Indian islanders sound strange to English ears, it is impossible that the intervals of our scale should strike gratefully on the Indian ear drum. But perhaps Mr. Payn, whose story, though dated 1835, is ingeniously contrived to open at the Inventions Exhibition of 1885, may have been misled by the never-to-be-forgotten attempt of the Siamese band at that time to play "Auld Lang Syne" under the title of "The Pegu Affliction," or by the horrors of that Oriental version of the soldiers' chorus from M. Gounod's "Faust" which they sprung on an unsuspicious public as "Glory of the Universe."

These are but trifles, however; and the book remains, in spite of them, a proof of the infinite adaptability and inexhaustible interest of the desert island in fiction. It is the novelist's ace of trumps; and now that Mr. Payn has played it, one can only wonder what other honours remain in his hand for our future entertainment.

Editor's Notes

▪ Shaw received this novel on 16 November 1887. His diary entry for 18 December 1887 begins "Reading Payn's *A Prince of the Blood* for review." He continued reading it for three more days, finishing it on the twenty-first. On 6 January he began a review of three novels (one of which was Payn's); on the eighth he "finished and sent off review of Payn's *A Prince of the Blood*" (*Diary*, 324–25, 332, 336).

▪ James Payn (1830–98), English novelist. His early education was unhappy, and he left school to study with a tutor, and finally entered Oxford. He contributed an article to *Household Words*, then edited by Dickens, with whom he became friendly. He graduated from Oxford and married, supporting his family by journalism and by becoming editor of *Chambers Journal*. From 1859 he wrote a great many novels, including *Lost Sir Massingberd* (1864), *A Woman's Vengeance* (1872), *By Party* (1878), *For Cash Only* (1882), *Some Literary Recollections* (1884), *The Mystery of Mirbridge* (1888) [see page 421 below for Shaw's review], *The Modern Dick Whittington* (1892), and *The Backwater of Life* (1899). His final years were spent in failing health.

▪ [3rd Viscount Henry John Temple] Palmerston (1784–1865), English statesman. His "experience in foreign affairs" came from his being foreign secretary, first in the Whig government formed in 1830, and later in Lord John Russell's government in 1846. He was a self-opinionated foreign secretary, frequently acting without consultation, and was eventually dismissed in 1851 for expressing his disapproval of the *coup d'état* by which Louis Napoleon became Napoleon III.

▪ Merdle is a London banker in Dickens's *Little Dorrit* who turns out to be a common swindler; Veneering absorbs both his business partners in *Our Mutual Friend*; the "Finches of the Grove" are quarrelsome members of a club (including Pip) that meets fortnightly in a Covent Garden hotel in *Great Expectations*; the Barnacles are a notorious family who run the government's "Circumlocution Office" (dedicated to strangling progress with red tape) in *Little Dorrit*, in which novel the Marshalsea prison features as the birth- and dwelling-place of the principal character.

▪ Major Pendennis is the uncle of Arthur Pendennis, who wrongly advises the latter to marry for worldly reasons in Thackeray's *The History of Pendennis* (1848–50), and Morgan is his blackmailing servant.

▪ It is, of course, well known that Defoe's interviews with Alexander Selkirk, who had been marooned on one of the Juan Fernandez group of South Pacific islands from 1704 to 1709, prompted him to write *Robinson Crusoe*; but it is also true that in that book Crusoe is wrecked while heading for "the Caribee islands" resolved to "stand away for Barbadoes."

▪ *Foul Play* (1869), a novel by Charles Reade in which a ship, supposed to be carrying gold, is scuttled in the Pacific by order of its owner, who does not realize that his sweetheart is also on the ship. She is cast away on a Pacific island with a supposed convict who turns out to be innocent, and finally, when rescued, she marries him.

▪ *The Swiss Family Robinson* (1813), a romance by Swiss author Johann Rudolf Wyss (1781–1830) in which a family is wrecked on a desert island.

▪ Gulliver, seeking to impress the giant King of Brobdingnag with an account of the excellence of European manners and morals, is quizzed on the subject by the King; after which the latter concludes:

> by what I have gathered from your own relation, and the answers I have with much pain wringed and extorted from you, I cannot but conclude the bulk of your natives to be the most pernicious race of

little odious vermin that nature ever suffered to crawl upon the surface of the earth.

- Of the manner of the death and burial of the Houyhnhnms Swift tells us in Part IV of *Gulliver's Travels:*

> If they can avoid casualties, they die only of old age, and are buried in the obscurest places that can be found, their friends and relations expressing neither joy nor grief at their departure; nor does the dying person discover the least regret that he is leaving the world, any more than if he were returning home from a visit to one of his neighbours.

- Woorali is a South American climbing plant, from the root of which one of the ingredients of the poison curare is obtained.
- Queen Victoria herself was the distinguished example: the "widow of Windsor" was devoted to the memory of her dead husband, Albert.
- Shaw had contributed an amusing but sympathetic note on the court band of the King of Siam to *Our Corner* in September 1885.

20 February 1888

MRS. OLIPHANT'S NEW NOVEL* [C405]

THERE is a memorable passage in Cobbett's "Advice to Young Men" on the incompatability of family property with frank and healthy social relations between the expectant heirs and the testator whose shoes they are waiting for. Now, Mrs. Oliphant, either from reading Cobbett, or sitting at the feet of Mr. William Morris, or independently working out her own merciless observation and criticism of class life in England, has succeeded in producing a novel which will almost persuade the roughest navvy (navvies are great novel readers nowadays) that he is sufficiently blest in not being a member of a county family. It is a story to freeze one's blood, and yet it is true to everyday nature—even commonplace. Four idle men—a widower and his three grown sons—live in a country house as four well-bred mastiffs might live in a cage, though rather less sociably. Certain supersti-

---

*"The Second Son." By Mrs. Oliphant. Three vols. (London: Macmillan and Co. 1888.)

tions as to what is becoming to men of their standing and kinship restrain them from preying bodily on each other, and even compel them to a gloomy and jealous recognition of one another's rights to civility and toleration. But each man keeps such affairs as he has to himself with a reticence which is only the gentlemanly expression of fear, mistrust, defiance, diffidence, and every other symptom of perverted and stunted social instinct. Yet only one of them, the youngest, is a rascal. His two brothers are good fellows, with no sort of natural relish for their duty of keeping up their position by keeping all the work-a-day world at arm's length, yet submitting to that duty like heroes, and bearing as best they can the consciousness of being, in practical effect, a pair of morose and useless blockheads. The father, naturally choleric, and armed with an unentailed property which he can dispose of as he pleases, is curbed only by the dogged obstinacy of the family temperament in his elder sons, the youth and superior smartness of the youngest, and a salutary dread of apoplexy. He is certainly not a respectable character; but he, too, is no worse than the spoiling of a fairly good citizen. And so the four get through life as best they can, killing partridges and foxes rather more cleverly than they kill time. One can imagine a frivolous reader indignantly asking Mrs. Oliphant whether she considers these men amusing. If she deigned a reply, it would probably be: "No; but they are actual, instructive, and therefore interesting." Anyhow, there they are; and if there is nothing but discomfort in their lives most of us can console ourselves with the reflection that we are too humble to be invited to share it even for a single dinner party. The grapes really and truly are sour, after all.

The story begins to move when Nature, jealous of the eldest son's allegiance to the county, plunges him head over ears in love with the gamekeeper's pretty daughter, who, to her own unspeakable futilization, has been brought up as a lady. The false relation between her and her mother, the honest and useful working woman, is shown as unsparingly as the false relation between the squire and the three rivals for his property. She prefers the youngest of the three, and has a very narrow escape indeed of coming terribly to grief through him. How it all ends may be ascertained by the curious from the book itself. Suffice it here to say that the upshot is so far happy that it indisputably makes the best of a bad job. As Mrs. Oliphant states it, "That strange injustice which lies underneath the surface of life, which gives the lie to all the optimisms of philanthropy, which is restrained by no law, and is so often permitted to establish itself in absolute impunity, gains the upper hand; and the stars in their courses fight for the unworthy." But is Mrs. Oliphant quite sure that they do, even in such cases as she puts? An absolute power to dispose of half an English county is given to a hot-headed and ignorant man, with the narrowest class sympathies and the narrowest class education. Naturally, he makes a deplorable mess of the business, and finally bequeaths his powers to the basest member of his family. If the stars in their courses permitted anything better to come of such monstrous malversation of a national trust, we might well turn cynical, like Mrs. Oliphant, and nerve ourselves with all the strength of our minds to show misery without showing any way out. But surely the way out of such miseries as we are shown in "The Second Son" is simply to give up throwing our counties as private property to country gentlemen and their heirs to play pitch and toss with. The right use of Mrs. Oliphant's novel is to show that the country gentlemen themselves have nothing to lose in point of domestic happiness by such a readjustment.

Editor's Notes

- There is no indication in his diary of when Shaw received this book. It is first mentioned on 29 January 1888, when he is "reading a novel of Mrs. Oliphant's for review." He next mentions it on 15 February, and the following day he "wrote and sent off review of A Second Son by Mrs. Oliphant" (Diary, 344, 349).
- [Mrs.] Margaret Oliphant [née Wilson] (1828–97), Scottish novelist. She was the cousin of Laurence Oliphant [see page 150 above]. While yet a teenager she began to write, and her first novel was published when she was twenty-one. It was Some Passages in the Life of Mrs. Margaret Maitland of Sunnyside (1849), and it won the approval of the critic Francis Jeffrey. After three more novels were published, David Moir, a local physician-poet, introduced her to Blackwoods, who became the publishers of all her subsequent novels. In 1852 she married her cousin Francis Oliphant, a designer of stained glass, and went to London, where she had a son and a daughter. Her husband died in 1859, leaving his wife not only with the task of bringing up his two children and a third about to be born, but also of caring for his brother and his family. Mrs. Oliphant's children all predeceased her: her daughter died in 1864, her eldest son in 1890, and his younger brother in 1894. Her literary output was prodigious, her published books consisting of fiction, criticism, guidebooks to Italian cities, translations, and biographies of such people as the Brontës, St. Francis, Cervantes, etc. She also published innumerable articles in Blackwood's and The Cornhill Magazine. A representative

selection of her books would include *Salem Chapel* (1863), *Miss Marjoriebanks* (1866), *The Beleaguered City* (1880), *The Ladies Lindores* (1883), *The Days of My Life* (1868), and *Autobiography* (1899).
- Cobbett's *Advice to Young Men* was published in 1829.
- A "navvy" is a laborer, usually employed in heavy construction work. The word is an abbreviation for "navigator," a colloquial term for a workman engaged in excavating and constructing a canal.
- A "county family" is one that belongs to the nobility or gentry, possessing estates and a "seat" in the county.
- The word "county" in the first sentence of the second paragraph was misprinted "country" in the *Pall Mall Gazette*. Shaw corrected it by a stroke of the pen in his book of press cuttings.

19 March 1888

*PINE AND PALM** [C413]

A NOVEL by Mr. Moncure Conway is not as other novels are. Many who ask for it at the library will do so for the writer's sake, and, if it proved as dull as a sermon, would forgive it for the sake of many sermons that were as lively as novels. The movement of which Mr. Moncure Conway's ministry at South-place Chapel was part is breaking up rapidly enough now. It may be said to have begun with Hobbes, and to have made its way in England as a sort of negative philosophy, materialistic, empirical, and utilitarian, up to 1880 or thereabout; but it was always far less a school of philosophy than a campaign against Church and State for free thought and free contract; and that side of it which struck the popular imagination most strongly was its association with militant Atheism—or what used to be called Atheism in the days when open disapproval of duelling or promotion by purchase marked the objector as at least a Dissenter, if not a downright sceptic. It was the party of progress during the struggle of individualism against feudalism; but the moment its antagonist went under, its own lack of any binding social principle became apparent in the havoc of anarchical industrial competition; and now we are in full revolt

---

*"Pine and Palm." By Moncure D. Conway. Two vols. (London: Chatto and Windus.)

against it either as reactionists or Socialists. It still survives in the theories of Mr. Herbert Spencer and the unpractical politics of Mr. Auberon Herbert; Mr. John Morley and Mr. Bradlaugh do it precarious mouth honour occasionally in a vague spirit of Voltairian Benthamism; it is the moral basis of Mr. Balfour; and it is a living influence with the party of Woman, whose personal liberty is not yet wholly achieved. But the new party of progress is just now full of the discovery that personal liberty, conceived as a right of individual self-assertion against social order, leads to the very worst form of economic slavery for the individual, and to disintegration and consequent retrogression for the community. In the heyday of Mr. Moncure Conway's activity at South-place Chapel, this was a view quite strange even to his "advanced" congregation. Social order was only known there as a system of dogmatic persecution, having the State for its official organ. Revolt against it was a duty. The more modern idea that social organization is paramount, with the resultant sense that a State against which it is a duty to revolt is the worst of social evils, and must at all hazards be converted into a State which commands by sheer desert the moral support of all, was then confined to the Positivists, whose practical solution was, however, little more than a proposal to break up the civilized world into a cluster of miniature Holy Roman Empires, with their temporal and spiritual interests in charge of a moralized feudality and a moralized Church. Hegelianism was also in the field in the form of German Socialism; but its positive side had never been adapted and translated into practical English politics, and it remained, in the hands of Marx, chiefly effective as a scathing but quite negative criticism of industrial individualism. In brief, the advanced people of those days were in the main individualists, fighting against the State for women's rights, readjustment of the marriage laws, and a rational as opposed to the accepted idolatrous view of the Bible. "What we want," said a sincerely religious clergyman, who scandalized his Bishop by holding out his hand to the freethinkers, "is to get rid of the Bible for a hundred years." On these lines Mr. Bradlaugh hammered away at the unbelievers of St. Luke's; the Dialectical Society held discussions in which women took part, and neither religious nor sexual questions were tabooed; John Stuart Mill's Essays on Liberty and on the Subjection of Women attained scriptural authority; and Mr. Moncure Conway held together at Finsbury those who appreciated a milder method, somewhat genteeler company, and a more Emersonian and artistically conscious doctrine than Mr. Bradlaugh offered at the Hall of Science. Probably no Englishman could have succeeded half so well at South-place as Mr. Moncure Conway. He was an American, and had been a Methodist; and nobody else could—or, at any rate, nobody else did—hold so fervently to what was vital in conventional orthodoxy, or blaspheme so quaintly at what was mere dry rot in it. And withal he had what was hardly then to be hoped from an American or Methodist—a full equipment of the literary and artistic culture of the London of his day.

The whole movement went to pieces at the beginning of the present decade before the assault of Mr. Henry George. It made a desperate stand against him for its one economic tenet—Malthusianism; but the discussion only confirmed both sides in the new idea that the real problem of modern society was an economic problem, and that essays on Liberty had nothing to do with it. The clergyman who made that remark about the Bible became an ardent Georgite, and fell out with his Bishop more than ever. The Dialectical Society dwindled almost to nothing. Secularists, sick of negation, rushed into Socialism; and Mr. Henry George was left behind in the general enthusiasm as a "mere land nationalizer" in politics, and in economics as arrant a vulgarizer of Ricardianism on the proletarian side as Bastiat or the Liberty and Property Defence League on the side of property. And, among other signs of the times, Mr. Moncure Conway, his warfare accomplished, left South-place, and wrote the book now under notice.

"Pine and Palm" deals with times that are now old times—chiefly with the struggle for the abolition of negro chattel slavery which had to precede our own struggle for the abolition of white wage slavery. It is natural that Mr. Moncure Conway should go back to that most exciting modern episode in the campaign for personal liberty. It would be idle to criticise the result of his essay as a novelist according to the canons of the three volume time killer. He is not *the* novelist of his movement: George Eliot was that; but he contributed many books as well as many sermons to it; and in this last he has indulged himself in the novel form for the sake of the freedom it gives to his fancy. It is a novel for those who have lived the life of their time rather than for the great army of casuals who have accidentally "done their bit" of the nineteenth century without knowing how or asking why. And it has a foregone interest for those who remember South-place, and miss the spoken word that used to place them in friendly and helpful communication with one of the most remarkable London preachers of our time.

Editor's Notes

▪ Shaw received this book for review on 18 November 1887. On 27 February 1888 his diary reports that he "began review of *Pine and Palm.*" The following day he "added a few words to review," and on 29 February he "finished and sent off review of Moncure Conway's *Pine and Palm*" (*Diary*, 332, 352–53).

▪ Moncure D[aniel] Conway (1832–1907), American freethinker, biographer, and essayist. Born in Virginia of a strict Methodist family of slaveowners, Conway was educated at Fredericksburg Academy and Dickinson College, Pennsylvania. Under the influence of Emerson, Carlyle, and Coleridge, his views began to change. He studied law in Warrenton, Virginia, served for two years as a Methodist minister in Virginia, and entered Harvard Divinity School against his family's wishes. He graduated in 1854, returning home an outspoken abolitionist. He became pastor of the Unitarian Church in Washington, D.C., but was dismissed in 1856 after an antislavery sermon. In 1858 he married, while he was minister of the First Congregational Church of Cincinnati. He had begun to contribute articles to *The Atlantic Monthly* and in 1860 edited a magazine called *Dial,* to which Emerson and W. D. Howells contributed. In 1862 he moved to Concord, Massachusetts, and edited the Boston literary and antislavery paper *The Commonwealth.* The following year, Conway went to England to advocate the cause of the North in the Civil War. He became minister of South Place Chapel in Finsbury, London, which— although ostensibly Unitarian—became a forum of freethought as Shaw describes it above. There he remained until 1884, preaching, writing articles for *Fraser's Magazine* and *The Fortnightly Review* and acting as correspondent for American newspapers. He returned to America in 1884, now a confirmed freethinker. He visited Europe again, however, and from 1892 to 1897 was again minister of South Place Chapel. He died in Paris. Among his many books, Conway wrote *Tracts for Today* (1858), *The Rejected Stone* (1861), *The Golden Hour* (1862), *The Earthward Pilgrimage* (1870), *Demonology and Devil-Lore* (1879), *Thomas Carlyle* (1881), *Emerson at Home and Abroad* (1882), *George Washington and Mount Vernon* (1889), *Life of Nathaniel Hawthorne* (1890), *Life of Thomas Paine* (1892), *Centenary History of South Place Chapel* (1895), and *Autobiography, Memories and Experiences* (1904).

▪ Auberon [William Edward Molyneux] Herbert (1838–1906), English politician and social philosopher. Born in London and educated at Eton and Oxford, he interrupted his university career for a brief gallop with the 7th Hussars in India before graduating in civil law in 1861, and resigning his commission the following year. Defeated in 1864 as Conservative candidate for Newport, Isle of Wight, he turned Liberal and was elected to represent Nottingham in 1870. Four years later he resigned from Parliament because of philosophical doubts about liberalism and took up farming. However, he returned to Parliament in 1880, and saw out the Liberal term in office. Thereafter, he never sought reelection. Increasingly, however, strongly influenced by the writings of John Stuart Mill and Herbert Spencer, he became obsessed with individual freedom and unequivocally opposed to anything that smacked of uniformity. In 1885 he published *The Right and Wrong of Compulsion by the State*—a statement of the moral principles of the Party of Individual Liberty and the political measures founded upon them. For some years he edited *Free Life*—the journal of the Liberty Party, which, however, exerted only moral pressure, and never contested a parliamentary seat. Not surprisingly, in the 1890s Herbert was associated with the Anarchists, and repudiated the connection in print. He spent his declining years as an amateur geologist, traveling the world, and preaching in print the gospel of "freedom." Having attended one of Shaw's lectures on 24 August 1890, Herbert misunderstood Shaw completely, saying "He [Shaw] disapproves of God, Reason, Duty, Self-Sacrifice, and Discipline. He regards self-interest as the only commendable mainspring of human action" (*Free Life*, 17 October 1890). This so far falsified Shaw's beliefs that he was moved to reply to the effect that Herbert clearly did not understand Shaw's politics, and that

> my objection to what you call a free life is that it offers no solution whatever of economic problems which, if left unsolved, would produce, not a free life, but a free fight, ending in the enslavement of the vanquished.

- John Morley (1838–1923), English author and politician. Born in Blackburn, educated at University College School, Cheltenham College, and at Lincoln College, Oxford, where his loss of Christian faith alienated his father and led to his leaving with only a pass degree. Thereafter he became a journalist in London, writing articles for the *Saturday Review*, articles that brought him into contact with the most prominent men and women of letters of the day. In 1866 he became editor of the *Fortnightly Review*, which, under his anticlerical influence became the voice of the English Positivists, and increased its circulation to some thirty thousand readers. In 1869 he ran unsuccessfully as M.P. for Blackburn. In 1880 he again ran unsuccessfully for Parliament, and in this year he became editor of the *Pall Mall Gazette*, changing the paper's politics from conservatism to liberalism [see Introduction]. In 1882 he resigned his editorship of the *Fortnightly* and ran a third time for Parliament, this time successfully, and was elected M.P. for Newcastle-upon-Tyne. In 1885 he became Gladstone's chief secretary for Ireland, and was one of the authors of the first Home Rule bill. From 1905 to 1910 Morley served as Secretary of State for India. He became Viscount Morley of Blackburn in 1908, and remained in politics until 1914 when he resigned from Asquith's cabinet in protest against the country's drift towards war. He wrote about ten biographies, perhaps his most famous being his three-volume *Life of William Ewart Gladstone* (1903).
- Charles Bradlaugh (1833–91), English author and politician. Born in London, he was self-educated (his formal education finished at the age of eleven), and in 1848, as a fifteen-year-old Sunday school teacher, he quarreled with his priest over disparities between the Gospels and the Articles of

the Church. This experience began his career as a free thinker, and by seventeen he was leading debates, to arm for which he taught himself French, Hebrew, Greek, and Arabic. In 1850 he published a pamphlet denouncing Christianity, which further alienated him from his family, spent three years in the army (until his family purchased his discharge) after which he obtained work with a solicitor. In addition to producing antitheological pamphlets, he was also concerned with social and political issues, lecturing in support of Garibaldi, visiting Italy and Spain to help their struggles for independence, and taking the part of the French in the Franco-Prussian War. He was always a controversialist, many times appearing in court, his challenge to ancient edicts against blasphemy and his atheism resulting in changes to court practice in allowing freethinkers to give evidence. In 1861 he founded the *National Reformer,* a weekly journal that championed the issues mentioned above. Notwithstanding his radical views, he was never in favor of Socialism (largely because he associated it with violent revolution), and even wrote a pamphlet denouncing it in 1887. In 1868 and 1874 he ran unsuccessfully for Parliament, as the member for Northampton, but was finally successful in 1880. Ironically this moment of victory also saw his greatest controversy; for as an atheist he was unable to take the oath, and this led to a six year struggle over his right to take his parliamentary seat, which he finally did in 1886.

▪ Jeremy Bentham (1748–1832), English philosopher. He is chiefly remembered for his doctrine of "utilitarianism," derived from his *Fragment on Government* (1776), and *Introduction to Principles of Morals and Legislation* (1789). Simply put this contends that an action is moral to the degree that it is useful, the usefulness in question being its capacity to give pleasure or prevent pain. This leads to the notion that the end of all legislation should be "the greatest happiness of the greatest number." In 1824 he cofounded (with James Mill) *The Westminster Review,* to disseminate his political views.

▪ [Arthur James, 1st Earl of] Balfour (1848–1930), Scottish statesman. Although born in Scotland, he was educated at Eton and Cambridge. He was elected to Parliament, representing Hertford from 1874 to 1885, and Manchester from 1886 to 1905. However, Shaw is less concerned with his politics here than with his *A Defence of Philosophic Doubt* (1879). Much of Balfour's writing has a philosophic bent: *The Religion of Humanity* (1888) and *The Foundations of Belief* (1895) take up the same themes. Politically, Balfour later went on to become prime minister (in 1902). In 1906 his Unionist Party received a convincing defeat and he himself lost his seat, but he returned to politics (elected in the City of London), and in World War I joined first Asquith's coalition as First Lord of the Admiralty and then, under Lloyd George, joined the Foreign Office. It was here that he made his greatest mark, continuing to represent Great Britain on the diplomatic stage until 1929. Today perhaps he is best remembered for the "Balfour Declaration," which in 1916/17 expressed sympathy with Jewish aspirations for a homeland in what was then Palestine.

26 March 1888

THREE NEW NOVELS* [C415]

A GENERATION which read "The Scalp Hunters" in its boyhood cannot be trusted to tolerate cold-blooded scientific criticism of Captain Mayne Reid. It was he who first made known to us the romance of the Wild West, the scalping, the shooting, the Navajoes and Apaches who settled their differences with palefaces by stake and faggot—just like Christians, the raptures of Mississippi steamboat racing and boiler bursting, with countless other madly exciting things; and shall he be himself scalped by the very critics in whom he implanted a taste for fiction. Impossible! Captain Mayne Reid's novels were ever "jolly"; and this one—posthumous, alas!—has all the qualities that made them so. There are duels, adventures, a beautiful fair girl with a beautiful dark sister, scenery of the right sort, hill and valley, forest and moor, no streets except with gates and sentinels, no houses except fortified ones, all put in with the old inimitable touch. If he who wrote could thus keep up the spirit of youth to the end, why should not we who read? Let us try, at all events.

Captain Mayne Reid, it is said, became a bit of a politician in his last years, and fluttered the Kensington amateur parliament by his republicanism. In "No Quarter," which deals with the English Revolution of the seventeenth century, he borrows many an illustration from contemporary politics. Here is one of them:

> On this night Nathaniel Fiennes was unusually excited; angry at the difficult task left him by his predecessor, just as might the Earl of Ripon be with Lord Lytton, that ass in lion's skin—now politically defunct—for demising him the legacy of Afghanistan.

What would the gallant Captain have said had he lived to see Lord Lytton resuscitated and sent to Paris as the representative of England? But indeed that would have been a trifle to him had he lived to

---

*"No Quarter." By Captain Mayne Reid. Three vols. (London: Sonnenschein. 1888.)
"Lady Grace, and other Stories." By Mrs. Henry Wood. Three vols. (London: Bentley and Son. 1887.)
"Better Dead." By J. M. Barrie. (London: Sonnenschein. 1888.)

witness the doings of the present Government. Writing after the Liberal victory of 1880, he says:

What do we see now? what hear? A new Parliament entering on power under circumstances so like those that ushered in the "Long" as to seem almost the same. And a Ministry gone out who have outraged the nation as much as did the Straffords, Digbys and Lauds. But how different the action taken towards them! No Bill of Attainder talked of, no word of impeachment, not even a whisper about voting want of confidence. Instead of being sent to a prison, as the culprits of 1640, they of 1880 walk out of office and away, with a free, jaunty step and air of bold effrontery, blazoned with decorations and brand new titles bestowed on them—a very shower, as the sparks from a Catherine wheel.

If these notions spread, what will become of Mr. Balfour, and Mr. Matthews, and Mr. Justice Stephen, and Sir Charles Warren, not to mention Lord Salisbury, after the next general election? Imagine a nation of outraged Captain Mayne Reids impeaching fallen Ministers and their creatures for political profligacy, corruption, mendacity, folly, and cowardice! How the *Daily News* would rat, and how Messrs. Buckle, Pollock, and Greenwood, with their political staffs, would hurry to Geneva, and issue the *Times,* the *Saturday,* and the *St. James's* cheek by jowl with the *Sozial Demokrat!* Mr. Matthews may depend on it, these doctrines are dangerous; and a censorship is needed—from a Conservative point of view—for novels. Captain Mayne Reid is beyond the reach of coercion; but the publishers and printers are extant and plankbedable. Why not prosecute them for seditious libel, or for blasphemy?

Another posthumous novel from the hand of an old favourite is Mrs. Henry Wood's "Lady Grace." Her stories were women's stories, as Captain Mayne Reid's were men's; and they were meant to be read, not criticised. The characters and situations of which she made her books are indeed beyond all criticism: their interest has been proved by the experience of many generations. In permuting and combining them she had a happy facility which, with her good sense and good feeling, made her very popular at Mudie's. If her novels will not survive her long it is not because they are worthless, but because each generation can manufacture such work for itself with the advantage of the newest fashions. Shakspere himself would have been discarded long ago could we have produced an equally clever man every half-century or so.

Friendly hands have rolled the log of Mr. J. M. Barrie, the author of "Better Dead"; and it must be confessed that friendship has not been without its excuse in so amiably doing; for the little book is amusing enough. It is not always intelligible: little can be confidently inferred from such a sentence as, "The horsehair chairs were not torn, and you did not require to know the sofa before you sat down on it that day thirty years before, when a chubby minister and his lady walked to the manse between two cartloads of furniture, trying not to look elated." But the annals of the S.D.W.S.P., or Society for Doing Without Some People, have a laugh or two in them, and they have the attraction of being extremely personal. "Every day," says Mr. Barrie, "the Flying Scotchman shoots upon London its refuse of clever young men who are too ambitious to do anything." One of these Scotchmen joins the society, and has various adventures in its service—among others an interview with Mr. Labouchere, whom he vainly urges to commit suicide. And so on. Mr. Barrie is rather too conscious that a shilling skit is nothing if not smart; and his literary workmanship is very crude indeed; but his joke is not a bad one as jokes go.

Editor's Notes

- Shaw received Mrs. Wood's *Lady Grace* on 11 October, Mayne Reid's *No Quarter* on 18 November, and James Barrie's *Better Dead* on 3 December 1887. On 6 January 1888, his diary records that he "began review of 3 novels (Payn, Mrs. Henry Wood, and Mayne Reid)." However, as we have seen, his review of Payn's novel was finished separately from the others, on 8 January, and on the tenth we read, "finished and sent off reviews of Mayne Reid's *No Quarter*, Mrs. Henry Wood's *Lady Grace*, and Barrie's *Better Dead*" (*Diary*, 331, 332, 335, 337).
- [Captain Thomas] Mayne Reid (1818–83), Anglo-Irish novelist. Born in Northern Ireland, the son of a Presbyterian clergyman, although himself educated for the ministry, Reid was uninterested in theology, and in 1840 left home for the United States, where he was by turns trader, trapper, storekeeper, actor, poet, newspaper correspondent, and editor. In 1845 he accepted a commission and participated in the war with Mexico, playing a distinguished role in the storming of Chapultepec, where he was wounded, and supposed dead. While recovering from his injury he wrote his first novel *The Rifle Rangers*, which was published in 1850. Reid then went to London,

where his stories began to be popular. In 1853 he fell in love with the thirteen-year-old Elizabeth Hyde, whom he married two years later, and who was the inspiration for his novel *The Child Wife: a Tale of the Two Worlds* (1868). He suffered a financial reverse in 1866; and in 1867, on a trip to the United States, he became ill due to a recurrence of an old war wound, which left him crippled. Both his powers of invention and his popularity waned as a consequence, and he died in London in 1883, survived for many years by his widow, who wrote his biography. Among his better known works are *The Scalp Hunters* (1851), *The Boy Hunters* (1852), *The Quadroon* (1856), *Ran Away to Sea* (autobiography) (1859), *The Boy Slaves* (1865), *The Headless Horseman* (1866), and *The Free Lances* (1881).

- Mrs. [Ellen] Henry Wood (1814–87), English novelist. She was brought up by her maternal grandmother, and while still a girl was afflicted with curvature of the spine, which affected her health permanently and forced her to write most of her novels in a reclining chair with the manuscript on her knees. In 1836 she married Henry Wood, a banker, who had been for some time in consular service. She spent the next twenty years abroad, mainly in France, returning in 1856 to settle in Norwood. She had been contributing short stories (for which she received little payment) to *Bentley's Miscellany* and to Colborn's *New Monthly Magazine*, but her first remunerative work was the novel *Danesbury House* (1860), for which she won a prize of £100 from the Scottish Temperance League. In 1861, her story *East Lynne* was serialized in the *New Monthly Magazine*. Published independently in the fall of that year, the book became an enormous success, was translated into many languages and adapted as a very successful drama. After two more highly successful novels, Mrs. Wood became the proprietor of *The Argosy* magazine (with Bentley as publisher), and to this she contributed the better portion of her work. Her husband died in 1866, and Mrs. Wood moved from Kensington to St. John's Wood, where she lived for the rest of her life, working busily on her novels. A selection of her over forty works would include *The Channings* (1862), *The Shadow of Ashlydat* (1863), *Lord Oakburn's Daughters* (1864), *Mildred Arkell* (1865), *Lady Adelaide's Oath* (1867), *Anne Hereford* (1868), *Within the Maze* (1872), *Edina* (1876), *Pomeroy Abbey* (1878), *Court Netherleigh* (1881), and *About Ourselves* (1883). *Lady Grace*, the book reviewed above, was running in *The Argosy* at the time of Mrs. Wood's death.

- [Sir] J[ames] M[atthew] Barrie (1860–1937), Scottish playwright and novelist. Educated at Edinburgh University, from which he graduated in 1882, he began as a writer and reviewer for the *Nottingham Daily Journal* in 1883, in which year his first one-act play *Caught Napping* was produced in that city. Later he moved to London as a freelance journalist. In 1894 he married, but was later divorced. His first novel (reviewed above) was first privately printed in 1887, and thereafter a succession of novels followed: *When a Man's Single: a Tale of Literary Life* (1889), *The Little Minister* (1891), *Two of Them* (1893), and perhaps his most famous *The Little White Bird; or Adventures in Kensington Gardens* (1902), which was dramatized two years later as *Peter*

Pan; or, the Boy who Never Grew Up. Barrie wrote numerous other plays, both one act and full length, some of the most memorable being *Richard Savage* (1891); *Ibsen's Ghost; or, Toole Up to Date* (1891); *Walker, London* (1893); *The Professor's Love Story* (1902), first performed, as some others were, in the United States; *The Wedding Guest* (1900); *Quality Street* (1901); *The Admirable Crichton* (1902); *What Every Woman Knows* (1908); *Dear Brutus* (1917); and *Mary Rose* (1920). He also wrote many collections of short stories. He was made a baronet in 1913, was rector of St. Andrews University from 1919 to 1922, and was chancellor of Edinburgh University from 1930 to 1937.

▪ Henry Matthews [Viscount Llandaff] (1826–1913), English lawyer and politician. Educated at London University, he was called to the bar in 1850. In 1868 he was elected as a Conservative for the borough of Dungarvan. In 1874 he lost his seat and was unsuccessful in winning it back in 1880. However, he was elected for East Birmingham in 1886, and his personal friendship with Lord Randolph Churchill led to his appointment as Home Secretary. Among the difficult cases he had to deal with as Home Secretary was that of Lipski in 1887 [see page 336 above]. His decisions were occasionally attacked by W. T. Stead in the *Pall Mall Gazette,* but Lord Chief Justice Coleridge considered Matthews the best Home Secretary he had known. Reelected in 1892, he was in the opposition for the three years of the next Parliament, and when the Conservatives were returned again in 1895, he was elevated to the peerage as Viscount Llandaff.

▪ [Sir] Justice [James Fitzjames] Stephen (1829–94), English judge. Son of the English lawyer and abolitionist James Stephen (1758–1832), he was professor of common law at the Inns of Court from 1875 to 1879, at which time he became a judge of the High Court of Justice for twelve years. He also made the first attempt (since Blackstone) to explain the principles of English law in his *General View of the Criminal Law of England* (1863) and *History of the Criminal Law* (1883).

▪ Sir Charles Warren (1840–1927), English general and archæologist. Educated at Cheltenham College, Sandhurst, and Woolwich, he passed a distinguished military career, mostly on the African continent before being recalled in September 1886 to succeed Sir Edmund Henderson as chief commissioner for the London metropolitan police. The job was fraught with difficulty, and although he carried out the police arrangements for the Queen's Jubilee in 1887 with complete success, the "Jack the Ripper" murders and the police's treatment of political dissent in Pall Mall, Oxford Street, and Trafalgar Square [see "Bloody Sunday," page 372 above], led to charges of police incompetence, and caused strained relations between Warren and Home Secretary Matthews [see above] that culminated in Warren's resignation in 1888. Shaw had lent his name to the debate in a letter to the *Pall Mall Gazette* on 16 November 1887 in response to a leader in the *Daily News* that praised Sir Charles Warren for his courage in handling the "Trafalgar Square riots." After speaking of the outrageous behavior of the police on "Bloody Sunday," Shaw goes on

Now as to the soldierly qualities of Sir Charles Warren. I have always understood that the first quality of a soldier is courage, yet Sir Charles Warren has, by his extraordinary cowardice, turned an ordinary political meeting, which every experienced constable in the force knows to be as easy and harmless an affair for the police as the regulation of the traffic at Oxford-circus, into a formidable riot. It is ridiculous to speak of the hero of such an exploit as a capable commander merely because he was frightened into attacking peaceable citizens with all the brute force, military and civil, placed at his disposal for the gravest national emergencies. The secret of the whole matter is that Sir Charles is by temperament subject to delusive panic. Last year he got hydrophobia on the brain, and set his men to bludgeon our dogs. This year he has got revolution on the brain; and he sets his men to bludgeon ourselves, under the impression that we are all dynamiters. Last Sunday, apparently frantic with imaginary terrors, he ordered Superintendent Dunlap to stop the South London men and women "at any cost," and was prepared to exterminate them with bayonet and ball cartridge if they had got into the Square in spite of Mr. Dunlap. Personally, he deserves pity rather than angry denunciation. His particular form of poltroonery is a disease, and is quite compatible with tactical skill, conscientiousness, physical hardihood, and many amiable private qualities. But the terrible edged tools with which he is at present playing so wildly must be taken out of his hands at once. (Bernard Shaw, *Pall Mall Gazette*, 16 November 1887)

After resigning as Police Commissioner, Warren returned to his military career, commanding the post at Singapore until the outbreak of the South African war in 1899, when he joined Sir Redvers Buller [see page 199 above] in successful operations against the Boers. Returning to England in 1900, he was promoted general in 1904, and colonel commandant of the Royal Engineers the following year.

▪ Robert Arthur Talbot Gascoyne-Cecil, Third Marquis of Salisbury (1830–1903), English statesman. Educated at Oxford, from where he graduated in 1849, he first made a name for himself writing articles for the *Quarterly Review*, was twice secretary for India (from 1866 to 1867, and from 1874 to 1878), then Foreign Secretary. He became leader of the opposition in the House of Lords in 1881, and Prime Minister and Foreign Secretary from 1885 to 1886, from 1886 to 1892, and from 1895 to 1902, at which point (at the end of the Boer War) he retired in favor of his nephew A. J. Balfour. An old-style Tory, he was the polar opposite of Shaw in his political thinking.

▪ George Earl Buckle was editor of *The Times* from 1884 to 1912. W. H. Pollock [see page 345 above] editor of *The Saturday Review* from 1883 to 1894, and Frederick Greenwood (with H. D. Traill and Adam Gielgud) editor and joint proprietor of *The St. James's Gazette* from 1880 to 1888.

16 April 1888

SONGS OF A REVOLUTIONARY EPOCH* [C425]

To that section of manly England which in its golden youth went to Eton, the name Joynes is connected with Revolution much as the Bishop of London's name is connected with the ballet. Whenever the collision between the inertia of established law and the restless urgency of change found a painful concrete expression in a collision between the Reverend Mr. Joynes and the British schoolboy, it was Mr. Joynes who represented forceful law and order, and the schoolboy who, as personified Revolution, got the worst of it. But Force, as Karl Marx said, is the midwife of progress; and there arose another Joynes at Eton, who was in course of time transmuted with considerable academic distinction at Cambridge from Eton scholar to Eton master, and seems to have for a time conducted himself in a manner worthy of his antecedents. Now Eton expects, among other things, that every master shall keep out of the hands of the police. In 1882, or thereabouts, Mr. James Leigh Joynes was discovered travelling in Ireland with no less dangerous an associate than Mr. Henry George. The two were promptly incarcerated. But the days of Mr. Balfour were not yet; and the prison doors opened abashed to the Eton master. Mr. Joynes wrote to the *Times*, of course, and presently published a book of Irish travel; but the expected note of contrition was absent. Eton began to suspect that she was harbouring a sympathizer with Land Nationalization. Dr. Hornby called upon Mr. Joynes to purge himself of heresy or else withdraw. Further correspondence in the *Times* ensued; and Mr. Joynes, under protest, renounced the substantial mammon of Eton, and burned his boats by joining the Democratic Federation, then a united body facing the world hopefully with an unblemished record and unbounded prospects. Whilst this state of things lasted, he wrote a Socialist catechism; conducted a monthly magazine called *To-day* jointly with Mr. Belfort Bax; and contributed articles and poems to the new paper *Justice*, founded by Mr. William Morris and Mr. Edward Carpenter, under the editorship of Mr. H. M. Hyndman. Shortly before the reign of fraternity in the Socialist camp came to an end, Mr. Joynes left England, and in the course of a lengthy European tour continued a series of translations from the revo-

---

*"Songs of a Revolutionary Epoch." By J. L. Joynes. (London: Foulger and Co. 1888.)

lutionary poems of Freiligrath and Herwegh already begun in the pages of *To-day*. Some of these were sent to Mr. Hyndman and published in *Justice*. Others, sent to Mr. William Morris, appeared in the *Commonweal*. Finally, Mr. Joynes returned; collected his translations in the volume now under notice; engaged in the study of medicine at a metropolitan hospital—perhaps with an eye to the surgical exigencies of the next revolution; and settled down once more as a sober and respectable student.

Mr. Joynes has been the first to translate any considerable portion of the revolutionary poetry of the '48 period into vernacular English. The translations collected by Mrs. Freiligrath-Kroeker, and published in a fairly well known Tauchnitz volume, were of very unequal merit. The revolutionary spirit of a few of the poems had come safely through the hands of Ernest Jones; but the examples selected were for the most part purely romantic, and had been chosen on that account by the German-reading poets and men of letters of the romantic school. Mr. Joynes stands to Ernest Jones in the close relationship of Social Democrat to Chartist; and he hints in his preface, with refreshing frankness, that Ernest Jones is the only rival whose pretensions seem to him of any importance. This is perhaps a little hard on Bayard Taylor, whose vigorous version of "Die Todten an die Lebenden" will bear comparison with the original in point of metre better than Mr. Joynes's, though it is hardly as sincere in feeling. The most touching poems in the collection are those of George Herwegh. They are distinguished by a woeful sense of the chronic poverty of the people, expressing itself in a characteristic note of pathos, sometimes ironic, sometimes poignant and hopeless. This note has been imitated by many of the writers whose songs are grouped at the end of the volume. It is treated with special felicity and delicacy by Mr. Joynes—for example, in his Englishing of such poems as "Der Arme Jakob" and of Püttman's "Fliege, Schifflein, fliege." A more difficult achievement is his version of Herwegh's "Midnight Walk," which might pass for a fine piece of original work.

Editor's Notes

- Shaw's diary does not indicate when he received Joynes's book. On 13 March 1888, his diary records that he "began review of Joynes's translations in the afternoon at the Museum." The following day he "added a few words to the Joynes review," and on the fifteenth he wrote a review of the book for *The Star* newspaper, which was shorter than the above, and contained several quotations from the translations. On 19 March he "finished and sent off review of Joynes's *Songs of Revolution* to the *PMG*" (*Diary*, 356, 357, 359).

▪ J[ames] L[eigh] Joynes (1853–93), English Socialist, teacher, and poet. Shaw's above account serves as a pretty accurate biography of Joynes up to this date. Like Shaw, Joynes was both a vegetarian and a Shelleyan, and the two men were close friends, attended meetings and exhibitions, cycled and dined together (in fact he spent the day with Joynes only three days after he dispatched this review to the *Pall Mall Gazette*), and corresponded frequently in the 1880s. Joynes had already written *The Adventures of a Tourist in Ireland* (1882) and *The Socialist Catechism* (1884). *To-Day,* co-edited by Joynes and Belfort Bax, had serialized two of Shaw's early novels, *An Unsocial Socialist* (March to December, 1884) and *Cashel Byron's Profession* (April 1885 to March 1886). There was irony in the manner of Joynes's death: as Shaw records above, Joynes cherished the desire of becoming a doctor; yet, according to Shaw, he himself

> was slaughtered by a medical treatment so grossly and openly stupid and ruinous that I have never forgiven the medical profession for it since. (Letter to Archibald Henderson, *Collected Letters 1898–1910,* 490).

Interestingly, Joynes died in the year that Shaw wrote his second play, *The Philanderer,* with its savage attack on the medical pretensions of "Dr. Paramour."

▪ [Ferdinand] Freiligrath (1810–76) and Georg Herwegh (1817–75) were German poets of the popular uprising and expression of German nationalism in 1848, writing patriotic war songs and political poems, such as the former's *Glaubensbekenntnis* and *Ça Ira!,* and the latter's *Gedichte eines Lebendigen.*

▪ Ernest [Charles] Jones (1819–69), English Chartist reformer and poet. He was the author of *The Battle Day, and other Poems* (1855).

▪ Bayard Taylor (1825–78), American journalist and author. Born and educated in Pennsylvania, for four years he traveled in Europe as correspondent for the *Saturday Evening Post,* the *United States Gazette* (of Philadelphia), and the New York *Tribune,* whose literary manager he became in 1848. He also traveled widely in the Middle and Far East and Europe, and lectured on his travels, until 1856, when he settled on a farm near his birthplace. During this long period he had been writing poems, plays, and adult and children's fiction. In 1862 he became secretary (later chargé d'affaires) for the American legation in St. Petersburg, Russia. It was when he returned in 1863 and until 1867 that he worked on translating German texts, and became nonresident professor of German at Cornell University. In 1878 he became United States Ambassador to Germany, but died the same year.

24 April 1888

MR. GRANT ALLEN'S NEW NOVEL* [C428]

WHENEVER we change our creed—and we change its content, if not its form, oftener than we think—those of us whose chief delight lies in the fine arts cannot but feel concerned as to the artistic fertility of the new faith. There are leaders of opinion to an appreciable number at present whose first act of spiritual independence was the rejection of the Mosaic cosmogony and Ussher's chronology in favour of the theories of Herbert Spencer, Darwin, and Professor Tyndall. It occurred to many who watched that change to wonder what, if the new hypothesis prevailed, would be the equivalents of the great epics, oratorios, and altar-pieces of the age of faith. Shallow people, holding on to the outside of their religion, were ready enough to declare that the fall of supernaturalism must involve the extinction of art. The deeper and broader minds had no fear of that: they rather tended to the opposite extreme of denying that Darwinism had anything essential to do with either religion or art except to clear the atmosphere about both. All the same, it was evident to analytic thinkers that there would be, if not progression or retrogression, improvement or decay, at least a difference. Had Bunyan been an evolutionist he would no doubt have written a pilgrim's progress; but it would not have been *the* Pilgrim's Progress, though it might have been neither better nor worse.

It is from this point of view that Mr. Grant Allen, as a novelist, is specially interesting. He is a fair example of the Spencer-Darwin-Tyndall culture, with its abiding consciousness of a remorseless competitive struggle for existence, and its hopeless conception of organized life as a mere vagary of the energy stored in an earth predestined to finish its aimless whirl about the cooling sun by tumbling back again into it only to melt into a cloud and start off for another spin with the same inevitable end. With such uncomfortable, pessimistic notions, the mere physicist nowadays may find existence interesting: he can hardly think it encouraging. The only men still hopeful in spite of being up to date in physics and biology are the metaphysicians, who know better than to accept the physicists' knowledge of "science" as a science of knowledge; and the economists and sociologists, who see that the competitive struggle for existence, far from being necessarily eternal,

*"The Devil's Die." By Grant Allen. Three vols. (London: Chatto and Windus. 1888.)

must in time evolve its opposite, either by convicting itself of defeating its own end, or by eliminating the incorrigibly competitive in the long run as least fit to survive. Now, Mr Grant Allen is not a metaphysician; and he is not an economist. He is a physicist as purely and simply as it is possible for a man to be—which is happily not saying much, even in the Laputa of noveldom.

The result, as apparent in "The Devil's Die," is startling. There are three principal men in the story; and one of them, a very clever physicist, with a philosophy of empiric materialism, is a diabolical villain. The other two are amiable; but if the reader anticipates that they are therefore respectively metaphysician and economist he is mistaken: Mr. Grant Allen has no idea of any such alternative. One of them, Ivan Royle, is simply a fool, and the other an Indo-Arab believing in the inscrutable goodness of an over-ruling Allah as Gordon believed in God. From the Spencer-Tyndall point of view their amiability has not a leg to stand on, whereas the two murders committed by Harry Chichele are perfectly justifiable. Nay, the first of them is highly meritorious, since it consists in killing a miserably vicious, drunken and disreputable old woman in order to establish a germ theory of great importance. Clearly, if a dog may be vivisected on a calculation of the preponderance of the benefits of science over those of respect for the victim's will to live, why not a woman also? Modern biology knows no difference between the life of the human and that of the canine animal. Dr. Chichele next tries his hand on his wife, not without utilitarian warrant, since her death will produce positive results of happiness to two much more highly organized individuals—himself and a famous novelist—at the cost of a negative result involving no unhappiness to the solitary subject of the operation. One does not exactly see why Mr. Grant Allen calls his scientific hero a villain, especially as all his virtuous characters, with one exception, are either fanatics or idiots. The one exception is the novelist, a gifted and beautiful lady who owes her exemption to the fact that, though she begins, realistically enough, as a vulgar egotist and an intolerable twaddler, she afterwards becomes a purely romantic figure, outside the realm of scientific naturalism.

It would be ungrateful to Mr. Grant Allen to enjoy so good a story as "The Devil's Die" and then say nothing for it except that its philosophy is hopelessly inadequate. The turns and doublings of Harry Chichele's destiny, when once he lets loose from his laboratory the terrible cholera germs with which his researches arm him, make a novel and enthralling melodrama. When the end of that comes there is still another volume to hold the reader with the story of the crossing of the sage brush by the two outcasts from Eagle City. The horrors of this American desert, and the disappointments, more cruel than any Arabian mirage, which it has for the thirsty traveller, are worked into a capital third volume of adventure. In point of literary workmanship the book would have been better had the author taken more pains; but Mr. Grant Allen has recently confessed to the world that competitive bookmaking leads to the survival of the fastest rather than of the fittest, and the plea of necessity must be allowed.

In one of the later chapters, by-the-by, England is eulogised as "the land where, 'girt with friends or foes, a man may speak the thing he will' in public or in private." Is this a joke, or merely a roundabout way of conveying that Mr. Grant Allen never reads the newspapers?

Editor's Notes

▪ Shaw's diary makes no mention of the receipt of this book. On 10 April 1888, he reports, "Reading Grant Allen's novel *The Devil's Die* for review," and that evening, when he went with Archer to see J. F. Nisbett's play *Dorothy Gray* at the Princess's Theatre, he reports that it was "very long and dull. Read the novel between the acts." He did the same again, during a performance of Seebohm's *Little Lord Fauntleroy* at the Prince of Wales Theatre on 13 April. He finished the novel on the fifteenth; on the eighteenth he reports, "Still at the review of *The Devil's Die*," and the following day, after tea, he "finished, revised, and sent off reviews of Heyse [see pages 413–15 below], and Grant Allen to the *PMG*" (*Diary*, 365, 366, 367, 368).

▪ [Charles] Grant [Blairfindie] Allen (1848–99), Canadian-born novelist, philosopher, and scientific writer. Born near Kingston, Ontario, he was at first educated by his father (a minister of the Irish church), then by a tutor from Yale (while the family resided briefly in Connecticut), next at the College Impériel, at Dieppe, France, completing his secondary education at King Edward VI School, Birmingham, England. From there he went to Merton College, Oxford, where he graduated in 1871. While still at the university, Allen married a woman who was an invalid and worked hard to support her. He taught at Brighton, Cheltenham, and Reading for three years, and accepted a post as professor of mental and moral philosophy in an abortive university venture in Jamaica. This scheme collapsed in 1876, and Allen returned to England determined to be a writer. He had married again on his first wife's death in 1873 and had a son. In 1877 he published *Physiological Aesthetics* (he espoused an evolutionary theory of philosophy, based on Spencer), and this was followed by a number of "popular" scientific works such as *Colin Clout's Calendar* (1883), which was praised by Darwin and Huxley, and *Force and Energy* (1888), which was not received by the scientific community with the admiration Allen anticipated. He had also begun to write fiction, often of a powerful kind, including *Strange Stories* (1884), *This Mortal Coil* and *The White Man's Foot* (1888) [for reviews of which see page 453 below], *The Woman Who Did* (1895), which achieved a *succès de scandale,* and *The British Barbarians* (1896). He published a volume of poetry, *The Lower Slopes,* in 1894, and his *Evolution of the Idea of God* in 1897. He also wrote a number of essays and journalistic pieces.

- There is little doubt that Shaw remembered this book when writing *The Philanderer* (1893). Its two principal characters, the diabolical, yet clinically efficient Dr. Harry Chichele, and his friend the tenderhearted, ever faithful Dr. Mohammed Ali, are almost self-parodies. The former resembles Shaw's Dr. Paramore in that he wants to beat cholera independently of Pasteur:

> Germs! Why I can have whole gallons and bucketsful of them if I choose. I shall simply settle the whole cholera question.
>
> (*The Devil's Die,* 1:60)

Their bravery in the face of disease causes one of the companions to soliloquize thus:

> If you want to see what cowards men can be upon occasion, just ask them to face an unknown epidemic. Most men are brave enough in the presence of a danger that you can fight with thews and muscle and active energy; but when it comes to a danger that you have to oppose passively and unresistingly, the best of them will back out of it as gracefully as possible. We medical men are the only ones who will take a risk of this sort upon ourselves without a moment's hesitation.
>
> (*The Devil's Die,* 1:37)

Small wonder that Shaw put this attitude to comic use in *The Philanderer;* while his comments on justifying the vivisection of humans in the name of Science are repeated in the preface to *The Doctor's Dilemma* (1911).

7 May 1888

FOR FREEDOM [C436]

"For Freedom." By Tighe Hopkins. Two vols. (London: Chatto and Windus. 1888.) Among Mr. Tighe Hopkins's gifts are a certain lightness of heart and quaintness of touch which make him comparatively independent of solid subject matter. In this last novel of his he takes the Garibaldian expedition of 1860 for his scene, and trifles with it in a pleasantly audacious humour for two volumes. Sometimes he starts a piece of historical storytelling in Carlyle's unsurpassed way. Then, weakening on that, he dashes off into duels and escapades in the manner of Captain Mayne Reid. Finally, he is himself again, either chaffing over his puppets in the easiest and airiest fashion or suddenly melting and dropping a tear of heartfelt sentiment over some comically inadequate bit of pathos. However, if he is not a deep historian, he is not a dull one either. Garibaldi troubles him far less than he troubled Cavour. The irresponsible novelist takes his turn out of the red-shirted hero with a happy unconcern which the equally irresponsible reader may share without fear or reproach. If the upshot of the battle of Volturno was not as largely influenced by the pluck of an English tailor as Mr. Tighe Hopkins represents it to be, yet the novel is all the better and history none the worse for so patriotic an invention. On the whole, "For Freedom," which is evidently the result of an Italian trip, must not be taken as a test of what its author can do in his most strenuous intellectual mood. It is a piece of holiday work, and a bright and engaging piece at that; but it leaves Mr. Tighe Hopkins's reputation much as it stood before.

Editor's Notes

- There is again no indication of when Shaw received or read *For Freedom*, but his diary entry for 26 April 1888 reads in part, "Wrote and sent off review of Hopkins's *For Freedom*" (*Diary*, 370).
- T[] Tighe Hopkins (1856–1919), English journalist and writer. Educated at St. John's School, Leatherhead, Surrey, and Oundle Grammar School, he was later employed on the literary staff of *The Daily Chronicle* and *The Nation*. Among other works, he wrote *'Twixt Love and Duty* (1886), *Nugents of Carriconna* (1890), *The Incomplete Adventurer* (1892), *Lady Bonnie's Experiment* (1895), *Kilmainham's Memories* (1896), *Pepita of the Pagoda* (1897), *Dungeons of Old Paris* (1898), *An Idler in Old France* (1899), *The Man in the Iron Mask* (1901), *The Women Napoleon Loved* (1910), and a number of books on prison and penal reform. Hopkins was an acquaintance of Shaw's; and his marriage, in 1881, to a clergyman's daughter, Ellen Crump, and the arrival of *their* daughter, does not seem to have prevented Hopkins from having a roving eye. For on the day Hopkins and Shaw first met, 12 January 1886, each determined to seduce Jenny Patterson and played a waiting game at her house to see who should outstay the other. Shaw won.

▪ Giuseppe Garibaldi (1807–82), Italian nationalist, who devoted his revolutionary zeal to Italian unification and freedom. With the support of Conte Camillo Benso di Cavour, he led an expedition of one thousand men in 1860 from Genoa to Sicily, then governed by the king of Naples. His men were distinctively dressed in red shirts and became known as the "Red Shirts" or "The Thousand." He defeated the Neapolitans decisively on the banks of the River Volturno on 26 October 1860.

18 May 1888

A NOVEL WITH A HEROINE* [C442]

IT is a delicate question whether a novelist's utmost capacity is best tested by his heroes or his heroines. The highest literary feat of the constructive imagination is certainly the description either of the best conceivable man or the best conceivable woman. If woman be higher than man, then the creator of the highest heroine must take precedence of the creator of the highest hero: if not, the hero-maker sets the record. It is not an alternative upon which a wise man would publicly commit himself, however emphatic his private opinion might be. Paul Heyse, in "Der Roman der Stiftsdame," says nothing on the point, but sets himself with all his might to depict a noble woman. He attacks the work as a poet—as a realist in the true sense, whole skies above the naturalists who offer you a photograph of Polly Jones, guaranteed "real," and obviously a flagrant rag doll, though with a woman somewhere in the stuffing, no doubt, if the writer were only realist enough to get at her. In England, photographic naturalism does not greatly prevail: we rather throw ourselves heart and soul into the manufacture of faultless ideal heroines. It would be vain to pretend that the average result is encouraging. If a composite photograph from the all heroines in Mudie's could be taken, it might be hung in the British Museum beside Mr. Holman Hunt's "Light of the World," in order that future generations might possess two priceless historical documents concerning the Victorian conception of

*"The Romance of the Canoness," By Paul Heyse. Translated by J. M. Percival. (New York: Appleton. 1888.)

perfect respectability in humanity and divinity severally. Such a composite photograph must be stamped on the mind's retina of every reviewer. The golden hair, the blue eyes occasionally changing to green, hazel, or brown, the plain white dress, the one simple flower at her throat, the steadfast ignorance of all her social functions and duties, and the well-regulated heart beating in perfect synchronism with Mrs. Grundy's!—is it to be wondered at that cynics sometimes, in a frenzy of reaction, rush away to write books for the sole purpose of scandalizing that intolerable young lady; or that their readers, instead of being shocked, cry, "Come to our bosoms, gentlemen and lady naturalists; and if you cannot give us a better woman, then in the name of oppressed England give us a worse one. Anybody you please—Jezebel or Rahab—anybody but Rowena!"

This is well enough for a change; but Jezebel soon becomes ten times duller than Rowena; and some at least of us find that after all we do crave for somebody better and not worse. When this fit is on us, Mudie is seldom equal to the occasion; and we are fain to look at home for some book that we have read twenty times already. This is the point at which to take up Paul Heyse's "Romance of the Canoness." It is a charming story. The Canoness, a woman to whom neighbourly love is a necessity of the heart, and who doubts whether one can be happy in heaven without having been happy on earth, has occasion to protect from insult an actor. He is a magnificent simulacrum of a natural noble man; he condescends to desire her for his wife; and she generously gives herself to him. But the unfortunate man, with the ideas and the fine physical qualifications of a stage hero, has the will of a vain drunkard. As the woman with the lofty soul moves beside him among the mummers, one can hardly resist the fancy that these latter are the heroes and heroines of ordinary fiction brought to the touchstone and found counterfeit. Weissbrod, a student of theology, who occupies the place usually allotted to the hero of a novel, only becomes worthy of the Canoness when she unmasks him to himself after his first and last attempt to pose before her as a spiritual influence.

Heyse, in the person of this student, drops one criticism on English noveldom. "Thackeray," he says, "was my special favourite, whilst Dickens seemed to me a sentimental mannerist, striving for effect, with no correct ideas of women." The reproach is hardly as just to the Dickens of "Little Dorrit" as to the Dickens of "Bleak House;" but the truth is that the heroines even of our best novelists are by no means the mastercreations of English literature. No English novelist seemed able to conceive such women as George Sand drew for us. Those who have felt this will not regret devoting a few hours to "The Romance of a Canoness[*sic*]." Admirers of Henrik Ibsen will also be interested by the traces of his influence in the book; and they will hardly fall into the mistake made by certain German critics who have attempted to hold up Heyse as a rival to Ibsen. The two writers, who both reside in Munich, are good friends; and the influence of the great Scandinavian dramatist is certainly not felt in Heyse's pages with any malign touch of the competitive spirit upon it.

Editor's Notes

- There is no indication in Shaw's diary as to when he received this novel for review. However, on 2 April 1888 he stayed "at home all day, writing letters and reading Heyse's *The Romance of the Canoness*." He was reading it again the next day, and on the fifth "began review of Heyse's novel." On 9 April, he "went to the Museum after dinner to finish the review of Heyse. Got on very slowly . . . leaving the review unfinished." In the meantime he began the review of the Grant Allen novel reviewed above, and finally, on 19 April, "finished, revised, and sent off reviews of Heyse and Grant Allen to the *PMG*" (*Diary*, 362, 363, 365, 368).

- Paul [Johann Ludwig von] Heyse (1830–1914), German novelist, short fiction writer, and poet. He was born in Berlin, specialized in Romance Philology at the University of Bonn, achieved his doctorate in 1852, and traveled to Italy in search of unpublished Provençal manuscripts. Italy had a great influence on him and his later works. In 1854, enthusiastically recommended by the poet Emanuel Geibel, who praised his verse, Heyse received an invitation from King Maximilian II to settle in Munich (with a substantial salary), with no obligations but to attend the King's symposia. Heyse married and, on the death of his first wife, married again in 1866. He was a most prolific author, producing approximately 120 *Novellen*, sixty plays, and six novels. Most of his *Novellen* concern love, and his protagonists are usually women. He concentrated upon the presentation of beauty, ignoring the sordid aspects of life. His plays were less successful, although *Hans Lange* (1866) and *Maria von Magdala* (1899) enjoyed popularity when they were first performed. He received the Schiller Prize in 1884. His best novels are probably *Kinder der Welt* (Children of the World, 1873) and *Im Paradies* (In Paradise, 1876). His work was translated into English by various authors, including M. Wilson, L. C. Sheip, J. Philips, A. W. Hinton, and G. W. Ingraham. In 1910 Heyse became the first German writer to win the Nobel Prize.

- [William] Holman Hunt's (1827–1910) didactic painting of Christ, "The Light of the World," proved enormously popular, and its rather heavy symbolism very powerful, not only when it was first exhibited at the Academy Exhibition of 1854, but later when its replica toured the English-speaking world.
- Rahab was the harlot of Jericho mentioned in Joshua 2:1 who hid Joshua's spies, and had her and her family's lives spared as a consequence.
- Rowena is the beautiful and noble heroine of Scott's *Ivanhoe* (1819).

11 June 1888

*A BOOK OF VERSES** [C448]

WHEN a gentleman of respectable literary standing introduces himself to the public as the author of "a book of verses," certain tedious explanations are needed to settle whether he has really been writing verses, or merely cutting prose into lengths. If the latter, one intimates the fact with finesse, laying much stress on incidental achievements that are not to the point, in order to cover as far as possible the failure that so fatally is to the point. But with Mr. Henley one can make short work. The verses are verses; and the book does not contain a scrap of evidence that the author could write prose if he tried. And though some of his verses are shaped like others that have been brought forth before (notably by Heine), yet many of them take shapes of their own; and none can be mistaken for the mere images of verse made by running words into the assortment of second-hand moulds which are the equipment of "a master of form." Hence the learned will not call Mr. Henley by that leathery name, and so happy man be his dole. Yet happy man is not exactly a phrase that fits Mr. Henley; for it is no exaggeration to say that he sings as if the world were a rack, and he stretched taut on it, with every power absorbed by the effort to endure, and every nerve and sense so strained that there is no passing shadow or insignificant sound but starts a new mood, which is sometimes a mood of feverish exultation or pity, but never a tranquil one. Imagine lying listening to a cistern leaking:

*"A Book of Verses." By William Ernest Henley. (London: David Nutt. 1888.)

At the barren heart of midnight,
When the shadow shuts and opens
As the loud flames pulse and flutter,
I can hear a cistern leaking.

Like the buzzing of an insect,
Still, irrational, persistent . . .
I must listen, listen, listen
In a passion of attention;

Dripping, dropping, in a rhythm,
Rough, unequal, half-melodious,
Like the measures aped from nature
In the infancy of music;

Till it taps upon my heartstrings,
And my very life goes dripping,
Dropping, dripping, drip-drip-dropping,
In the drip-drop of the cistern.

This, it is true, was in hospital; but even in the country, in the most irreproachable bank holiday weather, Mr. Henley lies and listens until he is tortured into song instead of prosaically cursing the noise, as any one else would, and dismissing it for a good tough reverie on bi-metallism. Like Mr. R. L. Stevenson, who has collaborated with him in many an unacted play, he exploits the boy in us—the boy that loved pirate stories, and secretly bought pistols and lanterns. "Out of the night that covers me," he cries, "black as the pit from pole to pole, I thank whatever gods may be for my unconquerable soul." We whose souls hardly held out to the end of our schooldays may well wonder at that echo of our forgotten selves. The chord may be a twangling one with no tone left in it with most of us, but it is finely struck in that verse. Then says Mr. Henley suddenly, "Let us be drunk, and for a while forget." This is the whole philosophy of drunkenness, never before so happily put into a single line, even for Christopher Sly. With such home thrusts as these Mr. Henley probes you until, however brutally sound and sane you may be, you are touched to the quick and must laugh savagely at yourself or at him or both. In fact, the heading of the fifth poem—"Operation"—does not ill describe the reader's state of mind throughout. Altogether, it is a horrible, fascinating, and wrong, yet rightly done, little book—a book which no one should be advised to read, and which no one would be content to have missed.

Editor's Notes

- Shaw's diary does not record when he received this book. On 3 June 1888, however, Shaw "looked at Henley and Stevenson's *Macaire* which I borrowed from Archer." This was, no doubt, as Stanley Weintraub has said, in preparation for seeing *The Amber Heart* the following day, a play that contained Robert Macaire as a character; but it also served Shaw's review. The next day he "wrote review of Henley's verses" (*Diary*, 381–82).

- William Ernest Henley (1849–1903), English poet and critic. He attended the Crypt Grammar School in Gloucester, whose headmaster, Thomas Edward Brown, the poet, befriended the boy. Henley, from the age of twelve, suffered from tuberculosis of the bone and spent many years in hospitals. One leg had to be amputated just below the knee. His other leg was saved by the intervention of Joseph Lister (founder of antisepsis). Henley wrote the poems *In Hospital* while he was a patient in Edinburgh Infirmary. In 1878 he married Ann Boyle (his roommate in the infirmary), with whom he had one daughter, who died in childhood, to be immortalized as "Wendy" in Barrie's *Peter Pan*. In Edinburgh Henley had also made the acquaintance of R. L. Stevenson, with whom he was to collaborate on such plays as *Deacon Brodie, Beau Austin*, and *Admiral Guinea* (1892). After a few months in Edinburgh, in which he wrote French biographies for the *Encyclopædia Britannica*, Henley went to London, where he became editor of a magazine called *London*, to which he himself contributed stories and poems. The magazine lasted only two years, however, and Henley continued as a freelance journalist, writing criticisms for *The Athenæum, St. James's Gazette, The Saturday Review*, and *Vanity Fair*. From 1882 to 1886 he was editor of *The Magazine of Art*, and after more freelancing he finally became editor of the *Scots* (later *National*) *Observer*. Although a Conservative journal, the literary pages were iconoclastic and contained the early work of many promising young writers, including Shaw. Henley's principal works include poetry like *The Song of the Sword* (1892), *London Voluntaries* (1893), *For England's Sake* (1900), and *Hawthorn and Lavender* (1901); essays such as *Views and Reviews* (1890); and many editions of English classics—Shakespeare, Fielding, Smollett, and Hazlitt, among others. Shaw was introduced to W. E. Henley after the first night of G. P. Hawtrey's *The Pickpocket* at the Globe Theatre, on 24 April 1886, but thereafter saw little of him. His view of Henley was amplified in a letter he wrote to Archibald Henderson on 3 January 1905:

> [Henley] could appreciate literature and enjoy criticism. He could describe anything that was forced on his observation and experience, from a tomcat in an area to a hospital operation. Give him the thing to be expressed, and he could find its expression wonderfully either in prose or verse. But beyond that he could not go: the things he said—or the things he wrote (I know nothing of his conversation)—are always conventionalities, all the worse because they are selected from the worst part of the great stock of conventionalities—the conventional

unconventionalisms. He could discover and encourage talent, and was thus half a good editor, but he could not keep friends with it; and so his papers finally fell through. This is my opinion of him for what it is worth. My only review of him—that of his poems in the old Pall Mall Gazette under Stead's editorship—was written before I had formed my view of him. I have read it through since I wrote what I have scratched out here, and find I was mistaken in supposing that it contained anything likely to shew him that I did not think him a fertile writer. (*Collected Letters 1898–1910*, ed. Dan H. Laurence [New York: Dodd, Mead & Company, 1972], 482–83)

A cancelled passage following "editorship" in the letter reads, "So perhaps it was natural that we did not overcome the very slight obstacles that existed to a close personal acquaintance between us."
- "Happy man be his dole" is Falstaff's cry in Shakespeare's *Henry IV, Part One*. Christopher Sly is the drunken tinker in the Induction to *The Taming of the Shrew*, a play, incidentally, which Shaw saw at the Gaiety Theatre two days before he wrote the above review.

4 July 1888

FOUR NOVELS AT ALL THE LIBRARIES* [C460]

THE clever and amiable man, with an imaginative turn and no conscience, can do very well indeed in this England of ours (though it is mostly somebody else's) as a society novelist. Being clever and amiable, he gets invited among pleasant people for his own sake—the easiest of easy terms. The weaknesses of the pleasant, well-to-do people amuse him; and he soon gets the knack of serving them up in fiction, with here a dash of the cynic by way of sauce, and there a tribute to truth and virtue by way of grace before and after partaking. Having no conscience, he does not feel bound to dive into what one may call the political economy of the concern, and inquire whether

---

*"The Strange Adventures of a House Boat." By William Black. Three vols. (London: Sampson Low and Co. 1888.)
"The Mystery of Mirbridge." By James Payn. Three vols. (London: Chatto and Windus. 1888.)
"A Woman's Face." By Florence Warden. Three vols. (London: Ward and Downey. 1888.)
"The Fatal Three." By Miss Braddon. Three vols. (London: Simpkin and Marshall. 1888.)

the beautiful young lady, his heroine, who has nothing to do but wear delicious dresses and break hearts at river and garden parties, must not in the nature of things involve an extra dose of drudgery somewhere for unlovely people who have to keep her going—who stitch her "tailor-made" dresses, for example, at three farthings an hour. Now, it may be that we are all more or less dimly conscious of this stitching perpetually going on round the corner; or, perhaps, it is only the natural inferiority of fact to fiction: anyhow, house boats and garden parties in real life are failures, bores, haunts of the A's, who are snobs, and the B's, who are cads; of C, who is a beastly fool, and D, who is an infernal idiot; of Mrs. E, who declasses herself once for all by painting her face; of Miss F, who admires you and whom you don't admire, and Miss G, whom you admire and who doesn't admire you. The few nice people hate the whole wearisome pretence of enjoyment: the rest would hate it if they had a scrap of niceness in them. The only people—besides Mr. William Black—who really believe in such laborious unspontaneous festivities are girls looking forward to their first season. Why Mr. William Black believes in them it is not easy to guess. But it is certain that his imagination feeds full on cut flowers, shopping in High-street Kensington, and parties up the river. It is impossible to conceive anything more West-endish than his "Strange Adventures of a House Boat." Like a diary of a London season, it can be read either forwards, backwards, or in skips without the slightest confusion as to what it is about; for the fact is, it is about nothing. It is not even neat trifling; it is trifling and water, without the least change of flavour from the first drop to the last. Mrs. Threepenny-bit and the Person without a Character, sparkling as they promise to be, are vapid beyond belief; and their one little conversation palls perceptibly at the hundred and fifth repetition or so. Mr. Black is no doubt a delightful author; but one feels concerning his "strange adventures," as the philosopher felt concerning virtue, that the line must be drawn somewhere.

Mr. James Payn has a much juster appreciation of the dull vanities of high life above stairs than Mr. Black. He seldom forgives a man for being rich, and hates a snob; whereas Mr. Black's army of heroes, if not exactly an army of snobs, is one wherein the purchase system prevails; for the heroes who cannot behave expensively are invariably non-commissioned. And certainly nothing can be more genial than Mr. Payn's sense of humour, his frank and easy literary manners, and the pleasant perfunctoriness that saves him from any suspicion of

suffering from severe mental application. Underneath it all, too, there is a foundation of naïve piety—modern ungodly piety perhaps, but still unmistakable piety. He insists on virtue; and he likes to see a rascal kicked downstairs. Fortunately, he also insists on a story of some sort—a mystery, a shipwreck, a desert island, or a Chinese execution. This time it is a mystery—the "Mystery of Mirbridge." He is a long time getting to it; dawdles over it when he does get to it; and lets it go rather abruptly at the end; but still it serves its turn. The parts about Clara Thorne, who fills her conversation with spirited ironic Payniana, are good to read. Some other parts are good to skip if the reader is in any hurry.

"A Woman's Face" is an engrossing tale of a beautiful lady who is a very bad lot, and a pretty woman who is everything she ought to be except proof against mesmerism. Miss Warden seems to have written from hand to mouth, in the sense of not knowing what the next chapter was to bring forth; for there are several incidents—jewel robberies, somnambulistic expeditions, and other items in the daily routine of an English village—evidently meant to lead to something in the dénouement, but eventually abandoned as no-thoroughfares. They are none the worse, as far as they go, on that account. The charm of the book is that it is a romance without any of the stale stock characters of romance, and consequently not vulgar and tiresome, as romance in three volumes is apt to be.

It would be an insult to Miss Braddon to hesitate to praise "The Fatal Three" before reading it. It is well put together, interesting from cover to cover, equal in workmanship, and not lacking in sensible and humorous remarks on society and manners. For a year past the provinces have hung on it from week to week in its serial form; and now London and the libraries have their turn. Happy London!

Editor's Notes

▪ Again there is no indication of when Shaw received the above novels for review; but on 10 June 1888, Shaw "finished reading Warden's *A Woman's Face,* which took me all day." On 25 June, he was "reading Payn's *Mystery of Mirbridge* for review. Began review of a set of novels for the *PMG.*" This he finished and sent off on the twenty-eighth (*Diary,* 384, 388, 389).
▪ William Black [see page 262 above].
▪ James Payn [see pages 388–89 above].
▪ Florence [Alice] Warden [née Price] (1857–1929), English novelist. Born in Middlesex, she was educated in Brighton and France, her last five years of formal education (from 1875–80) being with a "finishing-governess." In 1880 she went on the stage for five years. She married James Warden in 1887. The British Library lists over 140 books by her, a random sampling of which includes *The House on the Marsh* (1877), *A Prince of Darkness* (1887), *A Witch of the Hills* (1888), *Those Westerton Girls* (1891), *Ralph Ryder of Brent* (1892), *The Inn by the Shore* (1897), *Tom Dawson* (1904), *Mad Sir Geoffrey* (1907), *The Man with the Amber Eyes* (1907), *Blindman's Marriage* (1907), *The Wiles of Wilhelmina* (1913), and *The Grey Moth* (1920). She also authored three plays, one of which was produced at the St. James's Theatre in 1900.
▪ Miss Braddon [see page 362 above].

23 July 1888

TWO UNIMPRESSIVE PAMPHLETS* [C468]

Sir Edwin Arnold's prose is one of the literary wonders of the age; and the largest circulation in the world is no more than it deserves. The zest with which he decorates trivial subjects and vulgar prejudices by magnificent platitudes and impetuous alliterations is as extraordinary as his power of saying, with perfect and sincere gravity, things that make an ordinary man lie down on the hearthrug and scream himself breathless with merriment. One single grain of susceptibility to the ridiculous would spoil him for ever, as irremediably as it would have spoiled Mr. Pecksniff. Not that Sir Edwin Arnold is here likened on his moral side to the Salisbury architect; but there certainly is between them a resemblance in descriptive genius that ought to— and doubtless does—make the *Daily Telegraph* very popular with the Pecksniffian section of the island.

For example, who but Seth Pecksniff or Sir Edwin Arnold could have described a young woman in the Health Exhibition, looking at a showcase containing the ingredients of human flesh and bone, as "the bright maiden who contemplated with unconvinced smiles those alleged materials of her being"? Who else could offer us "as a curious proof of the surviving propriety and self-respect of the very desperate, that forlorn women jumping from Waterloo Bridge almost always fold their shawls quite neatly; lay them on the parapet; and place their bonnets carefully atop, *as if the fatal balustrade were but a boudoir for the disrobing soul*"? Balustrade—boudoir! Is it not inimitable? Harvey is the discoverer of "how the loving, aching heart of man does its work:" Simpson, of "how the measureless flood of human anguish could be largely controlled by the ridiculously simple chemical compound of C_2HCl_3." "When we regard the stars of midnight we veritably perceive the mansions of Nature, countless and illimitable; so that even our narrow senses reprove our timid minds." And again, baffling all critical methods except quotation: "Nature is rather like the henwives in Essex. When a pullet will not sit, these good women" [note the condescension of the phrase] "pluck off the breast feathers from

*"Death—and Afterwards." By Edwin Arnold, M.A., C.S.I. (London: Trübner and Co.) Preface to a new Edition of "A Romance of Two Worlds." By Marie Corelli. (London: Richard Bentley.)

the recalcitrant fowls and whip the bare space lightly with nettles, whereupon the hens go straight to the nest to ease their skin against the nice cool eggs; and habit keeps them there, to the benefit of the farmyard and poultry market. Pride, doubt, fear, ignorance, ambition, fashion, bodily needs, are all in turn the nettles of nature."

To address oneself seriously to the discussion of the immortality of the soul in the face of utterances like these is more than can reasonably be expected of a reviewer who is, after all, only dust. The hee-haw which rises unbidden at their unconscious fun may be asinine; but it is irrepressible. In short, it is useless for Sir Edwin Arnold to expect anybody with a sense of humour to read his essay sympathetically. Suffice it to say that the main argument advanced is that if the secrets yet unrevealed by science are half as amazing as those already discovered, they may well include a demonstration of personal immortality. The essay appeared in the *Fortnightly Review* for August, 1885; and many correspondents earnestly urged Sir Edwin Arnold to republish it. He has complied, and the result is an undeniably amusing little one-and-sixpenny book.

Miss Marie Corelli sends a preface to a new edition of her first novel, "A Romance of Two Worlds." That work, as was pointed out in these columns at the time, was partly the outcome of a real gift for romance, and partly a naïvely presumptuous attempt to apply this gift to the invention of a fictitious religion entitled "Electric Christianity"—just such an attempt as might be expected from a very imaginative young lady without the slightest training in philosophy or science. It appears that a number of foolish persons, including perhaps a few practical jokers, have sent Miss Corelli testimonials as to the spiritual efficacy of her new religion. On the other hand the Electric Creed has been by some deemed blasphemous. "I know not why," says Miss Corelli. But the reader knows why when she proceeds: "Its tenets are completely borne out by the New Testament, which sacred little book [!] however has much of its mystical and true meaning obscured nowadays through the indifference of those who read and the apathy of those who hear." Again: "My creed has its foundation in Christ alone . . . only Christ, only the old, old story of Divine love and sacrifice." "The proof of the theories set forth in the 'Romance' is, as I have already stated, easily to be found in the New Testament." "I merely endeavoured to slightly shadow forth the miraculous powers which I *know* are bestowed on those who truly love and understand the teachings of Christ"— including, according to the romance, the power of remaining beautiful and young for ever; of electrically knocking down gentlemen who try to snatch kisses; and of extemporizing on the pianoforte. If all this is not blasphemy, and very outrageous blasphemy, then there is no such thing as blasphemy—a Secularist position not tenable from Miss Corelli's point of view. Further, the creed of Miss Corelli's second novel had its foundation in M. Alexandre Dumas alone. It carried his "Tue-la" doctrine to the extent of exhibiting a husband deliberately murdering his unfaithful wife under circumstances of diabolical cruelty as a matter of duty. This looked as if Miss Corelli had given up both electricity and Christianity as material for fiction; and her third novel contained no attempt to pose as the prophetess of a new religion. The new preface to the old book therefore comes as an unwelcome surprise; and though it would be absurd to take too seriously what is evidently only a passing folly on the part of an ill-advised young lady, who is perhaps a little upset by her deserved success as a romancer, still, since the document has been submitted for criticism, there must be no mistake about the verdict. In Miss Corelli's interest, her publishers should suppress it without delay and do their best to dissuade her from any future step likely to recall it to her critics or the public.

Editor's Notes

- Shaw received the preface to the new edition of *A Romance of Two Worlds* on 23 October and Arnold's pamphlet on 18 November 1887. There is no indication in the diary of when he read the two pieces, but on 9 January 1888 he "finished and sent off reviews of Arnold's *Death—and Afterwards* and M. Corelli's preface to *A Romance of Two Worlds*" (*Diary*, 332, 337).
- [Sir] Edwin Arnold (1832–1904), English journalist and poet. He was educated at King's School, Rochester, King's College, London, and University College, Oxford, receiving the Newdigate Poetry Prize in 1852 for his poem "Belshazzar's Feast." He himself taught briefly at King Edward VI School, Birmingham, until in 1856 he became principal of Deccan College, Poona. Bombay University awarded him a fellowship, and he studied the languages of India, as well as Persian and Turkish, also winning a commendation from the Indian government for his conduct during the Mutiny of 1857–59. In 1861 he returned to London and began writing for the *Daily Telegraph*, a newspaper with which he was to be associated for forty years, becoming its chief editor in 1873. He became a Knight Companion of the Indian Empire in the very year of the above review and also in 1888 traveled with his daughter to the East, writing picturesque accounts of his travels. In addition to quantities of journalism and the above pamphlet, Arnold produced a great deal of verse and translations, including *Poems, Narrative and Lyrical* (1853),

Griselda, a Tragedy and other Poems (1856), *The Book of Good Counsel: from the Sanskrit of the Hitopadesa* (1861), *History of the Administration of India under the late Marquis of Dalhousie* (1862–64), *Hero and Leander: from the Greek of Musæus* (1873), *A Simple Transliteral Grammar of the Turkish Language; with Dialogues and Vocabulary* (1877), and *The Light of Asia; or The Great Renunciation (the Life and Teaching of Gautama, founder of Buddhism) as told in verse by an Indian Buddhist* (1879). In 1891 he undertook a successful lecture tour of the United States, and, although his eyesight was failing, he continued to write. His last work *Ithobal* was published in 1901, two years before he died.

- Marie Corelli [see page 134 above].

26 July 1888

A BATCH OF BOOKS* [C471]

MR. W. J. ASHLEY's introduction to English history meets admirably the requirements of the modern view that the well springs of history and sociology are to be found in the old communal life, and not in King Alfred's cakes, King Charles's head, the battle of Waterloo, and the Great Exhibition of 1851—a general notion of which, applied to strictly modern conceptions of nationality, still forms the historical equipment of British childhood. Certainly, boyhood brings us to our Macaulay, with his original discovery that history was not a thing of kings and battles, but a commentary on Hansard, enlivened with character sketches in the style of Robinson Crusoe's diary, and touches of nature from obsolete street ballads. Our manhood, too, has in store a leading article, volumes long, containing the history of our own times as it struck the *Daily News*. But King Alfred, Macaulay, and the *Daily News* have left us, after all, in the densest ignorance of the real history both of our own times and those of our forbears; and now, being certain that

---

*"An Introduction to English Economic History and Theory." By W. J. Ashley, M.A. (London: Rivingtons. 1888.)

"A Popular History of Music from St. Ambrose to Mozart." By James E. Matthew. (London: H. Grevel and Co. 1888.)

"Ancient Legends of Ireland." By Lady Wilde. (London: Warde and Downey. 1888.)

"David Poindextre's Disappearance, &c." By Julian Hawthorne. (London: Chatto and Windus. 1888.)

"The Dusantes." By Frank R. Stockton. (London: Sampson Low. 1888.)

"The American Marquis." By R. H. Sherard.

whatever may or may not be true of Kings, battles, and debates, the people at least always worked for a living, we are setting to work to find out how and on what terms they worked—that being by far the safest index to how and on what terms they lived. A good foundation for such study, as far as England is concerned, will be found in Mr. Ashley's book which contains an excellent account of the old English manor, the occurrence of the towns, and the evolution of the merchant guilds and craft guilds of the Middle Ages.

Mr. James E. Matthew, the translator of M. Pougin's "Verdi," has provided a popular history of music from St. Ambrose to Mozart—Mozart not included. It is a brave red and gold volume, with well-executed and interesting illustrations, engraved on wood by manual skill in the old fashion—none of your "processes." The reproductions of seventeenth century French opera title-pages are especially to be commended. Mr. Matthew has supplied a straightforward list of works and composers, cataloguing them as chattily as the restrictions of space permitted, and dividing the honours judiciously between the Italian, French, English, and Dutch schools. He does not seem to be acquainted with Mr. Rowbotham's recent ingenious analysis of the music of the middle ages and its notation; but as his history mainly begins where Mr. Rowbotham left off there is no great harm done. It must not be inferred that Mr. Matthew's history, like Mr. Rowbotham's, is in itself a work of art; but it contains a sufficiency of information, compiled with due care and intelligence.

It will be as well not to affect impartiality in passing an opinion on Lady Wilde's collection of Irish stories and superstitions, the first edition of which was noticed here when it appeared. Her position, literary, social, and patriotic, is unique and unassailable. If any reviewer finds the book dull, it is extremely unlikely that he will have the hardihood to say so. However, it is not dull, although it contains such a length of matter that a hack writer would have made three books of it. Lady Wilde can write scholarly English without pedantry and Irish-English without vulgarity or impracticable brogue phonetics. She has no difficulty in writing about leprechauns, phoukas, and banshees, simply as an Irishwoman telling Irish stories, impelled by the same tradition-instinct, and with a nursery knowledge at first hand of all the characteristic moods of the Irish imagination. Probably no living writer could produce a better book of its kind.

"David Poindextre's Disappearance" is only one of a sheaf of short tales by Mr. Julian Hawthorne. The appetite for artifical fiction to which such tales minister is itself a thing so desperately fictitious that the unfortunate reviewer is tempted to turn to the publishers who have submitted David for rational criticism, and address them, with laboured politeness, in these terms: "Pray, gentlemen, what—as between man and man, and bearing in mind that I have no right to waste the public time and attention—do you expect me to say about these inventions?" To which it is conceivable that Messrs. Chatto and Windus might reply: "Sir, so clever a person as you cannot be at a loss for an entertaining remark, were it but that, unpretentious as our author's tales are, it is not every one could have written them." Which the reviewer hastily admits, and passes on.

Mr. Frank Stockton has ventured to take another turn out of Mrs. Lecks and Mrs. Aleshine in "The Dusantes." These two ladies get snowbound on a mountain, and discover their mysterious hosts of the desert island in the same predicament. They escape by taking a hint from the legend of the barbarians who, looking from the Alpine ridges on the fertile plains of Italy, sat down on their shields and swooped upon Rome in one multitudinous toboggan. The Dusantes and their former guests sit down on carriage cushions and attempt to make history repeat itself, with some success; but Mrs. Lecks and Mrs. Aleshine get rather worn in the process; and Mr. Stockton will probably let them rest for the future.

"The American Marquis" is by an author who has taken his task of writing a shilling shocker with commendable seriousness, adding a preface in which he professes intentions of a comparatively weighty kind. The intentions are not exactly fulfilled, partly because Mr. Sherard's powers are undeveloped; partly because, as an art student in Paris, he seems to have studied the world chiefly in one of its most pernicious little corners. But there is a promising touch here and there in his attempts at character sketching. Accordingly, it is not surprising to recall that Mr. Sherard is a great grandson of Wordsworth, and has come safely through "early poems," a three-volume novel, and other complaints not uncommon at his time of life.

Editor's Notes

▪ There is no mention in Shaw's diary of when he received any of the above books, and only one of them is listed as having been read for review. Shaw's diary for 12 July 1888, begins, "Reading Ashley's *Economic History*." On the thirteenth he went to the Museum and "spent the rest of the day finishing

Ashley." On the eighteenth he "wrote review of Ashley's *Economic History.*"
On 19 July, however, he "finished and sent off a set of six reviews for the
PMG" (*Diary*, 393, 394).

- [Sir] W[illiam] J[ames] Ashley (1860–1927), English economist, scholar,
and author. He was educated at St. Olave's School, Southwark, and Balliol
College, Oxford, where he read history. In 1885 he was appointed Fellow and
Lecturer of Lincoln College, Oxford. In 1888 he married and subsequently
had one son and two daughters. In the same year he became professor of
political economy at the University of Toronto, a post he held for four years. In
1892 he became professor of economic history at Harvard, where he remained until 1901, at which point he accepted the chair in Commerce at
Birmingham University, England, which he held for twenty-four years until
his retirement, for the last eight years of his academic life combining the
duties with those of vice-principal of the University. He also served on a great
many councils and government committees, joint-authoring the Report of the
Unionist Social Reform Committee on Industrial Unrest in 1914 and serving
on the Royal Commission on Agriculture (1919). In addition to the book
reviewed above (whose full title is *An Introduction to English Economic
History and Theory; Part I: The Middle Ages*) and its sequel *The End of the
Middle Ages* (1893)—a book which was translated into German, French, and
Japanese—Ashley also wrote *Surveys, Historic and Economic* (1900), *Adjust-
ment of Wages* (1903), *The Tariff Problem* (1903), *Progress of the German
Working Classes* (1904), *The Rise in Prices* (1912), *Gold and Prices* (1912),
The Economic Organization of England (1914), and *The Christian Outlook*
(1925).
- James E[] Matthew (n.d.), English author. In addition to translating A.
Pougin's *Verdi: an anecdotic history of his life and works* (1887) and writing
the book reviewed above (whose full title is *A Popular History of Music,
Musical Instruments and Opera, from St. Ambrose to Mozart*), Matthew also
translated F. Masson's *Napoleon at Home* (1894) and Charles van den
Borren's *The Sources of Keyboard Music in England* (1914) and compiled a
valuable *Manual of Musical History and Bibliography* (1898).
- Lady [Jane Francesca Agnes] Wilde [née Elgee] (1823–96), Irish poet and
folklorist. Born in Dublin, in 1851 she married Dr. (afterwards Sir) William
Wilde and had two sons, William (born in 1852) and Oscar (born in 1854),
the latter becoming the famous man of letters. There was also a daughter
Isola, born in 1859, who died at the age of eight. After her husband's death in
1876 Lady Wilde moved to London. In 1864 she published a volume of poems
under the pen name "Speranza," and later, under the name Lady Wilde, she
published a number of works on folklore such as *Driftwood from Scandina-
via* (1884), and *Ancient Cures* (1891); she also wrote *Men, Women and Books*
(1891), and *Social Studies* (1893). She conducted a salon in London, and
Shaw had first visited her house in Park Street in November 1879, probably at
the instigation or invitation of his sister Lucy, a promising singer.
- Julian Hawthorne [see page 78 above].
- Frank [Francis] R[ichard] Stockton (1834–1902), American novelist and

short fiction writer. Although he began as a wood engraver, his writing ability was evident from his schooldays, and by 1867 he was writing children's stories for the *Riverside Magazine for Young People*. In 1869 he began writing for *Hearth and Home*, and this led to the publication of a household handbook (in collaboration with his wife, whom he had married in 1860). He also contributed to *Scribner's Monthly* (afterwards the *Century Magazine*), and became assistant editor of the *St. Nicholas Magazine*. In addition to the novel reviewed above, Stockton wrote a number of popular works, including *Rudder Grange* (1879), *The Floating Prince and Other Fairy Tales* (1881), *The Casting Away of Mrs. Lecks and Mrs. Aleshine* (1886) to which Shaw refers above—a story of two widows shipwrecked on a desert island in the Pacific— *The Late Mrs. Null* (1886), *The Man of Orn and Other Fanciful Tales* (1887), *Personally Conducted* (1889)—a description of his European travels—*The Squirrel Inn* (1891), *Pomona's Travels* (1894), *The Adventures of Captain Horn* (1895), *Buccaneers and Pirates of our Coasts* (1898), and *Kate Bonnet: the Romance of a Pirate's Daughter* (1902). He was a great traveler and wrote about his trips to the Bahamas and to Europe. This was the second review of Stockton's work that Shaw had written; but the first, a notice of *The Late Mrs. Null*, reviewed in April 1886, was never published.

▪ R[obert] H[arborough] Sherard (1861–1943), English author. Educated in the Channel Islands, at New College, Oxford, and at the University of Bonn, he became a journalist, writing as a "special correspondent" for English, American, and Australian newspapers. He was a friend of Oscar Wilde, to whom he dedicated his first book of poems, *Whispers* (1884), and was very kind to Wilde after the latter's imprisonment. He published a *Life of Oscar Wilde* in 1906. Other publications include a collaboration with Alphonse Daudet, *Rogues: My First Voyage* (1893), *The White Slaves of England* (1897), *The Story of an Unhappy Friendship* (1902), *Twenty Years in Paris* (1905), *After the Fault* (1907), *The Real Oscar Wilde* (1912), *Guy de Maupassant* (1926), *Why?* [a novel] (1939), *Romances of the Table* (1939), *Ultima Verba* [a reply to Bernard Shaw] (1940), and *Memoirs of a Mug* (1941). His chief quarrel with Shaw was over the latter's endorsement of Frank Harris's book *The Life and Confessions of Oscar Wilde* (1920), which Shaw claimed to have read "at one shot," and which Sherard considered full of "perfidious slanders." But that Shaw's perfunctory review of his novel (above) still rankled fifty years later is clear from a paragraph in his book *Bernard Shaw, Frank Harris and Oscar Wilde* (1937):

> Had it been anybody else but George Bernard Shaw, I should have imagined that as there is reading *and* reading, his annihilating conviction about Oscar Wilde, as derived from this book, showed that he could only have read this ponderous work "at one shot" by reverting in a green old age to those "smelling the paper-knife" methods of perusal which he must inevitably have practised in the lean *Flegel-Jahre* when he was reviewing novels for the newspapers. (*Bernard Shaw, Frank Harris and Oscar Wilde* (London: T. Werner Laurie, 1937), 39)

16 August 1888

THE MAN WHO MIGHT HAVE AVERTED THE FRENCH REVOLUTION* [C475]

TURGOT is known to the general reader as a man of heavy qualities, but wise withal, who might have averted the French revolution if he had been given his own way in 1776. As any such licence would have been nothing less than a breach of natural law, it is hardly worth speculating what might or might not have been the sequel of it. Essayists raise the question for no better reason than that the world still confounds history with story telling, and thinks Marie Antoinette an important historic personage because she is invaluable as a heroine of romance. The great point which the events of 1776 afford to your fictionist historian is that when Marie Antoinette induced her husband to give his controller-general what the dignity of history forbids us to call the sack, though her action merits no graver word, she signed her own death warrant and that of many other women who had no share in the dishonest and heartless expenditure against which Turgot put down his foot. She was right from her own point of view, which, though she was only twenty, was substantially that now taken by the Duke of Cambridge, who is somewhat more experienced. Why should she not look after her own interests? Turgot was thinking only of the people, who were nothing to her. In their interests—and partly, perhaps, for the sake of putting into practice his pet economic doctrine—he would have thrown down the ramparts of feudalism and mediævalism behind which she was comfortably living beyond her income. Besides, everybody said he was wrong: the people themselves rose starving against his Free Trade enactments, and besieged the royal castle until law and order was restored by the famous "new gallows, forty feet high." On the whole, since Marie Antoinette gained fourteen years more of the old Versailles life by getting rid of the "homme à système"; and enjoyed, into the bargain, experiments in assertion of privilege, resolute government, and standing no nonsense generally which were quite in the iron manner of Mr. Balfour, she perhaps made as lucrative a bargain as the circumstances allowed. Even if Turgot had been able to show her the future, it is conceivable

---

*"Turgot." By Léon Say. (London: Routledge and Sons. 1888.)

that she, tempted by a Mephistophelean bond for thirteen years more of Versailles and then chaos, might have held to her choice.

To us nowadays this little by-comedy between the philosophic moralist and the self-willed and extravagant fine lady, is of no moment whatever: what concerns us is his unlucky position between the old order and the new. No Englishman ever had to face such a task as was set to Turgot. He had to attempt the work of Adam Smith and of Wat Tyler at the same time—not only to set trade free from the outgrown swaddlings (with a "vested interest" in every one of them) which survived from the mediæval guild system, but to abolish villenage. There was not only the difficulty of fighting the "Parliament," which was all for the guild methods; and the Court, which was all for the feudal system: there was also the question of what new regulation should take the place of the old. We can see clearly enough now that the only finally possible new order was complete democracy; but Turgot was no Democrat: in spite of his Whig economics he was a Tory in his notions of authority. He had to accept the alternative, temporarily possible, but finally disastrous, of anarchy, which seems startling and even reprehensible: wherefore it is well to remember that we also accepted it, and the whole civilized world after us, *faute de mieux*. What is more, we are not yet clear of it; and as it does not work well, and never did, the whole interest of the present situation to those who can see further than the end of their noses (which are now just touching Home Rule) lies in the problem of the new order that is to supersede anarchy. Mr. Balfour and Lord Salisbury, as one may mention by way of an illustration and a snap-shot, are trying to dragoon us back into feudalism; and Mr. Ruskin leans to the opinion that a new feudalism under highly moralized barons would settle the question. And so it would; but unfortunately the Balfourian barons are not highly moralized.

On the outside it seems curious that Turgot should in any extremity have faced and even preached industrial anarchy. But he did it willingly—enthusiastically, even. He was the disciple of Gournay, full of the hopes raised by the newly discovered science of modern political economy. Like all the economists of his day, he saw that there existed in free competition a powerful automatic natural regulator of production and distribution. What he did not see was that this regulator worked with no regard whatever to human welfare, and that its final benefits were, by the very theory of it, confined to the proprietors of the sources of production, so that it must in the long run come to the vesting of those sources in the whole nation, if only because competition would make life intolerable for the multiplying proletariat of outsiders. Such a solution was of course as impossible in eighteenth century France as it has proved in comparatively democratic nineteenth century England. The twentieth century will have enough to do to complete it. Meanwhile it is odd how anarchic we still are—how we cling to our faith in the spontaneity of social harmony, and the captivatingly simple method of Mr. Worldly Wiseman's friend for getting the burden off our back. Buy in the cheapest market and sell in the dearest, and everything will come right; why, and how, the professor of political economy can explain. And though the unfortunate professor has for some time past borne these references with growing uneasiness, and even with downright repudiation in a bold instance or two, we still carry our capital to Capel-court, and ask, not which is the stock of the valiant captain of industry and which that of the sweater, but simply which is the more lucrative investment. If Turgot were alive now, he would still be able to show that the individual can do very little better under the circumstances; but he would probably feel in some haste to change the circumstances.

M. Léon Say, as the grandson of his grandfather, and a member of the Academy to boot, has given, in a clear, unimpassioned, classic monograph, and from the Manchester school point of view, a precise account of Turgot's views; of the decrees which brought about his dismissal; and of the remarkable letters to Louis XVI in which he held up Charles I of England as a warning to weak kings. Such meagre details of his life as the dignity of the academic style permits are also given. Unfortunately, Messrs. Routledge entrusted the translation of the work to a Frenchman, arguing apparently on the lines taken by prudent ladies who buy a stock of foreign post-cards before they start for a trip on the Continent. M. Masson is incapable of the blunders of "English as she is spoke"; but his careful prose, though its grammar save for a pardonable slip or two, might make an ordinary lady novelist blush—if any literary consideration could—is nevertheless English as she is not spoke.

Editor's Notes

- There is no indication in his diary of when Shaw received Say's book. However, on 30 July 1888, Shaw reports "reading Say's *Turgot* for review at the Museum, but very discursively. For instance, I not only spent much time turning over Voltaire, but I read a couple of [G. W.] Foote's pieces and part of Sheridan's *Critic*." On the thirty-first he was "still reading Say at the Museum but not got very far when stopped to write a leaderette for *The Star*." On 1

August he "finished reading Say's *Turgot.*" On the second he began the review, which he finished on the third at the Museum (*Diary,* 399, 400).

▪ [Jean-Baptiste] Léon Say (1826–96), French journalist, statesman, and political economist. Shaw calls him "the son of his grandfather," because Jean Baptiste Say (1767–1832) was also a famous French political economist, who was secretary to the minister of finance during the French Revolution. His grandson, in addition to *Turgot* (which first appeared in French the previous year), also wrote *Examen critique de la situation financière de la bille de Paris* (1866), *La Politique financière de la France* (1882), *Finances publiques, liberté du commerce* (1896) and *Contre le Socialisme* (1896).

▪ [George William Frederick Charles, 2nd] Duke of Cambridge (1819–1904) was at this time a very elderly military commander who had commanded a division in the Crimean War of 1854, become commander-in-chief two years later, been made a field marshal in 1862, and subsequently had dogmatically opposed such innovations as the formation of an army reserve, and the creation of short-service commissions. At the time of Shaw's writing he was the chief personal *aide-de-camp* to Queen Victoria (a position he held from 1882 to 1895).

▪ Wat Tyler (d. 1381), English revolutionary. With Jack Straw he led the peasants of Essex and Kent to London in the Peasant's Revolt of 1381, and was killed by the Lord Mayor of London while in conversation with King Richard II at Smithfield.

▪ [Seigneur Jean Claude Marie Vincent de] Gournay (1712–59), French economist. He was *intendant* of commerce in France in 1757, encouraging free trade and opposing monopolies. The phrase *laissez-faire* (or, in full, *laissez faire, laissez passer*) is attributed to him.

▪ Mr. Worldly Wiseman's friend (dwelling in the village of Morality) was Legality,

> a very judicious man, and a man of a very good name, that has skill to help men off with such burdens as thine are from their shoulders.

Christian took his advice and was almost killed by fire and earthquake, until he was rescued by Evangelist.

20 August 1888

MARAHUNA [C476]

"Marahuna." By H. B. Marriott Watson. (Longmans). No lack of enterprise can be imputed to Mr. H. B. Marriott Watson for his "Marahuna."

By way of preparation for it, he must have shut himself from the world into the library of some pleasant country house, with Darwin's "Voyage of the *Beagle*," Coleridge's "Ancient Mariner," William Morris's "Sigurd," or perhaps the score of Wagner's "Nibelung's Ring," with "Elsie Venner," "Frankenstein," and Poe's tales thrown in. Imagine a new *Beagle*, driven by an invincible north wind straight for the South Pole, chancing on a perilous opening in the barriers of that dreadful region, and coming at last to a great wall of fire. Encircled by this wall there is a Brynhild; and, according to precedent, the new Darwin should sail fearlessly through and wake her with a kiss. But his scientific turn of mind rather leads him to conclude that the enclosure is too warm for anyone but a salamander; consequently Brynhild has to take the initiative and come out, at which he is extremely taken aback. Now, this is a spirited start for a modern novel; but the worst of it is the difficulty of keeping it up. When Brynhild-Marahuna comes to England and takes her place in the giddy society of that island, neither the author nor his naturalist hero know exactly what to do with her. When the house catches fire, she proves more than equal to the occasion, as a woman with her early advantages naturally would; but before the more awful emergency of a baronet falling into a pond she, being preoccupied just then in plucking water-lilies, takes no more trouble about him than if she were a great shipowner, and he only a common sailor. Consequently he is drowned; and though Marahuna encouragingly assures his disconsolate relatives that they will get over it in the course of the drive home she is dropped by the county as a social failure; and Mr. Watson shortly afterwards takes a hint from Mary Shelley and deposits his heroine in a volcano, where the climate and the importance of baronets are better suited to her constitution and prejudices.

Editor's Notes

- There is no indication in Shaw's diary as to when he received the above novel: however, on 20 May 1888, his diary records that he "wrote review of *Marahuna* and sent it off." (*Diary*, 377). Shaw also omitted this review from his scrapbook of press cuttings.
- H[enry] B[rereton] Marriott Watson (1863–1921), Australian journalist and writer. Born near Melbourne, at the age of nine he was taken by his family to New Zealand, where he was educated at Christ Church Grammar School and Canterbury College. In 1885 he went to England, and took up

journalism. Later he was to become for a time assistant editor of both *Black and White* and the *Pall Mall Gazette,* and also served on the *National Observer* staff under W. E. Henley. In 1895, when Shaw was on the staff of *The Saturday Review* under the editorship of Frank Harris, he reports in his diary that "Harris tried to establish a regular lunch every Monday for choosing members of the Saturday Review staff at the Café Royale. I attended them for some time. Harold Frederic, Mrs. Devereux, Marriott Watson and others used to come" (*Diary,* 1059, 1060). *Marajuna* (1888), reviewed here, was Watson's first novel: it was followed by nearly forty more, among the more notable being *Lady Faintheart* (1890), *The Web of the Spider* (1891), *Diogenes of London* (1893), *Galloping Dick* (1896), *The House Divided* (1901), *Twisted Eglantine* (1905), *A Midsummer Day's Dream* (1907), *The King's Highway* (1910), *Rosalind in Arden* (1913), *The House in the Downs* (1914), *The Affair on the Island* (1916), and *Aftermath* (1919). He also coauthored J. M. Barrie's play *Richard Savage.*

▪ *Elsie Venner; a Romance of Destiny* (1861) is a novel by Oliver Wendell Holmes (1809–94); in it Elsie herself is something of a child of destiny, a mesmeric figure who occupies the mind of the protagonist.

5 September 1888

PROLETARIAN LITERATURE* [C479]

THE literary leaders of proletarian thought seldom find their works noticed in the reviews and literary journals. They are cut off from the amenities of log-rolling; for their fame is won in the low-priced and cheaply-printed literature of working class Republicanism, Socialism, Secularism, Salvationism, and what not, which polite journals ignore, and polite individuals consequently never hear of. Such literature has all the faults and does all the mischief of work that never receives skilled and educated criticism. When its readers had no votes, this did not matter to the classes. Now that the franchise is more democratic, it does matter a great deal; and it is time to reconsider the old editorial policy—or rather habit—of giving a page and a half of vapid comment

---

*" 'Ça Ira!' Or, Danton in the French Revolution." By Laurence Gronlund. (Boston, Mass.: Lee and Shephard.)

"Insufficiency of Henry George's Theory." By Laurence Gronlund. (New York: Labour News Company.)

to a book destined to be forgotten without having influenced the con-duct or opinions of a single human being; whilst pamphlets that circu-late by thousands, dealing with vital questions of national economy and private morals, are tossed into the waste-paper basket after a glance at the name of the publishers—usually a "Freethought" or "Progressive" or "Universal Labor" or other vulgarly democratic sort of "Society." The best of these pamphlets contain much truth of which the classes are deplorably ignorant; and the worst of them much falsehood which the masses accept because the newspapers never condescend to refute it. But now that the wage-worker is beginning to count for something in the circulation of the daily papers, and for a good deal at General Elec-tions, it is becoming worth while to bestow upon his "best hundred books" at least as much notice as is lavished on insignificant three-volume novels. Perhaps the chief practical difficulty would be to induce the reviewers to learn enough political economy to avoid breaking down disgracefully over the little works towards which they instinctively assume an attitude of condescension. When Mr. Henry George's "Prog-ress and Poverty" forced itself upon their notice, they made wild work of it, attacking his old-fashioned cut-and-dried orthodox Ricardian deduc-tions and physiocratic canon of taxation as mad innovations; and either missing his weak points altogether or cautiously endorsing them as true but not new. Mr. Laurence Gronlund's "Co-operative Common-wealth" also made its way into notice, with a like result. Even in the solemn lines of the leading article, newspaper economics often leave much to be desired. If the truth must out, the average editor knows no more than Mr. John Bright or those Whigs who got just far enough into the subject to misunderstand Free Trade and to imagine that the func-tions of Government should be sternly restricted to putting rebellious members of the lower orders in prison. The writer of the money article is usually a frank mercantilist of the ante-Sir James Stewart [*sic*] pe-riod; and the reviewer modestly gives in his allegiance to what Profes-sor Sidgwick describes as "the kind of Political Economy sometimes called orthodox, though it has the characteristic, unusual in orthodox doctrines, of being repudiated by the majority of accredited teachers of the subject."

Mr. Gronlund's book on the French Revolution, though its style outrages English canons of literary taste, is much more concise, and less afflicted with italics, explosions of asterisks, and notes of admira-tion, than his "Co-operative Commonwealth." Its chief merit is the clearness and consistency with which it presents the Social-Democratic interpretation of the Revolution as a completely success-

ful self-assertion of the French *bourgeoisie* against the feudal aristocracy. That this is the true historic and economic significance of the
change is now admitted; but it certainly is not yet familiar to the
ordinary reader, to whom the Revolution is still a melodrama with
sensation scenes of the demolition of the Bastille, the hanging of
Foulon, the march from Versailles, the murder of the Princesse
Lamballe, the flight to Varennes, the guillotining of Marie Antoinette
and everybody else, and, in proof of the futility and wickedness of all
revolutions, the final restoration of the *status quo ante* by Napoleon
with his whiff of grapeshot. All of which, when described by such a
pen as Carlyle's, is excellent reading, and at least a part of history. Mr.
Gronlund is no Carlyle; but he has learned from the Hegelians something of the philosophy of history, and from Marx the radical importance of economic development in national movements. Hence, although he has failed from lack of strength and completeness of equipment fully to reconcile all the facts with his doctrine, and has allowed
himself to be seduced into a forced hero-worship of Danton, his book
is well worth reading by those who only know the sensational side of a
chapter of history the sequel of which is "to be continued in our next"
newspaper, and just at present shows signs of becoming rather exciting. He follows Mr. John Morley in regarding the instigation of the
September massacres as not proven against Danton, and is as
sceptical of his hero's shortcomings as he is credulous of the comprehensiveness of his statesmanship. He actually attempts to defend the
financial skill of the Jacobins, apparently believing that the policy of
issuing paper money against a reserve of unproductive land was sane
because the land had an estimated market value. He admits depreciation of assignats, but declares that extensive forgery by the party of
reaction had produced the effect of over-issue, and maintains that the
laws of maximum brought up the assignats to par. It is not, however,
difficult to bring paper money to par by fixing the prices of commodities in it: the difficulty is to induce people to produce commodities
when the price so fixed will not really pay for them. Other questionable passages are those in which Lloyd Jones is said to have died "of a
broken heart" from the failure of co-operation; the inevitable statement that four hours' daily work would supply all our needs under
Socialism; and a number of minor points which clash with particulars
given by Mignet, Louis Blanc, Claretie, and other writers.

Mr. Gronlund's smaller work is an attempt to demonstrate the insufficiency of Mr. Henry George's theory of interest, and of his consequent misconception of the function of the capitalist. He makes several points as against Mr. George, but throws no light whatever on the

real nature of interest; and his statement that "in Great Britain land is the *first* 'means of labour' to revolutionize" is rather astonishing to any one practically acquainted with the conditions of English industry.

Editor's Notes

- Shaw received Gronlund's *Ça Ira* on 25 November 1887, though there is no mention of the receipt of his pamphlet. On 11 December 1887, Shaw was "reading Gronlund's *Ça Ira* for review," and again on the twelfth. He finished reading it on the fifteenth. On 10 January 1888, he "read John Morley on the French Revolution and Danton (for the Gronlund review)." On the seventeenth he rose at 8:30 A.M., and "began review for Gronlund's book and pamphlet." On the eighteenth, he "finished and sent off reviews of Gronlund's books." Seven months later, on 18 August 1888, Shaw "corrected proofs of review of Gronlund for *PMG*" (*Diary*, 322, 323, 332, 337, 339, 340, 403).
- Laurence Gronlund (1846–99), Danish Socialist writer and lecturer. He received an M.A. from the University of Copenhagen in 1865, intending to study law, but before completing his work he emigrated in 1867 to the United States. Here he taught German in Milwaukee public schools and continued his law studies in his spare time. He was admitted to the Chicago bar in 1869, and was a practicing attorney for some years. Interested in social questions, he became a Socialist under the influence of Pascal's *Pensées,* and his first work, published in 1878, was *The Coming Revolution: Its Principles.* His most influential work was published six years later, *The Co-Operative Commonwealth in Its Outlines: an Exposition of Modern Socialism.* In the fall of 1884, Shaw, offered £5 by Henry Hyde Champion of The Modern Press to rewrite this work, should the book ever produce "anything over the cost," "set to work to edit [it] for an English issue" (*Diary,* 33). This took him into the new year, and the book was published in May of 1885 [see Dan Laurence's *Bernard Shaw: A Bibliography,* 2 vols. (Oxford: Clarendon Press, 1983), 483]. Gronlund's book was widely read and discussed, and its popularity led Gronlund onto the lecture circuit, traveling extensively in America, and also visiting England. On 3 July 1885, Gronlund addressed the Fabian Society for the first time. Shaw was disappointed:

> Gronlund has evidently no adequate notion of the spread of Socialism in England, or of the extent to which the ideas he evidently regards as startling novelties have become common property here.

Shaw, on this occasion

> somewhat maliciously set the Fabians laughing at the expense of Mr. Gronlund, who complained of the incident with unexpected bitterness at the close of the debate. (Bernard Shaw, *Justice,* 11 July 1885, no. 2, 7:1)

Subsequently, for the next two years, Shaw met Gronlund at various meetings, and lent him money fairly regularly. In 1888 Gronlund was elected to the executive committee of the American Socialist Labor Party. In 1891 he published *Our Destiny; the Influence of Nationalism on Morals and Religion*. At this time Gronlund began a movement to organize a secret society of college students to be called the American Socialist Fraternity, with the object of speeding the advance of Socialism. In 1895 he married. His last two works, *New Economy; a Peaceable Solution of the Social Problem* (1898) and a paper, *Socializing a State* (1898), advocate gaining control of the political machinery to initiate social change. At the time of his death he was in charge of the labor section of the *New York Journal*.

- John Bright (1811–89), English statesman and an eloquent public speaker, who, in 1838, was an outspoken advocate for the repeal of the Corn Laws, which had kept the price of bread artificially high, to the distress of the working population.
- Sir James [Denham] Steuart (1712–80). Either Shaw or the *Pall Mall Gazette* misspelled the surname of this Scottish mercantilist who published his great treatise *An Inquiry into the Principles of Political Economy* in 1767, nine years before Adam Smith's *Wealth of Nations* revised the thinking on mercantilism and condemned Steuart's book to oblivion.
- [Patrick] Lloyd Jones (1811–86), Irish reformer. Born in Dublin (of Welsh descent), he moved to Lancashire and, under the influence of Robert Owen, opened a cooperative store in Salford. He became a leader in the Owenite movement, mostly in the north of England, and was politically active in working class journalism, Christian Socialism, trade unionism, and labor representation. The cooperative movement, however, lay nearest his heart, which was certainly not broken by his sporadic disagreements with fellow Owenites who had, he thought, too narrow a view of the cooperative life. He died of cancer at the age of seventy-five.

25 September 1888

A CRIB FOR HOME RULERS* [C486]

THIS book of Mr. Robert Oliver's is 233 pages long. It is the record of a single conversation on a single subject between James and Andrew. For three hours and a quarter, as one calculates, these two gentlemen

---

*"Unnoticed Analogies. A Talk on the Irish Question." By Robert Oliver. (London: Kegan Paul and Co. 1888.)

debate the question of Home Rule with a self-control, a strict keeping to the point, and an undulled sense of literary form, that are beyond all praise. Weaker men would have sacrificed propriety to dramatic opportunity, but not these. James does not sneer nor Andrew swear. There are none of those gusts of wrath in which the raised voice and scornful accent arrest the passer-by with promise of a fight. The result is that James and Andrew personally impress the reader as a pair of well-conducted and well-informed members of the middle class, whose arguments and analogies will serve at second-hand in private wranglings over the question of the hour. Indeed, with Andrew's speeches at his tongue's end, a man might become a finished Gladstonian. But he might also become a finished bore. For the truth is, Andrew, though conclusive, is not convincing. One feels that James, the nether millstone of the debate, might make short work of him by quoting Hegel's dictum that all mistakes are made for good reasons.

To the mere literary reviewer, admiring from his study windows the omniscience, the readiness, the energy of his political contemporaries, it seems a strange thing that any human being should discuss Home Rule as if its accomplishment depended on the upshot of a utilitarian discussion of its probable results. Nationalism is surely an incident of organic growth, not an invention. A man discusses whether he shall introduce a roasting-jack into his kitchen, but not whether he shall introduce an eye-tooth into his son's mouth or lengthen him as he grows older. If men did discuss such things, the result would undoubtedly be a consensus of opinion to the effect that thirty teeth are quite sufficient for modern purposes, and that every inch of stature above five-feet-six inches is a waste of the world's industry in providing clothing fabrics, carrying power, uselessly high rooms, and so on. But as it is clear that this decision, however scrupulously rational, would not have the slightest effect on the proceedings of the power which arranges our teeth and our inches for us, we have to accept the inevitable average son of five-feet-eight, with thirty-two teeth; and provide for him accordingly. We shall have to accept the growth of nationalism in exactly the same way. In any purely abstract utilitarian discussion, where the historical method is excluded, and political and social institutions are treated as inventions of the roasting-jack order, Home Rule must stand condemned, as Mr. Chamberlain or any utilitarian-materialist-republican can show. Is not federation the most economical—the most social course? Is it not an advance in complexity of structure and order of organism—a step further towards the Parliament of Man, the Federation of the World? The conviction that all these questions must be answered in the affirmative lurks now disquietingly in the consciousness of many a Home Ruler who was wont, when Ireland was not the theme, to indulge imperial dreams of a federated Greater Britain. In the meantime, Ireland and Poland are as deaf to academic discussion as Italy was in her evil days. Go to the Cork mechanic and point out to him that the condition of the Parisian ouvrier who works as a Frenchman under a French Republic is in no way superior to his own under the tyranny of the Castle. Show him that when he works as an Irishman under an Irish republic, and Irish industry develops by leaps and bounds, he will assuredly find the bread of freedom as bitter and scarce under King Capital as ever it has been under Mr. Balfour. Then advise him to vote against Mr. Parnell and Mr. Maurice Healy at the next election. He will be about as much impressed as Garibaldi would have been by a discourse on the advantages of a united Austria and Italy. What Mr. Oliver calls an "unnoticed analogy" is to be found in the slavery struggle in America. The advantages of being a chattel slave were proved over and over again by the friends of the South. The master who bought a man valued him as something in which his capital was locked up. Just as a tramway company now takes more care of its horses than of its men, so did the planter take more care of his slave than the employer of his free wage worker. Slaves were cared for in their old age instead of being abandoned to the discomfort and disgrace of a pauper ward. In short, who would not be a slave rather than a free proletarian? Who indeed, except a man in whom the instinct towards personal liberty was as a burning fire shut up in his bones, so that he was weary with forbearing and could not stay? History tells us that it is usless to cross these instincts—tells us so dogmatically, and will not argue the point for a moment, with James or Andrew or any one else. The slave, equally unreasonable, sees nothing ahead of him but his freedom. He may be a moth flying towards a candle; but he has the moth's power of making it impossible for us to attend to our own business if we undertake the task of keeping him out of the candle by any other means than killing him. Here then we have to face an inevitable order of social growth. First, the individual will have his personal liberty, in pursuit of which he will at last weary out and destroy feudal systems, mighty churches, mediæval orders, slave-holding oligarchies, and what else may stand in his way. Then he will enlarge his social consciousness from his individual self to the nation of which he is a unit; and he will have his national liberty as he had his personal liberty, nor will all the excellent reasons in the world avail finally against him. He will rarely take the two steps at a time: he will never take the second before the first or the third before the second. The third step is the federation of nationalities; but you cannot induce him to forego the achievement of national independence on the ground that international federation is a step higher. He knows by instinct that if his foot missed that one rung of the ladder, he would not reach the higher rung, but would rather be precipitated into the abyss; and so it comes that there is no federating nationalities without first realizing them. And as the slave destroyed great hierarchies in his fight for freedom, so the conquered subject races will destroy great empires when their time comes, if the empires persist in opposing them. It may be that Providence has specially exempted the British Empire from these readjustments to social growth. The English middle class has always been more or less of that opinion. Indeed, history teaches us that the middle class always held that opinion. History also teaches us that the middle class is invariably wrong. For, to quote another Hegelian dictum, we learn from history that men never learn anything from history.

Editor's Notes

- There is no indication in his diary as to when Shaw received this book. On 12 September 1888, he records that he "began review of a book on Home Rule by R. Oliver." The following day he is "working at the review of the Home Rule book," and on the fourteenth he "finished and sent off the review of the Home Rule book and wrote to Cooke of the *PMG* remonstrating about the sort of books sent me for review" (*Diary*, 411, 412). An extract of this letter [C481] sent to subeditor C. Kinloch-Cooke was printed in the *Pall Mall Gazette* on 17 September 1888, under the following heading:

> Here is a bitter cry from a reviewer who is exasperated at the long continuance of the silly season in the publishing trade:
> Have————or————been yet disposed of? If not, I should be glad to get them as a relief to the slow murder of the cursed parcels of rubbish with which you blast my prime. Surely it must be dawning on editors at last that any sort of live copy is better than the mechanical literary stuff poured out on ordinary novels and minor poetry. Why condemn me to read things that I can't review—that no artistic conscience could long survive the reviewing of! Why don't you begin notices of boots, hats, dogcarts and so on? They would be fifty times as useful and

interesting as reviews of the last novel by Miss Braddon, who is a princess among novel manufacturers. There ought to be legislation against this sort of thing—on the lines of the Factory Acts. I believe the mortality in hospitals is perceptibly increased by the books distributed through reviewers by the Kyrle Society.

- Robert Oliver (n.d.), English political writer.
- The Congress of Vienna in 1815 had created a Kingdom of Poland; not, however, before it had divided the country up between Austria, Prussia, and Russia and made the Russian emperor king. Polish nationalism soon initiated a powerful movement for independence that culminated in an insurrection on 29 November 1830. This was unsuccessful and merely led to more repressive measures being taken by the ruling Russians. Nevertheless, this did not prevent further (equally unsuccessful) insurrections from taking place in 1846, 1848, 1861, and 1863.
- Maurice Healy (1859–1923), Irish lawyer and politician. He was the younger brother of the famous Irish Nationalist leader Tim Healy (1855–1931), M.P. for Cork City from 1885 to 1900, and later Irish Nationalist candidate for Cork from 1910 to 1918.

13 October 1888

SOME POETS* [C490]

MR. GEORGE BARLOW is to be congratulated on having produced a good fat epic in five books without the strain and travail which drove Carlyle to declare that no man can write a book without making himself ill. If the author of "The Pageant of Life" is not in robust health it is certainly not the fault of his work, which is obviously a collection of occasional poems, parcelled into "books" and supplemented with an epic framework and a preface. Thus Mr. Barlow has done for himself what time and tradition are supposed by some to

---

*"The Pageant of Life." By George Barlow. (London: Swan Sonnenschein and Co. 1888.).—"A Lay of Two Cities." By Jesharelah. (London: Passmore and Alabaster. 1888.).— "Dorica." By E. D. S. (London: Kegan Paul and Co. 1888.).—"Southern Songs." By D. C. F. Moodie. (Cape Town: J. C. Juta and Co. 1887.).—"Perla." By E. W. Bewley. (London: Wyman and Sons. 1888.).—"Darkness and Light." By Noel Vandal. (London: Swan Sonnenschein and Co. 1888.).—"Woodland and Dreamland." By Rowe Lingston. (London: Griffith, Farran, and Co. 1888.).—"My Jewels." Selected by Rowland Hill. (London: Williams and Norgate. 1888.)

have done for Homer. What he has done for others may be summed up as the provision of a sort of metrical commonplace book for persons who are not commonplace. For example, when once the commonplace idea of Christ's divinity is rejected, it becomes a commonplace to say with Mr. Barlow:

> My Christ is the Christ of Shelley and Hugo, not the Christ of St. Augustine or of Dr. Manning; the Christ who in the centuries to come will gain inconceivably more (both as a grand poetic figure and as an object of religious veneration) from the right apprehension of his manhood than he has gained (or shall we not rather say lost?) during the centuries that are past through the mistaken theory of his Godhead; the Christ who was loved by the men and women who were his companions, with honest, warm, human love, and never approached by them in the Christian Church's subsequent attitude of cringing awe and superstition.

Again, when one gets advanced views on the woman question, it becomes a commonplace to sing:

> All have praised our lips and tresses,
>   Golden locks or black:
> All have sought our love-caresses
>   All have held us back.
>
> All have checked our souls' aspiring
>   All have dreaded this.
> This has tired men, never tiring
>   Of the lips they kiss.
>
> All have dreaded lest the morning
>   Which should find us free
> Would be wild with note of warning
>   Rung by land and sea!
>
> Not one noble soul has trusted;
>   Roman, Jew, or Greek.
> Many and many a sword had rusted
>   Had they let us speak!

Here is a stanza from the section entitled "Chant of Positivists":

> Man first made God, but now retakes
> The sceptre from God's hand, -unmakes
> What once with fiery thought he made.
>
> God is a dream of mankind's brain
> But man dethrones God; man must reign;
> Not God, but man must be obeyed.

This would be quite a coruscation if emitted by an Evangelical grocer: from a Positivist it is a mere platitude. Further on comes a stanza which would be a platitude even from the grocer:

> And woman too is left to love:
> She brings us dreams of things above
> The common daily life she scorns.
>
> Woman makes all things beautiful;
> For from the hedge her hand can pull
> The blossoming rose, and leave the thorns.

Here is a sample of Mr. Barlow's energetic style:

> I mass my conscripts drawn from strange far regions;
>   I range my squadrons on time's boundless plain;
> I hurl the force of my imperial legions
>   Against thee, Death, again and yet again.

It will be seen that Mr. Barlow is no ridiculous poetaster. He is, in fact, a man of ideas, a propagandist, up to the latest move in Materialistic pessimism and sentimental optimism. The more benighted section of the community will be roused and refreshed by his numbers. And as Mr. Barlow comes to call, not the righteous, but sinners, to repentance, he will probably not mind our venturing to remark that those who know beforehand what his book contains will find nothing new in it.

Jesharelah, author of "A Lay of Two Cities," writes of the typical Babylon and Jerusalem with a naïve piety which contrasts as strongly with Mr. Barlow's strenuous freethinking as with the library "culture" of E. D. S., who sings ho! the daffodil and other matters in that strain of vapid quaintness and correct sprightliness which we at once associate with a bookish turn, a university education, and an independent income.

From Cape Town comes the third edition of D. C. F. Moodie's "Southern Songs." No words can express the wild hope with which the reviewer emphasizes the fact that there is a remote colony in which minor poetry runs through three editions. Here is a sample of D. C. F. M.'s lighter manner:

The Zebras bound o'er shaking ground in many a wild stampedo;
The Blesbok too, and sportive Gnu, make noise as much as they do.

The serious style is less difficult to manage:

Lo! where on Erin's land gaunt Famine stalks,
And thro' each stricken household grimly walks—
See the poor mother with her ghastly child,
In her bare home that once with plenty smiled—
Some chance has blown a morsel near her door.
She strives to reach it—struggling o'er the floor.
In vain, alas! the enfeebled limbs decline;
Death rattles in her throat—she falls supine—
And the poor child, with Famine's silent stare,
Falls down and dies where now no men appear.

The following impressive description of a waterfall is from Mr. Edward White Bewley's "Perla: a Legend of Tequendama":

GRAND TEQUENDAMA FALL. At birth the leap
It took o'er rock six hundred feet was deep;
And there it has leaped roaring ever since
Nor sign of failing years does it evince.

This passage, however, does not do justice to the elasticity of Mr. Bewley's metre, which will be better appreciated in such a passage as—

Some hunters, leaving highlands which afar
Stretch broadening inland toward the southern star,
Canoed downriver, lake and strait of Maracaibo;
Their leader, manly, young, a chief well known as Ibo;
The whole a party picturesque of bright dark hues
Well matching those of their mahogany canoes.

Noel Vandal, in "Darkness and Light," is reflective and edifying. He turns him home; no system, creed, or land, he fears, can teach the duties of the heart, or well direct the labour of the hand, or to the mind the secret deep impart. Rowe Lingston, author of "Woodland and Dreamland," has a modest measure of the genuine poetic melody and fancy. The translation called "Magali" is one of the prettiest things in the volume.

Mr. Rowland Hill's "Jewels" will be read and recited for many a year wherever the English language is spoken. This gratifying result will be due to Mr. Hill's forethought in getting his poetry done for him by "ghosts." The ghosts of Macaulay, Poe, and Shakspeare, in particular, will feel indebted to him for introducing their works to the public under the title of "his jewels."

Editor's Notes

- There is no indication in his diary as to when Shaw received any of the books reviewed above: there is only this entry of 19 September 1888: "In the afternoon, at the Museum, read Barlow's poem for review" (*Diary*, 413). On 26 September, Shaw writes "finished review of Barlow's epic." The following day he "got up before 8 and finished and sent off a page of reviews of minor poets to the *PMG*" (*Diary*, 415).
- George Barlow (1847–1913?), English poet and librettist. He was educated at Harrow School and Oxford. He wrote the English version of Gounod's *Ave Maria* at the request of the composer. In addition to the book reviewed above, he also wrote about fifteen other books, among them *Poems and Sonnets* (1871), *A Life's Love* (1873), *Under the Dawn* (1875), *The Two Marriages: a Drama* (1878), *Time's Whisperings: Sonnets and Songs* (1880), *Song-Spray* (1882), *An Actor's Reminiscences, and other Poems* (1883), *Love's Offering* [by "James Hinton" pseud.] (1883), *An English Madonna* [by "James Hinton" pseud.] (1884), and *Love Beyond Words* (1885).
- "Jesharelah" (n.d.), pseudonym for unidentified poet.
- [Reverend] E[dward] D[aniel] S[tone] (1832–1916), English clergyman, classical scholar, and poet. He graduated from King's College, Cambridge, in 1857 and was ordained in 1860. He was an assistant master at Eton College from 1857 to 1884. In addition to the above book, he also wrote a schoolbook, *Ionedes: Exercises in Greek Iambics: with Vocabulary* (1872), edited a second, *The Hannibalian, or Second Punic War: extracted from the Third Decade of Livy; with Notes* (1873), and translated a third, *A Philological Introduction to Greek and Latin by F. Baur* (1876). He also wrote *Iambic Verse based on the Prometheus Vinctus* (1878).

- D[uncan] C[ampbell] F[rancis] Moodie (n.d.), South African poet. The son of a retired English naval officer who emigrated to South Africa after the peace of 1815. In addition to the book reviewed above, Moodie also wrote *The History of the Battles and Adventures of the British, the Boers, and the Zulus in Southern Africa* (1879).
- E[dward] W[hite] Bewley (n.d.), English poet. In addition to the book reviewed above, Bewley also wrote *Dudley Castle in the Black Country* [verse] (1871), *Little Mabel's notebook and Lucy's album* (1884), and *Idonea; a Tale of the Twelfth Century* (1890).
- Noel Vandal (n.d.), possibly a pseudonym for an unidentified poet.
- Rowe [Rose] Lingston (n.d.), English poet. In addition to the book reviewed above, Lingston also wrote *Verses of Country and Town* (1886), and *Seven of Us* [children's verse] (1888), *John Chinaman* (1891), *A Sleeping Beauty, and other Tales in Verse* (1894), *Not Warranted Sound* (1902), *The Coming of Spring and Other Poems* (1906), *Molly's Book* (1908), *The Grey Mare and Other Verse* (1922), and *Round the Zodiac* (1922).
- Rowland [G.] Hill (n.d.), anthologist and minor poet. He came from Bedford; and Shaw knew Hill personally, having met him at the home of his friend James Kingston Barton in the late fall of 1885.

14 November 1888

THREE NEW NOVELS* [C500]

Mr. G. W. Cable's "Bonaventure" is a delightful book. The naïvetés of Accadian [*sic*] society, the oddities of the Louisianian lingo, the novelty of the scenery, the simplicity without brutality of life on a generous soil and in a soft climate among fairly socialized but utterly uncivilized people: all these make pleasant holiday for the cockney novel reader. As to how far it forms a true picture of anything that exists or ever has existed, one cannot at this side of the water pretend to judge. But if it be not faithfully recorded, it is at any rate well invented; and Mr. Cable's books will surely be received here for a long time to come without question as to how he came by them. Even Mr. Tarbox,

---

*"Bonaventure." By G. W. Cable. (London: Sampson Low and Co. 1888)
"The Man with a Shadow." By G. Manville Fenn. Two vols. (London: Ward and Downey. 1888.)
"Eve." By the author of "John Herring." Two vols. (London: Chatto and Windus. 1888.)

though he has done duty in fiction a hundred times before, has quite a new air in his "Cajun" surroundings.

"A Man with a Shadow," whoever he may be—conscientious perusal of Mr. Fenn's novel discovers no clue to his identity—is a man without a shadow of an excuse for being the occasion of three volumes of letterpress. If it were not for an amusing rascal of a sexton, who ekes out his wage by practising as a resurrection-man, the book would sink under the odiousness of all the other characters. Not that they are false to nature; there is not even the consolation of being able to deny that the clergyman-hero abounds in England, apparently sent by Nature for the purpose of popularizing Disestablishment. Here is a characteristic speech of his concerning his sister, who strenuously objects to his interference—"I stand to her in the place of a father, and I will do my duty by her, even if I have to keep her under lock and key." The worst of it is that Mr. Manville Fenn seems to consider him rather a fine fellow—an intolerable assumption. The most interesting part of the story takes place by night in a mausoleum under the following circumstances. The village doctor woos the parson's rebellious sister, who promises him her hand on condition of his achieving eminence in his profession. The squire happening just then to break his neck, it occurs to the doctor that such a feat as raising the squire from the dead might possibly bring him into some prominence as a medical man. Having, through the good offices of the resurrectionist sexton, procured nightly access to the squire's mausoleum, he proceeds to treat the body galvanically. But strangely enough (considering that the experiment is part of a novel) the squire does not come to; and the reader is left wondering why the book was ever written. It is difficult to believe that Mr. Manville Fenn deliberately contemplated so abortive an ending when he began the story.

Mr. Baring Gould's "Eve," a story of Dartmoor, has all the illusion and all the unreality of a very vivid dream. The tale has that in it that defies criticism; you see as you read, and will remember when you have done reading. You know of course that no real doctor ever walked into a strange house and said "He is suffering from concussion of the brain; if he does not awake to-morrow order a grave to be dug;" and that no mortal policeman ever moralized in such a strain as: "What is time to us police? It is made to be killed, like a flea." Further, you may strenuously object to such a very ambiguous ellipsis as "Barbara thought these chairs handsome, Eve detestable," meaning, not that Barbara liked the chairs and hated Eve, but that she liked the chairs which Eve hated. But these are trifles in a genuine piece of storytelling. Mr. Baring Gould has often spoiled a tale by some marring incongruity—some failure of imaginative vision at a critical point; but this time he has been lucky to the point of suggesting a comparison with Scott or Defoe. As to the characters, it is sufficient to say that no novel in this sheaf gives in anything approaching the degree attained in "Eve," the sensation of reading about living people.

Editor's Notes

▪ There is no indication in his diary as to when Shaw received the above novels. On 7 August 1888, he reports that he is "reading a novel of Cable's— *Bonaventure*," and again on the thirteenth, "read Cable's *Bonaventure* for review at Museum." On 22 October, we are told he "finished reading *Man with the Shadow* [*sic*] by Manville Fenn for review." On the twenty-third he notes in his diary that he must "call on Mrs. Home's in the evening to get the volume of *Eve* I left there." It is possible that he had left the book as far back as 13 July, which is when his diary lists his last call on the Homes's "to meet the Bells, over from America." On 24 of October, having retrieved the volume, Shaw "read away at *Eve*," as he did again on the twenty-fifth. On the twenty-seventh he "began a review of 5 novels . . . at the Museum" and "in the evening sat at home and finished the review." On the twenty-eighth, in the afternoon, he "corrected MS of review," and on 13 November, we read "corrected proof for *PMG*" (*Diary*, 401–2, 424–427, 433). The fact that Shaw originally reviewed five novels is borne out in the review by his comment that "no novel *in this sheaf* [except *Eve*] . . . gives the sensation of reading about living people." Three novels is hardly "a sheaf." The missing novels were probably the two by Grant Allen, a review of which was printed separately on 20 November. Shaw's list of "Books for Review" includes numerous titles that, it seems, were not reviewed at all, an example of which is Manville Fenn's *Bag of Diamonds,* received on 13 April 1887; however, in the present instance the books were reviewed, and the reviews not printed together. Presumably, paragraphs were deleted, and the heading FIVE NOVELS changed to THREE NOVELS by the editor (or subeditor) of the *Pall Mall Gazette.*

▪ G[eorge] W[ashington] Cable (1844–1925), American author and social and religious leader. Born in New Orleans of an old Virginian family and educated in public schools until 1859, he served in the Civil War (in the 4th Mississippi Cavalry), was twice wounded, and contracted "breakbone fever" at the war's end, which necessitated a slow process of recuperation. During this time he began to write journalism. He then obtained a post as an accountant for a cotton manufacturer, but immediately began a process of self-education in his spare time, rising at 4:00 A.M. to study. Having learned French, he discovered in the city archives old records of the Creoles, and in

them subject matter for his stories. He also prepared reports for the government on the condition of the people in parts of Louisiana. In 1869 he married
Louise Stewart Bartlett, by whom he had six daughters and one son. In 1885
he left the South for Northampton, Massachusetts, where he established the
Home Culture Clubs, a social movement which eventually was carried into
thirteen states. At this time, too, he toured with Mark Twain, each man
reading from his works. In 1904 his wife died; two years later he remarried.
In addition to the book reviewed above, he also wrote more than a score of
others, including *The Grandissimes: a Story of Creole Life* (1880), *The Creoles of Louisiana* (1884), *Dr. Sevier* (1885), *Strange True Stories of Louisiana*
(1889), *The Cavalier* (1901), *Kincaid's Battery* (1908), *The Flower of the
Chapdelaines* (1918), and *Lovers of Louisiana* (1918). He also wrote short
fiction and books on religious and social issues, like *The Busy Man's Bible*
(1891). In 1923 his second wife died, and he married a third time, two years
before his death.

- G[eorge] Manville Fenn (1831–1909), English novelist. He was educated
at the Battersea Training College for Teachers and from 1851 to 1854 was
master of a small school in Lincolnshire. He was also a private tutor. In 1855
he married, and had two sons and six daughters. He moved to London, where
he became a printer. Returning to Lincolnshire, he bought a press and began
a poetry magazine *Modern Metre*, in 1862. A foray into the world of newspapers as an editor was abortive; and it was not until Dickens accepted a story of
his for *All the Year Round* that he began to succeed as a writer. He wrote in all
more than 170 books, most of them novels and books for boys. In 1870 he
became editor of *Cassell's Magazine,* and from 1873 to 1879 published a
journal called *Once a Week.* He was also dramatic critic of *The Echo,* and in
1887 and 1888 produced farces at the Comedy Theatre.
- Sabine Baring-Gould (1834–1924), [see pages 153–54 above].
- Shaw's irritation with Manville Fenn's book (which, however, was *two* not
three "volumes of letterpress") may well have sprung from his impatience
with its old-fashioned clergyman-hero. By the 1880s, reaction against the
heroic parsons and curates of writers like Trollope and W. G. Wills was very
pronounced: W. S. Gilbert led the way with "The Fairy Curate" and "The
Bishop of Rum-Ti-Foo" in his *Bab Ballads* (1869), and later with his stage
work. By the 1880s, the comic clergyman was much more the fashion than
the serious one, particularly on the stage: he is to be found in Pinero's *The
Squire* (1881) and *Dandy Dick* (1887); and in James Albery's revival of *The
Crisis* as *The Denhams* in 1885, he did not merely alter the title: he altered
the character of Lord William Whitehead, a foolish suitor for the rich banker's
daughter, to the *Reverend* Lord William Whitehead, a long-haired clergyman.
Shaw, who had already supported this late Victorian convention by adding
the blushing curates Mr. Josephs and Mr. Fairholme to the collection in his
novel *An Unsocial Socialist* (1883), was shortly to create the more sinister
Reverend Samuel Gardner in *Mrs Warren's Profession* (1893). One notices
that Shaw received E. G. Egomet's *Only a Curate* for review on 29 July 1887.
The review was never written. At the time of Shaw's writing the above review,

too, following the brutal "Jack the Ripper" murders in Whitechapel, *The Star* newspaper was publishing letters on the subject under the heading "Is Christianity a Failure?" Shaw contributed two pseudonymous anticlerical letters to the debate, neither of which was published.

20 November 1888

TWO NEW NOVELS BY MR. GRANT ALLEN*
[C503]

IN spite of many drawbacks, "This Mortal Coil" is, for a rapidly written book, a wonder of inventiveness and vivacity. In one of its chapters we are told that "it is the curse of the purely literary intellect that it never looks at things, but always at phrases." From this Mr. Grant Allen's scientific training has saved him; and so, with all his haste, he is free from the ordinary writer's desperate ignorance of all but the literary aspect of things—especially things that have been much written about. He often succeeds in raising real questions of conduct; and it is the more to be regretted that he has not time to work out more adequate answers than the conventional ones he has to snatch at in passing.

"The White Man's Foot" was evidently inspired by those curious New Ireland feather masks in the British Museum which rank next to the mummies in the esteem of the casual patrons of that institution. As it is luridly illustrated, and describes sensational adventures in a volcano, it may be relied on as a safe present for a boy at the stage when his dreams of being a pirate are sobering into a moralized aspiration towards the navy.

Editor's Notes

▪ The diary gives no indication when Shaw received these novels. On 14 October 1888, however, he "read Grant Allen's *The White Man's Foot.*" On the

---

*"This Mortal Coil." By Grant Allen. Three vols. (London: Chatto and Windus. 1888.)
"The White Man's Foot." By Grant Allen. One vol. (London: Hatchards. 1888.)

seventeenth he went "to the Museum after dinner and read the first volume of Grant Allen's *Mortal Coil.*" The next day he "finished Grant Allen's novel." Since there is no account of the review being written or completed, one assumes that it was part of the "review of 5 novels" that Shaw began on 27 October (*Diary,* 422, 423, 426). The review of the first three novels was printed on 14 November. This would account for the brevity of the above piece; although a further reason for that is to be found in Shaw's shorthand note in the margin of his scrapbook of cuttings, which reads, "This is only a fragment of a long review. The first part has been omitted as being unfavorable to G. A. who has friends at the office of the *PMG.*"

- Grant Allen [see pages 410–11 above].

26 December 1888

THE GOSPEL ACCORDING TO ST. JUDE'S*
[C520]

I. By a "Practical Socialist."

One of the embarrassments of inquiry into Socialism arises from the fact that everything benevolent, eleemosynary, humble-minded, and beautiful on the one hand, and everything murderous, envious, dishonest, and reckless on the other are ticketed off-hand as "Socialistic." If Mr. Barnett were to circulate an examination paper containing the question, "Give an example from history of practical Socialism," half the answers would probably refer him to the People's Palace and the other half to the Gunpowder Plot. If another question ran, "Why does the Rev. Mr. Barnett call himself a Socialist?" all the answers would be, "Because he is a very benevolent man who spends his life in Whitechapel trying to improve the condition of the people there." But whoever reads this book of Mr. Barnett's will lay it down with a distinct impression that there is some other sort of Socialist whom he mistrusts and dislikes, the natural inference being that this other sort is the Gunpowder Plot sort, and that he himself only adopts the People's Palace half of the Socialist programme. Now, the book will be

---

*"Practicable Socialism: Essays on Social Reform." By the Rev. and Mrs. Samuel A. Barnett. (London: Longmans and Co. 1888.)

dealt with here from the point of view of a Socialist who regards *panem et circenses* (Mansion House Fund and People's Palace) as bribery, and the Gunpowder Plot as a form of war effective only for the purpose of stimulating and developing the other abomination. For since *panem et circenses* are never really distributed lavishly except from fear of the people, and since explosives are the only weapons against which the distributors can never thoroughly police themselves, nothing is more likely than that in the long run the almoner is the closest ally of the dynamitard. Consequently the practical Socialist is more afraid of the almoner than of the dynamitard because Society helps him to keep down the dynamitard, whereas it encourages and adulates the almoner. Besides, the almoner is often a good man, and therefore personally a power; whereas the dynamitard is usually a bad one, and personally a futility.

The first question that Socialists ask about Mr. Barnett is whether he means business when he calls himself a Socialist, or whether he is merely a preacher of charity. A Socialist who means business is one who means that the payment of all incomes derived from "private property"—to wit, those consisting of rent or interest—shall be discontinued. If a man means less than this, it is, to say the least, inconvenient to call him a Socialist. There is room for difference as to method: there is none as to the end aimed at. A careful study of Mr. Barnett's essays leaves no doubt that although his method of social reform—that is, the organization of the labour of the very poor by town councils with capital raised by taxing ground values—is exactly that of the Socialists, yet he clings to a quite unintelligible distinction between municipal and "State" action, and does not propose that the process shall be carried further than is necessary to make the lot of the poor decent and bearable. He speaks of "binding classes by friendship"; of making "links between the classes, and leading both rich and poor to give up habits which keep them apart"; of putting rent collecting into the hands "of volunteers with the time to make friends and the will to have patience with the tenants." It is clear, then, that there are to be classes—that rich and poor are to exist side by side, in Mr. Barnett's Utopia. If so, how is it possible for them to give up the habits that keep them apart, since the habit that keeps the rich man apart from the poor man is just the habit of being rich, and nothing else? And as to binding classes together otherwise than by the nexus of cash payments, what is to be the bond between, for example, Lord Cadogan and, not the Whitechapel costermonger, but even the professional gentleman in Sloane-street, whose rent is going to be raised on the strength of his own repairs and the goodwill of his own practice? As to multiplying university settlements, are our universities places in which young gentlemen are taught the true relation in which they stand to the poor? As for Mrs. Barnett's thoroughly well meant "at homes to the poor," let the following passage depict the desperation of such expedients: " 'Why! she said she was glad to see me,' said a low, coarse fellow, taking as a personal compliment to himself the conventional form of expression." Are we to understand that a "link" was thereby established between the classes of the lady (not Mrs. Barnett, by the by) who told the rough a lie, and the rough who was sufficiently unversed in "the knowledge, the character, the happiness, which are the gift of God to this age," to believe her?

It is not pleasant to throw these terribly practical considerations at the head of such a man as Mr. Barnett. The genuine Socialist can never regard Toynbee Hall as anything but a place where a few of the rich may learn something from the poor—can never for a moment forget that class art and class education are as powerless as class "wealth" to aid the workers. But the genuine Socialist is all the more conscious of the immense value of a man who will turn his back on his class so far as to go down among the poor, see how they live, and tell the world what he sees. Such a man is Mr. Barnett.

II. BY A "PRACTICABLE SOCIALIST."

There is, perhaps, no such body of doctrine in this book of "Practicable Socialism" as its title might lead us to expect. But practical people, who have had about enough of systems, will be grateful for the shrewd observation, the intelligent sympathy, the really bold though sober and unostentatious policy which Mr. and Mrs. Barnett put before us. It is true that they have no patent and universal remedy for the poverty, the misery, the cheerlessness of the life around them. Who but quacks have? But they do at least recognize clearly its true causes, and point to the direction in which amelioration and ultimate rescue is to be sought. What is the matter with the poor? It is not vice, or idleness, or want of thrift. These are consequences rather than causes, though, like all secondary maladies, they help to aggravate the evil from which they spring. What really ails the poor is their poverty. By all means let them practise temperance, thrift, "abstinence"—all the virtues, in fact, which the bourgeois philosopher is always preaching to them from his armchair. But give them all moral perfections, and they will still be poor (at least if they live in East London and can only earn twenty shillings a week per family), too poor to live a reasonably happy life, to enjoy wholesome pleasures, to cultivate refining tastes, to provide rest and decent comfort for old age. Individual merit is unable to bear up against the pressure of merciless conditions weighing down a whole community. With such a situation ordinary charity is ludicrously inadequate to deal. Charity may help the 5 or 10 or 20 per cent. of absolute paupers, but how about the 80 or 90 per cent. of cheerless and prospectless lives—the every-day condition of the "respectable poor" in a crowded city? No plaster will be of any avail here, for there is no external ailment. The cure, if cure there be, must be radical.

And it is the constant seeking for a radical cure, the dissatisfaction with mere palliatives, which so honourably distinguishes the aims of Mr. and Mrs. Barnett. This characteristic attaches to all their suggestions, including those which might at first sight appear small, or even trifling. What good can come, it may be asked, of a few well-to-do people being "at home" to the poor, as Mrs. Barnett is anxious to see them? Yet the idea is right. It is not the necessaries, but the refinements of life, which can be freely given without degrading the recipients. It is the same principle, though on an infinitely larger scale, which Mr. Barnett is advocating when he speaks in striking rather than happy phrase of the "nationalization of luxury." The essence of Mr. Barnett's Socialism is that the community should provide, not the means of life, but the higher goods and pleasures of life, for these whose narrow circumstances only suffice to give them food and clothing. Town councils with wide rating powers, freely used to provide great public institutions, which shall be open to all, not as a matter of grace but as a right—this is the agency by which he hopes to achieve his object. The plan looks well enough, but practical experience seems to show that we shall not get much beyond absolute necessaries by means of rating. We will, therefore, venture to put the matter in a different way, which we hope may meet the approval of Mr. Barnett. Of fifty rich men who die worth upwards of £100,000, or if you like £200,000 each, about one on the average leaves a substantial portion of his wealth for some public object—to found, or to enlarge, a church, a school, a park, a museum, a polytechnic. In some cases the object is ill-chosen, yet, on the whole, such bequests do an infinity of good. Only we want fifty times as many of them. How, then, about the other forty-nine rich men, who leave nothing, or next to nothing, to the community? Why shouldn't they? And if they won't, why shouldn't the law do it for them by means of a good wholesome local death duty on large estates?

It will be seen that Mr. Barnett's Socialism is confined to the distribution of wealth, and that it does not go beyond the demand for a larger contribution from private affluence to public purposes, coupled with the more intricate intermingling, the closer social relationship of different classes. Going thus far but no further, he will, of course, be open to attack from two opposite quarters. The out-and-out Socialists will turn up their noses at any man wearing their colours who is yet not prepared to go in blind for the nationalization of all the means of production, land, mines, houses, workshops, machinery, &c., &c., and for the unparalleled economic smash which would infallibly result from it. On the other hand, the Philistines will have at him on the ground that he is simply seeking to take part of the wealth of the rich and give it to the poor, thereby injuring the former, and benefiting the latter, if at all, to an inappreciable extent. But this criticism, of course, is based on a complete misconception. Mr. Barnett's policy is not to take from one in order to give to another, but to make those who can afford it help to enlarge the common possessions of all. His aim is to increase the birthright of the community, the number of possessions and advantages, the means of education and culture, which at present the rich only can command. To achieve this in any large measure would surely be to bestow upon the masses no inappreciable but the highest benefit. Enormously increased opportunities of physical and mental development—this is the most fruitful ideal for the Socialistic reformers of this present age. By pursuing it, moreover, they are laying the only possible foundation for that more thoroughgoing Socialism into which some zealots would like to plunge us at once, but which would be disastrous if it came to-day, and which fortunately is not going to come to-day nor yet to-morrow, the ghosts of Marx and Lassalle and the bodily presence of Mr. Cunninghame Graham notwithstanding.

Editor's Notes

- There is no indication in Shaw's diary as to when he received the above book. Its first mention is on 11 October 1888, when Shaw "began reading Barnett's *Practicable Socialism* for review. In the evening stayed at home and began review of Barnett." The following day he "finished and sent off review of Barnett's essays" (*Diary*, 421).

- Reverend Samuel A[ugustus] Barnett (1844–1913), religious leader and social reformer. Born in Bristol, he was educated privately, and at Wadham College, Oxford, where he studied law and history. He was curate at St. Mary's, Bryanston Square, from 1862 to 1872, at which date he became vicar of St. Jude's, Whitechapel, a post he held for twenty-two years. In 1873 he married Henrietta Rowland [see below]. He was one of the founders and warden of Toynbee Hall, Whitechapel, from 1884 to 1906, when he became its president. In addition to the above book he also wrote *The Service of God* (1897), *Religion and Progress* (1907), *Towards Social Reform* (1909), and *Religion and Politics* (1911).

- [Dame] Henrietta [Octavia] Barnett [née Rowland] (1851–1936), social reformer. She was a tireless and lifelong worker, particularly in areas pertaining to the welfare of women and children. After marrying the Reverend Barnett (above), she became manager of Forest Gate District Schools from 1875 to 1897. In 1881 she was one of the founders of the Whitechapel Art Exhibition. She promoted homes for workhouse girls, welfare for the feeble-minded, and country holidays for poor children. She was the vice-president of the National Union of Women Workers. In 1884 she founded and became president of the London Pupil Teachers' Association. She served on numerous committees and founded the Henrietta Barnett School. She was also a lecturer on housing, the Poor Law, and social subjects. In addition to the book she coauthored, reviewed above, and numerous magazine articles, she also wrote *The Making of the Home* (1885), *How to Mind the Baby* (1887), a children's book on anatomy *The Making of the Body* (1894), *Worship and Work* (1913), *Vision and Service* (1917), *Canon Barnett, His Life, Work, and Friends* (1918), and *Matters that Matter* (1930). She was made a Companion of the British Empire in 1917 and a Dame of the British Empire in 1924.

- The People's Palace in Mile End Road was a center for the social, educational, and recreational benefit of East Londoners. At the opening ceremony in 1887, Queen Victoria also laid the foundation stone of the East London Technical College, which eventually became Queen Mary College, University of London.

- The Gunpowder Plot was the failed conspiracy of a few Roman Catholics to blow up the Houses of Parliament on 5 November 1605, while King James I, the Lords, and the Commons were all assembled there.

- The Mansion House Fund (more properly the East London Church Fund) was instituted by Bishop Walsham How [see page 347 above] in 1880 to help the "cruelly undermanned" Church bring the "bread of life" to the vast numbers of the poor in that quarter of London. The annual meeting of the Fund took place at the Mansion House.

- Shaw's lurking awareness of the incongruity of the notion of "at homes to the poor," surfaces comically in *Pygmalion* (1912), when Eliza is a guest at Mrs. Higgins's "at home."

26 December 1888

*UNIVERSITY ECONOMICS** [C521]

To any one who is behind the scenes of political economy, such a title as "The University Economics" is fraught with promise of amusing reading. The path of the professor of the dismal science is not what it was. In the old days he had but to prove out of Ricardo that everything was for the best in the best of all possible worlds. But the advance of Democracy has created a State of which Ricardo knew nothing—a State into which the masses have been received, and which has already interfered with private property in all directions, limiting the hours of labour, quashing contracts, imposing unforeseen responsibilities on proprietors, dividing up shares of the landlord's interest among his tenants, educating Dick and Harry at Lord Tomnoddy's expense, forcibly taking private rent and interest by taxation from which the working class is exempt, and with the capital so taken organizing great industries for the public benefit. Consequently the professorial economist of the day is chiefly interesting for the ingenuity with which, addressing himself to the rising proprietors at Oxford and Cambridge, he may shade them from the rude glare of the economic obligation upon them to earn what they eat, in spite of independent incomes and fruitful rent-rolls.

Mr. Gonner has not quite sunk to the occasion. Though he does not rudely declare that the land should be made the property of the nation, he remarks that if he were concerned to find arguments for a proposal of that nature it would be "feasible to assert" that such a monopoly should be disallowed. He evades other burning questions by disclaiming all obligation as an economist to advocate or defend anything whatever; but this does not restrain him from taking a side unblushingly when the question is of Protection, Fair Trade, or the like. He saves himself from a world of controversial trouble by adopting that orthodox ground plan of abstract distribution by which rent is held not to enter into price, and commodities to exchange normally at their cost of production. This plan may be accepted with the double reservation that as a matter of fact rent does enter into price,

---

*"The University Economics." By E. C. K. Gonner. (London: R. Sutton and Co. 1888.)

and commodities do not exchange at their cost of production. It has the great convenience for university purposes of disguising the true relation between the haves and the have-nots, and, consequently, allowing wages to appear as the result of a free contract. Its main disadvantage for the purposes of the citizen and statesman is that it dismembers the whole economic synthesis of distribution by separating and removing the theory of rent which is its very backbone: after which operation there is nothing to do but to theorize, emptily and unhistorically, as to how profits, interest, and wages would hang together invertebrate. The startling result is that the "orthodox" economist finds himself landed on the same platform with the "individualist anarchists" of America and the Proudhonist "mutualists" of France, both of which bodies have arrived at their doctrinaire absurdities simply and directly by ignoring the fact that rent enters into the price of all commodities except those produced at the margin of cultivation.

Still, since Mr. Gonner had to provide, not a criticism of political economy, but a university student's introduction to the standard treatises, it is hard to see what other line he could have taken; and it would be unjust to deny him an acknowledgment of the clearness and conciseness of his primer, which is quite abreast of the march of university economics. His beginning by a statement of the assumption upon which the laws of the science are deduced, to wit, "that the industrial actions of men are determined by the desire of obtaining as much wealth as possible with the least possible exertion," marks a stage in the growing self-consciousness of economics. He states a second assumption; but it is only a particular case of the first. He follows Malthus as to wealth generally, Ricardo as to rent, Jevons as to value, Mill as to international trade, and Walker as to profits. As to capital, it has not yet emerged from the confusion into which Mill plunged it; so Mr. Gonner may be excused for not always using the term in the same sense. On the whole, the effect of the book (which is a handy little two-shilling volume with new-fangled rounded corners) is to make one wish that Mr. Gonner had had room enough and (professorially speaking) rope enough to express his full mind with that caustic pleasantry which distinguishes him as a lecturer, and the too decorous absence of which from "The University Economics" is a deplorable sacrifice of the humours of the science to the stiff proprieties of the class room.

Editor's Notes

- There is no mention in the diary of when Shaw received this book for review; but on 13 June 1888, he spent the day at the British Museum "reading Gonner's economics." The following day he went to the Museum and "fagged away at Gonner's book." He was still reading it on the sixteenth, and finished it on the eighteenth. The following day he began the review, which he finished and corrected on 20 June (*Diary*, 385, 386, 387). He wrote another review of Gonner's book (which in the *Diary* he calls *Political Economy*) on 11 July for the August issue of *To-Day* (*Diary*, 393). This review is shorter and more succinct than the one above, written, as it is, for a more partisan and economically aware audience; but it again stresses the folly of claiming that rent does not enter into price, excusing Gonner only on the ground that "university economics" are not "real economics," and praising him for producing a capable textbook. It concludes by saying

> From the point of view of Socialism or even pure economics, his way is only a way of "holding a candle to the devil"; but it is due to him to point out that he holds it steadily and is acquainted with all the latest improvements—except perhaps the extinguisher. (Bernard Shaw, (unsigned) review of *The University Economics*, in *To-Day*, August 1888, 10:63)

- [Professor] [Sir] E[dward] C[arter] K[ersey] Gonner (1862–1922), English professor of economics. Educated at Merchant Taylors' School, London, and Lincoln College, Oxford, he was first a lecturer for the London Extension Society in 1885, in which year he also became a lecturer at University College, Bristol. In 1888 he became a lecturer at University College, Liverpool. He married in 1890 and had one daughter. In 1891 he became a professor at University College, Liverpool. He was also president of numerous economics associations, and during World War I he was advisor to and director of statistics of the Ministry of Food. In addition to the book reviewed above, Gonner also wrote *Commercial Geography* (1894), *The Socialist State* (1895), *The Social Philosophy of Rodbertus* (1899), *Interest and Saving* (1906), *Common Land and Inclosure* (1912), and *The Economic History of Germany in the Nineteenth Century* (1912). He was knighted in 1921. Shaw knew Gonner well in the middle 1880s. His diary records his spending the evening with him on 13 September 1886; Gonner looking him up at the Museum on 1 and 15 November that year, and discussing economics with him twice in February of 1887. On 11 June 1888, Gonner persuaded Shaw to "write a textbook on Socialism for Sutton's University series. Terms—a royalty of fourpence a copy. I agreed, so far." The book was not started until 1891; but two days after talking to Gonner about it, Shaw was "at Museum all day reading Gonner's economics," no doubt as much to familiarize himself with the format of a university textbook, as to consider it for review. On 29 June 1887, Shaw "seconded" Gonner's motion to dissolve the Browning Society on the grounds that "it had ceased to exist," but managed to get only one other vote for their cause!

- Francis A[masa] Walker (1840–97), American educator, economist, and statistician. Born in Boston, he matriculated at Amherst College at fifteen, obtained his A.B. in 1860, and during the following nine years studied law, fought in the Civil War (where he rose from private to brevet brigadier-general), taught classics at Williston Seminary in Easthampton, and wrote editorials for the *Springfield Daily Republican*. He married in 1865 and there were seven children of the union. In 1869 Walker was appointed chief of the Bureau of Statistics, which he reorganized and improved. He also obtained a wealth of information on the economic and social situation of the United States, which assisted in his becoming professor of political economy and history in the Sheffield Scientific School of Yale (from 1873 to 1881), and as president of the Massachusetts Institute of Technology from 1881 until his death. He was a firm believer in competition, yet he advocated reduced working hours for labor; he was a free trader and an internationalist, and this may have made him better known and respected as a theoretical economist in England than at home. He wrote *The Wages Question* (1876), *Money* (1878), *Land and its Rent* (1883), and *Political Economy* (1883); but for his comment above Shaw may have been remembering Walker's article "The Source of Business Profits," which he had read when reviewing the first volume of the *Quarterly Journal of Economics*, published for Harvard University [see page 355 above].

INDEX

All entries that have been uppercased are articles or authors reviewed by Shaw.